American Reference Books Annual

Volume 47

2016 Edition

American Reference Books Annual
Advisory Board

2016
EDITION

AMERICAN REFERENCE BOOKS ANNUAL

Volume 47

Juneal M. Chenoweth, Associate Editor

 LIBRARIES UNLIMITED™

An Imprint of ABC-CLIO, LLC

Santa Barbara, California • Denver, Colorado

LIBRARIES UNLIMITED
An Imprint of ABC-CLIO, LLC
130 Cremona Drive
P.O. Box 1911
Santa Barbara, California 93116-1911
www.abc-clio.com

Library of Congress Cataloging-in-Publication Data

American reference books annual, 1970-
    Santa Barbara, CA, Libraries Unlimited.

        v. 19x26 cm.

Indexes:
    1970-74. 1v.
    1975-79. 1v.
    1980-84. 1v.
    1985-89. 1v.
    1990-94. 1v.
    1995-99. 1v.
    2000-04. lv.
    2005-09. lv.
    2010-14. 1v.

I. Reference books--Bibliography--Periodicals.
I. Chenoweth, Juneal
Z1035.1.A55 011'.02
ISBN 978-1-4408-4701-1
ISSN 0065-9959

Contents

Preface

Here is the interesting and challenging landscape for reference resources today. On the one hand, we clearly see the reference book diminished in the work of students, and the priorities of libraries. Going or gone are the vast collections of bound volumes in designated reference reading rooms. The disruptive element of course is technology: instantaneous access to online information. And reference seems to be the loser.

On the other hand, technology makes reference activity a winner too, but so seamlessly that the connection to old-fashioned reference work can be overlooked. All of us enjoy and use online tools to find airline ticket prices and flight schedules, weather forecasts and current conditions, currency exchange rates, stock prices, hotel and restaurant reviews, street maps, and foreign language translators. In the past we turned to print tools to meet these needs, with less convenience and less currency. Thanks to technology, we now have alternatives that match, and often surpass, yesterday's print reference works: timetables, weather almanacs, financial reports, tourist guidebooks, atlases, and bilingual dictionaries. So if reference is alive and well, but living under another name, where is the crisis? Which is to say, where is the change taking place?

Scholars have defined reference works in administrative, description, and functional terms. The administration definition was something like this: "a reference book is a book located in a non-circulating reference collection." Today, we no longer focus on printed books (though we may work with their e-book descendants), and resource access is no longer confined to a specific place. The descriptive definition has been more durable: a reference work incorporates elements of organization and presentation that reflect and promote its intended use … consultation as quickly and easily as possible. Hence subject indexes, alphabetical order for entries, or numerical coding, as well as newer features like cross-reference hot links. The functional definition perhaps has held up the best: while many sources can conceivably be used to answer a "reference question," a reference work is created for that purpose, and its form (those elements in the descriptive definition) follows that function. As long as readers seek information, that function has value.

Nor have the characteristics of "good" reference tools changed: when we want information, we want information that is accurate, objective, authoritative, current, and complete, as well as reliably accessible, clearly presented, and easily understood. Online reference sources meet these requirements just as thoroughly as do print-format classics like the the *Oxford English Dictionary,* the *World Book,* the *National Geographic World Atlas,* or the *Statistical Abstract of the United States* (all of which have expanded to online versions).

One final element makes modern life tough for reference: the general discounting of authority. Reference tools rely on the notion that important information is stable and therefore can be discovered, described, and evaluated. Behind the pursuit of "facts" to answer a reference query is an assumption that "facts" exist, that one answer is true and "best," that the "right" answer is available to us, and that reasonable people will agree about the "correct" answer when they see it. We may expect to argue about the best 10 American novels, but we expect to agree about the melting temperature of copper. In a world of relativism, conspiracy theories, and Heisenberg's uncertainty principle, not only are authorities in doubt, but even the facts themselves. And without the concept of correct facts, reference has no leg to stand on.

It is encouraging to see this aphorism widely quoted: "Everyone is entitled to his own opinion, but not to his own facts." When most of us can agree about facts, reference can thrive. Incidentally, this quotation itself illustrates the reference value of truth-seeking and fact-checking. Generally attributed to Daniel Patrick Moynihan, the *Dictionary of Modern Proverbs* (Yale, 2012) also documents similar statements extending back to Bernard Baruch in 1946.

If there are four participants in the ecology of reference—readers, authors, publishers, and librarians—then perhaps it is fair to say that two are leading and two are catching up. Readers still have plenty of questions to answer, and authors still eagerly turn out resources to meet that need. The challenges seem greatest for publishers and librarians, as value-added contributions shift from presentation in print to presentation in online form.

—Steven Sowards, Michigan State University Libraries

Introduction

We are pleased to provide you with volume 47 of *American Reference Books Annual* (ARBA), a far-reaching review service for reference books and electronic resources. As Steven Sowards points out in the preface, the reference landscape has changed considerably since the publication of ARBA's first volume in 1970. Reference users no longer need to spend hours in a library consulting bound volumes, microfiche, or microfilm when much sought-after information is available online. As the preface also highlights, this easy accessibility does not eliminate the need for well-curated, professionally produced reference material and the guidance of trained librarians.

ARBA strives to provide comprehensive coverage of English-language reference resources, both digital and print, published in the United States and Canada during a single year. We review both subscription-based and free Websites, as well as dictionaries, encyclopedias, indexes, directories, bibliographies, guides, concordances, atlases, gazetteers, and other types of ready-reference tools. Generally, encyclopedias that are updated annually, yearbooks, almanacs, indexing and abstracting services, and other annuals or serials are reviewed at editorially determined intervals. Reviews of updated publications attempt to point out changes in scope or editorial policy and comparisons to older editions.

Certain categories of reference sources are usually not reviewed in ARBA: foreign-language titles, books of fewer than 48 pages that are not part of a larger set, those produced by vanity presses or by the author as publisher, and those generated by library staff for internal use. Highly specialized reference works printed in a limited number of copies and that do not appeal to the general library audience ARBA serves may also be omitted.

For nearly two decades, ARBA has also been a go-to source for reviews of new literature written specifically for the library professional; this year's ARBA features approximately 100 reviews of professional development titles. These include monographs and handbooks that address the concerns of library and information specialists and can be found in chapter 11, titled "Library and Information Science and Publishing and Bookselling."

In 2002, Libraries Unlimited launched ARBAonline, an authoritative database designed to provide access to all reviews published in the print version of ARBA since 1997. The editorial staff updates ARBAonline monthly, giving librarians evaluations of the most up-to-date materials along with depth of coverage as they make purchasing decisions.

Reviewing Policy

To ensure well-written, balanced reviews of high quality, the ARBA staff maintains a roster of more than 400 scholars, practitioners, and library educators in all subject specialties at libraries and universities throughout the United States and Canada. Because ARBA seeks to be a comprehensive reviewing source, the reviews are generally longer and more critical than other review publications to detail the strengths and weaknesses of important reference works. Reviewers are asked to examine books and electronic resources and provide well-documented critical comments, both positive and negative. Coverage usually includes the usefulness of a given work; organization, execution, and pertinence of contents; prose style; format; availability of supplementary materials (e.g., indexes, appendixes); and similarity to other works and previous editions. Reviewers are encouraged to address the intended audience but not necessarily to give specific recommendations for purchase.

Arrangement

ARBA 2016 consists of 37 chapters, an author/title index, and a subject index. It is divided into four alphabetically arranged parts: "General Reference Works," "Social Sciences," "Humanities," and "Science and Technology." "General Reference Works" is subdivided by form: almanacs, bibliography, biography, and so on. Within the remaining three parts, chapters are organized by topic. Thus, under "Social Sciences" the reader will find chapters titled "Economics and Business," "Education," "History," "Law," "Sociology," and so on.

Each chapter is subdivided to reflect the arrangement strategy of the entire volume. There is a section on general works followed by a topical breakdown. For example, in the chapter titled "Literature," "General Works" is followed by "Children's and Young Adult Literature" and "National Literature." Subsections are based on the amount of material available on a given topic and vary from year to year.

Users should keep in mind that many materials may fall under several different chapter topics. The comprehensive author/title and subject indexes found at the end of the volume will assist users in finding specific works that could fall under several different chapters. Additionally, readers seeking out reviews of digital resources can find these quickly using the Website and Database Review Locator (p. xxiii).

Acknowledgments

In closing, we wish to express our gratitude to the many talented contributors without whose support this volume of ARBA could not have been compiled. Many thanks also go out to our distinguished Advisory Board members whose contributions greatly enhance ARBA and ARBAonline. We would also like to thank the members of our staff who were instrumental in its preparation.

Contributors

Anthony J. Adam, Director, Institutional Assessment, Blinn College, Brenham, Tex.

January Adams, Asst. Director/Head of Adult Services, Franklin Township Public Library, Somerset, N.J.

Michael Adams, Reference Librarian, City Univ. of New York Graduate Center.

Donald Altschiller, Librarian, Mugar Memorial Library, Boston Univ.

Mary Alice Anderson, Online Professional Development Instructor, Univ. of Wisconsin-Stout, Menomonie, Wis.

Adrienne Antink, Medical Group Management Association, Lakewood, Colo.

Karen Bagne, Wildlife Biologist, Kenyon College, Gambier, Ohio.

Thomas E. Baker, Assoc. Professor, Department of Criminal Justice, Univ. of Scranton, Pa.

Joshua Barton, Head of Cataloging and Metadata Services, Assistant Head of Technical Services, Michigan State Univ. Libraries, East Lansing.

Joshua Becker, Information Literacy and Assessment Librarian, Assistant Professor, Southern New Hampshire Univ.

Michael Francis Bemis, Asst. Librarian, Washington County Library, Woodbury, Minn.

Laura J. Bender, Librarian, Univ. of Arizona, Tucson.

Claire Berg, Information and Technology Literacy Specialist, Riverview Elementary School, Farmington, Minn.

Barbara M. Bibel, Reference Librarian, Science/Business/Sociology Dept., Main Library, Oakland Public Library, Calif.

Daniel K. Blewett, Reference Librarian, College of DuPage Library, College of DuPage, Glen Ellyn, Ill.

Alicia Brillon, Reference Librarian, James E. Faust Law Library, Univ. of Utah.

Georgia Briscoe, Assoc. Director and Head of Technical Services, Law Library, Univ. of Colorado, Boulder.

John R. Burch Jr., Dean of Distance Learning and Library Services, Campbellsville Univ., Ky.

Frederic F. Burchsted, Reference Librarian, Widener Library, Harvard Univ., Cambridge, Mass.

Joanna M. Burkhardt, Head Librarian, College of Continuing Education Library, Univ. of Rhode Island, Providence.

Vincent Burns, PhD, ABC-CLIO, Santa Barbara, Calif.

Diane M. Calabrese, Freelance Writer and Contributor, Silver Springs, Md.

Theresa Calcagno, IT & Engineering Librarian, George Mason Univ., Fairfax, Va.

Delilah R. Caldwell, Online Services Librarian and Adjunct Instructor, Southwestern College, Winfield, Kans.

Alice Chaffee, Freelance Editor, Carpinteria, Calif.

Bert Chapman, Government Publications Coordinator, Purdue Univ., West Lafayette, Ind.

Boyd Childress, Reference Librarian, Ralph B. Draughon Library, Auburn Univ., Ala.

Robert Clark, Reference/Research Librarian, O'Quinn Law Library, Univ. of Houston Law Center, Houston, Tex.

Rosanne M. Cordell, (formerly) Head of Reference Services, Franklin D. Schurz Library, Indiana Univ., South Bend.

Gregory A. Crawford, Head of Public Services, Penn State Harrisburg, Middletown, Pa.

Gregory Curtis, Regional Federal Depository Librarian for Maine, New Hampshire, and Vermont, Fogler Library, Univ. of Maine, Presque Isle.

James D'annibale, Technology & Learning Commons Librarian, Wilson College, Chambersburg, Pa.

Norman Desmarais, Professor Emeritus, Providence (Rhode Island) College.

Linda DeVore, Media Center Director, Casa Grande (Arizona) Middle School.

R. K. Dickson, Asst. Professor of Fine Arts, Wilson College, Chambersburg, Pa.

Scott R. DiMarco, Director of Library Services and Information Resources, Mansfield Univ., Mansfield, Pa.

Joe P. Dunn, Charles A. Dana Professor of History and Politics, Converse College, Spartanburg, S.C.

Bradford Lee Eden, Dean of Library Services, Valparaiso Univ., Valparaiso, Ind.

Sheri Edwards, Assistant Univ. Librarian, Florida Atlantic Univ.

Lorraine Evans, Social Science Research and Instruction Librarian, Univ. of Colorado, Denver.

Richard Fanning, Library Media Specialist, Spring Forest Middle School, Houston, Tex.

Autumn Faulkner, Asst Head of Cataloging and Metadata Services, Michigan State Univ. Libraries, East Lansing.

Judith J. Field, Senior Lecturer, Program for Library and Information Science, Wayne State Univ., Detroit.

Josh Eugene Finnell, Reference Librarian, Ohio.

Tracy A. Fitzwater, Teacher-Librarian, Crescent School District, Joyce, Wash.

Valerie Byrd Fort, Library Media Specialist, New Providence Elementary School, Lexington, S.C.

Julia Frankosky, Government Information Librarian, Michigan State Univ., East Lansing.

Brian T. Gallagher, Access Services Librarian, Head of Access Services, Univ. of Rhode Island, Kingston.

Zev Garber, Professor and Chair, Jewish Studies, Los Angeles Valley College, Calif.

Denise A. Garofalo, Systems and Catalog Services Librarian, Curtin Memorial Library, Mount Saint Mary College, Newburgh, N.Y.

John T. Gillespie, College Professor and Writer, New York.

Caroline L. Gilson, Coordinator, Prevo Science Library, DePauw Univ., Greencastle, Ind.

Michael W. Handis, Assoc. Librarian for Collection Management, CUNY Graduate Center,

New York.

Ralph Hartsock, Senior Music Catalog Librarian, Univ. of North Texas, Denton.

Muhammed Hassanali, Independent Consultant, Shaker Heights, Ohio.

David Hawksworth, Wildlife Biologist, Albuquerque, N.Mex.

Lucy Heckman, Reference Librarian (Business-Economics), St. John's Univ. Library, Jamaica, N.Y.

Laura Herrell, Writer/editor, Santa Barbara, Calif.

Mark Y. Herring, Dean of Library Services, Winthrop Univ., Dacus Library, Rock Hill, S.C.

Ladyjane Hickey, Reference Librarian, Austin College, Tex.

Jennifer Brooks Huffman, Serials/ILL Librarian, Univ. of Wisconsin, Stevens Point.

Jonathan F. Husband, Program Chair of the Library/Reader Services Librarian, Henry Whittemore Library, Framingham State College, Mass.

Amanda Izenstark, Asst. Professor, Reference and Instructional Design Librarian, Univ. of Rhode Island, Kingston.

Valerie Jankowski, Library Media Specialist, Washington Middle School, Washington, Mo.

Melissa M. Johnson, Reference Services, NOVA Southeastern Univ., Alvin Sherman Library, Ft. Lauderdale, Fla.

Donna J Kearns, Professor, Psychology Department, Univ. of Central Oklahoma, Edmond.

Craig Mury Keeney, Cataloging Librarian, South Caroliniana Library, Univ. of South Carolina, Columbia.

Andrea C Kepsel, Health Sciences Educational Technology Librarian, Michigan State Univ. Libraries, East Lansing.

Sue Ellen Knowlton, Branch Manager, Hudson Regional Library, Pasco County Library System, Hudson, Fla.

Amy Koehler, Support Services Librarian, Moody Bible Institute, Chicago, Ill.

Lori D. Kranz, Freelance Editor, Chambersburg, Pa.

Natalie Kupferberg, Biological Sciences/Pharmacy Library, Ohio State Univ., Columbus.

Robert V. Labaree, Reference/Public Services Librarian, Von KleinSmid Library, Univ. of Southern California, Los Angeles.

Shireen Lalla, Coordinator, Academic Affairs, Florida Atlantic Univ., Davie.

Peter Larsen, Physical Sciences and Engineering Librarian, Univ. of Rhode Island Libraries, Kingston.

Rob Laurich, Acting Chief of Technical Services, Collection Department, Cohen Library, The City College of the City Univ. of New York.

Martha Lawler, Assoc. Librarian, Louisiana State Univ., Shreveport.

Shelly Lee, National Board Certified Library Media Specialist, Central Junior High, Moore, Okla.

Kristin Kay Leeman, Adjunct Faculty Instructor, Univ. of Maryland, Univ. College, Largo.

Richard Nathan Leigh, Metadata & Digital Resources Developer, Ball State Univ. Libraries, Muncie, Ind.

Robert M. Lindsey, Instruction and Reference Librarian, Pittsburg State Univ., Pittsburg, Kans.

Megan W. Lowe, Reference/Instruction Librarian, Univ. Library, Univ. of Louisiana at Monroe.

Tyler Manolovitz, Digital Resources Coordinator, Newton Gresham Library, Sam Houston State Univ., Huntsville, Tex.

Sara Marcus, Asst. Professor of Education, Touro Univ. International, N.Y.

Michelle Martinez, Librarian, Newton Gresham Library, Sam Houston State Univ., Huntsville, Tex.

Judith Matthews, Physics-Astronomy Subject Librarian, Michigan State Univ., East Lansing.

Melinda F. Matthews, Interlibrary Loan/Reference Librarian, Univ. of Louisiana at Monroe.

John Maxymuk, Reference Librarian, Paul Robeson Library, Rutgers Univ., Camden, N.J.

Kevin McDonough, Reference and Electronic Resources Librarian, Northern Michigan Univ.—Olson Library, Marquette.

Jessica Crossfield McIntosh, Reference Services Coordinator, Asst. Professor, Otterbein Univ., Westerville, Ohio.

Lawrence Joseph Mello, Asst. Reference and Instruction Librarian, Florida Atlantic Univ., Boca Raton.

Amy Merrill, Reading Specialist, Calvin Coolidge Elementary School, Binghamton , New York, Binghamton.

Rachel Meredith Minkin, Head of Reference Services, Michigan State Univ. Libraries, East Lansing.

Janis Minshull, Library Consultant, Phippsburg, Maine.

Sara Mofford, Youth Services Librarian, Catawba County Library System, Newton, N.C.

Alda Moore, Head Librarian, Matoaca High School, Chesterfield, Va.

Lisa Morgan, Branch Manager, Pasco County Library System, Hudson, Fla.

Kat Landry Mueller, Electronic Resources Librarian, Sam Houston State Univ., Huntsville, Tex.

Paul M. Murphy III, Director of Marketing, PMX Medical, Denver, Colo.

Madeleine Nash, Reference/Instruction Librarian, Molloy College, Rockville Center, N.Y.

Mary Northrup, Reference Librarian, Metropolitan Community College-Maple Woods, Kansas City, Mo.

Thomas O'Brien, Librarian, Florida Atlantic Univ., Boca Raton.

Herbert W. Ockerman, Professor, Ohio State Univ., Columbus.

Lawrence Olszewski, Director, OCLC Library and Information Center, Dublin, Ohio.

Cynthia Ortiz, School Librarian, Hackensack (New Jersey) High School.

Amy B. Parsons, Metadata Librarian/Assoc. Professor, Courtright Memorial Library, Otterbein Univ., Westerville, Ohio.

Rares G. Piloiu, Information Literacy Librarian, Otterbein Univ., Westerville, Ohio.

Arthur Quinn, Library Director, St. Vincent de Paul Seminary, Boynton Beach, Fla.

Leslie Greaves Radloff, Licensed Library Media Specialist, The Heights Community School, St. Paul (Minn.) Public Schools.

Ellen Range, Media Specialist, Harding Senior High School. St. Paul, Minn.

Jack Ray, Asst. Director, Loyola/Notre Dame Library, Baltimore, Md.

Allen Reichert, Electronic Access Librarian, Courtright Memorial Library, Otterbein Univ., Westerville, Ohio.

Richard Salvucci, Professor, Economics, Trinity Univ., San Antonio, Tex.

Bruce Sarjeant, Reference, Documents & Maps Librarian, Northern Michigan Univ., Marquette.

Lisa Schultz, Instructional Services Research Librarian, Univ. of Colorado School of Law, Boulder.

Mark Schumacher, Art and Humanities Librarian, Univ. of North Carolina, Greensboro.

Ralph Lee Scott, Professor, Assistant Head of Special Collections for Public Services, and Curator of Printed Books and Maps, East Carolina Univ. Library, Greenville, N.C.

Colleen Seale, Humanities and Social Sciences Services, George A. Smathers Libraries, Univ. of Florida, Gainesville.

Susan E. Searing, Professor Emerita, Univ. of Illinois, Urbana-Champaign.

William Shakalis, Assistant Librarian, Worcester State Univ., Worcester, Mass.

Ravindra Nath Sharma, Dean of Library, Monmouth Univ. Library, West Long Branch, N.J.

Stephen J. Shaw, Library Director, Antioch Univ. Midwest, Yellow Springs, Ohio.

Kay Shelton, Instructor, Kishwaukee College, Malta, Ill.

Brian J. Sherman, Head of Access Services and Systems, Noel Memorial Library, Louisiana State Univ., Shreveport.

Breezy Silver, Collection Coordinator and Business Reference Librarian, Michigan State Univ. Libraries, East Lansing.

Todd Simpson, Assistant Professor/Catalog Librarian, York College, City Univ. of New York, Jamaica.

Holly Skir, Librarian, York College, City Univ. of New York, New York, Jamaica.

Kay Stebbins Slattery, Coordinator Librarian, Louisiana State Univ., Shreveport.

Mary Ellen Snodgrass, Freelance Writer, Charlotte, N.C.

Lee Sochay, Head of Acquisitions, Michigan State Univ. Libraries, East Lansing.

Steven W. Sowards, Asst. Director for Collections, Michigan State Univ. Libraries, East Lansing.

John P. Stierman, Reference Librarian, Western Illinois Univ., Macomb.

Martha E. Stone, Coordinator for Reference Services, Treadwell Library, Massachusetts General Hospital, Boston.

Eric Tans, Environmental Sciences Librarian, Michigan State Univ. Libraries, East Lansing.

Joseph E. Taylor III, Professor of History, Simon Fraser Univ., Burnaby, BC, Canada.

Susan E. Thomas, Head of Collection Development/Assoc. Librarian, Indiana Univ., South Bend.

David Tipton, managing editor, ABC-CLIO, Santa Barbara, Calif.

Diane J. Turner, Science/Engineering Liaison, Auraria Library, Univ. of Colorado, Denver.

Linda M. Turney, E-Resources Cataloging Librarian, Walker Library, Middle Tennessee State Univ., Murfreesboro.

Catherine Vinson, Instructional Strategist, L G Alleman Middle School, Lafayette, La.

J. E. Weaver, Dept. of Economics, Drake Univ., Des Moines, Iowa.

Karen T. Wei, Head, Asian Library, Univ. of Illinois, Urbana-Champaign.

Holly Whitt, Librarian, Walnut Grove Elementary, New Market, Ala.

W. Cole Williamson, Instruction Librarian, Sam Houston State Univ., Huntsville, Texas.

Julienne L. Wood, Head, Research Services, Noel Memorial Library, Louisiana State Univ., Shreveport.

Susan Yutzey, School Library Media Specialist, Upper Arlington High School, Columbus, Ohio.

Website and Database Locator

Reference is to entry number.

Part I

GENERAL REFERENCE WORKS

1   General Reference Works

Almanacs

1. **The American Book of Days.** 5th ed. Bronx, N.Y., H. W. Wilson, 2015. 1062p. illus. index. $195.00. ISBN 13: 978-1-61925-469-5.

This is the fifth edition of the *American Book of Days,* first published in 1937 under the editorship of George W. Douglas. This new edition updates and revises entries from the fourth edition and includes approximately 200 new essays, including pieces on the 9/11 terrorist attacks, the assassination of Osama bin-Laden, the Patient Protection and Affordable Care Act, the Boston Marathon bombing, the wars in Afghanistan and Iraq, and the 2008 financial crisis.

The book begins with a list of days and events; each day of the year (including February 29th) has at least one entry. These entries are accompanied by page numbers, so users can skip to the page directly. Months and dates serve as guide words at the top of every page for those who want to browse the entire volume. To accommodate moveable events such as Thanksgiving and Passover, the *American Book of Days* uses the date the event occurred in either the 1970 or 1997 editions. Each moveable event is so indicated. Entries range in length from about half a column on May 10th for Fort Ticonderoga Falls to nearly eight pages containing the text of George Washington's Farewell Address, which he delivered on September 19th. Altogether, the entries cover American history and culture from the colonial period to the present. Black-and-white photographs sprinkled throughout add interest.

The end of the book is packed with nine appendixes: The Calendar, The Era, The Days of the Week, The Signs of the Zodiac, the United States Constitution, the Articles of Confederation, the Mayflower Compact of 1620, and Important Public Holidays and Events. An index rounds out the work, which is recommended for school and public libraries.—**ARBA Staff Reviewer**

2. **The World Almanac and Book of Facts 2016.** New York, Infobase Publishing, 2016. 1008p. illus. maps. index. $34.95. ISBN 13: 978-1-60057-199-2.

Having begun publication in 1868, *The World Almanac and Book of Facts* remains a staple of reference collections in almost all libraries. The 2016 edition continues the excellence of the series. Of added interest are the special features and year in review for 2015. This section includes the top 10 news topics for the year, notable quotes, US Supreme Court decisions, obituaries of famous and infamous individuals who died during the year, and the year in pictures among other topics. Two special features are also included. The first focuses on the 2016 election and provides information such as the dates for presidential primaries and caucuses and the dates of the nominating conventions. The second is entitled, "Coming to America: Immigration in History and Today," and provides good background information for the ongoing debate about immigration and its impact on the United States. The volume also includes the standard statistical data found in earlier editions such as sections on the economy, crime, science and technology, US facts and history, world maps and flags, world history and culture, and sports. As a ready reference tool, *The World Almanac and Book of Facts* is indispensable and should be on the reference shelves of every school, public, and academic library.—**Gregory A. Crawford**

Biography

3.   **Current Biography Yearbook, 2015.** Bronx, N.Y., H. W. Wilson, 2015. 723p. illus. $199.00. ISBN 13: 978-1-61925-707-8.

Current Biography Yearbook 2015 is the 76th annual reference offering a select collection of over 200 biographical sketches of contemporary newsmakers from a variety of professions. It also includes a number of compact obituaries marking the passing of other notable persons between the later months of 2014 and into the publication year.

The collection emphasizes true diversity in choosing its subjects, who hold a range of professions such as, among many others, ecologist, actor, king, fashion designer, philosopher, mixed martial artist, and chef. Each biography lists the birth date and occupation of its subject before its main essay which touches on their early life, career trajectory, notable achievements, and personal life. The biographies also include a list of suggested reading about the subject and selected works as appropriate. Many, but not all, biographies come with a black-and-white photograph of their subject. Readers up on current events will recognize names such as writer and musician Carrie Brownstein, baseball player Madison Bumgarner, journalist Ta-Nahisi Coates, and U.S. Navy Admiral Michelle Howard.

The obituaries section lists birth date, death date and profession; it then offers a brief memorial including details of the death if known. They also include a reference to the subject's particular volume of *Current Biography* in which they are included.

All biography and obituary subjects are listed at the beginning of the volume and biographies are classified by profession at the volume's end.—**ARBA Staff Reviewer**

4.   Davis, Anita Price, and Marla J. Selvidge. **Women Nobel Peace Prize Winners.** Jefferson, N.C., McFarland, 2015. 238p. illus. index. $45.00pa. ISBN 13: 978-0-7264-9917-5; 978-1-4766-2212-5 (e-book).

Living through many of the regional conflicts that would lay the groundwork for the First World War, Bertha von Suttner was fervent in her work as a pacifist and novelist and is thought to be the inspiration behind Alfred Nobel's Peace Prize. In fact, Bertha won the prestigious award herself in 1905. This second edition of *Women Nobel Peace Prize Winners* (see ARBA 2007, entry 11) collects efficient but satisfying biographies of all female Peace Prize winners in one enlightening book.

With the addition of the three latest female winners, this edition now presents 15 total entries and covers such dignitaries as Emily Green Balch, Mother Teresa, Aung San Suu Kyi and the award's youngest female recipient, Malala Yousafzai. Each biography includes a black-and-white photograph, as well as excellent background focusing on interesting details of its subject's lives, a bit of historical context, and each woman's award-winning work. For example, we read how the senseless deaths of Mairead Maguire's young niece and nephews propelled her and a fed-up Betty Williams to create the Community of Peace People, which fought to address the violence raging in 1970's Northern Ireland.

Including a list of all Nobel Peace Prize winners by year, a bibliography for each entry, and a piece on Alfred Nobel himself, this book provides an important way for readers to connect with these determined figures devoted to the idea of a peaceful world.—**Laura Herrell**

Dictionaries and Encyclopedias

5.   **Encyclopedia of Deception.** Timothy R. Levine, ed. Thousand Oaks, Calif., Sage, 2014. 2v. illus. index. $370.00; $296.00 (e-book). ISBN 13: 978-1-4522-5877-5; 978-1-4833-8898-4 (e-book).

There is nothing more shocking to parents than the first time their child deceives them. Deception has the potential to shake us to the core. Yet there are times when we do not even know we have been deceived. The *Encyclopedia of Deception* does an excellent job providing readers with a thorough background of how deception has had powerful impacts on events in the past, is being used in the present, and even how it is used in nature with plants and animals.

With an introduction that captivates the reader's interest, Timothy R. Levine, Ph.D., explains that this field is so interesting to our society that we have network television shows dedicated to the science of deception as well as very regular national news coverage of deceptive current events. Levine points out the invalid nature of some of the lie-detecting myths that swirl through society while making the case that the real lie detection techniques will be found in the encyclopedia.

This encyclopedia does not disappoint. The reader's guide found at the beginning of volume one shows which articles fall under the overarching topics such as advertising, communication, psychology, the military, etc. The reader's guide coupled with the index will make this encyclopedia very easy to use. The content of the articles is appropriate for the many audiences ranging from upper-level high school to college students and beyond. The articles are well organized and very informative, yet still understood by the layman. The "Further Readings" section of each article will assist those looking for further depth.—**James D'annibale**

6.   **Famous First Facts: A Record of First Happenings, Discoveries, and Inventions in American History.** 7th ed. Bronx, N.Y., H. W. Wilson, 2015. 1425p. illus. index. $195.00. ISBN 13: 978-1-61925-468-8.

Famous First Facts, now in its seventh edition, was first published by editor Joseph Kane for H.W. Wilson in 1933. The sixth edition appeared in 2006 (see ARBA 2008, entry 26). The current edition has almost 8,000 entries, more than 100 illustrations, 4 indexes, and 16 chapters covering firsts in several arenas—scientific, medical, technological, political, legal, social, and financial—from the colonial period to the present. Entries can be as short as a sentence, but most are several sentences in length.

The book begins with a preface, notes on how to use the book, and "Expanded Contents." Chapters are organized into alphabetized subsections; "firsts" in these subsections are presented in chronological order. The chapters are as follows: Arts and Entertainment, Business and Industry, Daily Life, Education, Engineering, Media and Communications, Medicine and Health, Military and War, Nature and Environment, Population and Settlement, Religion, Science and Technology, Society, Sports and Recreation, and Transportation. Four indexes—subject, index by years, index to personal names, and a geographical index—facilitate searches.

This book of first facts would be a welcome addition to a public or school library.—**ARBA Staff Reviewer**

Directories

7. **AllAreaCodes.com. http://www.allareacodes.com/.** [Website] Free. Date reviewed: 2016.

AllAreaCodes.com is a freely available, easily searchable, and regularly updated resource of area code information within the North American Numbering Plan.

There is a prominent search screen in the middle of the home page that allows searches by number, area code, city, or state—this serves the function of a basic search screen for the entire site. Users can also use an area code search box or a city search box. On the right side of the screen, there is a list of area codes (from the 200s to the 900s) next to the name of the city with which the area code is associated. For example, 505 is listed with Albuquerque, New Mexico. Clicking on Albuquerque takes users to another page with a map of the region associated with the area code (this is printable), the names of other cities and towns in the area code, a full-number search screen, and time zone information.

The newest feature of the site is a reverse phone lookup. Simply typing in a number will produce (if available) the name of the person associated with the number along with city and zip code information. The site provides information about for-fee services that can find information about unknown numbers. For those who want to protect their privacy, there is a form that allows users to remove their personal information from this site. Other site offerings include a list of international dialing codes plus basic instructions on placing an international call, as well as an infographics and articles section.—**ARBA Staff Reviewer**

8. **Associations Canada, 2016.** 37th ed. Amenia, N.Y., Grey House Publishing, 2016. 2026p. index. $449.00pa. ISBN 13: 978-1-61925-957-7; 978-1-61925-958-4.

This edition of *Associations Canada* provides the most current directory of nonprofit associations. It includes over 20,000 associations which are either headquartered in Canada, headquartered elsewhere but house a branch in Canada, or entirely foreign but of potential interest to Canadians. All entries have been meticulously verified in terms of providing the most up-to-date information as of publication, including association name change, event dates, etc. Introductory information is conveyed in both English and French. Individual listings may be conveyed in either or both languages.

Opening pages provide a wealth of insightful information: a page on how to read an entry; a list of abbreviations and translations; "Canadian Associations at a Glance";

historical and organizational association information; several essays regarding timely and applicable topics (e.g., social media usage); and a comprehensive subject index.

Canadian associations, ranging from the Abbeyfield Houses Society of Canada to the Zurich & District Chamber of Commerce are profiled first, followed by foreign associations. Entries are alphabetized within each section and may include an association's current and former names and acronyms; address and other contact information; social media; overview; mission; affiliation; executives; membership; conferences; awards, grants or scholarship information; and more.

Entries are followed by a number of supplemental indexes which are necessary and helpful in regard to the great volume of information. All indexes are arranged alphabetically. There is an acronym index, providing a listing of acronyms and their corresponding associations; a budget index, organizing associations within eight budget categories; a conferences and conventions index, covering dates scheduled between 2016 and 2023; an executive name index; a geographic index; a mailing list index; and, finally, a registered charitable organization index.

This essential and well-curated source will prove a valuable addition to libraries.— **ARBA Staff Reviewer**

Quotation Books

9.   **Oxford Dictionary of Quotations.** 8th ed. Elizabeth Knowles, ed. New York, Oxford University Press, 2014. 1126p. index. $50.00. ISBN 13: 978-0-19-966870-0.

Surely with the Internet now so firmly ensconced in every inch and fiber of our lives, we no longer need bulky, tree-killing tomes like this one? Moreover, even this text is on the godalmighty Internet. Coming in at over five pounds and more than 1,100 pages, what could possibly possess any publisher, especially one as reputable as Oxford, to undertake such an expensive and laborious undertaking for what we might call a publishing *paralipomenon*?

Accuracy of phrase, ease of use, and profound assurance of source are just three reasons that come to mind, any one of which justifies the existence of the volume but all three make it *a fortiori,* or QED, as the philosophers might say. Yet apart from these reasons, the inclusion in this edition of the history of the volume and the introduction to the first edition by Berenard Darwin should make the matter incontestable even for tree-huggers. Well, okay, for everyone but them. Begins Darwin, "Quotation brings to many people one of the intensest [sic] joys of living." He goes on to point out that some will be disappointed at what is both included *and* what is left out, and he even points out one of his favorites that did not make that first edition cut. To which he muses, "Can it be, I ask myself, that this is due to the fact an Oxford scholar put several of the Master's [William Hepworth Thompson] sayings into his Greek exercise book and attributed them to one Talirantes? Down, base thought! I only mention this momentary and unworthy suspicion to show other readers the sort of thing they should avoid as they would the very devil." Alas, no one writes like this anymore but it is so charming to be reminded once again that elocution and felicitous expression used to be not only taught and practiced, but also admired.

The Oxford Dictionary of Quotations brings together thousands (and thousands) of quotations with their sources matched and their phrasing parsed as pluperfectly as possible. As with all other editions the arrangement is by author with birth and death dates, when applicable, in place. The author's nationality and occupation is noted and the original language of the quotation given. Cross-references, when appropriate, are given. A most expansive keyword index is included. What makes this edition so important is that many contemporaries, for better or for worse, are given their place in the sun. Thus, Frank Zappa, Joan Baez, Bob Marley, John Lennon, and Paul McCartney are all included as well as scores of others one has never heard of.

While it may not always be true that the Internet will give you several million answers in a few nanoseconds but a librarian the right one, when it is true, it is because of books such as this one are still published and still used. *Lauditor temporis acti.*—**Mark Y. Herring**

10.   **The Quotable Amelia Earhart.** Michele Wehrwein Albion, ed. Albuquerque, N.Mex., University of New Mexico Press, 2015. 255p. illus. index. $24.95. ISBN 13: 978-0-8263-4562-2; 978-0-8263-4563-9 (e-book).

A remarkable, dense little tome, *The Quotable Amelia Earhart,* edited by author, Michele Wehrwein Albion, who is known for similar collections of other historical notables like Eleanor Roosevelt and Henry Ford, is a thematic arrangement of quotations by the celebrated aviatrix. Albion's preface/acknowledgement provides a brief biography of the famous lady but stresses that the book has no intentions of exploring Earhart's disappearance. In addition to the fascinating collection of wise and witty words, Albion includes a chronology of major events in Earhart's life. This title would be an excellent fit for a public library and fans of the amazing female pilot. Highly recommended.—**Megan W. Lowe**

Websites and Databases

11.   **Academic Video Online: Premium. http://alexanderstreet.com/products/academic-video-online-premium.** [Website] Alexandria, Va. Alexander Street Press. Price negotiated by site. Date reviewed: 2016.

Academic Video Online: Premium provides a vast database of film and video clips from documentary, newsreel, entertainment, and television sources. The range of material is deep and broad, organized into eight "disciplines" more appropriately understood as general themes that range from history to arts, literature, social science, and science and engineering but also the idiosyncratic categories of "diversity" and "personal interest." The oldest clips are 1894 footage of Sioux Indians performing "ghost dances." Much of the oldest footage comes from the Edison Company and Library of Congress. As of this review the newest videos date from late 2015.

The collection will appeal to researchers for several reasons. Users can browse generally or through discipline folders. Browsing the health science category produced a number of public service announcements and interviews with scientists and doctors, while personal interest videos included many railroad aficionado films. Keyword searches can quickly identify useful resources if the terms are selective enough, but the user must take care and be lucky to avoid a vast data dump, most of which is not useful. The advanced search function enables much more targeted queries by author, title, date, subject, and other typical categories singly or in combination. These searches were much more successful for ferreting out specific items and themes.

The materials are useful for teaching high school and college-level courses. The thematic range and temporal span make the collection relevant to many disciplines, courses, and student levels. Subjects and events can be teased out easily using the search functions, making the clips accessible for students conducting assignments or for accentuating lectures. Teaching with these clips is trickier. Large items load slowly, and lecturers will want to boot up the material ahead of time to avoid awkward delays while presenting material in the classroom because none of the items can be downloaded to a computer desktop. Older films are also grainy, making them poor choices for projection.

Many of the older clips are in the public domain and accessible through the Library of Congress or *Internet Archive,* but some older items are not easily available and most of the newer material is still copyright protected, including feature film and television shows such as several Ken Burns documentaries. Silent films sometimes have little documentation about the context of footage, but sound-era clips are better documented and usually include searchable transcripts. This feature is particularly notable and useful.—**Joseph E. Taylor III**

12.   **Canada In Context http://solutions.cengage.com/InContext/Canada/.** [Website] Farmington Hills, Mich. Gale/Cengage Learning. Price negotiated by site. Date reviewed: 2016.

Canada In Context is an online research resource dedicated to Canada. It pulls together reference information, academic journals, news, videos, maps, critical essays, and primary documents from a variety of sources to help researchers learn more about Canadian people, history, and contemporary issues from a Canadian perspective. It spans a range of subjects from technology to literature and sports to business. The database includes video and audio from CBC, NPR, and other authoritative sources. Articles from more than 370 Canadian publications including *Maclean's, The Toronto Star,* and *Globe and Mail* are continually added to the site.

Samples of topics include Lucy Maude Montgomery (author of *Anne of Green Gables*), Canada under British Rule, and Hockey. There are many topics that do not appear to be germane to Canada (e.g., Leonardo DaVinci, Nigeria, and the American Civil War), but these are included because study of or reference to them is made in a Canadian publication or by a Canadian author or politician. This is useful for examining the Canadian perspective on the world.

The resource can be searched by keyword or browsed by topic. There are so many topics to browse, that a helpful filter for category (e.g,. geography, government, sports, social issues, etc.) is also included. An advanced keyword search option allows users to combine keywords with title and/or publication title. Users can also limit their search to full-text or peer-reviewed journals or specify a desired document type or content type. Teachers will appreciate the ability to search by content level (beginner to advanced) and Lexile level. Educators will also appreciate the curriculum standards provided in the site which include Canadian standards among those from other English-speaking countries.

The database integrates with Google apps including Google Drive and Google Classroom. This makes it easy for both students and teachers to save documents to their own Google Drive. The ability to save to a central location is very useful. Any highlights and notes made in the database can be retained when the document is saved to Google Drive. Teachers have the added ability to save a document to their Google Classroom as an announcement or an assignment.

This dynamic resource is recommended for school and public libraries in Canada or to libraries that serve large populations with Canadian research interests. It provides an engaging way to study Canada with a wide variety of resources including multimedia.—**Kristin Kay Leeman**

13.   **Internet Archive. https://archive.org/.** [Website] Free. Date reviewed: 2016.

Internet Archive is a 501(c)(3) nonprofit Website that stores millions of books, movies, and music that can be downloaded for free. They provide "universal access to all knowledge" and offer a variety of genres for each type of media provided on the site. From animation and cartoons to spirituality and religion, *Internet Archive* is truly comprehensive.

Because this Website was founded to build an Internet library, the creators of this site have librarians, historians, scholars, and researchers in mind when broadening their collection of literature and media. *Internet Archive* creators are in charge of overseeing one of the world's largest book digitization projects and are based in three Californian cities. These digitally formatted files, of which there are more than 15 petabytes worth, can be both uploaded and downloaded directly.

Students in particular will find the clean layout welcoming and easy to use. Tabs at the top of the page allow users to choose the form of media they would like to browse and, upon selecting a form, they can choose a specific category. A search tab is beneficial for users looking for information on a particular subject. Users can hover over the *Internet Archive* symbol to find information about the organization, browse blog posts, contact the library with questions, and discover what new projects *Internet Archive* is investing in. Users can access information in multiple languages and though the site may seem advanced for those new to the internet, the intuitive design will appeal to novice and expert alike.

Librarians, students, and the general public will find this site useful. Both academic and entertainment sources can be accessed, and there is likely information on any subject users can think of. This resource is relevant and highly recommended for all.—**ARBA Staff Reviewer**

14.   **Very Short Introductions. http://www.veryshortintroductions.com/.** [Website] New York, Oxford University Press. Price negotiated by site. Date reviewed: 2015.

This online assemblage of over 400 books from Oxford's Very Short Introductions (VSI) series covers topics in the arts and humanities, law, medicine and health, science and mathematics, and social sciences. The material is easy to navigate from the home page via a quick search or a browse by subfield of all available books. For example, clicking on Human Geography under Social Sciences returns a list of five books. This search can be narrowed further by the use of a buildable search query on the left side of the screen. For example, once a book like *Modern Ireland: A Very Short Introduction* is selected, researchers will see an abstract of the book, clickable keywords that link to other publications in the VSI database, and bibliographic information including the ISBN, a digital object identifier, and online and print publication dates. A clickable table of contents below this allows users to move around in the book, while the left-hand side of the results page has links to quick reference terms like Orange Order and land tenure. Once the full text of a chapter or a book is accessed, users can take advantage of tools that enable the creation of a personal profile or citations. Citations are provided in the MLA, APA, Chicago, or AMA formats and are exportable to EndNote, ProCite, RefWorks, and more. Use of the Oxford Index Underbar allows users to find related Oxford University Press content.

The VSI database comes equipped with other special features. Under the About tab on the main page, librarians will find a variety of resources, including online support for K-12 librarians in using VSI material to meet Common Core Standards. Thirty-nine author videos and 98 author-written reading guides are also offered under the About tab, along with links to the OUPblog and VSI Facebook page. Institutional subscribers can purchase access to all or part of the VSI content, depending on library needs. This comprehensive, easily navigable collection of products is recommended for academic libraries, especially for those that do not already own print copies of the sources included in the database.—**ARBA Staff Reviewer**

Part II

SOCIAL SCIENCES

2 Social Sciences in General

General Works

Dictionaries and Encyclopedias

15. **Encyclopedia of Diversity and Social Justice.** Sherwood Thompson, ed. Lanham, Md., Rowman & Littlefield, 2015. 2v. index. $225.00/set; $224.99 (e-book). ISBN 13: 978-1-4422-1604-4; 978-1-4422-1606-8 (e-book).

One of the first of its kind, this two-volume encyclopedia wants to, "...reveal the unique nature of the language of diversity and social justice in our everyday lives..." Bringing together contributors from around the world and from different occupations this set is a good beginning to the dialogue on this topic. That being said the encyclopedia has a few shortcomings; for instance, sometimes there are two entries for the same topic for no reason. There are, for example, two entries for "Protestant Ethic" written by different contributors. There is an entry for "Appalachia" in the A section and a separate entry for "Education in Appalachia" in the E section. There is a very good entry for Creole, but lackluster entries for Genocide and Ethnic Cleansing. Entries vary in length from a few paragraphs to multiple pages. The entries are signed and contain a reference section. The volumes are hardback and have sturdy binding. The subject index is confusing because it inexplicably lists people mentioned in entries without context. As is, the set is a good addition to academic library collections. It will probably evolve into a better resource as it is updated.—**Melissa M. Johnson**

16. **Encyclopedia of Humor Studies.** Salvatore Attardo, ed. Thousand Oaks, Calif., Sage, 2014. 2v. illus. index. $370.00/set. ISBN 13: 978-1-4129-9909-0.

This wide-ranging work of over 300 entries prepared by 200 contributors explores truly diverse topics, e.g., Akan humor, Christianity, ritual clowns, Sanskrit humor, humor in psychotherapy, puns, and Molière. Eleven articles examine various periods of the "History of humor," while a 16-page chronology covers 2600 B.C.E. to 2014! The entries are "designed to be comprehensive but not exhaustive treatments" (p. xxxii) and accessible to college students. The articles examine a dozen types of humor theory and the psychology of humor and comedy, as well as the sociological dimension of the field. Each article has cross-references and a list of further readings.

Organized along the same clean lines as a number of other Sage encyclopedias published recently and edited by a scholar of the linguistic theories of humor, this set is clearly most suited to academic libraries, but could also be useful for larger public libraries.—**Mark Schumacher**

17.   **The SAGE Deaf Studies Encyclopedia.** Genie Gertz and Patrick Boudreault, eds. Thousand Oaks, Calif., Sage, 2016. 3v. illus. index. $495.00/set. ISBN 13: 978-1-4522-5956-7.

This comprehensive set of over 320 entries (in over 1050 pages) explores topics from deaf history (18 articles) and assistive technology to sign language (30 articles), linguistics, and legislation. Scores of scholars from around the world have contributed to this undertaking. Certain articles require some background knowledge of the subject matter; discussions of, for instance, Japanese Sign Language or fingerspelling suppose prior exposure to/understanding of the topic.

Some articles seem to present a distinct viewpoint on selected issues surrounding deaf studies. For instance, there are no articles on "lip reading" or "American Sign Language." An article on the latter could, for instance, provide the reader with information about its creation, development, and evolution. There is, however, an entry entitled "American Sign Language, Positive Psychological Effects of." The article on "Oralism" is quite severe at times, concerning its effects on children.

This work provides a great deal of information, on an international scope, about the world of the deaf. All libraries with students/patrons/scholars interested in the topic would benefit from acquiring this set.—**Mark Schumacher**

18.   **The SAGE Encyclopedia of Alcohol: Social, Cultural, and Historical Perspectives.** Scott C. Martin, ed. Thousand Oaks, Calif., Sage, 2015. 3v. index. $475.00/set. ISBN 13: 978-1-4833-2525-5.

The *SAGE Encyclopedia of Alcohol: Social, Cultural, and Historical Perspectives* is a unique documentation of the uses of alcohol in human societies. Taking a sociocultural approach rather than a medical stance warning against the use and abuse alcohol consumption, this title examines various cultures and their affinities for certain types of alcohol. Because alcohol has strongly impacted societies for millennia, there is much to explore in the social, cultural, historical, economic, and political realms of human history.

Included in the text is a lengthy glossary and detailed subject index for quick reference. A chronology traces the use of alcohol back to 5400 B.C.E. and the appendixes include social trends of toasting and a per capita alcohol consumption study. There are 550 entries that are organized alphabetically and are authored and signed by academics with cross-references and further readings, in addition to a helpful resource guide that highlights classic books, journals, and Websites for more specialized study.—**ARBA Staff Reviewer**

Handbooks and Yearbooks

19.   Cumo, Christopher. **The Ongoing Columbian Exchange: Stories of Biological and Economic Transfer in World History.** Santa Barbara, Calif., ABC-CLIO, 2015. 393p. illus. index. $89.00. ISBN 13: 978-1-61069-795-; 978-1-61069-796-5 (e-book).

This book (8-by-10-inch hard cover with 395 pages) covers stories of biological and economic transfer in world history. The author is well qualified. The book starts with an alphabetical list of approximately 100 entries that covers animals, plants and their derivatives, insects, and diseases. A topical list of entries is followed by the 12 primary documents utilized in writing this book. Next, the book presents a preface, introduction, and then a timeline of events from 1492 to 1943. The major portion of the book is an alphabetical discussion that explains the historical importance of each entry; discussions range from a short paragraph to several pages. A further reading of primary documents follows the discussions. The book concludes with a bibliography, index, and brief author biography.

The book is an interesting read, and it explains many of the historical events that have shaped where we are today. A few photographs illustrate the written material. The binding and paper is average, but the font is a little small for long-term reading. I would recommend this book for any agricultural, food, or history library.—**Herbert W. Ockerman**

20.   **The Gallup Poll: Public Opinion** 2013. Frank Newport, ed. Lanham, Md., Rowman & Littlefield, 2015. 524p. index. $135.00; $134.99 (e-book). ISBN 13: 978-1-4422-4132-9; 978-1-4422-4133-6 (e-book).

Here is a complete gathering of more than 500 Gallup Poll reports for the year 2013. A seminal reference, it is home to an abundance of interesting data covering topics such as patriotism, personal wealth, foreign sympathies, optimism, job engagement, presidential approval, and much more.

Reports are presented chronologically, and may include a number of charts in addition to narrative summaries providing context for the data, drawing conclusions and noting survey methods. Furthermore, reports can reflect general information gleaned from the surveys, such as how stressed Americans felt, or very specific information, such as how depression increased in areas hit the hardest by 2012's Superstorm Sandy.

As the entirety of the Gallup Poll reports date back to 1935, it would be fascinating to compare this volume with prior volumes. Users would be able to discern the trends and sharp detours in public opinion throughout the decades.

Supplementary information includes a 2013 chronology, explanations of Gallup economic indexes, and a volume index particularly relevant in terms of identifying the many topics broached by the polls. Recommended for academic and public libraries.—**Laura Herrell**

21.   **Human Rights Studies Online. http://alexanderstreet.com/products/human-rights-studies-online.** [Website] Alexandria, Va. Alexander Street Press. Price negotiated by site. Date reviewed: 2016.

Developed by an editorial board at Alexander Street Press, Human Rights Studies Online is a collection of research and learning databases. With a diverse assemblage of content types including multimedia formats, options for human rights studies are plentiful.

The worldwide database covers a broad array of human rights violations and atrocities between 1900 and 2010. The expanse of more than a century will prove useful for students seeking historical perspective. Overall, the comparative documentation, analysis, and interpretation are rich with human rights information. The databases include: 137 hours of visual media on 272 videos and 3,992 documents and books as well as related Web sources which are easily assessed. Information can be found as both primary and secondary sources.

The online collection is organized with a sidebar which will provide access from four different entryways; Browse, Discipline Perspectives, Human Rights Themes, and

Featured Playlists will provide paths to human rights data. Each area segues to other topics—for example, under the heading of Discipline Perspectives, subtopics are many and incorporate areas of diplomacy, law, and sociology, just to name a few. For those who want to narrow their search and already know their topic, search and advanced search options will give a more direct route. Filtering is key to using these online resources, and the organization is a clear advantage. A very comprehensive list of organizations is another superb option as is the Human Rights Events Content. References are easily garnered by clicking the citing tab.

Grueling subject matter, *Human Rights Studies Online* offers insight into the human struggle and horrors of the 20th century. The multiplicity of human suffering and the personal stories bring the greatest meaning to this collection. For example, authentic documentation (UNAMIR Evening Sitrep: June 12, 1994) on a daily basis from the Rwandan civil war and genocide (1994) bring not only real life data, but also the harsh realities of such atrocities. Titles such as *What We Knew: Terror, Mass Murder, and Everyday Life in Nazi Germany, An Oral History* repeatedly expose the tragedy of each individual experience and the larger implications. High quality of content is very consistent though there were instances of inferior work; *Threat of the Faithful* has dynamic information about Orthodox Jews in Israel but the double layering of subtitles is distracting.

Unfortunately, there is a vast amount of human rights tragedy in this world and this collection provides plentiful documentation of that tragedy and also the resilience of the human spirit. *Human Rights Studies Online* is a very solid online resource for high school and undergraduate students, as well as for general research. Areas of study might include: human rights, social sciences, history, or global politics.

Highly Recommended.—**Janis Minshull**

22.   **The International Handbook of Political Ecology.** Raymond L. Bryant, ed. Northampton, Mass., Edward Elgar, 2015. 699p. index. $297.00. ISBN 13: 978-0-95793-616-5.

This reference work from Edward Elgar brings together some of the best recent work in the growing field of political ecology—the study of how political, economic, and societal factors affect environmental issues. Editor Raymond L. Bryant, Professor of Political Ecology in the Department of Geography at King's College London, writes in his introductory section that "for most political ecologists, a deep ethical commitment, sometimes but not always tied to a radical personal politics, means that what really matters to them are the constraints placed by an 'unsympathetic socio-economic milieu'... on human agency and creativity, as well as on healthy environments and biodiversity." Many of the articles in this volume discuss postcolonialism, the North-South divide, and efforts to combat the exploitation of the resources of have-not communities by the rich and powerful. The 67 contributors feature many scholars from European and US universities but also from Latin America, Asia, Africa, and Australia. The articles in part two, "Issues and Approaches," include an appreciation of the foundational work of the Marxist theoretician Antonio Gramsci. The articles in part three, "Governance and Power," deal with power relations in regard to natural resources—forests, mining, water—as well as intriguing contributions on the political ecologies of religious pilgrimages and on the Fukushima nuclear disaster, the latter from a feminist perspective. Parts four, five, and six cover, respectively, knowledge and discourse, method and scale, and connections and transformations. The articles are supported by notes and references. There is a helpful list of abbreviations and an intelligently prepared index. This book is recommended for academic libraries and will be of use to both academics and activists in the field of political ecology.—**ARBA Staff Reviewer**

23. **Issues in U.S. Immigration.** 2d ed. Carl L. Bankston, III and Danielle Antoinette Hidalgo, eds. Hackensack, N.J., Salem Press, 2015. 2v. illus. index. $195.00/set. ISBN 13: 978-1-61925-708-5.

This hefty, retitled, second edition of *Immigration in U.S. History* (see ARBA 2007, entry 735) contains 215 essays, all signed by the contributors and arranged alphabetically, on "the many issues surrounding immigration—from the earliest settlement of British North America in the seventeenth century to the latest twenty-first century legislation," (p. xiv) including 75 new articles and rich supplementary material such as recent state and federal immigration statistics. Each article includes a title, brief definition, list of issues covered, dates and places if relevant, a note on significance, explanatory text, annotated "Further Reading" list and *see also* cross-references to related articles. Volume one contains a complete list of contents and of all contributors as well as a publisher's note. This volume presents 114 articles ranging from "Affordable Care Act and Undocumented Immigrants" to "Alien and Sedition Acts," "Federal Riot of 1799," "Hull House," and "Indentured Servitude." Volume two yields 101 additional articles such as "International Adoptions," "Ku Klux Klan," "Little Havana," "Sikh Immigrants," and "War Brides Act," plus "U.S. State briefs," individual essays on all 50 states together with New York City, and Washington, D.C. These state and city essays each present a profile table showing number and percentage of immigrants in each area's population and the largest immigrant groups, based on 2013 U.S. census data, an analysis of the area's significance, and an annotated book list for "Further Reading." Together, the two volumes offer more than 200 black-and-white illustrations.

The appendixes consist of an annotated bibliography (books only) and a "Time Line of U.S. Immigration History" through 2014 and are followed by the new, 100-page "Immigration Statistics" (1820-2012) section with 41 detailed tables of U.S. Department of Homeland Security, Office of Immigration Statistics data current as of 2012. Finally, the category index of topics groups related articles into 37 broader categories while the more traditional alphabetical subject index provides page numbers for specific keywords including names, events, laws, places, groups, and organizations.

Readers may quarrel over specific topic selections or omissions, but this well-designed set is broad in scope and content and deserves a place in high school, public, community college, and many university libraries. Given the great current interest in U.S. immigration issues, these two volumes should help stimulate and support additional research on many, diverse, immigration-related topics.—**Julienne L. Wood**

24. **Procon.org. http://www.procon.org/.** [Website] Free. Date reviewed: 2016.

Procon.org is a Website that provides comprehensive information about controversial topics popular in contemporary discourse. The homepage has links to discussions about each issue clearly divided into topics such as health and medicine, education, politics, science and technology, and more, including a section featuring the most popular issues. When a link is selected, a wealth of information about each issue becomes available to view, including an introduction, a "did you know" set of facts, ample arguments in favor of and opposed to arguments, a thorough background essay about the issue, and videos featuring news clips and speeches. Additional features include a teacher's corner, reader comments, in-the-news articles, and access to the bulletin board of the procon.org office. Overall, the site provides a wealth of information to teenagers and adults interested in educating themselves about hot-button issues and polarizing topics.

This resource is especially useful to students who are writing persuasive essays, as well as individuals who want to learn as much as possible about an issue before casting a vote for a candidate or a ballot measure. This is due to the accessible nature of the writing, and the visual layout of the Website, which enables the researcher to easily access any relevant and accurate information. There is some variation in format between topics, in that some issues have a straightforward and color-coded pro/con layout, and other topics have links to essays that explore the topic but do not include the color-coded visual graphic. There is also the issue of providing false balance to topics such as vaccines, though the treatment on the Website remains overwhelmingly unbiased.

Procon.org is easy to navigate, filled with a near-overwhelming amount of content, and curated in a manner that makes information easy to access and cite. It is highly recommended to public and academic libraries, individual users, and schools.—**ARBA Staff Reviewer**

25. **The SAGE Handbook of Research Management.** Robert Dingwall and Mary Byrne McDonnell, eds. Thousand Oaks, Calif., Sage, 2015. 631p. illus. index. $175.00. ISBN 13: 978-1-4462-0318-7.

The SAGE Handbook of Research Management is recommended to "early to mid-career researchers in the social sciences and humanities who are looking to scale up their work and create research groups, or who are being asked to do this by the research organization, usually a university, for which they work." Others who would benefit include doctoral students or postdoctorals "who are thinking about their career strategy." This handbook is comprised of essays designed to assist research managers, written by experienced research leaders and specialists. The essays in the book are arranged within the following categories: Getting Started; Developing the Proposal; Getting Organized; Managing in Different Environments; Managing the People; Planning for Impact; Delivering Impact; and Beyond the Current Project. The essays progress from preparing for a research career to getting funded through developing the budget through promoting teamwork through dissemination of the results and analysis of the qualities of successful research management. The contributors are from agencies and organizations which include the Social Science Research Council, the Sociometrics Corporation, University of Michigan, Tulane University, Cardiff University, and George Mason University. According to its editors, the book is "not designed to be read cover to cover" but it can be used as a reference guide or the basis for a series of workshops "organized around each block of chapters." Case studies are included throughout the book and bibliographic notes and an index are provided. Overall, *The SAGE Handbook of Research Management* should prove to be a valuable guide to researchers, grant writing, developing proposals, and teamwork. It is recommended to academic and research libraries.—**Lucy Heckman**

26. **The Statesman's Yearbook 2015: The Politics, Cultures and Economies of the World.** Barry Turner, ed. New York, Palgrave Macmillan, 2014. 1588p. illus. maps. index. $350.00. ISBN 13: 978-1-13732-324-8.

This long-standing title, begun during the American Civil War, remains extremely useful today for its political, economic, and sociocultural information. Its organization is straightforward, presenting information first on scores of international organizations (both worldwide like the United Nations and regional like the Organization of American States), then entries on the 194 countries of the world, with geographical subdivisions for the United Kingdom, India, Canada, and the United States, among others. From biographies of the current political leaders (e.g., the president and prime minister of France) to population tables by region within a country and summaries of social institutions, this volume provides concise but accurate details about many aspects of the world's nations. A brief "Further Reading" section provides other resources, and occasionally Internet sites. Highly recommended to those libraries who can afford to purchase it. It is also available in an online format at **http://www.statesmansyearbook.com/**.—**Mark Schumacher**

3 Area Studies

General Works

Handbooks and Yearbooks

27.   **Nations of the World, 2015: A Political, Economic, and Business Handbook.** 14th ed. Amenia, N.Y., Grey House Publishing, 2015. 2153p. maps. $180.00pa. ISBN 13: 978-1-61925-288-2.

This comprehensive handbook profiles every country and self-governing territory in the world from Afghanistan to Zimbabwe with the goal of providing readers with a clear view of the country's political, economic, and business situations. The book provides an abundance of useful details in an easy to follow format. This 14th edition has been updated with new information relative to changing political climates.

Each country's entry opens with an overview of the current political environment, covering nation-specific topics such as corruption in Bosnia and Herzegovina, Hong Kong's strained relationship with mainland China, or the strong demand for fishing licenses in Kiribati, for example. A Country Profile section presents a general timeline of significant political events followed by a breakdown of a country's governing and civil structures, such as form of state, legal system, political parties, education, ethnicities, media, agriculture, tourism, and banking. Information is ample and the directory employs many headings and subheadings for clarity. Some country profiles include a category new to this edition—People to Watch—which highlights individual newsmakers. Each country's entry concludes with a business directory listing contact information for a number of ministries, chambers, organizations, news agencies, and more.

Shaded sidebars house key facts where readers can find data and statistics fast, like land area, head of state, official language, etc., as well as economic data like exchange rate, GDP, and unemployment rate. Most every profile has a country map and two tables reflecting risk assessment and key economic indicators.

The work concludes with the essay "The World in 2014," which provides a generalized, global, and rather "gloomy" outlook, then moves on to five regional profiles providing summaries, a regional map, and two tables displaying currency values against the U.S. dollar and key indicators.

An invaluable reference for business travelers, government officials, researchers, and more.—**ARBA Staff Reviewer**

United States

General Works

Dictionaries and Encyclopedias

28.   **Worldmark Encyclopedia of the States.** 8th ed. Farmington Hills, Mich., Gale/ Cengage Learning, 2016. 2v. index. $370.00/set. ISBN 13: 978-1-4144-3396-7; 978-1- 4103-3344-5 (e-book).

A familiar component of undergraduate reference, Gale's latest edition of the *Worldmark Enyclopedia of the States* continues to provide a detailed overview of each state as well as the District of Columbia, Puerto Rico, and the U.S. dependencies in the Caribbean and the Pacific Ocean.

The information one would expect to find about each state is available in this text: maps, flags, state seals, etc. However, this set is more than just an almanac of ready reference facts. This set also provides information on a range of topics from mining to securities, health to social welfare, from press to tourism. Each entry also contains its own bibliography, a hallmark of all encyclopedias published by Gale/Cengage. Most helpful, though, is the way both the print and online versions are arranged within each entry. Each entry has the same 50 subheadings, always arranged in the same order. These subheadings have a small number next to them so that patrons can quickly skim multiple entries for the same subject. As an example, number 43 always refers to Libraries and Museums and so readers can quickly find just that specific information.

A compact two volumes in print, this set is a good addition to any undergraduate, community college, and public library reference collection, providing a lot of information but not taking up too much shelf space. Overall, whether in print or online, the *Worldmark Encyclopedia of the States* is useful for ready reference and for readers at the beginning of their research.—**Rachel Meredith Minkin**

Handbooks and Yearbooks

29.   **Profiles of America: Facts, Figures, Statistics for Every Populated Place in the United States.** 3d ed. Amenia, N.Y., Grey House Publishing, 2015. 4v. maps. index. $795.00pa/set. ISBN 13: 978-1-61925-105-2.

This ready reference set of facts, figures, and statistics is thorough in its treatment of each place and comprehensive, including every populated place in the United States. Twelve data fields are new to this edition, including health insurance, median travel time to work, and median age. Each data field can be easily traced back to its source using the "Data Explanation and Sources" in the "User Guide" in every volume. Sources include the Census Bureau, other government agencies, and nongovernment sources. Places that the U.S. Census Bureau designates as Census Designated Places, Minor Civil Divisions, or unincorporated communities are included. The "Regional and Comparative Statistics" section of each volume takes 14 data fields and ranks them for the 100 largest cities in the region. "Regional Rankings" provide rankings for those same pieces of data. Information that may be a column in "Regional and Comparative Statistics" will be a page of data in the "Regional Rankings." To properly analyze the information and understand how these fit together, the "Data Explanation and Sources" in the user guide should be consulted. "Regional Rankings" assists individuals from a particular background to find communities that share that background.

The set has four regional volumes: Southern Region, Western Region, Central Region, and Eastern Region. Within each region, information is organized alphabetically by state, by county, and by place. Each state includes an index of the places in that state with their county and page number. In volume one, Southern Region, is the master index for all four volumes giving the volume, county, and page number.

Although the listings for each place are easy to use and understand by the general public and undergraduate students, other portions, such as the "Regional and Comparative Statistics" and the "Regional Rankings," require more expertise to properly interpret and analyze the data. Highly recommended for all academic and public libraries.—**Ladyjane Hickey**

California

30.   **Compare 50. http://compare50.org/.** [Website] Free. Date reviewed: 2015.

Compare 50 is a Next 10 Project, which is "focused on innovation and the intersection between the economy, the environment, and quality of life issues for all Californians." It is a data tool that allows users to compare all 50 states and gauge differences in the topics of Economy, Innovation, Jobs, Income & Equity, and Demographics. Users simply select a topic and the states they wish to compare, then click the "submit" button for a graph chart that displays the information. It is also possible to select states to compare to the national average. All graphs can be downloaded in PNG, JPEG, and SVG image forms as well as in a PDF document, a useful feature for students who need visuals for presentations.

Overall, the site is simple and does not overwhelm the user. Apart from the bar at the top of the page including the main categories for search, there is not much else to click on. An index page provides shortcuts to all searchable subcategories and applicable data series, but this feature is best used for users who don't have a specific search in mind and are simply curious about the variety of information available on the Website. Otherwise, the topics on the bar at the top of the page contain the same information and would be more useful for users who want to carry out a specific search. To provide clarification, there is a technical notes tab below each graph that users can click on to obtain more information about statistical measurements and terminology, as well as general clarification for users who are less familiar with statistics.

While this site contains visually appealing and easy-to-read statistics and graphs, it unfortunately only includes data from 1990 to 2011, making it outdated enough to hinder users. Those who require updated information beyond 2011 will have to find another source. Another drawback is the format of the information, which is limited to the graph. Students who need to compare multiple states or record multiple numbers will have to hover the mouse directly over the state and the year on the graph in order to obtain the number they want, and then record it independently. This is time consuming, and it would therefore be helpful to have the numbers and any other relevant chart information recorded in document form somewhere else on the page, perhaps directly under the chart.

Compare 50 is a free Website and may be useful for students, academics, and researchers who need comparative reference sources.—**ARBA Staff Reviewer**

31.   **Profiles of California.** 4th ed. Amenia, N.Y., Grey House Publishing, 2015. 988p. maps. $149.00pa. ISBN 13: 978-1-61925-815-0; 978-1-61925-816-7 (e-book).

Based on data from the 2010 U.S. census and the American Community Survey, demographic data includes all geographic areas for which the U.S. census provides individual statistics. It is the "most comprehensive portrait ... published." The user guide starts with a data explanation of the sources used, the rankings, and the information presented in each section of the material. It has seven sections: About California, Profiles, Comparative Statistics, Community Rankings, Education, Ancestry and Ethnicity, and Climate. Most of the material is alphabetical by place; other parts of the material are lists by rank. This is one of the best sources for those considering relocating to California.

The first section of this reference work, About California, is an overview that can be found in many reference works. Education compares public school district rankings and the state test results. This section is by rank while the listing includes the school district with the place-name. The Climate section has a descriptive overview and relief map; however, most of the material is organized by the weather station with its location and the data it collected. Profiles has descriptive information on the usual demographic data; and, it includes air quality, ancestry, health care, health insurance, religion, and transportation. The communities within each county vary in what information is provided. The counties are in alphabetical order; the communities within each county are in alphabetical order; and an alphabetical place index is here. The Profiles comprise a third of the content. Comparative Statistics compares specific characteristics, such as health insurance, from the 100 largest cities in easily read tables. The cities are in alphabetical order. This is followed by the Community Rankings section that compares data for incorporated places having a population of 10,000 or more. For areas with larger populations, users will look at both; but, smaller places are included in the Community Rankings only. In this section, the arrangement is by rank while the listing is by place-name with the county. For example, population with health insurance, population with private health insurance, population with public health insurance, population with no health insurance, and population under 18 years old with no health insurance are new data in this edition. In the Comparative Statistics, these health insurance data are column headings. In the Community Rankings, they are separate lists by rank. In Ancestry and Ethnicity, Place Profiles includes demographic information for the state, counties, and cities. Ancestry Group Rankings lists the place of ancestry in alphabetical order with the top 10 places in California whose population is from that place. Each place has three separate lists, sorted differently. Hispanic Origin Rankings and Racial Group Rankings are presented similarly. The Ancestry and Ethnicity section is another third of the content.

Highly recommended for high school libraries in California and for public and academic libraries throughout the nation. High school students may need assistance using the Ancestry Group Rankings section of the data; but, they should easily negotiate searches in all the material listed by place or rank.—**Ladyjane Hickey**

Massachusetts

32. **Profiles of Massachusetts, 2015.** 4th ed. Amenia, N.Y., Grey House Publishing, 2015. 800p. maps. $149.00pa. ISBN 13: 978-1-61925-573-9; 978-1-61925-574-6 (e-book).

The fourth edition of this expansive regional resource covers over 600 places, including 351 incorporated municipalities, 104 unincorporated communities, and other lesser-known population centers within the Commonwealth of Massachusetts. This edition derives most of its information from the U.S. Census Bureau's 2010 census, but enhances this data from other sources as well, such as the U.S. Census Bureau's American Community Survey 2009-13, Five Year Estimates, County Business Patterns 2012, U.S. Geological Survey, and several others. The extensive amount of data gathered for this publication makes it the "most comprehensive portrait of the state of Massachusetts ever published."

The material is organized into seven clearly demarked sections. The four-color About Massachusetts section employs maps, charts, a photo collection, and more to give users an overall sense of the state's history, government, geography, and demographics. The main Profiles section, organized by county, offers current government statistics in addition to original research for each place in the state (as outlined above) reflecting data on such topics as ancestry, housing, economy, education, and religion. The fourth edition of *Profiles in Massachusetts* includes new categories concerning health insurance, languages spoken at home, military veterans, and residents with disabilities. There is also a helpful place-name index at the end of this section.

Other sections address Comparative Statistics, Community Rankings (also new to the fourth edition), Education, Ancestry and Ethnicity, and Climate. Key to understanding all of this data is the vastly helpful user guide found at the beginning of the book. It, too, is separated into four sections and provides information, such as definitions and sources, for all covered data items.

Readers looking for historical, demographic, and statistical insight into this New England state will find abundant information in this hefty, recommended resource.— **Laura Herrell**

Michigan

33. **Profiles of Michigan, 2015.** 4th ed. Amenia, N.Y., Grey House Publishing, 2015. 835p. maps. $149.00pa. ISBN 13: 978-1-61925-567-8; 978-1-61925-568-5 (e-book).

This reference book (one of 15 titles in Grey House Publishing's Profiles of series) contains the sort of geographical statistical data you would have referred to before the Internet came around and now might write off because of that—don't be fooled. While most of this data has been gathered from disparate freely available online sources (mostly the U.S. census), its value lies in being presented here in one organized volume. New for this fourth edition is an expanded Profiles chapter containing statistics on health insurance coverage, language spoken at home, people with disabilities, and veterans, as well as a place-name index. An entirely new section, Community Rankings (for populations of 10,000 or more), has been added, covering topics such as occupations, income, ancestry, rent, and race, ranked in ascending and descending order for the top (or bottom) 150 communities. The user guide explains and cites the data sources used for each chapter. The handful of color reproductions are of good quality, but most of those in black and white are poor quality.—**Bruce Sarjeant**

New Jersey

34. **Profiles of New Jersey, 2015.** 4th ed. Amenia, N.Y., Grey House Publishing, 2015. 800p. illus. maps. $149.00pa. ISBN 13: 978-1-61925-571-5; 978-1-61925-572-2 (e-book).

The fourth edition of this expansive regional resource covers over 800 places, including 565 incorporated municipalities, 93 unincorporated communities, and other lesser-known population centers within the state of New Jersey. This edition derives most of its information from the U.S. Census Bureau's 2010 census, but enhances this data from other sources as well, such as the U.S. Census Bureau's American Community Survey 2009-13, Five Year Estimates, County Business Patterns 2012, U.S. Geological Survey, and several others. The extensive amount of data gathered for this publication makes it the "most comprehensive portrait of the state of New Jersey ever published."

The material is organized into seven clearly demarked sections. The four-color About New Jersey section employs maps, charts, a photo, and more to give users an overall sense of the state's history, government, geography, and demographics. The main Profiles section, organized by county, offers current government statistics in addition to original research for each place in the state (as outlined above) reflecting data on such topics as ancestry, housing, economy, education, and religion. The fourth edition of *Profiles in New Jersey* includes new categories concerning health insurance, languages spoken at home, military veterans, and residents with disabilities. There is also a helpful place-name index at the end of this section.

Other sections address Comparative Statistics, Community Rankings (also new to the fourth edition), Education, Ancestry and Ethnicity, and Climate. Key to understanding all of this data is the vastly helpful user guide found at the beginning of the book. It, too, is separated into four sections and provides information, such as definitions and sources, for all covered data items.

Readers looking for varied historical, demographic, and statistical insight into the state of New Jersey will find abundant information in this hefty, recommended resource.—**Laura Herrell**

New York

35. **Profiles of New York State, 2015/2016.** 11th ed. Amenia, N.Y., Grey House Publishing, 2015. 968p. illus. index. $149.00pa. ISBN 13: 978-1-61925-565-4.

This fascinating 11th edition of *Profiles of New York State—History, Statistics, Demographics for 2,574 Populated Places in New York including Comparative Statistics & Rankings,* provides the reader the statistics and demographics of the populated areas of New York, and the ability to compare one place to another. Published by the award-winning Grey House Publishing, this title is useful on so many levels.

Organized for the best possible effect, the material is reliable and interesting in 968 pages. *Profiles of New York State* has a useful table of contents that enables the user to navigate the vast amount of data available; a helpful user's guide; key facts about New York; a photo gallery; a timeline of New York State history; demographic information; government information; land and natural resources information; profiles of place and comparative statistics; community rankings; ancestry; climate; and education.

A great example of a typical New York State place is the village of Herkimer in Herkimer County with a 2000 Census population of 7,743. This village is world-renowned for Herkimer Diamonds (actually clear quartz). The average per capita income was $19,207, the poverty rate was 24.9%, and the average household income was $41,494. Of the total population, 82.9% of people commuted to work by car; 47.6% of people owned their homes that carried a median value of $80,200 and had a median build date of 1940. The school district of 1,177 students is the Herkimer Central School District.

This title, by Grey House Publishing, is a companion piece to the *New York State Directory;* the two titles are available as a set.—**Scott R. DiMarco**

North Carolina

36.   **Profiles of North Carolina & South Carolina, 2015.** 3d ed. Amenia, N.Y., Grey House Publishing, 2015. 1055p. $149.00pa. ISBN 13: 978-1-61925-138-0; 978-1-61925-157-1 (e-book).

The third edition of this expansive regional resource provides data for over 1,300 populated places within the states of North Carolina and South Carolina. These places are comprised of incorporated municipalities, Census Designated Places (CDPs), and unincorporated communities (or postal areas). Most of the data has been gathered from the U.S. Census Bureau's American Community Survey, 2009-2013 in addition to the long-form 2010 census, but other focused surveys are used as well. The addition of new data categories, rankings, and supplemental historical and general information helps to make this volume the "most comprehensive portrait of the states of North Carolina and South Carolina ever published."

Within each state's report (North Carolina's precedes South Carolina's), the material is organized into seven clearly demarcated sections. The four-color About North (South) Carolina section employs maps, timelines, charts, a photo collection, and more to give users an overall sense of the state's history, government, geography, and demographics. The main Profiles section, organized by county, offers current government statistics in addition to original research for each place in the state (as outlined above) reflecting data on such topics as ancestry, housing, economy, education, and religion. This third edition includes new categories regarding public and private health insurance, veterans, language(s) spoken at home, and people with disabilities. There is also a helpful place-name index at the end of this section. Other sections include Comparative Statistics, Community Rankings (new to this edition), Education (including state profile and school district rankings), Ancestry and Ethnicity, and Climate.

Key to understanding all of this data is the vastly helpful user guide found at the beginning of the volume. It, too, is separated into four sections and provides information such as definitions and sources for all covered data items.

Readers looking for historical, demographic, and statistical insight into these two southern states will find abundant information in this generous and well-researched resource.—**ARBA Staff Reviewer**

Ohio

37.   **Profiles of Ohio, 2015.** 4th ed. Amenia, N.Y., Grey House Publishing, 2015. 640p. maps. $149.00. ISBN 13: 978-1-61925-569-2; 978-1-61925-570-8 (e-book).

This is the fourth edition of *Profiles of Ohio* (see ARBA 2007, entry 75; ARBA 2009, entry 79; ARBA 2013, entry 83). This title presents data on the history, statistics, and demographics for all the populated communities and counties in Ohio for which the U.S. census provides statistics in addition to data on 132 unincorporated places in the state.

The book begins with a general user guide and three sectional user guides for education, ancestry and ethnicity, and climate. These are followed by About Ohio, section one, where users can find information about key facts and state emblems; color photographs that represent the state; a brief history of Ohio; information on government, land, and natural resources; and full-color demographic maps. Following this is the second section, State Profiles, organized alphabetically by county and based on data from the 2010 census and American Community Survey along with current government statistics and original research. This section presents information about a county's geography, ancestry, economy, housing, transportation, industry, education, population, health insurance, religion, climate, national and state parks, and schools. An alphabetical place index wraps up this portion. Section three, Comparative Statistics, uses dozens of data points to compare Ohio's 100 largest communities. Next, a new section called Community Rankings looks at places with population of over 10,000 and ranks the top 150 and bottom 150 in dozens of categories like population density, black/African American population, population under age 18, and rental vacancy rate. Those interested in education statistics will find school district ratings in the fifth section, along with National Assessment of Education Progress and State Report Card data. The sixth part, Ancestry and Ethnicity, provides a wealth of information about ancestry and ethnicity in the Buckeye State. The final section, Climate, includes maps, a list of weather stations by county, weather station rankings, and more.

This title, densely packed with vital information, is recommended for libraries in Ohio. Free online access is available to buyers of this fourth edition.—**ARBA Staff Reviewer**

Puerto Rico

38.   Méndez-Méndez, Serafín, and Ronald Fernández. **Puerto Rico Past and Present: An Encyclopedia.** 2d ed. Santa Barbara, Calif., Greenwood Press/ABC-CLIO, 2015. 449p. illus. index. $100.00. ISBN 13: 978-1-4408-2831-7; 978-1-4408-2832-4 (e-book).

The first edition of this work (see ARBA 2009, entry 93) was one of the earliest reference works to exclusively focus on Puerto Rico. This edition, which contains more than 185 entries, provides an overview of the island's history and culture from the twentieth century to the present. The depth of coverage within each of the essays varies widely. Educational topics, for example, are extremely detailed. Others, like "Economy," provide the bare essentials. Although the economy article does not paint a pretty picture, it does not address the depths of Puerto Rico's economic calamities which have its leadership exploring legal means to declare bankruptcy. Another significant weakness is its lack of attention to Puerto Rico's history prior to it becoming a possession of the United States. For instance, there is no entry for the Spanish American War. That conflict saw Puerto Rico invaded by the United States military. Important economic engines from the past, like the coffee industry, are likewise forgotten. Despite these shortcomings, this work is appropriate for public and school libraries.—**John R. Burch Jr.**

Africa

General Works

Dictionaries and Encyclopedias

39.   **Africa: An Encyclopedia of Culture and Society.** Toyin Falola and Daniel Jean-Jacques, eds. Santa Barbara, Calif., ABC-CLIO, 2015. 3v. index. $294.00/set. ISBN 13: 978-1-59884-665-2; 978-1-59884-666-9 (e-book).

African culture and society is as rich and diverse as the African continent itself, from its indigenous development to the internal and external forces that have permanently shaped its varied sociocultural landscape. While many of those transformations have been at great cost to human life and treasure, the achievements of African socioculture continue to evolve at a pace that is unbridled in both stride and form. It is fortuitous, then, that this three-volume encyclopedia is geared specifically toward students and nonscholars who are just beginning to learn about African society and its corresponding culture.

The three volumes total 54 entries written by scholars who are from institutions spanning three continents and who are either African themselves or who have lived in Africa. Each entry describes an African country and any associated islands and includes a corresponding black-and-white map (with major cities plotted). The entries are ordered alphabetically, beginning with Algeria and ending with Zimbabwe, and include brief snippets of factual information (capital cities, types of government, and the like). Each entry is divided into 15 culturally relevant subtopics, ranging from the typical (religion, social customs, and literary and oral traditions) to the specialized (cuisine and accompanying recipes, sports and games, and media). Included with each entry is a brief introduction of its respective country's geography, ethnic communities, and language(s). On that note, the first volume includes a comprehensive introduction in which Africa's geographical and historical background is explicated according to its five regional divisions (North, East, West, Central, and Southern); a comprehensive but concise chronology of African history (40,000 B.C.E. to 2014); and one map each of the continent's topography and geography, although, as with the other maps throughout the encyclopedia, both are in black and white and thus rather one-dimensional. Duly, the third volume includes an extensive index and complete bibliography.

Given the editors' stated purpose of placidly introducing students and readers to the scope and essence of African socioculture, a useful addition to the front matter in the first volume could be a small section that explains how to use and interpret the encyclopedia beyond its A to Z arrangement. Moreover, a wider selection of photos might lend the encyclopedia a more dynamic tone than do the current black-and-white photos, of which there are a modest amount. Nonetheless, the encyclopedia is all-inclusive, well-organized, informative, and expressed in a straightforward and easy-to-digest writing style.—**Sheri Edwards**

Handbooks and Yearbooks

40.   **Countries, Peoples & Cultures: Eastern & Southern Africa.** Michael Shally-Jensen, ed. Hackensack, N.J., Salem Press, 2015. 586p. illus. maps. index. (Countries, Peoples & Cultures, Volume 6). $125.00. ISBN 13: 978-1-61925-782-5.

This sixth volume in the nine-volume Countries, Peoples & Cultures series focuses on 23 distinct countries in eastern and southern Africa, including Botswana, Djibouti, Kenya, Rwanda, Somalia, Tanzania, and Zimbabwe to name a few, aiming to provide readers with a sound understanding of a large amount of material.

An introduction provides a good overview which helps readers grasp the scale of the information concerning economics, politics, cultures, and more in the very different countries described in this volume. The material for each country is well organized into several categories: General Information, Environment and Geography, Customs and Courtesies, Lifestyle, Cultural History, Culture, Society, Social Development, Government, and Economy. These categories are further subdivided. For example, the Cultural History section discusses art, architecture, drama, music, and literature.

Readers will also find the country's flag, as well as fast facts, statistics, and maps depicting major cities, landmarks, and regional location. Color photographs sprinkled throughout the volume add interest. Country essays, at approximately 15 pages each, provide current details about youth culture, food, women's issues, and language, among other things.

Two extensive appendixes, World Governments and World Religions, close out the volume (the same appendixes appear in each volume of the series). World Governments describes 21 different forms of government and includes a list of current examples and a bibliography. The second appendix provides information about faiths like Islam and Christianity, explaining basic tenets, religious leaders, and religious philosophy. These essays also include bibliographies. An index rounds out the work.—**ARBA Staff Reviewer**

41.   **Countries, Peoples & Cultures: Western & Central Africa.** Michael Shally-Jensen, ed. Hackensack, N.J., Salem Press, 2015. 618p. illus. maps. index. (Countries, Peoples & Cultures, Volume 7). $125.00. ISBN 13: 978-1-61925-784-9.

This offering from Salem Press is the seventh volume of a nine-volume series on cultural, social, economic, and religious practices of "nearly every country around the globe," as the publisher's note says. Twenty-five nations in West and Central Africa are examined, from Angola to Togo. Each country profile includes two color maps, one of the country itself and another showing it in its regional setting; a picture and description of its flag; and one or more color pictures of art objects or natural features. A brief introduction to the profile is followed by general information such as the country's population, currency, ethnic groups, languages, and climate. Then come the following sections: Environment and Geography (topography, plants, and animals); Customs and Courtesies; Lifestyle; Cultural History; Culture; Society; Social Development; Government; and Economy. There is a shaded box giving the principal cities by population, and another box providing a few factoids specific to the country. Finally there is a fairly brief bibliography on each country and a list of works cited. There is an index and two appendixes totaling some 110 pages, the first on world governments and the second on world religions—the same appendixes appear in all the volumes of this series. The book is attractively designed and could be of interest to general readers, travelers, and students seeking a quick synopsis of the life and culture of Western and Central Africa.—**Alice Chaffee**

Nigeria

Handbooks and Yearbooks

42.   Falola, Toyin, and Bukola Adeyemi Oyeniy. **Nigeria.** Santa Barbara, Calif., ABC-CLIO, 2015. 412p. maps. index. (Africa in Focus series). $89.00. ISBN 13: 978-1-59884-968-4; 978-1-59884-969-1 (e-book).

This book from ABC-CLIO's Africa in Focus series provides a richly textured account of the history, peoples, culture, and struggles of Africa's most populous nation. Authors Toyin Falola, professor at the University of Texas at Austin, and Bukola Adeyemi Oyeniyi of Missouri State University draw on their deep knowledge of Nigeria in describing the country's enormous strengths and human, cultural, and economic resources while acknowledging its weaknesses. Nigeria, which the British established as a single state by force in the 1860's in order to facilitate their economic position, gained its independence in 1960. The decades since have been marked by periods of conflict between and among the three major peoples—Igbo, Hausa, and Yoruba. There is a major religious divide, as the Hausa are predominantly Muslim and Christianity is widespread among the other ethnic groups. The book outlines Nigeria's history, delineates its various types of civil and military rule, describes its economic development, and delves deeply into its society and culture. Chapters on social classes and ethnicity, women and marriage, language, and the arts give the reader a great deal of detailed information. The book's last section discusses the continuing problem of integrating widely different ethnic groups, the threat posed by the terrorist movement Boko Haram, the prevalence of bribery and corruption, and other contemporary issues. The book has numerous black-and-white photographs, 35 pages of statistics, a glossary, a holiday chart and a list of country-related organizations, an annotated bibliography, and an index. One minor shortcoming is the lack of a chronology. Students and general readers will find this book a most valuable resource on a country of growing world importance.—**Alice Chaffee**

Asia

General Works

Handbooks and Yearbooks

43.   **Countries, Peoples & Cultures: Central, South & Southeast Asia.** Michael Shally-Jensen, ed. Hackensack, N.J., Salem Press, 2015. 630p. (Countries, Peoples & Cultures, Volume 2). $125.00. ISBN 13: 978-1-61925-788-7; 978-1-61925-789-4 (e-book).

Increased globalization has pulled in its wake increased travel and interaction between people from different countries and backgrounds. The increase in travel may be due to economic or political factors, and may stimulate greater leisure travel. As a result, the leisure travel industry now offers travelers more locations and options. Travelers, in turn, need specific information about potential vacation destinations and some may even be looking for overviews about the countries they are considering.

This work is the second of nine volume series and covers 20 countries which include the Asian former Soviet republics, Indian subcontinent, and Southeast Asia (from Burma to East Timor). Each country is covered in about 20 pages focusing on the geographical, economic, cultural, social, historical, and political profile. Each of these sections is clearly titled, and each section is further divided into subsections. For most of these countries the focus is after independence, and, more specifically, the early twenty-first century. Plant and animal life receive a special focus under the Geography section. An entire section called Customs and Courtesies covers popular greetings, gestures, etiquette, popular dishes and eating customs, and socializing. In addition, water conservation, women's rights, and human rights are covered in their respective subsections. One appendix summarizes the types of governments in the world devoting two pages per category. Another appendix outlines major world religions devoting six to seven pages per religious belief.

This reference is geared towards providing travelers (specifically leisure travelers) an overview of the countries they wish to visit. Everyday greetings and gestures, common meals and eating traditions, social structure, cultural norms, tourist sites, and a bias towards contemporary developments provide travelers with a good foundation. Recommended for those who love to travel or want to evaluate several vacation destinations.—**Muhammed Hassanali**

44.   **Countries, Peoples & Cultures: East Asia & the Pacific.** Michael Shally-Jensen, ed. Hackensack, N.J., Salem Press, 2015. 534p. illus. maps. index. (Countries, Peoples & Cultures, Volume 9). $125.00. ISBN 13: 978-1-61925-790-0.

This book is part of a new nine-volume series exploring the social, cultural, historical, religious, and economic story of most every country in the world. This ninth volume focuses on six distinct countries in East Asia (China, Japan, Mongolia, Taiwan, and the Koreas), in addition to the large country of Australia and 13 island countries (New Zealand, Samoa, Fiji, etc.) spread throughout the waters of the Pacific. Overall, the volume conveys the stories of 20 countries within the area.

The introduction provides a good overview which helps readers grasp the scale of the information concerning the very different countries described in this volume. The book then presents the essays on the East Asian nations, followed by the essays covering Australia and the island nations. Within each country's essay, readers will find a variety of umbrella ideas which do well to organize the material: General Information, Environment and Geography, Customs and Courtesies, Lifestyle, Cultural History, Culture, Society, Social Development, Government, and Economy. Particular topics then fill in the narrative under each umbrella idea. For example, the Economy section begins with an overview, followed by discussions on industry, labor, energy, agriculture, and tourism, among other topics. Readers will also find the country's flag, as well as fast facts, statistics, and maps depicting major cities, landmarks, and regional location. Color photographs are used sparingly throughout the volume. Each country's essay concludes with a thorough bibliography. Essays average about 15 pages long, and truly provide an informative snapshot of each country, filled with current details about youth culture, food, women's issues, language, and much more.

Two rather lengthy appendixes close out the volume (and are the same in all volumes of the series). World Governments describes 21 types of governments employed throughout all regions of the world today, including parliamentary monarch, communist, and so forth. Each description exposes the guiding premise behind the government, its typical structure, and the role of the citizen. Each essay also includes a list of current examples and a bibliography. The second appendix, World Religions, presents essays on 10 of the world's most-practiced faiths like Islam, Christianity, and Jainism. Each essay offers a general description of the faith in addition to a number of topics like basic tenets, major figures, and philosophical basis. These essays also include bibliographies.

The structure and scope of this series makes it ideal for secondary school students across several disciplines, including history and geography.—**ARBA Staff Reviewer**

Afghanistan

Handbooks and Yearbooks

45.   **Afghanistan   Online: http://www.afghan-web.com/.**   [Website]   Free.   Date reviewed: 2015.

Afghanistan Online is a privately owned Website that provides news and information about everything Afghanistan. It was launched in 1997 and claims to be the most-used Afghan Website on the Internet today. It provides information on numerous topics and is updated frequently to stay relevant.

While the Website offers access to a variety of information, advertisements clutter the look and make navigation difficult; ads are usually pertinent to the Website content, forcing users to question whether or not clickables will lead to spam or relevant external pages. Users can look to the left side of the homepage to find dozens of links to locate legitimate informational pages about entertainment, culture, history, education, travel, health, Islam, and much more. Each link provides something different and exciting. The weather link informs the reader about current weather in various locations throughout Afghanistan, while the food link provides access to dozens of delicious recipes. Though there is no glossary, a search tab allows users to type in inquiries and subjects of interest, and questions can be directed to the Website host via email under the "contact us" tab.

The Website has received many awards of excellence since its launch and continues to provide comprehensive information about Afghanistan, which is its main appeal. Though it will undoubtedly appeal to those interested in the culture, it is not recommended for use as an academic resource.—**ARBA Staff Reviewer**

China

Handbooks and Yearbooks

46.   Li, Xiaobing. **Modern China.** Santa Barbara, Calif., ABC-CLIO, 2015. 419p. illus. maps. index. (Understanding Modern Nations). $89.00. ISBN 13: 978-1-61069-625-8; 978-1-56720-761-3 (e-book).

This interdisciplinary work focuses mainly on China's rise to become the second largest economy in the world during the 1980s through the 2010s. The author closely examines China's transformation from a third-world country to a modernized nation, taking into consideration Chinese values and attitudes towards social transition and economic growth, as well as identifying key elements behind China's modernization. Following a brief introduction, the book is organized into 16 chapters addressing topics ranging from history, politics, and government to economy, media, and popular culture. Each chapter contains an overview, followed by entries on important events, major issues of contemporary relevance, biographies pertaining to the chapter's theme, and ending with cross-references and further readings. The volume concludes with a selected bibliography, an alphabetical index, and four appendixes, consisting of a day in the life, a glossary of key terms, facts and figures, and a holidays chart. By exhibiting a Chinese perspective, this well-researched and well-presented book has attained its goal of introducing the complex nature of the tremendous changes in China that have occurred during the past 30 years to a wide audience. This comprehensive work is particularly suitable for high school and undergraduate students and the general public who are interested in understanding the incredible transformation of modern China.—**Karen T. Wei**

Canada

Dictionaries and Encyclopedias

47.   **The Encyclopedia of Saskatchewan. http://esask.uregina.ca.** [Website] Free. Date reviewed: 2016.

The *Encyclopedia of Saskatchewan* published by the Canadian Plains Research Center at the University of Regina, launched online in 2007. The encyclopedia contains approximately 2,300 entries arranged alphabetically and over 1,000 charts, graphs, maps, tables, and photographs. The entries vary in length and some have suggestions for further readings. Cross-references within entries are highlighted. The site offers several search options: browsing by subject, an A-Z entry list, an image list, and a contributor index.

A "related subjects" link on the left-hand side of the page takes users to related entries. The names of contributors appear with each entry, and a list of the editorial board and encyclopedia sponsors is available. This freely accessible encyclopedia is easy to use and will serve as a source of basic information or a starting point for further research.—**ARBA Staff Reviewer**

Europe

General Works

Handbooks and Yearbooks

48.   **Countries, Peoples & Cultures: Eastern Europe.** Michael Shally-Jensen, ed. Amenia, N.Y., Salem Press, 2015. 652p. illus. maps. index. (Countries, Peoples & Cultures, Volume 4). $125.00. ISBN 13: 978-1-61925-794-8.
    This is the fourth volume of a projected nine-volume series. The volume provides 20-page profiles of the 25 countries that comprise Eastern Europe. Each begins with a colorful map of the country's location in the world, the country itself that highlights major cities and natural landmarks, and the nation's flag. The common format includes General Information, Environment & Geography, Customs & Courtesies, Lifestyle, Cultural History, Culture, Society, Social Development, Government, and Economy, each with several topical subdivisions. Full-color photographs, tables of information that include important statistics and useful facts, "Do You Know" fun facts, and a bibliography augment the profiles. Two lengthy appendixes, th*at* I assume are included in each volume, address the 21 types of governments found in the world and extensive introductions to 10 of the world's religions.
    This is an exceptionally beautiful and useful source, but as with all such volumes, online sources are readily available and much less expensive for libraries.—**Joe P. Dunn**

49.   **Countries, Peoples & Cultures: Western Europe.** Michael Shally-Jensen, ed. Hackensack, N.J., Salem Press, 2015. 657p. illus. maps. index. (Countries, Peoples & Cultures, Volume 3). $125.00. ISBN 13: 978-1-61925-796-2; 978-1-61925-797-9 (e-book).
    This statistical and descriptive overview covers the nations of Western and Central Europe, including Scandinavia, as well as Greece because of its affiliations with NATO and the European Union. There is no entry for the United Kingdom, but individual articles deal with England, Scotland, Wales, and Northern Ireland. Each of the 27 entries provides an introductory statistical summary, a simple map, an illustration of the flag, and commentary about geography and the environment, customs and lifestyle, culture and cultural history, society and social development, government, and the economy. Articles end with lists of additional print and online resources. Entries average some 20 pages in length, with shorter pieces for smaller states such as Monaco and Vatican City. Two appendixes make up the last 100 pages of the volume, one on world governments and the other on world religions, describing types of regimes (such as democracy or theocratic republic) and major faiths (such as Christianity or Hinduism) without direct reference to

Western Europe. The index notes the recurring subdivisions within the articles, as well as cultural figures or landmarks.

This work brings together information that also can be found (sometimes in greater depth) in other sources such as the *Europa World Year Book* (see ARBA 2013, entry 34), *Statesman's Yearbook* (see ARBA 2012, entry 74), and the *CIA World Factbook* (see ARBA 2015, entry 24) for current political and economic summaries; and in resources focused on cultural differences such as *Ethnic Groups of Europe* (see ARBA 2012, entry 377); *Kiss, Bow, or Shake Hands*; NGO Websites; and guidebooks for tourists. Readers will encounter statistical tables and lists, notes that convey the "flavor and feel" of contemporary social conditions and practices (p. vii), and discussion of historical highlights in the arts and culture, with less coverage of political, historical, or economic trends.

The presentation is marred by typographical errors, misstatements of fact, and omissions. Italy was not a member of the World War I Central Powers (as stated on p. xi). The scale on a sketch map of Andorra suggests that this ministate is larger than France or Spain (p. 5). A misprinted number states that the "legal age for marriage is 1" in Austria, rather than the actual 18 (p. 36). The writer Franz Kafka is identified variously as Austrian (p. 30) and German (p. 150): while he wrote in German, he lived and worked in Prague, now in the Czech Republic. The fall of the Berlin Wall is misdated as November 1990, not 1989 (p. 157). In general, the historical explanations behind some fundamental conditions in modern European life (such as the impact of the Spanish Civil War or the Holocaust) are thin, scattered, or absent.—**Steven W. Sowards**

50.   Thompson, Wayne C. **The World Today Series,** 2015-2016: Western Europe. 34th ed. Lanham, Md., Rowman & Littlefield, 2015. 454p. illus. maps. (World Today series). $21.00 pa.; $19.99 (e-book). ISBN 13: 978-1-4758-1884-0; 978-1-4758-1884-0 (e-book).

Since 1982, the World Today Series has provided an annually updated, comprehensive snapshot of countries within the context of their national and regional milieu. This particular volume in the series surveys seven major regions in Western Europe: the United Kingdom and the Republic of Ireland, Benelux, The French Republic, The Eastern Mediterranean, The Alpine Democracies, The Italian Peninsula, and the Iberian Peninsula. Note that "western" is used in this series in a geographic sense rather than a political one.

Whether tiny like San Marino, or possessing longstanding regional power like the United Kingdom, the book presents each entity's essay respectfully and informatively. Each entry opens with a map(s) and a number of quick facts for easy reference, such as GDP per capita, capital city, official language, etc. All entries are then subdivided into a number of standard topics, such as history, economy, culture, and education. The narrative does well to emphasize significant characteristics of a nation's story, giving broad space to subjects like tolerance in the Netherlands or the tensions rendered by the competing Turkish and Greek ethnic groups on the small island of Cyprus. Readers may also delight in the random odd facts peppered throughout, such as the fact that the Industrial Revolution began in Belgium earlier than almost anywhere else in Europe. Preceding the national entries is a section introducing the region in general terms, which provides good insight into the ways and means of governing apparatus like NATO and the European Union.

Complete with many black-and-white photos and an extensive Website directory and English language bibliography, this volume does an excellent job of surveying a region both immensely diverse, yet inextricably linked.—**Laura Herrell**

Spain

Handbooks and Yearbooks

51. López, Enrique Ávila. **Modern Spain.** Santa Barbara, Calif., ABC-CLIO, 2016. 427p. illus. index. (Understanding Modern Nations). $89.00. ISBN 13: 978-1-61069-600-5; 978-1-61069-601-2 (e-book).

The series, Understanding Modern Nations, furnishes titles written about countries around the world. Questions about cultures, societies, and customs in the twenty-first century are answered. In this book, Enrique Ávila López, professor of humanities and general studies at Mount Royal University in Calgary, Canada, focuses on modern Spain.

This book is available as an e-book or in hardcover and contains 450 pages. The collaged cover photo is inviting and exotic in feel. A table of contents is functional as are the references, appendixes, and index. Tables and figures support the text throughout and Appendix C (Facts and Figures) will be useful for those solely seeking data. Sourcing information follows charts but tends to be from the same sources, time and time again.

Sixteen chapters structure the text and chapters begin with a very useful overview for those looking for brief information. Black-and-white photos throughout are not engaging though they are well captioned. For deeper learning, chapters are well organized into subtopics. These key entries are followed by "cross-references" for easy access to related information elsewhere in the book and further reading suggestions, both print and digital. Chapters end with references.

In a few instances, paragraphs seem misplaced. For example, a paragraph in the geography chapter discusses fish and food production which could have been more easily accessed in chapter four under the topic section about agriculture and the fishing industry.

Modern Spain provides detailed data on contemporary culture and issues. López does well to intertwine facts with the multifaceted history and rich diversity of Spain. This book represents a fusion of many elements and in researching present-day Spain; López does well to expose the country and its issues while giving a succinct picture of what life looks like for Spaniards. Spain as part of the global community is introduced, but the focus is weightier on culture and modern life. This book is a solid overview of Spain today and will give readers a greater appreciation of the country. This book will be useful to high school and undergraduate students, and most practical to those who intend to travel to Spain. Not a travel guide, but a worthy tool for access to modern Spain.

Recommended.—**Janis Minshull**

Latin America and the Caribbean

General Works

Handbooks and Yearbooks

52. **Countries, Peoples & Cultures: Central & South America.** Michael Shally-Jensen, ed. Hackensack, N.J., Salem Press, 2015. 532p. illus. maps. index. (Countries,

Peoples & Cultures, Volume 1). $125.00. ISBN 13: 978-1-61925-788-7; 978-1-61925-789-4 (e-book).

This reference explores the countries of Central and South America, showing us similarities and differences. For each nation we are given general demographics as well as brief descriptions of its geography; customs; lifestyle; culture; the economy; social development to include standard of living, education, women's rights, and health care; government to include structure and foreign policy; as well as a bibliography for further reading. As an example of what we learn, Sao Paulo, Brazil, is the largest city in the Americas, surpassing Mexico City and New York City. Landlocked Bolivia is a plurinational state in which the constitution requires each "nation" or region to be recognized and respected. The Quechua and the Aymara, indigenous Amerindian peoples, represent 55 percent of the population. At least 39 official languages are spoken in Bolivia. The University of San Francisco Xavier in Sucre, Bolivia, is considered the oldest university in the Americas. It was established two years prior to the founding of Harvard. The appendixes include essays on the world's different forms of government and religions. This survey introduces the secondary student to this vibrant and diverse part of our globe.—**Adrienne Antink**

53. **Countries, Peoples & Cultures: North America & The Caribbean.** Michael Shally-Jensen, ed. Amenia, N.Y., Grey House Publishing, 2015. 544p. illus. maps. index. (Countries, Peoples & Cultures, Volume 8). $125.00. ISBN 13: 978-1-61925-786-3.

This book is a part of a new nine-volume series exploring the social, cultural, historical, religious and economic story of most every country in the world. This particular volume focuses on two very different regions: the expansive and complex populations of North America, and the small island nations of the Caribbean. Overall, the volume conveys the stories of 22 countries within the two regions.

The introduction provides a good overview which helps readers grasp the scale of the information; this is followed first by essays on the four countries of North America and then by essays covering the Caribbean nations. Within each country's essay, readers will find a variety of umbrella ideas which do well to organize the material: General Information, Environment and Geography, Customs and Courtesies, Lifestyle, Cultural History, Culture, Society, Social Development, Government and Economy. Particular topics then fill in the narrative under each umbrella idea. For example, the economy section begins with an overview, then discusses industry, labor, energy/power/natural resources, fishing, forestry, mining/metals, agriculture, animal husbandry and tourism.

Readers will also find the country's flag, as well as fast facts, statistics, and maps depicting major cities, landmarks, and regional location. Color photographs are dotted throughout the volume. Each essay concludes with a thorough bibliography. Essays average about 15 pages long, and truly provide a snapshot of each country, filled with current details about youth culture, food, women's issues, language, and much, much more.

The book includes two appendixes (approximately 100 pages), World Governments and World Religions, that are common to all the volumes in the series. World Governments describes 21 types of governments employed throughout all regions of the world today. Each description exposes the guiding premise behind the government, its typical structure and the role of the citizen. Each essay also includes a list of current examples and a bibliography. World Religions presents essays on 10 of the world's most-practiced faiths like Islam, Jainism, and Hinduism. Each essay offers a general description of the faith in addition to a number of topics and includes bibliographies. An index rounds out the work.—**ARBA Staff Reviewer**

Middle East

General Works

Handbooks and Yearbooks

54.   **Countries, Peoples & Cultures: Middle East & North Africa.** Michael Shally-Jensen, ed. Amenia, N.Y., Salem Press, 2015. 566p. illus. maps. index. (Countries, Peoples & Cultures, Volume 5). $125.00. ISBN 13: 978-1-61925-798-6.

Since ancient times, people have traveled to far-off lands. Leisure travel has increased in modern times, and reasons for leisure travel have ballooned. Whatever the reason, deciding where to go—especially if there are several options to choose from—requires specific information about potential destinations and the more savvy travelers may even be looking for overviews about the countries they are considering before embarking on their journeys.

This volume focuses on the Middle East and North Africa covering 21 countries from Iran to Morocco, and from Sudan to Turkey. Unlike other volumes, it does not consider the Middle East separately from North Africa. The regional map does not extend westward to show all the countries covered in this volume. Like the other volumes, each country is covered in about 20 pages focusing on the geographical, economic, cultural, social, historical, and political profile. Each of these sections is further divided into subsections. For most of these countries the focus is contemporary times. Plant and animal life receive a special focus under Geography. An entire section called Customs and Courtesies covers popular greetings, gestures, etiquette, popular dishes and eating customs, and socializing. In addition, water conservation, women's rights, and human rights are covered in their respective subsections. A larger percentage of references in this volume are Web links, and unfortunately a significant number of them have become dead links.

Appendixes providing a two-page summary of the types of world governments and a six-to-seven page summary of each major religious belief are replicated in this volume from previous ones. Like other works in this series, this volume is geared towards providing travelers an overview of the countries they wish to visit.—**Muhammed Hassanali**

4 Economics and Business

General Works

Dictionaries and Encyclopedias

55. **Encyclopedia of Business Information Sources.** 31st ed. Farmington Hills, Mich., Gale/Cengage Learning, 2014. 2v. index. $687.00/set. ISBN 13: 978-1-4144-7814-2.

The *Encyclopedia of Business Information Sources* is designed to assist researchers "in locating material relevant to today's rapidly changing business environment." The *Encyclopedia* contains nearly 25,000 citations covering over 1,100 business, financial, and industrial topics including accounting, personnel management, specific industries, foreign trade, and information industry topics. Types of sources listed and annotated include: abstracts and indexes; almanacs and yearbooks; bibliographies; e-books; financial ratios; online databases; periodicals and newsletters; handbooks and manuals; encyclopedias and dictionaries; trade and professional associations; and research centers and institutes. The *Encyclopedia* contains an outline of contents with listings of topics and cross-references; the entries for each topic, including cross-references; and a list of sources cited. The *Encyclopedia* covers a diverse range of topics among which are: directories of corporations in the United States and overseas; economic research; economic indicators, business history, mass media; marketing; telecommunications; and specific industries (e.g., cosmetics, fitness, and banks and banking). For each topic, items are arranged within categories including online databases, directories, handbooks and manuals, and trade/professional associations. For example the topic Savings and Loan Associations contains a *see also* reference to Savings Banks and information resources grouped under types of sources categories: bibliographies, CD-ROM databases, directories, Internet databases, online database, other sources, periodicals and newsletters, and statistics sources. Each entry includes name of publisher, cost, frequency of publication, and a brief description of content. Addresses of publishers are located in the sources cited section. Each entry in sources cited includes name and address of publisher, Website, contact information, and a description of resource. The *Encyclopedia of Business Information* is a good starting point to research in various topics in business and economics. It is recommended to public, academic, and special libraries. Students and faculty researching specific industries will find a wide range of resources available. Highly recommended.—**Lucy Heckman**

56.   **Gale Encyclopedia of U.S. Economic History.** 2d ed. Thomas Riggs, ed. Farmington Hills, Mich., Gale/Cengage Learning, 2015. 3v. illus. maps. index. $532.00/set. ISBN 13: 978-1-57302-753-3; 978-1-57302-757-1 (e-book).

I have contributed to or reviewed approximately two dozen encyclopedias. This is the most interesting that I have seen. This second edition added 257 entirely new topics from the first edition. The 987 alphabetically arranged entries are lengthy, substantive, and well written. Most items have a bibliography that is more than merely token entries. Even more impressive are the 200 sidebars, 60 text excerpts, and more than 450 images and drawings, most in color. It constitutes an impressive visual display. Possibly the most valuable features are the lengthy "think pieces" that treat socioeconomic issues of import in American history. An example is "The History of Economic Inequality in the United States." The volumes are full of statistical information presented in a very readable fashion. Among my favorite inclusions are essays on the economic history of each state, complete with a color map that incorporates the Interstate highways and all the national and state parks, forests, and wildlife areas. Standard encyclopedia features include a list of articles, a thematic outline of contents, a quite extensive chronology, and the list of contributors.

I am not a specialist on economic history and I found myself spending hours reading various topics at random through the volumes because the material was so interesting and informative. Printed encyclopedias are at a great disadvantage against the ready access of online reference sources, but this may be one printed source whose merits allow it to compete for users.—**Joe P. Dunn**

57.   **Government and the Economy: An Encyclopedia.** Dieterle, David A. and Kathleen C. Simmons, eds. Santa Barbara, Calif., Greenwood Press/ABC-CLIO, 2014. 552p. index. $100.00. ISBN 13: 978-1-4408-2903-1; 978-1-4408-2904-8 (e-book).

This textbook provides an in-depth examination of the American government and how it is affected by the United States economy and the global economies. Twenty-five economic scholars have contributed to this collection of essays that describe important Supreme Court cases that have impacted the economic infrastructure, the biographies of famous economists, and the seven key economic systems—socialism, democratic socialism, fascism, market capitalism, state capitalism, transitional, and welfare state. The alphabetic entries are in alignment with the 20 National Content Standards in Economics and the United States History Content Standards.

There are four appendixes. They cover the Constitution of the United States, the Supreme Court and its opinions, legislative acts with economic impact, and online resources for educators and researchers. A glossary of terms used in the text, a bibliography, and an index are provided.

I would recommend this book for the business and economic collections of high school and academic libraries. It provides a very insightful study of the world government and how the economy affects them.—**Kay Stebbins Slattery**

58.   Olson, James S., and Abraham O. Mendoza. **American Economic History: A Dictionary and Chronology.** Santa Barbara, Calif., Greenwood Press/ABC-CLIO, 2015. 695p. index. $89.00. ISBN 13: 978-1-61069-697-5; 78-1-61069-698-2 (e-book).

Captains of industry ("Ford, Henry;" "Rockefeller, John Davison"), historic events ("Gold Rush;" "Bank Holiday"), governmental policies ("Laissez-Faire"), and so-called alphabet agencies ("Federal Deposit Insurance Corporation"/FDIC) are a few of the subjects making their appearance among the approximately 1,200 concisely written entries of this volume. Authors stress the need for a resource providing basic facts concerning the background of American private enterprise and how the various threads of business, legislative oversight, and history are intertwined within the fabric of our nation (Preface, xxxix). Supplementary material includes a timeline of American economic history and a bibliography of pertinent literature.

Writing style is authoritative yet accessible, making this work appropriate for use by senior high school/undergraduate college students and members of the lay public at our nation's libraries. In keeping with a dictionary format, entries usually consist of one or two paragraphs, although important topics are lengthier; "Emergency Railroad Transportation Act of 1933" takes up nearly an entire page.

Olson holds a doctorate from The State University of New York at Stony Brook and is the distinguished professor of history at Sam Houston State University in Huntsville, Texas. Mendoza holds a master's degree in history from San Francisco State University. While these two have authored the majority of the entries, there is nevertheless the curiosity of a number of articles signed by contributors for whom no other information is given. Be that as it may, this volume represents a well-written and comprehensive overview of United States economic activity from the revolutionary era up to the present day.—**Michael Francis Bemis**

59.   Skrabec, Quentin R., Jr. **The 100 Most Important American Financial Crises: An Encyclopedia of the Lowest Points in American Economic History.** Santa Barbara, Calif., Greenwood Press/ABC-CLIO, 2015. 337p. illus. index. $89.00. ISBN 13: 978-1-4408-3011-2; 978-1-4408-3012-9 (e-book).

There are those that are obvious and fresh in our minds, like the Great Recession of the 2000s, and then there is the Boll Weevil Cotton Crisis of 1917. While clearly some American financial crises are quick to bring images of "For Sale" signs and long unemployment lines to mind, others that are more obscure may be just as important to their particular time. This engaging and substantial work brings together over 100 entries describing both the famous and not-so-famous economic debacles affecting American lives throughout our history.

The chronological arrangement of entries helps readers find particular examples easily and provides a linear picture of the crises. We note, for example, that the decade preceding the 1929 Wall Street Crash included a potentially foreboding National Steel Strike, Automotive Recession, British Rubber Embargo, and Peanut Import Crisis.

In looking at the book as a whole, readers are able to discern themes and patterns preceding crises and throughout their aftermath; observing, for example the commonalities surrounding natural disasters like Hurricanes Katrina and Sandy. Individually, the entries manage to be both concise and generous with their material. We learn of everything from the tumult affecting U.S. merchant shipping at the hands of early-nineteenth-century pirates (expenses related to dealing with this dangerous lot reached 20 percent of our new nation's annual expenditures), to the Labor Uprisings of 1936-39 which emanated from President Franklin D. Roosevelt's New Deal legislation and its attempts to improve working conditions and unionize important labor sectors. Further, the richness of detail within each topic (an entry on the 1977 Natural Gas Shortage Crisis, for example, refers to President Jimmy Carter, the formation of the Department of Energy, the record cold of 1976-77, and more) will certainly encourage readers towards deeper study.

Each entry is cross-referenced and provides suggestions for further reading. An appendix provides a glimpse into a small sample of relevant primary documents (such as Article One of the Federal Reserve Act), and is followed by a thorough bibliography. This book is recommended for high school and college libraries.—**Laura Herrell**

Directories

60.   **The Directory of Business Information Resources, 2015.** 22d ed. Amenia, N.Y., Grey House Publishing, 2015. 1976p. index. $195.00pa.; $495.00 (online database). ISBN 13: 978-1-61925-547-0.

The *Directory of Business Information Resources,* which covers 101 industries, is an annotated guide to associations, directories, databases, newsletters, journals, and trade shows. This edition has added two chapters: "Cyber Security" and "Social Media." Entries in the directory are arranged alphabetically by industry listings and industries covered include accounting, automotive, computers and data processing, communications and media, insurance, health care, chemicals, electrical, agriculture, sports and recreation, and broadcasting. Each resource entry is given a one-paragraph description. Within industry categories, entries are listed in categories of associations, newsletters, magazines and journals, directories and databases, trade shows, and industry Websites. Each association entry includes name, address, URL, officers' names, when founded, and number of members. For journals, magazines, and newsletters each entry contains title of publication, address, subscription cost, URL, and special issues information. For Websites the name and URLs are listed along with a description of the organization and its purpose. For trade shows, entries include name and address of agency, officers, membership, and frequency of trade shows. For directories and databases, entries contain name address, phone, URL, officers, and frequency of publication. Also included in the directory are a content summary of chapter listings; NAICS codes; cross-references; and two indexes. The *Directory of Business Information Sources* is a comprehensive guide to research resources and is recommended to practitioners and faculty and students in undergraduate and business programs. It allows researchers to thoroughly research specific industries and is a helpful finding aid to locating resources and associations. Recommended to larger public libraries and university libraries supporting a program in business administration.—**Lucy Heckman**

61.   **The Directory of Business Information Resources, 2016.** 23d ed. Amenia, N.Y., Grey House Publishing, 2015. 2013p. index. $195.00pa.; $495.00 (online database). ISBN 13: 978-1-6925-900-3.

This substantial volume offers a comprehensive collection of industry-specific resources that make for a one-stop business reference. This 23d edition has enhanced a number of industry categories with nearly 300 new listings, predominantly in the alternative energy, environment and conservation, food and beverage and health care sectors, although other sectors have been enhanced, as well.

One hundred and one industries are efficiently segmented into categories of affiliated associations, directories, databases, trade shows, magazines, journals, newsletters, and Websites. The number of listings within each category will vary with industry. Listings under each of the prior categories include key names, contact information, and a brief description. Social media (Facebook, Twitter, etc.) availability is also noted if applicable. Industries and listings within the industries are presented alphabetically.

Supplementary material helps make this resource extremely navigable, such as the user guide, a content summary of chapter listings (further segmenting industry categories into more specific businesses), the NAICS and SIC (industry classification systems) reference tables, and two indexes.

Whether desiring to research an industry from a scholarly or a commercial point of view, this book and its trove of well-organized information is an indispensable starting point.—**ARBA Staff Reviewer**

Handbooks and Yearbooks

62.   Business Statistics of the United States, 2014: Patterns of Economic Change. 19th ed. Cornelia J. Strawser, ed. Lanham, Md., Bernan Press, 2015. 573p. $165.00. ISBN 13: 978-1-59888-732-7.

Business Statistics of the United States is "a basic desk reference for anyone requiring statistics on the US economy. It contains over 3,000 economic time series portraying the period from World War II to December 2013 in industry, product, and demographic detail." Also, in 200 time series, the period from 1925 through 1948 is presented. New features for the 2014 edition are: a comprehensive revision of data back to 1925 on private and government fixed assets; comprehensive revision of the International Transactions Accounts and the international investment position; and expanded producer price indexes covering services as well as goods. *Business Statistics of the United States* is arranged as follows: Preface; an essay on cycle and growth perspectives; an essay with graphs on the U.S. economy, 1929-1948; general notes, including a list of data sources; and the following chapters which contain tables of data, sources of data, and definitions: "National Income and Product," "Industrial Production and Capacity Utilization," "Income Distribution and Poverty," "Consumer Income and Spending," "Savings and Investment," "Government," "U.S. Foreign Trade and Finance," "Price," "Employment Costs, Productivity, and Profits," "Employment, Hours, and Earnings," "Energy," "Money, Interest, Assets, Liabilities and Asset Prices," "International Comparisons," "Product and Income by Industry," "Employment, Hours, and Earnings by NAICS Industry," "Key Sector Statistics," and "Index." In addition to the data, there are essays analyzing historical economic events (e.g., what was the Great Depression?) and URLs for U.S. government statistics sources. *Business Statistics of the United States* is a valuable, thorough source of data and recommended for researchers, as well as business school faculty and students. This is an essential source for research and larger academic library business and economics collections.—**Lucy Heckman**

63.   Econ Lowdown. https://www.stlouisfed.org/education. [Website] Free. Date reviewed: 2016.

Econ Lowdown is a free online resource published by the Federal Reserve Bank of St. Louis for educators, parents, and consumers who want to learn about economics, personal finance, money and banking, and the Federal Reserve. Resources are conveniently organized by educational level: elementary, middle school, high school, college, and consumer. Within the elementary category, there are lessons appropriate for various ages. For example, K-Grade 1 learns about spending vs. saving, while Grades 5-8 are taught that money was an invention. Middle school lessons get into everything from debit cards to choosing a college, and high school students are warned about predatory lending and "alternative financial services" like pawn shops and payday loans, instructed in the basics of car buying, and introduced to capital markets and the characteristics of entrepreneurs. Consumers, by which they do not mean "adults," as one might have expected, are actually given lesson plans for all ages, including podcasts and videos. This category appears to include many (all?) of the lessons available in the other categories.

In each category, lessons are arranged alphabetically and a brief summary is provided. Some are available in Spanish. Users can also perform a keyword search, so it is not necessary to guess which categories contain which lesson plans. Pinned to the top of each list is "10 FRED Activities in 10 Minutes." FRED is the Federal Reserve Economic Data free online database, and the activities range from finding and graphing GDP data to creating custom graphs. There are videos and other online tutorials to help along the way.

By far the most interesting lesson plan to this reviewer is Barbie® in the Labor Force, intended for a high school audience. The goal is to teach students about changing career options for women in the past half century by encouraging a dialog about what careers were available to Barbie® as indicated by her outfits. (If you were unaware that Barbie® had any career options at all, other than the first one, fashion model (1959), you are not alone). Notwithstanding questions about whether popular culture reflects reality, or influences it, or lags far behind it, this lesson plan asks thought-provoking questions about women's choices in different eras in thoroughly engaging ways. It also provides suggested answers, saving teachers hours of Googling. It is no wonder that the developers of *Econ Lowdown* were awarded the 2015 Abbejean Kehler Technology Award by the National Association of Economic Educators and the Council for Economic Education. The variety and depth of the lesson plans and activities are highly recommended for students of all ages, their teachers and professors, school libraries as well as public libraries looking for materials for public workshops in financial and economic literacy.—**ARBA Staff Reviewer**

64.   Garbus, Julia. Corridor, Shawn, ed. **U*X*L Money: Making Sense of Economics and Personal Finance.** Farmington Hills, Mich., Gale/Cengage Learning, 2015. 3v. illus. maps. index. ISBN 13: 978-1-57302-979-7; 978-1-57302-983-4 (e-book)..

Connections between macroeconomics and the importance of establishing a good credit history can seem tenuous, but this excellent three-volume set makes the case that understanding economic theory, from international trade to the workings of the stock market, relates to being a savvy consumer. Each volume includes the complete index and table of contents for the set. Chapters include brief summaries of main ideas, study questions, glossaries, and recommended print and online sources for additional reading. Well-written entries interweave explanations of economic concepts such as Smith's invisible hand and the prisoner's dilemma with current events such as the Great Recession. The third volume will be of especial importance to many high school students because it focuses on the basics of personal finance, providing concrete examples to help young people understand such topics as the implications of various types of student loans and the basics of investing in stocks and bonds.—**Delilah R. Caldwell**

65. **Handbook of Choice Modelling.** Stephanie Hess and Andrew Daly, eds. Northampton, Mass., Edward Elgar, 2014. 720p. index. $295.00. ISBN 13: 978-1-78100-314-5.

The *Handbook of Choice Modelling* from Edward Elgar is a carefully selected compendium of articles on strategies used to analyze the choices made by individuals and groups and thus to predict their future choices. Choice modeling is increasingly important in today's world, where the ability to forecast what individual consumers and the public at large will need affects not only product manufacturers but local and state budgets and ultimately the global economy. Editors Stephane Hess and Andrew Daly, both from the University of Leeds, United Kingdom, have grouped the articles into seven parts: one, Foundations; two, Observing Preferences; three, Modelling Heterogeneity; four, Going beyond Simple Discrete Choice; five, Specification, Estimation and Inference; six, Analysis and Use of Results; and seven, Area-Specific Research Needs. The opening article, by Nobel Prize winner Daniel McFadden of the University of California at Berkeley and the University of Southern California—described by the editors as "the leading architect of developments in choice modelling in the past 50 years" —is titled "The New Science of Pleasure: Consumer Choice Behavior and the Measurement of Well-Being." The articles in part two deal with the observation of choice, both through stated preference data and revealed preference data. In part three, various approaches for modeling heterogeneity are examined. The authors in part four go in new directions to discuss such options as choices made by multiple individuals and the development of hybrid choice models. In part five, the issues involved in working with increasingly complex model structures are discussed. Part six brings a perspective from the field of economics and a discussion of forecasting, while the articles in part seven deal with what the editors consider "the most active disciplines" in choice modeling—marketing, environmental and resource economics, health economies, and transportation. All the chapters in the book rely heavily on sophisticated mathematical formulae and include a multitude of figures. Each chapter is followed by notes and references; a comprehensive index concludes the volume. The *Handbook of Choice Modelling* is designed for use by scholars and working professionals and is recommended for academic and institutional libraries.—**ARBA Staff Reviewer**

66. **Handbook of Qualitative Research Techniques and Analysis in Entrepreneurship.** Helle Neergaard and Claire M. Leitch, eds. Northampton, Mass., Edward Elgar, 2015. 464p. index. $225.00. ISBN 13: 978-1-84980-986-3.

Handbook of Qualitative Research Techniques and Analysis in Entrepreneurship is a book that works to build on the foundation established in the prequel *Handbook of Qualitative Research Methods in Entrepreneurship.* Techniques used by more experienced researchers to explore and understand the entrepreneurial phenomena are broken down in step-by-step explanations. With the contribution of 23 experts, this book explores the rarely discussed topic of qualitative research with a focus on entrepreneurship.

The book is divided into five parts: Constants Comparative Technique, Metaphor Methodologies, Critical Incident Technique, Focus Groups, and Repertory Grid Technique. These five parts are used to explain the three forms of research interviews that most of the current data uses as a way of collecting data. These three forms of interviews are as follows: unstructured/conversational interviews, semistructured interviews, and structured interviews. The book concentrates on interviews in qualitative research because it is the most common method of data collecting when conducting research on entrepreneurship.

At the beginning of each chapter, the book includes an introduction to the content within the chapter. The book's supplementary items include an index, tables, and graphs.

Not only does the book introduce the reader to how entrepreneurship research is collected but it also introduces the reader to the basics of entrepreneurship. The material starts with an introduction that explains the concept, objective, and structure of the book. The introduction clearly states that the objective of this book is to concentrate on the foundation for new researchers in the applied techniques in studying and researching entrepreneurship. This book would have the most impact on those that are new to researching entrepreneurship, which in itself is a fairly new research topic. Since entrepreneurship is a new research topic, the history of research and applied methods mainly concentrates on studies in the 1980s-90s. Furthermore, it concentrates primarily on entrepreneurship in the Western world. This book is great at breaking down terms, explaining history, and dissecting methods used in research, and assumes that the reader is a novice in entrepreneurship research. While this book would be a natural fit for an academic library with its main focus being research, it would also be appropriate for a public library for patrons who are interested in starting a business.

Handbook of Qualitative Research Techniques and Analysis in Entrepreneurship is highly recommended as a reference source for academic libraries and public libraries.—**Sara Mofford**

67.   **Handbook of Research on Entrepreneurship and Creativity.** Rolf Sternberg and Gerhard Krauss, eds. Northampton, Mass., Edward Elgar, 2014. 411p. illus. index. $225.00. ISBN 13: 978-1-78100-442-5.

This Edward Elgar handbook provides analyses of entrepreneurship and creativity as linked factors in driving the capitalist economic engine. After an introduction by the editors Rolf Sternberg and Gerhard Krauss on the relationship between these two phenomena, the three parts of the book cover the role of creativity for entrepreneurial activities, the local/regional environment's impact on entrepreneurship and creativity, and government policies to support both entrepreneurship and creative economic development. The pages on the 23 contributors, most of whom are associated with West European institutions (none currently work in the United States) are very informative, listing the authors' publications and describing their academic roles and achievements. All the chapters have reference notes and many have charts, graphs, and illustrations. The book also has a comprehensive index. There is a list of tables with intriguing titles such as "The Psychological Paradoxes of Creativity" and "Mean Differences between Self-Employed and Paid Employees." Chapter titles include "Knowledge Creation in Entrepreneurial Teams," "The Creative Environment as Stimulator for Entrepreneurial Opportunities," and "The Role of Education in Enterprising Creativity." One chapter provides a case study of the fashion industry in Milan, Italy, in relation to civic efforts to encourage it. American readers will note that there is little in the book on entrepreneurship in the United States, although as the editors state, entrepreneurship was first studied as an academic subject at Babson College in 1981. This book will serve as a valuable reference for graduate students and scholars examining the factors that may affect economic life and development.—**ARBA Staff Reviewer**

68.   **Handbook of Research on Islamic Business Ethics.** Abbas J. Ali, ed. Northampton, Mass., Edward Elgar, 2015. 318p. index. $190.00. ISBN 13: 978-1-78100-944-4; 978-1-78100-945-1 (e-book).

Most Muslims do not see religion as separated from other spheres of human activity, but see it as encompassing all spheres of human endeavor. A capitalist model strives to maximize profit—unlike an Islamic model that strives to leave the world better than it was before. While the two models are different, they are not incompatible. This work showcases how an Islamic perspective can be used practically in the contemporary business world, examining its underpinning and discussing how closely the lived reality mimics these ideals.

The book is divided into six parts, and each part consists of two to three essays. An introductory essay frames all 14 essays, and each essay makes up one chapter. The first part addresses the ethics of knowledge, focusing more on the duties of scholars in dispensing knowledge rather than the pursuit of acquiring knowledge. The second essay focuses on individual rights and responsibilities, thus covering themes broader than just knowledge. Part two covers ethical systems. The first essay covers the various institutions entrusted to interpret ethical conduct. The second essay focuses on businesses and the third on uncertainty. Part three focuses on marketing—more specifically marketing to a global marketplace in a post-9/11 world. The second essay in this section is a case study of Islamic banking in the United Kingdom. Part four addresses the ethics of leadership, authority, and power. Part five explores the ethics of financial reporting. The last part consists of case studies focused on work ethics in some of the Arabian countries.

Most of the literature on Islamic business is based on quoting religious texts and relating these quotes to contemporary business practices, or on case studies—specifically Islamic banking. This work differentiates itself by exploring the underpinnings of Islamic ethics—especially in business—by probing other quasi-religious and nonreligious sources. In this regard, it is a welcomed addition to the existing literature. Recommended for scholars interested in Islamic business.—**Muhammed Hassanali**

69. **InfoSci-Business and Management Information Science and Technology.** **http://www.igi-global.com/e-resources/infosci-subject-databases/infosci-business/.** [Website] Hershey, Pa., Information Science Reference/IGI Global. Price negotiated by site. Date reviewed: 2016.

The *InfoSci-Business and Management Information Science and Technology* database is a collection of over 625 scholarly e-books covering areas within business, management, and economics including accounting, finance, economic theory, human resources, hospitality, marketing, and more. The books have a copyright of 2000-2016. The e-books are edited volumes with chapters by different authors. The authors, editors, and reviewers come from academia, institutes, government entities, and businesses from across the globe giving the books an international perspective.

The database lets users browse or search the titles. When browsing the collection the only way to narrow it down is a keyword search of the titles. In order to do a search of the entire collection, users must use the Database Search which loads the books and chapters, and it includes basic, advanced, and expert search options. It would have been nice to narrow down the books by subject area within the business collection, but the current searching methods are satisfactory. The Database Search searches all available collections, and filters on the right side narrow to specific databases (i.e., the business database), content type, etc. The filters need to be used after the search as they are erased once the keyword is entered.

When browsing an individual title, the book opens to a table of contents. Each chapter is a separate file. The older titles are only available in PDF format, but starting in 2010 HTML versions were also included. When searching the database, the results show relevant titles but mostly individual chapters with a link to the PDF and HTML files if available. From the chapter profile page, a user must click on the source title to see the entire book. While looking at the PDF or HTML of the chapter, the book's table of contents is hyperlinked on the left making it easy to navigate the entire book. The organization of the e-books is simple with the table of contents showing the layout. The text is easy to read and images are included.

Overall, *InfoSci-Business and Management Information Science and Technology* is an easy-to-use e-book platform with some very minor annoyances. The format allows users to search scholarly content, and the format of the books allows a way to find similar pieces since they are organized by subject within the books. Recommended for libraries looking for resources in these subject areas.—**Breezy Silver**

70.   Knoop, Todd A. **Business Cycle Economics: Understanding Recessions and Depressions from Boom to Bust.** Santa Barbara, Calif., Praeger/ABC-CLIO, 2015. 391p. index. $58.00. ISBN 13: 978-1-4408-3174-4; 978-1-4408-3175-1 (e-book).

This is written as an undergraduate textbook on business cycles in a nontechnical, narrative style. Equations and graphs are kept to a minimum. The author presents different approaches to the topic, providing summary points in the chapters but leaving it to the reader to decide which is strongest. The book starts with a discussion of business cycles, followed by macroeconomic theories of business cycles (early; Keynesian; Austrian; monetarist; rational expectations; real business cycle; new Keynesian). The next section is on financial instability and forecasting. Business cycles in the United States and modern international recessions and depressions (East Asian crisis; Japan; sovereign debt crises; 2008) are the last two sections. The book reads partially like a short, basic history of thought text and a review article of major economic events of the last 20 years. There is confusion in the discussion about new Keynesian (to be found in the index) and post-Keynesian (not listed in the index). Alternatives to the gold standard before WWII are not given; nor is the importance of the rate at which a currency establishes itself to a fixed standard. The author clearly states what he believes is known and what is not known about business cycles and policies to prevent or correct the problems associated with them. There are additional reading suggestions at the end of each chapter, a bibliography, and an index.—**J. E. Weaver**

71.   Ladner, Sam. **Practical Ethnography: A Guide to Doing Ethnography in the Private Sector.** Walnut Creek, Calif., Left Coast Press, Inc., 2014. 210p. illus. index. $26.95pa. ISBN 13: 978-1-61132-390-0; 978-1-61132-741-0 (e-book).

Practical Ethnography: A Guide to Doing Ethnography in the Private Sector gives functional and insightful tips for business professionals who want to apply ethnographic methodologies in their personal trade. Written by Sam Ladner, a Senior User Researcher at Microsoft Office, *Practical Ethnography* brings a fresh perspective to the academic writings that apply sociological concepts to business practice. The book covers corporate and nonprofit environments and offers a wide knowledge base with various examples for real-life application for the business setting. Ladner uses personal references and examples to enliven her story and provide understanding for her concepts and ideas. She refers to private-sector ethnography as "culture change work" and inspires readers to pay attention to not only their end goals but also their process and participants.

Ladner splits this book into 11 chapters, with content ranging from "Managing Clients" to "Fieldwork" and "Reporting." Her general overview gives background knowledge that is applicable to the rest of the book in a humorous and interesting manner. She shares multiple report types and goes in-depth into the process of completing fieldwork in the business setting. She also discusses various types of sampling and leads the reader through the steps of selecting and examining samples. The book includes call-out boxes, figures, photographs, and tables—all of which aid in driving home her observations and points.

She finishes with a chapter that shares literature reviews, focus-group coverage, and usability labs. Ladner goes into just the right amount of detail about the ethnographic process and keeps the reading informative but also digestible and interesting. Overall, *Practical Ethnography* is a must-have for any academic library serving a business and/or research marketing program.—**Jessica Crossfield McIntosh**

72. **Psychology for Business Success.** Paludi, Michele A., ed. Santa Barbara, Calif., Praeger/ABC-CLIO, 2013. 4v. index. (Women's Psychology). $215.00/set. ISBN 13: 978-0-313-39803-2; 978-0-313-39804-9 (e-book).

Psychology for Business Success represents an essential four-volume academic and professional resource. Distinguished editor, Michele Paludi, provides management consulting to businesses, K–12 schools, and colleges and universities. Her impressive resume documents extensive expertise that includes facilitating training on equal-employment opportunity, diversity training, development of employee handbooks, development of performance appraisals, and investigations of sexual harassment and campus violence. In addition, she has edited 39 texts on workplace discrimination, sexual harassment, the psychology of women, workplace violence, and campus violence. The well-documented chapters focus on employee needs and suggest meaningful solutions to everyday workplace situations that require thoughtful and positive leadership strategies.

The developers and designers of *Psychology for Business Success* considered many options in their effort to produce a superior product. For example, individual book covers of the four-volume set are visually pleasing and appear enhanced by a color palette generator. Bold images capture recognizable workplace scenarios. The book titles are vibrant and the volumes serve as appealing additions to library collections. *Psychology for Business Success* fulfills the editor's stated sentiment that underlines major goals: valuing women, treating women as the norm, taking a non-Eurocentric view of women's experiences, and facilitating connections between readers' experiences and psychological theories and empirical research. Carefully chosen chapter articles address diverse human resource management topics that include leadership, management and employee relations. In addition, content that explores conflict management, employee performance evaluation, training, workplace violence, and numerous other matters inform readers. The entries are comprehensive and address current issues. Book chapters include clear charts and graphics that enhance understanding and retention. The appropriate use of bold section headings prepares readers for new topics and further discussion. The fonts are reader-friendly and illustrative case studies appear highlighted in text boxes for emphasis. The reference section at the conclusion of each chapter is extensive. Publication dates appear current and offer additional opportunities to peruse related content. Volume appendixes offer additional content that enhances opportunities for integration and application of concepts. Examples include: Sample Human Resource Policy Statements and Procedures; Conducting Investigations of Complaints of Equal Employment Opportunity; Sample Work-Life Integration Programs; Sample Syllabus for Seminar on Women, Work, and Families in Cross-Cultural Perspective; and Sample Training/Exam Questions in Human Resource Management. About the Editor and Contributors sections include short biographical sketches. Summaries enhance authenticity and document suitable acknowledgement for substantial author efforts. The volume titles are: *Juggling, Balancing, and Integrating Work and Family Roles and Responsibilities; Institutional Equity and Compliance; Managing, Leading, and Developing Employees;* and *Implementing Best Practices in Human Resources.* The volume chapters present practical solutions. Internationally recognized authors offer suggestions on how businesses can develop into resourceful and resilient organizations. The academic content offers leadership and management styles that benefit business leaders, managers, and supervisors. In addition, the volumes propose approaches that integrate management theories and leadership strategies. The principles highlight the significance of gaining an understanding of the strategic influences on managing and leading people. The editor's philosophical perspective endorses positive leadership strategies. Exceptional chapter examples include the introduction by Paludi; "Acts of Dignity: Women of Color Balancing Work and Family" by Lillian Comas-Diaz; "Intimate Partner Violence as a Workplace Concern" by Paludi; "Leadership Styles and Leader Effectiveness" by Bruce Klonsky; "Trainer Communication Styles and Training Outcomes" by Annette Towler and Gamze Arman; and" Workplace Incivility: What It Is, and What We Can Do" by Thomas G. Reio, Jr., Carolyn Meeker, and Stephanie M. Reio.

Career opportunities exist for readers of the *Psychology for Business Success.* The application of psychology principles to leadership enhances the possibility of successful employee rapport and development. Insight offers avenues that connect business vision and success. The following markets will benefit from the acquisition of the four-volume work: business and marketing agencies; individuals interested in enhancing their leadership skills and business relationships; government agencies that will find the volumes useful for training programs; international markets; public and private libraries; and high school, community college, and university libraries.

Michele Paludi accomplishes her overall objective to provide readers with effective management strategies to work strategically, ethically, honestly, and effectively with people.—**Thomas E. Baker**

73. **Research Handbook on Political Economy and Law.** Ugo Mattei and John D. Haskell, eds. Northampton, Mass., Edward Elgar, 2016. 583p. maps. index. (Research Handbooks on Globalisation and the Law). $305.00. ISBN 13: 978-1-78100-534-7; 978-1-78100-535-4 (e-book).

The global economic/financial crisis that began with the "housing bubble" in 2007 has continued to plague the world. There is no consensus about the causes of this crisis, what policies or directions are best to take, what should be done, what strategy to implement, or how to implement a strategy. In this book, the writers present three ideas that are emerging as a consensus: economic ideas of the last 40 years are not valid; any future analysis needs to think through conditions (not individuals or states); and, as stated on page three of the introduction, a "central problem of global governance revolves around … 'inequality' and 'production.'"

The book is organized into three parts: Money and Markets; The Relations of

Organization: Industry, Labour and the State; and Commodities, Land and Resources. Each substantive chapter is a starting point for further research and includes extensive notes and bibliographical references. The collection of signed articles presents a very different way of thinking about issues from a global perspective.

Essential for academic libraries preparing students for the future in a global economy. Highly recommended for all academic libraries supporting curriculum in business, economics, political science, and globalization.—**Ladyjane Hickey**

74. Roper, Kathy O., and Richard P. Payant. **The Facility Management Handbook. Fourth Edition.** New York, AMACOM/American Management Association, 2014. 675p. index. $79.95. ISBN 13: 978-0-8144-3215-0.

Facility management is an expansive field where multiple lines of expertise blur. From construction to zoning compliance to disaster preparedness and more, facility management demands a complex professional network. Add to this the rapidly evolving technology, design, and environmental issues of the modern workplace and there arises a clear need for a definitive resource for facility managers. This *Facility Management Handbook* corrals the necessary information from a variety of facility management sectors into one place.

Sections cover a wide range of umbrella issues, including budgeting, real estate, security, and maintenance. Information within each section is comprehensive: chapters in the Facility Emergency Preparedness and Business Continuity section cover topics such as threat assessment, communications, preparation, training, and emergency recovery. Furthermore, sections offer "pulse points" (where main ideas are distinctly distilled), review questions, and graphic exhibits to make information easily accessible and memorable.

This fourth edition seamlessly incorporates the latest technologies, trends, challenges, and strategies into the basic foundations of facility management. For example, Life-Cycle Cost analysis, wherein facility management expenditures are calculated over the life span of the facility, is still only an occasionally used best practice. As the public demands a greater sustainability mindset, Life-Cycle Cost analysis is becoming particularly relevant in contrasting "green" building to traditional design, construction, and operation.

A generous appendix offers options for quick reference, and includes Websites, education programs, a Life-Cycle Cost example, security and emergency best practices, and good examples of backup documents including service questionnaires, contractor evaluation forms, budget requests, and much more. The handbook also includes a substantial glossary focused on building functions and financial aspects of facility management. An index completes this extensive guide, which is highly recommended for institutions and libraries looking for a title on this important topic.—**Laura Herrell**

75. **World Economic Situation and Prospects 2014.** New York, United Nations, 2014. 181p. $42.00pa. ISBN 13: 978-92-1-109168-7.

This United Nations-sponsored report offers a summary outlook on the direction of the global economy. It succinctly assesses key areas such as growth, inflation, employment, trade, financing, risk, and international policy-making. Some specific analysis covers such topics as depreciating currencies, commodity markets, banking system reforms, and innovative financing options.

The report also summarizes development and outlook issues on a regional basis, so readers can easily understand, for example, Western Europe's emergence from recession in context with Japan's high public debt issue, as well as other regional projections.

This report makes solid use of text boxes, charts, tables, and summarizing sidebars for ease of reference. Data partly estimated or forecast is clearly marked as such. This report will find wide use in academic and research libraries.—**Laura Herrell**

76.   **Worldmark Global Business and Economy Issues.** Farmington Hills, Mich., Gale/ Cengage Learning, 2015. 2v. $310.00/set. ISBN 13: 978-1-4109-1756-8; 978-1-4103-1759-9 (e-book).

International business knowledge is growing with importance as globalization continues to make the world a smaller place. *Worldmark Global Business and Economy Issues* covers a wide range of relevant topics that include marketing, human resource management, finance/accounting, and development economics. Intended to reach the needs of students focusing on global studies, this collection provides users with an in-depth look at issues surrounding international business. This new collection is split into two volumes; volume one being Business and volume two being Economy. There are a variety of sections that include resources for more information, a list of key organizations, and an index, as well as thematic outlines for both volumes. Brief sidebars highlight additional relevant information, such as extended text on certain topics, biographical information, and pop culture topics. Graphics and images support the relevant information throughout the text and help keep the content engaging.

One of the more unique aspects of this collection is the inclusion of primary source information shared by way of subheadings in the main chapters. There is a Using Primary Sources section in volume one that discusses how and why to use primary sources. These additions help provide context and history for the reader. A glossary of terms is located in the beginning of each volume and both sections have a chronology of events, which are very useful for a newcomer to international business. These sections help put historical and current development into perspective. *Worldmark Global Business and Economy Issues* is an effective text for teaching relevant international business issues. It covers topics that affect consumers and business owners worldwide, and provides context for readers to analyze, understand, and apply important topics in the discipline. It can be used in the classroom or as a resource text. This set is a valuable addition to any academic or business-oriented library.—**Jessica Crossfield McIntosh**

Accounting

Handbooks and Yearbooks

77.   Shim, Jae K., Joel G. Siegel, Nick Dauber, and Anique A. Qureshi. **Accounting Handbook.** 6th ed. Hauppauge, N.Y., Barron's Educational Series, 2014. 1062p. index. $39.99pa. ISBN 13: 978-0-7641-6657-0.

Since accounting is a detail-oriented field, it is helpful to both students and professionals to have access to a desk reference to look up quick information. This handbook is from Barron's, a publisher known for their guides. The authors are professors, a former professor, and a lecturer at universities so they should have a strong understanding of the academic area and its needs.

The handbook is a large single volume which makes it handier than multiple volume competitors even if less detailed. The handbook is a combined encyclopedia and dictionary in one. It is organized by topic with descriptions and examples, and includes a section for a dictionary of accounting terms. It includes chapters on financial statements and analysis, financial reporting requirements, management accounting, individual income taxation, information technology, quantitative methods for accounting, auditing and internal control, personal financial planning, governmental and nonprofit accounting, international accounting and financial reporting standards, and forensic accounting. It also includes appendixes on a summary of the Sarbanes-Oxley Act of 2002 and a Sarbanes-Oxley Compliance Practice Aid.

This is not a handbook for beginners or people with no accounting or business experience. There are terms and concepts that they may not be familiar enough with to be able to understand this handbook fully. For example, there is not a good explanation of accounting standards and the types of standards. In addition, the organization of the handbook is not clear. For example, the accounting terms are stuck in the middle of the handbook. The table of contents and index are very helpful in navigating the book. It also has cross-references to be able to find additional information. The individual entries are concise and easily readable. While the content may be confusing to beginners, it could be a valuable resource for accounting or business students and some professionals needing a refresher or to look up something quickly.—**Breezy Silver**

Business Services and Investment Guides

Handbooks and Yearbooks

78.   **TheStreet Ratings' Guide to Bond and Money Market Mutual Funds, Spring 2015.** Amenia, N.Y., Grey House Publishing, 2015. 523p. $249.00pa. (single issue); $499.00pa. (4 quarterly issues). ISBN 13: 978-1-61925-597-5.

The stated purpose of *TheStreet Ratings' Guide to Bond and Money Market Mutual Funds* is "to provide investors with a reliable source of investment ratings and analyses on a timely basis." Coverage includes corporate bond funds, municipal bond funds, government bond funds, and money market funds. The ratings system is as follows: A (Excellent); B (Good), C (Fair), D (Weak), E (Very Weak), and U (Unrated). The plus and minus signs indicate the fund is at the top third or bottom third of its letter grade. Unrated is assigned to mutual funds if they are "too new to make a reliable assessment of its risk-adjusted performance." The guide has eight sections: Index of all Rated and Unrated Fixed Income Mutual Funds; Analysis of Largest Bond and Money Market Mutual Funds; Top 200 Bond Mutual Funds; Bottom 200 Bond Mutual Funds; Performance: 100 Best and Worst Bond Mutual Funds; Risk: 100 Best and Worst Bond Mutual Funds; Top-Rated Bond Mutual Funds by Risk Category; and Top-Rated Bond Mutual Funds by Fund Type. The appendix contains an investor profile quiz, fund descriptions, and more. The following information is included for each mutual fund in section one: fund name, fund type, ticker symbol, overall investment rating, phone, total return (three-month, six-month, etc), dividend yield, expense ratio, risk rating/points, net asset value, net assets, corporate bonds, manager tenure, average coupon rate, back-end load, and front-end load. Section two directory information includes name of fund, fund family, address, phone, major rating factors, annualized total return, services offered, and rating. The *Guide to Bond and Money Market Mutual Funds* should prove useful to investors seeking information and to researchers and students of business administration. Recommended for larger public libraries and academic libraries, particularly those supporting a program in undergraduate and graduate business.—**Lucy Heckman**

79. **TheStreet Ratings' Guide to Common Stocks, Spring 2015.** Amenia, N.Y., Grey House Publishing, 2015. 331p. $249.00pa. (single issue); $600.00pa. (4 quarterly issues). ISBN 13: 978-1-61925-581-4.

This guide to common stocks provides consumers, professionals, and institutions with high-quality advising information on common stocks traded on the NYSE, NYSE MKT, and NASDAQ. The book begins with a use guide, an explanation of how each stock is rated, the reasons the ratings in this title differ from other services, what the ratings mean, and important cautions and advice.

The data is presented in eight sections: Index of Common Stocks; Top 200 Common Stocks; Bottom 200 Common Stocks; Performance: The 100 Best and Worst Common Stocks; Risk: 100 Best and Worst Common Stocks; Top-Rated Stocks by Risk Category; Top Rated Common Stocks by Industry; and 200 Highest Dividend-Yielding Common Stock. For each stock, the guide provides information about such things as industry sector, company name, stock ticker symbol, overall investment rating, earnings, risk, and stock valuation as of 3/31/15.

Before purchasing a single volume, libraries will want to look into the Financial Rating Series offered by Grey House online at (http://www.financialratingsseries.com), which has financial strength ratings for more than 21,000 banks and insurance companies and investment ratings for over 6,000 stocks and 16,000 mutual funds.—**ARBA Staff Reviewer**

80. **TheStreet Ratings' Guide to Exchange-Traded Funds, Spring 2015.** Amenia, N.Y., Grey House Publishing, 2015. 852p. $249.00pa. (single issue); $499.00pa. (4 quarterly issues). ISBN 13: 978-1-61925-585-2.

The goal of the *Guide to Exchange-Traded Funds* is "to provide investors with a reliable source of investment ratings and analyses on a timely basis." Covered in this guide are: growth funds, sector or international funds, municipal bond funds, corporate bond funds, or other ETFs and closed-end funds. Excluded are open-end mutual funds; for information on open-end equity funds, refer to *TheStreet Ratings' Guide to Stock Mutual Funds* and for open-end bond or money market funds refer to *TheStreet Ratings' Guide to Bond and Money Market Mutual Funds*. Each Exchange-Traded Fund is rated on the following scale: A (Excellent, the top 10 % of funds); B (Good, next 20% of funds); C (Fair, middle 40% of funds); D (Weak, next 20 % of funds); and E (Very Weak, bottom 10% of funds). Pluses and Minuses indicate if it is in the upper or lower third of its letter grade. This guide is arranged within the following sections: Index of ETFs and other Closed-End Funds, an analysis of all rated and unrated Exchange-Traded Funds and Other Closed-End Mutual Funds; Analysis of ETFs and other Closed-End Funds, a summary analysis of all Exchange-Traded Funds and other Closed-End Mutual Funds receiving a TheStreet Investment Rating; Top ETFs and Other Closed-End Funds, a compilation of those Exchange-Traded Funds and Other Closed end mutual funds receiving the highest TheStreet Investment Ratings; Bottom ETFs and Other Closed-End Funds; Performance: Best and Worst ETFs and Other Closed-End Funds; and Top-Rated ETFs and Other Closed-End Funds by Fund Type; The appendix includes such things as fund type descriptions and exchange-traded funds summary data. Section one lists name of fund, fund type, ticker symbol, overall investment rating, price, 52-week high, 52-week low, total return (three-month, six-month, etc), dividend yield, expense ratio, beta, risk rating points, net assets, portfolio turnover rate, and manager tenure. Section two includes name of fund, fund family, fund type, inception date, major rating factors, rating, and annualized total return. *TheStreet Ratings' Guide to Exchange-Traded Funds* provides detailed information to help potential investors in exchange-traded funds. Students and faculty of business administration should also find this a helpful research source. Recommended.—**Lucy Heckman**

81.   **TheStreet Ratings' Guide to Stock Mutual Funds, Spring 2015.** Amenia, N.Y., Grey House Publishing, 2015. 837p. $249.00pa. (single issue); $499.00pa. (4 quarterly issues). ISBN 13: 978-1-61925605-7.

TheStreet Ratings Guide to Stock Mutual Funds condenses "all of the available mutual fund data into a single composite opinion of each fund's risk-adjusted performance." The mission of *TheStreet Ratings Guide to Stock Mutual Funds* "is to empower consumers, professionals, and institutions with high quality advisory information for selecting or monitoring financial investments." Included in the guide are growth funds, index funds, balanced funds, and sector or international funds; not included are pure bond funds or money market funds (for this data see *TheStreet Ratings Guide to Bond and Money Market Mutual Funds.* The following rating scale is used for Stock Mutual Funds: A (Excellent); B (Good); C (Fair); D (Weak) and E (Very Weak). Plus signs indicate that the fund is in the top third of its letter grade, the minus signs indicate that the fund is in the bottom third of its letter grade, and U (Unrated) indicates that it is too new to make a "reliable assessment of its risk-adjusted performance." The editors stress that there are important warnings and cautions involved in using the book: standards are more consumer-oriented than those of other rating agencies; "a rating alone cannot tell the whole story"; investment ratings in the guide were current as of publication date—for updates contact information is given, including the Website, www.thestreet.com/ratings; and decisions to buy and sell must be based on a wide variety of factors other than theStreet investment rating. *TheStreet Ratings Guide to Stock Mutual Funds* is arranged within the following sections: Index of Stock Mutual Funds, an analysis of all rated and selected unrated Equity Mutual Funds; Analysis of Largest Stock Mutual Funds, a summary analysis of the 183 largest retail Equity Mutual Funds, receiving TheStreet Investment Rating; The Top 200 Stock Mutual Funds; Bottom 200 Stock Mutual Funds; Performance: 100 Best Stock Mutual Funds; Top-Rated Stock Mutual Funds by Risk Category; and Top-Rated Stock Mutual Funds by Fund Type. The appendix contains a piece called "What is a Mutual Fund" and an investor profile quiz. Section one, the Index of Stock Mutual Funds lists each fund, its ticker symbol, overall investment rating, phone, total return, assets, minimums, and loads. Section two, Analysis of Largest Funds, includes name, address, phone, major rating factors, annualized total return (chart), rating, and services offered for each entry. *TheStreet Ratings Guide to Stock Mutual Funds* provides statistics and ratings of stock mutual funds and should serve as a useful guide to investors, consumers, and researchers. It is recommended to larger public libraries and academic libraries supporting a business program.—**Lucy Heckman**

Consumer Guides

Dictionaries and Encyclopedias

82.   **Real-World Decision Making: An Encyclopedia of Behavioral Economics.** Morris Altman, ed. Santa Barbara, Calif., Greenwood Press/ABC-CLIO, 2015. 499p. index. $100.00. ISBN 13: 978-1-4408-2815-7; 978-1-4408-2816-4 (e-book).

Economics is a multifaceted discipline which regularly subdivides into more specialized research areas. This book has been compiled as an attempt to provide the reader with a comprehensive set of definitions and explanations of key concepts used by researchers in the area of behavioral economics. The definitions have been written to be useful to the scholars doing research in this multidisciplinary area as well as providing insight for students, public policy experts, and journalists. Over 240 concepts are defined and over a dozen well-known experts in the field are profiled. A list of the contributors who provided the definitions for this encyclopedia has been included. Just reviewing the lists of terms shows the reader how diverse the field has become and the types of methodological tools that are used in developing their premises. The reader will find that each term includes a short, appended reading list.

This book will be useful in academic institutions that have economic departments.— **Judith J. Field**

Directories

83.   **The Directory of Mail Order Catalogs, 2015.** 29th ed. Amenia, N.Y., Grey House Publishing, 2015. 777p. index. $450.00pa. ISBN 13: 978-1-61925-286-8.

This, the 29th edition of *The Directory of Mail Order Catalogs,* is the latest installment of Grey House's longest-running annual reference directory. As the introduction points out, catalogs continue to play an important role in retail; in fact, the Direct Mail Association statistics show the number of catalogs mailed in 2013 represented the first increase since 2006. As proof, this directory contains 511 new catalogs across a wide number of categories.

The directory is organized in two sections. The first, Consumer Catalogs, has 43 chapters, starting with animals and covering such other areas as beauty, collectibles, educational products, gardens and lawns, hobbies, music, photography, shoes, toys and games, and travel and leisure, totaling 5,925 catalogs. The 2,761 catalogs in the 39 chapters from the second section, Business Catalogs, are aimed at business buyers. Categories of business catalogs include audio visual, building supplies, disability products, fire protection, lighting, packaging, sanitation, and work and apparel uniforms.

Searches are facilitated by the table of contents and five indexes: Consumer Catalog & Company, Business Catalog & Company, Consumer Geographical Index, Business Geographical Index, and Product Index. Users can find such details about companies as numbers and addresses, products sold, executive information, forms of payment accepted, number of employees, number of years in business, and sales volume. This data is also accessible electronically via Grey House's online database platform at http://gold.greyhouse.com. Recommended for larger public libraries and business libraries.—**ARBA Staff Reviewer**

Handbooks and Yearbooks

84.   **Weiss Ratings' Consumer Box Set.** Amenia, N.Y., Grey House Publishing, 2015. 9v. $499.00pa. (two biannual editions); $359.00pa. (single edition). ISBN 13: 978-1-61925-612-5.

Each title in the set, which is a part of the Financial Ratings Series, covers a topic with background information and step-by-step worksheets, making the content clear and easy to understand. Any graded entries receive a letter grade, with an explanation of what the grades mean, and the entries also contain contact information. A FAQ in each volume covers basic questions related to that volume's topic. The following volumes comprise the set: Automobile Insurance, Elder Care Choices, Homeowners Insurance, Long-Term Care Insurance, Medicare Supplement Insurance, Medicare Prescription Drug Coverage, Health Savings Accounts, Term Life Insurance, and Variable Annuities. Consumers seeking information on these topics may find them of use.—**Denise A. Garofalo**

Finance and Banking

Dictionaries and Encyclopedias

85.   **Encyclopedia of Education Economics & Finance.** Dominic J. Brewer and Lawrence O. Picus, eds. Thousand Oaks, Calif., Sage, 2014. 2v. index. $375.00/set. ISBN 13: 978-1-4522-8185-8.

The Encyclopedia of Education Economics & Finance is edited by Dominic J. Brewer, Gale and Ira Drukier Dean of New York University's Steinhardt School of Culture, Education, and Human Development and Lawrence O. Picus, professor of education finance and policy at the Rossier School of Education at the University of Southern California. These two, along with an editorial board of leading academics in the field of education policy and economics, solicited the more than 300 scholarly entries that comprise this two-volume work.

The entries are arranged alphabetically; however, a reader's guide at the beginning of each volume organizes topics thematically under such categories as "Accountability and Education Policy," "Production and Costs of Schooling," "Revenue and Aid for Schools," and "Teacher Labor Markets." Entries are several pages in length and each concludes with suggestions for further reading and *see also* references. The second volume includes three appendixes: a resource guide, an education chronology, and a glossary, followed by a subject index that contains *see* and *see also* references. The electronic version of the encyclopedia combines the index, reader's guide, and cross-references for easy searching.

A brief entry list is enough to indicate the scope of this encyclopedia in which users can find information on the Common Core, the benefits of higher education, *Brown* v.

Board of Education, early childhood education, education technology, for-profit higher education, general obligation bonds, property taxes, private contributions to schools, professional development, and much more. Public and academic libraries will want to own a copy of this well-researched, inclusive, and highly recommended title.—**ARBA Staff Reviewer**

86. **Personal Finance: An Encyclopedia of Modern Money Management.** Barbara Firedberg, ed. Santa Barbara, Calif., Greenwood Press/ABC-CLIO, 2015. 403p. index. $89.00. ISBN 13: 978-1-4408-3031-0; 978-1-4408-3032-7 (e-book).

Personal Finance: An Encyclopedia of Modern Money Management is a complete source that reports research and trends on sound financial decisions for the average person. Designed for researchers, scholars, and novices *Personal Finance* fills the need for personal financial education reference resources. Author Barbara Friedberg has previously published books on financial education and also has experience as an educator, chief financial officer, chief information officer, and chief executive officer. The book includes supplementary items such as an index, glossary, and suggested further reading on topics mentioned in the book.

The book is formatted akin to an encyclopedia but does differ in some aspects. The book is divided into three sections concerning personal finance—Ideas and Concepts, Events, and People. Within those three sections, topics are arranged alphabetically as one would find in an encyclopedia. Entries under those sections are neatly organized and typically include a general introduction followed by writings on specific topics. As an example Alimony is filed under the Ideas and Concepts section and has further sections on the history of alimony, alimony and gender, and more. This type of format is great for neophytes to the financial world because it provides a broad understanding of a subject as well as the option to dig deeper into the subject. The contents of this book, devoid of personal commentary from Friedman, provide the reader with a more research-driven and fact-driven reporting style. The reader will not necessarily be guided into making decisions about their own finances but will be educated in the process and history of the financial world. This book would be a solid addition to any academic or high school library and would correlate with the curriculum of any economics class. That said, the same lack of personal finance resources coupled with the general lack of knowledge surrounding personal finances also make this a great addition to a public library.

Personal Finance: An Encyclopedia of Modern Money Management is recommended for high school, academic, and public libraries.—**Sara Mofford**

Directories

87. **The Directory of Canadian Venture Capital & Private Equity Firms.** 5th ed. Amenia, N.Y., Grey House Publishing, 2016. 176p. index. $199.00. ISBN 13: 978-1-61925-969-0; 978-1-61925-970-6 (e-book).

This fifth edition of the directory profiles 185 financial firms and over 850 executives who work within the venture capital and private equity markets in Canada. In addition, the book contains reports and indexes which make the directory a user-friendly, invaluable resource for financial professionals.

The book opens with three technical reports detailing background of the Canadian markets and summaries of current activity, highlighting trends in particular sectors and more. In addition to a look at the geographical centers of venture capital interest, the reports share a number of charts and graphs offering a visual, data-driven overview.

The bulk of the directory arranges company listings alphabetically. Entries are numbered, and include contact information such as address(es), phone and fax numbers, email, and Web addresses. Entries also include a company's founding date, mission statement, geographic and industry-group preferences, investment criteria, portfolio companies, and key executives (with background and contact information if known).

Indexes make for easy reference, and include a college/university index aligning with executives' alma maters, an executive name index, a geographic index, an industry preference index, and a portfolio companies index.

This book can be a key publication for the business world, and would be handy in business libraries or for anyone researching the realm of Canadian venture capital.— **ARBA Staff Reviewer**

88. **The Directory of Venture Capital & Private Equity Firms: Domestic & International.** 19th ed. Amenia, N.Y., Grey House Publishing, 2015. 1352p. index. $395.00pa (library). ISBN 13: 978-1-61925-550-0.

Now in its 19th edition, *The Directory of Venture Capital & Private Equity Firms* provides information on over 3,000 firms, more than 1,000 branches, and more than 12,000 partners. This edition includes approximately 300 new firms and 1,000 new partners.

Like the other editions, this one is logically organized and easy to use. The information is divided into four major sections: Domestic Firms, Canadian Firms, Domestic Associations, and International Firms; information in each section is listed alphabetically.

The firm profiles include such necessary pieces of information as mission statements, geographic preferences, contact information, and investment criteria. Users will also find career and education information on partners. Each firm profile is assigned a number, which is referenced in the indexes.

The five indexes enhance the usability of this resource. The college/university index lists approximately 800 schools and the executives who attended them. The executive index lists the key partners (more than 12,000). For those who want to search by area, the geographic index organizes firms by state in the case of domestic listings and by country for international listings. These three finding aids are followed by the industry reference index—this lists more than 200 industry segments alphabetically along with the names of the firms that invest. The final index, the portfolio companies index, lists in alphabetical order more than 15,000 companies that receive venture capital from a firm listed in the directory.

Those buyers interested in purchasing this as an online database should consult http://gold.greyhouse.com. Larger public libraries and academic libraries will want a copy of this valuable reference resource.—**ARBA Staff Reviewer**

Handbooks and Yearbooks

89. Downes, John, and Jordan E. Goodman. **Finance & Investment Handbook.** 9th ed. Hauppauge, N.Y., Barron's Educational Series, 2014. 1152p. index. $39.99. ISBN 13: 978-0-7641-6751-5.

The purpose of this *Finance & Investment Handbook* is not to advise, but to "join in one volume the different elements" that together make up the world of finance and investment. This one-volume handbook provides a comprehensive presentation of terms and concepts of financial and investment terms that will enable the investor to talk knowledgeably with their broker, or as a broker, to be a better source of advice.

The handbook is divided into five parts: how to invest your money, which defines 30 key personal investment opportunities; how to read annual and quarterly reports; how to understand the financial news; the dictionary of finance and investment terms; and a finance and investment reference that provides a listing of organizations and government agencies, financial institutions, mutual funds, historical data, and publicly traded companies.

The definitions are concise and are accompanied by graphs and sidebars of additional information. Cross-references are minimal. The finance and investment ready reference lists provide names and contact information for financial sources. There is an appendix that provides a bibliography of financial and economic books, currencies of the world, and abbreviations and acronyms used in the book.

I would recommend this handbook to public and academic libraries business sections.—**Kay Stebbins Slattery**

90.   **Household Finance.** Michael Haliassos, ed. Northampton, Mass., Edward Elgar, 2015. 3v. (The International Library of Critical Writings in Economics). $1520.00/set. ISBN 13: 978-1-78347-604-6.

Economists today know much more about household assets and debt market participation and holdings than they did in the 1990s. Before 1990, many households had a bank savings account, a mortgage, and maybe an IRA for retirement. Throughout the 1990s more and more workers and retirees began investing in the various markets—stocks, bonds, mutual funds, and real estate. The papers presented in these three volumes provide in-depth insight into private household participation rates in various asset and debt categories, across countries and demographic groups.

Financial innovation has provided households with an increasing set of financial options from ever-expanding financial firms that provide a tremendous amount of financial information. The consumer gathers all of this financial information and becomes a "do it yourself" investor. Investors are expected to make decisions about their pension plan contributions and their payouts and to choose from an array of credit instruments to fund everything from home purchases to autos to short-term cash needs. The researchers found that many household portfolios did not have a high percentage of stocks and were not well-diversified in other areas of investments. The rich investor tended to invest in riskier investments than the poorer investor, and individual investors lacked trust in the investment firms as a whole. The researchers found that if private households used a broker, they were sold lines of investments whose distributions fees were higher, and that the consumer failed to consider the costs and benefits of the investor/broker relationship.

The third part of the papers presented is a discussion of credit card behavior, credit limits, and borrowing restraints and bankruptcy by private citizens. The puzzle to the researchers was the number of households that had high-interest loans, coupled with low-interest liquid assets that would not be sufficient to pay off the loans.

This publication is an exhaustive and insightful study of personal finance during the last 25 years. It is an essential work for business and economics researchers and students. Recommended for academic and large public library business collections.—**Kay Stebbins Slattery**

91.   Lehu, Pierre A. **Living on Your Own: The Complete Guide to Setting up Your Money, Your Space, and Your Life.** Sanger, Calif., Quill Driver, 2014. 232p. index. $18.95pa. ISBN 13: 978-1-61035-212-3.

Perhaps you've recently graduated from college. You've landed your first real job and mom is eyeing your bedroom for a new yoga studio. You're geared up to move out and move on, but where do you start and what should you expect? This book provides much of what you need to know in terms of planning, financing, and maintaining a life away from the nest.

The book is divided into sections covering home, personal, and financial aspects of life on one's own. Initial chapters help determine budgets and moving and living expenses, followed by the brass tacks of day-to-day life such as home furnishings, house cleaning, and utilities. The latter half of the book gets personal regarding issues of medical care, diet, and relationships. The book concludes with basic but important financial and legal advice.

Chapters are brief with generous headings, bulleted lists, and sidebars which make the information highly engaging and accessible. The author includes an ample supply of personal anecdotes, money-saving tips, and helpful community resources as well. From advice on air-drying laundry (saves money and smells nice) to the contemporary issues surrounding managing one's life via smart phone, *Living on Your Own* is the book for any adult taking their first baby steps out into the real world.—**Laura Herrell**

92.   **Life and Career Skills Series.** Miranda Herbert Ferrara and Michele P. LaMeau, eds. Farmington Hills, Mich., Gale/Cengage Learning, 2015. 4v. index. $600.00pa./set; $660.00 (e-book). ISBN 13: 978-1-4103-1760-0; 978-1-4103-1765-0 (e-book).

The Life and Career Skills series covers many topics with the aim of clearly conveying sound information regarding basic aspects of adult life. The four volumes are designed to offer the most up-to-date, pertinent information in a logical and engaging way.

The first volume focuses on the topic of personal finance. The book organizes its material into four main sections: Personal Decision Making and Shopping, Why People Go into Debt, Saving and Investing Money, and Insurance and Government Protection. Subsequent chapters within each section are concise and use an easy-to-follow question-and-answer format to convey information on such topics as the benefits of a budget and the consequences of not paying a bill. Volume two on employment has the following four main sections: Take Action on Your Job Search, Identify and Target New Opportunities, Getting a Job, and Keeping a Job or Knowing When It's Time to Move On. The question-and-answer section covers basics like how to get a job with no work experience and job search fundamentals. Volume three focuses on health and wellness. It is important to note that the information in this volume is meant to be general and educational; however, it is not definitive and cannot replace discussion with physicians or other healthcare practitioners. The four main sections are: Nutrition, Exercise and Personal Care and Hygiene; Preventative Health Care, Medications and Alternative Medicine; Health-Care System; and Personal Identity, Mental Health and Behavior. A key highlight from the Health-Care System section is the excellent report on the current U.S. government health programs, including the Affordable Care Act. Information conveyed in the question-and-answer portion includes the importance of physical activity, ways to teach good hygiene, and lifestyle advice. The final volume on social skills has four main sections: Interpersonal Communication Skills; Organizational, Problem-Solving and Decision-Making, and Conflict Resolution Skills; Entering the Workplace: Professional Ethics, Etiquette and

Conduct; and Teamwork, Collaboration and Leadership Skills. In the question-and-answer section users will learn about such things as obstacles to good communication, the benefits of face-to-face communication, and presentations.

The material is enhanced by a number of eye-catching extras, such as shaded sidebars housing case studies, professional profiles, etc.; visual iconography pointing to key terms, concepts, and helpful hints; charts; photographs; and more. Additionally, the four sections in each volume begin with an overview that supplies foundational information. At the end of each chapter within the four sections, readers will find a listing of books, periodicals, and Websites for further information. A more comprehensive list of resources is found at the end of the volume, in addition to a list of such key organizations as the American Financial Services Association, the Centers for Disease Control and Prevention (CDC), and the Center for Creative Leadership. Concept, name, and term indexes appear at the end of each volume.—**ARBA Staff Reviewer**

93. **Weiss Ratings' Guide to Banks: A Quarterly Compilation of Financial Institutions Ratings and Analyses, Spring 2015.** Amenia, N.Y., Grey House Publishing, 2015. 343p. index. (Financial Ratings Series). $249.00pa. (single edition); $499.00pa. (4 quarterly editions). ISBN 13: 978-1-61925-577-7.

This volume in the Financial Ratings Series provides a comprehensive listing and rating of U.S.-based commercial and savings banks as a way to assist readers with the selection and monitoring of their financial institution. It employs an objective, easy-to-follow ratings system marked by an A-F grading scale (A "U" rating denotes that the institution is unrated) and provides users with nine steps of clear instruction on how to best approach and use its information.

Ratings reflect a summation of rigorous analysis which considers a company's financial solvency relative to both favorable and adverse economic situations. Mainly deriving its analysis from company financial statements, Weiss Ratings then considers that information against a number of different indexes in order to assign its grade.

The main content of the guide presents an alphabetical listing of over 6,000 U.S. commercial and savings banks. In addition to the institution name, location, and grade, each listing includes information such as total assets, asset growth, net income, asset base investments, prior ratings, and much more, all of which are clearly defined preceding the listings. Subsequent listings in the guide compile recommended banks by state (those which have received a grade of B+ or above), as well as those institutions whose ratings have been downgraded or upgraded from the previous quarterly review.

An appendix includes information regarding recently failed institutions, a glossary of terms, and a basic but enlightening comparison between credit unions and banks. This guide would be extremely useful for consumers or professionals seeking broad-based financial institution information. Recommended for public libraries.—**Laura Herrell**

94. **Weiss Ratings' Guide to Credit Unions, Spring 2015: A Quarterly Compilation of Credit Union Ratings and Analyses.** Amenia, N.Y., Grey House Publishing, 2015. 326p. (Financial Ratings Series). $249.00pa. (single edition); $499.00pa. (4 quarterly editions). ISBN 13: 978-1-61925-615-6.

Weiss Ratings has created this volume in its Financial Ratings Series in order to provide readers with a solid analytical tool for use in selecting and monitoring their credit union. It employs an objective, easy-to-follow ratings system marked by an A-F grading scale (A "U" rating denotes that the listed institution is unrated) and provides users with nine steps of clear instruction on how to best approach and use its information.

Ratings reflect a summation of rigorous analysis which considers a company's financial solvency relative to both favorable and adverse economic situations. Mainly deriving its analysis from company financial statements, Weiss Ratings then considers that information against a number of different indexes in order to assign its grade.

The main content of the guide presents an alphabetical listing of over 6,000 credit unions. In addition to the institution name, location, and grade, each listing includes information such as total assets, asset growth, net income, asset base investments, and much more, all of which are clearly defined preceding the listings. Subsequent listings in the guide compile recommended credit unions by state (those which have received a grade of B+ or above), as well as those institutions whose ratings have been downgraded or upgraded from the previous quarterly review.

An appendix includes information regarding recently failed institutions, a glossary of terms, and a basic but enlightening comparison between credit unions and banks. The guide is also available for subscription as part of the Financial Ratings Series Online. This guide would be highly useful to consumers or professionals seeking broad-based financial institution information.—**Laura Herrell**

Industry and Manufacturing

Dictionaries and Encyclopedias

95.   Tortora, Phyllis G., and Ingrid Johnson. **Fairchild Books Dictionary of Textiles.** 8th ed. New York, Bloomsbury Academic, 2014. 711p. illus. $210.00; $188.99 (e-book). ISBN 13: 978-1-60901-535-0. 978-1-60901-950-1 (e-book).

This eighth, and 100th anniversary, edition updates the dictionary that has been published since 1915. The dictionary provides a basic reference tool for those working in or studying the textile industry and related fields and contains some 14,000 entries on fabrics, fibers, inventors, organizations, and other textile-related topics. Entries all focus on the definitions relevant to textiles rather than those more common in standard dictionaries. For example, "austria" is defined solely as a "twilled silk fabric used for covering umbrellas." Pronunciation guidance, alternate spellings, historical background, and *see* and *see also* references are provided for terms as the editors feel appropriate. The dictionary also includes black-and-white illustrations to clarify some terms. Geographical references throughout the book have been updated in this edition to reflect current terminology. An appendix listing U.S. and international trade, educational, and professional organizations and associations is also included. This is a useful reference that will be of primary importance for patrons researching historical or contemporary aspects of the textile industry and related subjects.—**Mary Bagne**

Directories

96.   **Food & Beverage Market Place, 2016.** 15th ed. Amenia, N.Y., Grey House Publishing, 2015. 3v. index. $695.00/set. ISBN 13: 978-1-61925-732-0.

The *Food & Beverage Market Place* is a huge three-volume directory which has been updated from the previous edition with more company profiles and updated entries. The first volume contains food and beverage manufacturers. The first section of this volume lists common products and ingredients and the corresponding categories used throughout the rest of the works. The second section lists the manufacturing companies by those categories, and the third section lists all of the profiles of those companies in alphabetical order. Then there are four indexes: by brand names, ethnic food, geography, and parent/subsidiary. The second volume contains equipment, supplies, and services companies. It too has a product category and company profiles sections. There are two indexes—brand names and geography. The third volume contains broker companies, importers/exporters, transportation firms, warehouse companies, and wholesalers/distributors. There are 11 indexes that allow the user to search by company, region, type, and brands.

The entire directory can be a little confusing when trying to use it the first time. However, the table of contents and user guides with examples at the front of each volume help. The sections were also difficult to differentiate without flipping, and it would benefit to add tabs or colored pages at the edges to visually help distinguish the various sections. The cover also shows that there is content on organic and gluten-free, but this was difficult to find in the directory. The product category listing shows where to find organic but not gluten-free. They were listed alphabetically in the product category section "Specialty & Organic Foods" which may not be intuitive. Since it is a print resource, one cannot search the data in all the ways users may be interested. For example, users are unable to search for a specific product in a state. If a user wanted to find bread manufacturers in Michigan she would have to browse the product page that includes all states to look for those located in Michigan. The individual company entries included basic information and varied in the amount of information available. The directory does not describe the criteria used to determine what companies make it in the directory as it does not include every company. As an added note, there is an online version available via the Grey House Online Database (GOLD) which may make it easier to search.

Overall, while navigating the content can be a challenge at first, this directory provides access to useful information in one spot for anyone interested in locating companies and brands within the distribution and supply chain of the food and beverage industry.—**Breezy Silver**

Insurance

Handbooks and Yearbooks

97.   Heckman, Lucy. **The ALA Guide to Information Sources in Insurance, Risk Management and Actuarial Science.** Chicago, American Library Association, 2016. 213p. index. $70.00pa.; $63.00pa. (ALA members). ISBN 13: 978-0-8389-1275-1.

Lucy Heckman (Head of Reference, St. John's University Library and author of several business-related guides to information sources) has focused her expertise on the insurance industry, creating a detailed bibliography covering all aspects of insurance and actuarial science. Written for a wider audience than librarians, this book is organized intuitively, with materials for general insurance information, and textbooks comprising the first two chapters, and then delving deeper into the many subspecialties of insurance, risk management, and actuarial science. Within those chapters, sources are broken out by format, allowing readers the option to locate materials most conducive to their reading preferences. Heckman finishes her bibliography with chapters dedicated to information sources geared towards education and finding careers in insurance and then a chapter of miscellaneous sources. Particularly helpful for librarians in smaller institutions, or in institutions without dedicated reference for business and related disciplines, Heckman provides several appendixes, covering an alphabet soup of abbreviations and acronyms, lists of associations and agencies with their Websites, select journals with ISSN numbers, school and university departments supporting insurance, risk management and/or actuarial science, and selected major libraries (academic and public) supporting business and management. A small but detailed reference work, this paperback could function as the one insurance, risk management, and actuarial science resource for academic libraries with smaller collections or for public libraries with a strong business focus. For larger institutions, this text would provide a handy quick guide in a reference collection.—**Rachel Meredith Minkin**

98.   **Weiss Ratings' Guide to Health Insurers, Spring 2015.** Amenia, N.Y., Grey House Publishing, 2015. 535p. $249.00pa. (single issue); 499.00pa. (4 quarterly issues). ISBN 13: 978-1-61925-589-0.

The purpose of *Weiss Ratings' Guide to Health Insurers* is "to provide policyholders and prospective policy purchasers with a reliable source of insurance company ratings and analyses on a timely basis." The guide covers medical reimbursement insurance; managed health care (PPOs and HMOs); disability income; and long-term care (nursing home) insurance. It includes ratings for commercial for-profit insurers; mutual insurers; Blue Cross/Blue Shield plans; and for-profit and not-for-profit insurance. Companies are rated as follows: A (Excellent)—the company offers excellent financial security; B (Good)—the company offers good financial security and "comfortably exceeds " the minimum levels for all rating criteria; C (Fair)—the company offers fair security and is currently stable but may have difficulties during economic downturn and other financial pressures; D (Weak)—company has significant weaknesses and in unfavorable economic conditions, the weaknesses could be magnified; E (Very Weak)—company has significant weaknesses, failing the basic tests Weiss uses to demonstrate fiscal stability; F (Failed)—this occurs when the company is either "under supervision of insurance regulatory authority, in the process of rehabilitation; in the process of liquidation or voluntarily dissolved after disciplinary or other regulatory action by an insurance regulatory authority;" and U (Unrated Companies), which includes companies whose total assets are less than $1 million; premium income for current year is less than $100,000; the company functions mostly as a holding company rather than an underwriter; and not enough information is available for Weiss to issue a rating. Plus or minus signs indicate if companies are at the lower or upper end of letter grade ratings. The *Guide to Health Insurers* is arranged in the following sections: Index of Companies, an analysis of 1722 rated and unrated companies; Analysis of Largest

Companies; Weiss Recommended Companies; Weiss Recommended Companies by State; Long-Term Care Insurers; Medicare Supplement Insurance; Analysis of Medicare Managed Care Complaints (analysis for complaints filed against U.S. Medicare Managed Care Plans); and Rating Upgrades and Downgrades. The appendix includes a long-term care insurance planner, a Medicare prescription drug planner, and more. Section one, Index of Companies, provides name of insurance company, domicile state, financial strength rating, data date, total assets, total premiums, health premiums, and capital and surplus. Section two, Analysis of Largest Companies, includes name of company, major rating factors, principal business, member physicians (number), medical loss ratio, enrollment (total number of policyholders, group affiliation, principal investments, historical data, address, and phone. *Weiss Ratings' Guide to Health Insurers* contains a wealth of information for consumers, health care professionals, and students and faculty of colleges and universities supporting an insurance program. Recommended.—**Lucy Heckman**

99.   **Weiss Ratings' Guide to Life and Annuity Insurers: A Quarterly Compilation of Insurance Company Ratings and Analyses. Spring 2015.** Amenia, N.Y., Grey House Publishing, 2015. 322p. (Financial Ratings Series). $249.00pa. (single edition); $499.00pa. (4 quarterly editions). ISBN 13: 978-1-61925-593-7.

This volume in the Financial Ratings Series provides a comprehensive listing and rating of U.S.-based life and annuity insurance companies as a way to assist readers with the selection and monitoring of their policyholder. It employs an objective, easy-to-follow ratings system marked by an A-F grading scale (A "U" rating denotes that the institution is unrated) and provides users with 14 steps of clear instruction on how to best approach and use its information.

Ratings reflect a summation of rigorous analysis which considers a company's financial solvency relative to both favorable and adverse economic situations. Mainly deriving its analysis from company financial statements procured from state insurance commissioners, Weiss Ratings then considers that information against a number of different indexes in order to assign its grade.

The first section of the guide presents an alphabetical listing of over 800 life and annuity insurance companies. In addition to the institution name, location and grade, each listing includes information such as total assets, capital and surplus, net premium, and invested assets, all of which are clearly defined preceding the listings. Section two offers a summary analysis of the largest companies (with capital over $25 million) and includes information such as principle business, principle investments, and licensing. Particular to this section are customized graphs detailing a company's net income history, rating indexes, and policy leverage among other things. Subsequent sections compile recommended companies by state (those which have received a grade of B+ or above), all companies indexed by rating, and those institutions whose ratings have been downgraded or upgraded from the previous quarterly review.

An appendix includes a chart detailing coverage of state guaranty funds, a listing of recently failed institutions, a glossary of terms, and more. This guide would be extremely useful for consumers or professionals seeking broad-based insurance institution information.—**Laura Herrell**

100.   **Weiss Ratings' Guide to Property and Casualty Insurers, Spring 2015.** Amenia, N.Y., Grey House Publishing, 2015. 436p. $249.00pa. (single issue); $499.00pa. (4 quarterly issues). ISBN 13: 978-1-61925-601-9.

The purpose of the *Weiss Ratings' Guide to Property and Casualty Insurers* is "to provide policyholders and prospective policy purchasers with a reliable source of insurance company ratings and analyses on a timely basis." This guide covers homeowners insurance, business insurance, auto insurance, workers' compensation insurance, product liability insurance, and medical malpractice and professional liability insurance. Companies are rated according to the following scale: A. Excellent; B. Good; C. Fair; D. Weak; E. Very Weak; F. Failed; and U. Unrated. Plus and minus signs indicate whether the company is on the upper end or lower end of the letter grade. The guide is arranged within the following sections: Index of Companies; Analysis of Largest Companies; Weiss Recommended Companies; Weiss Ratings Recommended Companies by Type of Business; Weiss Ratings Recommended Companies by State; All Companies Listed by Rating; and Rating Upgrades and Downgrades. The appendix, which includes information on state guaranty funds, recent industry failures, and more. Each company listed in section one includes insurance company name, domicile state, financial strength rating, total assets, capital and surplus, net premium, reserve adequacy index, profitability index, liquidity index, stability index, stability factors, loss ratio, expense ratio, and net premium growth. Largest company entries in section two include, name, address, phone, NAICS code, rating factors, principal business, principal investments, and rating. The *Weiss Ratings' Guide to Property and Casualty Insurers* provides detailed information to consumers, practitioners, students, faculty, and researchers. Recommended to larger public libraries and to university libraries supporting programs in insurance, actuarial science, and risk management.—**Lucy Heckman**

International Business

Handbooks and Yearbooks

101. World Trade Organization Dispute Settlement Decisions. Volume 102: Decisions Reported 27 April 2009-14 May 2009. Jackson C. Pai, Mark Nguyen, and Bryan Cave, eds. Lanham, Md., Bernan Press, 2015. $175.00. ISBN 13: 978-1-59888-771-6.

This book represents a comprehensive chronological collection of all decisions of the World Trade Organization Dispute Settlement Body, which includes full cases heard by World Trade Organization panels and/or its Appellate Body. This volume (102) covers two decisions reported within April and May of 2009: *Colombia—Indicative Prices and Restrictions on Ports of Entry* and *United States—Laws, Regulations and Methodology for Calculating Dumping Margins ("Zeroing").*

Each report begins with an Annotations section which includes the identities of the complaint and respondent nations, the date the decision was issued, procedural history, summarized conclusions, annotations, and an informational market implication section (new to this volume).

The volume then presents the World Trade Organization report issued for each case in its entirety. A detailed table of contents precedes each report and outlines its structure by including the following sections: Introduction, Factual Aspects, Parties' Requests,

Arguments of the Parties, Arguments of the Third Parties, Interim Review, Findings, and Conclusions and Recommendations. The table of contents also includes numerous subsections listing executive summaries of each party's submissions and rebuttals, and more.

Following both reports are helpful tables noting an update of disputes recorded during the timeframe of this volume, updated dispute settlement activity by country (noting whether the country is a complainant or respondent), the specific World Trade Organization agreements interpreted within the two cases of this volume, and a listing of other subsidiary World Trade Organization materials such as decisions, protocols, announcements, and more applicable to these cases.

This thorough publication provides an accessible way for readers to closely study World Trade Organization mechanisms and decision-making analyses and would be of great interest to students or professionals involved with international trade.—**Laura Herrell**

Labor

Career Guides

102.   **Careers in Building Construction.** Michael Shally-Jensen, ed. Hackensack, N.J., Salem Press, 2015. 351p. illus. index. $95.00. ISBN 13: 978-1-61925-862-4; 978-1-61925-863-1 (e-book).

This book provides a compact resource for examining the many career possibilities in building construction. Readers will learn general information about this growing and changing sector, as well as more targeted information regarding specific jobs. Particular mention is made of "green" construction and its emphasis on sustainability, energy efficiency, and environmental awareness.

Alphabetically arranged chapters guide readers through 26 diverse jobs, such as brickmason, electrician, plumber, surveyor, and landscape architect. Within each chapter, readers will find ample and varied information detailing specific work duties, the expected work environment, occupation specialties (a heavy-equipment operator may specialize in a particular vehicle, e.g., a crawler-tractor, scraper, or fine-grade bulldozer), educational requirements, earnings and advancement potential, and much more. The use of bullet points, shaded sidebars, tables, and photographs make the material easy to navigate. Some special features include "Fun Facts," "Famous Firsts," projected employment trends, interviews with professionals, and a listing of applicable organizations readers can consult for further information.

Appendixes explain the Holland Code, which provides a useful tool to help potential job seekers match their personalities with career possibilities, and provide a bibliography.

Compiled in a positive, straightforward manner, this book will appeal to young readers just beginning to considering their career path or even older readers mulling a shift into this job sector. An index makes for quick searching for those interested in a particular career.—**ARBA Staff Reviewer**

103.   **Careers in Human Services.** Michael Shally-Jensen, ed. Hackensack, N.J., Salem Press, 2015. 357p. illus. index. $95.00. ISBN 13: 978-1-61925-778-8; 978-1-61925-779-5 (e-book).

Human Services is a broad career category that includes many compelling and surprisingly diverse jobs that call for attention and study. This well-organized, easy-to-use reference can help job seekers learn general information about Human Services and perhaps narrow their choices within the field.

Alphabetically arranged chapters guide readers through 25 different specialties, ranging from activities therapist to vocational rehabilitation counselor. Within each chapter, readers will find ample and encouraging information detailing specific job duties, the expected work environment, occupation specialties, educational requirements, earnings and advancement potential, and much more. The use of such devices as bullet points, shaded sidebars, and tables makes the material easy to navigate. Some special features include a brief history of a particular job, a typical day in the life on the job, interviews with professionals, a "snapshot" of the job, and a listing of applicable organizations readers can consult for more information.

The book also includes a helpful overview providing a general sense of the types of people who might pursue a career in Human Services, the types of people who might benefit from these jobs (e.g., the elderly, military veterans, immigrants, etc.), the types of professional Human Services organizations available, and more. In addition, an appendix provides a useful tool to help potential job seekers match their personalities with career possibilities, followed by a bibliography and an index.

Compiled in a positive, comprehensive manner, this book will appeal to those embarking on their first job search as well as those considering a shift into this fulfilling job sector. Recommended for students at the high school and undergraduate level.—**Laura Herrell**

104.   **Careers in Technical Services & Equipment Repair.** Michael Shally-Jensen, ed. Amenia, N.Y., Grey House Publishing, 2015. 326p. illus. index. $95.00. ISBN 13: 978-1-61925-780-1; 978-1-61925-781-8 (e-book).

This guidebook is a go-to source for those considering entering the broad field of technical services and equipment repair. It not only educates readers as to what types of jobs are available, but also provides ample information regarding the greater job environment in an engaging way.

Alphabetically arranged chapters guide readers through 25 different jobs, ranging from aircraft mechanic to vending machine repair. Within each chapter, readers will take a straightforward and thorough look at specific job duties, elements of the work environment, occupation specialties, educational and training requirements, earnings and advancement potential, and much more. The use of bullet points, shaded sidebars, tables and more makes the material easy to follow. Some special features include "Famous Firsts," a typical day in the life on the job, conversations with professionals, a "snapshot" of the job, and a listing of applicable organizations readers can consult for more information.

The book also includes a helpful overview providing a general sense of the types of people who might pursue a technical career, an employment outlook, and information about training, skills, and certifications. In addition, an appendix provides a useful tool based on the Holland Code to help potential job seekers match their personalities with career possibilities.

Compiled in a positive, comprehensive manner, this book will appeal to those embarking on their first job search as well as those considering a shift into this fulfilling job sector.—**Laura Herrell**

105.   **Encyclopedia of Careers and Vocational Guidance.** 16th ed. New York, Infobase Publishing, 2015. 5v. $249.95/set. ISBN 13: 978-0-8160-8503-3.

The Encyclopedia of Careers and Vocational Guidance has been in print for more than 45 years and is now in its 16th edition. This edition includes more than 50 new job articles, over 15 new career field and industry articles, hundreds of new photographs, and updated career information about 820 jobs in 120 fields in five volumes. This edition also includes such new sections as Career Ladders and Tips for Entry.

The first volume's Career Guidance section provides chapters on preparing for a career, finding a job, applying for a job, and what job seekers need to know once hired. In each of these chapters, users will find an annotated list of related Websites. Career Guidance is followed by Career Fields and Industries, which has overviews of 120 career fields or industries such as book publishing, computer and video game design, insurance, railroads, trucking, and waste management. The first volume concludes with two appendixes, the first of which, "Career Resources and Associations for Individuals with Disabilities," supplies Web and physical addresses, phone numbers, and other information. The second, "Internships, Apprenticeships, and Training Programs," has been completely updated for this edition and gives names, physical and Web addresses, and phone numbers for government and other organizations. Four indexes conclude the first volume.

The career articles are arrayed in four alphabetically organized volumes; each starts with a list of the career articles it contains and concludes with a job index that pertains to the whole set. Black-and-white photographs and sidebars with quick facts enhance these entries. Individual job descriptions convey a wealth of information about earnings potential, required education and training, advancement prospects, and much more.

This reference makes accessible a large amount of career-related information and is recommended to public and school libraries.—**ARBA Staff Reviewer**

106.   **Employment, Hours, and Earnings 2015.** 10th ed. Ryan, Mary Meghan, ed. Lanham, Md., Bernan Press, 2014. 726p. $105.00; $104.99 (e-book). ISBN 13: 978-1-59888-787-7; 978-1-59888-788-4 (e-book).

Employment Hours, and Earnings: States and Areas 2015, a special addition to Bernan Press's *Handbook of U.S. Labor Statistics: Employment, Earnings, Prices, Productivity, and Other Labor Data* "is a consolidated wealth of employment information, providing monthly and annual data on hours worked and earnings made by industry across America for the years 2005 through 2014." This resource covers the 50 states, the District of Columbia, and America's 75 largest metropolitan statistical areas (MSAs). *Employment, Hours and Earnings* is divided into sections: Part A, State Data, and Part B, Metropolitan Statistical Area (MSA) Data. Part A contains data for individual states; coverage includes: population (2005 estimate, 2010 census, and 2014 estimate); percent change in population for 2005-2014 and 2010-2014; percent change in total nonfarm employment; industry with the largest growth in employment, 2005-2014; industry with the largest decline or smallest growth in employment, 2005-2014; civilian labor force for 2005, 2010, and 2014; unemployment rate and rank among states for 2005, 2010, 2014; over-the-year change in employment rates 2011-2012, 2012-2013, 2013-2014; employment by industry (pie chart); and tables for employment by industry, 2005-2014 and average hourly earnings by selected industry, 2010-2014. Part B contains MSA data including employment by industry 2005-2014. Additionally the book includes a table of 75 MSAs ranked by population; in the overall rankings list, each MSA provides employment and unemployment rates. Specific

MSAs covered include: New York-Newark-Jersey City, NY-NJ-PA; Los Angeles-Long Beach-Anaheim, CA; Denver-Auroroa-Lakewood, CO; and Raleigh, NC. The appendix contains the 75 largest MSAs and components (as defined February 2013). Each MSA entry includes core based statistical area; state/county FIPS code; and a list of counties included within each MSA. This reference resource fills a need for employment data by state and MSA and provides approximately 300 tables. An explanation of concepts and terms is included in the Overview section. Recommended to larger public and academic libraries.—**Lucy Heckman**

Management

Handbooks and Yearbooks

107. Alexander, Geoff. **The Nonprofit Survival Guide: A Strategy for Sustainability.** Jefferson, N.C., McFarland, 2015. 212p. index. $29.95pa. ISBN 13: 978-0-7864-9844-4; 978-1-4766-2050-3 (e-book).

The big picture challenges of the nonprofit organization are many. How do you attract funding from limited pockets? How does your cause stand out above the crowd of equally worthy organizations? And how do you and your mission stay afloat during tough economic times? This book helps readers gain control of the smaller challenges behind running a nonprofit so that they can keep their focus on the big picture and keep their nonprofit running smoothly.

Short but informative chapters organize a variety of topics geared around the overall theme of success. Information details how to set up an office, how to create and maintain an online presence, the importance of volunteers, pursuing sponsorships and nontraditional modes of income, managing publicity, and thinking alternatively, among other things. Prevalent use of subheadings, checklists, real-life examples, and more helps make the material memorable and actionable.

There are two appendixes. The first provides case studies of three successful nonprofits and the second a sample checklist that organizes a nonprofit's inventory (down to software particulars) and important access information. There are also extensive notes, a good bibliography, and an index.

Written in an experienced and encouraging tone, this book is the right choice for those interested in running or working within the growing nonprofit sector.—**ARBA Staff Reviewer**

108. Bolton, Robert, and Dorothy Grover Bolton. **What Great Trainers Do: The Ultimate Guide to Delivering Engaging and Effective Learning.** New York, AMACOM/American Management Association, 2015. 304p. index. $45.00pa. ISBN 13: 978-0-8144-2006-5; 978-0-8144-2007-2 (e-book).

Even the best job trainers need training, and this book offers a warehouse full of the latest, most effective tips and tools for helping readers become the best corporate trainers they can.

The book addresses the many elements of successful training in a way that allows readers to comprehend the importance of utilizing these elements together. Key sections highlight the overall importance of fusing solid content with active training, with particular emphasis on developing a dynamic workshop, the trainer as facilitator, and maturing as a trainer.

Singular topics under these umbrella concepts include how to best use flip charts and PowerPoint slides, how to actively engage workshop participants, how to keep training positive, and how to improve things in training that don't work well.

Material is broken down into small, headed sections for ease of reference, and the authors use lists, bullet points, charts, and other devices as well. Appendixes offer worksheets to help trainers prepare a course, tips on how to adapt workshops to their audience, and advice on how to "install" one's training program.

With its positive tone and solid selection of best practices, the book will set readers off on the right path to enhance job training to the point of vastly improved corporate result.—**Laura Herrell**

109.   Doucette, Jill, and Lee Johnson. **Greening Your Office: Strategies That Work.** North Vancouver, B.C., Self-Counsel Press, 2014. 117p. (Green Series). $12.95pa. ISBN 13: 978-1-77040-208-9; 978-1-77040-964-4 (e-book).

This straightforward guide aims to help offices of all sizes minimize the amount of environmental resources used to conduct business. Chapter one lays out the case for going green at the office, while subsequent chapters discuss such things as a triple-bottom-line approach that takes people, the planet, and profit into account; the common barriers to creating a green office and ways to start the process; the benefits of a green office; ways to assess an office's environmental performance and engage team members; and marketing a business as a green company. The book uses case studies, quick tips, checklists, and tables that make the prospect of creating a green office less daunting. A download kit available via the URL provided in the book includes references and resources for further readings as well as checklists. This reference is recommended for public libraries.—**ARBA Staff Reviewer**

110.   **Handbook of Research Methods on Human Resource Development.** Mark N.K. Saunders and Paul Tosey, eds. Northampton, Mass., Edward Elgar, 2015. 424p. index. (Handbooks of Research Methods in Management series). $225.00. ISBN 13: 978-1-78100-923-9.

Handbook of Research Methods on Human Resource Development provides a great reference source if one is interested in data collection methodologies and analysis techniques in the ever-evolving field of human resource development. There is an in-depth introduction that summarizes the four parts of the book which are Conceptual Issues, Qualitative Research, Quantitative Research, and Methodological Challenges. With a total of 25 essays written by 42 authors, the essays provide perspectives from a scholarly point of view both past and present in collecting qualitative and quantitative measures in human resource development. In conjunction with the text content, visual learners will appreciate the abundance of supplementary resources including figures, images, tables, and graphs. An index enhances the overall usefulness of the work.

All of the essays are set up in a specific format that includes a summary, introduction, and a discussion after all of the content is presented. The discussion after the essay is beneficial because it includes how this research is important to the continuing research world of human resource development. Most of the history presented in the book only focuses on the last quarter of a century but this is mainly because research in human resource is a fairly new research topic. Another great feature of the book is that after every individual article there is an annotated further reading list. This annotated further reading list offers commentary by the individual authors on suggesting further research resources for the reader. The author provides a cited source and also a small summary on why a particular source would be of interest to the reader and its relevance to human resource development.

The content of this book is saturated with research, which is appropriate since the focus of this book is research in human resource development. The content is a plethora of both past and present research not only in this book but also in the emerging field of human resources. This book breaks down the different challenges that the field has had to deal with because of the wide range of different methodologies and techniques. This book could be used to teach those interested in the field of human resources but it could also be used to teach those that have a general interest in research methods. *Handbook of Research Methods on Human Resource Development* is available in hardback and paperback (significantly less expensive). Highly recommended as a reference source for academic libraries.—**Sara Mofford**

111.   **Handbook of Research on Management Ideas and Panaceas: Adaptation and Context.** Anders Örtenblad, ed. Northampton, Mass., Edward Elgar, 2016. 508p. index. $240.00. ISBN 13: 978-1-78347-559-9; 978-1-78347-560-5 (e-book).

Handbook of Research on Management Ideas and Panaceas concentrates on general management ideas such as, but not limited to, achieving competitive excellence, competitive intelligence, corporate social responsibility, Japanese management, social cognitive theory, strategic human resources management, total quality management, and transformational leadership. The book is comprised of 26 essays authored by 39 experts with experience ranging from management, human resources, political science, and communications to psychology and economics. The objective of this book is to teach readers about management ideas and the application of those ideas to organizational problems. The essays provide a wide range of supplemental illustrations as well as an index, figures, tables, and images. These supplementary items enhance the usefulness of the material. The work includes history, research, trends, comparative management, and methods to create a sustainable future for managing an organization. Most of the essays are written by academics; this is not a book in which subjects reflect on their experiences with management ideas.

The book is easy to navigate. The introduction briefly summarizes every essay, clearly stating the objectives of each piece. This book would be appropriate for someone who is looking for a specific management idea or someone who wants to grasp an all-encompassing knowledge of management ideas. Even though the content is written with academic standards, the text pertains to all levels and types of organizations. In general the book concentrates on the Western world but there is an inclusion of two essays, "The Curious Case of Japanese Management: A Nation as a Panacea" and "Global Wisdom: Not a Panacea, but Absolutely Necessary for Transcending Managerial Failures" that highlight management ideas in both Japan and South American countries. Most of the research cited in this volume is current and almost all of the content deals with management ideas that are conducive to a twenty-first-century society. *Handbook of Research on Management Ideas and Panaceas* is highly recommended as a reference source for academic and business libraries.—**Sara Mofford**

112.   **Handbook of Research on Managing Managers.** Adrian Wilkinson, Keith Townsend, and Gabriele Suder, eds. Northampton, Mass., Edward Elgar, 2016. 379p. index. $210.00. ISBN 13: 978-1-78347-428-8.

The three editors of this book state in their introduction that whereas there has been "an ever-growing mountain of research on management...much less attention has been paid to managers and still less to how they are themselves managed." Editors Adrian Wilkinson and Keith Townsend are professors of Employment Relations at Griffith University, Australia, and Gabriele Suder is Principal Fellow at the Melbourne School and Director of International Relations at The University of Melbourne. The 30 contributors come from Australia, France, the United Kingdom, India, Tanzania, Canada, and Scandinavia. The book is divided into three parts: "Processes Available to Managers within Organisational Boundaries," "Topics Cutting across the Roles of Managers," and "Contemporary Issues and New Directions." Subjects covered in part one include talent management, remuneration, and managing managerial careers. Part two deals with the role of leadership in developing innovative managers, the front-line manager, professions and managers, evidence-based management, and managerial work. The contemporary issues discussed in part three include the crisis in management education, women in management, and issues involved in managing across cultures and in developing countries. Each chapter has an extensive list of references and there is an index for the whole book. Recommended for academic libraries.—**ARBA Staff Reviewer**

Marketing and Trade

Handbooks and Yearbooks

113.   **International Trade and the New Global Economy.** Edward D. Mansfield, ed. Northampton, Mass., Edward Elgar, 2015. 543p. (International Library of Critical Writings in Economics). $310.00. ISBN 13: 978-1-78471-259-4.

This book consists of 18 articles published this century on international trade. It is divided into three sections; the first is on preferential trade areas (PTAs) which have increased considerably since World War II. The impact of PTAs on the openness of international trade is debatable. The six articles in this section address the economic sources of PTAs and the political economy of PTA formation. The next section covers public attitudes about open trade. Several articles look at whether the factor endowments or specific factors models help explain attitudes in different countries. Other factors that might influence attitudes about international trade, such as consumption-based theory, education, socio-tropic perceptions, and social/cultural consequences, are explored in several articles. The last section, four articles, looks at the impact of the 2008 financial crisis and the Great Recession on international trade. They investigate why the feared increase in protectionism did not occur. Except for a short introduction to the book, the articles are reprinted as originally published in journals.—**J. E. Weaver**

114.   VanAuken, Brad. **Brand Aid: A Quick Reference Guide to Solving your Branding Problems and Strengthening Your Market Position.** 2d ed. New York, AMACOM/ American Management Association, 2014. 352p. index. $29.95. ISBN 13: 978-0-8144-3473-4.

In the ultracompetitive world of business, it is your brand that sets you apart. And a brand, of course, is much more than a simple logo. *Brand Aid* is a perfect book for marketing novices or business veterans who are looking to strengthen their grasp of the elements behind building, sustaining, and maximizing a brand.

The author has condensed his many years of experience in the marketing and brand management world into this information-packed resource. He begins with the essentials by establishing the importance of brand management, a common branding vocabulary, and an overview of the total brand management process. The book then concisely explores numerous topics related to designing, building, and leveraging a brand. Chapters explore the need to understand consumers and competition, the effectiveness of nontraditional marketing approaches like contests or sponsorships, the ideas behind a "total brand experience," the ability to brand globally, and much more. The book further explores related topics such as legal issues and common brand problems.

This second edition includes expanded coverage of many of these topics, as well as more up-to-date brand examples throughout. It has also been updated with information related to how branding can be maximized online via multiple social media formats and blogs. The new edition further incorporates the latest ideas appealing to marketers and consumers, such as sustainability, neuromarketing, and brand storytelling.

The book incorporates case studies, charts, best practices, and detailed checklists. It includes three appendixes: Brand Audits, Online Brand Management and Advertising Resources, and References/Further Reading. Notes and an index round out the work. The book's ease of use and thorough coverage will satisfy readers from all aspects of the branding process—marketers, advertisers, and seasoned executives alike. Recommended for academic, business, and public libraries.—**Laura Herrell**

Service Industries

Dictionaries and Encyclopedias

115.   **The Sage Encyclopedia of Quality and the Service Economy.** Dahlgaard-Park, Su Mi, ed. Thousand Oaks, Calif., Sage, 2015. 2v. index. $340.00/set. ISBN 13: 978-1-4522-5672-6.

Aspects of quality management in the services industry are the subject of this unique encyclopedia. The services sector is now the largest sector of the U.S. economy and also makes up the largest part of the world's gross domestic product. In the introduction, the editor, Su Mi Dahlgaard-Park, Lund University, provides an historical overview of quality control as it was first applied in the manufacturing industry to its adoption in the services industry. Article contributors are from universities spanning the globe. Over 230 diverse topics are covered in an A-Z format, many of which reflect the changing digital environment: Blog, E-Business Models, Electronic Word of Mouth (eWOM), Google, Online Consumer Behavior, Wikipedia, etc. An alphabetical list of entries is provided in each of the two volumes and a reader's guide section classifies articles into 20 general topical categories to help readers locate related material. An index is provided in the second volume. All of the articles are signed and *see also* entries are provided. Further readings and an extensive bibliography and Website listing also significantly add to the content. Recommended for academic and large research libraries.—**Colleen Seale**

Handbooks and Yearbooks

116.   Miziker, Ron. **Miziker's Complete Event Planner's Handbook.** Albuquerque, N.Mex., University of New Mexico Press, 2015. 459p. illus. index. $34.95pa. ISBN 13: 978-0-8263-5551-5.

Written by the founder and director of the Miziker Entertainment Group in Los Angeles, this book packs an enormous amount of valuable information into more than 450 pages in a title compact enough to be truly portable.

There are approximately 300 pages of terminology entries arranged alphabetically for ease of use. The entries also contain cross-references; some entries are followed by further tips and suggestions. Throughout the terms section of the book users will find sidebars related to the author's event planning experiences. The definitions themselves are useful for all planners, from the novice to the experienced professional. The terminology section is followed by more than 150 pages of "Tables and Techniques," which detail beverage consumption per person, the temperature at which to serve different types of wine, a sample event budget, the proper flowers for theme dinners, flag protocol, food quantities, invitations, linens, napkin folding, wedding seating arrangements, room setup, and more. A list of Websites and a bibliography complete this offering.

This excellent and extensive guide will be useful to event planners, students studying hospitality or related fields, or anyone planning an event. Highly recommended.—**ARBA Staff Reviewer**

5 Education

General Works

Almanacs

117. **The Almanac of American Education 2014-2015.** 8th ed. Deirdre A. Gaquin and Gwenavere W. Dunn, eds. Lanham, Md., Bernan Press, 2015. 563p. index. $79.00pa. ISBN 13: 978-1-59888-736-5; 978-1-59888-737-2 (e-book).

The Almanac of American Education is a useful print compilation of statistics from the U.S. Census Bureau, the National Center for Education Statistics, and other sources. The book is broken down into three education statistics sections; national, region and state, and county. Each part opens with informative graphs and analysis followed by numerous tables of current and historical data. Each section ends with notes and definitions about the data. The statistics focus on enrollment, both current and historical, educational attainment, and county by county comparisons on a number of differing variables. Numbers can be found on per student expenditures, free or reduced lunch programs, unemployment rates based on educational attainment, dropout rates, and more. The almanac has a very useful appendix providing a guide to educational resources on the Internet for further research. This almanac is a must have in any educational research setting, and would be a good addition to any public or academic library collection. The scope of the almanac, stated clearly in the preface, makes it essential for anyone doing comparative research.—**Sue Ellen Knowlton**

Dictionaries and Encyclopedias

118. **Encyclopedia of Christian Education.** George Thomas Kurian and Mark A. Lamport, eds. Lanham, Md., Rowman & Littlefield, 2015. 3v. index. $340.00/set; $329.99 (e-book). ISBN 13: 978-0-8108-8492-2; 978-0-8108-8493-9 (e-book).

Libraries that serve students of the Christian faith, whether in the context of a seminary, undergraduate institution, or public library, are well advised to purchase a copy of the landmark, three-volume *Encyclopedia of Christian Education.* As attested to by each of the forewords, prologue, preface, and introduction (all written with pathos by leading theologians and practitioners), *Christian Education* aims to enrich the mind and faith of believers in the Christian gospel using the tools of all available disciplines and knowledge of how and what residents of the Christian world have learned over the millennia. In it, well-credentialed scholars from all over the globe describe the 2,000-year history of Christian education and its contemporary, global state in 1,200 articles. Entries detailing biographies, institutions, philosophies, praxis, and more fill a sizeable gap in reference literature, while most denominations that adhere to the orthodox, Trinitarian doctrine and most nations that feature some level of Christian education receive treatment. Naturally, we read much about the philosophies, pedagogies, curricula, and administration of education itself. We also learn about the settings of education, from institutions of higher learning to those of the Church and its organizations, or even the home. While the editors have included articles about the Christian faith and its doctrines, these are introductory compared to the length and breadth of the articles dealing with education itself (compare the length of "Jesus Christ" to "Learning and the Rise of Vernacular Languages").

In terms of accessibility, librarians might determine that effective use of the encyclopedia will require some assistance given some of its unique features. For example, the A-Z list of 1,200 entries corresponds to 19 lead-in introductions that are found after the last Z article. Articles dealing with Christian pedagogy, then, have a five-page introduction in the third volume, though the articles themselves can be found throughout the whole alphabet. For optimal searching, the user would wish to have all of the volumes present. Secondly, some of the entries are titled in ways that may confuse novice readers. "Diversity," for example, refers narrowly to ethnic diversity rather than multiculturalism, while "Special Needs" refers to special education or entries related to disability. "Deaf" and "Blind" receive their own entries. One could easily overlook some of these related articles because of the dearth of *see also* references in the articles themselves.

Yet these unique features detract only little from the value of this important addition. I found the set a treasure, from the front matter described above to the A-Z entries, the 17-page bibliography, and the appendixes with statistics on the global Christian community, its populations, and universities. The set closes with an index of names and entries and short biographies of the contributors. Highly recommended.—**Amy Koehler**

Directories

119.   **Educators Resource Directory 2015/2016.** 11th ed. Amenia, N.Y., Grey House Publishing, 2015. 765p. index. $145.00pa. ISBN 13: 978-1-61925-549-4.

Designed to allow busy education professionals easy and well-curated access to associations, publications, trade shows, workshops, and training programs, as well as educational resources for their students and schools, *Educators Resource Directory 2015/2016* is organized into three sections. Of the 6,408 entries in section one, 140 are new to this edition. Here users will find key contact names, fax numbers, e-mail addresses, and Websites arranged into 13 chapters: "Associations & Organizations"; "Conferences & Trade Shows"; "Consultants"; "Teaching Opportunities Abroad"; "Financial Resources"; "Government Agencies"; "Professional Development"; "Publications, Publishers"; "Research Centers"; "School Supplies"; "Testing Resources"; "Software"; and "Hardware & Internet Resources." Section two presents ample information on national and state statistics. Valuably, this section also includes international and Canadian data. The indexes—publisher, geographic, and subject—and a glossary comprise section three. This incomparable source is recommended for every school, public, and academic library.— **Melinda F. Matthews**

Handbooks and Yearbooks

120.   **Causation or Correlation? http://jfmueller.faculty.noctrl.edu/100/correlation_or_causation.htm.** [Website] Free. Date reviewed: 2016

This Website was created by a teacher in order to help his upper-grade students identify the differences between causal relationships and correlations. The Web page has a simple design and features two columns. The left column contains headlines of public press articles and clickable links that lead to external pages. If the articles are based on academic studies, those are also included. At the bottom of the column, "Related Resources" includes cartoons, graphs, and blogs that will better equip students to use and identify correlation and causal language. The right column is text-heavy and describes the purpose of this Website to users. A few links are included that lead to student activities most helpful for teachers to download and use in class. Teachers should be aware that the Website seems to be in an early stage of development and does not contain much content apart from the columns and is not comprehensive.

This resource is recommended for both high school students and teachers. Students will benefit most from the left column and the dozens of interesting articles that will teach them about correlations and causations. The activities would be helpful for middle school students as well, though some of the article content is mature; BBC's "Higher Beer Prices 'Cut Gonorrhea Rates'" is an informative read, but may be inappropriate for a younger audience. The right column will be useful for any teachers, especially those instructing a statistics course.—**ARBA Staff Reviewer**

121.   **Digital Public Library of America: Primary Source Sets. http://dp.la/primary-source-sets/sets?tags[]=law-government.** [Website] Free. Date reviewed: 2016.

Provides a wide selection (100 as of this review) of primary source sets designed to help educators promote critical thinking skills with their students. The sets, created by the Digital Public Library of America (DPLA)'s Educational Advisory Board, address a variety of topics related to American history, art, and literature including *Beloved, The Scarlet Letter,* the internment of Japanese Americans, the Underground Railroad, the 1878 yellow fever epidemic, school desegregation in Boston, the invention of the telephone, and the populist movement. Each set begins with a brief overview and a link to a teaching guide, followed by digital reproductions of 10 to 15 sources from the DPLA, and links to authoritative online sources on the topic for further research. The sets have all been assigned one or two subjects and a time period allowing users to easily narrow the array or find related source sets. Each source suggests that students consider the author's point of view, the author's purpose, the historical context, and audience, and includes a citation and links to the content record both at DPLA and the item's home institution. The digital scans are good quality and can be enlarged, but not always enough to read the fine print on some items. The teaching guides present discussion questions and classroom activities linked to individual primary sources. General suggestions for primary source analysis and links to information on using primary sources from the National Archives and the Library of Congress are also included. Overall this will be a useful and intriguing collection for educators in history and literature.—**ARBA Staff Reviewer**

122. **InfoSci-Educational Science and Technology. http://www.igi-global.com/e-resources/infosci-subject-databases/infosci-education/.** [Website] Hershey, Pa., Information Science Reference/IGI Global. Price negotiated by site. Date reviewed: 2016.

The *InfoSci-Educational Science and Technology* database provides full-text access to over 430 e-books on education and educational technology research. This academic reference collection also includes some teaching cases and appears to also be adding some video resources.

The collection represents the work of education and technology researchers on a wide range of topics from blended and mobile learning to gaming trends in education, and from educational administration and leadership to special education. These topics are covered from all perspectives from K-12 to higher education.

The search interface provides three different search options: basic, advanced, and "expert." The advanced search option allows full-text keyword searching as well as title, author, DOI, and publication date. The "expert" search option allows you to exclude and weight search terms. This is very interesting and the option is appreciated while not anticipated to see much use. The books are indexed and searchable at the chapter level.

The database delivers the e-books in a very usable manner. Each book has an annotated table of contents and a search box to search within the book. The text of each book is provided by chapter and available as both an HTML file and a PDF for easy download. The viewing pane also gives options for citing the book.

Teachers, education administrators, education policy-makers, researchers, and librarians will find this a rich resource. It is a trove of reputable and timely research on everything concerning the intersection of technology and education—a subject that will be of great importance for the foreseeable future. IGI provides these titles in both print and electronic format, but database subscribers receive the digital versions much faster.—**Kristin Kay Leeman**

123. Kwon, Samuel M., Daniel R. Tomal, and Aram S. Agajanian. **Technology for Classroom and Online Learning: An Educator's Guide to Bits, Bytes, and Teaching.** Lanham, Md., Rowman & Littlefield, 2015. 187p. index. $38.00pa.; $37.99 (e-book). ISBN 13: 978-1-4758-1544-3; 978-1-4758-1545-0 (e-book).;

In *Technology for Classroom and Online Learning* the authors provide a succinct overview of hardware, software, and computer networks for the classroom teacher. Chapter one starts out with brief histories of electricity, electronic devices, and computer technologies, before defining key hardware and software components. Chapter two discusses the fundamentals of electricity and electronics. Chapter three covers computer peripherals (e.g., printers, scanners, external hard drives), connection hardware, supporting software, and troubleshooting. The remaining chapters focus more on traditional educational technology concepts such as computing platforms for schools, teaching and learning with technology, and online and blended learning. Finally there is a chapter on security and maintenance. Each chapter starts out with stated objectives and concludes with a case study, exercises, and discussion questions, thereby serving as both a textbook and reference work. There are also four short appendixes that include a list of Websites for school technology resources, common technology acronyms, technology standards for educators, and trademark sources for products mentioned in the book. Upon initial review it appeared this was going to be an academic text and hard to understand. On the contrary, although one of the authors is an engineer, the text was clearly written, making the concepts very accessible. That said, there are not many images, and some of the concepts discussed, such as electronics and electricity are hard to understand, even when simplified. As a whole, the appendixes don't offer much value. Even with these shortcomings this short book (187 pages) is an important introductory text for future classroom technology professionals or as a succinct reference source for practicing educators.—**Kevin McDonough**

Elementary and Secondary Education

Bibliographies

124.   **EL-HI Textbooks & Serials in Print 2015: Including Related Teaching Materials K-12.** 143d ed. Amenia, N.Y., Grey House Publishing, 2015. $540.00/set. ISBN 13: 978-1-61925-625-5.

This is the 143rd edition of a title that first started as part of *Publishers Weekly* and has been known as *EL-HI Textbooks & Serials in Print* since 1985. The title focuses on school textbooks but also includes reference books, periodicals, maps, pedagogical books, tests, teaching aids, and programmed learning materials that appear in book form. Seven indexes comprise this two-volume, 4,000-page set, starting with the main subject index, which is arranged into broad subject areas, including art, education, literature, drama, and social science, with specific subdivisions. Searches in this index are facilitated by *see* and *see also* references, guide words, and the table of contents. Subject index listings typically include title, series affiliation, author, coauthor, editor, translator, grade publication date, education level, binding, price, related supplementary materials, ISBN, imprint, and publishers. When available, the index lists a separate price for schools. Asterisks are used at the beginning of a listing to indicate if the book is newly added to this year's edition. Volume one also contains an author index, which provides page references to the relevant listing in the subject index.

The second volume has a title index that includes page references to the subject index, followed by a series index, a serials-subject index, a serials-title index, a publisher name index, and a wholesaler & distributor name index. The latter two indexes provide necessary contact data along with ISBN prefixes and other pertinent information.

For busy librarians and teachers, this will serve as an important and comprehensive reference source, combining in one easy-to-use volume access to information on titles from every conceivable publisher.—**ARBA Staff Reviewer**

Handbooks and Yearbooks

125.   Brooks-Young, Susan J. **Creating Content with Your Tablet.** Thousand Oaks, Calif., Corwin Press, 2015. 121p. index. $26.95pa. ISBN 13: 978-1-4522-7183-5.

This book is a perfect guide to using iPads and tablets in the classroom. The book begins with a tutorial on choosing the right apps for the classroom and moves to taking photographs and videos for student publishing. Each of the chapters includes strategies for classroom use and suggested activities to get things started. The text is easy to follow and well-organized. For teachers who are looking for a way to start using hand-held technology, this book is a wonderful place to begin. A bibliography and index round out the work.—**Catherine Vinson**

126.   **Handbook of Urban Educational Leadership.** Muhammad Khalifa, Noelle Witherspoon Arnold, Azadeh F. Osanloo, and Cosette M. Grant, eds. Lanham, Md., Rowman & Littlefield, 2015. 677p. index. $120.00; $119.99 (e-book). ISBN 13: 978-1-4422-2084-3; 978-1-4422-2085-0 (e-book).

This giant tome—and it is a hefty one—takes a look at urban education leadership. Its articles by education experts tackle the tough questions facing principals in urban schools: poverty, white flight, social justice, activism, poor teacher quality, segregation, failed reform efforts, advocacy, education policy, global perspectives, and local and federal government influences. The array of scholars is wide, impressive, and long. It is a book for graduate educational leadership or a reference tool for education collections. The voices are critical, pensive, rabble-rousing (as much as one can use that term in connection with educrats) and, by and large, honest, at least to a degree.

The trouble is there is nothing new here.

I don't mean that the authors are rehashing old material. Rather, the problems have not changed in 40 years. Look again at the list in the opening sentences: white flight, poverty, segregation, poor teacher quality, and so on. The book may as well have been written in 1970. W. B. Yeats once famously wrote that education is not the filling of a pail but the lighting of a fire. Apparently, education experts thought he said that whenever you see a student start to catch fire, douse a pail of water on him or her, quickly. After trillions of dollars and dozens of reforms, all we have to show for our efforts are the identical problems those trillions and those reforms were meant to ameliorate.

What the book doesn't cover may be more telling than what it does. While government gets some of the blame, as do uninvolved parents, both of which deserve it, the National Education Association (NEA) is not mentioned at all, and the National Council for the Accreditation of Teachers is mentioned once, if the index is any indication. True, the book's focus is leadership, not so much those matters connected with problem-solving per se. But it does strike one as odd that the decline in American K-12 education, whether urban, rural or public, coincides almost precisely with the now 40-year rise of the hold (or stranglehold, some critics might argue) that both of these organizations have on schooling in these United States. That nothing happens in American education without the express written consent of either of these organizations is well-known. While the advent of home-schooling has lessened that influence somewhat, both remain formidable forces; and the influences, good and bad, deserve some mention in every education context.

Still, this book is a useful one for what it does: bring together under one roof all the aspects of urban school leadership in its myriad contexts.—**Mark Y. Herring**

127.   Haven, Kendall. **Writing Workouts to Develop Common Core Writing Skills: Step-by-Step Exercises, Activities, and Tips for Student Success, Grades 7-12.** Santa Barbara, Calif., Libraries Unlimited/ABC-CLIO, 2015. 121p. index. $42.00pa. ISBN 13: 978-1-61069-868-9; 978-1-61069-869-6 (e-book).

This book is a collection of tips and activities intended to help teachers build basic writing skills and confidence in their students. Activities support core curriculum and state language arts standards. The focus is on the content of student writing rather than mechanics. The 30 workout topics are student-friendly. It would be helpful to have more about overall goals and requirements of the Common Core Writing Standards as a reference. Examples of specific standards each activity most specifically supports would also be helpful. These missing elements aside, the book is easy to use and very practical. An index rounds out the work.—**Mary Alice Anderson**

128.   Haven, Kendall. **Writing Workouts to Develop Common Core Writing Skills: Step-by-Step Exercises, Activities, and Tips for Student Success, Grades 2-6.** Santa Barbara, Calif., Libraries Unlimited/ABC-CLIO, 2014. 133p. index. $21.00pa. ISBN 13: 978-1-61069-866-5; 978-1-61069-867-2 (e-book).

Effective communication is the goal of writing. Like any other skill, success at writing requires practice. This book provides ample suggestions, and ways to engender enthusiasm, all geared toward supporting writing skills required by Common Core. The workouts focus mainly on the content skills rather than the mechanical skills. Engaging activities include building a scene, story starters, sequencing, revising and editing, persuasive writing, and varying point of view. The skills and activities presented could also be adapted for older students. A purpose, directions, and review and discussion for each workout are included. For some there is also evaluation and postdiscussion. The book contains a list of other sources of writing games and activities. An index rounds out the work.—**Cynthia Ortiz**

129.   Ivers, Karen S., and Ann E. Barron. **Digital Content Creation in Schools: A Common Core Approach.** Santa Barbara, Calif., Libraries Unlimited/ABC-CLIO, 2014. 251p. index. $50.00pa. ISBN 13: 978-1-61069-629-6; 978-1-61069-630-2 (e-book).

This is an update of the popular Multimedia Projects in Education, Fourth Edition (see ARBA 2011, entry 304) and emphasizes digital content creation. The ability to create and share content instantly and the formats for this content have changed. The authors have created a four-step model/process for digital content creation in the classroom; chapters are geared around each step of the model. Blackline masters, sample activities, reproducible handouts, rubrics, and worksheets are provided for each chapter. The authors include a list of recommended tools or applications for each step and project, but they don't address the time needed by the teacher to become comfortable with the tools. The authors have chosen current tools/apps which will date the book quickly. However, it is a great starting place for the teacher or librarian. The book's subtitle is misleading as the authors do not discuss how their book integrates into the new standards.—**Linda DeVore**

130.   **Research In Context. http://solutions.cengage.com/incontext/research/.** [Website] Farmington Hills, Mich, Gale/Cengage Learning. Price negotiated by site. Date reviewed: 2016.

Research In Context is an online database designed to support the learning and research needs of middle school students. It provides them access to a wide range of information in a variety of formats to address nearly every subject studied by students in grades 6-8. The homepage and navigation are dominated by images and encourage browsing and discovery in the following topics: Culture, Geography, Government, Literature, People, Science, Social Issues, and History.

Information on the topics in the collection is presented in a diverse array of formats including videos, audio, newspapers, books, and images. Content is drawn from *National*

Geographic, NPR, NASA, and Gale's own products. All of these sources are integrated on one page for a holistic view of the topic. This presentation approach creates a sort of information "command center" that has the potential to inspire and empower students to draw connections with the content.

Though the database is designed for browsing, it can be searched by keyword, and there is an advanced search option to allow searchers to combine keywords and limit searches to full-text or images. The advanced search menu is simplified for the intended audience. Educators will appreciate the curriculum standards provided in the site. State and national standards are included as is Common Core.

The database integrates with Google Drive and Google Classroom making it easy for both students and teachers to save documents to their own Google Drive. The ability to save research to a central location is a very useful feature. Any highlights and notes made in the database can be retained when the document is saved to Google Drive. Teachers have the added ability to save a document to their Google Classroom as an announcement or an assignment.

This is a fantastic resource to engage younger students in the habits of responsible, academic research at an early age. It is an excellent tool for encouraging information literacy especially as there are many different content formats and sources. It is highly recommended for school and public libraries.—**Kristin Kay Leeman**

131.   Sheninger, Eric. **Digital Leadership: Changing Paradigms for Changing Times.** Thousand Oaks, Calif., Corwin Press, 2015. 227p. $27.95pa. ISBN 13: 978-1-4522-7661-8; 978-1-4833-3996-2 (e-book).

This is a book for those people who are leading other teachers in how to use technology to enrich their instruction. It would be a great college text as well. The book is well-organized and easy to read. One of the most useful chapters is about the importance of PLNs, Professional Learning Networks. These networks provide support and the sharing that is necessary to quickly learn how to manage changing technology. As a book for leaders, there is also a chapter on coaching the reluctant teacher on how to use technology efficiently. An index completes the work.—**Catherine Vinson**

132.   **Student Resources In Context. http://solutions.cengage.com/InContext/Student-Resources/.** [Website] Farmington Hills, Mich., Gale/Cengage Learning. Price negotiated by site. Date reviewed: 2016.

Student Resources In Context is a multidisciplinary database that integrates a wide variety of content types from academic journal articles to interactive maps to inform on topics ranging from John Adams to Mark Zuckerberg.

Content is sourced from Gale publications and its partners. In addition to these reference sources, the database includes full-text access to many respected newspapers (e.g., *Newsweek, The Economist,* and the *New York Times*), images, videos, and audio clips from the BBC and NPR, among others. The content is aligned to curricular standards at state and national levels including Common Core.

All of the sources related to a topic are presented together, curated on one page for a holistic view of the topic in question—from news commentary to academic research. This approach creates an information "command center" experience and gives teachers and librarians a compelling argument to students on why they should never use Wikipedia again. There are also tools to highlight, bookmark, share, and cite resources.

The resource can be searched by keyword or browsed by topic. There are so many topics to browse that a helpful filter for category (e.g., Social Issues, Sports, Government, New and Updated, etc.) is also included. An advanced keyword search option allows users to combine keywords with article and/or publication title. Users can also limit their search to full-text or peer-reviewed journals, specify a desired document type (e.g., map, cover story, pamphlet, or video among many options), or content type (book, journal, experiments, Websites, etc.). Teachers will especially appreciate the ability to search by content level (beginner to advanced) and Lexile level. Educators will also appreciate the curriculum standards provided in the site. Curriculum standards for not only the United States (both national and state) are provided, but so are the standards for other English-speaking countries like Canada, Australia, New Zealand, Ireland, and the countries of Great Britain.

This Gale resource integrates with Google apps including Google Drive and Google Classroom. This makes it easy for both students and teachers to save documents to their own Google Drive. The ability to save to a central location is very useful. Any highlights and notes made in the database can be retained when the document is saved to Google Drive. Teachers have the added ability to save a document to their Google Classroom as an announcement or an assignment.

This is a fantastic resource, and it is highly recommended for school and public libraries. It brings a fresh and engaging perspective to research and breathes fresh air into the research process with engaging, multimedia resources. Students and teachers alike will find this a "go-to" resource for research on anything from Steve Jobs to steampunk. By including additional database tools (save and share search results, citation tools, etc.) this becomes a tool everyone will want to use. Rather than going to many different places to find this information, it is all now available in one powerful, user-friendly dashboard.—**Kristin Kay Leeman**

133.   **TeachUNICEF. http://teachunicef.org/.** [Website] Free. Date reviewed: 2016.

TeachUNICEF—an initiative of the United Nations Children's Fund (UNICEF)—is a free online resource for teachers and K–12 students that aims to foster global citizenship and intercultural awareness through education, advocacy, and leadership. Drawing from a "rights-based framework," *TeachUNICEF* doubles as both a reference and support site that can be easily navigated by teachers and students alike. Its offering of a wide range of support materials for students is useful for helping teachers approach often difficult topics of global concern through dynamic and engaging lessons and activities.

Armed conflict, children with disabilities, gender equality, and sustainable development are a just a few of among the more than 15 "global education" topics included on the site. For each topic, teachers can easily download units and lesson plans for their particular grade levels (PK-2, 3–5, 6–8, and 9–12). Each of these clearly states the objectives of the lesson, outline the relevant standards being touched upon, and include different ideas for activities (complete with handouts). These are all presented in a graphic, visually appealing, and easy-to-follow format.

Additional support-related materials include photos of the month, which provide questions for class discussion and background on a featured photograph; UNICEF's *ACT: Action for Children Today* student magazine (available in both a diplomat edition for students in grades 3–5 and an ambassador edition for students in grades 6–8); and global maps. Furthermore, each of *TeachUNICEF*'s lessons has been crafted to align to both national and state education standards.

A separate component of *TeachUNICEF*'s site includes workshops and information on making a change through action and leadership. Details on how to get involved in UNICEF's advocacy and volunteer programs (UNICEF LIVE, UNICEF global action, UNICEF kid power, and UNICEF Tap Project) is readily available on the site, as is information on how to get involved in fundraising and other campus initiatives. Additionally, the "Get Involved" section of the site offers links to social media, where students can share projects that they have undertaken, teachers can share lesson plans, and where interested parties can sign up for *TeachUNICEF*'s monthly newsletter.

With its engaging lessons and wealth of interactive, multimedia material, *TeachUNICEF* is a highly useful resource for guiding educators through teaching difficult global issues in a wide variety of formats across the K–12 spectrum. It is also a great resource for inspiring action, community building, global awareness, and leadership in students.—**ARBA Staff Reviewer**

134.   Thornburg, David, Norma Thornburg, and Sara Armstrong. **The Invent to Learn Guide to 3D Printing in the Classroom: Recipes for Success.** Torrance, Calif., Constructing Modern Knowledge Press, 2014. 178p. $24.95pa. ISBN 13: 978-0-9891511-4-6.

For anyone setting up a makerspace or adding a 3D printer to their engineering or technology classes, this book is essential. The authors have logically laid out what one needs to know before setting up the space. The book covers the basics necessary for safety, how consumer 3D printers work, and what features to look for when purchasing a 3D printer. They explore three pathways for creating designs and examples of programs and platforms. Finally, there is a wide variety of beginner to intermediate project ideas. Each project includes background information, Next Generation Science Standards, Common Core Math Standards, and connections associated with the project, a materials list, and construction details. This book will be a favorite with educators!—**Claire Berg**

Higher Education

Handbooks and Yearbooks

135.   Brooks, F. Erik, and Glenn L. Starks. **African American Student's Guide to College Success.** Santa Barbara, Calif., Greenwood Press/ABC-CLIO, 2015. 232p. index. $37.00. ISBN 13: 978-1-4408-2929-1; 978-1-4408-2930-7 (e-book).

Higher education professionals understand that the transition for many students from high school to college is difficult—hence the proliferation of first-year experience and "student success" programs at many colleges. Editors Brooks and Starks, both public policy specialists, have a general grasp of the difficulties faced by African American students as they begin their college careers and have sought to guide this population from the application process through integration into the network. Although the guide is informative, the intended audience itself is unclear—is the work written more for the parents/guardians of potential students or for the students themselves? Some of the information does not apply to all higher education institutions in all states—community colleges rarely require written essays and are often open admissions, for example—and some information seems almost quaint, such as "Appropriate Student Attire in Class" (how many male students wear single-breasted suits to class?). Roughly half of the book includes such advice, much of it good, but the volume is filled out with 87 pages of tables and another 32 of "How We Did It," success stories related by former African American students. Despite these issues, Brooks and Starks is a welcome update to earlier similar works, including Kunjufu's *Black College Student Survival Guide* (African American Images, 1998) and Black's *African American Student's College Guide* (Wiley, 2000). Recommended for all undergraduate and high school collections.—**Anthony J. Adam**

136.   **Coursera. https://www.coursera.org/.** [Website] Free. Date reviewed: 2015.

Coursera is an educational platform that has partnered with universities across the country to offer students free access to online courses. While it claims to provide "universal access to the world's best education," it is not a college and there is no way to obtain a degree. Students can, however, receive formal recognition for course completion and course certificates may be provided upon request. Students can study from anywhere as long as they have Internet connection, and will find their classes to be exciting and interactive. The Website layout is simple and intuitive, and users should have no trouble navigating it to select their courses and access material.

Each class includes online video instructions and lectures, quizzes, peer-graded assignments, and the opportunity to connect with others and delve deeper into the course material through online forums. Students can choose their schedules, making this platform perfect for working students, parents, teachers, and those interested in gaining skills and knowledge in a particular subject matter without the stress of enrolling at a formal academic institution. Still, students are required to put in the work to pass these classes and will find the material as challenging as it is enriching. Because *Coursera* partners with top universities, such as Yale, Stanford, and Northwestern, and offers classes taught by professors at these schools, students can expect top-notch instruction.

Coursera offers nearly 1,500 courses in the following subjects: Arts and Humanities, Business, Computer Science, Data Science, Life Sciences, Math and Logic, Personal Development, Physical Science and Engineering, and Social Sciences. It is a highly recommended source for busy scholars, curious intellectuals, and those who simply want to learn something new.—**ARBA Staff Reviewer**

137.   **History Departments Around the World: http://chnm.gmu.edu/history-departments-around-the-world/departments/.** [Website] Free. Date reviewed: 2016.

This is an interesting site that allows users to search for history departments from among thousands of U.S. and hundreds of non-U.S. universities and colleges. It has a simple, clean layout that contains only a search tab on the home page that allows users to narrow their search by university, city, state, and U.S. or non-U.S departments. The page states that it can help users "find ideas for creating departmental web pages, let you look in on or locate colleagues, conduct historical research, or help out with a graduate or undergraduate application." The latter seems to be the most appropriate way to use this site, and therefore it should prove useful for high school juniors and seniors interested in history, as well as former history majors scouting graduate schools for a potential fit. There does not seem to be a way to search for individuals; therefore, locating colleagues would be difficult.

Conducting historical research would also be difficult to do with this Website because it simply links to department Web pages, which contain more information about the history programs offered and less historical and academic information. Users would benefit from this site most as a tool for gauging what kinds of specializations and tracks are available at various universities and colleges. It is highly recommended for upper grade high school students and graduate applicants to get a feel for prospective schools.—**ARBA Staff Reviewer**

138.   Major, Claire Howell. **Teaching Online: A Guide to Theory, Research, and Practice.** Baltimore, Md., Johns Hopkins University Press, 2015. 296p. illus. index. (Tech. edu: A Hopkins Series on Education and Technology). $29.95pa. ISBN 13: 978-1-4214-1633-5; 978-1-4214-1623-6 (e-book).

Teaching Online serves as a compact introduction for faculty teaching online courses and instructional designers developing various types of online teaching courses. The volume functions more like a handbook for online course development and less as a reference work. This book would be appropriate for both a circulating library in any educational institution offering online instruction, from high school to graduate level work, and for corporations that train employees with online resources. It would not, however, be appropriate as a noncirculating reference library book. Its organization and topics compel the audience to read it cover to cover instead of using it as a quick reference book.

One valuable aspect of this handbook's content can be found at the beginning— should the delivery of a course be changed to online, and if so, what technology to choose? Educators should find the chapter entitled "Teaching Online as Instructional Change" helpful in making those decisions. Next, the insight provided by short vignettes written by nearly 50 educators and instructional designers interspersed throughout each chapter provide practical real-world advice. The placement of the vignettes, often in the middle of the chapters, breaks up the content and the reader might be better served had those sections appeared at the end of the chapters. Extensive annotated notes appear as a separate reference section and thus do not disrupt the visual flow of the content, adding to this handbook's effectiveness.—**Kay Shelton**

139.   Martin, James, and James E. Samels. **The Provost's Handbook: The Role of the Chief Academic Officer.** Baltimore, Md., Johns Hopkins University Press, 2015. 235p. index. $34.95pa. ISBN 13: 978-1-4214-1626-7.

What is a university provost? Or more specifically, what is a university provost today? This book clarifies the traditional responsibilities of the provost, or the Chief Academic Officer (CAO) in executive terms, in addition to examining the more contemporary demands upon the position through a series of scholarly essays written by diverse representatives from the ranks of higher education, including athletic directors, professors, research fellows, and, naturally, provosts.

The book's first section, The Academic Agenda, shares 10 essays which overall work to define the main duties a CAO must navigate as they strive to advance their school's mission. Essays here broach a variety of topics, such as designing a formal CAO training program, ensuring the most effective executive relationships, navigating the tough decisions behind curricula, and more. In his piece titled "Difficult Change in the Provost's

Domain in Curriculum, Faculty Appointments, and Teaching Strategies," for example, Robert M. Groves (Georgetown University) offers strategies to help CAO's choose the academic offerings on their campus.

Essential Partners takes the provost out of the office, so to speak, and focuses on their role in the broader university community. Essays in this section discuss best practices for working across the different academic departments. For example, Penny Rue and Suresh Subramani (UC San Diego) share best practices for CAO's working with the main university administrative connection to its students—i.e., the Office of Student Life. And William Scott Green (University of Miami) connects the CAO with the many needs of the university athletic program in his essay "Increasing Accountabilities: The Provost's Role in Intercollegiate Athletics."

Shaded sidebars mark key concepts, "lessons learned," and other insightful information. For example, one sidebar lists seven aspects of effective academic governance, which are each more thoroughly addressed in the accompanying essay. Notes conclude each essay. The book also includes a bibliography, generous information about the contributors, and an index. Recommended.—**ARBA Staff Reviewer**

140.   Polly, Drew. **Evaluating Teacher Education Programs through Performance-Based Assessments.** Hershey, Pa., Information Science Reference/IGI Global, 2016. 436p. index. (Advances in Higher Education and Professional Development Book Series). $164.00. ISBN 13: 978-1-4666-9929-8; 978-1-4666-9930-4 (e-book).

The 22 studies brought together in this volume explore various aspects of using edTPA (developed at Stanford University) to assess beginning teachers' (and their students') performance. Examples of projects and studies engaging this topic come from the U.S., Mexico, and Croatia. Focusing on the role of teacher education programs, these articles present a number of diverse approaches to training future teachers to analyze, plan, and assess their work with their students, so as to succeed in the certification process.

A useful feature is that the "detailed table of contents" at the front of the volume provides abstracts of all of the chapters, helping readers select the most useful parts of the volume. This work is clearly designed for academic libraries, with patrons conversant with the topics being presented, particularly those with schools of education. Any educator working in a state that has adopted edTPA standards for their teachers should look at this volume. (The editing process could have been done better, but distracts only slightly from the useful content.)—**Mark Schumacher**

Special Education

Handbooks and Yearbooks

141.   **Practicing Disability Studies in Education: Acting toward Social Change.** David J. Connor, Jan W. Valle, and Chris Hale, eds. New York, Peter Lang, 2015. 247p. $41.95pa.. ISBN 13: 978-1-4331-2551-5; 978-1-4539-1446-5 (e-book).

This book provides a kaleidoscope of information regarding the historical and current status of disability studies (DS) in education. Each chapter reflects on efforts to include people with disabilities in communities throughout the world from the early twentieth century to the early twenty-first century. Stories of real people become intertwined with examples of research, practice, and policies that have demonstrated confusion, prejudice, caring, and understanding regarding disabilities. Questions regarding the social construct of "disability" as well as the needs of individuals who have disabilities are raised and described from a variety of viewpoints. Feminist, cultural, and ethnic concerns have been described and leave the reader with questions about future DS issues. Not only does this book focus on the role of inclusion, teacher education programs, and higher education in disability studies within the United States and Belgium, it also provides details to help the reader consider not just physical disabilities but also mental health issues and transforms the reader's understanding of both.

Finally, the authors describe how policies in the United States, the United Kingdom, and New Zealand have affected disability studies and how they may limit changes needed for this field to improve. This compilation of material delivers nearly a century of information about disability studies from perspectives around the world. Whether the reader is an educator, a mental health worker, a social worker, or in some other related field, this book leaves one with the opportunity to reflect on disability studies of the past and questions about where we may need to go in the future. The scope of the work is broad enough to challenge the reader, yet organized well enough to clarify each topic. Well worth reading!—**Donna J Kearns**

6 Ethnic Studies and Anthropology

Anthropology

Archaeology

142. Springate, Megan E. **Coffin Hardware in Nineteenth-Century America.** Walnut Creek, Calif., Left Coast Press, Inc., 2015. 116p. illus. index. (Guides to Historical Artifacts). $29.95pa. ISBN 13: 978-1-59874-135-3; 978-1-62958-053-1 (e-book).

There is an amazing interest among people in old coffin hardware. Coffin hardware appears to have become an inspiration point for a new generation of artists. This volume explores nineteenth-century coffin hardware from a historical artifact perspective. The introduction of mass-produced coffin hardware in the nineteenth century provides insight into how individuals living in the period felt about themselves and the afterlife. Based on a British coffin hardware antecedent, the American hardware incorporated a unique new world vision of the afterlife. Through a series of topical chapters the book explores concepts such as: coffin typology, children's hardware, coffins as artifacts, safety and security (in case the person was buried alive), the coffin industry in America, and themes of design and social factors (status, religion, gender, ethnicity) in coffins. Appendixes included are: a list of coffin catalogs in public repositories, an excellent bibliography, and an index. The blurb on the back cover states that the book is "extensively illustrated" but this reviewer would rather say that it has some illustrations of coffin hardware and burial practices in the nineteenth century. Most reference collections will find this volume useful, especially around Halloween time. The book covers a topic about which not much is written in an excellent and informative manner.—**Ralph Lee Scott**

143. Webster, Chris. **Field Archaeologist's Survival Guide: Getting a Job and Working in Cultural Resource Management.** Walnut Creek, Calif., Left Coast Press, Inc., 2014. 157p. illus. index. $24.95; $24.95 (e-book). ISBN 13: 978-1-61132-928-5; 978-1-61132-930-8 (e-book).

Are you a librarian at a college or university that offers archaeology courses? Do you work in a college or university career office that maintains a collection of career resources? Do you want to help your college students find their dream job? If so, then consider adding this honest and straightforward guide to working in the field as an archaeologist to your collections.

Chris Webster's *Field Archaeologist's Survival Guide* covers advice on working as an archaeologist, from which classes college students should take, how to choose participating in a field school, how to prepare curriculum vitae (CV), to how to cook meat on a shovel on a campfire. Webster's guide begins with how to prepare for the working world as an archaeologist for college students and ends with what to do during the winter season when there is no outdoor fieldwork in the colder climates. There are detailed chapters on how to develop a CV, resumes, and cover letters, including how to describe various types of military experience on a CV or a resume. Webster provides advice on where to find job listings, how to respond to job advertisements, and how to send resumes and cover letters to companies that do not have current job openings listed.

Supplying invaluable career advice not usually discussed in archaeology classes, Webster describes equipment, projects, lodging, and other logistical considerations. Webster lists the type of equipment needed for archaeology and provides explanations as to why the gear is important. Next, the author describes different types of archaeological projects and jobs in cultural resource management so prospective employees know what to expect if hired. With real-world experience and a knack for storytelling, Webster gives a myriad of suggestions on types of lodging, such as living out of a van, camping, and staying in hotels. He includes several recipes and recommendations on how to cook in hotel rooms.

Additionally, the author explains how to use information to be successful as an archaeologist, with the perspective of a seasoned archaeologist imparting wisdom not learned in the classroom to future archaeologists. For example, he describes the University Transverse Mercator (UTM) grid, the township and range system, and the Smithsonian Trinomial System. He also introduces drawing maps, lumber sizing, and the *Munsell Book of Color* adapted to soil samples. Becoming successful may pose challenges, however, and the author devotes an entire chapter to unemployment. Although specific to the state of Nevada, he believes his information about the unemployment process can be applicable to other states.

The author closes with the reminder that becoming an archaeologist is really a dream job. Telling a story about a wealthy investment banker he met, the author wrote that the banker said that he wished he had the job as the archaeologist. Lastly, short but thorough appendixes correspond to the chapters and provide sample CVs, examples of cover letters, equipment and clothing checklists for fieldwork, sample interview questions to ask, and a checklist for what to do during the winter off-season.—**Kay Shelton**

Ethnic Studies

General Works

Dictionaries and Encyclopedias

144.   **Ethnic Dress in the United States: A Cultural Encyclopedia.** Annette Lynch and Mitchell D. Strauss, eds. Lanham, Md., Rowman & Littlefield, 2015. 326p. illus. index. $75.00; $74.99 (e-book). ISBN 13: 978-0-7591-2148-5; 978-0-7591-2150-8 (e-book).

This concise examination of the impact of foreign cultures on the dress of the United

States contains over 150 entries, ranging from lederhosen and djellaba to wingtips and polo shirt. Most entries have a short reading list for further exploration; many provide cross-references to related topics. The majority of the entries are comprised of three sections: a "history" section, which examines the origins of a type of clothing, hat, or footwear; a second section, the item "in the United States," which traces the evolution and development of the item within the American context; and a third section, "influence and impact," which looks at the current state of the garment, its customer base, and other contemporary aspects.

This volume would be most appropriate for interested readers in public libraries and for undergraduates seeking an introduction to the subject. From more well-known items, like muumuus, oxford shirts, and espadrilles to the more obscure jeogori and the Sibenik cap, this volume will provide the reader with intriguing information about their history.—**Mark Schumacher**

145.   **The SAGE Encyclopedia of African Cultural Heritage in North America.** Mwalimu J. Shujaa and Kenya J. Shujaa, eds. Thousand Oaks, Calif., Sage, 2015. 2v. illus. index. $375.00/set. ISBN 13: 978-1-4522-5821-8.

This set explores the numerous dimensions of Africa's cultural impact on North American society. Entries range from broad overviews (Education, Black Studies, Matriarchy and Patriarchy, Medicine) to narrower topics (Yoruba Symbolism, Bottle Trees, Quilts and Quilting, Pinkster Festival, Kwanzaa). Each entry includes cross-references to related entries and a brief bibliography. Some are very straightforward and easily understood, while others will require some background knowledge or consulting other related articles in this set. For example, the entry "Papa Legba," a spirit within the Vodu (voodoo) world, will probably attract specialists rather than casual readers.

Organized along the same clean lines as a number of other Sage encyclopedias published recently, and edited by a renowned scholar in the field of African and African-American Studies, these 250+ entries, from 140 authors around the world, present the multifaceted dimensions of African culture and how it has shaped lives in North America. Academic and public libraries will certainly benefit from this set.—**Mark Schumacher**

African Americans

146.   **Black Studies in Video. https://search.alexanderstreet.com/blsv.** [Website] Alexandria, Va., Alexander Street Press. Price negotiated by site. Date reviewed: 2016.

This collection of videos is an Alexander Street Press signature collection and contains award-winning documentaries, newsreels, interviews, and archival footage. California Newsreel has also allowed access to their African American Classics collection.

Black Studies in Video showcases 855 videos for a total of 55 hours of visual media on a spectrum of topics related to black culture in the United States. Video subject areas focus on black history, politics, art and culture, family structure, social and economic pressures, and gender relations. The films come in a variety of formats from drama and animation, to news clips and interviews. The majority of films would be classified as documentaries (336); 50 contain speeches and 69 include a panel discussion on the challenges of being an African American.

The opening search tools include sidebars called Browse, People, and Specialized Areas of Interest. These tools will be useful for those who are not sure of the direction of their research. The search box provides direct searching for researchers with a specific time, person, keyword, or topic in mind. When a movie is selected, the landing page has another useful sidebar for further details. Information provided in this sidebar relates to the production of the film and contain: Content Type, Persons Discussed, Organizations Discussed, Topic/Theme, Director/Producer, and Speaker/Narrator. This page also provides options for correct citing of the film, email and sharing of this visual media.

The collection covers a broad array of major events and people important to the study of African Americans, but there is a lack of balance in subject areas at times. For example, in browsing "historical events," the query finds 140 entries under U.S. Civil Rights Movement and only 3 entries listed under Slavery and Abolition. More-well-known people who have contributed to black culture and the struggle for freedoms are well documented in this collection, but it also includes coverage of lesser-known personalities.

Diversity, challenge, and passion have been a mainstay of the African American experience. The collection of visual media gathered in *Black Studies in Video* brings this experience to life. In many instances, remarkable footage (i.e., *The Black Eagles, Part 1-Clipped Wings*) not only shows the challenging history of African Americans, but makes visceral this time period and its concomitant discrimination. Because of the breadth of information pertaining to black culture, the diversity of this collection will be useful to students in both high school and college. General researchers seeking engaging footage and a multiplicity of options will benefit from this video collection. Recommended.—**Janis Minshull**

147.   **Black Women of the Harlem Renaissance Era.** Lean'tin L. Bracks and Jessie Carney Smith, eds. Lanham, Md., Rowman & Littlefield, 2014. 304p. illus. index. $80.00; $79.99 (e-book). ISBN 13: 978-0-8108-8542-4; 978-0-8108-8543-1 (e-book).

The role of women in the Harlem Renaissance has been well-documented throughout the years, with biographies of both individuals and women as a whole. What distinguishes the current volume, edited under the direction of Fisk University's Bracks and Smith, is the inclusion of African American women other than poets and fiction writers active during the period 1919-1940. The reader should note that a number of these women were not directly associated with the Harlem Renaissance activities in New York City, hence the "Era" at the tag-end of the book's title. However, that broad scope is not to take away from the general usefulness and scholarship of the collection. The editors include roughly 200 one-to-three page signed biographies arranged alphabetically of women in the fields of community leadership and activism, the arts, education, journalism, and entrepreneurship, although the preponderance of entries are for literary and entertainment individuals. But for every familiar name such as Bessie Smith or Nella Larsen, the editors have rediscovered women such as anthropologist Caroline Day and activist Lugenia Burns Hope. A short bibliography is included at the end of the volume, but there are no bibliographic references appended to the entries themselves. Some of the entries also include black-and-white photos, but those are few and far between. In sum, the scope and utility make this volume an excellent addition to all African American Studies collections, along with Wall's *Women of the Harlem Renaissance* (Indiana University Press, 1995) and Roses' and Randolph's *Harlem Renaissance and Beyond: Literary Biographies of One Hundred Black Women Writers, 1900-1945* (Harvard University Press, 1997).—**Anthony J. Adam**

148.   Drew, Bernard A. **Black Stereotypes in Popular Series Fiction, 1851-1955: Jim Crow Era Authors and Their Characters.** Jefferson, N.C., McFarland, 2015. 292p. illus. index. $55.00pa. ISBN 13: 978-0-7864-7410-3; 978-1-4766-1610-0 (e-book).

Drew, a prolific author of books delineating popular U.S. fiction, profiles 29 authors active between 1851 and 1955, both black and white, who featured stereotypical African American characters in their serialized short stories, newspaper columns, and other works. Although some of the authors are still remembered—Langston Hughes and Booth Tarkington, for example—many others such as Roark Bradford and Harris Dickson have become footnotes in American literature. Additionally, Drew supplements his work with brief single-paragraph biographies of another 72 authors such as Richard Wright and Zora Neale Hurston who used recurring black characters in their works. Black-and-white illustrations are scattered throughout (readers might find many of the period pieces offensive), and Drew is more than generous with providing examples of dialect conversation and humor from the cited authors. Drew's prose style takes some getting used to—he is a former newspaperman and retains the "short and sweet" style of that format—but his research is informative and extremely useful for those studying popular literary culture. Above all, readers will benefit greatly from Drew's primary and secondary bibliographies, which include lists of every serial appearance of the characters. Recommended for all popular culture collections and comprehensive collections of African-American studies and literature.—**Anthony J. Adam**

149.   **In Motion: The African-American Migration Experience. http://www. inmotionaame.org/home.cfm.** [Website] Free. Date reviewed: 2016.

This extensive and top-notch database from the Schomberg Center for Research in Black Culture presents the history of African American migration. The breadth of the site is immediately apparent. The African American migration narrative does not start in colonial Virginia but with migrations from Mexico and the Caribbean and includes everything in between up to contemporary African migrations. Taken altogether, *In Motion* shows the diversity of African Americans living in the United States and combines in one place all components of the African diaspora. Included in the approximately 35 million African Americans in the United States in the twenty-first century are African Americans, Africans, Afro-Caribbeans, Central Americans of African descent, and African and Afro-Cubans born in Europe. As the database demonstrates, all these groups are heirs to the migrations that have shaped U.S. history.

This well-curated site, written and organized by scholars and professionals, has 16,500 pages of text, 8,300 illustrations, and 60 maps arranged around 13 migrations: The Transatlantic Slave Trade (1450s-1867); Runaway Journeys (1630s-1865); The Domestic Slave Trade (1760s-1865); Colonization & Emigration (1783-1910s); Haitian Immigration: 18th and 19th Centuries (1791-1809); The Western Migration (1840s-1890); The Northern Migration (1840s-1890); The Great Migration (1916-1930); The Second Great Migration (1940-1970); Caribbean Immigration (1900-Present); Return South Migration (1900-Present); Haitian Immigration: 20th Century (1970-Present); and African Immigration (1970-present). Each migration has a narrative; hundreds of illustrations, each with a caption, bibliographical indexing, and ordering information; 20-40 research resources (books, essays, book chapters, article, manuscripts, Websites); maps; and lesson plans. Searching could not be more intuitive. Users can browse by migrations, geography, or timeline and choose what to do from there. All migration texts have highlighted words that link to a glossary, which can also be accessed from a glossary box on the bottom of each page. Better still for students and teachers, the text is available in a printer-friendly format and all images are downloadable. As explained in the rights and usages link from the main page, these resources are intended for scholarly and personal use. For these purposes, the quality of the images is sufficient; however, high-resolution copies of images are available from the library.

In the opinion of this reviewer, the best way to gain a true appreciation of the information on this database is to search it by migration. The Western Migration, for example, opens with a sound clip and images on the top of the page. From there, a user can explore the image gallery; read "The Way West: Migration and the African-American Search for Freedom and Opportunity in the Western United States" by University of Washington professor Quintard Taylor; study maps created for the project by Rutgers University cartographer Michael Siegel; or jump straight to the educational materials. The bibliography and links in this essay alone are enough to launch dozens of research projects. For example, one link takes users to *African Americans and the Old West,* an extensive database of text, images, and further links created by Long Island University. The provided curriculum covers grades 6-12 and includes the necessary resources for such lesson plans as "OK in Oklahoma? All-Black Communities" for grades 9-12.

In Motion is a resource of the highest value and quality that will prove useful to students, researchers, and teachers.—**ARBA Staff Reviewer**

150.   **Smithsonian National Museum of African American History and Culture Online Collections. http://nmaahc.si.edu/.** [Website] Free. Date reviewed: 2016.

The Smithsonian National Museum of African American History and Culture Website provides an excellent and accessible online resource dedicated to the rich and diverse history and culture of the African American experience. This site includes information about exhibitions and programs, events, collections, and education workshops and is a companion for the physical gallery, currently located at the National Museum of American History. In September 2016, the five-acre museum will open to the public on the National Mall in Washington, D.C. The foundational collection of African American culture and history now includes 1,000 items, including photographs, artifacts, documents, and art that are searchable on the Website.

The site provides tabs with information about visiting the gallery and opportunities for getting involved through volunteering, membership, collaborations, and internships and fellowships. A "Connect" tab links visitors to the blog and social media, and the "Newsroom" shares chronological stories on the upcoming museum opening as well as articles related to African American culture and history. Visitors have ample opportunity to donate their time, money, or artifacts or become NMAAHC members.

While this comprehensive resource benefits virtual visitors, many of the resources like the exhibitions at the gallery and the museum itself are available only to physical visitors. A handful of activities suitable for K-6 classrooms are available for download, but nothing is offered for students at the secondary levels. The education section provides a link to request materials for Black History Month, but resources are currently unavailable as they "have reached capacity of requests" at this time. Overall, the Website is slick, polished, and provides access to multiple social media outlets, opportunities to become involved, and information about other activities. Recommended for all audiences.—**ARBA Staff Reviewer**

Asian Americans

151. **Asian American Religious Cultures.** Jonathan H.X. Lee, Fumitaka Matsuoka, Edmond Yee, and Ronald Nakasone, eds. Santa Barbara, Calif., ABC-CLIO, 2015. 2v. illus. index. $189.00/set. ISBN 13: 978-1-59884-330-9; 978-1-59884-331-6 (e-book).

This two-volume encyclopedia provides a comprehensive, accessible overview of Asian American religious cultures and social customs. The set provides a broad historical context for understanding the great diversity found within these cultures. Both volumes include a contents section, thematic guide to related topics, and alphabetical entries. Each entry concludes with *see also* references directing readers to related entries and essays and a bibliography of suggestions for further reading. Volume one contains an informative introduction highlighting the complex interplay of history, religion, and race in Asian American cultures as well as 19 essays covering a wide range of topics including politics, law, gender and sexuality, and LGBT issues. Volume two includes an up-to-date bibliography of print, online, and film resources, biographical information about the editors, and a list of contributors and their associated organizations. In addition, volume two contains a 42-page index with essays and main entries indicated by boldface page numbers. This is a user-friendly resource enhanced by clear writing and the inclusion of black-and-white photos. With more than 100 contributors including academics, religious leaders, and community elders, this encyclopedia covers a wide range of topics and serves as both a starting point for scholarly research and a general source for the casual reader. This encyclopedia is recommended for academic and large public libraries.—**Lisa Morgan**

152. **Asian American Society: An Encyclopedia.** Mary Yu Danico and Anthony C. Ocampo, eds. Thousand Oaks, Calif., Sage, 2014. 4v. index. $625.00/set. ISBN 13: 978-1-4522-8190-2.

This 2,000-page set explores many diverse topics relating to the Asian American experience. The first two volumes contain 320 alphabetically arranged entries. Topics include broad areas such as Japanese Americans, hate crimes, and families (overview), but also more focused entries such as Charlie Chan, Bollywood, Lunar New Year, and picture brides. Americans from Hawaii, Japan, Korea, China, Thailand, the Philippines, Bangladesh, Cambodia, Vietnam and India are included in this comprehensive set.

Volumes three and four present primary documents covering the years 1849 to 2013. Earlier documents include court cases, articles in, and letters to, newspapers, and occasional legislation. Many of the recent items are government reports and congressional activities of various kinds, including declarations honoring Asian Americans and testimony before committees and subcommittees.

Any library with patrons investigating the Asian experience in America will find this reference work useful, although it may not fit, alas, into every budget. Copyediting needs work on occasion, but otherwise this is a very useful set.—**Mark Schumacher**

153. **Chinese Americans: The History and Culture of a People.** Jonathan H. X. Lee, ed. Santa Barbara, Calif., ABC-CLIO, 2015. 498p. illus. index. $100.00. ISBN 13: 978-1-61069-549-7; 978-1-61069-550-3 (e-book).

This is a reference book devoted to all aspects of the Chinese American experience in North America. It is divided into four alphabetical (by subject) sections. Part one deals with Chinese American immigration. Part two delineates Chinese American political and economic life. Part three covers Chinese American cultural and religious life. Part four covers Chinese American contributions to literature, the arts, popular culture, and sports. There are many biographical articles. Each article contains a short bibliography. There is an additional bibliography of more than 100 books and articles and a chronology of Chinese American history from January 18, 1778, to February 11, 2015. Editor Jonathan H. X. Lee is an associate professor of Asian American studies at San Francisco State University. There is an editorial board of six academics and a list of consultants. A detailed index is included. A 20-page section of primary documents and numerous black-and-white illustrations are also included.

Many articles treat little-known or unknown aspects of Chinese American life. The ongoing history of the treatment of Chinese Americans (and other minority groups) is often a shameful one, but Chinese Americans have pressured and even prevailed in many areas of American life. There has been no lack of breathtakingly wrong-headed judicial decisions and laws. This is a book that should be in every secondary school, academic, and public library especially those libraries serving a Chinese American population.—**Jonathan F. Husband**

154.   **Smithsonian Asian Pacific American Center.** http://smithsonianapa.org/. [Website] Free. Date reviewed: 2016.

The Smithsonian Asian Pacific American Center, established in 1997, is a virtual space dedicated to highlighting and appreciating America's Asian Pacific culture and heritage through innovative digital and museum experiences. The splash page for the site highlights an exhibit on Japanese American civil rights activist Yuri Kochiyama in celebration of Women's History Month. The drop down menu in the upper left corner directs readers to information about the center, exhibitions, events calendar, blog, employment, and a page for donations. At the top of the page, visitors can connect with the site's social media pages.

The organization provides a "museum for the 21st century"—an interactive online entity that connects Asian American communities nationwide through partnerships, technology, and experiences both in person and online. These experiences are created through "Culture Labs" that provide participants with opportunities for critical inquiry and dialogue, guided by storytellers, through which to explore Asian Pacific American history, culture, and art. The "About Us" page provides a downloadable two-year "Blueprint," or strategic plan, for strengthening the organization and programs, developing a collection acquisitions strategy, and experimenting with new in-person and online programs. The page also provides their mission statement and information about board and staff members.

Although the site is slow to load and navigate (likely due to the extensive digital content) the strongest area is the "Exhibitions" page. Viewers can access information about traveling exhibits as well as view the entire content of four digital exhibitions. Each exhibit includes full color images, videos, artwork, and narratives. Recommended for all audiences.—**ARBA Staff Reviewer**

Indians of Central America

155.   **Encyclopedia of the Ancient Maya.** Walter R.T. Witschey, ed. Lanham, Md., Rowman & Littlefield, 2016. 574p. illus. maps. index. $95.00; $94.99 (e-book). ISBN 13: 978-0-7591-2284-0; 978-0-7591-2286-4 (e-book).

The editor of this excellent reference work hopes to acquaint the reader with information regarding the ancient Maya, their architecture and writing, and the techniques used for gathering and analyzing archaeological information. The audience for this work is high school and college students.

The front matter begins with a table of contents and a thematic index containing 15 subject groupings such as Agriculture and Food, Ceramics, and Environment. This is followed by a list of maps, tables and figures. The preface includes a brief history of Maya archaeology. It outlines the fascinating story of how Maya glyphs were deciphered and discusses the ongoing nature of discovery in Maya archaeology. A brief Note to Readers supplies helpful information about cross-referencing, orthography of Maya words, tips for understanding the complex Maya language, a list of Maya rulers, and definitions of abbreviations and units of measure used in the book. A chronology of the Mayan civilization from 14,000 B.C.E. to A.D. 2012 includes notes explaining a variety of dating methods used to anchor the Mayan civilization in time. Finally, the book explains the archaeological naming conventions for various time periods in the Maya civilization.

The introduction offers a very brief explanation of Maya civilization and the people who made prominent discoveries in that realm. It defines the geography of the Maya area and outlines the history of settlement and development of MesoAmerica and the Maya area. A list of recommended readings completes the Introduction.

Eight maps of different types precede the alphabetical entries for the encyclopedia. The entries include archaeological sites, brief biographies of people, cultural concepts (Craft Specialization, for example), and the roles played by individuals in Maya life. Each entry gives a definition of the term with a description. For archaeological sites geographic coordinates are included. Each entry has cross-references as appropriate, provides a brief bibliography for further reading, and may include a photo or drawing. Entries range from a single paragraph to six pages in length.

The alphabetical entries are followed by a glossary, an essay describing critical resources for information about the Maya, a list of selected Internet resources (often Websites for specific archaeological sites), a list of research institutes working on Maya topics, a list of series and journals relating to Maya topics, and an extensive bibliography.

The work is completed with an index to investigators and explorers, a general index to the entire encyclopedia, and very brief biographies of the 81 authors.

This work provides a wealth of information on the topic of the ancient Maya, couched in terms that can be understood by the layperson. It includes information on very recent discoveries as well as those of the distant past. This is an excellent introduction to the ancient Maya, the people who study them, and the techniques used in the process. This book should be in all high school and college libraries and in appropriate special libraries.—**Joanna M. Burkhardt**

Indians of North America

156. American Indian Culture: From Counting Coup to Wampum. Bruce E. Johansen, ed. Santa Barbara, Calif., Greenwood Press/ABC-CLIO, 2015. 2v. illus. index. (Cultures of the American Mosaic). $189.00/set. ISBN 13: 978-1-4408-2873-7; 978-1-4408-2874-4 (e-book).

Edited by Bruce E. Johansen, Jacob J. Isaacson University Research Professor in Communication and Native American Studies at the University of Nebraska at Omaha and editor or coeditor of such works as *The Encyclopedia of Native American Legal Tradition* (see ARBA 1999, entry 388) and *Encyclopedia of the Haudenosaunee (Iroquois Confederacy)* (see ARBA 2001, entry 299), this is the most recent addition to Greenwood's Cultures of the American Mosaic series. It contains approximately 150 entries divided into 11 chapters: "Population and Demographics"; "Nations, Tribes, and Other Native Groups"; "General Historical Considerations"; "Arts"; "Family, Education, and Community Overview"; "Food"; "Language and Literature"; "Media, Popular Culture, Sports, and Gaming"; "Spirituality"; and "Transportation and Housing." Each of the entries contains bibliographic citation. Some include "Spotlights," which are utilized like sidebars, and cross-references to related articles. Sprinkled throughout the two volumes are black-and-white illustrations and reproductions of photographs. Concluding the reference are a 24-page "Selected Bibliography" and a general index. Written in language accessible to high school students, this work is recommended for high school, public, and undergraduate libraries.—**John R. Burch Jr.**

157.   **Creek (Muskogee) Texts.** Haas, Mary R., and James H. Hill. Martin, Jack B., Margaret McKane Mauldin, and Juanita McGirt, eds. Oakland, Calif., University of California Press, 2015. 819p. (University of California Publications in Linguistics, Volume 150). $65.00. ISBN 13: 978-0-520-28642-9.

This large volume contains over 150 Creek texts collected by renowned linguist and anthropologist Mary Haas (1910-1996) during the period 1936 to 1941. Her primary source was James H. Hill (1861-ca. 1953), a Creek Indian of the Atkayahchi clan living in eastern Oklahoma, who provided over 100 of the texts. The editors have carefully transcribed and translated these texts, which range in content from autobiography and history to native folktales. Each text has each line presented in four ways: the Creek spelling, a phonemic transcription, a word-for-word translation (given by Haas), and the editors' free translation.

Clearly an advanced text created for linguists and ethnologists studying Native American peoples, this volume is recommended for academic libraries supporting such programs. Interestingly, one can hear about 20 of these texts being read by Mauldin at http://lingspace.wm.edu/lingspace/creek/texts/haas-hill/.—**Mark Schumacher**

158.   Dennis, Yvonne Wakim, Arlene Hirschfelder, and Shannon Rothenberger Flynn. **Native American Almanac: More Than 50,000 Years of the Cutlures and Histories of Indigenous Peoples.** Canton, Mich., Visible Ink Press, 2016. 643p. illus. maps. index. $24.95pa. ISBN 13: 978-1-57859-507-5; 978-1-57859-608-9 (e-book).

Once pushed to the side by the Eurocentric version of new world events, Native Americans and their story have been lifted by dogged scholarship and patient dissemination. This story is, of course, a long one, beginning prehistorically and continuing through today even as cultures have blended. In this almanac, readers will find abundant and enlightening details of Native American life and history which fill in the account of many great and diverse tribes spread throughout the United States.

Three sections organize the material, following a historical overview of Indian-white relations in the United States in the opening pages. The essay here is generally chronological and touches on many of the events, treaties, and acts which have determined the course of relations since the Europeans began colonization. It mentions everything from the Doctrine of Discovery, adopted into U.S. law in 1823 and giving Christian people dominion of non-Christian, "heathen" people; federal assimilation policies enacted throughout the decades; and the 2010 Congressional Resolution of Apology which marked the U.S. government's remorse for centuries of neglect, manipulation, and violence towards the Native American peoples.

The second and largest section groups tribes geographically (e.g., Northeast, Southwest, etc.), and presents many topics within broader ideas of tribal history, cultural signifiers, and political struggles. Some examples of topics covered in this section include Art Traditions, Native Languages, and The Struggle for Citizenship and Land Rights, Select biographies chronologically profile tribal leaders, politicians, artists, and others of note.

A generous use of headings and subheadings helps readers navigate all the material throughout the two main sections. It is important to point out that topics within each regional section may differ from tribe to tribe and from region to region.

A final section carries numerous appendixes, including condensed native histories for Canada, Mexico, the Caribbean, and Greenland; a regional listing of all indigenous nations and groups throughout North America (alphabetized within regions); Indian Lands: Definitions and Explanations; a glossary of Indigenized English; Indigeneity From Sea to Sea, listing sacred sites throughout the United States; Selected Indigenous Firsts: People, Places and Things; Native Owned and Operated Museums; The Indigeneity of the Powwow; and finally Indigenous Ancestry Affiliation of Some Notable People.

While offering new and abundant information, the book is not meant to be comprehensive or encyclopedic, nor is it meant to be considered scholarly. The book also includes suggestions for further reading and an index. Recommended.—**ARBA Staff Reviewer**

159. **The Newspaper Warrior: Sarah Winnemucca Hopkins's Campaign for American Indian Rights, 1864-1891.** Cari M. Carpenter and Carolyn Sorisio, eds. Lincoln, Nebr., University of Nebraska Press, 2015. 329p. index. $75.00. ISBN 13: 978-0-8032-4368-2; 978-0-8032-7661-1 (e-book).

In *The Newspaper Warrior,* editor Cari M. Carpenter, professor of English at West Virginia University, and Carolyn Sorisio, professor of English at West Chester University of Pennsylvania, present hundreds of newspaper articles, letters to the editor, advertisements, book reviews, and editorial comments by and about Sarah Winnemucca Hopkins, covering the years 1864-1891 and focusing on the years 1879-1887. While well-known for her book, *Life among the Paiutes: Their Wrongs and Claims* (1883), *Newspaper Warrior* sheds new light on Sarah Winnemucca Hopkins and her work on behalf of Native Americans. The book begins with an introductory analysis, which is followed by three parts: West, 1864-1882, East, 1883-1884, and West, 1885-1891. The individual newspaper articles are listed chronologically; each has complete identifying information—newspaper name, article title, page and column numbers, and dates. The book also has notes and a complete index, so, for example, a user could look up articles that appeared in the *Daily Alta California* from San Francisco, the *Silver State* from Winnemucca, Nevada, or the *Boston Daily Globe.*

While this title will be more likely found in general circulation than on the reference shelf, it can serve as a useful and valuable reference for researchers and scholars looking for a single collection of primary documents on a well-known Native American woman and activist. Highly recommended.—**ARBA Staff Reviewer**

160.   Sekaquaptewa, Emory, Kenneth C. Hill, and Dorothy K. Washburn. **Hopi Katsina Songs.** Lincoln, Nebr., University of Nebraska Press, 2015. 421p. index. $65.00. ISBN 13: 978-0-8032-6288-1.

This unique book provides Hopi transcriptions, English translations, and explanatory commentary for 150 Hopi katsina songs, including songs from the Library of Congress and the Indiana University Archives of Traditional Music that have not been previously transcribed and translated. This work is the result of collaboration by the three authors under the guidance of Emory Sekaquaptewa.

The book begins with an introduction that explicates the katsinas and their role in Hopi tradition; Hopi principles of life; the corn metaphor; katsinas, katsina performances, and katsina songs; the metaphorical presentation of the song message; and the history of the project that resulted in this volume. It then describes the collections used for the project: the Natalie Curtis Burlin Collection (1903); the Samuel Barrett Collection (1911); the Jesse Fewkes Collection (1926); the Helen Roberts Collection (late 1920s); the Beaglehole Collection (ca. 1934); the Robert Black Collection (1957-1959); the George List Collection (1960); and those contributed by Sekaquaptewa himself. The transcribed and translated songs are presented in the chronological order of the collections. The songs are followed by three appendixes: Linguistic Comments, Compounds in the Songs, and Glossary of Hopi Words. An index rounds out this fine offering.

This book is highly recommended for academic libraries.—**ARBA Staff Reviewer**

161.   **Smithsonian National Museum of the American Indian Collections. http:// nmai.si.edu/explore/collections/.** [Website] Free. Date reviewed: 2016.

The Smithsonian's National Museum of the American Indian has two locations. The main museum, located in Washington, D.C., on the National Mall, houses one of the world's largest collections of some 825,000 items related to Native America. The second location is in New York City in the Alexander Hamilton U.S. Custom House. The "Visit" tab on the Website provides virtual visitors with information about both locations of the museum including hours, admission, parking, and directions for public transportation and driving. The "Explore" tab provides detailed descriptions about the current, upcoming, and past exhibitions at both locations, as well as details about traveling exhibits. This section also includes extensive information about the history, significance, conservation, repatriation, and use of the collections as well as an online search tool. The top of the collections page provides a "featured item" along with other collection highlights. The site offers a variety of ways for visitors to search by people, individuals, places, and objects.

In the "Education" section, educators and students will find information about programs and resources as well as past and present education e-newsletters. The museum hosts Native American film screenings and festivals and provides a searchable film and media catalog, blog, and live Webcasts. Other tabs on the Website give details about how visitors can connect to and support the museum through memberships, donations, internships, events, and programs for both American Indians and non-American Indians. The "Shop" tab allows visitors to view and purchase a wide range of books for all readers, children's books, Spanish language books, and CDs and DVDs. One drawback is that items can only be purchased by calling and ordering over the phone (available 24-hours) or downloading and faxing the order form.

Visitors can hover over a tab to see the available links. Upon clicking on one of the links, it not only opens to that page but also lists all of the available links for that tab on the left-hand side of the page for easy navigation. A "Share" link in the upper right hand corner links visitors with a variety of social media for the site. Overall, the Website is well-organized and filled with engaging, full-color images. Recommended for all audiences.—**ARBA Staff Reviewer**

162.   **Treasures from Native California: The Legacy of Russian Exploration.** Hudson, Travis, and Craig D. Bates. Blackburn, Thomas and John R. Johnson, eds. Walnut Creek, Calif., Left Coast Press, Inc., 2015. 231p. illus. maps. index. $99.00; $39.95 (e-book). ISBN 13: 978-1-61132-982-7; 978-1-61132-984-1 (e-book).

During the early nineteenth century, Russian collectors and researchers traveled to California, prior to its statehood, to collect material culture of native peoples on behalf of the Academy of Sciences. Those researchers deposited the materials and notes about them primarily in the Kunstkamera in St. Petersburg. This volume describes the cultural objects collected from California, along with brief chapters that contextualize the collectors themselves. These collections are older than the Smithsonian and the Kunstkamera's collection of early California material culture is the world's largest from that area during the early nineteenth century. Following California's statehood, native cultures changed rapidly. Il'ia Gavilovich Voznesenskii should be considered California's first collector, according to the authors, and the resulting collection in the Kunstkamera includes objects not found anywhere else. Although the authors include objects held in other museums collected by Russians besides the Kunstkamera, its collection is the focus of the volume.

Contextualizing the collectors, the authors describe the Russians who collected from California as having learned from previous Russian contact with native people further north. Harsh treatment by Russians toward the Tlingit compelled them to fight back and destroy Russian towns earlier in history. These later Russian descriptions of California's native people focused less on making derogatory comments about their physical appearance compared with contemporary and earlier European travelers and missionaries. Although not all of the Russian collectors praised the artistry of the objects they collected, a better attitude toward the native peoples resulted in far less hostile relations compared to their predecessors.

The authors' detailed descriptions and photographs of the objects held in Russian museums are a strong feature of this book. The photographic technique of showing the objects with dark backgrounds is particularly strong in Chapter eight, "Objects for Festive Occasions: Music, Gifts, and Games," which illustrates the intricate detailed work of baskets. Chapter seven, "Interacting with the Supernatural: Ritual Dress," focuses on the clothing and jewelry, although discussion about interacting with the supernatural is scant.

While not affecting the quality of the content, there is an oddity of the text layout, with numerous sections of blank space at the bottoms of pages in the middle of chapters. Nevertheless, this volume includes lavish photographic images of the objects in the collections and the sketches and paintings of the native people completed by Russian artists. Academic libraries that support museum studies, anthropology, American Indian, and Russian history should consider purchasing this book for reference collections. Additionally, larger public libraries in California may wish to add this book, which provides an unusual perspective on early California history, providing insight on material culture of native peoples, as seen through the eyes of Russian researchers.—**Kay Shelton**

Indians of South America

163.   **Encyclopedia of the Incas.** Urton, Gary and Adriana Von Hagen, eds. Lanham, Md., Rowman & Littlefield, 2015. 324p. illus. maps. index. $75.00; $74.99 (e-book). ISBN 13: 978-0-7591-2362-5; 978-0-7591-2363-2 (e-book).

At the peak of its influence the Inca Empire extended from Columbia to Chile, and from the Pacific Ocean into the Amazon rainforest. The empire covered a wide variety of terrain, including mountains, deserts, and tropical jungles. Keeping control over the many and diverse people in this far-flung empire relied on a fascinating mixture of cultural overlay and actual conquest. The workings of the empire were interrupted and eventually destroyed with the arrival of Spanish explorers in the sixteenth century.

The editors of this volume are well-known experts in Pre-Columbian Inca studies. Entries were written by the editors and by 35 other Inca experts from fields such as anthropology, archaeology, geography, and ethnohistory. The purpose of the work is to provide newcomers with an introduction to the Inca civilization and to place each of the subjects covered in the 128 entries into its larger cultural context.

The volume begins with a table of contents listing the individual entries in alphabetical order. This is followed by a thematic contents listing subjects and the individual entries that pertain to those subjects. The introduction that follows gives a brief description of the geographic boundaries of the Inca Empire. It goes on to explain the sources of information available concerning this nonliterate people and describes the pros and cons associated with the use of those sources. A very brief description of the history of the Incas and their rise to power is followed by an explicit rationale for the creation of this encyclopedia. The introduction ends with a note about the orthography of the Quechua language and the spellings used in this book. A map of the Inca Empire, its road system, its political boundaries, and the location of modern cities and capitals completes the introductory materials. The entries follow in alphabetical order. A comprehensive index allows an additional means of access. A brief section about the editors and the authors completes the volume.

A typical entry is two to three pages long. It explains the term, gives its history, and describes its cultural context. Many entries contain a photograph or a classic drawing relating to the subject of the entry. Entries contain cross-references to other entries in the encyclopedia, as appropriate. Each entry ends with suggestions for further reading. All entries are signed.

While the entries are relatively short and the total number of entries is limited, this volume will serve the stated purposes of providing an introduction to the Inca civilization and placing the entries in their cultural context. This volume will be useful to high school, public, and undergraduate libraries.—**Joanna M. Burkhardt**

Latin Americans

164.   **Leaders of the Mexican American Generation: Biographical Sketches.** Anthony Quiroz, ed. Boulder, Colo., University Press of Colorado, 2015. 368p. illus. index. $35.95; $19.95 (e-book). ISBN 13: 978-1-60732-336-5; 978-1-60732-336-5 (e-book).

This timely and important book shares the stories of the people who carved out the long road taken by millions of Mexican Americans on their journey towards social, political and economic acceptance in the United States. Focusing on the years between 1920 and 1965, the book presents interesting biographical sketches of the prominent thinkers and doers of the "Mexican American Generation."

The book divides its essays into two sections. The first section, Intellectuals and Ethnic Consciousness, shines a spotlight on the prime movers behind the Mexican American identity, such as José de la Luz Sáenz, World War I veteran and cofounder of LULAC (League of United Latin American Citizens), and Alice Dickerson Montemayor, who came to inject a feminist angle into LULAC's mission by working to advance women's issues. The second section focuses on Legal, Political and Labor Activists; identifying those who took the reins from the early thinkers and pushed Mexican American issues into the greater civil rights conversation. Chapters here feature biographies on John J. Herrera, Ralph Estrada, and others, including Dr. Héctor P. García, considered by his essay's author a "giant of the twentieth century." Detailed notes follow up each biography. Black-and-white illustrations enhance the book, which is rounded out by an index.

At a time when the topic of immigration has become a hot-button political issue, this book can acquaint readers with the trailblazers who helped their people surmount significant hurdles and establish themselves as a proud component of the American ideal.—**ARBA Staff Reviewer**

165.   **Smithsonian Latino Center. http://latino.si.edu/.** [Website] Free. Date reviewed: 2016.

The Smithsonian Latino Center, created in 1997, promotes Latino culture through research, public programs, exhibitions, education programs, leadership and professional development programs, and Web-based content. The center is not housed in a physical building but exists on a virtual platform in which participants collaborate with communities, institutions, and individuals around the country. This colorful site opens with engaging and constantly changing images of Latino culture and artifacts. Under the "About Us" tab, visitors will find contact information, social media links, an interactive events calendar, and at the center of the page, their Twitter feed. Visitors can hover over events to get additional information or click on the event title for even more detail. Most of the events are in various locations at Smithsonian institutions in Washington, D.C., and New York City. The overall feel is one of active engagement. Bold headings tell visitors that the mission of the center is to engage, inspire, and support Latino heritage.

Other tabs provide visitors with links to current, upcoming, and past exhibitions, public programs, education opportunities, press, resources, and ways to support the center. One of the most striking parts of the Website is found under the Virtual Museum tab that includes 2-D and 3-D collections, educational activities, and other simulations in the virtual world related to Latino culture and heritage. Visitors can click on the Virtual Museum tab and be transported to a virtual world where they'll find a simulated town square. Viewers can hover over parts of the town to find pop up images linked to a variety of exhibits, podcasts, galleries, and archived performances. Overall, this is an engaging and lively site with excellent virtual information on Latino culture and heritage. Recommended for all audiences.—**ARBA Staff Reviewer**

7 Genealogy and Heraldry

Genealogy

166. Baxter, Angus. **In Search of Your German Roots: A Complete Guide to Tracing Your Ancestors in the Germanic Areas of Europe.** 5th ed. Baltimore, Md., Genealogical Publishing, 2015. 125p. maps. index. $19.95pa. ISBN 13: 978-0-8063-2011-3.

This new fifth edition of *In Search of Your German Roots* is updated with new Websites, newly available records, and an expanded bibliography of resources for family history researchers.

This engagingly written piece provides a wealth of information on how to conduct research on family names and histories in Germany, including tips on letter writing to German entities. The author cautions novice researchers to be careful and not overly optimistic about finding complete records related to their family history in Germany. Genealogical information is, at best, fragmented and incomplete. Regardless, the book is chock full of helpful tips on getting started in family history research and finding the locations of the best resources. Chapters include starting the search, church records, immigration, archives in Germany, genealogical associations in Germany and North America, vital and other records, and, very important for armchair researchers, online resources. Jewish records and names are handled in a separate chapter due to the distinctive problem of researching Jewish names and history in any country. Website addresses are printed in bold making it easier to pick out the addresses buried in the text. This new edition is overall a very useful reference for family genealogy research in Germany.—**Linda M. Turney**

167. Bowen, Jeff, transcriber. **Cherokee Intermarried White, 1906. Volume I.** Baltimore, Md., Genealogical Publishing, 2014. 330p. $36.00pa. ISBN 13: 978-0-8063-5670-9.

168. Bowen, Jeff, transcriber. **Cherokee Intermarried White, 1906. Volume II.** Baltimore, Md., Genealogical Publishing, 2014. 330p. $36.00pa. ISBN 13: 978-0-8063-5671-6.

169. Bowen, Jeff, transcriber. **Cherokee Intermarried White, 1906. Volume III.** Baltimore, Md., Genealogical Publishing, 2014. 334p. $36.00pa. ISBN 13: 978-0-8063-5676-1.

170.   Bowen, Jeff, transcriber. **Cherokee Intermarried White, 1906. Volume IV.** Baltimore, Md., Genealogical Publishing, 2014. 326p. $36.00pa. ISBN 13: 978-0-8063-5677-8.

171.   Bowen, Jeff, transcriber. **Cherokee Intermarried White, 1906. Volume V.** Baltimore, Md., Genealogical Publishing, 2014. 328p. $36.00pa. ISBN 13: 978-0-8063-5678-5.

172.   Bowen, Jeff, transcriber. **Cherokee Intermarried White, 1906. Volume VI.** Baltimore, Md., Genealogical Publishing, 2014. 338p. $36.00pa. ISBN 13: 978-0-8063-5684-6.

173.   Bowen, Jeff, transcriber. **Cherokee Intermarried White, 1906. Volume VII.** Baltimore, Md., Genealogical Publishing, 2014. 343p. $36.00pa. ISBN 13: 978-0-8063-5686-0.

174.   Bowen, Jeff, transcriber. **Cherokee Intermarried White, 1906. Volume VIII.** Baltimore, Md., Genealogical Publishing, 2014. 342p. $36.00pa. ISBN 13: 978-0-8063-5689-1.

175.   Bowen, Jeff, transcriber. **Cherokee Intermarried White, 1906. Volume IX.** Baltimore, Md., Genealogical Publishing, 2014. 290p. $36.00pa. ISBN 13: 978-0-8063-5692-1.

176.   Bowen, Jeff, transcriber. **Cherokee Intermarried White, 1906. Volume X.** Baltimore, Md., Genealogical Publishing, 2014. 294p. $36.00pa. ISBN 13: 978-0-8063-5693-8.

This 10-volume series offers up an abundance of 1906 court transcripts regarding the application of white Americans to enroll as a citizen by intermarriage of the Cherokee Nation. The reasons for ensuring enrollment boiled down to land. In the late nineteenth century, an act of Congress established the Dawes Commission to redistribute long-held communal tribal lands into singular allotments assigned throughout the membership of the "Five Civilized Tribes," the Cherokee Nation one among them. This series represents the process by which white applicants could state their claim via intermarriage to a land allotment provided they had married into the Cherokee Nation prior to November of 1865. The year 1906 is indicative of the U.S. Supreme Court ruling which upheld Cherokee citizenship laws.

This series displays transcripts from 288 cases, or an average of 28 per volume. Volumes appear to be organized by order of transcription. Each volume is individually indexed by name (applicants, progeny, court representatives, etc.). Records reflect a number of court proceedings, including applicant and witness testimony, court acknowledgement of proceedings, letters of receipt between the court, applicants and Cherokee Nation attorneys, and more.

Readers can glean much from these records. They may enjoy this series' look at turn-of-the-century law and court processes in regards to matters of tribal land allocation. In addition, testimony often includes valuable geographical and familial information, such as birthplace, place of residence, numbers and names of progeny, and marriage details. It may include straightforward answers to basic questions concerning familial relations to more pointed interrogation regarding multiple marriages, scattered residences, etc. Such detail offers the researcher a genuine ear to the voices of the past.

Devotees of American history or anyone interested in genealogical information will find these volumes highly accessible, fascinating, and useful.—**Laura Herrell**

177.   Bowen, Jeff, transcriber **Choctaw by Blood Enrollment Cards 1898-1914, Volume I.** Baltimore, Md., Genealogical Publishing, 2015. 336p. illus. index. $35.00pa. ISBN 13: 978-0-8063-5731-7.

178.   Bowen, Jeff, transcriber **Choctaw by Blood Enrollment Cards 1898-1914, Volume II.** Baltimore, Md., Genealogical Publishing, 2015. 332p. $35.00pa. ISBN 13: 978-0-8063-5739-3.

The Dawes Commission, enacted under an act of Congress in the late nineteenth century, served the purpose of redistributing communal Indian tribal lands into individual allotments assigned throughout the membership of the "Five Civilized Tribes" (Cherokee, Choctaw, Creek, Chickasaw, and Seminole). Over 6,100 enrollment cards were registered for members of the Choctaw tribe alone (although it is to be noted that under the law members were only allowed to register under one tribe, even if they claimed relation to others). These volumes, the first two in a series, include Choctaw enrollment cards 1 through 300 and 301 through 600, transcribed by Jeff Bowen from microfilm in the National Archives.

Each card reports the age, sex, and degree of Choctaw blood applicable to each registrant, as well as the date of enrollment. Additional information may include parents' names, spousal information, and other miscellaneous notes. An alphabetical index helps readers find particular names with ease.

These volumes would be highly useful to students in many fields or anyone interested in pursuing genealogical histories.—**Laura Herrell**

179.   Bowen, Jeff, transcriber **Starr Roll, 1894 (Cherokee Payment Rolls), Volume One. Districts: Canadian, Cooweescoowee, and Delaware.** Baltimore, Md., Genealogical Publishing, 2014. 542p. $40.00pa. ISBN 13: 978-0-8063-5699-0.

181.   Bowen, Jeff, transcriber **Starr Roll, 1894 (Cherokee Payment Rolls), Volume Two. Districts: Flint, Going Snake, and Illinois.** Baltimore, Md., Genealogical Publishing, 2014. 332p. $40.00pa. ISBN 13: 978-0-8036-5701-0.

180.   Bowen, Jeff, transcriber **Starr Roll, 1894 (Cherokee Payment Rolls), Volume Three. Districts: Saline, Sequoyah, and Tahlequah; Including Orphan Roll.** Baltimore, Md., Genealogical Publishing, 2014. 348p. $40.00pa. ISBN 13: 978-0-8063-5703-4.

This three-volume set records the payment receipts issued as a result of an 1893 act of Congress which authorized the sale of lands west of the Cherokee Nation (known as the Cherokee Outlet). Volume one covers the Canadian, Cooweescoowee, and Delaware Districts of the nation; volume two covers the Flint, Going Snake, and Illinois Districts; and volume three covers the Saline, Sequoyah and Tahlequah Districts. Volume three also records receipts of payment for the disenfranchised, i.e., orphans and the mentally infirm.

As background, the Cherokee Outlet was created in 1835 as a "perpetual outlet west" for the Cherokee people. It occupied a 57-mile-wide section of what is present-day northwestern Oklahoma. A growing eastern population was instilled with the promise of land out west, and the federal government opened the land to homesteaders in Oklahoma's fourth and largest land run. A per-capita payment of $265.70 was made to eligible members of the Cherokee Nation in return for this outlet land.

The receipts reflect the names of the head of household and other household members, the name of the person receiving payment, and the name of a witness to the transaction. Amounts listed may reflect a total sum received for the household vs. individual payouts. Some rolls are marked by notes, which seem self-explanatory although it is not clear why they are transcribed in a different typeface than most of the information.

The payments were administered and documented by Ezekiel Eugene Starr, who was the elected Treasurer of the Cherokee Nation. His family tree is included in the book, as well as a fascinating black-and-white photograph of him in the midst of the fund allocation.—**ARBA Staff Reviewer**

182.   Boyle, Joseph Lee, comp. **"Apt to Get Drunk at all Opportunities." White Pennsylvania Runaways, 1750-1762.** Baltimore, Md., Genealogical Publishing, 2015. 485p. index. $45.00pa. ISBN 13: 978-0-8063-5782-9.

This volume continues the work of a previous volume (White Pennsylvania Runaways 1720-1749) in compiling records concerning the indentured white servants of the American colonial era. These servants may have represented convicts, political exiles, or those who could not afford passage to the New World. This book gathers advertisements placed in a variety of colonial newspapers requesting assistance in locating those servants who had escaped their masters. While originating in Pennsylvania, these ads may have been placed in newspapers throughout New England and the mid-Atlantic colonies.

The advertisements themselves, through simple in structure, are rich with telling details of servant and master. Clothing is clearly described. A servant named Robert Carlisle is described as wearing "a good brown homespun jacket, lined with striped flannel, ozenbrigs shirts, wide petticoat trowsers, buckskin breeches and an old castor hat." Many other interesting tidbits speak to the times, such as pock marked faces, swearing, horsewhips, raccoon hats, and more. Such other details may include native country, dialect spoken, aliases used, and physical characteristics (e.g., "very swarthy complexion, lisps and speaks broad Yorkshire").

While not providing a completely accurate record of runaways—many were perhaps of low worth to their owners and not reported—this collection is an excellent genealogical resource for many people, via the abundance of names, dates, and Pennsylvania locales. An alphabetical index lists names of both solicitor and runaway.—**ARBA Staff Reviewer**

183.   Boyle, Joseph Lee, comp. **"Lazy, loves strong Drink, and is a Glutton". White Pennsylvania Runaways, 1720-1749.** Baltimore, Md., Genealogical Publishing, 2015. 478p. $39.95pa. ISBN 13: 978-0-8063-5749-2.

This book gathers advertisements placed in a variety of colonial newspapers drawing attention to those indentured white servants who were noted to have run away from their masters. While originating in Pennsylvania, these ads were placed in newspapers throughout New England and the mid-Atlantic colonies.

The ads themselves, though simple in structure, are rich with telling details of servant and master. Clothing is clearly described—Richard Shelton, a 23-year-old runaway from Chester County, was apparently wearing "a felt hat, brown coat, light brown jacket, an grey Kersey Breeches with peices (sic) on the knees." Many other interesting tidbits speak to the times, such as pockmarked faces, beaver hats, wigs, pewter buttons, etc. Other details may include native country, dialect spoken, aliases used, notable characteristics (e.g., "swarthy, Thick and Gross"), and more.

While not providing an accurate number of runaways—many were perhaps of low worth to their owners—this collection is an excellent genealogical source for many people, via the abundance of names, dates, and Pennsylvanian locales.—**Laura Herrell**

184.   Carangelo, Lori. **The Ultimate Search Book: U.S. Adoption, Genealogy & Other Search Secrets.** Baltimore, Md., Genealogical Publishing, 2015. 85p. illus. $19.95pa. ISBN 13: 978-0-8063-5729-4.

A small volume that carries significant and specialized material, *The Ultimate Search Book* provides tips and resources designed to assist readers in their search for missing people. Adults who have been adopted as children, families seeking missing children, and many more may all find this material useful.

In chapters that are brief and to the point, the book does very well to take what may be an overwhelming endeavor and break it down into manageable bits. After listing 50 clear and actionable search tips (e.g., how to read a birth certificate, how to use Facebook, etc.), the book then targets its material to specific groups: families separated by adoption or divorce, missing or runaway children, missing adults, novice genealogists, and more. This 2015 edition conveys information on many of the most up-to-date organizations, websites, databases and other sources that readers can turn to in their searches.

A chapter providing tips on how to start one's own search business is an added bonus, as are the list of resources and Websites and samples of birth certificates and other documents useful to searches.—**ARBA Staff Reviewer**

185.   Dobson, David. **Scottish Highlanders on the Eve of the Great Migration 1725-1775: The People of Highland Perthshire. Volume 2.** Baltimore, Md., Genealogical Publishing, 2015. 116p. illus. maps. $17.50pa. ISBN 13: 978-0-8063-5725-6.

The many clans living in the rough and remote Scottish Highlands of the eighteenth century faced great change. As the long-held social and economic structures began to break down due to the advent of the Industrial Revolution as well as the political turmoil wrought from British overlords, families were either inspired or forced to migrate across the Atlantic Ocean. This book is the second volume on immigrants and their families from the Perthshire area in the Scottish Highlands; both volumes are part of the larger series, Scottish Highlanders on the Eve of the Great Migration, 1725-1775.

The volume presents an alphabetical listing of over 2000 individuals and their kin. The entries include first and last names, and any available relevant information regarding birth, death, marriage, children, profession, and more. Listings also include acronyms relating to the source of each individual's emigration information, as well as any known points of disembarkation. A sample entry reads: MCDONALD, PETER, born 1772, a farmer at Litigan, died 1864, husband of Jane Scrimgeour, born 1780, died 1853. [Fortingall MI], with the MI meaning monumental inscription. It was necessary for the author to find other information sources for Perthshire emigrants, as the parish registers in the area only include details on Presbyterians.

The book also includes a few charming illustrations and maps, and would appeal to anyone interested in pursuing genealogical histories.—**Laura Herrell**

186.   Henderson, Harold, Mary Leahy Wenzel, and Dorothy Germain Palmer, comps. **La Porte County Indiana Early Probate Records 1833-1850.** Baltimore, Md., Genealogical Publishing, 2015. 290p. index. $29.95pa. ISBN 13: 978-0-8063-5733-1.

This book presents one of the quintessential genealogical resources available to the researcher—probate records—for La Porte County, Indiana, during 1833-1850. Covering the earliest years of record for this county, the book organizes these transcripts into three sections. Probate Order Book A tracks daily activities of the particular court as recorded by its clerk. Probate Complete Record (Book) A provides full accounts of some of the cases upon their completion. The final section gathers the "loose papers," or random material submitted to the court such as receipts, bills, inventories, bonds, and letters, and records them according to estate. The volume has indexed all the names appearing in the records (aside from judges, clerks, and attorneys).

While providing no real context for the material, these records make an excellent foundational tool in pursuing a history of the area or information about the decedents and anyone conducting their legal affairs in La Porte County at that time.—**Laura Herrell**

187.   Jacobson, Judy. **History for Genealogists: Using Chronological Time Lines to Find and Understand Your Ancestors.** Baltimore, Md., Genealogical Publishing, 2016. 310p. $37.50pa. ISBN 13: 978-0-8063-5768-3.

The field of genealogy can be so much more than dusty archives and lists of names and places. Rather, the study of genealogy is like a black-and-white line drawing, and it is the accompanying history which fills in the colors between the lines. This book helps genealogists understand the need to incorporate historical research into their work to create a more contextualized and colorful picture of the people of the past. In particular, it points to the use of chronological timelines to help readers understand the times their ancestors were living in, in addition to pinpointing particular events or things which may have affected them.

Chapters mark information which may help users to organize and understand their searches. For example, they emphasize a large number of reasons for migration (e.g., wars, politics, religion, disease, etc.), how ancestors may have traveled, where certain groups of people went, and more. The author also touches on issues which readers may not have thought of in their genealogical searches, such as name changes of people and places, slaves, orphans, and shifting territorial boundaries. In addition, the book lists many ideas for focusing one's search such as historical books and diaries, or historical group affiliations, societies, and unions.

Dotted throughout all this information are specific timelines readers can use to hone and "color" their research. For example, there is a religion timeline which tracks global religious events which sparked migration and settlement. There is also a timeline marking the rise of labor unions which helps readers see the assembling of various groups (textile workers, railroad workers). And perhaps most importantly, there are state timelines covering settlement and major events such as natural disasters and military involvement.

In addition to the plentiful timelines, the author uses bullet points, quotes, lists, charts, an extensive timeline bibliography, and an index of people and places and wars and battles to make the information easy to navigate. This revised edition has been updated with an addendum reflecting editorial corrections to the 2009 edition, which appear to be the addition of an early-twentieth-century "hardship" timeline and a fashion and leisure timeline.—**ARBA Staff Reviewer**

188.   Martinez, Leroy. **From Across the Spanish Empire: Spanish Soldiers Who Helped Win the American Revolutionary War, 1776-1783 Arizona, California, Louisiana, New Mexico, and Texas Military Rosters.** Baltimore, Md., Genealogical Publishing, 2015. 269p. illus. index. $29.95pa. ISBN 13: 978-0-8063-5784-3.

This volume is the product of the author's close examination of myriad military records, which, taken together, help paint a clearer picture of Spanish involvement in the American Revolutionary War. While much has been said of French involvement, this book asserts Spain's contribution of finances and manpower to the American cause (as Spain, like other nations, held a stake in England's failure).

Opening chapters provide brief historical background noting the origins of Spanish assistance, a chronology of events beginning with Spain's colonization of Florida and working through Spain's covert role in the American Revolutionary War, a glossary of Spanish references, a list of Spanish regional governors, a list of Spanish presidios, and a copy of the 1783 Treaty of Paris (which in agreement with the King of Spain, ended the war). Following this historical background are transcriptions of military and presidio records mainly listing the names of garrisoned soldiers. Some records include financial information, denotation of officers and, in the case of the Louisiana Records chapter, service sheets denoting a soldier's age, country of origin, and associated campaigns. Some of the smaller details are truly interesting, such as the fact that Grenadier commander Francisco Bouligney, from Alicante, Spain, captured the enemy flag while under fire in Pensacola in 1781, or the fact that the Louisiana rolls convey a mixed Spanish and French garrison.

The author enhances his research with black-and-white photos of historical artifacts such as coins, maps, weapons, and other items of interest. His attention to detail makes the book valuable to historians as well as those seeking genealogical information. The book indexes all recorded names for ease of reference.—**ARBA Staff Reviewer**

189.   Morin, Gail, comp. **Manitoba Script.** 2d ed. Baltimore, Md., Genealogical Publishing, 2015. 330p. $39.95pa. ISBN 13: 978-0-8063-5727-0.

In the late nineteenth century, the Canadian government offered land allotments or cash scrip to Métis, or "half-breed" indigenous and white heads of family and children living within the province of Manitoba. The government made the same allotments to full white settlers and their descendants if they resided in Manitoba at time of scrip distribution (June of 1874) and also between the years 1813 and 1835. This book offers a record of scrip payment applications processed by the government beginning in 1875 and running through the early 1880s.

Receipts from nearly 7,000 applications hold the names, date of application, language spoken by applicant, nation of origin if applicable, birthdates, and other miscellaneous information. Readers can cull other interesting details from the records as well, such as professions, reasons for delayed applications, and more. Applications are presented alphabetically by last name and will include abbreviations which are keyed on the introductory page at the front of the book. The applications also include the Manitoba Scrip microfilm reel number from which the information was extracted.

These narrowly focused records provide little context but would nonetheless be valuable to those seeking genealogical information relative to the area of Manitoba.—**ARBA Staff Reviewer**

190.   **New York Historical Manuscripts: Dutch. Old First Dutch Reformed Church of Brooklyn, New York: First Book of Records, 1660-1752.** A.P.G. Jos van der Linde, editor and translator. Baltimore, Md., Genealogical Publishing, 2015. 297p. index. $32.50pa. ISBN 13: 978-0-8063-1049-7.

While it was the English who ultimately secured the strongest footing in what would eventually become the United States of America, it is common knowledge that the Dutch had a major presence as well, making the first land claim in 1609. It is a Dutch minister, Domine Henricus Selijns (1636-1701), installed in the church of what was then known as Breuckelen (Brooklyn), who began keeping a meticulous record of the noteworthy events occurring within and around his congregation. This book, a 2015 reprint of the 1983 edition, encapsulates all of his entries, and those of his successors, from 1660 through 1752 in full English translation.

Corresponding to the order established by Domine Selijns at first writing, this book is organized into seven major sections, covering the original protocol which established Domine Selijns as leader of his congregation, baptisms, financial transactions, an orphan registry, a cow registry, marriages, and a general registry of church members. Although there is little contextual insight to accompany the entries—the book mainly relays the formal and precise data collected by the Breuckelen church—the information can be fascinating. Records of the parish's expenditures, for example, allow readers to note the basic necessities of seventeenth-century "New Amsterdam:" tobacco, buttons, yarn, sugar, shoes, beer, and "planks and nails for a coffin," to name a few. Other interesting stories emerge as well. There is the young orphaned girl whose dead father was revealed to the minister as alive and living in Jamaica. And there is the minister's interpretation of a violent Native American raid as "the Lord's wrath burning severely against us."

The editor/translator has taken pains to provide the most accurate translation, including correct spelling of seventeenth-century Dutch names. The translation is smartly presented aside the original Dutch (transcribed) text. Including two appendixes, copious notes, and a thorough, cross-referenced index, this book is a treasure for those interested in history, Dutch-American genealogy, and more.—**Laura Herrell**

191.   **New York Historical Manuscripts: Minutes of the Mayors Court of New York, 1674-1675.** Kenneth Scott, ed. Baltimore, Md., Genealogical Publishing, 2015. 87p. index. $16.50pa. ISBN 13: 978-0-8063-1033-6.

This small but hugely insightful volume is a valuable measure of the provincial history of New York, at a time when the region was just over a century removed from American statehood. In unearthing and transcribing these records (specifically, summarized minutes of legal proceedings), editor Kenneth Scott has shone yet another light on this land's fascinating early years.

A mere decade away from its status as a Dutch colony, New York in the 1670's was now firmly in English hands. The Mayor's Court, also known as the Court of Common Pleas, served to conduct public business relative to both civil and criminal matters and generally consisted of the governor-appointed Mayor, Recorder, and Alderman. The court minutes gathered in this book reflect nearly 10 months of regional litigation and exemplify the common issues of the day, from disputes over payment for goods or services to estate inheritances and petty theft. While not far removed from issues courts might see in the modern world, it is notable how many cases evoke this particular time in history, when wounds were still fresh from the Dutch abdication of government under English force and when property disputes might actually pertain to people (i.e., slaves).

The transcriptions do well to honor seventeenth-century spelling and grammar, and also include biographical notes enlightening readers to individual and family names, occupations, and more. A treasure of biographical, legal, and social insight like this book is particularly vital as so many historical records of the age are lost or have been destroyed. It will appeal to any students of history, law, and genealogy.—**Laura Herrell**

192.   Ports, Michael A. **Georgia Free Persons of Color. Volume I: Elbert, Hancock, Jefferson, Liberty, and Warren Counties, 1818-1864.** Baltimore, Md., Genealogical Publishing, 2015. 266p. $26.95pa. ISBN 13: 978-0-8063-5762-1.

193.   Ports, Michael A. **Georgia Free Persons of Color. Volume II: Appling, Camden, Clarke, Emanuel, Jones, Pulaski, and Wilkes Counties, 1818-1865.** Baltimore, Md., Genealogical Publishing, 2015. 184p. $19.95pa. ISBN 13: 978-0-8063-5764-5.

194.   Ports, Michael A. **Georgia Free Persons Of Color. Volume III: Baldwin, Columbia, Lincoln, Lumpkin, Taliaferro, and Thomas Counties, 1799-1865.** Baltimore, Md., Genealogical Publishing, 2015. 186p. $19.95pa. ISBN 13: 978-0-8063-5777-5.

As a law passed in the Georgia legislature demanded, from 1818 on all free persons of color were required to register with the lower (inferior) court of the county within which they resided. Information such as their age upon registration, place of nativity, current county residence, and occupation was recorded. These volumes do well to transcribe these historical, handwritten records for interested readers and researchers.

Volume one collects over 2,000 registrations of all free persons of color within Elbert, Hancock, Jefferson, Liberty, and Warren counties in the state of Georgia, carried out within the years 1818-1864. Volume two covers over 1,500 registrants in Appling, Camden, Clarke, Emanuel, Jones, Pulaski and Wilkes counties from 1818 to 1865. Volume three consists of transcriptions of the free black registers for the Georgia counties of Baldwin, Columbia, Lincoln, Lumpkin, Taliaferro, and Thomas for 1799-1865.

Since the original records generally followed a clear, tabular format, most of the transcription is similarly clear and complete. However, where there is any confusion over the material, due to illegibility, wear, etc., the information is noted within brackets. Also, because registration may have been carried out differently from county to county, a brief introduction explains the structure and content for each one.

There is also a brief explanation of the Georgia laws behind the registration requirement, as well as the rarely enacted policy of manumission. Included in these volumes is a full listing of manumissions issued by the Georgia state legislature from 1798-1865.

The books offer little context for these records; however, they remain a fascinating record of the deep South during slavery, and an excellent starting point for one's research, genealogical or otherwise. The book also includes a surname index for ease of reference.—**Laura Herrell**

Heraldry

195.   **Coats of Arms. http://www.heraldry.ws/.** [Website] Free. Date reviewed: 2016.

This free-to-browse Website offers images of coats of arms for over 10,000 surnames, focusing on Ireland. The site is easy to search by an alphabetical index on the left side of the page. The site also offers a featured coat of arms. At the time of this review, the coats of arms were for the surnames (O) Healy, Hely, Haly, and Heeley, with a note on McHale. Besides images of the different coats of arms, there is a significant amount of genealogical research on the families. An additional link takes users to a history of heraldry that explains the parts, patterns, and colors used for coats of arms.

The information on the site is created and maintained by an individual. While there is a general bibliography of the sources he consulted to create the coats of arms, citations do not accompany the individual images. This for-profit Website has some nonintrusive advertising and offers high-quality graphics for sale. However, users can download images in GIF/JPG format; these images are smaller and at a lower resolution. Clearly this is not a place for advanced research, but it would be sufficient for a class project or for the casual user interested in coats of arms.—**ARBA Staff Reviewer**

196.   **European Heraldry. http://www.europeanheraldry.org/.** [Website] Free. Date reviewed: 2016.

European Heraldry is an online collection of hundreds of coats of arms from the early years of the seventeenth century to the present. The site is free to use, easy to navigate, and regularly updated (updates are clearly listed on the home page).

A series of tabs runs across the top of the home page: France, Iberian Peninsula, Italy, Germany, United Kingdom, Scandinavia, Eastern Europe, Central Europe, and Benelux. There is also a simple search link. These main categories are further subdivided, so a click on France pops up links to Royal, Maison du Roi, Great Officers of the Crown of France, Colonel Généraux, Duc-Paris, and Families. Spain and Portugal have separate links under the Iberian Peninsula. Italy has sublinks for Naples and Sicily, Modena, Masserano, Savoy, Parma, Tuscany, and Mantua. Coats of arms in Germany can be searched by clicking on Holy Roman Empire 1745, House of Hapsburg, House of Lorraine, Electoral Houses, Mediatised States, and Ecclesiastical States of the Empire. A search for coats of arms in the United Kingdom can be further refined by clicking on England, Scotland, Ireland, Great Britain, the United Kingdom of Great Britain and Ireland, and Families. Scandinavia includes links for Sweden and Denmark. Eastern Europe includes links for Russia, Poland and Courland; Central Europe has sublinks for Austria, Bohmia, and Hungary. A click on the last tab, Benelux, produces links to the Netherlands, Belgium, Luxembourg, and Hapsburg Netherlands.

The images of the coats of arms are clear, but not downloadable. Additionally, the site does not provide much in the way of context. Nevertheless, it is extensive and sufficient for someone looking to find a particular coat of arms or as a place to start further research.—**ARBA Staff Reviewer**

Personal Names

197.   Shane, Neala. **Inspired Baby Names from Around the World: 6,000 International Names and the Meaning behind Them.** Novato, Calif., New World Library, 2015. 712p. $21.95pa. ISBN 13: 978-1-60868-320-8.

This compilation of baby names from around the world provides information on name meanings, name origin, and pronunciation, but it also gives readers a spiritual affirmation for each name or variation of a name. For example, the description for the name Justina gives its meaning as just, judicious, and fair, its usage as English, and a quote from Proverbs. The spiritual affirmations are drawn from a large variety of such sources as the Bible (22 different versions), Buddhist sutras, and proverbs from Japan, Hawaii, and Africa. The book's introduction is followed by sections on naming customs from around the world, how to choose a name, and name changes; it concludes with lists of most popular names by decade from the 1910s, grandparent names (nana, memaw, papa, zaide, etc), the most popular names of kittens and puppies, an index of names by meaning, and a list of sources. This fun and informative book would be a welcome addition to public libraries.—**ARBA Staff Reviewer**

8 Geography and Travel Guides

Geography

General Works

Atlases

198.   **Atlases, Gazetteers, Guidebooks, and Other Books. http://digitalcollections. nypl.org/collections/atlases-gazetteers-guidebooks-and-other-books#/?tab=about.** [Website] Free. Date reviewed: 2016.

This collection from the New York Public Library contains atlases, gazetteers, guidebooks, and more from John H. Levine estate, received by the library in 1990. The easy-to-navigate site offers hundreds of clickable images from places worldwide from the seventeenth-nineteenth centuries. On the left-hand side of the page users will find a navigation tab which allows searches by region or type. Users will find a seventeenth-century map of Brazil, eighteenth-century maps of the coast of Norway, an eighteenth-century map of the solar system, an eighteenth-century map of Barbary (including Fez, Algiers, Tunis & Tripoli, and adjacent countries), and a nineteenth-century map of England and Wales (including principal roads), among so much more.

Each still image provides the user with the following information: type of resource, genre, date issued, division, publisher, cartographer, notes, identifiers, citations (in MLA, APA, Chicago, and Wikipedia), as well as additional descriptive information. A timeline shows when the creator of the image was born and died, when the image was issued, and when it was digitized. Users can also download the images in a variety of sizes and resolutions.—**ARBA Staff Reviewer**

199.   **Atlases of New York City. http://digitalcollections.nypl.org/collections/atlases-of-new-york-city#/?tab=navigation.** [Website] Free. Date reviewed: 2016.

The *Atlases of New York City* page in The New York Public Library Digital Collections is a compilation of real estate maps from William Perris who, during the mid-1800s, mapped the city building by building in order to help fire insurance companies appropriately price their customers' policies. The maps depict Manhattan and Brooklyn, and show streets, blocks, tax lots, and current use classifications. They also show streams and other natural features, earlier roads, lot lines, and more. Other items in this collection include aerial maps of New York City from 1924, topographical surveys of Central Park, and atlases that show surrounding regions such as Long Island and Queens.

Because these maps are extremely specific to one region, they would be most useful for professionals, including historians, architects, archeologists, and urban planners. According to the site, they can use the maps to research the history of particular buildings and neighborhoods, for social history and design, and also for ecological and engineering purposes. Though these maps are attractive, students who are not specifically studying New York City in the 1800s and early 1900s would not get much context.—**ARBA Staff Reviewer**

200.   **Atlases of the United States. http://digitalcollections.nypl.org/collections/ atlases-of-the-united-states#/?tab=navigation.** [Website] Free. Date reviewed: 2016.

This collection from the New York Public Library contains nearly four thousand historical atlases from many different states and regions in the United States. Most are atlases of New York, New Jersey, and other east-coast states. Upper-grade students in geography classes may benefit from viewing these maps to see how the regions have changed over time. Like many of the other online collections in the New York Public Library, this one would be most appropriate for professional historians, architects, engineers, and archeologists who would better understand these maps and be able to use them for professional study.

This page is recommended for students as an additional resource to geography studies, and highly recommended for professionals who could use these maps as tools to aid their work.—**ARBA Staff Reviewer**

201.   **World Atlas. http://www.worldatlas.com/aatlas/world.htm.** [Website] Free. Date reviewed: 2016.

World Atlas is a great resource for elementary and middle grade students. On the home page, a clickable world map allows users to search for information about all seven continents and the Middle East. Users simply hover the mouse over the region of their choosing and click the highlighted area, which leads to a separate page that provides a historical account of the countries and territories that comprise it. This site also includes a search bar at the top of the page for users to find famous natives, flags, fast facts, maps, symbols, and more. The layout is slightly cluttered with ads, but it is fairly easy to distinguish them from the page content. Filled with pictures and other clickables, this Website would be a perfect option for students new to the study of geography who need to gain experience with maps and general research.

Older students who are conducting research may not find this particular Website useful, as it provides a general overview of various regions, but does not contain a search tab for those looking for specialized information. On the home page, students can scroll down to find additional links to help them locate bodies of water, latitude and longitude, currency conversion, and populations. Still, this information will be more useful for younger students conducting beginner-level research.—**ARBA Staff Reviewer**

Dictionaries and Encyclopedias

202.   **Antarctica and the Arctic Circle: A Geographic Encyclopedia of the Earth's Polar Regions.** Andrew J. Hund, ed. Santa Barbara, Calif., ABC-CLIO, 2014. 2v. illus. maps. index. $189.00/set. ISBN 13: 978-1-61069-392-9; 978-1-61069-393-6 (e-book).

Antarctica and the Arctic Circle takes us on wide-ranging journey through our planet's most mysterious and challenging terrain: the Polar Regions. This two-volume encyclopedia holds well over 300 entries of various lengths which explore the history, science, animal life, politics, etc., of these particularly unique places. Entries are concise, but offer ample detail to conjure a clear portrait of topics ranging from the Adélie Penguin to the Yukon River. Sidebars and black-and-white illustrations enhance the content.

Taken together, the encyclopedia tells a story of seemingly inhospitable lands and waters which are nonetheless rich in life and intrigue. In cataloguing animal life, from fascinating penguin varieties to polar bears, orca whales, and more, we learn about the habits and adaptations which have enabled many species to survive in such hostile conditions. We also learn of the resilient peoples who have called the Arctic home, like the wide-ranging Inuits who have likely populated the northern regions for thousands of years, or the more recent Dolgans of northern Russia. We read of their unique techniques of survival, from storing food in permafrost, tending nomadic animal herds, and developing weatherproof clothing. With respect to current events, the encyclopedia points to such environmental concerns of the Polar Regions as overfishing and global warming in entries covering treaties, conventions, and protocols and the scientific research behind them.

Some of the richest narrative comes with the detailed descriptions of the audacious expeditions which opened, and continue to open, these frontiers to western civilizations. We learn of the triumphs and tragedies of sailors like Vitus Bering, who in the early eighteenth century charted the dark and cloudy passage between Asia and the northern American coasts with such accuracy that Captain Cook would later refer to his information with confidence. Then there is Ernest Shackleton, who in his quest to reach the geographical South Pole, made resounding discoveries and set navigational records while enduring a three-year expedition of unimaginable conditions in an attempt to cross the entire Antarctic continent.

Individual entries are followed by *see also* references and suggestions for further readings. Appendixes regarding glaciers around the world as well as select Arctic, Antarctic, and Northwest Passage Expeditions are followed by a select bibliography, a list of contributors, and an index.—**Laura Herrell**

203.   Quinn, Joyce A., and Susan L. Woodward. **Earth's Landscape: An Encyclopedia of the World's Geographic Features.** Santa Barbara, Calif., ABC-CLIO, 2015. 2v. illus. index. $205.00/set. ISBN 13: 978-1-61069-445-2; 978-1-61069-446-9 (e-book).

Earth's Landscape: An Encyclopedia of the World's Geographic Features is a two-volume encyclopedia that provides 460 articles that define the diversity of the world's continents and oceans. This geography encyclopedia discusses lesser-known, as well as, prominent geologic features of our planet Earth. The articles are alphabetically arranged. The format for each of the entries are an overview, the geographic coordinates, a description, its geologic history, the circulation and major currents (in entries for oceans and seas only), the biota, which is the animal and plant life of the region, protected areas, environmental issues, and a bibliography for further reading. There is a list of the entries by geologic location, and a list of abbreviations used in the text. Supplemental tables and black/white photographs are interspersed through the text. There is a "table of contents" for both volumes in volume one, but the index and glossary are only available in volume two. There are three appendixes at the end of volume two, entitled "The Highest, Lowest, Biggest, Deepest Places: 'Top Tens' and Other Global Comparisons," "Opposing Viewpoints:

Issues Related to Natural Features," and "Activities and Discussion Questions."

I believe this work would be a great purchase for the geology collections of high school and undergraduate libraries.—**Kay Stebbins Slattery**

Handbooks and Yearbooks

204.   **GeoBeats. http://www.geobeats.com/.** *[Website] Free. Date reviewed: 2016.*

GeoBeats is a fantastic free video Website, perfect for students of all ages and travelers. According to the About Us page, *GeoBeats* is essentially a video production company that produces and distributes professional content. Filmmakers for the company are located around the world. The site features close to 1,000 videos from approximately 80 countries, featuring specific tourist destinations, cultural sites, etiquette, restaurants, iconic foods, traditional performances, and much more. Videos range from around 1 minute 30 seconds to 3 minutes. The homepage of *GeoBeats* includes a section called "Hot Topics," which allows users to link directly to city-specific videos. There are also videos grouped into "Recently Popular," "Editors' Choices," and "New Releases." A feature video—on Balinese Dance—is also front and center on the homepage. Users can Browse All Videos, or can select a Category (the only available category is Travel), Sub-Category (a specific country and city), and Video (on a specific topic in a specific city).

GeoBeats would appeal to students of all ages, in particular middle and high school users. Travelers would also find the videos helpful. Due to their brevity, the videos are easy to watch and are presented in an accessible, engaging way, offering an alternative for students who benefit from more interactive ways of learning. Some—but not all—of the videos include a transcript, which users will find helpful. References and further readings are not listed, but some videos provide links to more information. For instance, in the Italy-Florence-Gelato video, the contact information for Perche No, a gelateria featured in the video, is provided. Some narrators are American hosts, while others are locals of the areas being presented. The site is easy to navigate, although it could benefit from a general search engine and alphabetical listing of all videos (when looking at the Browse All Videos link, they don't seem to be in any specific order). However, users can easily find a video by using the drop down category menus. Sample videos include: Austria-Salzburg-Top 5 Travel Attractions; Azerbaijan-Baku-Baku Government House; Cuba-Havana-San Cristobal Cathedral; Italy-Florence-Gelato; Japan-Tokyo-Cherry Blossom; South Africa-Kruger-Kruger National Park; and Yemen-Socotra-Socotra Island. Some videos are live action, with the host actually in the city, and some videos are collages of images with a voiceover narration. While some videos skew more toward tourists, cultural and historical content can be found for student users. School, public, and college libraries should keep www.geobeats.com in mind when patrons are looking for information on specific countries.—**ARBA Staff Reviewer**

205.   **Geographia. http://geographia.com/.** [Website] Free. Date reviewed: 2016.

Produced by interKnowledge Corp, *Geographia* is a free Website that provides users with a mix of cultural and travel information. The homepage of *Geographia* is set up with world regions, called "Destinations," in the left margin, along with a column called "Contents," which links users directly to the most recently added destinations, and another column called "Features," which links users to articles on specific topics in select cities and countries. The world regions under "Destinations" include Africa, Asia, Caribbean, Europe, and Latin America, and these link to approximately 50 country and territory profiles. In general, the profiles include information broken down into two main sections: Location, Geography, and Climate; and History and People. A majority of the profiles have a similar look and feel, but many are set up differently, and some—such as those under the Caribbean—include different information that is geared more toward travel, such as listings of activities, accommodations, and travel tips. The readability of the profiles is consistent and looks to be geared toward middle school and high school students, as well as general readers interested in travel. The "Features" include articles such as "Magnificent Mulu" (about a rainforest in Borneo), "Nelson in Nevis" (about war hero Horatio Nelson in the Caribbean), "Pirates of the Bahamas," "Land of Fire & Ice" (about Iceland) and "A Journey to Moscow."

Geographia provides users with good introductory material on the culture, history, and people of various countries and world territories. However, student users should proceed with caution, as articles are not cited, and there are no listings for further reading or research. Users might be confused by the inconsistency of the country profiles, since many look different from country to country. Some profiles, such as Botswana, are accompanied by beautiful photos of the land, people, and animals. Other profiles, such as Burma (Myanmar), have only one to two small photos. Additionally, some very key countries are missing, such as China, Japan, and most of Europe (though there are links to tourism sites for missing European countries).The site is easy to navigate, with clearly labeled links that take users around from the country profiles, back to the regions, and back to the homepage. Users should be warned that since the site is free, there are many ads on every page. At the bottom of the homepage is a Google Search engine that allows users to search the Web or the www.geographia.com site. A search for the term "cheetah" pulls up the appropriate pages on the Kenya, Namibia, South Africa, and Zimbabwe country profiles. A search for "great wall," however, pulls up an odd listing of pages, since China is not included on the site. Overall, *Geographia* can be used as a supplementary Website that might help give users a starting point in researching culture and travel.—**ARBA Staff Reviewer**

206.   **Maps of North America. http://digitalcollections.nypl.org/collections/maps-of-north-america#/?tab=about.** [Website] Free. Date reviewed: 2016.

This collection from the New York Public Library contains hundreds of private maps that were once part of Lawrence H. Slaughter's private collection. Some others belonged to the John H. Levine estate. Most of these maps focus on the Middle Atlantic region and are a nice accompaniment to the NYPL collection "Atlases, Gazetteers, Guidebooks, and Other Books."

The attractive and organized site offers a variety of clickable images from the seventeenth-nineteenth centuries. Users will find maps of New France, Mexico, the Caribbean, the young United States and its territories, and so much more. Each still image provides the user with the following information: type of resource, genre, date issued, division, publisher, cartographer, notes, identifiers, citations (in MLA, APA, Chicago, and Wikipedia), as well as additional descriptive information. A timeline shows when the creator of the image was born and died, when the image was issued, and when it was digitized. Users can also download the images in a variety of sizes and resolutions.—**ARBA Staff Reviewer**

207. **Old Maps Online. http://www.oldmapsonline.org/.** [Website] Free. Date reviewed: 2016.

Indexes over 400,000 maps that are available online from a variety of institutions including the New York Public Library, the USGS, the British Library, the Biblioteca Nacional de Colombia, and many others. Users of the site search by entering a place-name (Browse brings up maps for the user's location) to retrieve a window with a modern map of that location with a selection of older maps as search results to the right. Zooming the modern map or changing its focus will change the results accordingly. Users can also filter their results using a timeline or selecting specific attributes such as scale or keyword. Hovering over a map shows what portion of the modern map is included. The search results provide very basic information about each map (cartographer, date, scale, institution) and links to the map online at its home institution's Website. In some cases, users have the additional option of viewing the historic map as an overlay with a modern map of the same area.

This is a fascinating Website for finding, or just browsing, historic maps of regions throughout the world and will be useful for scholars, students, and the general public alike.—**ARBA Staff Reviewer**

Travel Guides

Handbooks and Yearbooks

208.   Baretz, Julie. **The Bible on Location: Off the Beaten Path in Ancient & Modern Israel.** Lincoln, Nebr., University of Nebraska Press, 2015. 344p. illus. maps. $19.95pa. ISBN 13: 978-0-8276-1222-8; 978-0-8276-1189-4 (e-book).

The Bible on Location, described by author Julie Baretz as an unconventional guidebook, moves tourists (or readers) in the footsteps of Biblical literary characters, drawing on stories from Joshua, Judges, 1 Samuel, 2 Samuel, 1 Kings, 2 Kings, Ezra, and Nehemiah. The stories from these books of the Bible all take place in Israel at sites that have been identified. The author has twin goals; to put readers/tourists in the landscape where the stories took place and to describe the narrative and chronology of Biblical action from the arrival of the Israelites to the Babylonian destruction of the temple and the return from exile.

The book begins with an introduction, a list of abbreviations, a timeline, and a map of Israel. Stories are prefaced by a historical introduction and followed by a short analytical commentary. Each chapter is also illustrated with maps and color photographs. An appendix "How to find the Biblical Sites," contains excellent colored maps, directions, hours, and other handy details. A bibliography completes the work.

While this guidebook's size and information make it an excellent choice for travel to Israel, it is also a fascinating look at the history of a people when read from cover to cover. Recommended for public libraries.—**ARBA Staff Reviewer**

209.   **Britannia. http://www.britannia.com/history/.** [Website] Free. Date reviewed: 2016.

Produced and maintained since 1996 by Britannia.com, LLC, a privately owned and operated American company, the *Britannia* Website is both a history and a travel resource. The site has no connection with *Britannia* Magazine, the British government, or any university or other organization. *Britannia* bills itself as a site run by Americans for Americans who are planning to travel to Britain, whether for formal study or for leisurely exploration. The site is currently funded by ad revenues, but plans are underway for creation of a "Reader Donation Program" to help finance future expansion. However, access to the site will remain free and open to all. Content is provided by contributors from around the world who are "experts in their field," and information is updated regularly, especially as regards the travel portion of the site. Many of the topic entries and biographies on the history side are drawn from older works—"Catherine of Aragon," for instance, comes from a 1909 publication by Emery Walker—and the larger overview pieces are signed by their contributors, though links allow readers to inquire about the author of any unsourced or unsigned piece.

Britannia covers the entire history of Britain, from the prehistoric period to the twenty-first century, with Arthurian Britain a particular emphasis. Besides King Arthur, major content sections include Monarchs of Britain, Church History, and Biographies of important Britons. Including about 200 individuals, from Caratacus to Margaret Thatcher, the biographies cover a good selection of political, military, and literary/cultural figures in essays averaging perhaps 200-300 words. Also provided are detailed narrative histories of England, Scotland, and Wales by Peter N. Williams, and of London by David Nash Ford. Timelines, narratives, topical essays of events and artifacts, bibliographies, and original sources—in many cases with relevant images—are offered for each broad period covered, i.e., Prehistoric Britain; Roman Britain; Anglo-Saxon Britain; Medieval Britain; Reformation and Restoration; Age of Empire; Modern Britain; and Myth, Legend, and Folklore. An Original Resources section offers further primary documents, timelines, and historical maps. The essays and biographies are generally well written and accurate and pitched to a level appropriate for high school and undergraduate students and interested general readers.

The travel side of the site allows users to search for hotels and lodging in London and across Britain and to find and book tours of all kinds. Links take the user to the site of the tour operator for full details and booking information. One can book tours of Arthurian sites; for Leeds Castle, Canterbury, and Dover in Kent, and for a tour of Downton Abbey sites in Oxfordshire. Would-be travelers can also obtain theatre tickets, attraction and event tickets, and airport transfers. The site also offers a series of virtual tours for such places as Hadrian's Wall, Northumberland's Battlefields, and Robin Hood's Yorkshire.

Britannia is highly recommended for anyone planning to travel to Britain, whether for study or for pleasure, who wishes to know more about the places he or she plans to see, and the best way to get to them.—**ARBA Staff Reviewer**

210.   Harris, Mike. **Olvera Street: Discover the Soul of Los Angeles.** Cheyenne, Wyo., La Frontera Publishing, 2015. 71p. illus. maps. $19.95pa. ISBN 13: 978-0-9857551-8-8.

This compact travel guide to Olvera Street and El Pueblo de Los Angeles by award-winning writer and editor Mike Harris takes users back in time to the city's founding by eleven families more than 230 years ago. The guide covers such sites as the Old Plaza

Firehouse, the oldest firehouse in Los Angeles; the Chinese American Museum; the painted booths (puestos), food, and shops along Olvera Street; the Avila Adobe House Museum; and the La Placita Church Cemetery. The book ends with a description of the actions taken by Christine Sterling to save and preserve the area in the early twentieth century. All of this is told with the aid of color and black-and-white photo reproductions and two maps.

This well-written title clearly expresses the author's love for a fascinating place that represents early California history and would be useful for those planning a trip to the area. Teachers of California history at the elementary level could also use the information in this book, especially if organizing a class trip to Olvera Street and El Pueblo. It is important to note, however, that the title is spiral bound and thus not likely to hold up to heavy use.—**ARBA Staff Reviewer**

211. Kaplan, Paul M. **Jewish New York: A History and Guide to Neighborhoods, Synagogues, and Eateries.** Gretna, La., Pelican Publishing, 2015. 240p. illus. maps. index. $24.95pa. ISBN 13: 978-1-4556-1968-; 978-1-4556-1969-6 (e-book).

Jewish New York: A History and Guide to Neighborhoods, Synagogues, and Eateries covers neighborhoods from south to north and is only about Manhattan; no other parts of the city are discussed. The introduction is a history of the Jews in New York. The book has end notes, a bibliography, and an index; the book is punctuated with black-and-white photographs. Each chapter has a one-page map marked with the places discussed. An average entry lists directions (by subway) on how to get to sites, along with the address, telephone number, Website, days open, and notes on why the place is historical, significant, and/or important. Some entries are longer than others. The Essex Street Market (p. 69), for example, has a little over a page of information while the former Café Royale (p. 125) listing is only two paragraphs. Many entries are subdivided into sections. The entry for the Triangle Shirtwaist Fire Site (p. 134) is over three pages and subdivided into three parts: the fire; the trial; and the legacy. Most eateries listed have short descriptions, although a few, like Sylvia's in Harlem (p. 206), are a bit longer. An informative book.—**Michael W. Handis**

212. Mitchell, Charles W. **Travels through American History in the Mid-Atlantic.** Baltimore, Md., Johns Hopkins University Press, 2014. 204p. maps. index. $24.95pa. ISBN 13: 978-1-4214-1514-7; 978-1-4214-1515-4 (e-book).

This book is both travel guide to historic sites and engaging historical narrative. It begins in the colonial period and moves through the Revolutionary era, Early Republic, antebellum period, and the Civil War. The 16 chapters cover, in order, Jamestown, Williamsburg, and Yorktown; St. Mary's City; Fort Frederick; Independence National Historical Park; Fort McHenry and the Star-Spangled Banner National Historic Trail; the Baltimore & Ohio Railroad Museum; the Chesapeake & Ohio Canal; Harper's Ferry; Civil War Richmond; Antietam; Civil War Washington; Gettysburg; Fredericksburg, Chancellorsville, the Wilderness, and Spotsylvania; Cedar Creek and the Belle Grove National Historic Park; and Petersburg and the road to Appomattox. Chapters include detailed maps, suggestions for side trips, and further readings; in some cases, the author separates his further readings section into recommendations for adults and children.

The chapters create an interesting tapestry by interweaving historical context, suggestions for how to best enjoy a visit, vivid physical descriptions, and quotes from letters and diaries of those who witnessed and/or made history in the places described. For example, readers will find in the chapter on Valley Forge George Washington's opinion of Congress's inability to provision his soldiers during the Revolutionary War, what is on offer in the visitor center, hiking information, driving directions, and much more. The detailed map is a fine visual aid. Suggestions for further readings include three titles for adults and one for children, Jason Cooper's *Valley Forge* (2003).

Information is easily locatable within *Travels through American History* due to the table of contents and index, but the artful renderings of each place and its history will compel a cover-to-cover reading. Highly recommended.—**ARBA Staff Reviewer**

213.   Triebel, Arthur. **Road-Tripping the South Atlantic League: A Guide to the Teams, Ballparks and Cities.** Jefferson, N.C., McFarland, 2015. 276p. illus. index. $29.95pa. ISBN 13: 978-0-7864-9811-6; 978-1-4766-2041-1 (e-book).

For die-hard baseball fans, there may be no greater pleasure than road-tripping the summer away following your favorite teams from ballpark to ballpark. This fun, thoughtfully presented guide provides ample information for fans of minor league baseball's South Atlantic League, an A-level league affiliated with Major League Baseball.

Melding a genuine love of the sport's history with key information one would find in a well-researched travel guide, this book fits the bill for those interested in observing up-and-coming talent, checking out historic ballparks and clubs, and rooting for the unsung heroes—the minor leaguers—of America's favorite pastime. The book covers 14 teams playing in a region bordered by New Jersey in the north, Georgia in the south, and Kentucky in the west. It engagingly takes readers back to the beginning of the league, tracing its development from a ragtag mixture of young D-level prospects and older ex-Major League players to the A-level, quality training ground it is today. It additionally offers a detailed profile of each current team in the South Atlantic League, from the Lakewood Blue Claws to the Charleston River Dogs, including stadium information, team and player highlights, and more. It is particularly interesting to trace the success of many current and recent Major League Baseball players to their time playing in the South Atlantic League.

With team and league information well in hand, the book then helps readers plan their epic baseball road trip by offering a number of travel routes, tips, cost-saving ideas, and other information. The author lists several enticing dining options as well as local non-baseball attractions near the home stadium for every team in the league.

Diligently gathered player and team statistics, black-and-white photos, and several sample itineraries point to the author's genuine desire to inspire true baseball fans to hit the road in enjoyment of America's favorite pastime.—**Laura Herrell**

214.   Van Ellis, Mark D. **America and WWI: A Traveler's Guide.** Northampton, Mass., Interlink Books, 2015. 432p. illus. maps. index. $22.00pa. ISBN 13: 978-1-56656-975-0.

With time passing rapidly and memories fading, this thoughtful, well-researched book traces the path of American involvement in the Great War of 1914-1918. While primarily serving as a guide to both domestic and foreign locales, the book nonetheless conveys a reverent narrative that leaves no street corner bypassed when following American "Doughboys" through their first great international crisis.

The book sets the scene at the outbreak of the war as Americans consider their European sympathies then begin to prepare with the establishment of domestic military training camps throughout the homefront. From here we travel to ports of embarkation, major battle theaters (including naval and air), museums, memorials, and final resting places of American fallen.

Found along this journey are the stories that elevate these places beyond mere points on a map. We read of the famous exploits of Pvt. Alvin C. York, an uneducated sharpshooter who almost singlehandedly captured over 100 enemy troops in the Argonne Forest, of the tragic loss of the troopship *Tuscania* off the remote Scottish Isle of Islay, and of the needless death of Henry Gunther, shot just one minute before the Armistice ended the war. Each of these tales leaves behind gravestones, memorials, and other markers serving to preserve their place in history. It is worth commenting that while coming in at 400 pages, the paperback is relatively compact and would be an easy travel companion.

The book's four appendixes provide information on overseas cemeteries, country museums and historic sites, historical societies and tourism authorities, and books and Websites on the American experience in the Great War. These are followed by an index of place-names.—**Laura Herrell**

9 History

American History

Chronology

215. America in the World, 1776 to the Present: A Supplement to the Dictionary of American History. Edward J. Blum, Cara Burnidge, Emily Conroy-Krutz, and David Kinkela, eds. New York, Charles Scribner's Sons/Gale Group, 2016. 2v. illus. index. $436.00/set. ISBN 13: 978-0-684-32502-6; 978-0-684-32505-7 (e-book).

The editor explains that this two-volume supplement is a reimagining of the 10-volume *Dictionary of American History,* (see ARBA 2003, entry 414). The former multivolume focused on the United States' national existence. The new source takes a transnational perspective concentrating on America's relationship with the globe. The more than 540 entries feature people, events, ideas, organizations, and geographical spaces that pursue this theme. As an example of the new approach, the editor cited the entry on Martin Luther King, Jr., that concentrates on how his early and later life shaped his global thinking and his impact on the world rather than merely the United States.

As with most encyclopedias, the entries include cross-references, a bibliography for each entry, and an index. A moderate number of black-and-white pictures are scattered through the volumes.

The entries are well done, although the editor's emphasis that they are written by younger, more globally oriented junior scholars is a weak reed. Most such encyclopedias call on junior individuals willing to undertake these assignments. Trying to draw a distinction between scholars with name recognition and graduate students and others new to the field is not only silly but borders on insulting.

The real question is why a library would invest in such an expensive printed source with constantly updated information from any perspective available in electronic forms. Contemporary technology has made encyclopedias such as this one rather obsolete, unless they are particularly unique. Despite the editor's contentions, this one does not meet the test of uniqueness, and thus isn't particularly necessary.—**Joe P. Dunn**

216. Mickolus, Edward. **The Counterintelligence Chronology: Spying by and Against the United States from the 1700s through 2014.** Jefferson, N.C., McFarland, 2015. 240p. index. $75.00pa. ISBN 13: 978-1-4766-6251-0; 978-1-4766-2240-8 (e-book).

This is an exhaustively detailed and thoroughly researched resource on spying for and against the United States from the Revolutionary period to 2015. In addition to well-known cases of espionage, this book chronicles lesser-known instances of spying. *The Counterintelligence Chronology* includes several charts that detail the motivations of spies and would-be spies, the American targets of foreign intelligence services, and more. In addition, two appendixes provide the names of American spies and the countries for which they operated and the names of alleged foreign espionage agents and the countries for which they spied. Valuably, the book concludes with a 141-item annotated bibliography by Howard Peake, curator of the Historical Intelligence Collection of the Central Intelligence Agency, and an accurate index. A recommended title for anyone wanting to find information on espionage conducted by or against the United States.—**Melinda F. Matthews**

Dictionaries and Encyclopedias

217.   **Abolition and Antislavery: A Historical Encyclopedia of the American Mosaic.**
Peter Hinks and John McKivigan, eds. Santa Barbara, Calif., Greenwood Press/ABC-CLIO, 2015. 446p. illus. index. $100.00. ISBN 13: 978-1-61069-827-6; 978-1-61069-828-3 (e-book).

This is an encyclopedia, in dictionary order, of the (mostly) pre-Civil War abolition and antislavery movement. One hundred thirty-six articles, from Abolitionist Women to Women's Anti-Slavery Societies, some more than 10 pages long, describe various aspects and personalities involved in the fight to end slavery in the United States. Each article includes a descriptive bibliography of one to several items. There is a 40-page section of excerpts from primary documents such as *Uncle Tom's Cabin* and the Emancipation Proclamation. Supplementary materials include an introduction, a chronology of events, a bibliography of more than 150 items, and an index. The editors are Peter Hinks, who is the author of *To Awaken My Afflicted Brethren: David Walker and the Problem of Antebellum Slave Resistance,* and John McKivigan, Professor of History at Indiana-Purdue University Indianapolis, the editor of the Frederick Douglass Papers and the author of books on abolitionism.

This encyclopedia covers its subject quite thoroughly. The text is accessible to readers at a high-school level and above. It would be a useful supplement to works such as the seventh edition of the *Encyclopedia of American History* (Harper, 1996), especially in academic libraries supporting courses in American history. However, its relatively steep price makes it a luxury for smaller libraries. The black-and-white illustrations add little reference value.—**Jonathan F. Husband**

218.   **American Civil War: A State-by-State Encyclopedia.** Spencer C. Tucker, ed. Santa Barbara, Calif., ABC-CLIO, 2015. 3v. illus. maps. index. $189.00/set. ISBN 13: 978-1-59884-528-0; 978-1-59884-529-7 (e-book).

ABC-CLIO is the acknowledged leader in military encyclopedias and Spencer C. Tucker has treated virtually every war in the American experience. He has already produced several encyclopedias on the Civil War, including the comprehensive six-volume product in 2013 also named *American Civil War.* In this new publication, he takes a different approach by addressing the war in separate chapters on each state and territory extant at the time. The format is a brief introduction to the state or territory; entries on the prominent cities; treatment of forts, navy yards, foundries or other installations with any connection to the war; the most prominent individuals related to the conflict; and wartime battles. Obviously, some states such as Virginia (where half of all Civil War battles occurred), North and South Carolina, and Tennessee are prominent. It is a stretch though to include the Utah and Dakota Territories, Maine, Wisconsin, and several other Northern states. For example, the two territories only connections to the war were that troops were drawn from outposts on the frontier to the South and Civil War veterans returned to the plains to fight in wars against the Indian populations.

The volume contains good maps, a few pictures, a very selective overall bibliography, and indexes. The extremely brief overview accounts of the war in the individual states, particularly in those where much of the war was fought, are unfulfilling. And the overlooking of the myriad of skirmishes that characterized the war in so many areas, Missouri as just one example, is a flaw. The Civil War is classic local history, a story that could be addressed virtually county by county throughout the South. Greater concentration on local history in the Southern states, where the war was fought, rather than the wider scope beyond the South arguably would have been a better organizational structure. Moreover, a fuller bibliography of citations of the vast number of historians, both professional and amateur local students, who have produced the exhaustive literature on the Civil War at the local level in every place in the South would have enhanced the value of the resource. Admittedly, one could fill volumes with these references.

The concept of the project had promise, but the product is a bit disappointing. Most libraries probably can pass on this publication in favor of earlier reference sources.—**Joe P. Dunn**

219.   Grossman, Mark. **Encyclopedia of the Continental Congress.** Amenia, N.Y., Grey House Publishing, 2015. 2v. illus. index. $245.00/set. ISBN 13: 978-1-61925-175-5; 978-1-61925-176-2 (e-book).

The Encyclopedia of the Continental Congress offers an in-depth look into the first Continental Congress in 1774, the second Continental Congress, 1775-1789, and the first Federal Congress in 1789. It is written by Mark Grossman, author of *Encyclopedia of the United States Cabinet: 1789-2010* and *Speakers of the House of Representatives, 1789-2009,* both published by Grey House Publishing. This 1,746-page, two-volume set does not merely focus on the men who answered the call to serve as delegates to the Continental Congress but also those who did not serve during the days leading up to and during the American Revolution and creation of the U.S. Constitution. Mark Grossman also sheds light on and confronts issues dealing with the Native Americans as a people, the role of women in society, and our nation's ability to handle diplomacy to name a few. A small but interesting piece of information that exposes the depth and quality of research that went into creating this multivolume set is found in the preface under the heading The Story Behind the Story. While some may regard this small segment as trivial information, it opens the reader to the creational framework of the resource that lays before them, which was in fact 25 years in the making. Grossman shares how his conceived concept for the *Encyclopedia of the Continental Congress* was born out of the coverage the *Miami Herald* ran in 1987, tied to the 200th anniversary of the signing of the U.S. Constitution; the series was called "We the People": The Constitutional Convention of 1787. He noted that the newspaper only focused on daily happenings at the Constitutional Convention. After collecting and reading all the articles put out by the *Miami Herald,* he concluded there was no one single volume that discussed what other events and persons were influential during this period of America's history; moreover, there was no real definitive work that covered the Continental Congress as well. Through the course of the preface, the reader is provided with a very short and concise depiction of the events that transpired in 1774. This gives the reader enough insight to understand why the Continental Congresses were called into being. Grossman also explains his in-depth research methods and acknowledges the various institutes where he obtained the material used to see this work come to fruition.

The uniqueness of *The Encyclopedia of the Continental Congress* is evident on the very first page of the preface (xvii) where he introduces the reader to quotes from primary resources. "William Eddis, the Surveyor for Annapolis, who had a front row seat for the conflict that was about to reach a tipping point, wrote to a friend in England on 28 May 1774: 'All America is in a flame! I hear strange language every day. The colonists are ripe for any measure that will tend to the preservation of what they call natural liberty.'" Grossman's use of direct quotes from firsthand accounts sets the narrative hook if that is even possible for a reference book. The use of and placement of the quote on the very first page of the preface is shouting to the reader/researcher that they are in for a grandiose experience, more so than they may have come to expect based on their use of an ordinary encyclopedia regardless of the subject matter. We live in a digital age where Wikipedia and one's need for instant gratification in finding a quick but often bland tertiary encyclopedia entry on a particular topic has seemed to lessen the value of the encyclopedia as a true reference tool. Mark Grossman's *Encyclopedia of the Continental Congress* will help shatter the user's misconception of just what an encyclopedia can bring to the research process.

This nicely hardbound set presents 509 detailed entries covering each delegate who served on either the first Continental Congress in 1774, the second Continental Congress from 1775 to 1789, or the first Federal Congress in 1789. Grossman focuses on both the more significant figures [historical household names] and those who may be lesser known or who were overshadowed by their more prominent counterparts. All of them regardless how large or small played a vital role in the Continental Congresses, and Grossman ensures the reader sees their importance. His focus shines light on all the delegates who attended these meetings, stressing the significant figures of the political social scene, as well as women and other figures involved at the time. In addition to these detailed biographies, this reference work includes comprehensive accounts of places, battles, laws, treaties, and court cases that were significant to the workings of the Continental Congresses.

The Encyclopedia of the Continental Congress is presented in a very straight-forward manner, regardless of whether the user is a novice first-year college student or ardent researcher. It offers a table of contents which lists the entries from Andrew Adams to John Joachim Zubly. Grossman provides the reader not only a descriptive entry pertaining to the delegate's time as a member of the Continental Congress, but a comprehensive history of the men prior to and after their time served. The reader will not only be impressed by the extensive list of delegates presented to him, but will be astonished by the incredible collection of topics, including the Bank of the United States, Relations with France, Lexington and Concord, Nassau Hall, and the Olive Branch Petition. Nearly all entries include either an image or a state seal, italicized excerpts from relevant primary documents, and footnotes.

Since Grossman clearly understands that events in history just do not happen randomly or haphazardly in some spatial plane, he added a historical timeline right after the table of contents. This timeline will help the researcher who may not be as in tune with America's history during the years leading up to and during the American Revolution. He begins the timeline in 1764 with the passage of the Sugar Act and the Currency Act, both of which led to protests in the colonies. The timeline ends in 1789, when the U.S. Senate and House of Representatives met in New York City, marking the official end to the second Continental Congress. The timeline will provide the backstory to the formation of the Continental Congress and first Federal Congress.

There is some validity in the old cliché "When History Comes Alive!" Mark Grossman's use of 31 primary documents transports the reader into this period of American history. The use of the selected primary resources helps provide additional insight into this turbulent period of American history, promoting an understanding of the general and the detailed workings of the Continental Congresses. Here readers will find familiar documents, such as Patrick Henry's "Give Me Liberty or Give Me Death" speech, as well as more obscure texts like a letter from John Adams describing his journey to the first Continental Congress. One of the more interesting documents comes from *The Massachusetts Spy* newspaper, which provides one of the initial reports on the first salvos between colonial militiamen and British soldiers at Lexington and Concord, 1775. All documents include a brief but illuminating introductory note. Again, the use of primary sources will truly entice the reader to delve deeper into the history that is the Continental Congress and the delegates who shaped this key moment in America's history.

The true essence of any good secondary or tertiary resource will come in the way it is indexed and the quality of its appendixes. *The Encyclopedia of the Continental Congress* offers the researcher both. It offers a detailed subject index, which will help the readers to quickly find just what they are looking for, including individuals, places, battles, acts, and other items of interest related to the Continental Congresses. Grossman provides six appendixes which offer some very interesting details in a straightforward format: Delegates to the Continental Congress by State; Signers of the Declaration of Independence by Occupation; Signers of the Articles of Confederation by State; Presidents of the Continental Congress; Places and Times of Sessions of the Continental Congress; and Statistics on the Thirteen Colonies. Regardless of whether the researcher wants to leisurely browse the resource through the table of contents or knows exactly what he needs and heads straight for the indexes and appendixes, Grossman's style and format will ensure they find what they are looking for.

The Encyclopedia of the Continental Congress is not only a valuable resource on the subject matter but offers the researcher a comprehensive bibliography by type, including books and articles; unpublished dissertations, masters theses, and other works; newspapers and magazines used; Continental Congress and other federal colonial documents; U.S. government documents post-1789; colonial and state government documents; other U.S. government documents; British government documents; and manuscript collections. Such a bibliography will provide a reader with the means to dive headfirst into further research on the men, events, and actions of the Continental Congress as well as the American Revolution. It is a clear must have for any academic library's reference collection, let alone a historian who specializes in this era of American history.—**Lawrence Joseph Mello**

220.   **Ideas and Movements That Shaped America: From the Bill of Rights to "Occupy Wall Street".** Michael S. Green and Scott L. Stabler, eds. Santa Barbara, Calif., ABC-CLIO, 2015. 3v. illus. index. $294.00/set. ISBN 13: 978-1-60169-251-9; 978-1-61069-252-6 (e-book).

This exemplary three-volume set provides accompanying text from primary source documents, sometimes as many as four, for each entry. The historical documents, frequently edited for brevity and clarity, feature introductions providing context and historical information about the authors. In some cases, the text is complete, as in the case of several speeches. Material for the encyclopedia includes a wide variety of perspectives in order to fully showcase the intellectual foundation for the movements being discussed, from George Lincoln Rockwell's arguments in favor of white supremacy to Valerie Solanos' manifesto for the Society for Cutting Up Men.

Although each of the three volumes includes a full table of contents, only the third volume provides an index and bibliography. Readers will sometimes face a challenge in finding information since the entries are movements and concepts rather than more easily recognized names of persons and events. High school libraries should have this set.—**Delilah R. Caldwell**

221.   **Imperialism and Expansionism in American History: A Social, Political, and Cultural Encyclopedia and Document Collection.** Chris J. Magoc and David Bernstein, eds. Santa Barbara, Calif., ABC-CLIO, 2015. 4v. index. $415.00/set. ISBN 13: 978-1-61069-429-2; 978-1-61069-430-8 (e-book).

This encyclopedia developed as an opportunity to examine how the United States moved from a colony to a global military power. Imperialism and expansionism are defined broadly by this four-volume work. The editors argue that one of the key strengths of this book is how it includes social and cultural elements, such as music, film, and literature. The overall structure of this work divides each volume chronologically. Each volume is further subdivided into three different chronological sections. While this grouping does make narrative sense to show how topics relate, it does make it harder to use as a reference source. Fortunately, the table of contents and the index help clear up confusion. The addition of numerous primary sources is another benefit of this encyclopedia.

Overall, this is a fine addition to the body of reference sources about American history. Each section has a clear historic overview and the signed articles all have bibliographies to learn more about the topic. At times, the entries could have been more clearly tied to the organizing theme of this encyclopedia and a little more information about the authors could have been provided. Those minor concerns aside, this is a valuable work and is recommended for most collections.—**Allen Reichert**

222.   **Irish Americans: The History and Culture of a People.** William E. Watson and Eugene J. Halus, Jr., eds. Santa Barbara, Calif., ABC-CLIO, 2015. 511p. index. $100.00. ISBN 13: 978-1-61069-466-7; 978-1-61069-467-4 (e-book).

This book offers an encyclopedic look at the indelible stamp of Irish immigrants upon American history and culture. Two great waves of emigration brought Irish numbers to American shores. Colonial times saw the arrival of Scots-Irish Presbyterians seeking relief from English persecution. Several generations later, and perhaps more famously, the burgeoning Industrial Revolution welcomed droves of Irish-Catholics fleeing starvation and willing to work cheaply. The book thoroughly details how these groups infiltrated and shaped American culture.

An excellent introduction provides the context—the reasons and initial impacts of Irish emigration to America. Then, in nearly 200 sectionally alphabetized entries, ranging in length from several paragraphs to several pages, we learn of people like Father Charles Coughlin, the firebrand priest who used the relatively new medium of radio to espouse his somewhat polarizing ideas for social justice, or events like the Dead Rabbits riots of 1857 which epitomized the violent conflicts between nativists (usually Protestant and anti-immigrant) and the newly arriving Irish. These entries are grouped into sections which corral the people, events, institutions, and more under the greater themes of politics and economics, culture and religion, and arts and sciences. Each section also includes a succinct historical overview providing key background regarding the subsequent subject matter. Entries conclude with a list of sources and *see also* references (where applicable). The generous use of black-and-white photographs and illustrations enhance the text.

A well-curated selection of primary documents concludes the encyclopedia and sheds further light on some of the most compelling subject matter. Some selections here include an anonymous account on an 1834 nativist attack on a Catholic convent, a newspaper article from the great Chicago Fire of 1871 (purportedly begun by Mrs. O'Leary's cow), and U.S. President John F. Kennedy's 1963 speech before the Irish Parliament. A bibliography and an index round out the work.—**Laura Herrell**

223.   **Jim Crow: A Historical Encyclopedia of the American Mosaic.** Nikki L. M. Brown and Barry M. Stentiford, eds. Santa Barbara, Calif., Greenwood Press/ABC-CLIO, 2014. 471p. illus. index. $100.00. ISBN 13: 978-1-61069-663-0; 978-1-61069-664-7 (e-book).

Jim Crow (created in the mid-1880s and running through the mid-1960s), the laws and customs supporting legally sanctioned discrimination in the United States, is covered in-depth. The title not only provides a few primary documents, but also covers the history, events, and institutions involved, and describes the effects on politics, people, and culture. An alphabetical list of entries, a guide to related topics, a chronology, black-and-white photographs, and a select bibliography comprise the title. High school students and anyone with an interest in learning more about this racial segregation will find this title of interest.—**Denise A. Garofalo**

224.   **Reconstruction: A Historical Encyclopedia of the American Mosaic.** Richard Zuczek, ed. Santa Barbara, Calif., Greenwood Press/ABC-CLIO, 2015. 435p. illus. index. $100.00. ISBN 13: 978-1-61069-917-4; 978-1-61069-918-1 (e-book).

This is a handy guide to the American Reconstruction period that provides a series of brief essays written "for the high school student and lower-level college student." The essays are written by (for the most part, some are unsigned), "the most prominent historians in the field." These essays are well written and provide a concise treatment of topics such as: the Kirk-Holden War in Tennessee/North Carolina, Nathan Bedford Forrest, Edwin Stanton, and Joseph Hayne Rainey. In addition to the essay topics there are 11 primary source documents reprinted in the book. These documents include: the Emancipation Proclamation, the 14th and 15th Amendments to the Constitution, the Civil Rights Act of 1866, Articles of President Johnson's impeachment, Mississippi Black Codes, and the so-called Ku Klux Klan Act (Enforcement Act of 1871). The book has an index, a list of essay entries, a classed guide to inter-related topics, a chronology of Reconstruction, a list of Reconstruction governors, and a list of dates of readmission for former Confederate States, as well as a small bibliography. A quick check between the authors listed in the bibliography, and the "prominent historians in the field" who wrote the essays in this work produced no matches alas. This leads the reviewer to wonder exactly how "prominent" these folks are. A number of topics/persons mentioned in the chronology fail to appear in the book: Posse Comitatus Act, Wormley House "deal," Hamburg Massacre, Homestead Act, John McEnery, and Zebulon Vance. The brief "acknowledgements" section in the front of the book contains this odd statement in italics: "The views expressed herein...are not to be construed as official or reflecting views of the Commandant or of the U.S. Coast Guard." While the editor of the book teaches at the U.S. Coast Guard Academy and has previously written a two-volume Greenwood *Encyclopedia of the Reconstruction Era* (2006), one could hardly make the leap that the book is a statement of Coast Guard policy. Overall this works does a good job of serving the audience for which is it was written.—**Ralph Lee Scott**

225.   **The World of the American Revolution: A Daily Life Encyclopedia.** Merril D. Smith, ed. Santa Barbara, Calif., Greenwood Press/ABC-CLIO, 2015. 2v. illus. index. $198.00/set. ISBN 13: 978-1-4408-3027-3; 978-1-4408-3028-0 (e-book).

This Greenwood Press series, The Daily Life Encyclopedias, addresses a very interesting concept—"What was life really like for ordinary people in different cultures throughout history? What did they eat, wear, believe, think?" "By examining the social, cultural, and material history topics—family life, political life, religious life, recreation and social customs...we can examine their emotional life, interactions, intimate relationships, opinions and beliefs, and the interactions between them and the greater world." Editor Merril Smith presents us the two-volume *The World of the American Revolution* as part of this series. The two volumes, Arts to Housing and Community and Politics and Warfare to Science and Technology, respectively, contain primary documents, a selected bibliography, and illustrations.

There are 265 individually authored, richly detailed entries that cover an eclectic array of subjects grouped into 10 topical areas. Examples of entries indicate the breadth of coverage: For the Arts: Books, Music, Intellectual Life, Oratory, and Political Pamphlets; Economics and Work: Artisans, Debt, Fur Trade, and Printers; Family and Gender: Breastfeeding, Celibacy, Fatherhood, Friendship, Old Age, and Orphans; Fashion and Appearance: Cross-Dressing, Hats, Jewelry, and Textiles; Food and Drink: Corn, Rum, Tea, and Wine; Housing and Community: Churches, Crime, Forts, Prisons, and Slave Housing; Politics and Warfare: The Boston Massacre, Citizenship, Pacifists, and Soldiers; Recreation and Social Customs: Duels, Etiquette, Libraries, Reading, and Theater; Religion: Bible, Catholicism, Fast Days, Quakers, and Sermons; and Science and Technology: Fires, Lightening, Mental Illness, and Ships.

Recommended for high school and undergraduate libraries.—**Scott R. DiMarco**

226.   **The World of the Civil War: A Daily Life Encyclopedia.** Frank, Lisa Tendrich, ed. Santa Barbara, Calif., Greenwood Press/ABC-CLIO, 2015. 2v. illus. index. $198.00/ set. ISBN 13: 978-1-4408-2978-9; 978-1-4408-2979-6 (e-book).

This handy Civil War encyclopedia is divided into 10 topical subject sections: arts; clothing, fashion, and appearance; economy and work; family life and gender roles; food and drink; housing and community; politics and warfare; recreation and social customs; religion and beliefs; science and technology. Each section is then divided into essays on the topic "written by more than 100 scholars and period specialists." The essays are aimed primarily at high school and lower-division college students as well as the general reader. For example, the science and technology section includes essay topics such as: cooking techniques; disease; education; factories; firearms; hospitals; inventions; medicine; Minié Ball; nursing; railroads; sanitation; steamboats; telegraph; time; transportation; transportation, medical; weapons, wounds. Some essays include appropriate topical sidebars. As a case in point, the essay on medicine includes a sidebar on "Using Southern Botanical Remedies." The nursing section includes photograph of a Civil War nurse in a field hospital in Nashville, a three-page essay on the topic, a small bibliography, and a list of related essays in the set. Some omissions are odd; for instance, despite a two-page essay on the Minié Ball, there is no photograph or drawing of the ball. The essay section concludes with 18 Civil War primary documents. These documents, which are rather general and subjective in nature (example: "Confederate Woman held in Old Capitol Prison"), are rather haphazardly tossed at the end of the book in a poorly formatted way that makes it hard for the general reader to make sense of their use or purpose. There is a selected bibliography at the end of the book along with a list of contributors. This reviewer did not recognize any of the authors as well-known Civil War historians, and no special qualifications are listed by the persons' names—only affiliations are provided (e.g., Columbus State Community College). The index provides some access to the essays but is sloppily constructed. For example, there are separate index references to the Fugitive Slave Law and the Fugitive Slave Act. In a well-constructed index, these two entries would have been combined for the benefit of the reader. Overall the two-volume set will provide the general reader with a glimpse into a turbulent time in American history.—**Ralph Lee Scott**

Handbooks and Yearbooks

227. **American Eras: Primary Sources: Early American Civilizations and Exploration to 1600.** Farmington Hills, Mich, Gale/Cengage Learning, 2015. 299p. illus. index. $177.00. ISBN 13: 978-1-4144-9823-2; 978-1-4144-9840-9 (e-book).

The American Eras Primary Sources series packs a generous amount of information into a compact, well-organized volume. This particular volume shares a plethora of primary sources representing the era of early American civilizations and explorations to 1600.

Introductory information includes a thorough essay breaking down the presentation of the primary sources and another essay discussing both benefits of and potential limitations to using primary sources within one's research. This section also provides a helpful general chronology of major world events within the era covered in this volume. Over 75 primary sources cover a wide selection of artifacts, memoirs, charters, artwork, maps, letters, and more. They are arranged into eight thematic chapters and presented chronologically. Chapters include: "The Arts, Fashion and Leisure"; "Business and the Economy"; "Communications and Education"; "Government and Politics"; "Law and Justice""; Lifestyles and Social Trends"; "Religion;" and "Science, Medicine and Technology." Each chapter opens with an overview of its theme and then a chronology including events directly related to the theme and primary sources as well as more general events of note.

In presenting the primary source, the book first lists basic information such as who created it, when it was made, etc. An essay, accompanied by a photograph of the artifact, document, excerpt, etc., provides good contextual information and explains the significance of the primary source. Other photographs may accompany the essay as well. The entry concludes with a listing of resources for further study specific to the entry. Some of the primary sources featured in this book include the 1492 charter granting Christopher Columbus funding for his trip in search of a sea route to Asia, an illustration, *Florida Indians planting Maize,* and Martin Waldseemüller's 1513 *World Map.*

The volume concludes with additional generalized resources, a primary source type index (with headings such as Architecture, Charters, etc.), and a general index.

Recommended.—**ARBA Staff Reviewer**

228.   **American Eras: Primary Sources: The Colonial Era, 1600-1754.** Farmington Hills, Mich, Gale/Cengage Learning, 2015. 438p. illus. index. $177.00. ISBN 13: 978-1-4144-9823-2; 978-1-4144-9839-3 (e-book).

The Colonial Era (1600-1754), is volume seven in the series American Eras: Primary Sources. Other titles in the series include the following: *Early American Civilization, Exploration to 1600; The Colonial Era (1600-1754); Revolutionary Era (1754-1783); Development of a Nation (1783-1815); Reform Era & Eastern U.S. Development (1815-1850); Westward Expansion (1800-1860); Civil War and Reconstruction (1860-1878);* and *Development of the Industrial United States (1878-1899). The Colonial Era (1600-1754),* much like the other titles in the series, can be used as a stand-alone item when studying the colonial era, or it can be incorporated alongside the other volumes in the series when teaching, researching, and understanding American history on a broader scope instead of a singular era isolated in time and space. The volume can be purchased individually or as a set.

According to the Gale Publishing Website, this resource is written to allow the average student in ninth grade, college, and beyond to read and extrapolate the information from it. Regardless of whether the researcher is a novice or a seasoned veteran, this source will prove to be highly valuable to all who open its cover and begin the research process. This resource pulls from select primary sources encompassing a wide range of documents and images, from recipes and diary entries to cartoons and photos, to government legislation and court rulings. This varied mixture creates a diversity of perspectives that will provide the reader with a fresh insight into key events and figures of the colonial era. This volume, as well as the rest of the series, is designed to make the content as accessible as possible to the reader. Each entry is organized by standardized rubrics that allow the user to find information quickly within an entry and facilitate comparisons across entries. The introduction and significance sections are kept brief and focused. It covers the historical background and contributing factors, importance, and impact of the primary source, while it encourages the reader to begin to think critically about the source and how it played a role in history. Besides the key facts about the primary source and its creator, it offers a "Further Resources" section as the end of the entry. This will ignite the researcher to delve deeper into an event or person who shaped our history.

The Colonial Era (1600-1754) opens with an era overview, which will set the stage for the primary sources the reader is about to engage. The primary sources provide unique perspectives and a wealth of understanding through the use of oral histories, songs, speeches, advertisements, letters, laws, legal decisions, newspaper articles, cartoons, and recipes. History and the historical events are brought to life for the researcher largely because of the primary resources presented across the following categories: the arts, business and the economy, education, fashion and leisure, government and politics, law and justice, lifestyles and social trends, media, medicine and health, religion, and science and technology. Because of the varied categories offered to the reader, there is a little something for everyone who turns to this work to learn about the colonial era.

The print format is consistent across all the categories. Regardless of the topic, the user is presented with 10 primary sources relating to the subject heading. There is a topical overview that will set the stage for the section, and this will provide the researcher with a starting point to the particular subject and how it shaped the colonial era.

There is also a chronology list of key dates as it pertains to any particular section and this proves very advantageous for the user who needs a linear timeline to better understand how the particular topic shaped this era in history. Just as each section is structured in a similar format, so too is every entry within this book. The entry is presented in the following format: primary source type and title, author, date, source (from which the entry was taken from,) a short biography about the author, an introduction (to set the stage for the primary source,) and significance (of the entry to history). This wealth of background information not only aids the reader in learning about a particular "Primary Source Entry," but it just may become the spark that will light the fire to go beyond that particular entry and even this particular book in their quest to learn about the "Colonial Era." It is important to note that regardless of whether the reader is a beginner or a veteran doing research, this volume, like others in the series, lays before the reader a thorough explanation and gives them a detailed example of the format that every entry will look like and why it is formatted this way. *The Colonial Era (1600-1754)* offers up a couple of different indexes. The first one is a "Primary Source Type Index" which will provide the user a list of based on the type of resource. This will allow the user the unique ability to see all entries based on a particular type such as but not limited to artifacts, charters, or government documents. There is also a general index which is sorted word-by-word and the index offers bold page numbers as indicators to main essays and italic page locators which indicate images. Both types of indexes will allow them to hone into an area of interest when they are researching and under a time constraint. While the printed format and structure is very important to the reader or teacher in learning the topic, the physical structure while often overlooked is just as important. The physical version is well put together and the hardcover version can withstand the daily use that it will find in any respectable classroom or library reference department. The title is clearly presented on the spine as well as the cover of the book. The book's rear cover provides a quick synopsis of what this work will provide along with the 10 different perspectives offered up to the reader. *American Eras: Primary Sources: The Colonial Era (1600-1754)*, like the rest of the series, is a valued resource for the classroom and library alike.—**Lawrence Joseph Mello**

229. **American Eras: Primary Sources: The Revolutionary Era, 1754-1783.** Farmington Hills, Mich, Gale/Cengage Learning, 2015. 435p. index. $177.00. ISBN 13: 978-1-4144-9823-2; 978-1-4144-9831-7 (e-book).

Primary documents are a unique way to study history, be they letters, newspapers, government documents, pictures, or books—all provide contemporary accounts that enrich one-of-a-kind insights into the people, places, and events of the period. The Gale American Era Primary Sources series targets primary sources with a sweeping array of materials revealing more details about period history. Covering pre-twentieth-century American eras, the series now numbers eight stand-alone volumes and the Revolutionary

War volume is a useful addition.

The volume is divided into 10 chapters representing broad topics such as the arts, education, business, government, social trends, and religion. After some brief explanatory material, a chronology, and historical overview, each chapter includes an overview, a useful chronology, and 10 documents. Each document is preceded by a description, an introduction and statement of significance, and the primary source, although "document" is misleading (excerpt is more accurate). Some sources are complete but most are not. For example two pages from Thomas Paine's *Common Sense* (1776) are reproduced. The introduction and significance are greater in length. A few recent references for further reading are added as are Websites. An example of a complete source is "The Tragical Death of Miss Jane McCrea," a 1778 poem that inspired militia enrollment in New York. A brief source listing, source type index, and general index conclude the volume. Although a useful reference work for the public or secondary school library, researchers of the war looking for a more comprehensive work will still turn to *The Spirit of 'Seventy-six,* first published in 1958 and reprinted for the Bicentennial.—**Boyd Childress**

230. Bender, Nathan E. **Historic Bottle and Jar Closures.** Walnut Creek, Calif., Left Coast Press, Inc., 2015. 107p. illus. index. (Guides to Historical Artifacts). $34.95pa. ISBN 13: 978-1-62958-199-6; 978-1-62958-201-6 (e-book).

This slim volume examines the history of American lids and other closures between the 1890s and the 1950s, using numerous illustrations from industry journals and patents. For scholars of this area of material culture, or collectors of these items, this volume provides a great deal of detailed information on the topic. Particular attention is paid to the evolution of the hermetic seal. An 87-item bibliography lists both primary and secondary sources. This volume is recommended for libraries with patrons interested in these areas.—**Mark Schumacher**

231. **California Digital Newspaper Collection. http://cdnc.ucr.edu/cgi-bin/cdnc.** [Website] Free. Date reviewed: 2016.

The freely accessible *California Digital Newspaper Collection* (CDNC) has over 600,000 pages of newspapers, all of which are in the public domain and thus not subject to use restrictions. A selection of more recent newspapers is also available. The CDNC is produced and curated by the Center for Bibliographic Studies and Research (CBSR) at UC Riverside with support from the U.S. Institute of Museum and Library Services under the provisions of the Library Services and Technology Act. Funding was provided by grants from the National Endowment for the Humanities.

Four links on the right-hand side of the page—Browse by Title, Browse by Date, Browse by Tag, and Browse by County—make navigation a snap. Under Title, users will find links to papers from the *Amador Ledger* (Jackson, 1900-1911) to the *Wide West* (San Francisco, 1854-1858). Browsing by date starts in 1846 and runs through May, 2015. Clicking on a month and year will take users to a calendar which has links to different newspapers for each day of the month. On April 19, 1861, for example, there are links to the *California Farmer and Journal of the Useful Sciences,* the *Daily Alta California,* the *Red Bluff Independent,* and the *Sacramento Daily Union.* The tag for " Salt Lake City-Mormons deserting" links to an August 12, 1857, article from the *Sacramento Bee.* If someone wants to investigate happenings in Madera County, a click on the county name goes straight to the 1861-1922 issues of the *Mariposa Gazette.* A right click on articles accessed produces further options, like the ability to clip the article or create a PDF file.

For those hoping to use historic California newspapers, the highly recommended CDNC will truly amaze.—**ARBA Staff Reviewer**

232.   Cameron, Christopher. **The Abolitionist Movement.** Santa Barbara, Calif., Greenwood Press/ABC-CLIO, 2014. 253p. index. (Documents Decoded). $79.00. ISBN 13: 978-1-61069-512-1; 978-1-61069-513-8 (e-book).

This title in the exceptional Documents Decoded series offers wide-ranging perspectives from the people and events surrounding the push to abolish slavery in America. It takes a close, chronological look through a wealth of primary source documents in context with a succinct, modern commentary. This book's unique approach in aligning key historical documents side-by-side with modern-day insight facilitates an active relationship between readers and the material at hand.

Gathering petitions, speeches, legal opinions, personal letters, and more from key figures ranging from slaves to presidents, the book traces the evolution of thought surrounding many aspects of the abolition movement. The first section, Slavery and Racial Thought in Colonial and Revolutionary America, explores the genesis of the movement and follows influences such as religion, colonial rebellion, and Native American alliances. The second section, Abolitionism and Pro-Slavery Thought in Antebellum America, carries readers through the heart of our young nation's major moral conflict, sharing documents such as the text of Frederick Douglass' rousing speech "What to the Slave is the Fourth of July?" and perhaps providing the capstone to the abolitionist movement in President Lincoln's Second Inaugural Address of 1865. Alongside each document, the author provides just the right amount of commentary to help readers pinpoint the most salient ideas and connect these ideas to other aspects of the movement.

The documents are followed by a historical timeline, beginning with the date and place where the first Africans were sold into slavery (1619 Virginia), an alphabetized list of sources for further reading, and an index. This unique, well-conceived book brings modern illumination to our very real, very compelling history, and would be an enjoyable and educational find for any scholar. Recommended for high school and academic libraries.—**Laura Herrell**

233.   **Colonial America. Module 1: Settlement, Expansion and Rivalries. http://www.amdigital.co.uk/m-collections/collection/colonial-america/.** [Website] Chicago, Adam Matthew Digital. Price negotiated by site. Date reviewed: 2016.

Colonial America is an extensive digital resource built using the Colonial Office document collection (mostly manuscripts) held by the National Archives in London. The collection includes original correspondence between the American colonial governments and the British government agencies responsible for administering them. This relationship dealt with all manner of subjects, and its archive documents a broad scope of issues encompassing political, economic, social, cultural, and military subjects. These topics are represented in both public and private documents ranging from letters and diaries to public notices, newspapers, and printed pamphlets. The collection also includes maps and some architectural drawings. All documents are available as high-resolution scanned images and can be downloaded, saved, and sent via email.

The full collection covers 1602-1822 and will be made available in five modules to be released over the next four years. (This review covers only Module 1 released in late 2015.) Module 1: Early Settlement, Expansion, and Rivalries focuses on the early development of and events in the American colonies including such major events as the 1688 Glorious Revolution and the French and Indian War of 1756-63.

Colonial America's primary navigation is organized by tabs, and the Document tab provides access to the manuscript collection. The collection has been scanned, indexed, and described at the document level allowing it to be searched and browsed by keyword, people or place-name, date, and theme. Dropdown menus at the top of the Document tab help users drill down to specific information and combine multiple search parameters. For example, a user can filter to show only diary entries on community organization in New York. The Popular Searches function provided by the editors highlights interesting topics in the collection.

Each document is described with a title, place-name, keyword, people, places, volume name, dates, and theme and is represented by a high-quality scan of the original. Users can zoom in several times without compromising the quality of the image. This is useful as some of the documents are faded or have difficult-to-read handwriting.

The Explore tab includes an interactive Government Chart, Essays, Biographies, Data Associations, and Popular Searches. The Government Structure Chart allows users to connect key information such as date, region, and office to key office-holders in time. This facilitates user's contextualization of the major players of this time period. Data Associations is a heatmap display illustrating the connections between people, places, and keywords.

The Map Gallery tab provides access to many interesting maps that can be filtered by image type, date, or keyword. Users can view full-size images of the maps, and images can be saved to a personalized collection (using "My Lightbox") or downloaded as a PDF.

Translating a manuscript archive of this size, scope, and historical importance into a usable online resource is an immense task. Great thought and care has gone into representing this body of material well. Emphasis has been placed on search, discovery, navigation, ease of access, and interpretation. Several different points of access have been provided and various methods have been employed to support specific searching and serendipitous browsing.

This resource is a treasure for scholars. It is immensely important for British and American history scholars, and any library or institution supporting this audience should consider this resource. It also has the potential to inspire young scholars by bringing them close to historical documents through digital media. This is a rich and extensive digital archive enhanced by thorough and thoughtful organization and judicious application of technology.—**Kristin Kay Leeman**

234.   **Defining Documents in American History: Civil Rights (1954-2015).** Michael Shally-Jensen, ed. Hackensack, N.J., Salem Press, 2015. 321p. index. $175.00. ISBN 13: 978-1-61925-856-3.

The fight for civil rights is no longer considered specific to an era; rather, it is an ongoing part of the American story. This volume in the Defining Documents in American History Series gathers a good variety of primary source documents revolving around the general theme of civil rights and couples them with contemporary analysis prepared by a host of knowledgeable scholars.

Five main sections focus on the most compelling areas of civil rights study: African American Civil Rights, Women and Equality, Latino Civil Rights, The Gay Rights

Movement, and Native American Rights. Within each section readers will find applicable primary source documents ranging from letters to speeches to court opinions and more. Some examples of the documents within this volume include Martin Luther King's "Letter from Birmingham Jail," the National Organization for Women (NOW) Founding Statement, and the Don't Ask, Don't Tell law.

Enriching these documents are well-organized essays providing background and contemporary insight into the challenges and implications wrought by the issues. Each essay is similarly constructed, with well-demarcated, concise sections providing a summary overview, defining moment, document author biography, document analysis, and essential themes. Other features within each essay include a glossary of selected terms from the primary document and a bibliography.

Appendixes offer further supplemental information, and include a chronological list of events relative to the volume's documents, Web resources, a bibliography, and an index.

Whether reaching back to the mid-twentieth century to hear the Women's Political Council of Montgomery, Alabama, ask for respectful treatment in public transportation to reading an impactful 2015 Supreme Court decision about defining marriage in *Obergefell* v. *Hodges,* readers will get an excellent sense of the complex fight for civil rights in the United States.—**ARBA Staff Reviewer**

235.   **Defining Documents in American History: Postwar 1940s (1945-1950).** Michael Shally-Jensen, ed. Hackensack, N.J., Salem Press, 2015. 308p. index. $175.00. ISBN 13: 978-1-61925-739-9; 978-1-61925-740-5 (e-book).

This title is the latest in a series of books that examines discrete periods of American history through a close reading of the primary documents produced therein. Previous volumes by Salem Press include the Reconstruction Era (1865-1877) and the decade of the 1920s.

A standard format allows the user of any one work to be familiar with the entire set. An "Editor's Introduction" sets the scene by giving an objective overview of the period in question. Each chapter takes an in-depth look at a single speech, government report, legislative act, or other document, and uses this as a springboard to discuss not only the primary source itself, but also the social, cultural, and political ramifications.

A "Summary Overview" gives the researcher a snapshot of the contents of the document, while "Defining Moment" fleshes out the background that led up to its creation. This is followed by "Author Biography" (if appropriate, as some documents are created by committees or other groups, as opposed to an individual writer), "Document Analysis," which is self-explanatory, and "Essential Themes," which discusses the significance and historical import of the document. Lastly, a "Bibliography and Additional Reading" section lists resources helpful for further research. The core of each chapter, however, is a shaded box that contains the verbatim text of the primary source under examination. Shorter pieces appear in their entirety; more lengthy pieces are excerpted but can still run to several pages.

Editor Michael Shally-Jensen holds a doctorate in cultural anthropology from Princeton University. He has assembled a competent crew of academics whom likewise hold advanced degrees and that have contributed to the contents of this work.

As with previously published volumes in this series, *Postwar 1940s* is well written, exhibits solid scholarship, and presents an engaging read. As an understanding of our nation's past is central to becoming a well-rounded citizen, this volume is strongly recommended for purchase by all public and academic libraries.—**Michael Francis Bemis**

236.   **Defining Documents in American History: The Vietnam War (1956-1975).**
Michael Shally-Jensen, ed. Hackensack, N.J., Salem Press, 2015. 288p. index. $175.00.
ISBN 13: 978-1-61925-852-5; 978-1-61925-853-2 (e-book).

The Vietnam War continues playing a critical role in U.S. history and national
security policy-making. References to its impact are regularly made by critics of proposed
U.S. military interventions in other countries. This work covers various documents on this
conflict between 1956 and 1975 representing a divergent spectrum of political views on
why the United States should or should not participate in this war.

This compilation is broken up into the following sections: Kennedy's War, Johnson's
War, The Antiwar Movement, Nixon's War, and Aftermath. Within these sections,
overviews are provided of individual documents and the individual involved in creating
them, the text of the document, analysis of the document's significance, and bibliographic
references. Examples of documents in these sections include: a January 14, 1961, letter
from John Kennedy to South Vietnamese ruler Ngo Dinh Diem; Lyndon Johnson's August
4, 1964, address on the Gulf of Tonkin incident; a July 21, 1965, meeting between LBJ
and advisors such as Secretary of Defense Robert McNamara, Secretary of State Dean
Rusk, and Undersecretary of State George Ball; a March 1965 call by the Students for
a Democratic Society for a march on Washington, D.C., to oppose the Vietnam War;
Robert Kennedy's February 8, 1968, speech "An Unwinnable War"; a September 1969
memorandum on Vietnamization from National Security Advisor Henry Kissinger to
Richard Nixon; excerpts from the 1973 Paris Peace Treaty ending U.S. participation in the
war; and Jimmy Carter's 1977 pardoning of draft evaders from this conflict.

This is a succinctly edited work which also features bibliographic references and
Websites such as the State Department's Historians Office covering American diplomatic
relations during the Vietnam War. It will serve as a useful introduction to undergraduate
students beginning to study the complexities and controversies of the Vietnam War and
their lingering impact in American foreign and national security policy.—**Bert Chapman**

237.   **Defining Documents in American History: World War II (1939-1946).** Michael
Shally-Jensen, ed. Hackensack, N.J., Salem Press, 2015. 2v. index. $295.00/set. ISBN 13:
978-1-61925-737-5; 978-1-61925-738-2 (e-book).

This installment in Salem Press's Defining Documents in American History series
focuses on World War II. Like the other titles in the series, the two volumes that comprise
this set contain the entire text of primary documents (80 in this case). Documents are
contextualized by an essay that contains a summary overview, a defining moment, a
biography of the document writer, document analysis, and discussion of essential themes.
The critical essays are signed by the contributors, all of whom are listed in the front
matter of volume one. Documents are arranged under the following nine categories,
each of which is prefaced by a brief introduction: The Lead-Up to War, Pearl Harbor,
Domestic Aliens, Other Demographics, Foreign Policy, War and Victory, The Holocaust,
Nuremberg, and The Atom Bomb. Readers will truly get a sense of the 1939-1946 period
from the documents, which include journal entries, letters, speeches, political sermons,
laws, government reports, and court cases. Glossaries, a bibliography, and an additional
reading section follow each entry.

The set concludes with a chronological list of documents and the pages on which
users can find the material, a list of Web resources, a bibliography, and an index. The set
offers students, especially those in need of historical facts and context, easy access to

primary sources.—**ARBA Staff Reviewer**

238.   Deppisch, Ludwig M. **The Health of the First Ladies: Medical Histories from Martha Washington to Michelle Obama.** Jefferson, N.C., McFarland, 2015. 232p. illus. index. $35.00pa. ISBN 13: 978-0-7864-7436-3; 978-1-4766-1766-4 (e-book).

Reaching back over two centuries, this book examines the known medical histories of each of the First Ladies. Three sections chronologically advance readers through the information, but individual chapters may unite First Ladies through their conditions (as in chapter seven which details the impact of the common nineteenth-century malady of tuberculosis upon several White House residents).

Taken as a whole, the book traces advancements in medical diagnoses and treatments, notes the ascendancy of certain medical conditions and the elimination of others, and observes shifting attitudes regarding whether a First Lady's medical issues should be of public or private concern. Individual accounts are frank, often highlighted by contemporary reports, and relayed with sufficient background information on the women's family histories, marriages, childbirths, and more. Among the chapters is an account of Mary Todd Lincoln's mental illness and the story of Betty Ford and her enduring legacy of the Betty Ford Center. Interesting themes appear; most notably, the impact of stress upon the health of the First Lady in addition to the impact their health may have had on their husband's ability to govern. The book concludes with discussion as to whether a First Lady's medical issues should be conveyed to the public, noting the effect of Nancy Reagan's announcement of breast cancer on the increased number of screenings, yet also reminding readers, as Laura Bush pointed out, that First Ladies are not elected officials. As traditional roles of first spouses change and expand, however, learning about more personal aspects of their lives becomes very compelling relative to comprehensive understanding of national leadership. The book includes detailed notes, an extensive bibliography, and an index.—**Laura Herrell**

239.   Derks, Scott. **Working Americans 1880-2015. Volume V: Americans at War.** 2d ed. Amenia, N.Y., Grey House Publishing, 2015. 685p. illus. index. $150.00. ISBN 13: 978-1-61925-743-6; 978-1-61925-744-3 (e-book).

Online sources have made many traditional printed reference volumes somewhat obsolete. However, that is not the case with this unique gem that cannot be captured electronically. The fifth contribution in a series that examines the lives of representative Americans, this volume addresses one of the occurrences in people's lives that affects them in the most dramatic ways—war. Beginning with the frontier conflicts of the 1880s, the volume extends through the present day. Organized by decades, the collection brings together personal stories, media excerpts, clippings, diaries, letters, cartoons, statistical information, and thousands of photographs, pictures, and other visuals. The inclusions are both traditional ones and segments of popular culture that include a wide range from song lyrics to mementoes of all kinds. The volume reminds me of both a truly excellent museum display and a Ken Burns documentary in printed rather than video medium.

Each of the 13 chapters begins with an overview of important events of the decade and contains personal profiles (a total of 38). The volume highlights individuals from a range of ethnicities and socio-economic levels to capture a snapshot of Americans from many perspectives. A common feature in each chapter is a chart of selected prices and average pay for jobs as one element that demonstrates statistical comparisons between the decades. The index is quite useful.

The volume is a tour de force, one that a reader can become absorbed in for hours on end. I recommend this compilation highly. It is an educational tool of impressive merit.—**Joe P. Dunn**

240.   DiNunzio, Mario R. **The Great Depression and the New Deal.** Santa Barbara, Calif., Greenwood Press/ABC-CLIO, 2014. 329p. illus. index. (Documents Decoded). $79.00. ISBN 13: 978-1-61069-534-3; 978-1-61069-535-0 (e-book).

This title offers a compelling, clearly conceived examination of the tumultuous issues surrounding the Great Depression and the New Deal legislation created to confront it. The book takes a close, chronological look through a wealth of primary source documents in context with insightful author commentary. Its unique approach in aligning key historical documents side-by-side with this commentary facilitates an active relationship between readers and the material at hand.

Gathering newspaper editorials, legal rulings, speeches, photographs, legislation, and more, this installment in the Documents Decoded series traces the rise of economic turmoil and the resultant national response. Document selections, such as a photograph of the army clearing out the camps of protesting World War I veterans, or the Republican Party platform of 1932, follow themes that truly encapsulate 1930s America, such as veteran's rights, women's rights, labor relations, federal regulations, and prohibition. The well-curated pieces allow readers to observe a variety of perspectives beyond the political: from that of the struggling American farmer to that of the watchful business owner.

Juxtaposed with the documents is succinct author commentary, providing background information for each piece as well as relevant insight into particular ideas. For example, we learn that Father Charles E. Coughlin—whose popular radio address included here stridently warns against the overreach of FDR's government—was at one time the president's ally.

The documents are followed by a historical timeline which begins with the 1928 landslide election of Republican Herbert Hoover and ends as President Roosevelt's request for increased military spending signifies the end of The Great Depression. The book also includes ideas for further reading and an index. Recommended for high school and academic libraries.—**Laura Herrell**

241.   **The Gilder Lehrman Institute of American History. https://www.gilderlehrman. org/.** [Website] Free. Date reviewed: 2016.

New York's Gilder Lehrman Institute of American History is devoted to the improvement of history education. Its Website offers a unique Web resource ideal for students, teachers, and general readers.

The core of the site is the Institute's "History by Era" section, under the editorial aegis of historian Carol Berkin. Organized chronologically, "History by Era" tells the story of American history, divided into 10 distinct periods: Colonization & Settlement, 1585-1763; The American Revolution, 1763-1783; The New Nation, 1783-1815; National Expansion & Reform, 1815-1860; Civil War & Reconstruction, 1861-1877; Rise of Industrial America, 1877-1900; Progressive Era to New Era, 1900-1929; Great Depression & WWII, 1929-1945; and 1945 to the Present.

Each of the 10 eras covered includes an historical overview essay written by some of the most distinguished historians writing today, including John Demos, Pauline Maier, Alan Taylor, Eric Foner, Richard White, and David M. Kennedy, among others. Each of these overview essays are complemented with three additional thematic essays and a set of featured documents or primary sources, including letters, government and legal documents, paintings, photographs, and songs—all drawn from the extensive holdings of the Gilder Lehrman Collection. For those interested in exploring important topics across chronology and periodization, users can also search for content organized by various historical "themes"—African American History, American Indian History, Literature and Language Arts, etc.

The site's Multimedia section offers more than a dozen video series on subjects ranging from "Studying the Constitution" to "GIs, Generals, and American Wars." The "Historian's Now" video series features conversations with major historians of US history, including Gordon Wood, David Reynolds, Richard Brookhiser, and Julian Zelizer, among other luminaries.

Helpful lesson plans and other classroom resources from master teachers are also included in the site.

As Carol Berkin says in her introduction, the site "…is not an online textbook. From the beginning, we set ourselves the task of providing the reader with a far richer texture than a textbook can offer…. A collection of fifty individual essays written by some of the most distinguished scholars of our day…speaks to the reader not in one voice, but in fifty different, unique voices as each of these renowned scholars interprets the important developments, people, events, and ideas of a particular era." The Gilder Lehrman Institute's impressive Website is highly recommended for high school and college students, for teachers, and for American history buffs.—**ARBA Staff Reviewer**

242.   **The Great Chicago Fire and the Web of Memory. http://www.greatchicagofire. org/.** [Website] Free. Date reviewed: 2016.

A joint project of the Chicago History Museum and Northwestern University Information Technology Department of Academic and Research Technologies, the Website presents a documentary history-in-miniature of the Great Chicago Fire of 1871—one of the most infamous disasters in nineteenth-century U.S. history.

The site is divided into two main parts. "The Great Chicago Fire" includes background material on Chicago's growth in the decades before the fire, a brief narrative of the conflagration, as well as an essay on the rapid reconstruction of the city during the "Great Rebuilding" of 1871-73. "The Web of Memory" includes contemporaneous accounts of the fire from eyewitnesses and from the popular press, as well as a brief examination of how the fire was later commemorated in poetry, fiction, drama, song, and visual works. A rich variety of images are available, as well as fascinating audio and video clips.

Users interested in touring significant sites related to the fire can find interactive maps with 10 suggested tours of more than 50 landmarks, including the O'Leary's cottage, which miraculously survived the surrounding devastation. A minimal selected bibliography points users at a half-dozen print sources for further information on the subject.

The Website would be a logical place for students and history buffs to begin research on this infamous disaster.—**ARBA Staff Reviewer**

243.   Hillstrom, Laurie Collier. **Defining Moments: The Cuban Missile Crisis.** Detroit, Omnigraphics, 2015. 240p. illus. maps. index. (Defining Moments). $60.00. ISBN 13: 978-0-7808-1348-9.

This well-written and engaging work takes an in-depth look at the two-week period during October 1962, when the world stood on the brink of nuclear war. The bulk of the book is presented in a tripartite structure, as are other titles in this series. A "narrative overview" tells the story itself chronologically in six concise chapters, which are amply illustrated with black-and-white photographs of the period. Shaded text boxes provide amplifying information. A second section consists of two- to three-page biographical sketches of major actors involved in this drama. This compact tome is rounded out with a third section of excerpts from primary sources, such as President John F. Kennedy's televised announcement of the discovery of Soviet missiles on the island of Cuba. Special features include a glossary, timeline, and bibliography.

One of the outstanding features of this volume is the balanced, objective, and authoritative style of writing. Although no author background blurb is to be found, it is obvious that Laurie Collier Hillstrom has done her homework and has an obvious mastery of the subject matter at hand.

Produced with students in mind, this title would be especially appropriate for high school and academic libraries, although public libraries with strong American history collections may also wish to acquire this volume.—**Michael Francis Bemis**

244.   Hillstrom, Laurie Collier. **Defining Moments: The Lewis and Clark Expedition.** Detroit, Omnigraphics, 2016. 240p. illus. maps. index. $60.00. ISBN 13: 978-0-7808-1417-2.

This title in the Defining Moments series brings together the most essential information regarding the courageous Lewis and Clark Expedition and conveys it all in a variety of intelligent, focused ways. Arranging the book into three well-delineated sections provides readers with easy access to this rich and engaging history.

Chapters in the narrative overview chronologically establish the story of the fortuitous Louisiana Purchase, President Thomas Jefferson's long-held desire to explore far beyond his new nation's western border, the enlistment of the Corps of Discovery under the leadership of Meriwether Lewis and William Clark and ultimately the daring journey and its legacy. The next section, biographies, shines a spotlight on a number of prominent figures in the complex story. Aside from Lewis and Clark themselves, we read of Sacagawea, George Drouillard, Patrick Gass, and others. The primary sources section allows us then to examine some well-curated documents, such as excerpts from the Louisiana Purchase Treaty, Captain Lewis' "shopping list" of items he thought he would need for the journey, or Thomas Jefferson's address to representatives of several Native American nations residing in Louisiana Purchase territory.

Supplementary material includes a glossary of the main people, places, and terms, a detailed chronology, black-and-white illustrations and photographs, a list of references for further study, and, perhaps most helpful to readers, a generous list of potential research topics. All in all, this Defining Moments title is sure to engage readers in the fascinating historical topic at hand.—**ARBA Staff Reviewer**

245.   Hillstrom, Laurie Collier. **Defining Moments: The Underground Railroad.** Detroit, Omnigraphics, 2015. 232p. illus. maps. index. $60.00. ISBN 13: 978-0-7808-1346-5.

The series, produced for a middle school and high school audience, follows a common pattern of preface, how to use the book, possible research topics/study questions from the volume, narrative, biographies, documents, terms, chronology, sources for further study, bibliography, and index. The writing is appropriate for the target audience and good pictures support the narrative. This volume is normative for the series, but like previous volumes in the series that I have reviewed, I question the market value for any other than a school library that can afford the entire series.—**Joe P. Dunn**

246.　　Hudson, David L., Jr. **The Handy American History Answer Book.** Canton, Mich., Visible Ink Press, 2016. 428p. illus. maps. index. $21.95pa. ISBN 13: 978-1-57859-471-9.

Condensing over 200 years of history is no easy task. While much information today may be only a computer click away, what is often lacking in many resources is context and connection. The success of the *Handy American History Answer Book* stems from its accessible and neatly organized chronological structure that melds the ease of a timeline with the satisfaction of significant research.

Three sections encompass the exciting eras and major events that shaped the United States into what it is today. The book begins with a chapter on pre-Revolutionary history followed by chronologically organized chapters that take readers into the early twenty-first century. This is followed by a chapter on sports history and a chapter on music and entertainment.

Uniquely, all information is presented as an answer to a question—a format both eye-catching and effective in terms of readability. Entries are generally brief, yet perfectly capture the essence of each topic. "What was the Teapot Dome Scandal?" is answered, for example, with the names, dates, and places relevant to this prime display of government corruption. Questions may be general ("What were the causes of the Civil War?") or intriguingly specific ("Who was Mrs. Catt?"), but all will encourage readers' curiosity and further their desire to learn more. Including nearly 1,000 entries exploring politics, social lives, literary contributions, military endeavors, and much more, this book is an excellent resource for history lovers, students, and others. The book includes a timeline of American history following the table of contents. The final chapter is followed by a short bibliography; a section that lists each state and its basic facts (date admitted to the Union, capital, largest city, state nickname, number of electoral votes, and population); a chronological list of US presidents including life dates, office dates, political party, election opponent, home state, and vice president; the full text of the U.S. Constitution; and an index.—**Laura Herrell**

247.　　Luhrssen, David. **Secret Societies and Clubs in American History.** Santa Barbara, Calif., ABC-CLIO, 2015. 290p. illus. index. $58.00. ISBN 13: 978-1-59884-903-5; 978-1-59884-904-2 (e-book).

This is a narrative history of secret societies in the United States from 1730 to 2011. Societies well-known to history such as the Masons, the Anti-Masons, the Knights of Labor, the Ku Klux Klan, Dianetics, the Molly Maguires, the Know-Nothings, and the Mafia are treated, as well as more obscure societies such as Knights of the Golden Circle and Ordo Templi Ordis. The Communist Party of the United States is not treated. Many of the societies were/are nativist and/or anti-Semitic, while others were simply screwball. Individuals such as L. Ron Hubbard, Al Capone, and Charles Manson are treated. More than 60 pages of primary documents are included. There are some 20 pages of notes, a bibliography listing 88 books, and shorter chapter bibliographies. The index is name only. There is a timeline from 1730 to 2011 and some two dozen black-and-white illustrations. David Luhrssen is the author and coauthor of several books, such as *Hammer of the Gods: Thule Society and the Birth of Naziism,* a lecturer at several colleges, and editor of a newspaper column.

The text is readable and accurate. However, there are typos galore, including one horrendous error in the timeline—"Andrew Johnson, instead of "Andrew Jackson." The book's reference value is limited, but public and academic libraries might want it for their circulating collections.—**Jonathan F. Husband**

248.   **Memories of the Enslaved: Voices from the Slave Narratives.** Spencer R. Crew, Lonnie G. Bunch, III and Clement A. Price, eds. Santa Barbara, Calif., Praeger/ABC-CLIO, 2015. 303p. illus. index. $48.00. ISBN 13: 978-1-4408-3778-4; 978-1-4408-4179-1 (e-book).

Memories of the Enslaved is based upon the Library of Congress collection titled "Born in Slavery: Slave Narratives from the Federal Writer's Project, 1936-1938." The "Born in Slavery" collection includes over 2,300 first-person slavery accounts that *Memories of the Enslaved* used for the content of this book. Essentially, *Memories of the Enslaved* is an edited and curated collection of excerpts from those 2,300 accounts intended to provide easier accessibility to the content while highlighting larger themes and topics.

Memories of the Enslaved is divided into seven main chapters of approximately 650 excerpts discussing community culture, childhood recollections, the enslaved family, enslaved women, slave labor, punishments, and escape attempts. Each chapter includes a descriptive introduction, followed by excerpts ranging from a few lines to a few paragraphs that exemplify the topic at hand. The text also includes a chronology of slavery in the United States, an appendix explaining historians' views on slavery, recommended resources, and an index.

Memories of the Enslaved is a useful resource in acting as a gateway into these remarkable stories, while also providing some narrative context and understanding. The full text of these excerpts is available online, but this book is much more accessible and likely to be used by those being introduced to the history of slavery.—**Tyler Manolovitz**

249.   Nichols, Bruce. **Guerrilla Warfare in Civil War Missouri, Volume IV, September 1864-June 1865.** Jefferson, N.C., McFarland, 2014. 453p. illus. maps. index. $39.95pa. ISBN 13: 978-0-7864-7584-1; 978-1-4766-0384-1 (e-book).

This is the fourth in a series of books covering guerrilla warfare in Civil War Missouri. The first focused on 1862, the second on 1863, and the third on January-August 1864. This volume supplies an in-depth study of all known guerrilla events from September 1864 to June 1865, a period that includes Confederate major general Sterling Price's regular army invasion of Missouri in September and October 1864. The author divides Missouri into geographical quadrants for this study, making exceptions where necessary, and uses county designations for location descriptions. The chapters are organized chronologically and geographically. For example, chapter four, "Fall 1864 in Northeast Missouri Including Centralia" begins with maps and general information, followed by such subheadings as Union atrocities; attacks by Bill Anderson's guerrillas on riverboats in the area; and guerrillas in Knox County during September.

The book uses a wide variety of primary sources, including the U.S. War Department's *Official Records of the Union and Confederate Armies,* newspapers, journals, and letters, along with secondary sources. Black-and-white photographs and illustrations are used throughout the book. The geographic organization, table of contents, and extensive index make it easy to find information on specific people, places, and events. Recommended for public and academic libraries.—**ARBA Staff Reviewer**

250. Phillips, Richard Hayes. **White Slave Children of Colonial Maryland and Virginia: Birth and Shipping Records.** Baltimore, Md., Genealogical Publishing, 2015. 393p. $39.95pa. ISBN 13: 978-0-8063-2030-4.

Few students complete any survey of colonial American history without learning something about the Atlantic slave trade and the practice of indentured servitude. The kidnapping and enslavement of white children, however, has been largely overlooked. In *White Slave Children of Colonial Maryland and Virginia,* historian and genealogist Richard Hayes Phillips tracks 1,400 white children (out of a total of 5,000) who were kidnapped and forced into labor by the county courts of Maryland and Virginia. Working from baptismal records, court order books, military pension files, and shipping records, Phillips seeks to identify each child's date of birth, parents, and home town or parish. The entries are arranged geographically.

White Slave Children serves as a continuation of Phillips's previous work, *Without Indentures: Index to White Slave Children in Colonial Court Records,* and as a companion piece to his other recent publication, titled *White Slave Children of Charles County, Maryland.* Phillips ably conveys the excitement of finding obscure and forgotten primary sources, and, more importantly, he provides an historical overview of the enslavement of white children in colonial Maryland and Virginia. He also offers a wealth of information on the shipping trade, including detailed descriptions of the ships that transported enslaved white children and biographical sketches of the men who profited from the trade.

As a contribution to genealogy and colonial American history, *White Slave Children* succeeds on all counts.—**Craig Mury Keeney**

251. **Railroads and the Making of Modern America. http://railroads.unl.edu/.** [Website] Free. Date reviewed: 2016.

Railroads and the Making of Modern America is a digital, social history of railroads focused on the intersection of social history and technology. The principal editor of the project is William G. Thomas, III, the John and Catherine Angle Professor in the Humanities at the University of Nebraska-Lincoln. Links on the left-hand side of the home page will take the curious to information about other project directors and support personnel, partnerships, funding, and copyright.

The top of the page has links to Topics, Views, Data, Search, Student Projects, and Teaching Materials. The topics—Slavery and Southern Railways; Railroad Work and Workers; The Civil War and Strategy; The 1877 Railroad Strike; Politics and Corruption; Land Sales, Migration and Immigration; The Origins of Segregation; William Jennings Bryan's 1896 Presidential Campaign; Tourism and Mobility; and Representing the Railroad—incorporate personal letters, newspaper articles, images, business documents, and more. The Views tab takes users to assemblages of data and interpretations. The views are also comprised of original documents, maps, and more and are linked to relevant sources; views can be searched several ways—by topic, by category, and by a browsable list. Two of many such views are Passenger Mobility in the 1850s and Northern Expansion in the 1850s.

Following Topics and Views, the Data tab links researchers to the freely available data, for which there is download functionality. The Search feature allows users to access documents and databases by a variety of means—by type, by topic, etc. For those curious to see the sort of railroad-related research being conducted by graduate students at the University of Nebraska-Lincoln, there is a link to Student Projects. Lastly, the Teaching Materials link, all created with free, open-source material, is designed for teachers at all levels, elementary through college and university. This section has links to frequently asked questions for teaching *Railroads and the Making of Modern America,* connections to interviews with teachers, and access to the site's blog.—**ARBA Staff Reviewer**

252.   Teed, Paul E., and Melissa Ladd Teed. **Reconstruction: A Reference Guide.** Santa Barbara, Calif., ABC-CLIO, 2015. 281p. index. (Guides to Historic Events in America). $63.00. ISBN 13: 978-1-61069-532-9; 978-1-61069-533-6 (e-book).

In the latest entry in ABC-CLIO's Guides to Historical Events in America series, Saginaw Valley State history professors Paul and Melissa Teed attempt to provide students relatively unfamiliar with the details of the era with basic facts and documents which could direct their further research. The current volume follows the series pattern: chronology, historical overview, topical chapters, biographies of chief players, selected essential primary documents, and an annotated bibliography. The six topical chapters comprise roughly half of the volume, followed by four brief analytical essays. Twenty-three single-paragraph essays and 22 short primary documents support the essays, and students will find the short bibliography helpful. Because of the introductory nature of the work, readers will not find great depth in the presentation of the material, but undergraduate students in particular should benefit. Although a number of excellent reference books on Reconstruction are available, including *Reconstruction: A Historical Encyclopedia of the American Mosaic* edited by Richard Zuczek (Greenwood, 2015), the Teed volume is useful for its collection of primary documents and well-written topical chapters. Recommended for undergraduate U.S. history collections.—**Anthony J. Adam**

253.   **This Is Who We Were: 1880-1899.** Amenia, N.Y., Grey House Publishing, 2015. 608p. illus. maps. index. $155.00. ISBN 13: 978-1-61925-755-9; 978-1-61925-757-3 (e-book).

This Is Who We Were: 1880-1899 joins the other *This Is Who We Were* books in providing students with primary-source information about a particular period in United States history. Section one begins with 29 profiles of individuals like that of telephone company executive Donald Rutherford in 1880; the profiles include snapshots of life at home and work and facts on life in the community (in the case of Rutherford, the community was Boston, Massachusetts). This section of profiles is generously illustrated and successfully immerses readers in the life and times of the person featured using various materials like historic documents and diaries. A list of historical snapshots of inventions, political events, women's rights, expansion, and more comprises the second section, while section three provides data on the annual income of blacksmiths, cigar makers, and others for 1883, 1890, and 1898, along with pricing information for such products as furniture polish, a typewriter, and coffee in 1883, 1890, and 1898. This section also has information on the value of a dollar from 1860 to 2014. Section four "All around

Us," uses 86 documents in chronological order (mostly reprinted in their entirety) from popular magazines and newspapers to give a sense of how people felt about a variety of topics like music, shopping, women's work, and education. The fifth and largest section, "Census Data," is comprised of six state-by-state ranking tables from 1880, 1890, and 2010 followed by reprints from the 1890 Census of Population and a reproduction of the report "Progress of the Nation: 1790-1890."

This will be a helpful resource for students from middle school through high school and beyond because it makes accessible in one place a wealth of interesting and useful information. A selected bibliography and index round out the volume.—**ARBA Staff Reviewer**

254. **This Is Who We Were: In the 1940s.** Amenia, N.Y., Grey House Publishing, 2015. 579p. index. $155.00. ISBN 13: 978-4-61925-741-2.

This is a derivative work, as the contents are based on a previously published 13-volume series entitled *Working Americans,* edited by Scott Derks. Said series presents a decade-by-decade snapshot of everyday American life as viewed through the lens of various demographic groups (women, the middle class, immigrants, etc.). Current title, therefore, is essentially a repackaging of the chapters from each volume regarding World War II and the postwar readjustment as the troops came home.

Current title under review presents material in five sections. "Profiles" consists of bulleted lists of facts concerning the lives of individual working men and women of the decade, such as "Glassblower," "Longshoreman," and so on. "Historical Snapshots" appears in the same format, but lists here are of "…significant people, places and things that dominated the 1940's" (page 191). "Economy of the Times" contains tabular data regarding consumer prices of various commodities, annual incomes, and a "Value of a Dollar Index, 1860-2014." Excerpts from primary source documents take up section four, entitled "All Around Us." Reprints of articles from newspapers, popular magazines, and books of the period give the reader a "you were there" perspective on issues of the day. The last section is a reproduction of the year 1950 census report.

From this reviewer's perspective, there are a number of problematic areas with this work. More factoid that factual, the bulleted lists give the appearance of randomly assembled bits and pieces of information with little historical relevance, as in "The production of soybeans rose as new uses for them were discovered" (page 57). While well-illustrated, the photographs and drawings are poorly reproduced and appear only in black and white. Many have no captions, leaving the reader to guess as to the activity depicted. The inclusion of the census report, which takes up almost half of the pages of this volume, amounts to so much filler; not only is table after table of statistics of limited value, but it's doubtful that modern-day researchers, with electronic access to all the figures they could desire, would even bother to consult this material in the first place.

A much more useful tool for understanding this eventful decade is the three-volume set *The Forties in America* (see ARBA 2011, entry 387). The 600+ alphabetically arranged articles in this encyclopedia are informative, engaging, and concisely written, all of which give the reader an historically accurate profile of this momentous 10-year period.—**Michael Francis Bemis**

255.   **U.S. History In Context. http://solutions.cengage.com/InContext/US-History/.** [Website] Farmington Hills, Mich., Gale/Cengage Learning, 2016. Price negotiated by site. Date reviewed: 2016.

The *U.S. History In Context* database provides access to a broad range of resources spanning America's history from the arrival of Vikings to the 2008 financial crisis, from the Mayflower to Barack Obama. It even includes updated documentation on the 2016 presidential election.

The collection's scope encompasses many facets of U.S. history: political developments, social movements, Supreme Court rulings, conflicts, culture, etc. These topics are represented with reference entries, academic journal articles, videos, images, and audio files (e.g., NPR clips). Magazine and news articles and Websites are also included. The collection additionally contains a substantial amount of primary documents to serve the history researcher such as JFK's papers, excerpts from Thoreau's *Walden,* and the personal account of General Cornwallis's surrender at Yorktown.

For each topic in the collection, all of these different information formats are presented together on one page for a holistic view of the topic from a variety of viewpoints. This presentation approach creates information "command center." The authoritative data provided in the site. Teachers and librarians can use this database to make a compelling argument to students on why they should never use Wikipedia again. There are also tools to highlight, bookmark, share, and cite resources.

The resource can be searched by keyword or browsed by topic. There are so many topics to browse that a helpful filter for category is included (e.g., Government Documents; Political Constructs, Movements, and Organizations; Hispanic Americans, Economic, etc.). An advanced keyword search option allows users to combine keywords with article and/or publication title. Users can also limit their search to full-text or peer-reviewed journals, specify a desired document type (e.g., map, cover story, pamphlet, or video among many options), or content type (book, journal, experiments, Websites, etc.). Teachers will especially appreciate the ability to search by content level (beginner to advanced) and Lexile level. Educators will also appreciate the inclusion of curriculum standards.

The resource integrates with Google Drive and Google Classroom making it easy for both students and teachers to save documents to their own Google Drive. The ability to save to a central location is very useful. Any highlights and notes made in the database can be retained when the document is saved to Google Drive. Teachers have the added ability to save a document to their Google Classroom as an announcement or an assignment.

This is an excellent and fun resource. It is highly recommended for school and public libraries. It brings a fresh and engaging perspective to the study of American history and presents it in a way that is familiar and appealing to students. This will be a staple resource for both students and teachers.—**Kristin Kay Leeman**

256.   Walters, Kerry. **American Slave Revolts and Conspiracies: A Reference Guide.** Santa Barbara, Calif., ABC-CLIO, 2015. 259p. illus. index. $58.00. ISBN 13: 978-1-61069-659-3; 978-1-61069-660-9 (e-book).

The institution of slavery in America sought to control the bodies, intellects, and ambitions of enslaved Africans and their descendants. It also created anxiety in the minds of white slave owners, many of whom feared violence at the hands of their slaves as much as they relied on them to maintain their households, farms, and businesses.

In *American Slave Revolts and Conspiracies: A Reference Guide,* author Kerry Walters examines 11 slave rebellions that occurred (or were rumored to have occurred) from colonial times through to the Civil War. He highlights the differences and similarities between events and individuals, and the contrasts are fascinating. Some rebel leaders, like Nat Turner, appear to have been motivated by religious convictions; others seem to have entertained no grand notions beyond the desire to escape their circumstances. Denmark Vesey, a free person of color, forfeited his career, and ,ultimately, his life for planning a slave revolt; other conspirators may have formerly been trained warriors in their native lands. Slave insurrections invariably failed, even in areas where slaves constituted majorities. White communities in response blamed outside agitators and acted with indiscriminate violence, seemingly without regard to the facts of the situation.

The subject matter aside, *American Slave Revolts* is strangely organized. The annotated bibliography and primary documents sections are valuable, but the biographies section only contains profiles of white leaders. The analytical essays seem to merely summarize the main ideas of the book without introducing new ideas. Despite its shortcomings, *American Slave Revolts* offers an informative introduction to an often neglected aspect of American history.—**Craig Mury Keeney**

257. **WPA Posters. http://www.loc.gov/collections/works-progress-administration-posters/about-this-collection/.** [Website] Free. Date reviewed: 2016.

Under the New Deal beginning in 1936, thousands of out-of-work artists began creating posters for the Works Progress Administration; the WPA Posters Collection on the Library of Congress's Website includes more than 900 of these posters. The WPA posters were created for everything from theater productions, to national health campaigns, to travel and tourism ad campaigns. As a whole, the WPA posters provide a window into the 1930s-early 1940s United States, including the artistic styles of the time, what sorts of theater productions and recreational activities were popular (posters promoting reading and public libraries may be of particular interest to librarians), and what some of the major public health concerns were.

The site features a section of collection highlights (grouped into seven categories: Health and Safety, Cultural Programs, Travel and Tourism, Educational Programs, Community Activities, Federal Project Number One, and World War II); the Federal Art Project calendar, created to showcase the art being produced for the benefit of government officials; and an interview with Tony Velonis, a master silkscreen printer who worked on the posters.

The collection would benefit from the addition of essays discussing the WPA poster project or additional interviews with those involved in the project. However, even without additional context, the WPA posters are fascinating and often striking.

Each poster in the LOC collection is accompanied by basic information regarding the poster (where available; includes name of the artist, year the poster was produced, and program the poster was produced for), along with hi-resolution TIFFs and JPGs of the posters. Users can search the collection, and there are a number of filters for viewing subsets of the collection (e.g., Federal Theatre Project posters, posters from individual states).

The WPA poster collection is appropriate for all audiences, but those who are researching the 1930s or are interested in the history of the arts in the United States will find it particularly useful.—**ARBA Staff Reviewer**

African History

Côte d'Ivoire

258.   Daddieh, Cyril K. **Historical Dictionary of Côte D'lvoire.** 3d ed. Lanham, Md., Rowman & Littlefield, 2016. 633p. (Historical Dictionaries of Africa). $150.00; $149.99 (e-book). ISBN 13: 978-0-8108-7186-1; 978-0-8108-7389-6 (e-book).

This third edition of the *Historical Dictionary of Côte d'Ivoire* (the Ivory Coast) by Cyril K Daddieh is a major update of the first two editions by Robert J. Mundt—the second edition was published in 1995. Daddieh, born in Ghana and currently professor of political science and director of graduate studies at Miami University of Ohio, has written extensively on government and conflict in the Ivory Coast and has consulted for USAID on the postconflict situation in that country. This edition of the dictionary includes an 18-page list of acronyms and abbreviations, necessary in part because so many international actors and agencies have been involved in the Ivory Coast's sometimes chaotic history. The chronology spans the period from ca. 1300 C.E. to late December 2014. The introduction gives a general overview of the land and people of the Ivory Coast, followed by an outline of its history from the precolonial era. It includes a major section on the 1960-1993 period, when the Ivory Coast emerged from French rule and was governed by Félix Houphouët-Boigny, and deals with the two civil wars that followed in the 2000s. Three maps show the country in the context of its West African region, the ethnic distribution of its people, and the division of power during the first civil war. The dictionary entries are extensive, readable, and informative. A most helpful aspect of this edition is the bibliography of works in French and English, spanning over 100 pages. The bibliography includes sections on culture, economics, history, politics, sciences, anthropology, ethnology and sociology, and regional studies. The section on culture includes a listing of works on the 27 languages that are or have been spoken in the Ivory Coast. This book serves as a valuable resource for scholars, policy-makers, and general readers with an interest in the Ivory Coast.—**ARBA Staff Reviewer**

Asian History

China

259.   Jian, Guo, Yongyi Song, and Yuan Zhou. **Historical Dictionary of the Chinese Cultural Revolution.** 2d ed. Lanham, Md., Rowman & Littlefield, 2015. 507p. illus. maps. (Historical Dictionaries of War, Revolution, and Civil Unrest). $130.00. ISBN 13: 978-1-4422-5171-7; 978-1-4422-5172-4 (e-book).

The Great Proletarian Cultural Revolution is a significant event in the history of the People's Republic of China. Lasting from 1966 to 1976 the movement severely disrupted millions of lives and radically changed the Chinese economy, society, and culture. It was a period of great confusion that necessitates the systematic collection and compilation of historical information such as the work under review. Armed with firsthand experience, the editors completed the first edition of the *Historical Dictionary* in 2006, followed by a paperback edition retitled *The A to Z of the Chinese Cultural Revolution* in 2009. The format of this new second edition follows the first edition closely, with main sections consisting of a chronology, an introduction, the dictionary, a glossary, and a bibliography. The excellent introduction highlights major events and includes an assessment of the legacy of the Cultural Revolution. The main body of the dictionary contains over 400 cross-referenced entries on key individuals, organizations, politics, economy, social issues, religion, and culture. A useful, bilingual glossary and an extensive 91-page bibliography complete the volume. There are no significant changes from the first edition except adding a couple dozen entries such as Xi Jinping and Bo Xilai, and making some corrections. As an alphabetically arranged dictionary, the book offers no index as a finding aid, which may present a challenge to users. The dictionary can be used alongside *The Cultural Revolution Database*. Recommended for reference collections.—**Karen T. Wei**

Japan

260.　Shimamoto, Mayako, Koji Ito, and Yoneyuki Sugita. **Historical Dictionary of Japanese Foreign Policy.** Lanham, Md., Rowman & Littlefield, 2015. 385p. (Historical Dictionaries of Diplomacy and Foreign Relations). $125.00. ISBN 13: 978-1-4422-5068-0; 978-1-4422-5067-3 (e-book).

Three Japanese scholars, all affiliated with Osaka University, have produced a quite useful work that covers the entire period of Japanese diplomatic and foreign relations. To accommodate its primary target audience, names are written according to Western rather than Asian practice, and all sources are exclusively English. Emphasis is on Japanese relations with the United States and Asia with lesser attention to the rest of the world. The volume begins with a quite complete chronology from the end of the centuries of Japanese national exclusion (by the 1854 Kanagawa Treaty with the United States) through 2014. A lengthy essay on Japanese foreign relations, broken down by periods, follows.

The bulk of the volume consists of several hundred alphabetically arranged entries on significant people, places, events, institutions, conferences, and statements that cover the entire range of Japan's interaction with the world. Bold-faced items within an essay indicate those that have their own entry, which makes cross-referencing convenient. *See also* references at the end of an entry provides supplemental references.

Other features include a lengthy list of acronyms and abbreviations; Japanese prime ministers, foreign ministers, and vice foreign ministers with their dates of service; and a very good bibliography arranged by time period.

In sum, this is a good addition for libraries that need such a reference.—**Joe P. Dunn**

Canadian History

Handbooks and Yearbooks

261.　**Canadian National Digital Heritage Index. http://cndhi-ipnpc.ca/.** [Website] Free. Date reviewed: 2016.

Canadian National Digital Heritage Index (CNDHI) is an index of digitized collections from universities and provincial and territorial libraries across Canada. Produced by the Canadian Research Knowledge Network with funding from Library and Archives Canada's Documentary Heritage Community Program, the CNDHI seeks to provide a tool for librarians and members of the public for finding and accessing digitized collections, both to promote awareness and use of these collections among researchers and to foster collaborative digitization efforts among librarians and archivists.

The main page of the site allows the user to search for collections by keyword, collection title, hosting institution, collection description, original language, and media type. There is no browse option. Search results can be viewed in a list, on a map, or downloaded in .csv format. Each entry includes a URL linking to the collection, a brief description, and collection contact information. Hyperlinked media type, language, and keyword fields facilitate finding similar items in the index. The search function is not as intuitive as it could be and would benefit from more explanatory text; for example, "diaries" in the main search box retrieves one result while the same search under format retrieves seven (and keyword retrieves zero). Users will also want to be aware that not all of the collections indexed are publicly available. Overall, however, this is a useful resource for those interested in finding online collections related to Canada's history and heritage.—**ARBA Staff Reviewer**

European History

General Works

Dictionaries and Encyclopedias

262.   Ermatinger, James W. **The World of Ancient Rome: A Daily Life Encyclopedia.** Santa Barbara, Calif., Greenwood Press/ABC-CLIO, 2015. 2v. illus. index. $189.00/set. ISBN 13: 978-1-4408-2907-9; 978-1-4408-2908-6 (e-book).

James W. Ermatinger, Dean of the College of Liberal Arts and Sciences and professor of history at the University of Illinois, Springfield, has devoted his career to Ancient Rome, as evidenced in the detailed information in these encyclopedias.

The World of Ancient Rome: A Daily Life Encyclopedia is a two-volume set with 864 pages in total, available in hard copy or e-book format. Following a preface, the table of contents is extensive and reads somewhat like an index, albeit in order by chapters. A chronology placed near the beginning of the book illustrates the timeline of important events in Roman history; the early placement of this listing in volume one is logical for those wanting to understand the timing of ancient happenings. Found at the end of volume two, there is a helpful bibliography of print and nonprint information resources for further research, and a more-than-suitable index. The subject index (p. 765) is an excellent access point to topics whether a common topic like Cleopatra or an elusive subtopic, such as florists or naming children. Because of the great indexing, topics from the minor to those of a larger scope are easily found.

These volumes on life in Ancient Rome primarily cover the period of greatest transformation, the Republican period (509-31 B.C.E.), with some entries from the Monarchy and Empire periods. There are 10 chapters that begin with an introduction and then address areas of daily life in this ever-changing society. Organization of information is excellent with each chapter having subtopics in alphabetical order. There are 24-27 entries for each chapter and each includes *see also* references and further reading suggestions. Black-and-white photos are ineffective but break up the text and are well captioned.

There are 11 primary documents along with other literary sources and archaeological information to bring together evidence of how this society lived. Focusing on the lives of everyday people in Ancient Rome, these texts also examine life of all social orders: slaves, rural peasants, urban poor, middle-class merchants, and aristocratic leaders. Entries allow researchers to understand the influence these citizens had on modern society.

Ermatinger has done an exceptional job in pulling together valuable and interesting research on the culture of Ancient Rome. In true encyclopedia fashion, the volumes and topics are easily accessible and the *see also* segment and bibliography lead students to more information. *The World of Ancient Rome: A Daily Life Encyclopedia* is a superior reference tool for high school and college students studying world history, Roman civilization, or how the people of Rome influenced modern life. General readers who are interested in ancient history will also find these volumes very useful.

Highly Recommended.—**Janis Minshull**

Handbooks and Yearbooks

263.   **United States Holocaust Memorial Museum. http://www.ushmm.org/.** [Website] Free. Date reviewed: 2015.

The United States Holocaust Memorial Museum offers a superb guide to scholars, students, teachers, genealogists, and the general public. This online resource fosters interest and understanding in the complex history of the Holocaust.

The clean and well-organized layout of the site allows for easy navigation and users can easily access hundreds of relevant articles with a simple search. The United States Holocaust Memorial Museum site is free to use and contains over 250,000 records in the Collections Search alone. Archival and primary source images are scanned and accessible to the public, providing information on people and historic events relating to the Holocaust.

At present, the site offers public access to over 35,000 images, a number that grows every year as the museum collects and publishes new information. Additional types of media available include art, audio and video interviews, three-dimensional objects, and works on paper. The *Holocaust Encyclopedia* resources are available in 14 different languages.

Videos from Holocaust survivors are particularly informative and provide a firsthand account of the Holocaust atrocities. To clarify or elaborate on information, users can view original documents written during World War II, access timelines, and even map the Holocaust via Google Earth to gain geographical knowledge of the concentration camps, battles, and important events. The museum provides documentation of events immediately following World War I through the closing of the displaced persons camps in the mid-1950s in order to maximize the historical context for the public.

This site is a perfect resource for students who are studying the Holocaust, and particularly for teachers who may struggle to find the best approach in teaching this complicated subject matter. An entire page is dedicated to resources for educators, providing worksheets, lesson plans, and tips on discussing the Holocaust with students.

Not only does the site offer a wealth of information for those seeking to learn more about World War II and the Holocaust, but the compelling stories and resources will undoubtedly encourage the public to visit the museum to witness artifacts and documents of the Holocaust in person.

The United States Holocaust Memorial Museum is a highly recommended reference source.—**ARBA Staff Reviewer**

264.   **Yad Vashem. http://www.yadvashem.org/.** [Website] Free. Date reviewed: 2016.

Yad Vashem (http://www.yadvashem.org/) has committed itself to the remembrance of the Holocaust through commemoration, documentation, research, and education. As part of this mission, they maintain a large collection of primary material, from oral histories to photo archives to primary document collections. In addition, they provide educational materials and exhibits to aid in interpreting the primary sources.

Whether trying to trace one person's story, or looking for an overview of the period, Yad Vashem's Website and digital archives can assist any student, researcher, or librarian. The collections include almost 180 million pages of documentation, including over 125,000 survivor testimonies (written, audiotaped, and videotaped), over 450,000 photographs, and over 2.7 million "pages of testimony" filled out by survivors, friends, and relatives of those who died. A section of the Website honors the "Righteous Among the Nations"—those who aided Jewish resistance.

The educational materials cover topics such as The Nazi Rise to Power, Jewish Resistance, and Antisemitism. The Website also provides a detailed chronology, glossary, and FAQs to aid in research. Teachers can access lesson plans, teacher's guides, sample ceremonies, and other educational resources.

Yad Vashem also offers conferences, seminars, online courses, publications, and other professional development materials. Use of this Website may inspire a trip to the Holocaust History Museum complex maintained in Jerusalem.

This site encourages users to delve into a wealth of information and witness the Holocaust through the eyes of historical and contemporary materials. Yad Vashem is a highly recommended reference source.—**ARBA Staff Reviewer**

Armenia

265.   **The Armenian Genocide: The Essential Reference Guide.** Alan Whitehorn, ed. Santa Barbara, Calif., ABC-CLIO, 2015. 425p. illus. maps. index. $89.00. ISBN 13: 978-1-61069-687-6; 978-1-61069-688-3 (e-book).

This is an extensive and valuable one-volume encyclopedia concerning the Armenian Genocide, published on the 100th anniversary of this atrocity. As noted in the preface, this is the first encyclopedia exclusively focused on this event. The overall structure of the book is concise and easy to follow. The editor Alan Whitehorn penned the seven introductory essays. These are two to four pages in length and look broadly at the genocide, featuring topics such as consequences, causes, and victims. They provide a helpful overarching view of the genocide. The main entries are all signed with short bibliographies. There are 23 primary sources, many of them coming from the British collection of documents *The Treatment of Armenians of Ottoman Empire, 1915-1916*, although there are also newspaper accounts and other letters. These documents serve as a useful gateway into studying the genocide. Of note is the relatively small, thought-provoking appendix that examines historical dilemmas surrounding the study of the Armenian Genocide, such as why it is not formally recognized by the United States, Israel, or the United Nations. A comprehensive bibliography and timeline round out this work. Well-sourced, concise, and clear, this is an immensely valuable work for understanding the Armenian Genocide. Highly recommended.—**Allen Reichert**

Belgium

266. State, Paul F. **Historical Dictionary of Brussels.** 2d ed. Lanham, Md., Rowman & Littlefield, 2015. 553p. illus. (Historical Dictionaries of Cities, States, and Regions). $130.00; $129.99 (e-book). ISBN 13: 978-0-8108-7920-1; 978-0-8108-7921-8 (e-book).

According to the compiler, even though Brussels serves as the headquarters of NATO and is located at the crossroads of major European influences, little is known about this small, but important city. The main text is an alphabetical listing of such things as place-names (in both French and Dutch), people, historical and political events, common expressions, etc. A brief note to the reader is followed by a list of abbreviations and acronyms, an extensive chronology, and a few simple maps. The introduction gives an overview of the history of Brussels and the text is enhanced with a system of cross-references. Although there are some interesting black-and-white illustrations, the quality is not very good. The presentation is wide-ranging, but the writing for the entries is sometimes awkward and could use some more editing. Sometimes the information presented is confusing—e.g., the entry on Notre-Dame de Laeken states that the church was never completed, although various Websites suggest that it was completed in either 1907 or 1909. The six appendixes are helpful and the bibliography (mostly French and Dutch sources) is extensive. This source would probably be most useful as a starting place for further research.—**Martha Lawler**

Chechnia (Russia)

267. Askerov, Ali. **Historical Dictionary of the Chechen Conflict.** Lanham, Md., Rowman & Littlefield, 2015. 285p. maps. (Historical Dictionaries of War, Revolution, and Civil Unrest). $95.00; $94.99 (e-book). ISBN 13: 978-1-4422-4924-0; 978-1-4422-4925-7 (e-book).

This work is a specialized resource for anyone reading about the war in Chechnya, and who needs to identify individuals, places, or episodes and set them in context. While many of the names found here appear in Wikipedia, entries in this source are more detailed, authoritative, and discoverable. The author is an academic expert on the topic, who has sought to report objectively on a conflict in which the same figure can be "a hero or freedom fighter for Chechnya, a terrorist for Russian officials." This is a volume in the series Historical Dictionaries of War, Revolution, and Civil Unrest.

Some 570 articles in alphabetical order vary in length from a few lines to a few pages: the longest, at six pages, covers "Separatist Tendencies in Russia" in the 1990s. Over half of the entries are short biographies of figures from the wars, especially on the Chechen side: rebel leaders, government ministers, military and police officers, victims of assassinations, human rights workers, and war correspondents. A significant number of entries describe specific battles, raids, or terrorist attacks. Related material ranges from the ethnic nationalities of the Caucasus, to the origin of friction in the eighteenth century, to the Chechen background of the 2013 Boston Marathon bombers.

The introduction is a history of the long conflict between those seeking Chechen independence and the rulers of the Russian Empire, followed by the Soviet Union, and now by the Russian Federation. Supporting material includes a chronology from 1567 to 2015 that strongly emphasizes the era since 1994, two small maps, a key to acronyms, texts of two cease-fire agreements, a list of presidents of the Chechen Republic during the 1990s, and a 20-page bibliography listing books, articles, films, and Websites. There are cross-references, but no index: keywords of course can be searched in e-book versions of the text.—**Steven W. Sowards**

Great Britain

268.   Bennett, Martyn. **Historical Dictionary of the British and Irish Civil Wars, 1637-1660.** 2d ed. Lanham, Md., Rowman & Littlefield, 2016. 321p. (Historical Dictionaries of War, Revolution, and Civil Unrest). $100.00; $99.99 (e-book). ISBN 13: 978-1-4722-6264-5; 978-1-4422-6264-5 (e-book).

This second edition of *The Historical Dictionary of the British and Irish Civil Wars 1637-1660* (see ARBA, entry 437) covers a complex war involving England, Scotland, Ireland, and Wales between King Charles I's unsuccessful attempt to bring the Scottish Protestant church in line with the Anglican form of worship in 1637 through a time of turbulence and parliamentarian government to the restoration of the monarchy in 1660. The dictionary section in this edition, comprising over 1,000 entries, has been significantly expanded from the first edition. The chronology at the front of the book provides a succinct history of the events under discussion. An introductory article by author Martyn Bennett, professor of early modern history at Nottingham Trent University, describes the rebellions against King Charles's religious policies in the four countries and the wars leading to the establishment and ultimate failure of the republic. Bennett, a leading specialist on the civil wars in the British Isles whose publications include several books on the British civil wars as well as a biography of Oliver Cromwell, provides a wealth of detail on the political, religious, and societal situation in all four regions, with a special emphasis on battles. The bibliography is divided into sections on printed primary sources for 1637-1660; general background texts on the four nations; political and religious histories of the civil war and the republican period; military history; and local studies. Unlike the first edition, this edition does not contain a map with battle sites and dates. This book would serve as a helpful reference for readers with a good general knowledge of the period wanting more information on specific events.—**ARBA Staff Reviewer**

269.   **Churchill Archive. http://www.churchillarchive.com/.** [Website] New York, Bloomsbury Academic. Price negotiated by site. Date reviewed: 2016.

First published in 2012 in collaboration with the Churchill Archives Centre, this massive digital collection contains more than 800,000 pages of original documents produced between 1874 and 1965, including personal and official correspondence, speeches, photographs, telegrams, manuscripts, and government transcripts. This archive can be used by everyone from interested members of the general public to high school students to seasoned researchers in history, politics, international affairs, military affairs, public speaking, and more. The site includes a wealth of education resources including specially commissioned essays and overviews of key topics linked to the appropriate files and documents. For secondary students and teachers, the Churchill Archive has resources based on four themes: key developments in modern British and empire history; key developments in modern world history; Anglo-American relations in the twentieth century; and, Churchill: discussion, debate and controversy. Six to eight documents from the archive accompany these themes along with interpretive data designed to help students truly understand the topic. For teachers, there are additional resources and guidance and advice about such things as getting students to care about modern history. This schools section is available free of charge via registration on the Website through the end of December 2020.

Various search tools make for easy navigation: the catalog can be browsed by topic, place, period, or people. There is also a quick search on each page and a more advanced search function. Moreover, users can easily print articles, export citations, access reading lists and bibliographies, view online exhibitions, and take advantage of special features like Action this Day. Librarians can download for free MARC records and utilize the site's technical support.

To be sure, much Churchill-related material is available on the Web—for example, browsers can find some of what they are looking for at the Churchill Archives Centre (https://www.chu.cam.ac.uk/archives/), but the completeness, functionality, search capabilities, and resources offered through this site make it highly recommended for libraries that can afford the purchase price.—**ARBA Staff Reviewer**

270.   **Foreign Office Files for the Middle East 1971-1974. http://www.amdigital. co.uk/m-collections/collection/foreign-office-files-for-the-middle-east-1971-1981/.** [Website] Chicago, Adam Matthew Digital. Price negotiated by site. Date reviewed: 2016.

Foreign Office Files for the Middle East 1971-1974 brings together files from the U.K. Foreign Office, Prime Minister's Office, and the Ministry of Defence and makes them available through an enhanced online portal. The collection covers a pivotal time period in a volatile part of the world and can shed light on the "policies, economies, political relationships and significant events of every major Middle East power." Major historical events such as the Arab-Israeli War, Qaddafi's regime in Libya, the Iranian Revolution, and the economic situation in Kuwait are documented through diplomatic correspondence, meeting minutes, reports, political summaries, and economic analyses.

This review covers Module 1: Middle East, 1971-1974: The 1973 Arab-Israeli War and the Oil Crisis. (The full resource is split into three modules, and the remaining modules will be released over the course of the next two years.) Module 1 documents the political situation in the Middle East in the build-up to the Arab-Israeli War and the related political, social, military, and economic impacts of the conflict.

Given the source of the materials, the collection naturally has a U.K. perspective and reveals the country's heavily vested interest in all facets of the Middle East during this time period. Not only was the U.K. involved in monitoring political and military activities, they also carefully assessed the economic impacts of Middle Eastern conflict, especially on oil prices. Additionally, they were influential in negotiating peace settlements. The military interventions and peace negotiations conducted by the United States and Russia are also represented.

Access to the collection is organized by tabs: Documents, Essays, Chronology, Popular Searches, and an Interactive World Map. The documents can be searched by simple or advanced keyword search, or they can also be browsed by date, collection, department, region/office. The Popular Searches option provides a starting point for users by providing the top 10 keywords most selected by users. The Interactive World map allows users to click a country and explore relevant content. The Chronology tab is an informative list of people and events through time. It can be searched by keyword, but it is not interactive in the sense that entries are linked to documents in the collection. This would be a nice feature. The Essays tab provides writings by leading scholars in the subject field. Helpfully, the essays are peppered with hyperlinks to relevant documents in the collection providing a nice demonstration of how the collection can be used. Users can save searches, documents, and images, and documents can also be downloaded as PDF files.

This resource is recommended for anyone interested in studying the development of the Middle East from the perspective of the people and offices that shaped and witnessed events first hand. It is a very unique primary resource tool that will be especially useful for serious scholars and teachers, but the enhancements and easy-to-use interface also make it suitable for novice students.—**Kristin Kay Leeman**

271.   **Richard III Society, American Branch. http://www.r3.org/).** [Website] Free. Date reviewed: 2016.

The Richard III Society was founded in England in 1924 as the Fellowship of the White Boar and took its current title in 1959. Today, branches of the Society are found in various countries worldwide, with the total membership of all branches put at about 4,000. The American Branch of the Society was founded in 1961 and today claims a membership of almost 400. The Society is dedicated to promoting study of the life and career of King Richard III, the history of the Wars of the Roses, and the history and culture of fifteenth-century England. The Society is also committed to securing a reassessment of the reputation of Richard III as he is portrayed in modern print and electronic media. Besides its primary audience of professional scholars and amateur enthusiasts who reject the traditional view of Richard III as a tyrant and child murderer, the site offers much to high school and college students and others interested in fifteenth-century English history.

The Website sponsored by the American Branch is maintained by volunteers. Portions of the site are password protected and restricted to members only, but the main links to news and information on Richard III and the Society itself are open to all. Links lead users to a wealth of current print and online scholarship regarding Richard III and life in fifteenth-century England. The Richard III link offers a detailed biography of the king and timeline of his life; a list of the 10 most common changes leveled at Richard and rebuttals for each; articles and bibliographies providing information on life in the fifteenth century; information on traveling to sites in England associated with Richard; and information on images of Richard. Of use to students and researchers is the Online Library Text and Essays link, which provides guidance for students on conducting research into the period and excerpts from various important primary documents (e.g., Crowland Chronicle, Cely

Papers) and well-known modern studies (e.g., "The History of Richard III" from Richard Marius' 1984 biography of Thomas More). The Ricardian and Medieval Fiction link lists novels, movies, and television programs on Richard and late medieval England. Also available are recent issues of the Society newsletter, the "Ricardian Chronicle" and news and notes about recent Society events, free online classes provided by various universities, and important stories relating to Richard III, most spectacularly, the discovery of his remains in a Leicester car park in 2012.

The most useful aspect of the American Branch site is the many links it provides to other sources of information, such as Websites for archaeological survey projects at various Wars of the Roses battlefields, including Bosworth Field; Websites of various other related organizations, such as the Heraldry Society; and various medieval and renaissance studies organizations and primary document Websites, such as the Internet Medieval Sourcebook and the Centre for Medieval Studies at the University of York. Although users must always remember that the Richard III Society seeks to promote a particular view of the king, and should view the information provided on the king himself in this context, they will find much current and accurate information on this site covering the broader topics of the Wars of the Roses and life in late-fifteenth-century England. Probably because the site is maintained by volunteers, some links have not been updated—there were, for instance, still notices in early 2016 for trips and events that occurred in late 2015, though this problem relates mainly to Society and other events. More troubling is the occasional broken link, such as that for the Richard III and Yorkist History Trust, which prevents access to some of the information. A must for users who share the Society's view of Richard III, the American Brach site is also recommended for those studying or interested in the Wars of the Roses or the history and culture of late medieval England.—**ARBA Staff Reviewer**

272.   **Tudorhistory.org http://tudorhistory.org/.** [Website] Free. Date reviewed: 2016.

Residing at this domain name since 2000, *Tudorhistory.org* is produced and maintained by Laura E. Eakins; the site is not affiliated with any university, organization, or company. The site, which Eakins began in the 1990s under the name *Tudor England,* was originally intended simply as a vehicle for Eakins to share her passion for Tudor history with like-minded individuals. However, Eakins soon discovered that a growing portion of her audience was school children who turned to the site for help with classroom projects. As a result, *Tudorhistory.org* has in recent years become more focused on meeting the needs of student users, particularly elementary and junior high students. To this end, Eakins has kept the content basic and wide ranging, not focusing in-depth on any one aspect of the period, but providing a good introduction to Tudor history as a whole. For those interested in more in-depth information on Tudor fashion, food, music, literature, etc., Eakins supplies lists of useful sites on many such topics under Links to Other Sites of Interest.

The site is simple and straightforward, opening with 20 links to broad themes and topics and to useful features for research and study, such as Tudor Monarchs; The Six Wives of Henry VIII, Topics in Tudor History, Chronologies of People and Events, Texts and Documents, Glossaries of Words and Terms, Reference Maps, and Image Gallery. The biographies of the Tudor monarchs and of Henry VIII's queens provide life dates, accession and coronation dates, and burial dates and sites. The biographical information is very basic, averaging perhaps 300-500 words, and, in some cases (e.g., Henry VIII himself), provides information on only a portion of the individual's life, something that appears the understandable result of one person attempting to maintain a large site in her spare time.

The Who's Who in Tudor History link leads to an impressive array of individuals, and, though most offer only very brief descriptions, e.g., "Physician of Henry VIII" for William Butts, most biographies also include images of the individual. Although often spare, the information in the biographical links is accurate and useful for the envisioned student audience.

The other research links also reflect the site's student audience. Texts and Documents contains about 20 items, which focus heavily on execution accounts and speeches, such as a description of Anne Boleyn's death and Edward Hall's version of her last words. The Reference Maps link offers thumbnails of seven historical and modern maps, information on their source repositories, and, in some cases, links to high resolution versions. The Images Gallery provides thumbnails of known images of many individuals, including such unusual renderings as the wax figure of Anne of Cleves at Madame Tussaud's in London. This link could be useful for more advanced students seeking particular Tudor images and their source repositories. The Movies and Television link has an extensive list of movies and television programs with Tudor settings, from the 1913 French silent film *Anne de Boleyn* to the 2007-2010 Showtime series *The Tudors,* though each individual link only sends the user to the *Internet Movie Database* (http://www.imbd.com) description of the work. In short, though there is little here for advanced students or those undertaking more detailed research, the site's target audience—pre-high school students who are just seeking a sound basic introduction to the subject—will be well served by *Tudorhistory.org* and the site is recommended for their use.—**ARBA Staff Reviewer**

273.   **Voices of Victorian England: Contemporary Accounts of Daily Life.** John A. Wagner, ed. Santa Barbara, Calif., ABC-CLIO, 2014. 298p. index. (Voices of an Era). $79.00. ISBN 13: 978-0-313-38688-6; 978-0-313-38689-3 (e-book).

An age of empire building, industrialization, and considerable scientific achievement, the Victorian Era encapsulated England at its boldest. This title from the fine Voices of an Era series presents a diverse array of primary source documents which serve to present a compelling portrait of a nation at the forefront of huge change.

Eight sections draw these documents together into themes such as Society and Economy, Religion and Science, and Empire and War. Within these sections readers find a generous selection of personal letters, scholarly papers, literary excerpts, first-hand news accounts, speeches, petitions, and more. Here we have actual excerpts from the Reform Act of 1867, which extended the vote to more of the male population, George Eliot's pointed and popular novel *Middlemarch,* a journalist's front-line account of a battle from the Crimean War, and many other varied and fascinating examples. Such intimate access—"My *life* as a *happy* one is ended! The world is gone for *me!*" exclaims the devastated Queen Victoria in a letter upon the death of her husband Albert—lends a genuine authenticity and very real effect of transporting readers to the bygone era.

The documents are enhanced by a generous number of contextual aides, including helpful information on how best to examine primary source documents. A chronology precedes these documents and notes the many key events occurring through the breadth of the Victorian era, from the future queen's birth in 1819 to her death in 1901 after a reign of 64 years. Additional tools highlight background information, important vocabulary, notable figures, and other resources for further information. Appendixes provide short biographies of other important people featured in the texts, a glossary, and a chart presenting the governing ministries working alongside the Queen during this remarkable era. An index rounds out the work.

This well-structured, expansive and engaging work would be a valuable resource for any student of history or Victorian society. Recommended for high school and academic libraries.—**Laura Herrell**

Russia

274. **Gulag: Many Days, Many Lives. http://gulaghistory.org/.** [Website] Free. Date reviewed: 2016.

Gulag: Many Days, Many Lives is an extensive study of the brutal system of forced labor camps in the Soviet Union endured by millions. Produced by the Roy Rosenzweig Center for History and New Media at George Mason University in association with the Gulag Museum at Perm-36 and the International Memorial Society in Moscow, the site features exhibits, archives, and resources. Funding came from several sources: The National Endowment for the Humanities, the Kennan Institute, and the Davis Center for Russian and Eurasian Studies at Harvard.

The home page of the site has links to the archives, exhibits, and resources in the upper-right-hand corner. Under the Archives link, users will find documents, photographs, art, and more. These can be browsed sequentially or by tag. A click on the Exhibits link directs users to the traveling exhibit produced by a partnership between the National Parks Service and the Gulag Museum of Perm. Called *Gulag: Soviet Labor Camps and the Struggle for Freedom,* this exhibit portrays life in Perm-36, a forced labor camp in the Ural Mountains. The exhibit recounts in vivid and painful detail conditions in the Gulag and the political system that put people there. The Resources link allows users to access an amazing bounty of material, including curriculum aimed at middle-and high-school students, a bibliography, and scholarly commentary on the Gulag system via sublinks. Under Teacher Resources users will find a downloadable curriculum entitled "GULAG: Soviet Prison Camps and Their Legacy," a Harvard-developed, three-day curriculum designed to accompany the traveling exhibition. Focusing on daily life in the camps, the Gulag system, and the legacy of the Gulag, the curriculum includes first-person accounts and artwork along with class assignments and homework. "Episodes in Gulag History'" presents conversations with scholars about the Gulag system and its legacy.

Highly recommended.—**ARBA Staff Reviewer**

275. **Russia at War: From the Mongol Conquest to Afghanistan, Chechnya, and Beyond.** Timothy C. Dowling, ed. Santa Barbara, Calif., ABC-CLIO, 2015. 2v. $189.00/ set. ISBN 13: 978-1-59884-947-9; 978-1-59884-948-6 (e-book).

This two-volume resource on the history of the Russian military from the Mongol Conquest to recent times is a gem. An important resource for understanding and interpreting the martial past and present of the Soviet Union/Russia is presented in the foreword by the editor, who provides the necessary background and deconstruction of the complex and sometimes strange behaviors of military cultures. Each entry consists of a detailed essay on the topic, with *see also* references and a further reading section. The entries are provided alphabetically, and are also listed in a guide to related topics where they are divided into individuals; events; ideas, movements, and policies; organizations; places; objects, artifacts, and weapons; treaties, acts, and other written materials; and other. Volume two includes a chronology at the end of the book, which is extremely helpful in providing an overview of Russian military history from 862 to 2014. Overall, this reference set would be an important addition on this topic in any academic library.—**Bradford Lee Eden**

276.   Smele, Jonathan D. **Historical Dictionary of the Russian Civil Wars, 1916-1926.** Lanham, Md., Rowman & Littlefield, 2015. 2v. (Historical Dictionaries of War, Revolution, and Civil Unrest). $250.00/set; $249.99 (e-book). ISBN 13: 978-1-4422-5280-6; 978-1-4422-5281-3 (e-book).

This two-volume work was compiled by Jonathan D. Smele, a scholar of Russian history who has focused his career on the civil wars. As part of the Rowman & Littlefield Historical Dictionary series, it is ostensibly written for high school and college students. While that audience does benefit, it also is a valuable addition to Russian scholars and specialists. Of particular note is the comprehensive, historiographic, 60-page essay which introduces this work. This essay details why this work incorporates a longer time frame in which to consider the civil wars and how the wars are more than just the Reds versus the Whites. Indeed, one of the key inclusions is the look at nationalist movements from the periphery of the Russian empire, such as in Latvia and Turkestan. The bulk of *Russian Civil Wars* is made up of 2,000 dictionary entries. These entries include bolded words to other entries. The extensive bibliography is broken out by region and broad subject areas and includes resources in English, Russian, or German. There is a chronology of events, and a few appendixes detailing the various governing institutions from this time. There are no images, including, unfortunately, no maps. The price may also be an impediment for some institutions. Recommended, highly so, for any libraries actively collecting in Russian history.—**Allen Reichert**

Latin America and the Caribbean

Dictionaries and Encyclopedias

277.   **Iconic Mexico: An Encyclopedia from Acapulco to Zócalo.** Eric Zolov, ed. Santa Barbara, Calif., ABC-CLIO, 2015. 2v. illus. index. $189.00/set. ISBN 13: 978-1-61069-043-0; 978-1-61069-044-7 (e-book).

If ever there were a need for an encyclopedia of Mexico aimed at a general audience, from high schools to public libraries, it is now. Obviously, electoral campaigns produce little serious analysis, but most honest observers agree that our relations with Mexico are in serious jeopardy. The reasons bear no repeating: everyone has heard too much nonsense about the country and its people.

Going to the Internet for help is hit and miss, because, honestly, the wisdom of crowds is not always apparent. Better an experienced guide and a number of tutored, if not quite impartial, sources to lead people to somewhere worth going. That is what makes these two volumes very worthwhile. My copy of the *Shorter Oxford English Dictionary* defines an icon as "a person or thing regarded as a representative symbol of a culture, movement, etc.," and that is a good description of what this encyclopedia provides. It is a compilation of 100 "iconic" Mexican persons, places, things, or events that open a window to the country's wider culture and history. It includes famous historical personages, well-known authors, material artifacts, rock groups, and events of really transcendent importance in the shaping of contemporary Mexico. The editor, Eric Zolov, is a respected historian, and while the limits of space make leaving a good deal aside, one can make the case that this encyclopedia is a reasonable starting point. For one thing, the entries are, for the most part, clearly and engagingly written and avoid that bane of good literature, academese. They are also accessible without being oversimplified, and cover a broad spectrum of obvious and not-so-obvious starting points for the interested reader. Each entry has a sidebar or, in some cases, the translation of a historical text as a supplement. Where photos are helpful, there are photos. There is a timeline, a bibliography of English-language works, and an index that runs to 50 pages. In addition, each entry has its own bibliography, and these are good guides to further enlightenment.

Some of the entries dealing with popular culture are especially entertaining. "Acapulco" leads off ("Zócalo" for the record, concludes), and I was happy to find a reference to Frank Sinatra's "Come Fly With Me" prominently featured as a quintessential 1950s plug for that still lovely, if not untroubled, city. There is a very nice discussion of the celebrated author Elena Poniatowska that prompted me to go out and buy one of her books that I had neglected to read. Essays on Father Las Casas and Antonio López de Santa Anna may not break any new historical ground, but they are accurate, although trying to say something nice about Santa Anna is akin to washing dirt: it can't be done. There is a good piece, well considered, on the significance of the earthquake of 1985 in Mexico City that was every bit as important as the author maintains. While I tend to think of the Mexican art form "papel picado" as bigger in San Antonio, Texas, than in Mexico City, I guess I will have to look more closely in the future. Omitting the Mexican political singer Oscar Chávez in favor of El Tri is generationally defensible—or a matter of taste. The entry on the Niños Héroes monument in Mexico City is actually pretty courageous, because calling the story of the military cadets in the War of 1847 a myth can still get you in trouble there. I went and looked up Truman's visit to it (mentioned in the entry) on You Tube as a result. That's a pretty good recommendation for an encyclopedia entry.

These volumes are well done and well worth the price. I recommend them to anyone interested in Mexico, because, literally, there is something for everyone, even long-time students of the country and its history.—**Richard Salvucci**

Middle Eastern History

Egypt

278.   **Voices of Ancient Egypt: Contemporary Accounts of Daily Life.** Rosalie David, ed. Santa Barbara, Calif., Greenwood Press/ABC-CLIO, 2014. 269p. (Voices of an Era). $79.00. ISBN 13: 978-0-313-39782-0; 978-0-313-39783-7 (e-book).

Voices of Ancient Egypt: Contemporary Accounts of Ancient Life paints a picture of life in Ancient Egypt as told by actual Ancient Egyptians. The book is based on 51 primary source documents spanning 3,500 years of Ancient Egyptian history. *Voices* presents translated excerpts from these documents and organizes them into seven categories addressing the full spectrum of daily life from domestic life and personal beliefs to intellectual life and recreational life. Specific topics include "How a Man Should Treat his Wife," "Behavior towards Superiors, Equals, and Inferiors," and "Worship through Dancing." The end result is a very multidisciplinary work of potential application in history, art history, economics, politics, anthropology, etc.

Each chapter includes an introduction, a translated excerpt from an historical document, and a "Further Information" section. Also included in each chapter are several sections designed to place the document in historical context and guide the reader to better understanding. These sections include "Keep in Mind as you Read," "Post-summary," "Aftermath," "Ask Yourself," and "Topics and Activities to Consider."

The book begins with an informative and thorough introduction that serves to orient the reader not only to Ancient Egypt and how its history is organized but also to the purpose and scope of the book. Also included after the introduction is a chronology of the history of Ancient Egypt and biological sketches of the major individuals.

This is a fascinating, thoroughly researched, and well-presented book. The writing and substance are at once academic yet very accessible for every level of scholar and reader. The selected excerpts represent authors not likely to be well known beyond serious Egyptian scholars, but David does readers a great service by introducing them through this book. David provides details to satisfy an advanced Egyptologist and enough "lay" explanation to enlighten a novice. Great effort is made to place the facts in not only Egyptian history, but also to connect the ideas to general ancient history and draw parallels with modern history.

This book is highly recommended for both academic and public libraries (especially public libraries serving teachers). It is especially recommended for anyone who wants to teach ancient Egypt or use primary documents in historical research. It is also recommended for students of history as a model for reading, interpreting, and using primary source materials.—**Kristin Kay Leeman**

Oceania

Fiji

279.   Lal, Brij V. **Historical Dictionary of Fiji.** Lanham, Md., Rowman & Littlefield, 2016. 293p. (Historical Dictionaries of Asia, Oceania, and the Middle East). $90.00; $89.99 (e-book). ISBN 13: 978-0-8108-7901-0; 978-0-8108-7902-7 (e-book).

This addition to Rowman and Littlefield's series of Historical Dictionaries of Asia, Oceania, and the Middle East provides a comprehensive and readable overview of the history of the small island nation of Fiji. Author Brij V. Lal, who was born in Fiji, is the professor of Pacific and Asian history at the School of Culture, History and Language at the Australian National University. He has written extensively on the politics and history of Fiji, notably in *Broken Waves: A History of the Fiji Islands in the Twentieth Century* (1992) and *In the Eye of the Storm* (2009). Lal's introduction to the *Historical Dictionary of Fiji* focuses on the modern era since 1874, when Fiji became a British Crown Colony, and the political, racial, and economic ramifications of the country's development. His explanation of the changing political scene in the past half century, culminating in the rule of Commodore Vorege Bainimarama, is enlightening. The chronology notes that the islands were settled circa 3500 B.C.E. and then moves directly to the seventeenth century, when the first European explorer sailed through the islands. Nearly all the chronology entries pertain to the nineteenth century through 2015. The items listed in the dictionary section provide considerable detail on the persons and events that shaped modern Fiji. These include a number of religious figures and institutions; missionary activity was strong and today the majority of Fijians are Christian. The book contains 10 maps of the Fijian archipelago and nine appendixes listing Fiji's governors, chief justices, presidents, prime ministers, opposition leaders, and main political parties as well as giving figures on the population and its religious distribution and on external trade. There is also a list of acronyms and abbreviations and a glossary of Fijian terms. Students of the Pacific area will find this book highly informative.—**ARBA Staff Reviewer**

World History

Dictionaries and Encyclopedias

280.   **Ancient History Encyclopedia. http://www.ancient.eu/.** [Website] Free. Date reviewed: 2016.

Ancient History Encyclopedia is a volunteer-run Website providing excellent and accessible resources on ancient history for high school and undergraduate students, teachers, and the general public. A team of specialists manages the site, which combines text content with a variety of digital resources. Overall it is well-organized and comprehensive. While the collection is more heavily weighted toward Western civilizations, a good effort has been made to be inclusive of global cultures. The search function works well: a search for "Roman Empire" called up 156 results, including articles, images, videos, and other resources, and results could be further limited by subject (such as daily life or warfare and battles). Users can also make a timeline search or use the "Explore" function to choose an area on a world map to research.

The heart of the site is made up of encyclopedia-style articles written by scholars in relevant fields. The articles are written in a clear and engaging style and are attractively presented, with images, maps, and videos accompanying the text. Other text resources include interviews with authors and scholars active in ancient history-related projects, features on current museum exhibitions, book reviews, and travel guides on locations of interest to ancient history enthusiasts.

This site provides maps of empires, cities, sites, and battle locations around the world. Finding the maps can be a bit tricky; however, clicking on "Maps" on the homepage takes the user to a page with just four large interactive maps, which is not the entire collection (to find other maps, the user can enter "maps" in the search bar and then select "images"). Nevertheless, the interactive maps are detailed and full of information; the map of the entire ancient world is especially impressive. The site's very extensive video collection draws from a variety of sources, including museums and other educational Websites. The site's large collection of high quality images can be found using a simple search on the

"Images" page. A tool to convert ancient measurements to their modern equivalents will be useful to students working with primary sources.

The quality of this site's content and presentation is outstanding, and it is highly recommended for students and general users.—**ARBA Staff Reviewer**

281.   **The Encyclopedia of the Industrial Revolution in World History.** Kenneth E. Hendrickson III, ed. Lanham, Md., Rowman & Littlefield, 2015. 3v. illus. index. $240.00/ set; $239.99 (e-book). ISBN 13: 978-0-8108-8887-6; 978-0-8108-8888-3 (e-book).

This three-volume set provides over 1,000 entries, written by 64 contributors (both academics and independent scholars), on a wide range of subjects related to the industrialization of the world. Individuals such as inventors, industry leaders, and politicians are profiled and their contributions discussed. Technological advances, such as the steam engine, the sewing machine, and refrigeration are explained within their historical context. Social topics like immigration, imperialism, and even romanticism are addressed. (The work at times seems more diverse or eclectic, as well as more selective, than a reader might expect. For instance, there are articles on "cell phones," "Gulf War (2003)," "Three Mile Island," and "superconductors," but none on India or any of the Middle East countries, despite reference to these areas in the introduction.)

A couple of remarks concerning the production of this work are necessary. Very few entries have references more recent than 2007 in the "Further Reading" section, possibly indicating a long gestation period for this complex work. Images seem to lack adequate contrast, giving them an overall grayish look. The writing, however, is clear; articles often contain cross-references to other entries which provide context for the original text being read. There is a comprehensive, 48-page index which is quite helpful, too. For students of the period and the evolution of industrialization around the world, this resource will be welcome. Public and academic libraries should consider.—**Mark Schumacher**

282.   **Oxford Classical Dictionary. http://classics.oxfordre.com/.** [Website] New York, Oxford University Press. Price negotiated by site. Date reviewed: 2016.

The *Oxford Classical Dictionary* (the "OCD" as it is always known) has been for more than a half century one of the great reference works of all time. Its clear writing, its authorship by hand-picked academics of the highest pedigree, and its coverage in one volume of the entire Greco-Roman world all made the OCD the "go to" resource for undergrads, buffs, graduate students, and scholars around the world. After its first edition (in 1949), new editions followed up to 2012 (the fourth edition, with 6,000+ entries, see ARBA 2013, entry 24). Now comes the digital OCD, launched formally in March 2016 as a member (probably the premier member) of the Oxford Research Encyclopedias suite. After spending a few hours with this new OCD, your reviewer (a constant user of the second edition many years ago in graduate school) considers the digital OCD an excellent and worthy successor to its dog-eared print ancestors. The two most important reasons this is so are, one, that a digitized OCD means that the simplest search can instantaneously retrieve all text mentions of the search term, freeing the user from relying only on the main entry and its official cross-references, and, two, OCD's promise of constant additions to and revision of the core material means the world will not have to wait a decade or more for important articles to reach their audience.

There are other reasons to love the new OCD. As expected, the new OCD contains both new and revised articles, everything from Gladiatorial Combat to Matriarchy. There is a commitment to add video in the near future. One can hardly wait! How does the digital OCD perform in testing? Entries are easily available via simple and advanced searches. For those keen on bibliography, most items are linked directly to their Google Books and World Cat pages. This is a huge boon for researchers wishing to dig deeper into the subject. To take advantage of the digital format, systematic browsing is enabled by drilling into the 25-odd subfields that the editors have determined best represent the OCD's summation of the classical world. Most of these categories cover expected topics such as Greek History and Historiography, Material Culture, Ancient Economy, and so on. But one category, Gender Studies, represents a field of scholarship that would never have appeared in the first editions of the OCD. Who says the field of Classics is a static one?

How does the subfield browsing work in practice? A sample drill-down into Roman History and Historiography retrieved 1,107 hits (fully a sixth of the entire database), beginning with Acclimation and ending with Zenobia (that's Zenobia of Palmyra, by the way, recently and sadly sacked by the Islamic State). What one does not find, unfortunately, is a major entry actually on "Roman History and Historiography" that might provide full context. (There is a "Roman Historiography" entry, but it took the reviewer some time to find it from within the subfield's list of entries.) This is a very minor quibble. The subfield organization is a legitimate way for OCD editors to tie together related entries as well as to enable the serendipitous browsing that has always been so irresistible a feature of print OCD.

Final verdict—the reviewer loves and highly recommends OCD's digital version to all libraries serving patrons and students who study and appreciate the classics. That said, the reviewer will also continue to own and treasure his print version of the OCD.—**Vincent Burns**

Handbooks and Yearbooks

283.   **Alpha History: http://alphahistory.com.** [Website] Free. Date reviewed: 2015.

Alpha History is a nonprofit online textbook and resource center that provides free information on 11 popular history subjects. It contains a simple and attractive layout with over 3,000 pages of historical sources, including topic summaries, documents, graphics, maps, timelines, glossaries, and even quizzes, essay questions, crosswords, and word searches for interactive fun.

The Website is based in Australia and is organized by several esteemed authors from around the globe. The targeted age group is 15 and older, so this Website would be a fantastic resource for high school students looking for concise and interesting content about a variety of historical events. The events included in *Alpha History* are: the American Revolution, French Revolution, World War I, Russian Revolution, Weimar Republic, Nazi Germany, The Holocaust, The Cold War, Conflict in Vietnam, Chinese Revolution, and Northern Ireland. Each subject can be found on the left side of the homepage; users will be able to navigate through the Website with ease to gather information on their desired topic. Each event has an extensive glossary that will benefit students who are unfamiliar with the content.

To further appeal to the student population, the homepage also includes *Alpha History's* Twitter feed, which provides blurbs of interesting historical information with links to external pages. Additional features include low-cost mobile apps for the iPad, iPhone, and iPod Touch, as well as e-book apps for different history subjects and advertisement-free quiz apps for iOS devices. This impressive collection of literature is continually updated, making the site an ideal and highly recommended resource for students, teachers, and history buffs alike.—**ARBA Staff Reviewer**

284.   Ciment, James. **How They Lived: An Annotated Tour of Daily Life through History in Primary Sources.** Santa Barbara, Calif., Greenwood Press/ABC-CLIO, 2015. 2v. illus. index. $205.00/set. ISBN 13: 978-1-61069-895-5; 978-1-61069-896-2 (e-book).

Scholar James Ciment's two-volume set focuses on a wide variety of primary sources related to daily life of ordinary people—the regular, repeated experiences that provide a historical context or provide knowledge about the economy, culture, or art of a time and society. An illustration or description of the source accompanies information that provides context for the source, and this context helps the reader understand the source and its relation to the society. Whether the entry is medicine practiced by a medieval Arab doctor, instructions on how an orator should dress from first century Rome, a description of Chinese foot-binding in the late nineteenth century, or Victorian mourning wear, these varied sources comprise this title of historical information. Each volume covers a different historical period; volume one deals with the ancient and medieval world, and volume two encompasses 1500 to the present day, and includes an index and a short bibliography of other daily life readings. Students and scholars of history, as well as teachers seeking sources to support the Common Core, will find this title of interest.—**Denise A. Garofalo**

285.   **The Crusades to the Holy Land.** Alan V. Murray, ed. Santa Barbara, Calif., ABC-CLIO, 2015. 330p. illus. maps. index. $89.00. ISBN 13: 978-1-61069-779-8; 978-1-61069-780-4 (e-book).

This guide to the history of the Crusades starts with three overview essays that set the context of the times, outline the origins, and describe the consequences of this epochal event that played such a major role in the history of Europe and the Near East from the late eleventh century until the end of the Middle Ages. The editor then moves into encyclopedic entries describing the key people, events, places, and ideas of the time, from Pope Urban II who initiated the Crusades to the Battle of Hattin when Saladin retook Jerusalem from the Latin kings, a discussion of the concept of penance and indulgences that was so crucial to the call to crusade, the development of the Templar and Hospitaller military orders—and much more. Peppered throughout are suggestions for further reading. Features include a chronology and a selection of primary documents that include, for example, a firsthand account of hearing Pope Urban's call to crusade in 1095 and a letter from one of the leaders of the First Crusade to his wife after the siege of Antioch. Another notable feature, Historical Dilemmas, presents three thought-provoking questions with responses from historians with different perspectives, giving a taste of current scholarly debate about the Crusades while pointing out the relevance this pivotal historical event still has for understanding our world today.—**Adrienne Antink**

286.   D'Efilippo, Valentina, and James Ball. **The Infographic History of the World.** New York, Firefly Books, 2014. 223p. illus. maps. $35.00. ISBN 13: 978-1-77085-316-4.

The Infographic History of the World is a terrific volume that examines our planet's history from the very beginning to modern times by analyzing data in graphical form.

The book is divided into four parts: In the Beginning, Getting Civilized, Nation Building, and the Modern World. The largest section is the Modern World by virtue of the fact that more data exists in present times than in the past. The book starts out in a primitive form and finishes with a modern flair from the quality of the paper to the color and style of the graphics to give the reader a sense of history's progress. The scope of the work is well stated on the "How to Read the Book" page. The authors are smart to state that they certainly could not include all aspects of world history. The authors are creative in matching the style of each graph to the data that is represented in a complementary fashion. *Infographic History* would do well in any library. The work is best suited for anyone middle school age and up who likes works of a visual nature. The graphical nature of the book gives perspective to data better than just stating statistics in a paragraph. A couple of good examples are the timeline of human existence (All in the Family, p. 46) that portrays the time and duration of many near-human species over the last 2.3 million years to the present or the comparison charts of current and historical carbon emissions (The world in Carbon, p. 160-161) per person and geographical area. The appendix explains where the authors got their sources and how they analyzed them. Timelines and graphs are certainly nothing new, but D'Efilippo and Ball create theirs in a fun, creative, and well-chosen way.—**Sue Ellen Knowlton**

287. **Defining Documents in World History: Ancient World (2700 B.C.E.-c.500 C.E.).** Michael Shally-Jensen, ed. Hackensack, N.J., Salem Press, 2015. 289p. index. $175.00. ISBN 13: 978-1-61925-771-9.

This primary source collection, another entry in the Defining Documents series published under the Grey House/Salem Press banner, represents the first title in a new subseries: *Defining Document in World History: Ancient World.* Like the original series' prior U.S.-focused titles, the present title is edited by Michael Shally-Jensen.

The core of this slim collection is the documents and their analyses. Documents excerpted originated in Mesopotamia, Egypt, Asia (China and India), Greece, Rome, and "Distant Lands" (which turn out to be Europe and modern-day Guatemala). The title contains 40 primary sources (running one to two pages to ten or more pages), prefaced with a scene-setting overview, "defining moment" description, and some basic data (date, region, author). After the primary source itself and a brief glossary (printed in a shaded box) come the analysis essay and "essential themes." Closing each section is a brief list of further readings.

Compilation of ancient documents in translation today presents particular challenges to teachers, students, and publishers: are the primary sources standard canonical texts or do they represent potentially new and unfamiliar texts to most students; are the translations fresh and recent or do they rely on early-twentieth-century translations (which sometimes require a translation of their own!); and do the primary sources well represent the entire "ancient" history of the world or do they largely come from well-studied Greece, Rome, Egypt, and Mesopotamia?

Judged by these criteria, this document collection fares relatively well in geographic diversity: eight of the forty documents originated in Asia. The document selection itself is relatively traditional: Code of Hammurabi, Epic of Gilgamesh, Sun Tzu, Bhagavad Gita, Thucydides, the funeral oration of Pericles, Cicero, and so on. The translations, alas, often can be traced back to out-of-copyright early-twentieth-century compilations which run the risk of being less than relevant or compelling to modern students. Fortunately, the analytical materials go some distance toward making the primary sources relevant to students.—**ARBA Staff Reviewer**

288.   **Defining Documents in World History: Middle Ages (476-1500).** Michael Shally-Jensen, ed. Hackensack, N.J., Salem Press, 2015. 253p. index. $175.00. ISBN 13: 978-1-61925-773-3; 978-1-61925-774-0 (e-book).

Another primary source collection in the Defining Documents series (*Defining Documents in World History: Ancient World*, 2016) this volume contains 40 sources of varying lengths (half a page to 10-12 pages, with shorter entries predominating). Each source is accompanied by a few pages of explanatory text, providing historical context, a glossary of terms, discussion of significant features of the source, and a short reading list. The entries are bookended by a short introductory essay (with its own reading list) and an index, bibliography, and lackluster list of Web resources. There are also a small set of badly reproduced but relevant maps presented without attribution. The collection is mostly restricted to Europe, with four sources relating to the Middle East and a few others connected to Byzantium. Like the previous collection, this volume seems to rely on public domain translations of the sources, encouraging less than up-to-date interpretations. Most of the text of the sources is easily available online. The explanatory text may be useful, but rarely goes into deep detail. This, along with the tendency of the sources to be excerpts from longer documents and the somewhat haphazard nature of the sources (e.g., while covering 1,000 years of history with 40 sources the editor chose to include two relating to the trial of Joan of Arc and another two from the work of Anselm), renders this collection extremely limited in use and a poor value compared to similar readers.—**Peter Larsen**

289.   Flynn, Hazel. **Missions Impossible: Extraordinary Stories of Daring and Courage.** New York, Firefly Books, 2014. 254p. illus. maps. index. $24.95pa. ISBN 13: 978-1-77085-422-2.

This book offers a thrilling survey of some of humanity's most courageous moments from prehistory through modern times. It cleverly and chronologically recounts many famous events, such as the Battle of Gettysburg, alongside lesser-known feats like the Lynmouth-Porlock Overland Lifeboat Rescue. The book engages readers from the get go via its crisp narrative and compelling visual style.

Each event is afforded two pages within seven tabbed thematic sections encompassing eras from the mythic "Age of Heroism" to the contemporary "Age of Terror." A section overview ties the events to the established theme. Each event entry is marked first with its date, location, objective, and a quick summary. Three paragraphs then detail the story of the event. In addition, each entry includes a numbered step-by-step tracking of the way the event plays out, a timeline including event-specific and contextual information, a map, and several evocative illustrations and/or photographs.

Events recounted in the book include The Trojan Horse, The Gunpowder Plot, the Pearl Harbor Attack, and the 9/11 Attacks. Since the book often focuses on militaristic events, the narrative is obviously more male-centric, though there are female-centered stories of bravery and daring, such as that of Allied spy Virginia Hall escaping the Nazis by hiking through the snow-covered Pyrenees on a prosthetic leg.—**ARBA Staff Reviewer**

290. **Histories of Everyday Life in Totalitarian Regimes.** Thomas Riggs, ed. Farmington Hills, Mich., St. James Press/Gale Group, 2015. 3v. illus. maps. index. (The Literature of Society Series). $550.00/set. ISBN 13: 978-1-55862-927-1; 978-1-55862-931-8 (e-book).

This three-volume set presents 300 articles, written by 43 contributors, on a diverse range of topics relating to the world of twentieth- and twenty-first-century totalitarianism. Focused on Nazi Germany and the Soviet Union, it also provides information on other countries, including China, Fascist Italy, North Korea, and Cuba. The volume titles reflect this broad coverage, too: *Personal Experiences, Effects of Totalitarianism,* and *Literary Approaches.*

Each of the entries is three to four pages long, and each follows the same format: "overview, historical and literary context, themes and styles, critical discussion, sources and further reading" (p. xviii). Therefore, although only small excerpts of the original texts are presented (in most cases), readers will have a clear understanding of the work's place and importance within a reflection on totalitarianism. Roughly two-thirds of the entries are biographical or autobiographical in nature; many are texts published since 2000. Classic texts, such as *Animal Farm, Fahrenheit 451,* and *The Trial* are also included, as are plays, poems, and songs.

A somber work by its topic, this set provides the reader a fine introduction to the literature exploring life under the harshest regimes of our recent past. The text is clear, organized, and easy to comprehend, so readers of all levels will benefit from it. Given the cost, however, purchase is most appropriate for large public and academic libraries.—**Mark Schumacher**

291. **Internet History Sourcebooks Project.** http://legacy.fordham.edu/halsall/. [Website] Free. Date reviewed: 2016.

The *Internet History Sourcebooks Project* (ISHP) collects primary source material in ancient, medieval, and modern historical topics. In addition, it provides subsidiary source materials on regional (African, Indian, Islamic, etc.) and thematic (science, women, LGBT, law, film) history. While designed for use by teachers, its resources can also assist students and researchers.

Each sourcebook begins with an introduction describing how and why to read and use primary sources, and then moves into thematically organized collections of primary documents. Some are hosted on the IHSP site; others are linked. Wherever possible, original citations are listed at the foot of the document. In addition, secondary sources introduce history, theory, and critiques. Where possible, the site links to additional archives including maps, music, and images.

This site offers access to primary sources on many topics that teachers can integrate into the classroom. ISHP is a highly recommended reference.—**ARBA Staff Reviewer**

292. **Modern Genocide: The Definitive Resource and Document Collection.** Paul R. Bartrop and Steven Leonard Jacobs, eds. Santa Barbara, Calif., ABC-CLIO, 2015. 4v. illus. maps. index. $415.00/set. ISBN 13: 978-1-61069-363-9; 978-1-61069-364-6 (e-book).

This 2,200-page set examines 10 major genocides of the twentieth and early twenty-first centuries: Armenia, Bosnia, Cambodia, Darfur, East Timor, Guatemala, Herero (Namibia), the Holocaust, Kurdistan, and Rwanda. Each section, ranging from 120 to 420 pages, includes a set of essays [Overview, Causes, Consequences, Perpetrators, Victims,

Bystanders, International Reaction].Those are followed by an A-Z list of entries discussing people, places, documents, and events of importance (each with "Further Reading" references), and a group of primary resources concerning the genocide, including legal documents, statements by political leaders, trial transcripts, and government declarations. Each section ends with an English-language bibliography and a list of contributors to that section.

The essays provide useful information to those beginning research into these tragedies. The entries and documents are more specialized and detailed for readers with some background on the subject. Any library with patrons investigating these events will benefit from having this set.—**Mark Schumacher**

293.   **1914-1918 Online: International Encyclopedia of the First World War. http://www.1914-1918-online.net/.** [Website] Free. Date reviewed: 2016.

1914-1918 Online: International Encyclopedia of the First World War is a collaborative English-language, Web-based reference encyclopedia resource covering World War I. The encyclopedia is project-managed in Germany, primarily at Freie Universität Berlin. Released in 2014, the project's approach looks at the First World War as a truly global conflict as opposed to the traditional emphasis on England, France, and Germany. The plan is to include more than 1,000 entries; as of this writing, the database includes 853 published articles. An additional 782 (listed as "unpublished articles" in the Articles A-Z section) remain unavailable, including such essential entries as Erich Ludendorff, Philippe Pétain, Joseph Joffre, the Battle of Amiens, and the Battles of the Marne, among others. While the current coverage of the war is good, clearly there remains much work to be done.

Submitted entries to the encyclopedia undergo academic review before they are accepted for publication. The project includes concise encyclopedic entries as well as broader thematic or regional essays tied to key topics or regions. Individual entries are generally very good, but in many cases tend more toward an academic audience than to general readers or students. Some of the project's published entries are shorter than one might expect considering the intended scope and depth of the project, leaving the reader to look elsewhere for more information.

The encyclopedia has a number of innovative approaches for accessing the content, including by themes, by regions, by subjects, and by timeline. The bibliography is excellent, with over 6,000 entries, which fortunately can be filtered by regions, themes, and languages. Similarly, an index with over 6,000 entries, filterable by name, place, and subject leads users to entries across the entire collection of content. The entries are connected with an impressive array of lists and graphs that provide many different ways to view the relations between entries. Entries can be exported in PDF, EPUB, and Kindle format, and can be linked to social media via buttons for Facebook, Google+, and Twitter. Images from the war are side-related to individual entries, but they are not integrated into the accompanying text for a closer association with the narrative.

In short, this is a useful but still in-progress scholarly resource on the First World War, with forward-looking technical, search, and social media features; those looking for an introduction to the war for students would be better served with other resources.—**ARBA Staff Reviewer**

294.   Price, Bill. **Fifty Foods that Changed the Course of History.** New York, Firefly Books, 2015. 223p. illus. index. $29.95. ISBN 13: 978-1-77085-427-7.

Presents 50 foods that have changed the world, discussing them in chronological order from the days of hunters and gatherers to the present. Entries vary in length from approximately two pages to eight pages. Each entry provides a place of origin, dates of origin, and type of food as well as sidebars and color photographs and illustrations. Readers will find historical context and brief introductions for each entry. Even though entries do not have notes or references, suggested further readings appear at the end of the book along with Website recommendations and an index. The 50 entries include several beverages—beer, tea, gin, American whiskey, Coca-Cola, and Starbucks coffee. Readers will find expected foods like bread, beef, corn, and the potato alongside foods that might not immediately come to mind, such as Spartan black broth, Roquefort cheese, madeleines, Anzac biscuits, and Swanson TV dinners. This eclectic mix, however, is partly what makes this a fun book to read.

This book does double-duty as both a good read and as food for thought for further research. Recommended for public and school libraries.—**ARBA Staff Reviewer**

295.   Redfern, Nick. **Secret History: Conspiracies from Ancient Aliens to the New World Order.** Canton, Mich., Visible Ink Press, 2015. 438p. illus. index. $19.95pa. ISBN 13: 978-1-57859-479-5; 978-1-57859-559-4 (e-book).

There is history and then there is *Secret History,* an analysis of nearly 60 global events which may not be what they seem on the surface. Revisiting ancient times and mulling over recent news, this book encourages readers to question everything they thought they knew about history as it has been reported. The book is organized into three sections—Ancient Aliens, Conspiracies, and New World Order—delving into the mysteries and potential conspiracies of a particular era, and begging readers to ask such what if questions as what if England's primitive stone circles are gateways between Neolithic times and the present or what if Abraham Lincoln's assassination was actually the work of British Freemasonry, the Jesuits, or even Vice President Andrew Johnson?

Ancient Aliens looks at a good cross-section of antiquity to find mysteries in the Bible, Native American legends, and Mesoamerica, as well as the aforementioned stone circles. Conspiracies focuses on a number of newsworthy events from more recent times, such as a variety of high-profile deaths and the proliferation of extraterrestrial conspiracies. The culminating New World Order brings readers into modern-day mysteries of events like 9/11, the Avian Flu outbreak, and the disappearance of Flight MH370. While certainly not providing definitive answers, the book nonetheless asserts a number of thought-provoking theories sure to keep readers engaged throughout.

Illustrations and an index enhance the usefulness of this work.—**ARBA Staff Reviewer**

296.   **U*X*L World Eras.** Carnagie, Julie, ed. Farmington Hills, Mich., U*X*L/Gale, 2016. 10v. illus. index. $780.00/set. ISBN 13: 978-1-57302-967-4.

This ambitious set attempts to provide a detailed overview of major periods of human history, organizing each volume into nine sections covering topics such as geography, art, family life, and science in periods such as ancient Mesopotamia, ancient Egypt, and the Industrial Revolution in Europe. Four additional volumes specifically focus on non-European periods: Ancient Mesopotamia, West African Kingdoms, Rise and Spread of

Islam, and Imperial China. A glaring omission in the set is the lack of any volume focused on great civilizations in the Americas such as the Aztecs, Incas, or Mayas.

Each volume in the set is self-contained with an introductory overview, volume-specific index, and the many maps, illustrations, and glossaries that render the UXL sets so readable and visually interesting for students. Sidebars contain copious quotations from original sources such as poems from the cultures being analyzed. The final volume ends with the onset of World War I.—**Delilah R. Caldwell**

297.   **Untold Lives Blog. http://britishlibrary.typepad.co.uk/untoldlives/.** [Website] Free. Date reviewed: 2016.

The Untold Lives blog, housed on the British Library Website, functions in an unusual way, in that its curation is very specific and unpredictable. It is not a comprehensive research tool, but rather a starting point that highlights otherwise obscure moments and facts. For example, a recent timely post featured an exploration of the leap year tradition of women proposing to men, and some of the varied perspectives on that tradition. Other recent features include pieces concerning Samuel Pepys, architect Sir Christopher Wren, Muslim burial ground design, and a slave governor. There are numerous others, with each piece providing a jumping off point to further discovery. *Untold Lives* also utilizes Twitter, which cleverly exploits the tidbit nature of the content.

From the blog: "The British Library's collections contain stories of people's lives worldwide, from the dawn of history to the present day. They are told through the written word, images, audio-visual and digital materials. The *Untold Lives* blog shares those stories, providing fascinating and unusual insights into the past and bringing out from the shadows lives that have been overlooked or forgotten…The blog contains many links to act as signposts to research information and online resources that you can explore for work or pleasure." There is a link to the History and Classics Web page, which does offer a traditional interface for research sources and topics. The blog functions as an appetizer for the history department of the British Library, offering a pop take on conventionally academic pursuits.

Untold Lives also has a tags section: you can click on a descriptor, such as "Philatelic," to land on a piece about stamps issued in the 1920s and 1930s in the Middle East. It is a distinctive approach to information dissemination. Though not recommended for pointed research efforts, the factoid roulette wheel design of the blog makes for an enjoyable visit for anyone interested in the daily life genre of history studies.—**ARBA Staff Reviewer**

298.   Weeks, John M., and Jason de Medeiros. **A Research Guide to the Ancient World: Print and Electronic Resources.** Lanham, Md., Rowman & Littlefield, 2015. 446p. index. $150.00; $149.99. ISBN 13: 978-1-4422-3739-1; 978-1-4422-3740-7 (e-book).

Divided into seventeen chapters and five substantial appendixes, this volume presents the study of the ancient world in the Mediterranean, Egypt, and southwestern Asia from the points of view of both the humanities and the social sciences. Chapters include, among others, dictionaries, handbooks, encyclopedias, biographical information, atlases, and theses and dissertations. The 136-page appendix on "Archaeological Site Reports" lists several thousand accounts of digs at hundreds of sites, from Algeria to Russia. Other appendixes focus on numismatics and paleography.

With its inclusion of a wide range of resources for those interested in this period, this volume could be useful in libraries in high schools to those in large academic institutions, whose users seek information on these topics. It should be mentioned that many entries in some categories, such as specialized libraries and specialized museums, may only list a name (and possibly a URL), while others will contain a longer description. It should also be noted that many of the entries in this volume refer to works in foreign languages, from French and German to Turkish and Greek.

Curiously, the "biography" section includes listings for Zeus and Aphrodite. In a work this vast, errors occasionally appear: several typos, and at one point, Mycenae is listed as being in Crete, Calvados in Italy, and a pottery collection at the University of Mississippi as being in Baltimore. The use of the University of Pennsylvania call numbers for books can also be a bit confusing, as both Library of Congress and Dewey numbers are used.—**Mark Schumacher**

299.   Westfahl, Gary. **A Day in a Working Life: 300 Trades and Professions through History.** Santa Barbara, Calif., ABC-CLIO, 2015. 3v. index. $310.00/set. ISBN 13: 978-1-61069-402-5; 978-1-61069-403-2 (e-book).

This three-volume set traces the various types of work that mankind has undertaken over the last 30,000 years, from cave painters and animal herders to video game and Website designers. Each entry is about four pages long, and provides a brief "Further Reading" list and a document, often a primary source, related to the job or profession. An extremely wide range of occupations is presented, from emperors, gladiators, and Islamic alchemists, to Victorian fire fighters, magicians, and twentieth-century dictators and astronauts. Readers can also examine the evolution of occupations, such as "soldiers" from the Hittite civilization to the Second World War.

Text editing is unfortunately sloppy at times: words are omitted or misused and occasional incorrect names and dates are included. This work is nevertheless recommended, primarily to high school and public libraries, whose readers will learn much about the work done across many centuries.—**Mark Schumacher**

300.   **World History Sources. http://chnm.gmu.edu/worldhistorysources/index.html.** [Website] Free. Date reviewed: 2016.

World History Sources is a Web-based resource intended to help teachers and students find and analyze primary sources for world history. The project was created by The Center for History and New Media (CHNM) at George Mason University. It is organized around four sections: Finding World History, Unpacking Evidence, Analyzing Documents, and Teaching Sources. The Finding World History section is a collection of reviews by a team of world history scholars of world history primary source archives, organized both by region and by time period. A helpful introductory framing essay in this section explores the myriad problems and issues involved with the use of online world history primary source materials: questions of authority, difficulties of translation, and more. Unpacking Evidence is a set of guides to the proper analysis of eight different types of primary sources: images, objects, maps, music, newspapers, official documents, personal accounts, and travel narratives. Each guide features an introduction to that type of source, provides sample questions to ask about that type, and a collection of resources designed to show how historians learn about the past using this type of source. The Analyzing Documents section features additional resources about each of those eight types of sources, including illustrated audio mini-lectures by the project's scholars. Teaching Sources is a collection of 16 case studies on how to use primary sources, ranging from Hammurabi's Code to Sgt. Pepper's Lonely Hearts Club Band. These case studies, written by world history high school and college instructors using their own experience, will be of greatest use to teachers looking for compelling ways to use primary sources in their own classrooms. The scholars who worked on the project throughout are excellent, and the content is thoughtful and of high quality. One caveat is that many of the reviews of the online source archives date as far back as 2003 and do not appear to have been recently updated; a matter of some concern considering the transitory nature of Websites.—**ARBA Staff Reviewer**

10 Law

General Works

Dictionaries and Encyclopedias

301.   **A Dictionary of Law.** 8th ed. Jonathan Law, ed. New York, Oxford University Press, 2015. 677p. $21.95pa. ISBN 13: 978-0-19-966492-4.

This dictionary was last updated in 2013; nevertheless, the aptly named editor promises that this new edition "reflects many recent changes in the law and legal system." Eighteen practitioners and legal scholars have contributed to this 8th edition. The editor's promise of an "easy-to-use format and emphasis on accessible language" is substantially fulfilled. The entries range in length from a single sentence to most of a page. One lengthy entry (appellate jurisdiction) is accompanied by a full-page diagram. There are numerous *see* and *see also* cross-references. In the center of the book there is a 10-page "Writing and Citation Guide." Additional features are a list of abbreviations and a directory of online legal resources. The chief drawback of this well-executed dictionary for an American audience is that it relates entirely to the current laws and legal system of the United Kingdom. Even entries on general topics that have universally applicable definitions (e.g., capital punishment) are treated only with reference to U.K. law. Hence, this dictionary can only be recommended for U.S. libraries that require legal information concerning this particular country. All others will continue to be well served by the venerable *Black's Law Dictionary* (10th edition, 2014).—**Jack Ray**

Handbooks and Yearbooks

302.   Epstein, Lee, Jeffrey A. Segal, Harold J. Spaeth, and Thomas G. Walker. **Supreme Court Compendium: Data, Decisions, and Developments.** 6th ed. Thousand Oaks, Calif., CQ Press / Sage, 2015. 840p. index. $195.00. ISBN 13: 978-1-4833-7660-8; 978-1-4833-7659-2 (e-book).

With the recent death of Justice Antonin Scalia and the controversy over the nomination of his successor, there has been heightened public interest in the Supreme Court. The larger part of this resource consists of 179 tables within nine chapters. Except for a general introduction and brief prefaces to each chapter, there is no text, making this a kind of statistical abstract. The topics include the Supreme Court as an institution; its review process, caseload, and cases; its opinions, decisions, and outcome trends; and its political and legal environments; the justices' backgrounds, nominations, confirmations, postconfirmation activities, departures from the Court, oral arguments, votes, and opinions; public opinion related to high-profile issues adjudicated by the Court; and the impact of the Court in American society. These last two topics do not present data on the Court per se, but draw on public opinion polls and statistical data on events related to areas in which the Court has been involved (e.g., "Legal Abortions, 1966-2008"). The editors provide source information for each of the tables. The greatest value of this compendium is in allowing researchers to see comparative data in specific areas; it is not the place to find a general overview of the court or its justices. The biographical information on the justices, while ample, is fragmented into numerous tables (e.g., family background; education and legal training; marriages and children). Some of the data is gleaned from social science research of an advanced nature (e.g., "Means and Medians in Economic Liberties Cases, 1946-2013 Terms"). This is a valuable resource, but will be best used by those seeking comparative information on specific topics. Recommended for large public, academic, and law libraries.—**Jack Ray**

303.   Hudson Jr., David L. Based on the prior edition by Kathleen A. Hempelman **Teen Legal Rights**. 3d ed. Santa Barbara, Calif., Greenwood Press/ABC-CLIO, 2015. 354p. index. (Contemporary World Issues). $89.00. ISBN 13: 978-1-61069-699-9; 978-1-61069-700-2 (e-book).

Teen Legal Rights, second edition, (see ARBA 2001, entry 541) is a straightforward volume that explains the rights of teens in a comprehensive manner, yet in language that teens (and their parents) can easily understand. It would be helpful to everyone, not just teens. For instance, it explains in understandable terms the theory of "no fault insurance," the legality of dress codes at work, what a "stop and frisk" search is, and a myriad of other everyday legal concepts.

Teen Legal Rights includes 19 chapters covering issues from young adult's rights at school, work, and home, to marriage, contracts, and conduct in the virtual world. Fifty state comparison charts are included as tables where applicable—for example, the table Marriage Laws by State specifies the age each state deems a teen able to consent to marry, both with and without parental consent. A list of the all the tables in the volume is provided after the table of contents.

Sprinkled throughout the volume are "Do You Have the Right?" segments which provide hypothetical legal situations, setting out a typical fact pattern and then providing questions designed to illuminate the intricacies of the problem. These would provide material for excellent discussions in a classroom setting.

At the end of each chapter a list of additional readings on the topics covered is provided, as well as other information sources, online sources, and hotline information where applicable. A comprehensive glossary and index are included at the end as helpful aids.

Teen Legal Rights is an accessible work that would be a valuable addition to any public library or academic library through the college level. Parents and teens alike would find it of interest and a highly usable resource when researching the legal rights of young people.—**Alicia Brillon**

304.   Kalyvas, James R., and Michael R. Overly. **Big Data: A Business and Legal Guide.** Boca Raton, Fla., CRC Press, 2014. 240p. illus. index. $59.95; $41.97 (e-book). ISBN 13: 978-1-4665-9237-7; 978-1-4665-9238-4 (e-book).

The topic of Big Data is becoming increasingly important for businesses and organizations worldwide. This book guides executives, managers, and counsel through the laws, regulations, and contracting practices that could impact the use of Big Data. Each chapter discusses an area of the law that affects how businesses and organizations use Big Data, providing readers with a way to think more broadly about its use and the creation of procedures that ensure legal considerations are part of any effort to harness the opportunities presented by Big Data.

The book is broken into 11 chapters and ends with a glossary and an index. The authors designed the book to allow individual chapters to stand alone, but more will be gained from a cover-to-cover read. The authors define Big Data in the first chapter and explain in everyday language how Big Data differs from traditional databases. The next 10 chapters address myriad vital considerations, including security and compliance, information and security in vendor and business partnerships, privacy, the implications of federal and state law for the creation and use of health information databases, the impact of Big Data on the insurance industry, the use of Big Data in the management of human resources, and the preservation of Big Data.

This guide is recommended for academic libraries, especially those that support business and/or law schools.—**ARBA Staff Reviewer**

305.   **National Survey of State Laws.** 7th ed. Richard A. Leiter, ed. Getzville, N.Y., William S. Hein, 2015. 829p. $225.00. ISBN 13: 978-0-8377-4026-3.

This smartly arranged book records the changes made to a wide variety of state laws since 2008. Covering eight general categories of law (Business and Consumer, Criminal, Education, Employment, Family, General Civil, Real Estate, and Tax), the book presents these changes in an easily referenced table format, wherein readers can compare each specific law from state to state.

Each category is further broken down into more specific topics. For example, the Education Law section details legislation concerning compulsory education, corporal punishment in public schools, prayer in public schools, and privacy of school records. Specific topics are arranged alphabetically. Each topic includes an overview which examines the history of the particular laws, national and state outlooks, and any current issues or debate concerning the law.

Specific topics are then examined in a table demarcated by state and applicable headings (so that headings will differ from topic to topic). For example, the topic of gun control within the Criminal Law section uses the headings of Code Section, Illegal Arms, Waiting Period, Who May Not Own, and Law Prohibiting Firearms On or Near School Grounds. The Code Section heading is particularly useful to readers who would like to peruse the actual text of the law. The table structure makes it extremely easy to compare laws across states. Using the same example of gun control, we can see how California law mandates a 10-day waiting period after the purchase of a gun, while Colorado mandates none.

The appendix of this recommended work references statutory compilations for each state and conveys abbreviations if applicable. This book would be put to great use by students of law, those just beginning their law careers, and more.—**ARBA Staff Reviewer**

306.   **US Constitutional Law.** https://global.oup.com/academic/product/us-constitutional-law-9780199363605?cc=us&lang=en&. [Website] New York, Oxford University Press. Price negotiated by site. Date reviewed: 2015.

US Constitutional Law is available as part of Oxford's Constitutional Law Product Family, which also contains *Oxford Constitutions of the World. US Constitutional Law* provides researchers with a comprehensive reference source that combines primary materials with expert commentary to offer a picture of the historical development of constitutionalism at the state and federal levels. Searches are available across both databases in the product family, even if a library only subscribes to one product. *US Constitutional Law* users can access the full text of current and historical state constitutions, as well as article-by-article commentaries on historical development from the Oxford Commentaries on the State Constitutions of the US series. New materials are added regularly and commentaries are amended as necessary. Additions planned for 2015 include the first volumes on the colonial era and founding period from Howard Gilman and Mark Graber's American Constitutionalism series, a documentary archive on the whole history of US constitutionalism, the updated new edition of Neil Cogan's *The Complete Bill of Rights,* and Bernard Schwartz's Unpublished Opinions series.

Searchers can use the quick search box from the home page or search using three main links: Browse All, Content Type, and State. Under these main links are advanced search options that allow users to narrow results. Once content is selected, tools to the right provide the ability to share results or to create personal profiles, among other things. Further tools on the left side of the screen include the Oxford Law Citator, which links to material form Oxford's online law resources and carefully selected third-party Websites. The citatory record contains citation details, links to content, and more, a service free of charge to subscribers of any of Oxford's online law products. Another interesting search feature is the interactive map of U.S. State Constitutions, which takes users from a simple click on Delaware, for instance, to the relevant secondary and primary sources.

Several features support librarians—direct object identifiers, downloadable MARC records, and ample help options. Subscriptions are available to libraries, organizations, and institutions; pricing depends on the size and type of institution and the number of users. This well-curated collection of primary and secondary sources is highly recommended to academic libraries and research institutions that need access to comprehensive, easily comparable, historical data pertaining to constitutional development.—**ARBA Staff Reviewer**

307.   **Whistleblowing Law.** Robert G. Vaughn, ed. Northampton, Mass., Edward Elgar, 2015. 2v. $695.00/set. ISBN 13: 978-1-78341-256-7.

The most commonly accepted definition of whistleblowing, quoted more than once in this resource, is "the disclosure by organization members (former or current) of illegal, immoral or illegitimate practices under the control of their employers, to persons or organizations that may be able to effect action." This source is not a textbook or treatise on whistleblowing, but rather a collection of 31 reprinted articles (primarily from law journals and the *Journal of Business Ethics*) and three book chapters. Vaughn's introduction is largely an overview of these various contents, which are thematically organized. Taken as a whole, these articles and chapters highlight many aspects of the history of and controversies surrounding the development of whistleblowing law, globally as well as in the United States. While whistleblowing has been more generally accepted in democratic societies that value individual rights than in societies in which loyalty to the group is the prevailing norm, the articles document how, even in the United States, protection of whistleblowers against retaliation that has been mandated by legislation often is not realized by courts and administrative agencies. While lip service is paid by organizations, their reactions are typically hostile. A number of issues and questions are explored in this collection: Should the whistleblower be required to report first to responsible superiors in the organization before going to external regulatory bodies or even the media? Should there be financial inducements to encourage whistleblowing or, conversely, penalties imposed for failing to report misdeeds? Is the public revelation of matters that may compromise national security, a la Edward Snowden, ever justifiable? Although governmental transparency is increasingly touted in the United States, one author's research surprisingly revealed that the more the public knows about government, the less they trust it. This collection is a thought-provoking and useful resource for academic and law libraries.—**Jack Ray**

Corporation Law

Handbooks and Yearbooks

308. **Research Handbook on Partnerships, LLCs and Alternative Forms of Business Organizations.** Robert W. Hillman and Mark J. Loewenstein, eds. Northampton, Mass., Edward Elgar, 2015. 504p. index. (Research Handbooks in Corporate Law and Governance). $290.00. ISBN 13: 978-1-78347-439-4.

This volume in the Edward Elgar series of research handbooks in corporate law and governance deals with the advantages and disadvantages of different types of business organization and their legal and financial ramifications. The limited liability company (LLC) was first introduced in 1977 as an alternative to the corporation and, as the introduction to this book states, "has increasingly become the business organization of choice in the United States." The rise of the LLC has led to much litigation and legal commentary, and this book attempts to present the issues involved in a broad and coherent perspective. Editors Robert W. Hillman, University of California at Davis, and Mark J. Loewenstein, University of Colorado Law School, have brought together essays by 30 professors and practitioners of business law that cover eight general topics: contractual freedom, internal relationships, relationships with third parties, tax and accounting, dissolution and fundamental change, specialized entities, judicial and legislative responses, and international perspectives on alternative forms or organizing a business. Each of the 27 chapters presents one or more conclusions, all have reference notes, and most also have either a bibliography or a list of references. The index is well thought out, as is the norm with offerings from Edward Elgar. This book will be of real value to practitioners and scholars concerned with business organization and business law and is recommended for academic and other professional libraries.—**ARBA Staff Reviewer**

309. **Research Handbook on Shareholder Power.** Hill, Jennifer G. and Randall S. Thomas, eds. Northampton, Mass., Edward Elgar, 2015. 628p. index. (Research Handbooks in Corporate Law and Governance). $350.00. ISBN 13: 978-1-78254-684-9.

This book from the Edward Elgar series of research handbooks in corporate law and governance examines shareholder power as it is exercised around the world. Editors Jennifer G. Hill, professor of corporate law at the University of Sydney, and John S. Beasley, II, professor of law and business at Vanderbilt University, have assembled here papers presented at two conferences, one at the Vanderbilt Law School in September 2013 and the other at the Faculty of Law at the National University of Singapore in March 2014. The first section of the book looks at the history of shareholder power in America from 1800 to 2000, agency capitalism, and images of the shareholder. The second section discusses shareholder categories: institutional investors, hedge funds, controlling shareholders, and the state (in this case China) as controlling shareholder. Articles in the third section deal with the evolving relationship between shareholders and the board of directors, which is often contentious. The fourth section assesses the operation of shareholder power in specific contexts: takeovers, executive pay, and shareholder litigation, while the fifth and final section provides international perspectives on shareholder power in Europe, Asia, and the Americas. The way the articles are structured, with each offering a conclusion and extensive reference notes, makes the information—and the author's perspective—easier to grasp. A number of the chapters include figures and tables and a few have appendixes. As is the norm with Edward Elgar reference works, the index is thoughtfully done and helpful to the reader. The book is recommended for reference libraries and will be of special interest to law and business school students as well as legal and corporate practitioners.—**ARBA Staff Reviewer**

Criminology and Criminal Justice

Dictionaries and Encyclopedias

310.   **Encyclopedia of Criminal Justice Ethics.** Bruce A. Arrigo, ed. Thousand Oaks, Calif., Sage, 2014. 2v. index. $370.00/set. ISBN 13: 978-1-4522-7411-9.

This two-volume set presents a diverse look at topics dealing with ethics in the criminal justice system. Entries include topics such as Postcolonialism, Jacques Lacan, Vice, Attorneys, Socrates, Insanity Defense, Public Shootings, and Pariah Underground Economy. The editor's introduction groups the 381 articles into eight categories: history, philosophical concepts, policing ethics, legal ethics, issues in offender treatment and rehabilitation, cases and controversies, science and culture, and politics and social justice. (This same categorization, with the articles in each section, is provided in the "Reader's Guide" at the beginning of the set.)

Entries range from one-and-a-half pages to seven pages, and each one has cross-references and a brief reading list. Three appendixes provide information on capital punishment, the FBI's code of ethics, and a document from the International Criminal Court. Organized along the same clean lines as a number of other Sage encyclopedias published recently, this set (also available online) provides much useful information on an important topic often in the news. It is highly recommended for academic and major public libraries; other libraries, if the cost is manageable, should consider it as well.—**Mark Schumacher**

Handbooks and Yearbooks

311.   Altschiller, Donald. **Hate Crimes: A Reference Handbook.** 3d ed. Santa Barbara, Calif., ABC-CLIO, 2015. 372p. illus. index. (Contemporary World Issues). $58.00. ISBN 13: 978-1-61069-946-4; 978-1-61069-947-1 (e-book).

Donald Altschiller is the distinguished author of eight reference books. In addition, he has published articles in the *Wall Street Journal, Chronicle of Higher Education, Boston Globe,* and the *Los Angeles Times.* Altschiller's impressive resume documents noteworthy contributions that include numerous essay entries in encyclopedias.

Hate Crimes: A Reference Handbook, third edition, represents an essential and comprehensive reference on bias-motivated violence committed in the United States. Debate, discussion, and legislation swirl around hate crime victims who suffer consequences because of their race, religion, ethnicity, skin color, or sexual orientation. *Hate Crimes* assists readers to explore and comprehend complex and divisive realities. This is an introductory, one-volume, academic and professional resource that provides an overview for scholars, researchers, lawyers, and students. Individuals interested in enhancing their expertise will find this text beneficial. Chapter themes integrate diverse approaches (historical, sociological, criminological, and victimology) that enhance understanding and in-depth examination of associated discussions and topics. Related legal issues expand inquiring minds and serve as another primary theme. For example, chapters document U.S. Supreme Court decisions and federal and state legislation regarding hate crimes.

Well-documented chapters focus on the recurrent and disturbing social dynamics of hate crimes. In addition, pertinent discussions address government and activist approaches to combat the hate crime phenomenon that ignites an atmosphere of prejudice and social restlessness. Furthermore, contemporary hate crimes committed on America's college campuses emphasize the need to acknowledge and combat this disturbing occurrence. According to the author's research, in multicultural America, the perpetrators occasionally resemble the diverse racial, ethnic, and religious spectrum of our society. Interestingly, the chronology chapter documents incidents that contradict the prevailing perception that hate crimes are almost solely committed by white racists. African Americans have harassed and abused Asian Americans; American Muslims have torched synagogues and physically attacked American Jews; Hispanics have beaten African Americans; and diverse minority groups harass and assault gays, lesbians, and transgendered individuals.

The developers and designers of *Hate Crimes: A Reference Handbook* considered many options in their effort to produce a superior product. For example, the photograph on the book's cover cover arouses strong emotions when one first observes the image of an impromptu memorial. The photograph represents a makeshift memorial and protest over the shooting of a gay man, Mark Carson, murdered by a stranger yelling anti-gay slurs in West Village, New York City on May 20, 2013. *Hate Crimes* presents a unique listing of audio-visual sources, including the most comprehensive annotated entries of magazine articles and other books on the topic; provides the most comprehensive source for U.S. congressional hearings and legislation on hate crimes and supplies a wide range of viewpoints on the philosophical and legal arguments both in support of and in opposition to hate crime legislation. The work also clarifies nomenclature in a helpful glossary; uses reader-friendly fonts; offers bold headings that prepare readers for new topics, enhance presentation, and facilitate content organization; documents the source and story behind authentic pictorial images that appear at the beginning of individual chapters; offers case studies that appear for emphasis and illustrate the significance of the problem; and offers extensive reference sections at the conclusion of each chapter.

Hate Crimes: A Reference Handbook includes seven well-appointed and organized chapters. The preface provides an overview of the book and highlights infamous hate crimes. The third edition offers new material and discusses controversies about related legal implications. Chapter one emphasizes the history of hate legislation and the Civil Rights Act of 1968. Significant legislative acts and Supreme Court decisions offer insight into the evolution of the legal requirements for prosecution. Chapter two, "Problems, Controversies, and Solutions," examines laws directed to punish and prevent hate crime and the opposition to these laws. Like many current issues, the topic of hate crimes draws diverse opinions ranging from the philosophical, legal, and ideological perspectives. Chapter three, "Perspectives," includes essays offering divergent viewpoints. Chapter four, "Profiles," introduces brief biographies of some notable experts on hate crimes, racial and religious bigotry, and political extremists. Chapter five, "Data and Documents," contains research materials on hate crimes. These include The Federal Bureau of Investigation Website provides an overview of the agency's mandate to investigate and prosecute hate crimes from the agency's Website and the excerpted reports, *Hate on the Internet* and *Vulnerable to Hate,* which document hate speech and violence touching the most vulnerable segments of society—children and the homeless. Chapter six, "Resources and Further Research," while unavoidably selective, provides students and researchers with annotated citations to significant and diverse publications on hate crimes. The number and documentation of individual hate crimes committed in the United States over the past few decades is too great to list. In chapter seven, "Chronology," carefully selected entries document the severity of the concern. The list also mentions international hate crimes that demonstrate the adverse impact on a global community. The appendixes (Glossary of Terms, Index System, and About the Author) offer additional content that enhances opportunities for integration and application of concepts.

Hate Crimes: A Reference Handbook highlights the significance of gaining an understanding of the social dynamics of hate crimes. The author's perspective endorses encouraging changes concerning the three branches of government that continue to evolve in combating these crimes. The FBI, state, and local law enforcement agencies have become more vigilant in enforcing hate crimes statutes. The following agencies will find this text of value: government agencies; law enforcement agencies; public and private libraries; and high school, community college, and university libraries. Donald Altschiller accomplished his overall objective to provide readers with an effective analysis and discussion of hate crime. The author offers insight into a topic that he acknowledges as being depressing. However, he proposes that one should never lose perspective about the basic goodness and humanity of our fellow citizens. Altschiller accomplishes his objective, remains focused, and offers a major contribution to understanding the role of hatred and violence in our society.—**Thomas E. Baker**

312.   Covey, Herbert C. **Crips and Bloods: A Guide to an American Subculture.** Santa Barbara, Calif., Greenwood Press/ABC-CLIO, 2015. 201p. index. (Guides to Subcultures and Countercultures). $37.00. ISBN 13: 978-0-313-39929-9; 978-0-313-39930-5 (e-book).

More so than any other gangs, Crips and Bloods have had the most significant impact on people's perceptions of what a gang is, what it's like to be in a gang, and the overall reach of the gangster subculture. Part of a series of books on American subcultures, the single-volume *Crips and Bloods: A Guide to an American Subculture* attempts to document the subculture of the two gangs forming first as a nonviolent, social entity in a time of social marginalization of young black men (particularly by law enforcement) who shared a common background and limited opportunities (Crips), and then as protection against the Crips (Bloods). The book begins with a timeline outlining the major events that have occurred since the formation of the Crips and the Bloods in the early 1960's to the first years of the twenty-first century. The many accounts of the early beginnings of the sets (gangs) is explored with its mix of first-hand accounts from current and prior members of both gangs, police accounts of the activities of both, and information gleaned from other research, the reader is exposed to the ideas and lifestyles that identify the Crip and Blood subcultures.

While not a complete account, *Crips and Bloods* provides a general overview of the gangs. The book devotes several early chapters to addressing whether or not Crips and Bloods are in fact gangs or are merely subcultures whose beliefs, values, and ways of life differ from mainstream society. These early chapters describe the characteristics of the Crips and Blood subcultures, the gangs themselves, and their members. In many cases, the reader is exposed to the social aspect of belonging to a family that looks out for the best interests of those affiliated, often becoming a de-facto neighborhood police that protects its people from outsiders. Later chapters explore the darker side of involvement with alcohol and drugs and the violence that so often accompanies it as well as the impact that Crips and Bloods have had on society through music, fashion, language, and movies which have disseminated the Crips and Blood subcultures nationwide. No exact membership numbers are given, as sets in one city generally do not have any affiliation with sets in another city or even sets within their own cities, including Los Angeles. The book's final chapter details how the Crips and Bloods will inevitably continue to thrive across the country as the two become involved in new types of crimes and continue to expand their territory and subcultural influence.

Each chapter includes brief "concluding observations" outlining major points followed by a bibliography for further reading. Because Crips and Bloods often use their own slang terms, the book also provides a glossary of terms; this glossary makes the book a less difficult read for those unfamiliar with the symbols, objects, words, colors, and images used to represent the gangs. The book also includes a comprehensive bibliography of print and nonprint resources from all chapters and an index for easy page references.

The book provides fascinating insight into two of the most influential street gangs in the world by referencing some of the most significant literature on gangs in a single volume. *Crips and Bloods: A Guide to an American Subculture* in an authoritative work for those wanting to get a well-rounded view of America's most famous subcultures.—**Thomas O'Brien**

313.   **Crime in the United States 2014.** 8th ed. Gwenavere W. Dunn, ed. Lanham, Md., Bernan Press, 2015. 824p. $105.00; $104.99. ISBN 13: 978-1-59888-717-4; 978-1-59888-718-1 (e-book).

Crime in the United States offers findings from the Federal Bureau of Investigation (FBI) of the offenses known to law enforcement, released annually from its Uniform Crime Reporting Program. The FBI no longer publishes these findings; however, Bernan Press continues to deliver this practical information in book format. This reference represents the most comprehensive official compilation of crime statistics in the United States and is an important addition to library reference collections. It serves the instructional and research needs of diverse patrons. The heart of a library is its collection.

At 824 pages, *Crime in the United States* is an intricately detailed source of statistics. Legal and law enforcement professionals, researchers, and those who are simply curious or have inquiring minds will discover violent and property crime data for the nation including—regions, states, counties, cities, towns, and even college and university campuses.

Crime in the United States includes statistics on the following: violent and property crimes; hate crimes; crime trends; victims by type; crimes cleared (those closed by arrest or other means); persons arrested (age, sex, and race); juvenile offenders; law enforcement personnel (including the number of sworn officers killed or assaulted); characteristics of homicides (including age, sex, and race of victims and offenders); victim-offender relationships; weapons used; and circumstances surrounding homicides. In addition to statistics, *Crime in the United States* contains supplementary content and illustrative figures that clarify the data and offer graphic perspectives of major offenses, among them murder and non-negligent manslaughter; forcible rape, burglary, and hate crimes. Data include the following: offense type, location, bias motivation, victim type, number of individual victims, number of offenders, and the race of the offenders.

Crime in the United States incorporates the following sections: Summary of the Uniform Crime Reporting (UCR) Program; Offenses Known to the Police; Offenses Cleared; Persons Arrested; Law Enforcement Personnel; Hate Crimes; and Appendixes.

Crime in the United States is the leading book on known criminal offenses and crime statistics. This book represents the ideal resource for library reference centers. Law enforcement agencies on the federal, state, and local level should have accessible copies for their personnel. Crime analysts require this resource for crime analysis and demographic comparisons. In addition, this superior contribution is the perfect addition to university, college, and high school libraries for use by researchers and criminal justice students. Library acquisition departments and decision-makers are duty bound to include *Crime in the United States* in their annual budget to enhance essential research collections.—**Thomas E. Baker**

314.   **Crime in the United States 2015.** 9th ed. Shana Hertz Hattis, ed. Lanham, Md., Bernan Press, 2015. 664p. maps. index. $105.00; $105.99 (e-book). ISBN 13: 978-1-59888-765-5; 978-1-59888-766-2 (e-book).

Using information provided by the FBI, the large volume of statistics provides detailed information on both crime and law enforcement in the United States. Following a brief overview of the nine categories of crime presented here and an explanation of the Uniform Crime Reporting Program, the book presents 94 tables of data, dealing with crimes committed, persons arrested, law enforcement personnel, and hate crimes. Several of the tables provide information at the local level, such as the 10-page "Offenses Known to Law Enforcement, by Selected State and University and College," outlining campus crime. For anyone seeking detailed, authoritative data on crime in America, this resource will be the place to look.—**Mark Schumacher**

315.   **Crimes of the Centuries: Notorious Crimes, Criminals, and Criminal Trials in American History.** Steven Chermak and Frankie Y. Bailey, eds. Santa Barbara, Calif., ABC-CLIO, 2016. 3v. illus. index. $310.00/set. ISBN 13: 978-1-61069-593-0; 978-1-61069-594-7 (e-book).

Over 500 of the most well-known American criminals and notorious events of the past 400 years, from the Salem Witch Trials to the Virginia Tech Massacre, are featured in an alphabetical listing of entries. The set begins with an introductory discussion of the history of crime in America, followed by a list of entries arranged into basic topics (such as "acquaintance homicides" and "organized crime") and a chronology which gives a brief listing of history of significant events. The individual entries present brief details of individuals (victims, perpetrators, and suspects), court cases, and specific criminal events. The writing is informative, but simplistic and gossipy and does not flow well. Also, some of the entries duplicate the same basic information. A brief bibliography appears at the end of each entry and a slightly larger general bibliography is included at the end of volume three. Following the main text of individual entries is an interesting section that features either the full text of or excerpts from primary documents (such as an arrest warrant from the Salem Witch Trials for Sarah Osburne and Tituba and an excerpt of the Jerry Sandusky sentencing decision). A listing of editors and contributors and an index complete the third volume. Black-and-white illustrations enhance the text, but more would have been better. According to the editors, this source "supports the National Standard's curriculum mandate" on current events education and is meant to be for secondary schools or for general readers.—**Martha Lawler**

316.   Hearn, Daniel Allen. **Legal Executions in Delaware, the District of Columbia, Maryland, Virginia, and West Virginia: A Comprehensive Registry, 1866-1962.** Jefferson, N.C., McFarland, 2015. 228p. index. $65.00pa. ISBN 13: 978-0-7864-9540-5; 978-1-4766-1825-8 (e-book).

Many Americans struggle today with the idea of capital punishment. Does it actually deter violent crime? Is it morally unjust? Does it provide victims with justice? It would seem that throughout most of the nineteenth and twentieth centuries that the subject was not quite as open to debate. This book catalogs each legal execution which took place in the mid-Atlantic region of the United States between the years of 1866 and 1962.

Organized by state, the entries are further arranged chronologically with the name, race, and age of the convicted, as well as the crime committed. The author has scoured court records, contemporary media reports, death certificates, and more to provide key information about each case. While some entries contain limited detail, others share riveting information about the perpetrator(s), their motives, and the crime itself.

There is, for example, the 1954 Maryland murder of Mrs. Dorothy Mae Grammer, bludgeoned to death by her husband so he could be with another woman. Mr. Grammer went as far as making it appear as if his wife had been killed in a car accident (he was executed on June 11, 1954). There is also the brief account of Mary Wallace, a black 17-year-old executed by hanging for poisoning a nine-month-old white infant reportedly out of spite.

Pouring through the entries allows readers a chance to consider a number of auxiliary issues, such as the pace of justice, racial relations, methods of execution, and economic realities. Including an appendix detailing a preliminary (incomplete) listing of executions held before 1866, this book elevates an otherwise grim report to the level of a highly respectable work of historical value. An index rounds out the work. This work is recommended to law, public, and academic libraries.—**Laura Herrell**

317.   Hearn, Daniel Allen. **Legal Executions in Georgia: A Comprehensive Registry, 1866–1964.** Jefferson, N.C., McFarland, 2015. 220p. index. $65.00pa. ISBN 13: 978-0-7864-9869-7; 978-1-4766-2000-8 (e-book).

This book is a one of a series documenting America's history of capital punishment. Focusing exclusively on the state of Georgia, the volume catalogs each legal execution—roughly 1000 of them—carried out over nearly a century from the post-Civil War era through the bulk of the twentieth century.

Culled from court records, government correspondence, newspapers and more, the registry is presented chronologically. Entries include the name, race, and age (if recorded) of the condemned, as well as the capital crime committed and method of execution (mostly hanging and electrocution). While some entries contain limited detail, others share interesting information about the perpetrator(s), their motives, and the crime itself. There is, for example, the 1911 murder of 19-year-old Green Key, senselessly shot in the head by one Ed Jones simply for laying drunk in the latter's path. An index enhances the usability of this resource.

Readers may note a number of auxiliary issues as they follow this chronology, such as alcohol use, domestic abuse, pace of justice, and racial issues. While little context is provided beyond the entries, the book is nonetheless hugely valuable to genealogical and historical researchers alike.—**ARBA Staff Reviewer**

318.   Hearn, Daniel Allen. **Legal Executions in Illinois, Indiana, Iowa, Kentucky and Missouri: A Comprehensive Registry, 1866–1965.** Jefferson, N.C., McFarland, 2016. 210p. index. $65.00pa. ISBN 13: 978-0-7864-9870-3; 978-1-4766-2001-5 (e-book).

This comprehensive registry of legal executions, the latest in a series from McFarland, presents information for Illinois, Indiana, Iowa, Kentucky, and Missouri in the first century following the end of the Civil War. The author has written several other books in the series, and, as in the case of the other titles, he clearly states that his intention is to provide a reliable reference free from politics and a slanted viewpoint.

The layout of the book makes information easy to find—the capital punishment cases are presented chronologically by state. Two columns comprise each page, and the length of the entries depends on the information available—the longest in this title is just over two full columns for Moses Canton of Kentucky, hanged in May, 1885, for murder. For each case readers will find the name, age, and race of the person involved in the crime, the date and location the crime was committed, details about the crime and the victim, and date of execution. Valuably, each entry contains the sources from which the author pulled his information. This gives researchers confidence in the information presented and points them in the right direction for further study. The case of Carl Otto Wanderer, a white, 24-year-old male convicted of murder, serves as a great example of the wealth of data this book provides. Wanderer committed his crime on June 21, 1920, in Cook County. He killed both his pregnant wife and a Skid Row vagabond. Wanderer may have been disillusioned by marriage, desirous of another woman, or a subliminal homosexual according to contemporary accounts. He killed the vagabond in an attempt to make it look like he himself had died in a murder-suicide. Wanderer was hanged on September 30, 1921. Hearn consulted a variety of newspapers, the 1920 U.S. Census, and other sources to describe this case.

While the author chose to focus on the century after the Civil War, his first appendix lists executions before 1866 chronologically by state, going back to the late eighteenth century; the list includes the name of the person convicted, the date the execution took place, the location of the crime, and the charge. This is followed by a name and subject index. There is a lot of information for historians, genealogists, and researchers in other fields packed into this recommended book.—**ARBA Staff Reviewer**

319.   Martinez, J. Michael. **The Greatest Criminal Cases: Changing the Course of American Law.** Santa Barbara, Calif., Praeger/ABC-CLIO, 2014. 266p. illus. index. $48.00. ISBN 13: 978-1-4408-2868-3; 978-1-4408-2869-0 (e-book).

In studying many of the landmark rulings that have changed the face of a law, scholars can often become mired in complex legal jargon and the technicalities a case may endure as it moves through a complicated court system. No major legal ruling has ever been considered straightforward and simply resolved, and yet it is imperative that such cases be clearly understood. This book strips away many of the complexities of some of the most groundbreaking and emblematic legal decisions and engagingly presents the human stories from which they emanate.

The author has chosen 14 cases spanning over a century and meeting compelling criteria. Readers can observe the origins and evolutions of legal principles we take for granted today, such as the Exclusionary Rule, whereby certain evidence becomes inadmissible in court, or the notion that criminal defendants have a "right to remain silent," aka the Miranda Right. The book also engages readers in the rich narrative behind the cases. An example is the story of "The Scottsboro Boys," where we see how the poverty and hopelessness of The Great Depression, along with vitriolic racial and regional divisiveness set the stage for the dubious court proceedings in *Powell vs. Alabama.* And there is the case of *Gideon vs. Wainwright,* which decided whether all defendants (as opposed to capital defendants only) had a right to counsel. This case included a cast of characters ranging from an irascible drifter to a future Supreme Court Justice.

Each chapter excellently captures the flavor of the times in which these cases were tried, demonstrates the delicate line between government authority and individual liberty, and provides a clear link between the initial ruling in the case, its precedents, and its impact today.

From an adultery-born street murder to our current "war on terror," this book delves into the vast historical milieu that has shaped our greatest legal rulings, and can genuinely be appreciated by history lovers and legal scholars alike.—**Laura Herrell**

320.   Sheridan, Matthew J., and Raymond R. Rainville. **Exploring and Understanding Careers in Criminal Justice: A Comprehensive Guide.** Lanham, Md., Rowman & Littlefield, 2016. 296p. index. $38.00; $37.99 (e-book). ISBN 13: 978-1-4422-5430-5; 978-1-4422-5430-5 (e-book).

Written by two people with extensive experience as practitioners in the criminal justice system and academics in college-level programs, this book is intended for use as a text in courses about jobs in the criminal justice profession but also as a reference for criminal justice program administrators as they guide undergraduates through their programs.

The book systematically covers an enormous amount of information in the following chapters: "Introduction: Why Another Book on Criminal Justice Careers?," "Exploring Careers in Criminal Justice," "Careers in Law Enforcement," "Careers in Corrections," "The Courts, Its Actors, and Its Functions," "The Federal Government," "Getting the Job, Entering the Field, and Career Advancement," "Criminal Justice Ethics," and "Life after the Career." The book also includes 16 valuable appendixes, the longest of which includes 16 profiles of people who have worked in the criminal justice system. In the appendixes, readers will find sample cover letters, a guide to interview questions, a sample resume, a list of federal law enforcement agencies in the United States, and much more. These appendixes are followed by notes and a bibliography of references and suggested readings. The index is particularly helpful for someone who wants to look up a specific topic like the CIA or Immigration and Customs Enforcement, as well as subjects like stress and tuition. There is a separate name index.

This practical guide to criminal justice careers is recommended for high school or college career counseling centers; high school, college, and public libraries; and for criminal justice practitioners or professors.—**ARBA Staff Reviewer**

321.   Ward, Harry M. **Public Executions in Richmond, Virginia: A History, 1782-1907.** Jefferson, N.C., McFarland, 2012. 223p. illus. index. $45.00. ISBN 13: 978-0-7864-7083-9; 978-0-7864-9259-6 (e-book).

Organized chronologically, *Public Executions in Richmond, Virginia* provides detailed information about hangings that prior to 1869 were attended by large numbers of spectators. During the period studied, hanged criminals were overwhelmingly poor and/or black. Chapters give readers a sense of the political, economic, and social conditions in the city, and highlight such things as the 1800 Gabriel slave conspiracy and criminal justice in both civilian and military realms during the Civil War. The appendixes offer selections from printed primary sources and the *Richmond Times Dispatch,* as well as a copy of a 1908 act by the general assembly of Virginia changing the mode of execution to death by electrocution. For reference users, Appendix G holds much value as it lists the names, race, gender, date of execution, and crime committed. This is followed by chapter notes, a bibliography sorted into primary and secondary sources, and an index.

Public Executions is an excellent source for students and researchers, especially when used in conjunction with the other McFarland books on executions in the United States.—**ARBA Staff Reviewer**

Employment Law

Handbooks and Yearbooks

322.   **Comparative Labor Law.** Matthew W. Finkin and Guy Mundlak, eds. Northampton, Mass., Edward Elgar, 2015. 491p. index. $285.99; $256.00 (e-book). ISBN 13: 978-1-7810-0012-0; 978-1-7810-0013-7 (e-book).

The 37 authors of the various chapters are all academic professors and lecturers of law from 16 countries. Each chapter, though focused on a particular area, presents information based on labor law in the country under study. The objective was to identify theoretical or policy-oriented commonalities, or trends. It is not organized in a traditional county-by-country format, but the countries are included in the index. Authors used comparative methodology to explain legal diversity or to reveal differences. Some authors used "ideal types" and looked for these characteristics in the labor law of countries they compared. In chapter six, for example, the authors examine and compare autonomy, privacy, and dignity under technological oversight in the United States, Germany, and Japan, commenting on specific technology oversight, employers' access to employee social media, geolocation, and biometric identification.

Each chapter includes an introduction, conclusion, and bibliographical references. The editors do an excellent job of explaining the many different ways authors compare the information. What is lacking is analysis of the conclusions reached or trends to watch unfold in the future. The authors of each chapter present their findings, but these need to be summarized.

Highly recommended for academic law libraries and for government law libraries.—**Ladyjane Hickey**

323.　Feldacker, Bruce S,, and Michael J. Hayes. **Labor Guide to Labor Law.** 5th ed. Ithaca, N.Y., Cornell University Press, 2014. 625p. index. $89.95. ISBN 13: 978-0-8014-5225-3.

The *Labor Guide to Labor Law* is a comprehensive guide, written from the labor perspective. Originally intended primarily for union officials, it focuses on issues of particular concern to the labor movement. Topics covered include: the history and structure of federal labor legislation, collective bargaining, union organizing rights, employees' rights, union regulation of work, fair representation, equal employment opportunity, and the federal-state relationship in labor relations. Review questions, which can be used to facilitate in-class discussions, are provided at the end of each chapter. Additionally, each chapter includes a list of basic legal principles, which explains the law and provides citations to relevant case law and National Labor Relations Board (NLRB) decisions. Recommended readings give further opportunities to add depth to student understanding and class discussions.

Since its first edition, published in 1980, *Labor Guide to Labor Law*has provided a straightforward explanation of current labor law principles. The structure of the fifth edition remains essentially the same; however, the content has been substantially revised.—**Lisa Schultz**

Environmental Law

Handbooks and Yearbooks

324.　Burch, John R., Jr. **Water Rights and the Environment in the United States: A Documentary and Reference Guide.** Santa Barbara, Calif., Greenwood Press/ABC-CLIO, 2015. 442p. index. (Documentary and Reference Guides). $100.00. ISBN 13: 978-1-4408-3802-6; 978-1-4408-3803-3 (e-book).

The problem of water: it seems that there is either too much of it (flooding) or too little (drought). This work examines how we Americans have historically grappled with both ends of the aqueous spectrum, along with more recent issues, such as pollution and climate change. It does so by providing the verbatim text, usually excerpted, of court cases, legislation, treaties, studies, and other such primary source material detailing who gets what and why. Sixty-six written records are thus examined.

Each document is presented in a standard four-part format. A "Snapshot" section gives the reader a bulleted list of basic facts, such as date of creation, geographic location, and the reason for its inclusion in this collection. This is followed by the actual record concerned, the title of which doubles as a chapter heading. An "Analysis" segment helps to digest and interpret the foregoing material, which is oftentimes written in "legalese" or other technical language. Furthermore, it places the material in its cultural and historical context, which goes a long way towards sense making. Lastly, a short bibliography entitled "Further Reading" provides additional pertinent literature regarding the matter at hand. Special features include an introductory essay that gives a well-written overview of the contents of the book, along with a series of sidebar articles entitled, "Did You Know?" that gives interesting ancillary information.

The author is well versed on this topic; included among his published works is *Encyclopedia of Water Politics and Policy in the United States* (Congressional Quarterly Press, 2011, which was coedited along with Steven L. Danver; see ARBA 2012, entry 773). Burch holds a PhD in history from the University of Kentucky and currently serves as Dean of Library Services at Campbellsville University.

Considering the vital importance of water distribution and usage in this country, this engaging and informative work would be an appropriate purchase for all public and academic libraries.—**Michael Francis Bemis**

Human Rights

Handbooks and Yearbooks

325.   Bouchet-Saulnier, Françoise. **The Practical Guide to Humanitarian Law.** 3d ed. Lanham, Md., Rowman & Littlefield, 2014. 797p. index. $88.00pa.; $87.99 (e-book). ISBN 13: 978-1-4422-2141-3; 978-1-4422-2113-0 (e-book).

Humanitarian law is certainly an important topic, what with natural disasters, deadly armed conflicts, millions of refugees moving across national borders, and correspondingly bitter debates over how they are to be helped and officially categorized. This scholarly encyclopedia has over 200 long entries that examine particular aspects of various important legal topics, and how the interpretation of and implementation of humanitarian law has evolved over time. The author notes in the introduction that this work emphasizes "the perspective of victim's rights and aid organizations [,]" and that the weakest need to be protected "from interpretation of the law by dominant actors such as States and armed forces."(p. xvi) The entries include many references to international agreements, official documents, court decisions, and procedures of organizations, so that one can track down the original source material. Boxed sections of text highlight other important points of information that should be considered for an issue. *See also* indicators are located throughout the text. At the end of the entry there are cross-references to other parts of this guide, and a bibliography of resources for additional information, such as the United Nations Office for the Coordination of Humanitarian Affairs (http://www.unocha.org/). The work was originally published in 2002, and had a second edition in 2007. It provides more discussion than Connie de la Vega's *Dictionary of International Human Rights Law* (Elgar, 2013). The author is the legal director of Medecins Sans Frontieres (http://www.doctorswithoutborders.org), which sponsored this work. The book is also available in electronic format through various platforms. This easy-to-use reference book is useful for both practitioners and policy-makers, those working in governments, Non-Governmental Organizations or Inter-Governmental Organizations, law libraries, and collections serving graduate students and upper level undergraduates.—**Daniel K. Blewett**

326.   **Sexual Harassment in Education and Work Settings.** Michele A. Paludi, Jennifer L. Martin, James E. Gruber, and Susan Fineran, eds. Santa Barbara, Calif., Praeger/ABC-CLIO, 2015. 347p. index. (Women's Psychology). $79.00. ISBN 13: 978-1-4408-3293-2; 978-1-4408-3294-9 (e-book).

Sexual Harassment in Education and Work Settings: Current Research and Best Practices for Prevention is a volume in the series on Women's Psychology that examines sexual harassment in K-12 classrooms, in higher education institutions, and various workplace settings. The contributors of this book intend it to be a resource for those who want to make education institutions healthier places for women. The volume is arranged into sections that allow the reader to understand the nature of sexual harassment, the workplace organizational culture, pervasiveness of sexual harassment, Title IX, prevention programming, and coping strategies.

This text expands the definition of sexual harassment to more than that of males in the workplace telling inappropriate jokes and giving unwanted advances to female coworkers. Rarely do we think of sexual misconduct in education spaces occupied by children and young adults. According to Paludi, "the incidence of sexual harassment among undergraduate students by their peers ranges between 20% and 80% each year." According to the contributors it is the responsibility of the educational institutions to develop policies and procedures that deal with sexual harassment and that it is imperative that student's complaints are taken seriously with little stereotyping.

This volume is a valuable resource for college students, parents, and members of the workforce that need ongoing training and education in order to minimize and eradicate sexual harassment. This book can also be utilized by educators and education administrators who wish to develop policies and procedures for dealing with sexual harassment. Readers can have access to recent studies completed on the subject and the valuable data retrieved. The contributors expose the reality of sexual harassment in both K-12 and higher education institutions.—**Shireen Lalla**

Insurance Law

Handbooks and Yearbooks

327.   **Research Handbook on the Economics of Insurance Law.** Daniel Schwarcz and Peter Siegelman, eds. Northampton, Mass., Edward Elgar, 2015. 541p. index. (Research

Handbooks in Law and Economics). $290.00; $261.00 (e-book). ISBN 13: 978-1-78254-713-6; 978-1-78254-714-3 (e-book).

Research Handbook on the Economics of Insurance Law is a unique volume in that it brings together two concepts that are related, but are not generally discussed in tandem: insurance law and insurance economics. The book is a compilation of 20 authors who have written on the topics.

The handbook is divided into four parts. Part one deals with why insurance is purchased. This may seem to have an obvious answer but the chapters deal with nuances that the average practitioner may not think of—bias, motivation, and the moral hazards of economically analyzing health insurance.

Part two discusses the roles played by non-individuals in the insurance markets, namely state governments. Government insurance programs and insurance regulation by those governments are covered in depth. Part three continues the analysis of regulation, while part four focuses on how particular aspects of insurance law are handled by the courts. An extensive index is included at the end.

Research Handbook on the Economics of Insurance Law would be a useful resource for a practitioner or researcher interested in either insurance law or insurance economics. There are many insights to be gained by both groups from the other and this volume achieves that goal. It would be a valuable addition to any research library.—**Alicia Brillon**

International Law

Handbooks and Yearbooks

328. **International Labour Law.** Barbara J. Fick, ed. Northampton, Mass., Edward Elgar, 2016. 882p. (International Law). $430.00. ISBN 13: 978-1-4422-4500-6.

This compendium of articles, the ninth volume in the Edward Elgar International Law series, focuses on the role of the International Labour Organization (ILO) in protecting core labor rights and on efforts to enforce those protections amidst a changing world economic and political environment. Editor Barbara J. Fick, Associate Professor of Law at the University of Notre Dame Law School and an acknowledged authority in the field, has selected 27 articles from the *International Labour Review,* the *Comparative Labor Law and Policy Journal,* the *European Journal of International Law,* and other journals, plus some book chapters and working papers. She points out in her introduction that globalization "has inserted a new player into the international labor regime" and that multinational corporations have had a growing influence on domestic labor policies. The task of the ILO has thus become more difficult as nations compete for foreign investment. The book aims to provide the reader with an understanding of the ILO's policies and practices, the core labor standards, and the ways that labor rights can be protected in the context of the many current challenges. Part one focuses on the ILO's role in international labor law, part two on the substantive content of the core labor rights, part three on enforcement mechanisms outside the ILO, and part four on the future of international labor law. Insofar as possible, the articles have been reproduced as they were originally published, using facsimile reproduction. All the articles are footnoted; there is no index. The earliest article dates from 1977 but the great majority are from 2010 or later. This volume, pulling together as it does relevant and significant scholarship on labor rights and the ILO, will be a valuable reference for students, researchers, and policy-makers concerned with labor rights and international law.—**ARBA Staff Reviewer**

329. **Research Handbook on International Financial Crime.** Rider, Barry, ed. Northampton, Mass., Edward Elgar, 2016. 797p. index. (Research Handbooks in Financial Law). $345.00. ISBN 13: 978-1-78347-578-0; 978-1-78347-579-7 (e-book).

This is the sixth volume in the series entitled Research Handbooks in Financial Law and has been compiled to be of interest to both scholars and practicing lawyers in this increasingly important field of financial crime. The majority of the contributors were educated in the United Kingdom.

The articles deal with matters related to the commission and the resulting consequences of economically motivated crime especially financial crime as impacted by different legal systems and traditions.

The articles have been grouped into seven topical areas which include: the enterprise of crime, business crime, the financial sector at risk, fraud, corruption, the proceeds of financial and economic crime and the enforcement and control of financial crime. The length of these 60 articles varies from 11 to 15 pages. A list of the cases cited in all the articles will be found at the front of the book.

Considering the number of financial crimes that have been in the headlines recently, this book will serve as a useful framework in providing the reader with practical information on what constitutes a financial crime and how it impacts society.—**Judith J. Field**

330. **Research Handbook on International Marine Environmental Law.** Rosemary Rayfuse, ed. Northampton, Mass., Edward Elgar, 2015. 492p. index. (Research Handbooks in Environmental Law). $265.00. ISBN 13: 978-1-78100-476-0; 978-1-78100-477-7 (e-book).

This research handbook from Edward Elgar deals with a timely and important topic—the conservation and sustainable use of marine biological diversity beyond areas of national jurisdiction. As the foreword by David Freestone, executive director of the Sargasso Sea Commission, points out, oceans beyond areas of national jurisdiction "are the last great global commons areas on Earth" and cover nearly half the surface of the planet. The book, intended to provide a critical survey of current legal research relating to protection of the marine environment, has six parts: the legal framework for protection of the marine environment, pollution, seabed activities, protection of marine diversity, regional approaches to legal protection, and climate change. Editor Rosemary Rayfuse, professor at UNSW Australia (formerly called The University of New South Wales) and conjoint professor at Lund University, Sweden, has pulled together contributions from 24 distinguished legal scholars from five continents to tackle these subjects. Chapters include "Principles of international marine environmental law," "Protection of the marine environment from offshore oil and gas activities," "Protecting marine species," and much more. Each chapter has explanatory notes, and a comprehensive index enables the reader to locate the pertinent information sought. This book is recommended for libraries serving scholars and practitioners dealing with international law as well as government agencies and readers concerned with the environment and preservation of marine biological diversity.—**ARBA Staff Reviewer**

331. **Research Handbook on Jurisdiction and Immunities in International Law.**
Alexander Orakhelashvili, ed. Northampton, Mass., Edward Elgar, 2015. 545p. index.
(Research Handbooks in International Law). $255.00. ISBN 13: 978-1-78347-217-8; 978-
178347-218-5 (e-book).

What are the legitimate uses of state power? When and how should that power be
restricted? These are the basic questions of jurisdiction and immunities, two of the most
fundamental aspects of international law. The essays in this book, while united by a legal
positivist methodology, represent a number of different perspectives on these questions,
with contributors drawn from seven countries and four continents. As befits such a
fundamental subject and diverse group of authors, the book covers a wide range of specific
issues. Among these are universal jurisdiction, jurisdiction of states and the law of the sea,
immunity from the criminal jurisdiction of national courts, treaties on state immunity, the
status of armed forces in public international law, immunity from execution, international
criminal tribunals, and jurisdictional immunity of international organizations. The
arguments in these essays are well developed and supported by thorough documentation
of sources, and the index provides the reader with easy access to information on specific
cases, treaties, and legal doctrines.

Given the importance of jurisdictional matters in an era of increasing globalization,
this book will be of particular interest to scholars of international law, lawyers in
international practice, and those working in civil service or nongovernmental organizations
at the international level. General readers, however, are likely to find that a more concise
introduction to the subject is better suited to their needs.—**Robert Clark**

Private International Law

Handbooks and Yearbooks

332. **Intellectual Property and Private International Law.** Paul Torremans, ed.
Northampton, Mass., Edward Elgar, 2015. 853p. (Critical Concepts in Intellectual Property
Law). $425.00; $385.50 (e-book). ISBN 13: 978-1-78347-142-3.

Intellectual Property and Private International Law is the 12th installment in the
Edward Elgar Critical Concepts in Intellectual Property Law series. The volume is a
collection of 33 journal articles dating from 1991 to 2013 that discuss the private law
issues that have come up in the area of intellectual property and vice versa.

The book is divided into five parts—from issues of territory and jurisdiction to choice of
law and enforcement of foreign judgments, *Intellectual Property* covers the topics involved at
the intersection of intellectual property and private international law issues. The law review
articles themselves delve into their specific issues in-depth, and, at well over 800 pages, the
volume is a substantial compilation of information on the topics at hand.

An introduction by Paul Torremans provides an accessible summary of the five parts and
the larger issues that each will cover. There is a table of contents but no index or other finding
tool.

Intellectual Property would be a good addition to any law library, and would be useful
for attorneys or government officials working in the area of intellectual property or private
international law.—**Alicia Brillon**

11 Library and Information Science and Publishing and Bookselling

Library and Information Science

General Works

333. Gorman, Michael. **Our Enduring Values Revisited: Librarianship in an Ever-Changing World.** Chicago, American Library Association, 2015. 256p. $45.00pa.; $40.50pa. (ALA members). ISBN 13: 978-0-8389-1300-0.

Michael Gorman has an extensive list of publications on librarianship, and this title updates his 2000 publication of *Our Enduring Values: Librarianship in the 21st Century,* which was published before such significant world events as 9/11, the Afghanistan and Iraq wars, the Great Recession, and other events and trends that have affected public perception of libraries and the challenges we face. Gorman sees patterns in wide-ranging phenomena and discusses their significance in light of topics such as "The Value of Libraries," "The Library as Place," "Stewardship," "Service," "Intellectual Freedom," "Literacy and Learning," "Equity of Access," and "Privacy," among others. The 14 relatively short chapters (most under 20 pages) present much to contemplate on the values librarians attempt to uphold. His views are not black and white; rather he delights in exploring the areas of nuanced decision-making in libraries. At times he seems objective, and at other times, merely argumentative. Highly recommended for circulating and professional collections in all libraries, but not a reference book.—**Rosanne M. Cordell**

334. **Information Services Today: An Introduction.** Hirsh, Sandra, ed. Lanham, Md., Rowman & Littlefield, 2015. 514p. $55.00; $54.99 (e-book). ISBN 13: 978-1-4422-3958-6.

This textbook provides an extensive overview of the many fields and specializations of information services, the wide variety of careers available, and the expanding roles of information services. A variety of management and technical skills needed and information issues such as ethics are discussed. School media specialists will be interested in the chapters on school libraries, teaching users, the creation culture and Makerspaces, and concepts such as the learning commons. A lengthy guide to abbreviations and a thorough glossary help the reader appreciate the increased depth of the field. Tables, pull quotes, and discussion topics within chapters add to its value.—**Mary Alice Anderson**

335.   Rubin, Richard E. **Foundations of Library and Information Science.** 4th ed. Chicago, American Library Association, 2016. 628p. index. $85.00pa.; $76.50pa. (ALA members). ISBN 13: 978-0-8389-1370-3.

Since its first edition (Neal-Schuman, 1998), this work has served as a standard introductory textbook in many LIS graduate programs. Rubin, retired from Kent State University, where he directed the School of Library and Information Science before serving as associate provost, is well informed about the latest developments and issues in the field. Compared to the third edition (see ARBA 2011, entry 492), the latest update is almost 60 pages longer, although some of the added length may be accounted for by a larger, easier-on-the-eyes typeface. Rubin's purposes, as outlined in the preface, remain constant: to describe the field of library and information science; to identify and systematically review major issues in the LIS professions; to place LIS in a larger social, economic, political, and cultural context; and to point the way for deeper explorations. Although he writes primarily for new LIS students, Rubin also explicitly addresses readers already practicing in the field and those as yet undecided about entering it. Archives are accorded somewhat more attention in this edition, and the first chapter discusses the increasing convergence of libraries, archives, and museums, but libraries remain firmly at the center of the text; other information professions are barely covered. The order of chapters is slightly altered, but otherwise the basic organization of the volume is little changed from the previous edition. However, nearly every page shows evidence of significant revision. Rubin updates terminology (for example, replacing the cumbersome phrase, "educational, recreational, and informational (ERI) infrastructure," with "knowledge infrastructure") and adds current background on a wide range of relevant topics, including digital publishing, tribal libraries, the common core learning standards, BIBFRAME, mobile devices, cloud-based computing, linked data, discovery systems, diversity, disabilities, demand-driven acquisition, the semantic Web, virtual reference, social Q&A services, and much, much more. Key historical and contemporary documents, laws, and standards are cited and quoted throughout. The extensive chapter endnotes and lists of recommended readings reference up-to-date printed and online resources. Throughout the text, facts and statistics are framed by the theories, models, and values that shape the field. Appendixes identify LIS associations and ALA-accredited degree programs and reprint the ALA accreditation standards and the IFLA/UNESCO Public Library Manifesto. This information can be easily found on the Web and merely adds unnecessary length to an already sizeable volume. The book concludes with a detailed index. LIS faculty who teach introductory courses in LIS should consider assigning Rubin's text as the primary reading. No textbook can perfectly match every instructor's desired learning outcomes, but this one may serve well with just a few supplementary readings. Competing titles include *Introduction to the Library and Information Professions,* 2nd ed., by Roger C. Greer, Robert J. Grover, and Susan G. Fowler (see ARBA 2014, entry 479), and *Information Services Today: An Introduction,* edited by Sandra Hirsh (Rowman & Littlefield, 2015).—**Susan E. Searing**

Reference Works

Bibliography

336.   **Children's Core Collection.** 22d ed. Corsaro, Julie, Kendal Spires, and Gabriela Toth, eds. Bronx, N.Y., H. W. Wilson, 2015. 2v. index. (Core Collection Series). $240.00/

set. ISBN 13: 978-1-61925-705-4.

This is the 22d edition of *Children's Core Collection* (CCC) and comes for the first time in two volumes, considerably helpful because it now runs over 3,100 pages. For those who prefer to search CCC online, it is available through EBSCOhost, where it is updated weekly. The CCC is comprised of fiction and nonfiction books recommended for children from preschool through sixth grade. An advisory committee of public and school librarians (listed on page ix of the front matter) selects books for inclusion. This edition has over 15,000 titles at the most highly recommended or core collection book level.

The book is designed to help librarians with purchasing, user service, curriculum support, collection development, and professional development and is divided into two parts. The first, Classified Collection, uses the Dewey Decimal system and starts with nonfiction followed by easy books, fiction, and story collections. Entries have full bibliographical descriptions, price information, recommended subject headings based on the *Sears List of Subject Headings,* a suggested classification number from the *Abridged Dewey Decimal Classification and Relative Index,* a short description, and an evaluation from a quoted source like *School Library Journal.* A star at the beginning of the entry indicates that the book is highly recommended. The second part is comprised of the author, title, and subject index. This list is alphabetical; classification numbers in bold help users locate the main entry for the book. The index employs "*see*" and "*see also* references." This title is a valuable tool for children's librarians.—**ARBA Staff Reviewer**

337.   **Guide to Reference: Essential General Reference and Library Science Sources.** Whitlatch, Jo Bell and Susan E. Searing, eds. Chicago, American Library Association, 2014. 248p. index. $65.00pa. ISBN 13: 978-0-8389-1232-4.

This book covers general reference and library and information sciences. It has sections on bibliography, biography, geography, dissertations, encyclopedias, genealogy, government publications, dictionaries, newspapers, periodicals, general reference works, and professional resources. While it is intended primarily for libraries serving institutions of higher education, some segments will also be helpful to public and school librarians, independent researchers, publishers, and book dealers. Selected works are broadly focused and favor titles published within the last 20 years and online sources. The sections on general reference works do not include discipline-specific sources. The numbered entries give brief descriptive annotations. The entries for Google Earth, Google maps, MapQuest, and Yahoo! Maps indicate that they are comparable to each other but there's no discussion of their strengths and weaknesses. The work includes an index.—**Norman Desmarais**

338.   **Middle & Junior High Core Collection, 12th ed.** Julie Corsaro, Kendal Spires, and Gabriela Toth, eds. Bronx, N.Y., H. W. Wilson, 2015. 2413p. index. (Core Collection Series). $295.00. ISBN 13: 978-1-61925-706-1.

This standard collection development tool includes over 11,000 book titles recommended for young people in grades 5-9, and professional aids for their school media specialists or public librarians, all chosen by an Advisory Board of librarians, consultants, and library school educators. The Core Collection series are intended to serve for purchasing, reader's advisory, verification of information, curriculum support, collection maintenance, and as instructional aids. All books listed are published in the United States or are published in Canada or the United Kingdom and distributed in the United States. The titles include graphic novels but now exclude classic literature as well as non-English language (except bilingual), dictionaries, adult fiction not typically read by young people, textbooks, or topics that quickly become outdated such as computer program manuals. Part one of the work is arranged by abridged Dewey (a summary table is provided), with each entry listing bibliographic information, the grades for which the title is recommended, the specific classification for the title, its Sears subject headings, ISBN and LC numbers, and descriptive, critical, and special features notes. Highly recommended titles are starred. Part two is the author, title, and subject index to the entries in part one. The current title of this work (Core Collection, rather than Catalog) emphasizes that it can be subscribed to via EBSCO, where one has access to weekly updates and features unavailable in print. Given the massive and unwieldy size of this work, investigating the e-book format should be considered. Essential.—**Rosanne M. Cordell**

339.   **Public Library Core Collection: Nonfiction.** 15th ed. Neal Wyatt, Kendal Spires, and Gabriela Toth, eds. Bronx, N.Y., H. W. Wilson, 2015. 2787p. (Core Collection Series). $420.00. ISBN 13: 978-1-61925-473-2; 978-0-8242-1445-6 (e-book).

This volume in the Core Collection Series (formerly known as the Standard Catalog Series) offers an up-to-date listing of recommended adult nonfiction and reference titles. It contains older titles which may be updated (provided they are considered the standard of their topic) as well as new titles which may either explore more recent areas of interest or reflect new understanding of a given topic.

This substantial volume includes over 12,000 titles naming books published in the United States or abroad (with a US distribution). Organized into two parts, this volume initially lists the Classified Collection (part one), with titles arranged according to the Dewey Decimal System, then follows up with an Author, Title and Subject Index (part two) which serves as a key to the first part.

Information detailed in the Classified Collection mainly includes a full bibliographical description (number of pages, etc.), recommended subject headings, Dewey Decimal classification numbers, a brief summation of the book's contents, pricing information, and more.

Part two is arranged alphabetically and indexes all titles in the Classified Collection. The boldface classification number guides readers to the location of the title's main entry in part one. This index is particularly helpful if a title may be classified in more than one area.

Including directions for understanding the book's organization as well as the best ways to use it (e.g., as an aid to purchasing etc.), this large and vital reference is a must for both public and academic libraries.—**Laura Herrell**

340.   **Young Adult Fiction Core Collection.** Julie Corsaro, Kendal Spires, Gabriela Toth, and Christi Showman Farrar, eds. Bronx, N.Y., H. W. Wilson, 2015. 1000p. index. $295.00. ISBN 13: 978-1-61925-866-2.

A manual of YA classics, Wilson's iffy reference guide compresses into data-filled entries suggestions for teen reads by author, title, publisher, year, length, price, and grade level. Works the quality of Ursula Le Guin's *The Lathe of Heaven* and Gary Paulsen's *Nightjohn* share space with Paul Zindel's *Pigman* and Sherman Alexie's *The Absolutely True Diary of a Part-Time Indian.* Wilson's selection criteria cling to the faded glory of Robert Lipstyle's *The Contender* and SE Hinton's *The Outsiders* while overlooking more appealing fiction. Surprising omissions include Walter Dean Myers's Vietnam War classic

Fallen Angels, Richard Peck's humorous *A Long Way from Chicago,* Avi's girl-centric *The True Confessions of Charlotte Doyle,* and the works of Irene Hunt, Cynthia Rylant, Ellen Raskin, and Isabel Allende. A pricey work that picks and chooses without regard to teacher and reader preferences. Not recommended.—**Mary Ellen Snodgrass**

Libraries

College and Research Libraries

341.   **ACRL Insider. http://www.acrl.ala.org/acrlinsider/.** [Website] Free. Date reviewed: 2016.

The mission of ACRL Insider is to keep the world current and informed on the activities, services, and programs of the Association of College & Research Libraries (a division of the American Library Association), including publications, events, conferences, and eLearning opportunities.

With this mission, it's important that the Website be up to date, and this one is. Its main feature is a set of posts that range in topic from the ACRL member of the week to announcements about the latest issue of *Keeping Up With...,* ACRL's online current awareness publication, featuring concise briefs on trends in academic librarianship and higher education. Other recent posts include an ad looking for new mentors for the ACRL Dr. E.J. Josey Spectrum Scholar Mentor Program, which links library school students and new librarians with established academic librarians for mentoring and professional guidance. The blog highlights professional workshops and profiles board-of-director candidates.

The format of the site is clear and attractive, with a set of main links across the top and a large scrolling photo banner underneath. The main page features a link to the newest blog content; a "Libraries in Transition" video, created for the 75th anniversary of the ACRL; a link to ACRL publications; Instagram photos; archives; a link to the ACRL's Twitter feed; and a delightful link to *Goodreads,* where ACRL members of the week share what books they're reading.

While a link to a Google calendar is available, no events show up. The blog appears to be a better place to find information. Clicking the "About" link takes users to the same Web page as the "Posts" link. What you see on the home page is basically what you get; the site doesn't have much depth, but most users will be interested in the information found on the blog, and a "subscribe" link makes it easy to get publications and information by e-mail or RSS feed.

In short, *ACRL Insider* is the go-to resource for librarians and others who want to stay abreast of the ACRL's varied activities and resources.—**ARBA Staff Reviewer**

342.   **Creating Leaders: An Examination of Academic and Research Library Leadership Institutes.** Irene M.H. Herold, ed. Chicago, American Library Association, Association of College and Research Libraries, 2015. 380p. index. (Publications in Librarianship series). $78.00pa. ISBN 13: 978-0-8389-8763-6.

This is the first book to systematically examine leadership training institutes for academic librarians, some of which have been running for decades. The 18 chapters each focus on a single program, including five that are defunct, and are written by librarians who participated in them. The authors, who are nearly all university library directors, associate directors, or department heads, are ideally positioned to provide insights into the benefits of preparation for leadership roles. In addition to reflecting on their personal experiences, the authors recount the institute's history, outline its curriculum, suggest ways to improve the program, and discuss specific leadership theories, if any, that underpin it. Most chapters also review publications about the institute, although the literature is generally scant, which reinforces the value of this collection. The book is divided into six parts. In part one, an institute open to all academic librarians is described. In part two, four institutes aimed at specific populations within academic librarianship are profiled—theological librarians; college library directors; librarians at historically black colleges and universities; and medical librarians. Part three focuses on four programs that develop leaders for Association of Research Libraries and large research libraries. Part four examines six institutes that span multiple types of libraries, including academic. Part five covers three programs that are open to a broad spectrum of academic personnel including librarians; two of the three are specifically for women in administrative roles. Across the categories, the majority of the institutes are intended for mid-career librarians, but a few target entry-level librarians or those already in senior positions. The formats vary widely, from intensive workshops to Webinar series to residential programs lasting one to three weeks. Many build in a strong mentoring component; several revolve around campus visits. Most of the chapters report the results of formal or informal surveys of program graduates. In part six, editor Irene Herold presents tabular comparisons of the 18 programs on several dimensions, including how they were formed, size, longevity, enrollment process, and curriculum. Although she uncovers little evidence that such programs actually develop leadership skills, it is clear from participants' testimonies that they increase librarians' self-knowledge, instill confidence, and create supportive collegial networks. Librarians who are considering applying for one of the still-active programs can benefit from the information and first-hand accounts gathered together in this book, as can directors who may be pondering the value of supporting a librarian's participation. Therefore, *Creating Leaders* is recommended for all academic libraries.—**Susan E. Searing**

343.   **Difficult Decisions: Closing & Merging Academic Libraries.** Sara Holder and Amber Butler Lannon, eds. Chicago, American Library Association, Association of College and Research Libraries, 2015. 253p. $58.00pa. ISBN 13: 978-0-8389-8791-9; 978-0-8389-8793-3 (e-book).

During three branch library consolidations, McGill University librarians sought advice and best practices from colleagues and library literature during the process. They discovered that while many librarians have experienced change and transition, their experiences are not shared in the literature. The McGill University librarians decided to gather case studies and other research from American libraries about their institutional experiences on library restructuring. This edited volume compiles case studies from 11 institutions, including McGill University Library, University of Illinois Library at Urbana-Champaign, Welch Medical Library, Purdue University Libraries, Columbia University Libraries, University of California-San Diego, University of California-Berkeley, University of Idaho's University Libraries, University of British Columbia Library, Georgia Regents University Libraries, and University of North Georgia Libraries. These institutions are mostly large, research libraries with some consortia. The case studies document transitions and illustrate a variety of problems including staff morale, collection weeding, and logistics. Twelve of the 14 chapters are case studies of mergers, downsizing, weeding, branch closings, service consolidations, and staff and budget reductions. One chapter outlines a failed merger of a library and IT department. This unusual case study describes where the failure occurred and what could have been different to ensure a better outcome. Chapter 12 describes the planning and implementation of a consolidated library Website and a section of chapter 3 describes how a cohesive library Website was created from several, unique library Websites. All chapters include bibliographical references. The text also includes tables, charts, graphs, illustrations, and planning documents. These case studies are valuable for administrators, librarians, and change agents in university settings. Smaller-size institutions may find nuggets of information that would assist in preparation for change. The keys to success are planning and communication.—**Linda M. Turney**

344.   **Digital Humanities in the Library: Challenges and Opportunities for Subject Specialists.** Arianne Hartsell-Gundy, Laura Braunstein, and Liorah Golomb, eds. Chicago, American Library Association, Association of College and Research Libraries, 2015. 287p. $68.00pa. ISBN 13: 978-0-8389-8767-4.

Although there are other books on digital humanities scholarship, this edited work is intended to help subject librarians understand the possibilities in this area and navigate relationships among faculty, students, and fellow librarians. The book is divided into four parts. Part one explores the reasons why subject specialists should acquire digital humanities skills. Part two provides examples of how librarians can become involved in digital humanities. Part three discusses successful library initiatives involving collaborations or in establishing spaces to accommodate digital humanities projects in the library. Finally, part four provides case studies on individual projects from start to completion. In most chapters, examples are given of actual projects or collaborations. Each chapter has a bibliography of about two dozen resources, and collaborators do a good job of mentioning other resources that can be helpful to librarians new to digital humanities. An appendix includes a list of tools and resources referenced in the book, followed by brief biographies of the contributors. Overall, if you are looking for a handbook on digital humanities, this isn't it. Rather it provides a "here's what we did" approach to understanding how subject librarians can become more involved in digital humanities. At close to 300 pages the book is sufficiently descriptive, and most librarians new to the topic will learn something. Recommended for all academic libraries.—**Kevin McDonough**

345.   Nelson, Bryce. **The Academic Library Administrator's Field Guide.** Chicago, American Library Association, 2014. 224p. index. $72.00pa. ISBN 13: 978-0-8389-1223-2.

Being in an academic library administration requires a diverse set of skills in leadership, management, communication, and supervision. Administrators often find a lack of time and resources to develop and improve on their skill sets. The purpose of *The Academic Library Administrator's Field Guide* is to provide an overview of the topics and decision-making approaches that fit the role of an academic library administrator. Administrators at any level of experience will find this book useful in exploring areas that they may not have previously thought about or realized the importance of in the fulfillment of their responsibilities within the college or university environment. The book is divided into three parts: being politically active where the director has a role in positioning the library as a part of the college or university's mission; managing and leading staff to the fulfillment of the library's mission; and supervising operations where the library's services are managed at a high level. Each chapter provides an assertion, commentary, and application examples for the relevant topics that administrators face in their roles. Each chapter also provides recommended reading materials for a more in-depth study on a particular topic. This book succeeds in its purpose, in both layout and content, of providing overview information that can be examined on an individual topic level or as a whole study. An administrator would find it simple to pick up this book, find a particular item of interest, and obtain an overview of its importance and how to apply it to daily activities.—**Lee Sochay**

346.   **Practical Strategies for Academic Library Managers: Leading with Vision through All Levels.** Frances C. Wilkinson and Rebecca L. Lubas, eds. Santa Barbara, Calif., Libraries Unlimited/ABC-CLIO, 2015. 168p. index. $65.00pa. ISBN 13: 978-1-61069-889-4; 978-1-61069-890-0 (e-book).

In this highly practical guide, experienced managers share their wisdom on traditional as well as emerging functions in academic libraries. Steven Mandeville-Gamble (University of California, Riverside) advises on communicating and implementing an organization's vision, with an emphasis on internal audiences. The volume's editors, Rebecca L. Lubas (Claremont Colleges) and Frances C. Wilkinson (University of New Mexico) contribute an essay on reorganizations, in which they identify common impetuses for revamping library organization structures and outline basic strategies for successful "reorg" processes. Pat Hawthorne (University of Nevada, Las Vegas) provides a primer on the core functions of human resources management: recruitment; orientation of new employees; supervision; management of teams; retention and staff development; and self-improvement as a manager. Susan E. Parker (UCLA) demystifies the complex topic of budgeting, which perplexes and frightens many first-time managers. Loreen S. Henry (University of Texas, Dallas) takes a broad view of marketing, publicity, and outreach; she focuses on clarifying the purpose of a marketing campaign, defining the target audience, and understanding what users want before framing the message. Mary Ellen Spencer (University of Oklahoma) and Sarah Barbara Watstein (University of North Carolina, Wilmington) offer a wide-ranging yet detailed overview of issues involved in conceptualizing, planning, and managing library facilities. Nina Davis-Millis (MIT) shares succinct wisdom on managing library information technology and IT staff. The relatively new concept of blended librarianship is explained by Anne E. Pemberton (University of North Carolina, Wilmington), who not only elaborates the benefits of combining traditional library expertise with instructional technology skills, but also illustrates how blended librarianship requires systems thinking that can be applied to many aspects of management. Finally, consultant Nancy Bolt analyzes the Colorado Digitization Project as a case study of collaboration between an academic library and other cultural heritage institutions, paying particular attention to managerial and leadership roles. Although the nine chapters vary in length, approach, and quality, taken as a whole this volume will be a lifesaver for new managers in academic libraries. As Maureen Sullivan notes in her foreword, most academic library managers are hired or promoted because of their record in a functional area of library practice, and the transition to a managerial role often feels daunting. This volume both informs and reassures new managers, and thus is an excellent choice for any academic library professional collection. In addition, many of the chapters would be useful in courses on library administration.—**Susan E. Searing**

347.   Puckett, Jason. **Modern Pathfinders: Creating Better Research Guides.** Chicago, American Library Association, Association of College and Research Libraries, 2015. 156p. $42.00pa. ISBN 13: 978-0-8389-8817-6.

Research guides are a mainstay in today's academic libraries. Whether they are developed online using proprietary software or created via word processors, librarians have adopted these guides as a communication tool for their patrons. *Modern Pathfinders: Creating Better Research Guides* by Jason Puckett provides background knowledge, theory, and application to help librarians design and implement more effective guides for their patrons. The book is not software specific and uses proven ideas supported by user experience design that anyone can apply.

This compact book includes a descriptive table of contents and introduction followed by six chapters that cover a variety of relevant topics with an important focus on learning objectives. Lengthy notes and references provide additional resources for those wanting to dig deeper. Puckett uses best practices, examples, and screenshots from various research guides to support the content. All stages of designing a guide are covered from pre-planning to design, development, and assessment.

In addition to providing specific examples for application, Puckett incorporates and applies learning styles and instructional theory while focusing on student outcomes. The book includes a terminology list which is helpful for librarians new to the concept of research guides. Puckett acknowledges common issues or mistakes and includes how to use Web analytics to increase efficiency and user experience. This book is highly recommended for academic libraries, and librarians of all experience levels will find the material relevant, useful, and accessible.—**Jessica Crossfield McIntosh**

Public Libraries

348.   Farlow, Jonathan M. **I've Seen It All at the Library: The View from Behind the Desk.** Jefferson, N.C., McFarland, 2015. 185p. illus. index. $35.00pa. ISBN 13: 978-0-7864-9684-6; 978-1-4766-1874-6 (e-book).

In the engagingly written *I've Seen It All at the Library: The View from Behind the Desk,* public librarian Jonathan Farlow recounts his entrée into the profession, many of his colorful encounters and experiences, and relationships with colleagues, imparting words of wisdom for fellow librarians throughout the text. Part autobiography, part advice book, the title ends with three appendixes. The first, "Library Stories" relays tales about myriad situations, like the time a patron brought a bug to the reference desk for identification—the bug wound up being a poisonous assassin bug. The second index contains an open letter to patrons from the perspective of librarians, asking for such things as basic hygiene, a desire to find information, and polite manners. "A Letter to My Fellow Librarians," the third appendix, reminds others in the profession of the importance of libraries and the work of librarians. There are black-and-white photographs scattered throughout the book, a one-page bibliography, and a short index.—**ARBA Staff Reviewer**

349.   Nichols, Joel A. **Teaching Internet Basics: The Can-Do Guide.** Santa Barbara, Calif., Libraries Unlimited/ABC-CLIO, 2014. 143p. $22.50pa. ISBN 13: 978-1-61069-741-5; 978-1-61069-742-2 (e-book).

This is a guide designed primarily for public librarians who teach Internet literacy. The guide is well-organized and designed to move learners from the basics of browsers through more advanced tasks such as online communities. Each chapter is a complete workshop plan that includes lesson outcomes, hands-on activities, and potential problems along with suggested solutions. Appendixes include free online courseware, additional resources, and sample handouts, as well as a reproducible glossary of key concepts. A few of the lessons may not be appropriate in a school setting; many can be found in other formats online.—**Alda Moore**

350.   **Public Library Video Online: Premium. http://www.alexanderstreet.com/ products/public-library-video-online-premium.** [Website] Alexandria, Va., Alexander Street Press. Price negotiated by site. Date reviewed: 2016.

The Alexander Street *Public Library Video Collection* provides video streaming access to over 42,000 videos with the aim to "serve the needs of today's public library patrons." This is certainly a vast and varied audience; hence, the collection includes a wide, diverse, and multidisciplinary selection of content including documentaries, newsreels, commercials, how-to videos, and performances. Subjects represented include American and world history, current events, art, science, cooking, etc. Content is provided from a wide range of sources including major, well-known providers (such as A&E, ABC, PBS, and NBC), to lesser-known independent and private filmmakers.

The video collection can be searched by keyword and browsed by title, discipline, people, and series. Searches can be refined by several criteria including persons and places discussed, content type (i.e., documentary, interview, performance, instructional material, etc.), subject, and date.

Users are allowed to add their own bookmarks to the videos, and they can cite and share the videos, save favorites to a playlist, and generate a permalink embed code—an option very useful for teaching or research. Users are also able to make and save their own video clips allowing many different and useful applications for both teachers and students such as building an engaging lesson, presentation, or report. Each video has a visual table of contents to help users easily navigate the videos by memorable scene.

All of the videos are fully transcribed. The transcript is synced with the video time code allowing users to click on any word or phrase in the transcript and jump to the corresponding place in the video. While still very useful, the transcripts were noted to contain several flaws, misspellings, and incorrect words choices. This can likely be attributed to machine/algorithm-based transcription.

This resource is recommended for public libraries interested in expanding their video offerings. It is a high-quality, user-friendly resource that can serve a large and diverse audience. There is a lot of content that will appeal to patron's recreation and entertainment needs, but the majority of the content is geared for more educational and research pursuits. Libraries looking for a more recreation/entertainment-oriented service might need to supplement with other materials.—**Kristin Kay Leeman**

School Libraries

351.   Cavanaugh, Terence W. **eBooks for Elementary School.** Santa Barbara, Calif., Libraries Unlimited/ABC-CLIO, 2014. 206p. index. $45.00pa. ISBN 13: 978-1-61069-849-8; 978-1-61069-850-4 (e-book).

The time for using e-books is here and educators need to embrace the technology that allows using different kinds of reading to engage and teach. Cavanaugh lays out a list of possibilities for different kinds of teachers, and different readers. There are many sources and good ideas for all teachers in this book. The suggestions for getting started provided lots of help and encouragement. Many of the Web addresses listed might be familiar, but the author also includes step-by-step ways to use them. It would be helpful if a district orders several copies to circulate. This is a book librarians can pore over again and again, taking away something each time. An index rounds out the publication.—**Leslie Greaves Radloff**

352.   Harvey, Carl A., III, and Linda L. Mills. **Leading the Common Core Initiative: A Guide for K-5 School Librarians.** Santa Barbara, Calif., Libraries Unlimited/ABC-CLIO, 2014. 230p. index. $22.50pa. ISBN 13: 978-1-61069-491-9; 978-1-61069-492-6 (e-book).

This text begins with a brief history of the Common Core State Standards and connections to the AASL standards. The next three chapters address the impact of Common Core on the administration, instruction, and growth of the library. The chapters on administrative, professional development, and advocacy impacts will be helpful to librarians and school administrators still struggling to figure out the role of the library. Budgeting, collection development, technology, facilities, policies, procedures, and professional development are each covered with sound advice and insight. Sample lessons for each grade level provide models for integrating Common Core Standards in collaborative and independent instruction. Appendix materials include student and staff surveys, bibliographies of print and electronic resources, and graphic organizers.—**Holly Whitt**

353.   Hopwood, Jennifer L. **Best STEM Resources for NextGen Scientists: The Essential Selection and User's Guide.** Santa Barbara, Calif., Libraries Unlimited/ABC-CLIO, 2015. 279p. index. (Children's and Young Adult Literature Reference Series). $65.00. ISBN 13: 978-1-61069-721-7; 978-1-61069-722-4 (e-book).

STEM (science, technology, engineering, and math) is a clearly defined emphasis in schools today. How do school librarians integrate STEM into their programming? *Best STEM Resources for NextGen Scientists: The Essential Selection and User's Guide* gives an overview of materials to support STEM curriculum.

Author Jennifer L. Hopwood currently works as a training coordinator for the Southern Maryland Regional Library Association and an online adjunct professor for Rasmussen College. A former youth services librarian, Hopwood has depth in her STEM experiences as she has carried out programs on a regular basis and contributes information to STEM publications.

This resource is available in print or e-book format. The cover is inviting and suggestive of exploration and innovation. A clear table of contents enables the user to find specific resources with ease. Chapter headings are clear making the information accessible. The indexes are particularly valuable; an Author Index, Title Index, and STEM index provide three access points to resources and information. The STEM index is divided into the four subjects, allowing librarians to focus on just some or all of the topics.

The first two chapters define and explore the library's role in STEM curriculum. As the title states, the primary purpose of this text is as a collection of STEM resources. Most chapters are listings of books, both fiction and non-fiction, from preschool through young adult, and Chapter 10 relates to professional development titles. There are no graphics within the book, save useful tables for each resource to show which of the four study areas the book pertains to (science, technology, engineering, or math). The tables are practical as they allow the user to quickly surmise the usefulness of a resource. Largely, the book lists are well annotated and contain strong titles both current (*Parrots Over Puerto Rico,* 2014) and from the distant past (*The Voyages of Doctor Doolittle,* 1923). Chapter nine, "New Media for STEM Education" is a collection of apps and Websites, but it is questionable whether CDs could be considered "new media."

Hopwood has done due diligence with *Best STEM Resources for NextGen Scientists: The Essential Selection and User's Guide.* Age groupings of resources that are suitable for STEM programming are valid and applicable to this curriculum. This book has programming ideas but that is not the focal point; school librarians trying to find resources to accentuate their STEM curriculum will find this collection supportive of learning plans and library programs. Recommended.—**Janis Minshull**

354.   Kelsey, Mark. **Cataloging for School Librarians.** Lanham, Md., Rowman & Littlefield, 2014. 316p. $44.00pa.; $43.99 (e-book). ISBN 13: 978-1-4422-3246-4; 978-1-4422-3247-1 (e-book).

Many school media specialists have never had a cataloging class; they rely on MARC records from vendors. Not only is this book a valuable refresher for professionals who aren't sure how to catalog a Web page, etc., it is a clearly written, step-by-step, easy-to-understand handbook for the many clerks and paraprofessionals in school libraries who have never had a cataloging class. This handbook explains where to get complete records, how to correct your current records, and includes a "what if" critical thinking section at the close of each chapter to help expand the reader's understanding. This book should be in every school library, read by every person who manages the local catalog, and kept nearby as a handy reference. Two appendixes, a glossary, and a bibliography complete the work.—**Claire Berg**

355.   **School Library Management.** 7th ed. Gail K. Dickinson and Judi Repman, eds. Santa Barbara, Calif., Libraries Unlimited/ABC-CLIO, 2015. 335p. index. $60.00pa. ISBN 13: 978-1-61069-140-6; 978-1-4408-3456-1 (e-book).

This is a compilation of articles from *Library Media Connection,* and is aimed at anyone in the library profession, from preservice library students to beginning librarians, as well as experienced practicing librarians. Five chapters cover establishing the library's place in the school; how librarians are putting into practice the concepts of intellectual freedom, access, and equity; current practices including ISTE technology standards and Common Core; keeping libraries current and relevant in difficult economic times; the future of school libraries; and the profession in general. This edition includes more writing about technology, and offers "TIPS and Other Bright Ideas" from the print publication. Each chapter starts with an Editor's Note. This is a reflective look at current practices that make school libraries relevant and necessary. This is a great reference book for all school librarians.—**Tracy A. Fitzwater**

356.   Spisak, Jen. **Multimedia Learning Stations: Facilitating Instruction, Strengthening the Research Process, Building Collaborative Partnerships.** Santa Barbara, Calif., Libraries Unlimited/ABC-CLIO, 2015. 223p. illus. index. (Tech Tools for Learning). $45.00pa. ISBN 13: 978-1-4408-3517-9; 978-1-4408-3518-6 (e-book).

The Tech Tools for Learning series introduces K-12 teachers and librarians to innovative technologies for the classroom and school media center. In this new volume, award-winning middle school librarian Jen Spisak provides detailed instructions for setting up learning stations to support standards-based curricula and to encourage students to take responsibility for their own learning. Students develop information literacy skills, acquire content knowledge, and hone their critical thinking ability as they rotate among stations to explore diverse resources on a topic, including databases, Websites, books, videos, podcasts, educational apps, manipulatable objects, and more. In the first third of the book, Spisak carefully lays out everything a librarian needs to know to implement multimedia learning stations and reap positive effects on student learning and librarian-teacher collaboration. Boxed testimonials from students and teachers further attest to the value of the station approach. Spisak emphasizes that learning stations appeal to students with diverse learning styles, facilitate both individual and group work, align well with any stage of research, and can be applied to a wide range of topics. One chapter is devoted to framing questions to propel and demonstrate learning, based on Bloom's taxonomy. Other chapters address the logistics of rotating students among the stations and designing assessments. Spisak provides a step-by-step guide to designing stations and recommends techniques for organizing and implementing them. The final two-thirds of the book contain 15 examples of stations for curricula in English (e.g., contextualizing the novel, *The Giver*), history (e.g., the Harlem Renaissance), math (e.g., fractions), and science (e.g., cells). Each example identifies the appropriate grade range, from middle school through high school, and relevant state standards (Virginia is given as an example) as well as the American Association of School Librarians (AASL) standards. Modifications for special education students are suggested. The number of stations per topic varies from three to eight. Each individual station is described in detail, including what students do, the questions they must answer, and what level of Bloom's taxonomy is addressed. Lists of the specific online and physical materials needed at each station follow, and assessment strategies for the unit are spelled out. Although learning stations are not a new concept, in this book Spisak blends traditional approaches with multimedia content and online interactivity to provides a start-to-finish recipe for success. A librarian who has not previously experimented with learning stations can take the plunge by adapting one of Spisak's detailed models. Those already using the station method will find inspiration to update their practice. This work is recommended for all secondary school librarians' professional reading shelves, as well as academic libraries that support the education of K-12 librarians and classroom teachers.—**Susan E. Searing**

357.   Weisburg, Hilda K., and Ruth Toor. **New on the Job: A School Librarian's Guide to Success.** 2d ed. Chicago, American Library Association, 2015. 223p. index. $40.00pa. ISBN 13: 978-0-8389-1264-5.

This book is an update to the earlier edition published seven years ago. Written by two retired school librarians with a great deal of experience between them, this book is excellent for new school librarians or veterans who are switching schools or just want to refresh their "game." The book is well-organized; an appendix includes Essential Resources and a list of Jobbers and Vendors. This title will help a new school librarian prepare for everything that first year—from advice for getting ready for the job interview, to organizing and cleaning out that first space, to getting along with a new school community. This book seems to have everything you need to know that you did not learn in library school. The book includes a useful glossary, table of contents, and index.—**Valerie Byrd Fort**

Special Topics

Archives

358.   Bastian, Jeannette A., Megan Sniffin-Marinoff, and Donna Webber. **Archives in Libraries: What Librarians and Archivists Need to Know to Work Together.** Chicago, Society of American Archivists, 2015. 146p. $69.95pa. ISBN 13: 1-931666-87-3.

The ideal reader of this slim volume, its trio of highly qualified authors suggest, is the director of a library that houses and manages, or is planning to start, an archives program. Their sage advice pertains to academic libraries that serve as repositories for their institution's historical records, as well as public libraries with local history rooms. Three decades have passed since *Archives and Library Administration: Divergent Traditions and Common Concerns,* edited by Lawrence J. McCrank (Haworth Press, 1986) laid out the differences and commonalities of the work that librarians and archivists do, so this new work is an important step toward increased mutual understanding and collaboration. As the authors note, the evolving digital environment for information management and access creates increased dissonance in some areas, while also fostering opportunities for convergence between the two professional cultures. A special feature of this work is the 15 vignettes scattered throughout the text, based on real-life scenarios. Verbatim responses of interviewees to questions about their work practices are also included, and it is enlightening to read the perspectives of front-line archivists as well as library directors on topics such as resource allocation and the value of the archives to the library overall. The book is organized in three parts, each with three brief chapters. Part one sets the stage with discussions of each field's foundational concepts (mission, professional roots, identity, and values), language, and educational pathways. Here, and throughout the book, side-by-side charts reveal where librarians and archivists are similar and where they differ. Part two explains the work that archivists do and how it diverges from the work of librarians, particularly in the realm of records management. One chapter is devoted to recommending a process for planning and managing a new archives. Part three looks at professional ethics and considers aspects of librarianship and archival practice that offer opportunities for collaboration: information literacy, digital access, and digital preservation. A two-page appendix points to published standards for archives, and a bibliography suggests avenues for deeper exploration. While aimed at library directors, this book can serve as a good introduction for professionals on either side of the librarian-archivist divide who wish to better understand the challenges their colleagues face.—**Susan E. Searing**

359.   **Encyclopedia of Archival Science.** Luciana Duranti and Patricia C. Franks, eds. Lanham, Md., Rowman & Littlefield, 2015. 454p. index. $125.00; $124.99 (e-book). ISBN 13: 978-0-8108-8810-4; 978-0-8108-8811-1 (e-book).

This first-time encyclopedia for archival science brings together archival concepts, principles, and practices into a single source. Contributions include an initial 200 entries from 100 contributors with oversight by an international editorial group of 20 archives experts on 154 topics. These cover all aspects of archival science and practice. Editors include Luciana Duranti (University of British Columbia) and Patricia C. Franks (San José State University), in addition to an Editorial Advisory Board of seven leading archivists and archival educators covering a spectrum of institutions.

Topic entries are arranged in alphabetical order, and each includes keywords, related entries, and a simple bibliography. An index and biography of each contributor in included. The 15-page index covers a multitude of subtopics and is an excellent finding aid to this broad field.

The *Encyclopedia* covers topics in archival theory, principles, and practice. Coverage of broad topics includes fundamental archival principles: Archival Description, Archival Fonds, Diplomatics, Documentary Evidence, Principle of Pertinence; and the more technical or practical: Metadata Application Profiles, Information Policy, Collecting Archives, Archival Preservation, Electronic Document and Record Management Systems, Photographic Records, or Records Inventory.

The work could benefit by the further separation of concepts (Archival Description could break down into Finding Aids, etc.). There is room for considerable expansion with additional topics of importance in the field of Archives Science.—**William Shakalis**

360.   Marks, Steve. **Module 8: Becoming a Trusted Digital Repository.** Chicago, Society of American Archivists, 2015. 68p. index. $29.99pa. ISBN 13: 1-931666-84-9; 1-931666-86-5 (e-book).

Published in 2015 by the Society of American Archivists (SAA), Module 8 of the series Trends in Archives Practice continues the explanations of best archival practices and will help archival librarians hone their skills with user-centered information. Each module in the series addresses a specific topic to ensure students, practicing archivists, and others seeking archival knowledge have filtered and synthesized information for their repository work. Each module can be a stand alone, available in print or electronic formation.

Author Steve Marks is a digital print librarian at the University of Toronto and a highly regarded professional in digital archives. Marks wrote *Module 8: Becoming a Trusted Digital Repository* to provide succinct definition to ISO 16363 which is the international standard for an "Audit and Certification of Trustworthy Digital Repository." A slim, soft cover guide is divided into five sections with an introduction to each. Sections three through five contain the details of ISO 16363 followed by two appendixes. Appendix A provides a case study from the University Archives, University of Illinois at Urbana-Champaign, and Appendix B is a useful addendum of resources for further research.

Approved in 2014, ISO 16363 measures the credibility of repository preservation programs and standards. The information age brings a tremendous level of digital content which brings into question the reliability and authority of documents. Staff working on a repository audit will find Marks' interpretations practical. The self-assessment helps with program measurement, identification of strengths and weaknesses, development of a plan of action, and preparation for final certification review.

The complexity of repository assessment is not for those who are faint of heart, and Marks breaks ISO 16363 into digestible bites. Trained auditors evaluate information storehouses for final certification, and Module 8 gives archivists, preservation specialists, administrators, and technical and support staff the clarity needed to undertake this process. Becoming a Trustworthy Digital Repository (TDR) means accountability and transparency in handling digital archives and the author clearly explains the expectations of ISO 16363. Each metric is met with disclosures on what each portion is about within the context of the whole assessment. Case in point, Section 3.5 of the standard is Contracts, Licenses and Liabilities, and Marks takes this weighty topic and breaks it down into the individual metrics which makes it an easy, albeit dry, read. *Module 8: Becoming a Trusted Digital*

Repository is a useful tool for archival staff seeking to pursue an audit and certification of TDR. Recommended.—**Janis Minshull**

361. Schull, Diantha Dow. **Archives Alive: Expanding Engagement with Public Library Archives and Special Collections.** Chicago, American Library Association, 2015. 324p. index. $79.00pa. ISBN 13: 978-0-8389-1335-2.

Despite the omnipresence of emphasis on digital projects and digitization in Library and Information Science (LIS) literature, building, maintaining, and expanding traditional print archival collections, sometimes with digital augmentation, remains a key role for academic and public library archives and special collections. This compendium of case studies demonstrates that the desire to highlight and expand public access to and engagement with unique local collections remains a critical part of public library operations nationwide.

It opens with an introduction describing using digital technologies and programming to make unique archival and special collections more accessible to local, national, and even international users. This work is broken up into 10 thematic sections covering art and archives, community archives, educational initiatives, emerging institutional models, exhibitions and related programs, interactive archives, lectures, conferences, and broadcast programs, national and international programs, oral history and community documentation projects, and tours, commemorations, and special events.

Examples of specific initiatives covered within these thematic sections include discoveries from the Free Library of Philadelphia's Fleisher Collection of orchestral music; the Community Archivist Program at the Austin, Texas, Public Library's Austin History Center; the Pittsburgh Iron and Steel Heritage Collection at Pittsburgh's Carnegie Library; the Jerome Robbins Dance Division at the New York Public Library's Performing Arts Division; a history of Kansas City, Missouri, stockyards in the metropolis' public library; the Allen County Community Album of genealogical information made by this Fort Wayne, Indiana, library's renowned collections in the field; the Central Arkansas Library System's Korean War Project; the Madison, Wisconsin, Public Library inviting individuals to bring 8 and 16 mm home movie for free onsite film inspections by experts and for public screenings; a Nashville, Tennessee, Public Library project documenting the impact of major 2010 flooding on Tennessee's capital city by creating a digital portal repository; and the La Crosse, Wisconsin, Public Library creating interpretive tours of community buildings and neighborhoods characterized by scripted walking tours, a stage production, self-guided online tours, and trolley tours.

These examples show that local libraries are seeking to expand public access to their unique archival and special collections by creative marketing and taking advantage of emerging digital technologies. Recommended for libraries interested in expanding and promoting regional history collections.—**Bert Chapman**

362. Wang, Chengzhi, and Su Chen. **Archival Resources of Republican China in North America.** New York, Columbia University Press, 2015. 255p. index. $125.00; $124.99 (e-book). ISBN 13: 978-0-2311-6140-4; 978-0-2315-4045-2 (e-book).

Historical archives are notably difficult for users to discover and access. Chinese archival material from the Republican era (1911-1949) is complex and voluminous, and records creation has been complicated by historical processing standards and use restrictions, leading to challenges in patron service. This timely bilingual resource guide, presented in both English and Chinese, brings together 329 hard-to-find archival resources of Republican China selected from academic institutions across North America with a goal of providing easy access to the scholarly community in the United States and abroad. The source materials, covering correspondences, diaries, memoirs, personal papers, and photographs, are selected based on their significance, uniqueness, and rarity of the primary resources. Examples of the prominent collections annotated in this volume include Columbia's Wellington Koo Papers, Harvard's Papers of John K. Fairbank, and Stanford's Chiang Kai-shek Diaries. Resources in the volume are alphabetically arranged by the names of the creators of the archival collections. Each entry begins with a title, followed by creator, physical description, finding aid, biographical note and historical background, language, provenance, location, content summary, and note. The thoughtfully described entries also indicate if a title has been digitized for online access. Three appendixes, an extensive references list, and an alphabetical index complete the volume. This well-researched, well-organized, and extremely useful reference work is published both in print and online and is highly recommended for all academic libraries supporting programs in East Asian Studies, history, and political science. The authors are two dedicated Chinese Studies Librarians who deserve commendation for initiating and contributing to the field of China Studies.—**Karen T. Wei**

Cataloging and Classification

363.   Broughton, Vanda. **Essential Classification, Second Edition.** Chicago, American Library Association, 2015. 421p. index. $95.00pa.; $85.50pa. (ALA members). ISBN 13: 978-0-8389-1369-7.

Broughton (Information Studies, University College, London) updates the first edition (2004) while maintaining its basic structure. The first part reiterates the theoretical basis of classification: types of classification schemes, content analysis, and controlled indexing languages. The book then discusses the three major classification schemes used in the world today: Library of Congress (LC), Dewey Decimal Classification (DDC), and, in a bow to her European colleagues, Universal Decimal Classification (UDC). The author also devotes two chapters to the structure and application of Library of Congress Subject Headings. The text ends with chapters devoted to faceted classification, managing classification, and classification in the digital era respectively. This last chapter, the one major update to this edition, delves into contemporary classification digital topics like information architecture, folksonomies, visualization tools, and the semantic Web. A practical glossary and a comprehensive bibliography round out the text.

The two other classics competing for attention in this arena also discuss subject access and analyze the major classification systems. However, Daniel Joudrey, Arlene Taylor and David Miller, *Introduction to Cataloging and Classification* (Libraries Unlimited, 2015, 11th ed.) add a discussion of Sears' List of Subject Headings and include other classification systems like Bliss and National Library of Medicine, which one would expect in an introductory text. Lois Chan and Theodora Hodges, *Cataloging and Classification* (Scarecrow Press, 2007, 3rd ed., see ARBA 2008, entry 528; fourth edition due 2016) treat subject headings more fully by including Sears, Faceted Application of Subject Terminology (FAST), and NLM's Medical Subject Headings (MeSH) and deal with even more alternative classification systems. Both give UDC short shrift.

Broughton is a noted contributor to the field, having authored most recently *Essential Library of Congress Subject Headings* (Neal-Schuman, 2012) and *Essential Thesaurus Construction* (Facet, 2013). She serves a leadership role on the editorial teams of the Bliss Bibliographic Classification and Universal Decimal Classification.

The book's greatest strengths are its focus exclusively on classification (i.e., without the descriptive cataloging element), a strong theoretical component, and greater focus on UDC. The additional inclusion of profuse examples, exercises (with answers), and bulleted summaries makes the book useful as an introductory library science text, a self-learning manual, or a refresher.—**Lawrence Olszewski**

364.   Coyle, Karen. **FRBR, Before and After: A Look at Our Bibliographic Models.** Chicago, American Library Association, 2016. 179p. index. $50.00pa.; $45.00pa. (ALA members). ISBN 13: 978-0-8389-1345-1.

In *FRBR, Before and After* Karen Coyle provides a critical look at the Functional Requirements for Bibliographic Records, more commonly known as FRBR. The book is divided into two parts; the first is an overview of the evolution of cataloging theory, data models, and technology. In the second part Coyle takes a close look at FRBR and the entities the model describes and provides a compelling argument for how bibliographic models must move to an integrative approach as data and technology continue to evolve. Coyle, drawing on over 30 years expertise, exposes some of the weaknesses of FRBR and the concept of the "work" in libraries within an ever-changing landscape of what library resources look like and how users try to find them. Written at a technical level this book is best for those with experience in cataloging or who would like to brush up on their knowledge of bibliographic data theories.—**Andrea C Kepsel**

365.   Golub, Koraljka. **Subject Access to Information: An Interdisciplinary Approach.** Santa Barbara, Calif., Libraries Unlimited/ABC-CLIO, 2014. 165p. index. $60.00pa. ISBN 13: 978-1-61069-577-0; 978-1-61069-578-7 (e-book).

The purpose of this book is to explore the relationship between library science and computer science. The book is an introduction to the topic and does not delve too deeply into the technical aspects of either discipline. Of particular interest is the last chapter, which considers future perspectives. Overall, this book provides a solid introduction to a complex aspect of both library and computer science and would be a worthwhile resource. An index rounds out the work.—**Valerie Jankowski**

366.   Hart, Amy. **RDA Made Simple: A Practical Guide to the New Cataloging Rules.** Santa Barbara, Calif., Libraries Unlimited/ABC-CLIO, 2014. 176p. index. $22.50pa. ISBN 13: 978-1-61069-485-8; 978-1-61069-486-5 (e-book).

In clear, concise language and well-organized chapters, this manual provides information for cataloging librarians moving to RDA. Hart has written an introduction to RDA specifically for general catalogers and not specialists. The book provides the basics, with bulleted points, charts, and lists that make it easy to find information. The book provides succinct descriptions, and deals with special topics such as MARC bibliographic fields impacted by RDA and collaborations/compilations. A final chapter provides a variety of real cataloging examples; they quickly show what has changed. While it contains much information, each chapter includes an introductory paragraph and a conclusion. This handbook would be helpful as an introduction to RDA for working catalogers or library students taking cataloging classes. Library directors may also find it useful, especially the chapters on planning and implementation. A bibliography and an index round out the work.—**Mary Northrup**

367.   Higgins, Colin. **Cataloging & Managing Film and Video Collections: A Guide to Using RDA and MARC 21.** Chicago, American Library Association, 2015. 240p. index. $85.00pa.; $76.50pa. (ALA members). ISBN 13: 978-0-8389-1299-7.

While there are quite a few guides available to catalogers related to film and video access and description, this one has been written by a true aficionado of these genres and accurately reflects current cataloging standards. The author indicates that the book is a primer on understanding the history, formats, vocabularies, and participants of film. Chapter one focuses on a history of film and its formats, a history of audiovisual librarianship, and why Blu-ray is the preferred medium for sales of films. Chapters two through four get into the nitty-gritty of cataloging DVDs and Blu-ray discs, with in-depth coverage of topics rather than MARC or RDA fields. This includes people, content, and technical features. Chapter five details cataloging of television programs, chapter six discusses older formats like VHS, and chapter seven contains a sequential list of the MARC21 bibliographic fields and how AACR2 practice differs from RDA. Chapter eight focuses on collection development and management and issues such as censorship, storage, and classification. Chapter nine explains the future of film through video streaming and why optical disc will slowly go away. A large Further Resources section, along with an appendix containing four sample cataloging records, closes a very useful book geared towards those involved in cataloging and purchasing film collections in libraries.—**Bradford Lee Eden**

368.   Moulaison, Heather Lea, and Raegan Wiechert. **Crash Course in Basic Cataloging with RDA.** Santa Barbara, Calif., Libraries Unlimited/ABC-CLIO, 2015. 164p. index. (Crash Course Series). $45.00. ISBN 13: 978-1-4408-3776-0; 978-1-4408-3777-7 (e-book).

Crash Course in Basic Cataloging with RDA provides both students and professionals with the adopted RDA procedures. This volume is designed for readers who are interested in cataloging but not experts in cataloging. This book describes the basic needs and reasoning behind the RDA rules and everything that accompanies RDA cataloging. Authors Heather Lea Moulaison and Raegan Wiechert both have extensive experience in teaching information organization and cataloging. The authors wrote this book to provide "a practical standpoint for non-catalogers," and the book succeeds admirably in this. Supplementary items include figures, sidebars, tables, images, three appendixes, and an index.

Since the book assumes the reader has had no prior history or knowledge with cataloging, information starts from the ground up. The 10 chapters in this book cover computer systems, different formats, MARC, encoding library data, RDA, access points, subject headings, Dewey Decimal Classification, and Library of Congress Classification. The inclusion of visual items such as images and figures is a great addition, given the target audience. These visual items range from screenshots of the Web interface of a catalog to a comparison of Bibframe version record versus MARC version record to MARC fields along with their explanations of use. These visual aids are beyond beneficial to those just starting their cataloging career as the material can be overwhelming. For example, the included flowchart on the decision and reasoning of adding access points enhances the understanding of readers with no cataloging experience and is much more effective than a text-only explanation. Finally, the book's appendixes provide examples of MARC record, RDA record, free and subscription-base Web resources, and other professional resources to further the readers' cataloging knowledge. The authors acknowledge that cataloging rules, protocols, and products can (and most likely will) change in the future, but presently this would be a great resource for students and nonprofessionals who need to learn the basics of cataloging.

This resource is highly recommended for academic and public libraries.—**Sara Mofford**

369.   **Sears List of Subject Headings.** 21st ed. Barbara A. Bristow and Christi Showman Farrar, eds. Amenia, N.Y., Grey House Publishing, 2014. 946p. $165.00. ISBN 13: 978-1-61925-190-8.

This 21st edition of the *Sears List of Subject Headings* presents a large collection of subject cataloging specifically for use in small and medium-sized libraries. Since 1923 this reference has been published with the express intent of making library collections as accessible as possible.

This edition includes over 250 new subject headings since the last publishing date (2007), which emerge from rapidly expanding STEM, computer technology, economics, education, and sports topics. It has also incorporated the full body of the *Sears List of Subject Headings: Canadian Companion* and, perhaps most significantly, conforms to the latest Resource Description and Access (RDA) cataloging standards. Finally, this 21st edition revises certain vocabulary to mesh with current norms (e.g., Latinos as opposed to Hispanic Americans, etc.).

This reference specifically includes an alphabetical rendering of nearly 9,000 subject terms most likely to be searched and thus patterns and examples which may then provide a foundation for future headings. New headings may be developed via new terminology demanded by current times (see above) and/or subdividing currently listed headings.

An excellent section titled Principles of the Sears Lists precedes the listings and covers topics such as purpose, grammar, types, subdivisions, difficult application (e.g., collective vs. individual biographies), catalog maintenance, and more. Information is also included regarding "key" headings, the use of subject subdivisions, and symbols used.

With a range from "Abacus" to "Zulu," this large reference is the necessary standard for the average-sized subject-cataloging collections.—**Laura Herrell**

Children's and Young Adult Services

370.   Alessio, Amy J., and Heather Booth. **Club Programs for Teens: 100 Activities for the Entire Year.** Chicago, American Library Association, 2015. 165p. index. $49.00pa.; $44.10pa. (ALA members). ISBN 13: 978-0-8389-1334-5.

Club Programs for Teens: 100 Activities for The Entire Year is a hands-on guide for development of young adult clubs at school or public libraries. Authors Amy J. Alessio and Heather Booth share years of experience as teen librarians in the public sector and have published other books on teen services.

This paperback's cover is bold and engaging though photos are gender limiting; girls are shown baking and sewing, boys are using technology. Turning inside, this American

Library Association (ALA) publication is comprised of a table of contents with 14 chapters representing teen club themes. The introduction is worthy of reading as it imparts overview tips such as "groups generally require four to six months to catch on," and the introduction also includes thoughts on how to handle a teen club scenario that isn't working. The book concludes with an effective index.

With club themes including "Crafting for Charity" and "Green Teens," each section offers multiple program suggestions. Some ideas overlap with other themes, and are duly noted in the CROSSOVER listing for each activity. Each activity may incorporate the following: a summary, the crossover, a shopping list, "make it happen" (the process), variation, online, and resources. The resource sections are slight, and only very rarely include books. The index is in-depth so it makes it an easily used book. Clear organization makes this a "go-to" guide for anyone doing club programming with teens. An evaluation process for programming, rated leveling for difficulty, or estimated preparation time are not part of this guide; such added information would save busy librarians time in deciding which activities best suit their planning time and their teen community.

Activity write-ups are generally all-inclusive but some are lacking, particularly for novice librarians. For instance, "A Picture's Worth..."(p 104) is an activity in using photography as a newsworthy story. Nowhere does it mention the need for permission in certain photographic settings. Author events are quite common and, yet, only get a brief mention. The "Traveling App Showdown"(p 145) neglects to include a shopping list whether it be a hand-held device or a computer and projector. The final chapter on more ideas for clubs is only four pages and is more of a listing of club themes and lacks activity details. It does reference *A Year of Programs for Teens* (see ARBA 2008, entry 534) and *A Year of Programs for Teens 2* (see ARBA 2012, entry 601), both coauthored by Alessio, which offer additional support for staff who organize teen programming.

Overall, *Club Programs for Teens:100 Activities for the Entire Year* gives the nuts and bolts of young adult programs from planning, to budget, through "how to make it happen." Suggestions are timely, engaging, and have potential to build a strong teen presence in school and public libraries. Activities can be modified for other age groups and program resources adjusted according to budgetary restrictions which makes this guide a flexible programming tool. Useful to librarians and educators seeking new ideas for teen engagement, this book will be the catalyst for your own club whether using one theme or intertwining many. Recommended.—**Janis Minshull**

371. Alessio, Amy J., Katie Lamantia, and Emily Vinci. **A Year of Programs for Millennials and More.** Chicago, American Library Association, 2015. 194p. index. $49.00pa.; $44.10pa. (ALA members). ISBN 13: 978-0-8389-1332-1.

Defining millennials as "young adults in their late teens, 20s, 30s, and 40s," the authors strive to fill a gap in the literature on public library programming, which tends to focus on children, younger teens, and seniors. Alessio, LaMantia, and Vinci provide detailed outlines for program planning, promotion, set-up and delivery keyed to the 12 months of the year. Alessio and LaMantia are teen librarians and Vinci is a readers' advisory specialist; all work at the Schaumburg Township District Library in Illinois. Alessio is coauthor, with Kimberly A. Patton, of *A Year of Programming for Teens* (see ARBA 2007, entry 510) and *A Year of Programming for Teens II* (see ARBA 2012, entry 601); this new work focused on an older demographic mimics the format of her earlier titles. The authors describe four or five programs for each month. Some of the suggestions are calendar-dependent (e.g., Un-Valentine's Day, Oscar Night, and Mardi Gras programs in February), but others seem designed to fill in months without major holidays or happenings (e.g., '80s Night in April and Microwave Magic in July). For each event, they specify the preparation time, length of program, optimal number of participants, and suggested age range. They also provide shopping lists, planning timelines, variations to appeal to different ages or to incorporate an online component, suggestions for marketing, and tips to guarantee the events run smoothly. The introduction to the book differentiates among the needs and interests of the age groups within the millennial generation. A final chapter describes 10 "clubs that keep them coming back" for ongoing programs about fitness, trivia, crafts, movies, and more. The index aids in identifying programs that, for instance, involve food or target parents. Overall, this is a well-organized and easy-to-consult sourcebook. Librarians can use it in conjunction with Brett W. Lear's *Adult Programs in the Library,* 2d ed. (ALA, 2013), which likewise presents program exemplars along with deeper discussions of mission, fundraising, publicity, and evaluation. Both works are excellent additions to public library professional collections; *A Year of Programs for Millennials and More* might also inspire academic librarians who wish to engage traditional-aged and older students.—**Susan E. Searing**

372.   Ernst, Linda L. **The Essential Lapsit Guide: A Multimedia How-To-Do-It Manual and Programming Guide for Stimulating Literacy Development from 12 to 24 Months.** Chicago, American Library Association, 2015. 276p. index. $72.00pa.; $64.80pa. (ALA members). ISBN 13: 978-1-55570-761-3.

In this exhaustive guide, the author, an expert children's librarian, compiles and updates practical information from her two earlier works, *Lapsit Services for the Very Young* (Neal-Schuman, 1995) and *Lapsit Services for the Very Young II* (Neal-Schuman, 2001). Like the earlier books, this guide presents a wealth of suggestions for storytime programs enhanced with movement and creative activities, all designed to foster language development in infants and pre-toddlers (12 to 24 months) through interactions with their parents or caregivers. Part one provides important context by presenting concise background on early childhood development, identifying adult program participants (e.g., bilingual families, teen mothers, grandparents), and recommending ways to make all components of library services, from facilities to collections to outreach, responsive to the needs of the very young. The heart of the book is part two, which focuses on programming. Detailed tips deal with everything from planning and publicity to room set-up and program pacing. An annotated bibliography of some 180 titles for reading aloud is arranged by author, but the topical index that follows immediately allows one to discover stories about, for instance, animals or seasons or stories that rhyme. Over 30 pages are devoted to nursery rhymes, finger plays, and short songs that audiences can perform along with the librarian. Ernst recommends combinations of stories and activities for more than 20 themes (e.g., animals, bedtime, food) but stresses that non-themed programs also succeed. As models for program planning, she offers sample outlines for 20-30 minute sessions that alternate listening to stories with active play. A chapter on "enhancements" adds ideas for incorporating music, flannel boards, puppets, crafts, and more, as well as displays and handouts for the adult participants. Librarians with small budgets will appreciate Ernst's instructions for making materials such as rhythm instruments from scratch. An appendix offers 21 reproducible handouts and templates, most intended to encourage adult participants to initiate similar activities at home with their little ones. The complete set of materials is also available for downloading/printing at http://alaeditions.org/Webextras, along with a compilation of the bibliographies and resource lists that appear throughout the book, a copy of the rhyme lyrics from part two, and nearly 50 video clips of the author performing rhymes and finger plays. Since Ernst began sharing her wisdom over 20 years ago, library programming for babies and toddlers has grown in popularity, making this new work an essential purchase for public libraries that serve this age group.—**Susan E. Searing**

373.   Lyons, Reneé Critcher. **Teaching Civics in the Library.** Jefferson, N.C., McFarland, 2015. 224p. illus. index. $39.95pa. ISBN 13: 978-0-7864-9672-3; 978-1-4766-2092-3 (e-book).

This timely work by Reneé Critcher Lyons, Assistant Professor in the School Library Media Program at East Tennessee State University, arrives on the heels of various new K-12 standards initiatives that place a renewed emphasis on civic readiness. The book pairs a basic background on the connection between libraries and civic education with practical activity ideas for a public or school library setting. While passing mention is made of "Socrates Cafés" and other programming ideas for adult patrons, public libraries considering this title for purchase should be aware that this book will be of interest primarily for a youth services audience. Chapters one–five provide an excellent, accessible introduction to the subject of democracy education and the critical leadership role the library has historically played in this field—a role the library should, the author contends, continue to play. Of particular interest to school librarians will be Chapter five, "21st Century Role of School and Public Libraries," which connects the dots between the American Association of School Librarians' Standards for the 21st-Century Learner and civic learning goals from social studies standards, such as those outlined in the College, Career, and Civic Life (C3) Framework. Chapter six offers readers an annotated list of clustered titles for students grades K–12 "for collection development modeling purposes." While readers may appreciate the list of titles vetted by an expert here, of even greater use will be the superb list of title evaluation criteria on page 69, which librarians will want to consult when considering any effort to develop a civics collection for youth. Subsequent chapters provide dozens of creative, ready-to-use activity ideas and resources organized by grade level. Lyons' passion for the Founding era resonates throughout this book and is contagious. However, Lyons' focus on this period comes at the expense of other essential moments in American history—with a few exceptions, those looking for civics-related resources and activity ideas set against the backdrop of later periods will need to look elsewhere. Readers wading for the first time into the treacherous waters of discussing political issues in the classroom may also have benefitted from additional guidance on building stakeholder support for their efforts to make the library a hub of civic learning and on anticipating and preparing for potential challenges to materials and programs. The work overall remains a vital contribution to an important and underexplored topic which has seen few book-length studies and none with as practical an approach as Lyons' book. Given the renewed emphasis on civic skills in K-12 standards, the book is recommended for purchase for libraries that support LIS education, school libraries, and those public libraries interested in initiating or growing civics-related programs for young patrons.—**ARBA Staff Reviewer**

374.   Torres-Roman, Steven A., and Carson E. Snow. **Dragons in the Stacks: A Teen Librarian's Guide to Tabletop Role-Playing.** Santa Barbara, Calif., Libraries Unlimited/ABC-CLIO, 2014. 212p. index. $45.00pa. ISBN 13: 978-1-61069-261-8; 978-1-61069-262-5 (e-book).

Public and school librarians who are thinking of adding tabletop role-playing games (RPGs) to their collection or programming will find this book to be an invaluable reference. Role-playing games create a structured and imaginative environment for players to complete quests, engage in storytelling, solve problems, and play make-believe. This book introduces readers to the genre and general vocabulary of RPGs; it suggests a core collection of RPGs for libraries and offers a more comprehensive list of game reviews and additional resources. It also includes ideas and considerations for cataloging, shelving, advertising, and programming. This book offers a tremendous single volume introduction to the world of tabletop RPGs and their potential place in the library. An index rounds out the work.—**Ellen Range**

375.   Velásquez, Jennifer. **Real-World Teen Services.** Chicago, American Library Association, 2015. 116p. index. $50.00pa.; $45.00pa. (ALA members). ISBN 13: 978-0-8389-1342-0.

This engaging title is directed at teen services librarians and library science students, but administrators and generalists can also benefit from its guidance and advice for real-world situations. In six fun-to-read chapters, Velásquez covers a wide range of topics inspired by her own experiences and by the questions she has received from practicing teen services librarians and from students in her introductory course on teen services. She focuses on the why of teen library services and demonstrates the importance of trusting teen ideas and desires regarding library experiences.

In the first chapter, "Teen Library Space," Velásquez discusses the importance of creating a designated place for teen library users, highlighting pitfalls and remedies, incorporating youth ideas in space development, and providing real world examples of how to claim space. For example, one space-claiming tactic allows teens to customize bookshelves and book carts. "Programming for Teens," chapter two, addresses myriad issues such as why teens don't attend programs, the difficulties of obtaining funding, and the resistance of colleagues, suggesting that successful teen programming not only responds to what teens want but also involves teens in program planning. The next chapter, "Crafting Service Dynamics and Modeling Service Strategies," examines the need for teen services librarians to educate all library staff about serving teens and addresses the creation of a reader's advisory strategy. Chapters four and five, "Rules, Conduct Codes, and Behavior," and "Access, Control, and Privacy" provide valuable guidance for the development of library use rules and the policies regarding how the library treats its users. In these chapters, readers will find ideas about maintaining professionalism, knowing when to call in the authorities, establishing library policies about teen privacy and truancy issues, and much more. The final chapter uses a question and answer format to address common situations like teaching colleagues how to answer teen services questions at the reference desk or the impulse to give teen patrons money, rides, a place to stay, etc.

All chapters begin with bullet point lists of key considerations and end with "soapbox moments" and references. An index rounds out the work. Highly recommended for anyone interested in the real world of teen librarian services.—**ARBA Staff Reviewer**

Collection Development

376.   Arndt, Theresa S. **Getting Started with Demand-Driven Acquistions for E-Books: A LITA Guide.** Chicago, American Library Association, 2015. 99p. index.

$65.00pa. ISBN 13: 978-0-8389-1314-7; 978-0-8389-1322-2 (e-book).

Demand-driven acquisitions has been a hot topic within the library industry in recent years. Published for ALA's LITA division, Ardnt has crafted a brief yet thoughtful introduction to demand-driven acquisitions (DDA). While many library professionals have heard the acronyms and perhaps have even had exposure to this acquisitions method, Arndt's guide provides explanations and helpful checklists of considerations, as well as her library's recent experience with implementing demand-driven acquisitions.

This guide is geared towards libraries or librarians who are investigating demand-driven acquisitions for the first time (although experience with purchased or subscribed e-books is assumed and is stated as such in the introduction). However, this book may also be useful for library school students and recent graduates.

The author begins with an overall explanation of demand-driven acquisitions as well as alternate names and acronyms for terms frequently referenced in the context of DDA. The next five chapters are divided by topics such as budgeting, cataloging aspects of DDA, DDA within a consortium, etc. Some considerations—inclusion of DDA records in the library catalog, in the discovery layer, or both—are repeated in multiple chapters, assumedly due to increased importance of these particular issues. Within the appendixes of this guide, a sample DDA implementation schedule is provided as is a glossary and index.

Inasmuch as the author states her own experience of desiring a comprehensive checklist of considerations when implementing demand-driven acquisitions (and does provide this divided throughout the book) nowhere are these checklists provided in entirety. The complexity and difficulties of de-duplication are somewhat over-simplified. Furthermore, the author's perspective seems to be limited to DDA via a library service provider, thus some topics would benefit from additional details and/or perspectives.

This concise (99 pages) guide's affordable price ($65) and availability in both print and eBook formats make it a worthwhile addition for many technical/access services departments' professional literature collections. It is appropriate for all libraries who have not yet implemented demand-driven e-book acquisitions at their libraries and are interested in a holistic view of the considerations this process entails.—**Kat Landry Mueller**

377.   Wilkinson, Frances C., Linda K. Lewis, and Rebecca L. Lubas. **The Complete Guide to Acquistions Management.** 2d ed. Santa Barbara, Calif., Libraries Unlimited/ABC-CLIO, 2015. 208p. index. (Library and Information Science Text Series). $60.00pa. ISBN 13: 978-1-61069-713-2; 978-1-61069-714-9 (e-book).

A great deal has changed in the more than a dozen years since the first edition of this book (see ARBA 2005, entry 626). The text has been completely revised and updated to reflect shifts in publishing and library processes. A new chapter on choosing vendors is one of the longest chapters; it includes recommendations for writing a request for proposal (RFP) and evaluating vendor performance. Previously separate treatments of serials and electronic resources are combined into a single chapter on acquiring continuing and electronic resources through subscriptions and licenses. Other chapters cover: the organization of acquisitions departments; the publishing industry; outsourcing; acquisitions systems; monographic content; used and antiquarian materials; gift and exchange programs; "decisions of permanence" (i.e., preservation and binding); and professional ethics. The authors conclude by asserting the value of acquisition librarians' perspectives as libraries choose and implement discovery and delivery services. The appendixes contain a wealth of useful reference material, including: a list of companies that offer automated acquisitions systems; acquisitions-related conferences and seminars; electronic discussion lists; Internet sites; journals; organizations; Web-based reference tools; and a glossary. Although the volume fits in the textbook genre, few LIS schools these days offer courses devoted to acquisitions librarianship. Librarians forced to learn the business of acquisitions on the job, however, will find this new edition invaluable. Although the authors are all academic librarians, any large library faces the challenges outlined here and will benefit from their sage, clearly presented advice. The detailed table of contents and subject index makes this a handy desk reference for anyone working in this area or desiring to learn more about it.—**Susan E. Searing**

Customer Service

378.   Goldsmith, Francisca. **Libraries and the Affordable Care Act.** Chicago, American Library Association, 2015. 98p. $24.00pa.; $21.60pa. (ALA members). ISBN 13: 978-0-8389-1288-1.

In terms of responding to user questions and needs following the rollout of the 2010 Patient Protection and Affordable Care Act, this book aims "to engage and encourage the awareness and service planning of public libraries in every state in supporting local community health." (xiii) Rather than a traditional index, the book uses an analytical table of contents and a question-based chapter guide. This decision was made to facilitate release prior to open health care enrollment in November 2014.

The first chapter begins with a contextualizing overview of the Affordable Care Act, moving on to chapters on health exchanges, knowing your community, tactical guidance, ethics and legal matters related to health-care information services, how to communicate with customers, and more. The book includes an appendix that lists the oversight agency regulating each state's health insurance marketplace, an appendix of Web-based resources, and an appendix that tells users where in the book to find certain information. Highly recommended for public libraries.—**ARBA Staff Reviewer**

379.   Hands, Africa S. **Successfully Serving the College Bound.** Chicago, American Library Association, 2015. 168p. index. $50.00pa.; $45.00pa. (ALA members). ISBN 13: 978-0-8389-1272-0.

American public libraries play an important role in filling the information needs of their users. New immigrants from different countries with different cultures, religions, languages, and little knowledge of computers come to the United States every year and use public libraries. Therefore, the role of librarians serving them has changed in the twenty-first century; this role includes helping immigrants prepare for college. This new book written by Africa S. Hands will fill the needs of college-bound students of all ages. The book has eight well-written chapters full of information for public librarians who have to play a new role in the present information age. The new law passed by the President Obama administration to give free education to all students in community colleges will further encourage college-bound students to seek more information through public libraries and librarians. The book includes four appendixes which will further help all interested parties find more information on going to college with the help of public libraries and academic libraries. The book also provides good suggestions for librarians to develop collections on the subject in all formats in order for their libraries to help library users of all ages. This book is certainly well written and fills a major gap in the library literature. It is recommended for all public and academic libraries.—**Ravindra Nath Sharma**

380.   Hernon, Peter, Ellen Altman, and Robert E. Dugan. **Assessing Service Quality: Satisfying the Expectations of Library Customers.** 3d ed. Chicago, American Library Association, 2015. 218p. index. $75.00pa.; $67.50pa. (ALA members). ISBN 13: 978-0-8989-1308-6.

First published in 1998 and revised in 2010 (see ARBA 2011, entry 590), the third edition of this indispensable guide reflects the latest developments in library service assessment theory and technique. Peter Hernon is a professor emeritus at Simmons College and a pioneer in the field of library assessment. Ellen Altman, who collaborated with Hernon on the earlier editions, is also a retired LIS professor. The new member of the authorial team, Robert E. Dugan, is the dean of libraries at the University of West Florida and has also published previously about library metrics. The organization of the book closely follows the first two editions, although some content is repositioned within the volume; for example, descriptions of techniques for eliciting user feedback are gathered into a new chapter titled "Different Ways of Listening to Customers." The authors begin with an essay on the concepts of customer service and service quality and then probe several key factors that affect service, e.g., customers' desire for self-sufficiency. They expound on mission, vision, goals, and values in the context of the library-as-system. The meaty chapter on "Measuring and Evaluating the Components of High-Quality Service" suggests 11 core questions to guide service evaluation, such as "how much?," "how prompt?," and "how reliable?" Under "how valuable?" the discussion of ROI (return on investment) is considerably expanded from the previous edition, as befits the current popularity of this metric. The authors make a key distinction between "countable" and "evaluateable" measures, and they present a conceptual framework that regards library service from the perspectives of the library, customer, decision-makers, and society. A brief chapter cautions about the pitfalls of working with quantitative data. Special emphasis is given to customer comment and complaint channels, surveys, and focus group interviews, with a chapter devoted to each mode of data collection. Another chapter recommends specific customer-related metrics for both academic and public libraries. The remainder of the book addresses techniques to measure customer satisfaction (which, the authors stress, is not the same as service quality), methods for interpreting and presenting data, and ways to incorporate service quality assessment into strategies for continuous improvement through engagement with customers. The book has a very detailed index but, unlike the earlier editions, lacks a bibliography. However, each chapter includes endnotes which cite both classic and recent publications. Over 60 charts, figures, and sample forms have been redesigned for greater visual impact. While most of the information is recycled from the last edition, every page shows evidence of careful revision to the text. Some older examples and quotations have been dropped, while new material has been added and content updated as needed. With the recent creation of assessment librarian positions in many academic libraries, as well as increased attention to the user experience across both physical and virtual library services, this new edition should find a wide readership among all types of librarians as well as LIS students.—**Susan E. Searing**

Digitization and Digital Libraries

381.   **Cultural Heritage Information: Access and Management.** Ian Ruthven and G. G. Chowdhury, eds. Chicago, American Library Association, 2015. 253p. index. $110.00pa.; $99.00pa. (ALA members). ISBN 13: 978-1-8389-1347-5.

This volume, first published in the United Kingdom by Facet Publishing and simultaneously issued in the United States by ALA/ Neal-Schuman, brings together 11 contributions on varied aspects of digital information systems for cultural heritage content. The level of discussion is appropriate for students or practitioners without specialized knowledge of the domain, but a general familiarity with digital information management is helpful. Nearly all the contributors are affiliated with university departments of information studies or computer science in the United Kingdom, Japan, South Africa, Germany, Canada, and the United States All cited works are in English; the perspective overall is Euro-centric. As should be expected in such a work, the chapters vary in their approach. Some serve as a state-of-the-art review of the research literature and reports from the field, while others highlight particular research projects that addressed specific challenges, such as developing a framework for analyzing user interactions with cultural heritage information online. Each chapter addresses a particular aspect of curating and managing digital cultural heritage information, including formulating policies, choosing digitization technologies, developing metadata, designing systems architecture, and designing for usability. While some contributors appear to encompass only visual resources in their definitions of cultural heritage digital content, others take a more expansive view. Digitized, rather than born-digital, resources take center stage throughout the book. Two of the more interesting chapters raise issues usually overlooked by more practical, how-to publications: Chris Alen Sula's call for an "alt-history" of digital humanities that recognizes the influence of cultural heritage institutions; and Gobinda Chowdhury's overview of economic, social, and environmental sustainability challenges which affect Internet-based services generally but are especially concerning for cultural heritage institutions, which through digitization aim to both preserve cultural content and make it widely available. This book is appropriate for libraries that support LIS or museum studies education, and for any cultural institution engaged in managing digital content, as many libraries are.— **Susan E. Searing**

382.   **Queers Online: LGBT Digital Practices in Libraries.** Rachel Wexelbaum, ed. Sacramento, Calif., Library Juice Press, 2014. 239p. index. (Gender and Sexuality in Information Studies). $35.00pa. ISBN 13: 978-1-936117-79-6.

A dozen contributions explore varied approaches to representing and preserving online the history and culture of LGBTIQ communities (lesbians, gay men, bisexuals, transgender, intersex, and queer). In section one, "Queering the Online Realm," four chapters situate digital information projects within the larger contexts of LGBTIQ theory and archival practice. Setting the tone for the rest of the book, the first chapter draws on the author's own experiences of using the Internet to explore his gay identity. He asserts that online spaces have supplanted physical spaces as the nexus for gay community-building and should therefore be preserved as historical artifacts. The following chapter makes a persuasive, theory-steeped argument that a particular pornographic Website has value as a public history repository. A survey of Web directories by and about transgendered people from 1994 to the present exposes multiple barriers to seeking transgender information on the Web; the author offers practical recommendations for meeting the online information needs of transgendered people. Acknowledging the dominance of Wikipedia as an information source, the final chapter in this section describes (with photos) Wikipedia edit-a-thons sponsored by the Tom of Finland Foundation and advocates for holding such events to improve access to accurate queer information. Section two focuses on the digitization of print and realia collections. A long-time volunteer at the Lesbian Herstory Archives in New York City explains how decisions about digitization are guided by the archives' principles. Included in the chapter are interviews with other volunteer staff who lead efforts to digitize photographic and audio materials and to create a Web-based catalog. The other chapters in this section address the legal and ethical nuances of copyright and privacy rights that affected digitization projects in Canada and Australia. Section three, titled "The Nuts and Bolts of Queer Digitization Projects," recounts the goals, challenges, and outcomes of three innovative projects: Open Up!, a Dutch effort to collect and digitize materials from Central, Eastern, and Southeastern Europe; the Matthew Shepard Web Archive at the University of Wyoming that captured and preserved Websites about the gay student's murder and its impact on the local community and worldwide movement for LGBTIQ rights, 10 years after the event; and the LGBT Religious Archives Network, which serves as a portal to existing archival collections and provides direct access to biographical profiles and oral histories of LGBTIQ religious leaders of many faiths. Section four offers two short chapters by editor Wexelbaum that bring to light continuing obstacles to information access: censorship in libraries, and the paucity of LGBTIQ e-books. The discussion of e-books is informed by her recent survey of LGBTIQ reading habits as well as background on how libraries acquire electronic content. Taken together, these dozen chapters make a compelling case for the centrality of the Web as a platform for LGBTIQ information. They advocate strongly for LGBTIQ communities to shape online spaces that meet their information needs, document their histories, and counter misinformation and prejudice. This work is recommended for all academic and public libraries.—**Susan E. Searing**

Evaluation and Assessment

383.   **Putting Assessment into Action: Selected Projects from the First Cohort of the Assessment in Action Grant.** Eric Ackerman, ed. Chicago, American Library Association, Association of College and Research Libraries, 2015. 216p. $52.00pa. ISBN 13: 978-0-8389-8813-8.

Putting Assessment into Action contains the earliest fruits of the Association of College and Research Libraries' (ACRL) Assessment in Action Grant Program. This casebook, edited by Radford University librarian Eric Ackermann, describes the campus projects of 27 institutions from the first cohort of this program. A diverse group of schools, from large research universities to small liberal colleges, is represented here. Each institution carried out their research during the 2013-2014 academic year.

Campus projects are concentrated in three broad areas: Information Literacy, Outreach and Library Services, and Longitudinal Studies. Information Literacy contains the bulk of the projects, with sections focusing on the assessment of first-year students, second-to-fourth-year undergraduates, and graduate students. Both traditional as well as authentic assessments are well represented. There is also significant variation in the types of assessment instruments (surveys, quizzes, annotated bibliographies, tutorials, etc.) used.

This casebook emphasizes the practical over the theoretical. Sections are concise and aimed at academic librarians with a limited background in assessment. The content is narrative based, though some original assessment instruments are also included. Chapters are written by the campus librarians that spearheaded their projects. In each chapter authors describe the successes and challenges of their projects, often with recommendations for future iterations. Despite the brevity of certain sections, a useful reading list allows for further exploration of these topics. Many of these campus assessments appear scalable to fit a broad range of institutions. This casebook will be highly useful to librarians trying to incorporate similar library assessments on their campuses.—**Joshua Becker**

384.   **Reviewing the Academic Library: A Guide to Self-Study and External Review.** Eleanor Mitchell and Peggy Seiden, eds. Chicago, American Library Association, Association of College and Research Libraries, 2015. 334p. $66.00pa. ISBN 13: 978-0-8389-8783-4.

This collection of 16 essays addresses the practical needs of academic librarians called upon to serve during reviews and self-studies involving their libraries, whether for internal purposes or as part of institutional accreditation. A mix of conceptual background and specific advice covers librarian roles whether as local managers, representatives of campus units, or members of visiting review teams. Content speaks to formal assessment and review, standards and accreditation, methods and process, and cultivation of a local culture of self-examination. Chapters fall into three parts, dealing with the rationale behind reviews, the process itself, and library-oriented metrics. Chapter 7 breaks down the elements of campus-level review in detail, with an appendix that provides a template for scheduling a two-day visit by external reviewers. Chapter 8 discusses the specific experience of Texas A&M University with the LibQUAL+ instrument. Chapter 13 reports on the use of the MISO Survey by librarians at Hamilton College. Each essay is followed by supporting citations: in some cases, these are extensive and may include books, articles, ERIC documents, and online resources. There are more than 20 tables and figures illustrating measurement systems and typical results.

Mitchell (library director at Dickinson College) and Seiden (library director at Swarthmore College) have assembled an impressive set of authors that includes officers from regional accrediting bodies, library deans and directors from large and small institutions, and data analysts from important libraries and library organizations in the United States. Many librarians will recognize contributors such as James G. Neal, University Librarian Emeritus at Columbia University; Martha Kyrillidou from the Association of Research Libraries; James Rettig, currently Library Director at the United States Naval Academy; and Kara Malenfant, a leader in the "Value of Libraries" project at ACRL.

Some modest steps by ACRL as publisher would have improved this volume. There is no index: in the e-book version, readers can search by keyword, but in the print format it is difficult to find, for example, all references to the ARL Statistics. Chapters end with cited references, but there is no combined bibliography or list of suggested core readings. We are given no affiliation or credential information for the two dozen contributing authors: a few pages devoted to background sketches would have enriched readers' appreciation of the expert advice on hand.

No recent work offers a comparable level of attention to both the details of library assessment and the potential for library contributions toward institutional accreditation. *The Challenge and Practice of Academic Accreditation: A Sourcebook for Library Administrators* edited by Edward D. Garten presents a similar breadth of views by multiple authors, but dates from 1994. The more concise *Preparing for Accreditation: A Handbook for Academic Librarians* by Patricia Lou Sacks and Sara Lou Whildin was published in 1993. *Library Assessment in Higher Education* by Joseph R. Matthews (2d ed., 2015) emphasizes the assessment side. A 2012 SPEC Kit, *Library Contribution to Accreditation* by Holly Mercer and Michael Maciel (who also is a contributor to the work under review) provides examples of accreditation documentation, but without as much conceptual background.—**Steven W. Sowards**

Fundraising

385.   Maxwell, Nancy Kalikow. **ALA Book of Library Grant Money.** 9th ed. Chicago, American Library Association, 2015. 348p. index. $180.00pa. ISBN 13: 978-0-8389-1211-9.

This book aims to provide librarians, fundraisers, and researchers with quick, convenient access to information on the major US funding sources for library grants. They include private and corporate foundations, corporate direct givers, library and nonprofit organizations, and government agencies. Each entry is arranged alphabetically and includes the pertinent information a grant seeker would need to begin researching a potential funder. A section on grant-related organizations and resources offers grant seekers help to do their research, write proposals, administer, and evaluate a project. Indexes include grantors by total grant value, grantors by state, named grants/programs, and professional library organization grantors. The introduction takes the novice grant seeker through the essential steps of becoming "grant ready." The book will pay for itself with the first grant and should be part of any library grant seeker's collection. Four indexes round out the book.—**Norman Desmarais**

Information Literacy

386.   Bowles-Terry, Melissa, and Cassandra Kvenild. **Classroom Assessment Techniques for Librarians.** Chicago, American Library Association, Association of College and Research Libraries, 2015. 118p. $36.00pa. ISBN 13: 978-0-8389-8775-9.

Although there is no dearth of material on assessing information literacy instruction (see, for example, *A Practical Guide to Information Literacy Assessment for Academic Librarians* by Carolyn J. Radcliff et al., ARBA 2009, entry 568), this new book is unique in its depth of treatment of a single method, classroom assessment techniques, or CATs. Bowles-Terry, Head of Educational Initiatives for the University of Nevada, Las Vegas, library, and Kvenild, Head of the Learning Resource Center at the University of Wyoming library, define classroom assessment as "a learner-centered, formative assessment practice that allows instructors to find out what students are learning in the classroom and how well they understand it" (p. xi). The authors illustrate how academic librarians can employ CATs to promote student learning and improve their own teaching. Their examples span the spectrum from one-shot class sessions to librarian-taught credit courses. The authors include techniques well suited to situations when librarians are temporarily embedded in courses for the duration of an assignment, and they illustrate the use of CATs in online as well as face-to-face teaching. Two dozen different techniques are grouped in six categories depending on the characteristic to be assessed: prior knowledge and understanding; skill in analysis and critical thinking; skill in synthesis and creative thinking; skill in application; attitudes and self-awareness; and learner reactions. The authors describe the particular strengths of each CAT and when to employ it. For example, the Defining Features Matrix CAT is recommended when students must compare different information sources, whereas Concept Maps are useful when students are selecting a topic to research. Concept Maps is just one example of a familiar tool that is often used for pedagogical purposes, but

Bowles-Terry and Kvenild zero in on its strengths for assessing learning. Some of the CATs included in this book, such as the Minute Paper and Think-Pair-Share, are widely practiced in library instruction, but others, such as Chain Notes, will be new to most readers. Bowles-Terry and Kvenild provide several examples of employing each CAT with different types of students, learning outcomes, and instructional frameworks. For many of the CATs, they also suggest variations on the basic technique. A cornerstone of their approach to classroom assessment is scoring the responses and providing feedback to the students, either by immediately sharing the results and modifying the session's agenda as needed to focus on areas where confusion lingers, or by analyzing responses after the class and following up with research guides, email messages, additional sessions, and the like. The sheer variety of CATs described in this practical, well-written guide guarantee that any instruction librarian, no matter what her teaching style, will be inspired to incorporate CATs into her classroom lessons. For this reason, every academic library should own at least one copy, and many instruction librarians will want personal copies.—**Susan E. Searing**

387.   Kaplowitz, Joan R. **Designing Information Literacy Instruction: The Teaching Tripod Approach.** Lanham, Md., Rowman & Littlefield, 2014. 201p. index. $55.00; $54.99 (e-book). ISBN 13: 978-0-8108-8584-4; 978-0-8108-8585-1 (e-book).

The Tripod approach focuses on the interrelationships between student learning outcomes, learning activities, and assessment. It is a tool for librarians who want to dig deeply into their teaching methods, learn more about how their students learn, and how to develop effective instructional strategies. Each chapter includes questions and checklists to help the individual instructor carefully look at what they are doing. The information literacy standards familiar to K-12 school librarians are not addressed, nor are there any student activities. The book offers many good ideas; it will be most useful for educators who provide staff development courses in their schools or teach future school librarians.—**Mary Alice Anderson**

388.   **Metaliteracy in Practice.** Trudi E. Jacobson and Thomas P. Mackey, eds. Chicago, American Library Association, 2016. 224p. index. $70.00pa.; $63.00pa. (ALA members). ISBN 13: 978-0-8389-1379-6.

This collection of case studies is a companion to the coeditors' recent influential book, *Metaliteracy* (see ARBA 2015, entry 416), which articulated four goals for developing metaliterate learners: evaluate content critically, including dynamic, online content that changes and evolves, such as article preprints, blogs, and wikis; understand personal privacy, information ethics, and intellectual property issues in changing technology environments; share information and collaborate in a variety of participatory environments; and demonstrate ability to connect learning and research strategies with lifelong learning processes and personal, academic, and professional goals. (For objectives associated with each goal, see https://metaliteracy.org.) Students no longer merely discover and consume information but actively create, repurpose, and share it. Jacobson, Head of the Information Literacy Department of the University of Albany Libraries, and Mackey, Vice Provost for Academic Programs at SUNY Empire State College, therefore argue that librarians must progress beyond teaching traditional information literacy skills. They specify four domains within the concept of metaliteracy: behavioral, cognitive, affective, and metacognitive. Eight of the chapters in this collection present case studies by academic librarians (typically partnered with faculty from other disciplines) who have designed, revised, assessed, and/or analyzed strategies to incorporate metaliteracy as both a learning outcome and a pedagogical method. The contributors explore elements of curricular design, information politics, social media as teaching tools, students as information creators, and other topics, while thoughtfully and honestly reflecting on their own experiences as teachers. Techniques to foster student empowerment are foregrounded in several of the chapters. Of the four domains, metacognition is discussed most often; these teachers grappled with promoting and then assessing students' awareness of their own mental processes as they interact with information. The case studies provide sufficient detail about assignments, assessments, and the process of curriculum development for readers who may wish to adopt these innovative approaches. Lending context to their experiences, the authors review relevant literature on pedagogy from librarianship, higher education, and their academic disciplines, and several observe how the concept of metaliteracy parallels and enriches disciplinary or campus-mandated learning objectives and competencies. The final chapter departs from the case study format. Instead, it offers a reflection on the meaning of "metaliteracy-as-agency," drawing on the ideas of social theorist Pierre Bourdieu. This eight-page essay is peppered with rarified academic jargon, overloaded with quotations, and adorned with 102 endnotes. Yet placed at the end of the book, it adds thought-provoking depth to the scholarly, praxis-centered studies that precede it. *Metaliteracy in Practice* is a timely publication—first, because the notion of metaliteracy has captured the attention of many academics, and second, because metaliteracy learning goals dovetail with the new ACRL Framework for Information Literacy in Higher Education. This book can be a source for inspiration and practical ideas to refresh the information literacy program of any academic library.—**Susan E. Searing**

389. **Teaching Information Literacy: Threshold Concepts Lesson Plans for Librarians.** Patricia Bravender, Hazel McClure, and Gayle Schaub, eds. Chicago, American Library Association, Association of College and Research Libraries, 2015. 251p. $48.00pa. ISBN 13: 978-0-8389-8771-1.

The editors (all from Grand Valley State and all librarians with liaison responsibilities) have compiled 34 lesson plans on the six information literacy frames (Scholarship as Conversation, Research as Inquiry, Authority is Constructed and Contextual, Information Creation as a Process, Searching as Strategic Exploration, and Information has Value) identified by the Association of College and Research Libraries (ACRL) in its 2015 Framework document. The 43 contributors' lesson plans are formatted consistently to include Learning Goals, Anticipatory Set, Lesson Objectives, Input/Modeling, Check for Understanding, Guided Practice, and Independent Practice. The lessons are short enough to cover in a one-hour session such as is common for information literacy courses, and could be adapted to be part of a one-shot instruction session. Materials needed for each lesson are listed, and handouts are included as an appendix and online at www.ala.org/acrl/files/handouts.pdf. Other appendixes are a list of lessons with overlapping threshold concepts, the ACRL Framework document, "Implementing the Framework" which includes sections for faculty and administrators, "Background of the Framework Development" covering a history of its development, "Sources for Further Reading" about information literacy and threshold concepts, and "Recommended Reading" about the framework. This is not a traditional "reference" book but will be most useful in a professional collection, possibly with a second circulating copy. It will be invaluable to academic librarians incorporating the information literacy frames in instruction sessions and information literacy courses. Highly recommended.—**Rosanne M. Cordell**

Information Science and Information Systems

390.   Mitchell, Erik. **Metadata Standards and Web Services in Libraries, Archives, and Museums: An Active Learning Resource.** Santa Barbara, Calif., Libraries Unlimited/ ABC-CLIO, 2015. 290p. index. $75.00pa. ISBN 13: 978-1-61069-449-0; 978-1-61069-450-6 (e-book).

Mitchell, associate university librarian at the University of California, Berkeley, is well qualified to write a textbook on metadata standards and Web services from an LIS perspective. He has taught classes on these topics and has published widely in the scholarly and professional literature. He is no doubt familiar with the difficulties faced by LIS instructors who must introduce students, including those with scant prior exposure to computer science concepts or skills, to the core information organization principles, data models, standards, schemas, and exchange formats currently used or being developed by libraries. Although Mitchell tries hard to make it all comprehensible, novices may find his approach daunting. Mitchell begins with a highly condensed overview of digital information systems, touching on the most influential theorists. The basics of digital document structure and HTML are introduced early on. The content grows increasingly technical as Mitchell explores the design of Web-based information systems and information organization models. The central, and longest, chapter focuses on metadata standards, contents, and values. Mitchell outlines the structure of common metadata schemas and describes the differing schemas preferred by libraries, archives, and museums. This chapter also covers vocabularies, taxonomies, thesauri, and ontologies, concluding with a discussion of RDF. Another long chapter follows devoted to serialization; here Mitchell supplies background on both well-established formats (e.g. MARC and XML) and newer formats (e.g. RDFa), along with relational and graph databases. Linked data and Web services for metadata exchange are also covered. The final chapters focus on the creation and use of metadata and on future trends. Mitchell addresses issues of quality control and value measurement; describes various techniques for automated generation and management of metadata; and briefly surveys the leading digital information systems, digital libraries, and large-scale metadata repositories. The penultimate chapter explains foundational concepts in computer programming before delving into XSLT as a means of creating HTML displays from XML documents. The final chapter discusses the future of information systems, metadata, and information use in libraries, archives, and museums, highlighting trends toward increasingly open and linked data, as well as concerns about return on investment, metadata quality, changing user needs, and technological capabilities. The book concludes with an excellent index that doubles as an acronym decoder. Unfortunately (though perhaps inevitably, given the breadth of information it covers), this book is burdened with dense prose and long, acronym-laden sentences. Pages full of sample code, clearly intended to clarify difficult concepts and facilitate comparisons, instead feel overwhelming. In addition, almost every page contains typographical or syntax errors that reveal a lack of attentive copyediting and make it harder to digest the ideas. The subtitle, "An Active Learning Resource," is a bit misleading, as the volume itself offers no learning activities or prompts for further inquiry. Rather, a section of Mitchell's personal Website, which is mentioned just once at the end of Chapter one, presents a 14-week syllabus for a course that uses the book as its central (but not sole) text. Downloadable worksheets provide exercises for active in-class learning; some of them require other readings and common proprietary software, such as Microsoft Access. Answer sheets accompany each worksheet. This book might be of use for self-study by unusually diligent students, especially those already familiar with the basics of Web coding, and it may appeal to professional catalogers and metadata specialists who need a refresher and a summary of the most promising new developments in the field. However, the most likely (and thus limited) audience consists of LIS teachers who offer similar courses. They will evaluate this work for its potential in their own classes, and, if they judge its strengths to exceed its flaws, may adopt it as a text.—**Susan E. Searing**

Information Technology

391.   Connolly, Matthew, and Tony Cosgrave. **Using iPhones, iPads, and iPods: A Practical Guide for Librarians.** Lanham, Md., Rowman & Littlefield, 2014. 210p. index. (Practical Guides for Librarians). $65.00pa.; $64.99 (e-book). ISBN 13: 978-1-4422-2687-6; 978-1-4422-2688-3 (e-book).

The primary audience for this book includes librarians and library IT staff with clear, easy-to-follow instructions for using iDevices for a variety of purposes across all types of libraries. The authors open with a general introduction that examines the Apple advantage and its implications for libraries. The remaining chapters are divided into three parts: iDevices in the Hands of Library Patrons; Lending iDevices to Library Patrons; and iDevices in the Hands of Librarians and Staff. Within each, chapters provide step-by-step guidance to every conceivable situation. The appendix lists and describes a selection of useful apps. Figures and tables are interspersed throughout the text. Each chapter ends with key points as well as a list of references. This title is a good purchase if your school is considering iDevices. There is an appendix of recommended iDevice apps and an index.—**Susan Yutzey**

392.   Mitchell, Erik T. **Cloud-Based Services for Your Library.** Chicago, American Library Association, 2013. 161p. index. (A LITA Guide). $65.00pa.; $58.50pa. (ALA members). ISBN 13: 978-1-55570-878-8.

Written for IT staff and technology oriented librarians who are exploring the pros and cons of managing technology services "in the cloud," this volume in the LITA Guide series provides an overview of the technical and organizational challenges of virtualization and cloud computing in the library context. The author, a member of the faculty of the University of Maryland's College of Information Studies, addresses legal and policy issues as well as technical requirements and trade-offs. Chapter one explains the characteristics of virtualization and cloud computing and outlines three approaches that are covered in greater depth in subsequent chapters: software-as-a-service (SaaS), platform-as-a-service (PaaS), and infrastructure-as-a-service (IaaS). Chapter two presents a snapshot of library adoption of cloud computing, based on survey responses from 111 libraries. As of 2011, few libraries had transitioned traditional resources such as the ILS to virtualized or cloud-based services; more had opted for outsourcing newer, data-intensive services such as discovery tools, research guides, and OpenURL resolvers. Open-ended survey questions yielded insights into factors that influenced decisions to pursue various options. Mitchell analyzes these using two theoretical models of technology adoption, with cost-benefit analyses and impacts on "IT service productivity efficiency, flexibility scalability" topping the list of influences. Chapter three delves more deeply into factors that inform the selection and implementation of cloud, virtualized, or non-virtualized services. These factors are technical (administering infrastructure, platforms, and applications; security; library-specific support), organizational (budgeting and service subscription; disaster and recovery planning; service agreements; service capacity), and environmental (cost and return-on-investment calculations; legal and policy issues). The following two chapters examine SaaS, PaaS, and IaaS and present examples of each approach. For instance, the discussion of SaaS draws examples from next-generation integrated library systems, digital archival management systems, and user-facing services such as virtualized reference. The discussion of PaaS distinguishes between server-type hosting and application-based PaaS environments. Mitchell's discussion of IaaS is the most thorough and is based on his experience transitioning library IT services to cloud-based platforms at Wake Forest University. The final chapter illustrates best practices by describing four models of cloud-based services: single-vendor cloud deployment; mixed-cloud management with SaaS; redundant and scalable multicloud deployments; and distributed SaaS environments. Given the rapid developments in this market, Mitchell's comparisons of the capabilities and costs for cloud service providers are probably out of date. However, by highlighting key issues—including the expertise required, the complexity, sustainability, and durability of the service, the cost, and its portability/interoperability—Mitchell constructs a framework for informed evaluation that will remain relevant. Throughout the book, well-laid-out tables and occasional sidebars complement the text, but shrunken, barely readable screenshots add nothing to the content. This book will be most useful for readers already familiar with IT management concepts and practices. Librarians and administrators who lack such background may prefer to start with Marshall Breeding's *Cloud Computing for Libraries,* no. 11 in the Tech Set series (see ARBA 2013, entry 447) or Robin Hastings' *Making the Most of the Cloud: How to Choose and Implement the Best Services for Your Library* (see ARBA 2014, entry 554). An earlier LITA Guide, *Getting Started with Cloud Computing* edited by Edward M. Corrado and Heather Lea Moulaison (Neal-Schuman, 2011), may still be a useful source for case studies and real-life examples.—**Susan E. Searing**

393.   **More Library Mashups: Exploring New Ways to Deliver Library Data.** Nicole C. Engard, ed. Medford, N.J., Information Today, 2015. 362p. illus. index. $45.00pa. ISBN 13: 978-1-57387-498-4.

A follow-up to Engard's 2009 *Library Mashups,* this collection introduces 21 new mashup projects created by Engard and 24 library professionals from all types of libraries. Engard, the vice president of education at ByWaters Solutions where she educates librarians about open source software, brings together projects for the novice and the experienced programmer, for those who engage in systems and Web programming on a regular basis, and for those who are just starting to consider the idea of using mashups in their libraries of any size. Focusing solely on free, open-source products, the book is organized into five sections: the basics, library Websites, library catalog data, visualizing data, and value-added services. The book begins with four basics of mashups for libraries that can be done by any person such as data play, map mashups, visualizing library data, and delivery access; the volume next offers three chapters on library Websites, specifically using Drupal and APIs. The third part offers four chapters on enhancing the library catalog data such as searching databases through Twitter, putting library catalog data on the map, next generation cataloging, and delivering catalog records using Wikipedia current awareness.

The fourth part focuses on visualizing data over four chapters, while the final section offers six chapters in ways to integrate value-added services such as a book suggestion app, single sign-on integration, and developing custom workflows. Each chapter is written by practicing librarians who have implemented the mashup and offers guidance, tips, tricks, successes, and failures that have occurred during the creation and implementation at the specific library. While the extensive knowledge can be overwhelming to the uninitiated, the opening part will be approachable and achievable by anyone, offering a sense of accomplishment and hopefully a desire to go forward with more advanced mashups in time. Public, school, academic, and special libraries will benefit from the ideas and tips offered in this book.—**Sara Marcus**

394.   **Technology Disaster Response and Recovery Planning: A LITA Guide.** Mary Mallery, ed. Chicago, American Library Association, 2015. 114p. index. $59.00pa.; $53.10pa. (ALA members). ISBN 13: 978-0-8389-1315-4.

Like other volumes in the highly regarded LITA Guide series, this small book presents a succinct and practical introduction to an important topic for library IT managers and other library staff responsible for digital collections and services. The contributors are expert consultants and librarians with first-hand knowledge of disaster preparation and recovery. Part one focuses on planning for disaster response. As the editor's brief initial chapter points out, librarians who are developing or revising plans to protect physical collections and library facilities can draw on a relatively rich professional literature with detailed recommendations, policy templates, and checklists; see, for example, the third edition of *Disaster Response and Planning for Libraries* by Miriam B. Kahn (see ARBA 2013, entry 548). Planning to mitigate the effects of IT outages and prevent the loss of digital collections is more recent and less well documented. This book begins to remedy the disparity. Liz Bischoff and Thomas F.R. Clareson advocate for thoroughly inventorying digital collections and assessing the risks to both collections and technical infrastructure; they recommend tools to facilitate these tasks. Donia Conn explains how dPlan, an online tool from the Northeast Document Conservation Center, can be used to develop a disaster recovery plan that applies to IT resources. Stating that successful responses to library disasters depend on a well-wrought communications plan, Denise O'Shea delivers a basic lesson in crisis communication, but she notes that IT outages may interfere with using the library's Website, email, or social media to get the word out to employees and patrons. A template for communications planning is supplied as an appendix. In what may be the most valuable chapter in the guide, Marshall Breeding examines the role of cloud computing in disaster mitigation. He clearly explains various options for locating library services in the cloud and using the cloud for back-up data storage. Although Breeding's chapter is titled "Future Trends," most of the cloud-based options he describes are available today, and forward-looking libraries are already beginning to utilize them. Part two presents two case studies of how libraries recovered from disasters that interrupted their IT operations. Oddly, since the editor and other authors identify a wide spectrum of possible disasters that can befall libraries—including weather-related natural disasters, fires, local technology failures, Internet outages, and security breaches—both case studies revolve around floods. The lessons they present, however, are applicable to most emergency situations and plans. Paul A. Soderdahl recounts the severe flooding at the University of Iowa in 2008 that tested a brand-new plan. The plan was reactivated in 2013 when the river again threatened to breach its banks. Soderdahl shares insights from both occasions. Clareson briefly examines disaster responses by three libraries in the wake of Hurricane Sandy in 2012. The volume concludes with an index. Although aimed primarily at academic librarians and IT staff, this handy guide will be useful in almost all libraries with digital content and services to protect. It can also serve to introduce LIS students to an important and evolving area of practice.—**Susan E. Searing**

395.   Tidal, Junior. **Usability and the Mobile Web: A LITA Guide.** Chicago, American Library Association, 2015. 118p. illus. index. $65.00pa.; $58.50pa. (ALA members). ISBN 13: 978-0-8389-1301-7.

The use of mobile and tablet devices is ever increasing. Therefore, more than ever, it is important that today's librarian is able to meet patron needs both inside and outside of the library setting. Librarians must consider the compatibility of Websites when interacting with these types of devices.

This resource covers the basics of developing mobile Websites (Websites that are user friendly with mobile and tablet devices) so they appear in a format similar to typical Websites on computers. Information is shared on usability, especially the significance of mobile usability in libraries. The topic of usability includes the labels used on Websites for ease in locating information, length of URLs, hardware limitations, and redirection within Websites. This guide also incorporates mobile usability testing, including types of testing, testing methods, getting people to take the test, testing accommodations, and recording testing data. Tidal concludes by covering information regarding what can be done after collecting data to help insure the usability of the mobile Website. Although technology continues to change rapidly, this is a useful resource for anyone seeking information on how to make mobile Websites conducive to mobile and tablet usage.—**Shelly Lee**

396.   van Hooland, Seth, and Ruben Verborgh. **Linked Data for Libraries, Archives and Museums: How to Clean, Link and Publish your Metadata.** Chicago, American Library Association, 2014. 272p. index. $88.00pa. ISBN 13: 978-0-8389-1251-5.

In the age of information and technology many books have been written on the subject of libraries and technology but the book under review is very different. It has been written by two Europeans, a library educator and an engineer/researcher. The book has seven well-written chapters on the subject of linked data and its importance. Each chapter starts with learning outcomes and is focused on the practical steps which will help librarians and others to learn more about the global pool of linked data and its importance in creating a global database. Five chapters include case studies of libraries and museums which will further help librarians and others to understand the subject. The authors are of the view that in the age of technology even the car navigation systems, phones, and fridge will start consuming linked date in the near future. Therefore, it is possible that the linked data will create a global database for the benefit of all institutions. The book introduces readers to practical steps to understand how libraries can help their institutions to join and create a global database. It is the business of libraries, archives, and museums to collect and preserve information for their users. Therefore, it is important to maintain powerful URLs. The technology has certainly influenced the world and the humans can also leave a mark on the technology by creating the linked database. The book is an excellent addition to the library literature and is recommended highly for all libraries, archives, and museums.—**Ravindra Nath Sharma**

Intellectual Freedom and Censorship

397.   **Intellectual Freedom Manual.** By the Office of Intellectual Freedom. Chicago, American Library Association, 2015. 273p. index. $70.00pa.; $63.00pa. (ALA members). ISBN 13: 978-0-8389-1292-8.

Now in its 9th edition, the *Intellectual Freedom Manual* continues its goal of supporting and advocating the rights of library users to access information without scrutiny or examination from outside sources. In this edition, the Office for Intellectual Freedom has updated and expanded their previous volumes to provide guidance, assistance, and resources for libraries striving to provide free and equal access to information.

This manual is divided into three main sections discussing intellectual freedom and libraries, issues and best practices, and advocacy/assistance. Part one serves as an introduction and provides ALA documentation as well as guidance for creating library policies related to intellection freedom. Part two makes up the bulk of the text, and delves into specific topics like censorship, children, collection development, copyright, etc. Part three provides information about communication and how to contribute to the movement. The manual concludes with a glossary of terms, a bibliography of further reading, a list of core documents, and an index.

The text is very well written and provides a wealth of information about each topic, including specific situational examples and explanations of the law surrounding the different topics. The information is organized well and includes great details to make navigation as simple as possible. It is very helpful to have all of this information collected and organized in one simple resource. Proponents of intellectual freedom would benefit from having a copy of this manual on hand.—**Tyler Manolovitz**

Library Cooperation

398.   **Going Beyond Loaning Books to Loaning Technology: A Practical Guide for Librarians.** Sander, Janelle, Lori S. Mestre, and Eric Kurt. Lanham, Md., Rowman & Littlefield, 2015. 158p. illus. index. (Practical Guides for Librarians). $65.00pa; $64.00 (e-book). ISBN 13: 978-1-4422-4499-3; 978-1-4422-4500-6 (e-book).

Thirteenth in the series Practical Guides for Librarians, *Going beyond Loaning Books to Loaning Technologies* is a useful resource for librarians. Available in paperback and e-book formats, this text details the emergence of a loanable technology program at libraries.

Adaptable to school, public, and academic libraries, most of the information is based on the model for creating an expanding loanable technology program at the University of Illinois at Urbana Champaign (UIUC). The guide is a step-by-step process in eleven chapters, including two appendixes, tables, and figures. Additionally, shaded text boxes in each chapter highlight information and tips. Chapters close with key points and references, and the book concludes with an index.

Overall, the organization of this book is quite good, though a few organizational flaws exist. Black-and-white photos are helpful but lack engagement. In a few instances, "Figures" show forms (Equipment Loan Form, p.75 and 105) which would be best if placed in closer proximity. Or, more logically, another appendix with all forms would be more useful to librarians. Final evaluation of technology programming, as discussed in Chapter 11, lacks any assessment form examples.

Authors Sander, Mestre, and Kurt clearly outline the steps necessary for a technology loaning program expansion. Sequential information will be useful for librarians seeking expansion of loaning services in the realm of technological equipment. Topics from initial identification of community needs through final assessment of successes and failures give this topic the A-Z of program development.

Libraries are repositories for a vast array of items, many of which are for borrowing. Looking beyond traditional lending, this book embraces the future by encouraging and guiding staff in the new age of loaning. Librarians will find this guide useful in exploring a library's niche for loaning these technologies. From e-books to cameras, gaming devices to projectors, *Going Beyond Loaning Books to Loaning Technologies* provides a guide to everything from the initial concept to the training of staff. Written with purpose, librarians will want this title on the professional development shelf. Highly Recommended.—**Janis Minshull**

399.   **Library Consortia: Models for Collaboration and Sustainability.** Horton, Valerie and Greg Pronevitz, eds. Chicago, American Library Association, 2015. 202p. index. $65.00pa.; $58.50pa. (ALA members). ISBN 13: 978-0-8389-1218-8.

As Valerie Horton and Greg Pronevitz declare in their first chapter, libraries have a long history of forming consortia to support cooperative programs. Consortia come in many forms, and their activities are multifarious. This volume attempts to survey the entire landscape of consortial library endeavors and to hint at what the future holds. Horton, the director of Minitex, and Pronevitz, executive director of the Massachusetts Library System, authored or coauthored the initial six chapters, which constitute about half of the volume. In chapter one, the history of library consortia, their goals, and their typical activities are briefly discussed. Chapter two summarizes the results of a 2012 survey of U.S. library consortia. In addition to statistical data, the survey revealed the major challenges and opportunities facing library consortia today. The survey also spotlighted the great diversity among consortia when it comes to membership size, budget, and services. Chapter three, on managing consortia, blends specific information about governance and legal status with generic advice on managing finances, human resources, strategic planning, advocacy, and communication. Chapter four briefly examines 10 activities of library consortia: cataloging; consulting; continuing education and training; cooperative collection development; cooperative purchasing; digitization services; institutional repositories and publishing; integrated library systems; physical delivery; and resource sharing. Chapters five and six look in greater depth at two of the most prevalent programs—discovery, e-content delivery, and resource sharing; and physical delivery. The second half of the book is devoted to 16 case studies of consortial operations, each separately authored. Most are about four pages long. Each starts by listing the needs the program addresses and the benefits it creates. One program was discontinued; several were in early or pilot phases at the time of writing; and others are long-standing programs that have changed over time to respond to emerging technologies, fiscal constraints, or other pressures. Horton and Pronevitz add a short conclusion, sharing lessons they have learned from years of involvement in library consortia. Horton observes that funding for consortia is usually in flux, and thus strong visionary leaders must be able to discern opportunities to add innovative services. Pronevitz acknowledges the rash of mergers among library consortia in the early twenty-first century in response to the economic downturn, arguing that mergers and contractions, although painful, have had positive outcomes. Because there is little doubt that library consortia will continue to play critical roles in helping libraries fulfill their missions, this book will be of interest to almost any librarian involved in consortium-based activities, and in particular, consortium staff members. In the short-term, it offers models for cutting-edge collaboration across a wide spectrum of traditional and nontraditional library activities. In the long term, it will provide a historical snapshot of library collaborative strategies at a pivotal point in the transformation of the field.—**Susan E. Searing**

400.   Nyquist, Corinne. **Resource Sharing Today: A Practical Guide to Interlibrary Loan, Consortial Circulation, and Global Cooperation.** Lanham, Md., Rowman & Littlefield, 2014. 213p. index. $65.00pa.; $64.99 (e-book). ISBN 13: 978-0-8108-8803-6; 978-0-8108-8804-3 (e-book).

Living in an interspace between circulation, reference services, and acquisition departments, Interlibrary Loan –ILL (or Interlibrary Services –ILS as it is called in some institutions) is a highly utilized yet underpromoted division within the library world. Corinne Nyquist (librarian, Sojourner Truth Library at State University of New York, New Paltz) seeks to address this under promotion by means of a "how-to" text geared to both new and more experienced librarians. Because ILL is rarely covered within traditional library/ information science programs, Nyquist covers everything from the early history and philosophy of consortial services through the departmental politics of ILL- where do ILL librarians report? To circulation? To reference? To acquisitions? Are they their own unit? Nyquist closes with appendixes for local, state, national, and international ILL codes, open access agreement, and purchase on demand plan templates.

A well-written, comprehensive work on consortial library services, Nyquist certainly succeeds at educating all librarians on the necessity of ILL to patrons in all manner of libraries. As stated in the introduction (written by Collette Mak, Head of Access Services, Notre Dame University), Nyquist's book joins a small but growing number of texts geared towards excellent user service in an increasingly networked world. Of particular interest is Nyquist's chapter 9, "Conundrums" where she elucidates on the myriad of issues ILL runs into: journal cancelations forcing up patron requests while database licensing makes articles more difficult to acquire, problems with citations stopping ILL requests, and encouraging better metadata so that technology can better verify even partial citation, etc. Although chapter 9 was a particular standout, each chapter holds its own in this text, making Nyquist's book useful for any librarian working within ILL.—**Rachel Meredith Minkin**

Library Facilities

401.   Albrecht, Steve. **Library Security: Better Communication, Safer Facilities.** Chicago, American Library Association, 2015. 184p. index. $55.00pa.; $49.50pa. (ALA members). ISBN 13: 978-0-8389-1330-7.

Library Security: Better Communication, Safer Facilities author, Dr. Steve Albrecht, is an internationally known expert on workplace violence, safety, and security and an author, speaker, trainer, and consultant. Dr. Albrecht is retired from the San Diego Police Department and is also board certified in human resources, security, and employee coaching. In addition, Albrecht manages a consulting firm that specializes in high-risk customer service skills. His expertise in law enforcement and conflict resolution in libraries offers positive leadership responses. This experience combines with his sense of humor to produce a literary contribution that is helpful, unique, and timely. Readers will enthusiastically determine that the pages address essential learning lessons for library administrative personnel and staff. Law enforcement agencies will also gain an awareness of related library security concerns after reading this informative handbook.

This one-volume professional resource contains nine chapters that offer opportunities to evaluate and implement essential safety and security requirements. Furthermore, the author's candid comments empower readers and motivate colleagues to maintain a safe library community and environment. Chapters cover the library work environment; the enforcement of a library code of conduct; difficult patrons and the challenges posed by certain such patrons as teenagers, the mentally ill, and the homeless; how to assess and manage threats; workplace violence; conducting a site security survey; the cultivation of community partnerships; and staff development for a safer library.

Library Security offers essential reading for public libraries. High school, community college, and university library colleagues also benefit along with local enforcement and security agencies. Steve Albrecht makes a literary contribution that warrants praise for readability and vision that encourages safety and due diligence in libraries that once served communities as quiet refuges from the noise of the world.—**Thomas E. Baker**

402.   Charbonnet, Lisa. **Public Library Buildings: The Librarian's Go-To Guide for Construction, Expansion, and Renovation Projects.** Santa Barbara, Calif., Libraries Unlimited/ABC-CLIO, 2015. 220p. illus. index. $65.00pa. ISBN 13: 978-1-4408-3858-3; 978-1-4408-3859-0 (e-book).

Lisa Charbonnet, a public library director-turned-consultant with experience in both renovating a public library and constructing a new branch, covers an astonishing amount of detail in this dense but readable guide. In a reassuring, conversational tone, she leads readers along the path from the initial vision for a new or remodeled space to postconstruction maintenance. Each chapter is devoted to a major stage in the process: getting started (understanding the community and setting goals); site selection and acquisition; securing funding; forming a project leadership team; programming and space planning; preconstruction planning; construction; wrapping up and moving in; and postconstruction sign-off and ongoing maintenance. The eight-page table of contents lists every heading and subheading in the text, making it easy to zero in on essentials like the requirements for different spaces (meeting rooms, shelving, staff workspaces, etc.). Charbonnet stresses essential behind-the-scenes space for storage and technical processing that may be overlooked by architects. Rather than dictate solutions, she frequently highlights the pros and cons of decisions. For example, she explains how using volunteers to help with the physical move requires more managerial effort than contracting with a mover, but it can save money and increase community enthusiasm for the new facility. Bulleted lists of considerations and questions about the anticipated uses of new spaces are extremely helpful. Boxed quotations from a handful of public library directors are sprinkled throughout the book; they provide honest glimpses of what has worked and what can go wrong. There are a number of works in the library literature about planning and managing library building and renovation projects, yet this book surprisingly lacks a bibliography—perhaps its only significant flaw. However, the author does employ endnotes to point to published standards and formulas, as well as documents from the two projects she led. Additional model documents and policies are reproduced as appendixes, accompanied by a glossary of terms. *Public Library Buildings* sets a new standard for such guides, and therefore it belongs in most public library professional collections and in all libraries supporting LIS education. The second edition of *Countdown to a New Library: Managing the Building Project,* by Jeannette A. Woodward (ARBA 2011), which is similar in content and approach, is another excellent resource for library directors and building planners.—**Susan E. Searing**

403.   Mathews, Brian, and Leigh Ann Soistmann. **Encoding Space: Shaping Learning Environments that Unlock Human Potential.** Chicago, American Library Association, Association of College and Research Libraries, 2016. 176p. illus. $62.00pa. ISBN 13: 978-0-8389-8825-1.

People go to libraries because the space gives them something. That physical space can provide great significance. In the future, libraries will speak to the human experience, promoting a feeling of well-being and openness to learning. The subtitle of *Encoding Space* describes this vision well; "shaping learning environments that unlock human potential".

A paperback book of 175 pages, the deceiving cover uses subtle tones of black, grey, and white; light bulbs decorate the cover, alluding to inspiration. Inside, the book comes alive with insight on what library facilities can be and how the philosophy of space really does matter.

Authored by Mathews of the Virginia Tech Libraries and in collaboration with interior designer Soistmann, the structure of the book encourages thinking outside the box on library design. Beginning with an unusual visual Journey Map (table of contents), Mathews and Soistmann epitomize exploration of space as unique and without boundaries. The book engages librarians and administrators with invigorating text and intersperses Soistmann's black-and-white drawings and color renderings throughout. The book concludes with notes, references, and attributions, as well as acknowledgements.

Mathews suggests there is more to a physical library space than bricks and mortar, asking readers what library environments best inspire people and what spaces a library community needs. The author also challenges preconceived notions of what a library space must adhere to; boundaries are pushed and new physical spaces that inspire confidence and exude accomplishment are suggested. Section topics include the Importance of Place, Conceptual Transitions, and Well-Being.

The text broadens concepts of architecture with intellectual and stirring conviction using graphics that support the contention. The argument that providing space, collections, and service is no longer enough is supported by the case that library environments must be alive and changeable to accommodate the needs of the community. Mathews states "at its heart, the future of library buildings is rooted in stimulating the mind, and inviting people to pause, ponder, and produce" (154).

The book lacks concrete architectural designs but is successful as a springboard to facility development or expansion. *Encoding Space* is the spark to ignite conversation on how to best design engaging space. Mathews and Soistmann's publication tosses open the door to possibilities and provokes library staff and administration to imagine what an amazing space can bring to library users. This book ameliorates traditional ideas of how library design evolves and cleverly demonstrates the philosophy of library space as a catapult for great thinking. Highly recommended.—**Janis Minshull**

Library Instruction

404.   Artman, Julie, Jeff Sundquist, and Douglas R. Dechow. **The Craft of Librarian Instruction: Using Acting Techniques to Create Your Teaching Presence.** Chicago, American Library Association, Association of College and Research Libraries, 2016. 101p. $38.00pa. ISBN 13: 978-0-8389-8821-3.

An innovative and effective book, *The Craft of Librarian Instruction* creatively draws a parallel between the worlds of dramatic acting and library instruction with the intent of helping librarians enliven their teaching skills and cultivate a true educator persona. The authors are all experienced professionals. Julie Artman is the Chair of Collection Management at Leatherby Libraries, Chapman University, and also teaches in the Department of Theatre. Jeff Sundquist, Assistant Professor and Collection Management Librarian at Eastern Washington University, has a bachelor's degree in theater. Lastly, Douglas Dechow is the Digital Humanities and Sciences Librarian at Chapman University.

The material is divided into three sections, the first of which explains how to "Prepare and Rehearse" in terms of confidently welcoming students into the learning environment. Section two then focuses on how to "Perform and Connect" vis á vis maintaining student interest in a librarian's own unique teaching "characterization." The last section helps readers "Reflect and Sharpen" with mind to continual practice of the teacher role.

Each section presents tips, exercises, questions and answers, and more, all well-managed by subheadings, numbered bullet points, quotes, and other useful and engaging tools. Topics covered include vocal warm-ups, role-playing, and scene, among other things. Overall, this book does an excellent job of inspiring a more contemporary, dynamic librarian with the ultimate goal of creating a more stimulating learning environment.—**ARBA Staff Reviewer**

405.   Buchanan, Heidi E., and Beth A. McDonough. **The One-Shot Library Instruction Survival Guide.** Chicago, American Library Association, 2014. 136p. index. $48.00pa. ISBN 13: 978-0-8389-1215-7.

What a wonderful little book this is. It has information to help new and seasoned librarians work better with teachers, manage time, and evaluate the success of lessons and programs. There is an extensive bibliography included to further reading as well. The chapters are easy to understand and have case scenarios to help the reader understand what the lesson would look like in practice. This book just might be the ticket to jump-start a ho-hum library program. An index rounds out the work.—**Catherine Vinson**

406.   Markgraf, Jill, Kate Hinnant, Eric Jennings, and Hans Kishel. **Maximizing the One-Shot: Connecting Library Instruction with the Curriculum.** Lanham, Md., Rowman & Littlefield, 2015. 188p. $55.00pa.; $54.99 (e-book). ISBN 13: 978-1-4422-3866-4; 978-1-4422-3867-1 (e-book).

This book is a case study of how university librarians collaborated with faculty to integrate information literacy instruction in a selected curriculum. The authors address the challenges of institutional reality, instructing students, and collaborating with faculty. They initially developed lessons for students in composition classes; their approach was expanded for science and nursing classes. The narrative explains lesson goals, planning processes, lesson activities, helping faculty understand the importance, scaffolding, and assessment. Selected worksheets, research guides, and less on study outlines are featured. The information will be helpful to high school and postsecondary librarians implementing a similar program.—**Mary Alice Anderson**

Library Management

407.   Bizzle, Ben, and Maria Flora. **Start a Revolution: Stop Acting Like a Library.** Chicago, American Library Association, 2015. 208p. illus. index. $52.00pa.; $46.80pa. (ALA members). ISBN 13: 978-0-8389-1267-6.

An excellent book written by Ben Bizzle and Maria Flora, two nonlibrarians for the benefit of all public libraries and librarians, it not only shows librarians how to introduce changes successfully in public libraries with the help of technology and effective teamwork, but also how to present the proposed changes to administrators, decision-makers, and the library board for approval. It is based on a practical and successful experience of a technology expert who changed the face of a library in five years—the library won a national award from the American Library Association. The book has eight well-written chapters including the "Digital Library"; "Going Mobile: Face Book Advertising"; "Marketing in the Real World"; "Making Pretty Pictures"; "Convincing the Decision Makers"; and "Start Your Own Revolution." It also includes three very practical "Twitter," "Pinterest," and "More Convincing the Decision Makers." Every chapter is full of information based on the practical experience of one author who successfully suggested changes to introduce technology in a public library in Arkansas, including a Website for the library and an online catalog and access to the library information and holdings through smart mobile phones, to attract successfully more readers and members to the library. It also discusses a successful marketing campaign using technology and traditional means of advertising to make the library more popular and attractive. Finally, the book discusses how the good teamwork of librarians, staff, and administrators can convince the Library Board, the decision makers, to approve the proposed changes in public libraries for the benefit of all users. This book is highly recommended for all public libraries in the United States.—**Ravindra Nath Sharma**

408.   Doucett, Elizabeth. **New Routes to Library Success: 100+ Ideas from Outside the Stacks.** Chicago, American Library Association, 2015. 256p. index. $55.00pa.; $49.50pa. (ALA members). ISBN 13: 978-0-8389-1313-0.

Library director and marketing expert Elisabeth Doucett wonders if libraries, as presently constituted, will still appeal to potential patrons in the years ahead: "I have fretted about whether we library professionals are moving fast enough and being creative enough to move our institutions into the right place for the future ... [to] successfully [make] the transition to a technology-driven, digitally dominated future" (ix). She wants tomorrow's libraries to be more innovative, data-driven, and better integrated with their respective communities.

Doucett's solution was to speak to successful professionals in the private sector. She sought to "discover not just new ideas but also transformative ideas—ideas that will help libraries take a giant leap forward into the future" (x). She ultimately talked with 11 different nonlibrary professionals at 10 different corporate entities, all in her native Maine. Topics discussed included Entrepreneurship (with Josh Davis of Gelato Fiasco), Customer

Service (with Chris Wilson of L.L. Bean), Unconventional Thinking (with Kate Cheney Chappell of Tom's of Maine), etc. Doucett also explains her own experiences with content curation (at the Curtis Memorial Library in Brunswick, Maine).

Doucett is a passionate advocate, but no reader will agree with all of the conclusions herein. Thankfully, there are over 100 ideas to cherry-pick amongst, and there are many thought-provoking quotes (from both interviewer and interviewees) to muse upon.— **Richard Nathan Leigh**

409.   Giesecke, Joan, Jon Cawthorne, and Deb Pearson. **Navigating the Future with Scenario Planning: A Guidebook for Librarians.** Chicago, American Library Association, Association of College and Research Libraries, 2015. 118p. $36.00pa. ISBN 13: 978-0-8389-8751-3.

To update her useful guide, *Scenario Planning for Libraries* (ALA, 1998), Joan Giesecke, former dean of libraries at the University of Nebraska-Lincoln, was joined by three experienced library administrators: Jon Cawthorne, West Virginia University; Deb Pearson, University of Nebraska-Lincoln; and Tyler Walters, Virginia Tech. Together they give readers the conceptual tools to develop multiple plausible futures as a basis for strategic planning. Scenarios for library planning sometimes come ready-made, such as the *ARL 2030 Scenarios: A User's Guide for Research Libraries* (Association of Research Libraries, 2010), *Futures Thinking for Academic Librarians: Higher Education in 2025* by David J. Staley and Kara J. Malenfant (ACRL, 2010), or scenarios developed by the library's parent institution. However, the authors of this book argue that adopting externally developed scenarios misses the benefits of organizational learning and leadership development that result from a full-fledged scenario planning process. In part one, four short chapters explain the theory and history of scenario planning and the steps in the process, including writing scenario stories (several more or less standard "plots" are described) and developing strategies based on the scenarios. While this isn't rocket science, if a library is going to engage in scenario planning, it is worth doing well. This overview is sufficient to inspire such an undertaking and to set planners on a firm path forward. Part two consists of five chapters, each exploring a different complementary topic. One chapter recommends the incorporation of other research methods into scenario planning and briefly explains the Delphi method, semi-structured interviews, case studies, and stratified and purposive sampling. Another chapter reviews published scenarios on the future of higher education, research, and university libraries; this material is secondary to the book's central purpose but is nevertheless thought-provoking. A third chapter discusses the benefits of scenario planning for library leaders who strive to think deeply about organizational culture and to approach change creatively. The book concludes with two case studies. The first analyzes the responses of academic library human resources directors to scenarios that require changes in the workforce. The second revisits a case from the 1998 edition, where scenarios informed decision-making about the allocation of a student fee for information technology. The volume has a bibliography but no index. Although this book is slanted toward academic librarians' needs, scenarios can be a useful tool for public, school, and special librarians too. This book belongs in most professional collections, as well as libraries that support LIS education.—**Susan E. Searing**

410.   Hernon, Peter, Robert E. Dugan, and Joseph R. Matthews. **Managing with Data: Using ACRLMetrics and PLAmetrics.** Chicago, American Library Association, 2015. 216p. index. $85.00pa.; $76.50pa. (ALA members). ISBN 13: 978-0-8389-1243-0.

In these days of budgetary constraints, it is imperative that libraries present relevance, usefulness, and value to their stakeholders. In order to accomplish this, data and the methods in which to appropriately use the data need to be incorporated into the management process that guides the making of decisions and the application of policies. The purpose of *Managing with Data: Using ACRLMetrics and PLAmetrics* is to build a foundation for using these data services to foster the decision-making process to manage the facilities, collections, and services of the library.

The theme of the purposeful use of metrics in evidence-based management is developed in each of the 11 chapters to address the areas of concern of providing the resources and services to fit the needs of the institution (academic library) or community (public library). This book is a practical guide in gathering data from the appropriate data sets, compiling the data for the relevant study, and encouraging the reader to draw conclusions that can improve services, facilities, and collection development. Each chapter provides the opportunity to gain real experience through examples and exercises that utilize complimentary access to a subset of data from the two data services. This approach solidifies the ideas presented and encourages the reader to expand upon these themes to incorporate other sources of data to fashion a management process that addresses the mission and visions of the institution or the community. Libraries are localized to a community or institution, so this book does not aim to provide a set of standard analyses, but, by developing benchmarking and analysis of peer library best practices, strategies can be applied to improve efficiencies, services, and outcomes demonstrating relevance and value.

The book's coauthors bring many years of experience within the LIS management field and they have all been a part in award-winning publications concerning planning, assessment, evaluation, and management of libraries. This book would serve students in LIS masters programs studying library management as well as current and future department heads and directors in public and academic libraries looking to improve skills in assessment, decision-making, and communicating value to stakeholders.—**Lee Sochay**

411.   **Running a Small Library: A How-To-Do-It Manual for Librarians.** John A. Moorman, ed. Chicago, American Library Association, 2015. 276p. index. $80.00pa; $72.00pa. (ALA members). ISBN 13: 978-0-8389-1273-7.

This book was written to help administrators of small libraries run them. Small libraries are often run by individuals who did not train for the job of chief administrator. Small libraries are run with small budgets and small staffs. This book is written to help administrators of small libraries by providing explanations and best practices for the various operations of the library. The book consists of five parts (Introduction, Administration, Public Services, Collection Development, Computers and Automation) and a resource section. Each section is made up of chapters written by 14 library practitioners with expertise in the subject under discussion. Most chapters are 5-10 pages long and include a table of contents on the first page of the chapter. At the end of each chapter the author includes references and suggested further reading. Topics covered range from budget basics to book selection and weeding. The Sourcebook, completely updated from the first edition, contains lists of State Library Agencies, Book and Periodical Vendors, Library Furniture and Supply Vendors, Automation Vendors, Professional Organizations, and Professional Statements. Very brief biographies of the authors are included, followed by an index.

The information in the book is very basic. It would be most helpful to new administrators who come to the job with very little training or experience. It will also be useful to librarians taking on new duties in unfamiliar segments of library work. Recommended.—**Joanna M. Burkhardt**

412.   Todaro, Julie. **Mentoring A-Z.** Chicago, American Library Association, 2015. 153p. index. $58.00pa.; $52.20pa. (ALA members). ISBN 13: 978-0-8389-1329-1.

The author is the 2015-16 President-elect of the American Library Association, who wrote this book on mentoring prior to her election. This book includes a discussion of perceived opinions and the nature of mentoring in the twenty-first century. Then there is a discussion of how to design and implement a mentorship program, which provides scenarios to highlight some of the issues that need to be addressed in developing an effective program. The reader will find clear guidelines for mentors and people considering being mentors to consider. The author also addresses issues that might arise between mentors and mentees. The author includes a chapter on best practices to follow in measuring and evaluating a mentorship program. This is followed by a series of job descriptions, goals and outcomes for such programs, and checklists that can be used to monitor the process. The author concludes her book with a list of library organizations that have mentoring programs. My one problem with this list is she refers to the Special Library Association when the name is Special Libraries Association and its divisions have been very involved in developing mentoring programs.

Mentoring has been a topic of great interest to the business community and additional insights on successful programs can be found by consulting the business literature.—**Judith J. Field**

Library Outreach

413.   Stoltz, Dorothy and others. **Inspired Collaboration: Ideas for Discovering and Applying Your Potential.** Chicago, American Library Association, 2016. 183p. index. $50.00pa.; $45.00 pa. (ALA members). ISBN 13: 978-0-8389-1396-3.

During her long career as coordinator of programming and outreach services at the Carroll County (MD) Public Library, Dorothy Stoltz gained valuable insights into the benefits of collaboration, planning, and deep community engagement. She shares her wisdom and celebrates the transformative role of libraries through true stories, parables, photographs, and quotations. Her team of coauthors—Susan M. Mitchell, Cen Campbell, Rolf Grafwallner, Kathleen Reif, and Stephanie Mareck Shauck—are, like Stoltz, staunch advocates for early childhood literacy programs. Although the title and subtitle imply a very broad treatment, the book's advice is aimed squarely at public librarians. Most real-life examples are drawn from youth library programs in Maryland. Seventeen short chapters appear in four sections: Why Collaborate?; The Trials of Collaboration; A New Way to Plan and Implement; and Engagement—The Heart of Collaboration. The upbeat prose is reminiscent of a pep talk or motivational self-help guide. Stoltz provides entertainingly exaggerated fictional vignettes as well as true-to-life stories of successes and failures of libraries striving to serve their communities. She constantly poses questions that prompt readers to examine their own beliefs as well as the organizational culture of their libraries, like "What is the essence of collaboration?" and "How can I nurture the good in each situation?" Embedded in the text are 17 "discoveries" advising readers to, for example, "think things through," "cultivate discernment," and "use adversity to your advantage." The sources of wisdom upon which Stoltz draws range from Benjamin Franklin to Socrates, Andrew Carnegie, Helen Keller, Winston Churchill, and Mr. Rogers. She repeatedly states that the mission of libraries is "to enlighten humanity," a mission that transforms librarians into "media mentors" and creates the foundation for early literacy programs that empower parents to be their children's first teachers. Stoltz aims to inspire readers with brief descriptions of innovative programs, anecdotes from the lives of famous people, metaphors for collaboration, and a constant flow of questions for self-reflection, but she offers few concrete techniques for community needs assessment, effective planning, or program evaluation. Eight short appendixes partly make up for this lack, but these materials are not well integrated with the rest of the book. Similarly, four supplementary documents at http://www.alaeditions.org/Webextras are presented with little context. The short bibliography of suggested readings mixes popular works on management and leadership with studies of early childhood literacy and learning. Despite the author's enthusiasm and years of experience, this book seldom succeeds in being more than the sum of its jumbled parts. However, public librarians seeking inspiration might find in Stoltz's optimistic words enough encouragement to push them toward greater self-awareness and a commitment to collaborative programming. The book may also be useful for in-house professional development programs, especially for librarians and staff who serve the very young.—**Susan E. Searing**

Museum Studies

414.   George, Adrian. **The Curator's Handbook.** New York, Thames and Hudson, 2015. 333p. index. $29.95. ISBN 13: 978-0-500-23928-5.

British curator George provides curators and students of museum studies insights into the many aspects of curation, whether for museums, galleries, or other spaces. Presented in a chronological sequence, from the original idea and finding an appropriate location, to fundraising, contract negotiations, and pre-exhibition publication items, steps are clearly laid out. Creating the display space, from wall color to lighting, creating press releases, and scheduling events during the exhibition are all key elements of curating success. This volume also explores risks and possible problems—international shipping of objects, security planning, emergency situations, and regulations concerning gatherings (such as openings) in the international context. A comprehensive examination of the world of curation.

A very minor comment about the layout of the book: readers may be distracted by the use of colored pages, bolded words, and blocks of background color. All libraries interested in museum studies and the work of curators will find this reasonably priced volume very informative and useful.—**Mark Schumacher**

415.   Latham, Kiersten F., and John E. Simmons. **Foundations of Museum Studies: Evolving Systems of Knowledge.** Santa Barbara, Calif., Libraries Unlimited/ABC-CLIO, 2014. 155p. illus. index. $55.00pa. ISBN 13: 978-1-61069-282-3; 978-1-61069-952-5 (e-book).

As of early 2016 there are over 60 graduate degree programs in museum studies and museology in the United States, according to the American Alliance of Museums. This book is intended to serve as a core text for them. It is not a how-to manual for museum practitioners, but a classic introductory text that covers the history, structure, functions, and values of the field. The authors are well qualified to provide an overview of the field and its theoretical frameworks. Latham established the museum studies specialization within the School of Library and Information Science at Kent State University; like her coauthor Simmons, she has had a varied career in museum education and museum practice. Their combined experience spans history, science, and art museums; and both are published scholars. "Reality checks" highlighted in text boxes throughout the book draw on their experiences to illustrate the intersection of theory and practice. Following an introduction that defines "museum," discusses legal and ethical responsibilities of museums, explains what museum studies is, and outlines the historical development of museums, the core content is organized around the basic categories of how, what, who, where, and why. The "How" chapters examine museums through the lens of systems theory and explain their functions: preservation, which includes restoration, conservation, and collection management; research; and communication. The "What" chapters differentiate among types of museums and discuss their collections, focusing on what makes a museum object meaningful. As befits an LIS approach to museum studies, the authors ground this section in the concept of the "document" as articulated by Michael Buckland and Suzanne Briet. The "Who" chapter on museum workers identifies over 30 different tasks fulfilled by employees or volunteers, while the chapter on museum users looks not just at demographics but also at users' varied reasons for visiting museums and the challenge of universal design. The "Where" chapter discusses the effects of globalization on museums, and the final "Why" chapter explores perceptions of museums' value to humanity now and in the future. This concise textbook is intended to be supplemented by additional readings. This is an essential purchase for libraries that support museum studies courses. Most general LIS collections should acquire a copy as well, because students are increasingly interested in how LIS concepts and skills can be applied beyond traditional employment in libraries. Readers looking for a more practical introduction to museum work might prefer the concise *Museums 101* by Mark Walhimer (Rowman & Littlefield, 2015) or the more substantial *Museum Basics,* 3rd ed., by Timothy Ambrose and Crispin Paine (Routledge, 2012).—**Susan E. Searing**

Readers' Advisory

416. Alessio, Amy J. **Mind-Bending Mysteries and Thrillers for Teens: A Programming and Reader's Advisory Guide.** Chicago, American Library Association, 2014. 152p. index. $54.00pa. ISBN 13: 978-0-8389-1204-1.

This book offers an explanation of the mystery genre and all its subgenres of interest to teens. The author offers a cross-referenced annotated list of representative books in each subgenre, along with authors. While the lists are not exhaustive, the examples will get a YA or teen librarian up to speed quickly if he or she is not that familiar with mysteries. The author also includes booktalking examples and programming and marketing ideas. Also included is a book discussion guide over a variety of books. Titles are listed by subgenre and by author in the appendixes, making it easy to find something specific, and genres, titles, and authors are also listed in the index for quick reference.—**Richard Fanning**

417.   Cart, Michael, and Christine A. Jenkins. **Top 250 LGBTQ Books for Teens: Coming Out, Being Out, and the Search for Community.** Chicago, Huron Street Press/ American Library Association, 2015. 164p. illus. index. $21.95pa. ISBN 13: 978-1-937589-56-1.

The Top LGBTQ Books for Teens provides an annotated bibliography of the best fiction, graphic novels, and nonfiction for gay, lesbian, bisexual, transgender, and questioning teens in middle and high school, published for the most part since 1994. The authors formerly collaborated on *The Heart Has Its Reasons: Young Adult Literature with Gay/Lesbian/Queer Content, 1969-2004* (Scarecrow, 2006).

The current title opens by addressing the evolution of LGBTQ literature and the inclusion criteria, before presenting 195 titles from a variety of genres. The preface to this section includes an explanation of the codes given to each book in the bibliography, designed to help place the titles within the larger community of YA literature with LGBTQ content. HV stands for homosexual visibility, GA for gay assimilation, and QC for queer consciousness. The sections on graphic novels and nonfiction are followed by one on professional resources available to librarians, teachers, parents, counselors, and any adult who works with LGBTQ teens. An index rounds out this fine work that can be used to great effect by librarians at public, college, and middle/high school libraries.—**ARBA Staff Reviewer**

418.   Fichtelberg, Susan. **Encountering Enchantment: A Guide to Speculative Fiction for Teens.** 2d ed. Santa Barbara, Calif., Libraries Unlimited/ABC-CLIO, 2015. 392p. illus. index. (Genreflecting Advisory Series). $55.00. ISBN 13: 978-1-61069-113-0; 978-1-4408-3451-6 (e-book).

A guide to fantasy, sci-fi, and the paranormal, Fichtelberg's compendium delineates fictive subgenres and particularizes such modes as talking animals, futurism, aliens, demons, and zombies. The text covers famous authors—Joseph Bruchac, Rita Mae Brown, Dean Koontz, J.K. Rowling, Scott Card, Robin McKinley, Frank Herbert—but omits the landmark books of Octavia Butler, Madeleine L'Engle, and Ursula LeGuin. Fichtelberg's pop fiction works and series cover Outlander, Hunger Games, Modern Faerie Tales, Raised by Wolves, Lunar Chronicles, and Lord of the Rings. Appendixes specify audiobooks, DVDs, club titles, and awards. For ease of use, the author itemizes print and electronic sources and separates indexes into author, title, subject, and award.

To her credit, Fichtelberg delves into fringe topics that include twinning and orphaning, abductees, protagonists with disabilities, alien parentage, refugees and prisoners, Middle Eastern fairy tales, Asian lore, bulimia, and LGBT issues. Each entry cites author, title, publisher, reading level, pages, and ISBN. Commentary lacks pizzazz, but dutifully reports major elements of most works. Indexing features key topics—hostages, pixies, automatons, seelies, Shawnee, Salem—and subtopics, as with 13 examples under "characters from mythology." This reference source has value for the teacher, librarian, and home schooler who reach out to the reader of the outre and Gothic and who tempt the at-risk student with the spell-binding.—**Mary Ellen Snodgrass**

419.   Isaacs, Kathleen T. **Excellent Books for Early and Eager Readers.** Chicago, American Library Association, 2016. 264p. index. $52.00pa.; $46.80pa. (ALA members). ISBN 13: 978-0-8389-1344-4.

Isaacs's guide to intriguing works for young bibliophiles introduces transitional readers and classics by cover art, title, author, illustrator, publisher, and type as well as interest and reading level, for example, *The Librarian Who Measured the Earth* and *Where the Sidewalk Ends.* The selections reach back to old favorites as beloved as *D'Aulaires' Book of Greek Myths,* O'Brien's *Mrs. Frisby and the Rats of Nimh,* and Randall Jarrell and Maurice Sendak's *The Bat-Poet.* Beyond fiction, the compilation spotlights biographies of Louisa May Alcott and U.S. marshal Bass Reeves and nonfiction introductions to the Boston Tea Party, octopi, marsupials, dinosaurs, and Steve Jenkins's cross-category bestseller *The Animal Book.* Keys to the success of this work lie in its appealing book summaries and two-part indexing by title, author, and subjects as variant as the Galapagos Islands, Honus Wagner, and boarding schools. A must-have work for belabored public and school librarians and teachers, as well as home-schooling parents. Highly recommended—**Mary Ellen Snodgrass**

420.   **Recommended Reading: 600 Classics Reviewed.** 2d ed. Hackensack, N.J., Salem Press, 2015. 400p. index. $125.00. ISBN 13: 978-1-61925-867-9; 978-1-61925-868-6 (e-book).

This excellent reference houses 600 compact and current reviews of literary classics. Chosen at the discretion of Salem Press editors, selected works are those that presently and continuously draw the praise and study of both general readers and literary experts. The volume presents alphabetical (by title) entries which all include essential bibliographic information and a brief statement noting the work's content and influence. The review itself trades off between a succinct description of the basic plot and an overall assessment of the work's deeper contemplations. While clearly not intended to be comprehensive, the selection is nonetheless well-curated. The entries include fiction, non-fiction, poetry, and drama with many diverse "sub-genres" and forms represented, such as mystery, parody, diary, scientific, epic, and so on. Users of this reference will recognize writers such as William Shakespeare, Jane Austen, George Bernard Shaw, or W.B. Yeats, as well as titles like *The Importance of Being Earnest, Main Street, Paradise Lost,* or *War and Peace.* Readers will be further impressed by the inclusion of such ancient texts as Sophocles' *Antigone, Beowulf,* or the *Bible.* And of further note is the inclusion of a number of "young adult" titles such as *Anne of Green Gables, Charlotte's Web,* or *The Giver* in recognition of the growing influence of this literary category.

Several helpful indexes round out this resource—an author index, literary genre index, and a publication year index.—**Laura Herrell**

Reference Services

421.   **Reimagining Reference in the 21st Century.** David A. Tyckoson and John G. Dove, eds. Ashland, Ohio, Purdue University Press, 2014. 418p. (Charleston Insights in Library, Archival, and Information Sciences). $29.95pa. ISBN 13: 978-1-6124-9366-4; 978-1-5575-3698-3 (e-book).

"Is reference still a useful component of library services?" So begins this provocative and uber-current essay collection on one of the great questions of librarianship. Veteran librarian and reference scholar David Tyckoson teams with publishing consultant John Dove to assess the status of the reference service provided by librarians today and how it will be done in the future. Nine essays and 23 case studies are followed by Tyckoson and Dove's concluding "Where Do We Go From Here?" chapter. The core of this last is a list of key trends the editors see as critical to future reference and user services: 1) twenty-first-century literacies, 2) lifelong learning, 3) filter failure and filter success (an understanding of the "filters" necessary for modern information processing), 4) the hidden Web, 5) inclusivity, and 6) changing technology. The book is particularly noteworthy for chapters by Wikimedia Foundation board member (Phoebe Ayers), the general editor of ALA's Guide to Reference (Denise Bennett), and Jessica Moyer of the University of Milwaukee who proposes the combination of two traditional library services ("Readers' Advisory Services As Reference Services"). The case studies run the reference gamut: using LibraryThing for Libraries (https://www.librarything.com/forlibraries) as a discovery tool for patrons at a public library in Massachusetts, crowdsourcing reference, "peer reference" tutoring, 24/7 global virtual reference, embedded librarianship, and much more.

This title is published as part of Purdue's Charleston Insights in Library, Archival, and information Sciences series of Purdue University, overseen by Katina Strauch and Tom Gilson of the College of Charleston. The purpose of the series—like that of the Charleston Conference itself—is to provide a forum for discussion of issues of interest to librarians, publishers, and vendors. Likewise, the editors of this volume sought out contributions from all segments of the librarian and publishing community.—**Vincent Burns**

422.   **Reinventing Reference: How Libraries Deliver Value in the Age of Google.** Katie Elson Anderson and Vibiana Bowman Cvetkovic, eds. Chicago, American Library Association, 2015. 176p. index. $65.00pa.; $58.50pa. (ALA members). ISBN 13: 978-0-8389-1278-2; 978-0-8389-1286-7 (e-book).

The goal of Anderson's and Cvetkovic's book is to envision the future of the librarian profession and library reference services as libraries continue to face challenging times, and presumably become less relevant. In a conventional three-part format including nine chapters, the book's contributors present a deeper understanding of current trends in reference services and suggest how the future of these services will look based on historical events in the profession. In part one, contributors thoughtfully describe the history of reference, its professional standards and ethics, and the changes in reference services caused by advances in technology. Following in part two, writers provide descriptions of the current state of reference in academic, school, public, and special libraries; however, these chapters suffer from a lack of a consistent theme. Last of all, the writers in part three offer a vision for the future of libraries and, in particular, reference services. The first two chapters of part three offer useful discussions on topics ranging from the effects of digital rights management, artificial intelligence, crowd sourcing of information, and emerging technologies to descriptions of the seven categories of reference service "strategies." Part three's last chapter is quite optimistic by playfully outlining what reference services will look like in the year 2052. Finally, even though the editors recognized that the book would be out of date by the time it was published, the real value of the book will be found by library staff that isn't well versed in the historical and current trends of reference services. They should find this book as a good starting resource for the subject.—**Jennifer Brooks Huffman**

Research

423.   McAdoo, Monty L. **The Student's Survival Guide to Research.** Chicago, American Library Association, 2015. 218p. index. $50.00pa.; $45.00pa. (ALA members). ISBN 13: 978-0-8389-1276-8.

Primers that explain the processes of locating information and writing research papers are an enduring genre. Other recent works in this vein include *The College Student's Research Companion,* 5th ed., by Arlene R. Quaratiello and Jane Devine (see ARBA 2011, entry 595), *Concise Guide to Information Literacy* by Scott Lanning (Libraries Unlimited 2012), *Research and Documentation in the Digital Age,* 6th ed., by Diana Hacker and Barbara Fister (Bedford/St. Martin's, 2014), and the more advanced *Oxford Guide to Library Research,* 4th ed., by Thomas Mann (Oxford University Press, 2015). Several elements recommend this new work. First, McAdoo, an experienced instruction librarian and undergraduate teacher, targets his advice to first-semester college students with no library research experience whatsoever. Second, although he doesn't allude to them outright, the ACRL Information Literacy Competency Standards align with the guide's organization, as it progresses from understanding an assignment and choosing a topic to locating resources, evaluating them, and using them responsibly. Third, the narrative is frequently punctuated with bulleted "tips," and each chapter concludes with "reflections" that prompt students to extend their learning and explore local resources. (Some of the activities suggested in these sections could also be utilized to good effect by librarians during in-class instruction.). Fourth, a handy glossary defines library and research terms which are highlighted in bold in the text. And finally, the writing is lively and engaging. McAdoo focuses clearly on general strategies for managing a research project, searching the literature, and writing a term paper, scarcely mentioning specific databases or vendor platforms. Along with its strengths, however, this work also has weaknesses. The friendly, second-person prose at times seems to condescend to its audience. The pep-talk tone depicts the research and writing process as burdensome and unpleasant; in the first 20 pages, negative adjectives abound, including "intimidating," "challenging," "daunting," "time-consuming," and "stressful." McAdoo empathizes with students who "struggle" and feel "afraid" and "frustrated." While academic librarians readily acknowledge the affective dimension of information-seeking, McAdoo overdoes it in assuming all students have strong adverse reactions to research assignments. In addition, the guide recommends only manual methods for note-taking and focuses in a single-minded way on the term paper as the end product, at a time when an increasing number of college courses require students to synthesize their research in presentations, Websites, posters, videos, and other products. Lastly, screen shots of the sample search outlined in the final chapter are so reduced that they are, for the most part, unreadable. Despite its imperfections, most academic libraries and tutoring centers should have a copy of this work to share with motivated students who lack a grounding in library research. It is well written overall, its visual design is appealing, and McAdoo unerringly zeroes in on the most important elements of the process. Were it not for the $50 price tag, this guide could also serve as a supplementary text for research- and writing-intensive freshman courses.—**Susan E. Searing**

424.   Roemer, Robin Chin, and Rachel Borchardt. **Meaningful Metrics: A 21st-Century Librarian's Guide to Bibliometrics, Altmetrics, and Research Impact.** Chicago, American Library Association, Association of College and Research Libraries, 2015. 241p. index. $60.00pa. ISBN 13: 978-0-8389-8755-1.

In the academic world of researchers citing each other to increase impact factors, predatory publishers, and administrators searching for faculty that will bring the most prestige to their departments, what metrics are meaningful and can they really be measured with certainty? Assessment is the bane of all educators in this day and age, and librarians are being asked to aid faculty and administrators to assess their impact on the scholarly world and their campus communities. At the same time, librarians and library administrators must be able to do this for their own work. Authors Robin Chin Roemer and Rachel Borchardt provide a variety of excellent sources and activities to help the student librarian as well as the experienced practicing academic librarian answer the question above. Covering information about bibliometrics (the traditional tracking of influence through numbers and sources of bibliographic citations) and altmetrics (tracing influence by using alternative, often Internet-generated methods), and providing understandable descriptions of core tools, this book will be of use to students and academic writers as well as by the librarians for whom it was written. The glossary at the end is helpful for all three groups and would be worth the space for the acronym definitions alone. The various tools highlighted throughout the book will be very useful to the new and experienced information professional. An index would be a nice addition to a second edition. This practical how-to guide would also be a great help to anyone expected to measure the impact of written material, be it scholarly, social, political, environmental, or beyond.— **Diane J. Turner**

425.   Ye, Yunshan. **The ALA Guide to Researching Modern China.** Chicago, American Library Association, 2014. 218p. maps. index. $60.00pa.; $54.00pa. (ALA memebers). ISBN 13: 978-0-8389-1209-6.

Authored by the academic liaison librarian for anthropology, East Asian studies, and political science at Johns Hopkins University and chair of humanities on the Collection Development Council of the Sheridan Libraries and Museums of Johns Hopkins University and editor-in-chief of the Chinese American Librarian Association Occasional Paper Series, this volume funded by a Carnegie-Whitney Award from ALA in 2008 fills a gap in the existing reference resources on China studies, addressing the changing landscape of scholarly research and teaching information literacy concepts and skills in the field. Organized into 15 chapters, Ye first offers introductory materials of basic facts and figures about Modern China, although this is a bit dated as the most recent reference is from 2012, followed by a chronology of Chinese history and culture. The first two chapters offer a historical overview of Modern China studies in the United States and fundamentals of scholarly research in the digital environment. These two chapters are of most interest to serious scholars and librarians, while the next seven chapters address finding sources such as reference sources, books and dissertations, articles in English and in Chinese, related articles for literature reviews, government documents, and archives, statistical data, news, and images. These seven chapters can help any librarian or user in search of specific material formats regarding Modern China. The final six chapters address researching specific subjects rather than resource types, including humanities in art, film, and media studies; humanities in Modern Chinese history; humanities in literature, philosophy, and religion; social sciences in anthropology, sociology, and education; social sciences in economics and business; and social sciences in law, politics, and women's and gender studies. The two appendixes offer guides to buying Chinese books and films, and Chinese e-resources; of particular use to collection development librarians who might not be familiar with materials in this area and/or language. Each chapter opens with objectives and a brief overview, making this a useful tool for teaching research in the area of Modern China, while the materials within the chapters make this equally useful for librarians who will be helping patrons researching any aspect or area of Modern China.—**Sara Marcus**

Storytelling

426.   Freeman, Judy, and Caroline Feller Bauer. **The Handbook for Storytellers.** Chicago, American Library Association, 2015. 416p. $65.00pa.; $58.50pa. (ALA members). ISBN 13: 978-0-8389-1100-6.

Caroline Feller Bauer's groundbreaking *Handbook for Storytellers* (1977) was the definitive guide to library storytime programming until it was superseded by her *New Handbook for Storytellers* (1993). In collaboration with Bauer, who died in 2013, Judy Freeman has thoroughly revised, expanded, and split this classic into two separate works. (The companion volume, published simultaneously, is titled *The Handbook for Storytime Programs* (see ARBA 2016, entry 427). Freeman is a former school librarian, teacher of graduate courses in storytelling, and author of several books on storytelling and children's literature; anecdotes from her and Bauer's experiences with young listeners provide useful and amusing background. A third of the book deals with the basics of planning, publicizing, and conducting a storytelling event. Detailed practical information ranges from sources for purchasing puppets and other objects to augment storytime activities, to advice on avoiding common performance pitfalls. The other two-thirds highlight sources for stories. In a chapter on folklore, Freeman covers beast tales, trickster tales, humorous stories, pourquoi (how and why) stories, scary stories, fairy tales, fables, myths, and religious stories, following the model set out in Bauer's last edition. The subsequent chapter presents additional folk and fairy tales arranged by continent. A chapter titled "More Stories to Tell" is a grab bag of modern retellings and parodies of folk and fairy tales, literary tales, and biographical stories, plus a short section on crafting and telling family stories. The final chapter recommends Freeman's and Bauer's favorite storybooks, tags them by age level, and organizes the citations by subject. Here, and throughout the book, Freeman has significantly updated the source lists, eliminated most out-of-print titles, and provided one-sentence annotations for all entries. In addition, many illustrative stories are presented in their entirety, making this a handy first stop for anyone needing to quickly plan a story program. Although the book is aimed at beginning storytellers, even the most experienced tellers will be inspired and discover new sources because the handbook is brimming with ideas for engaging listeners through riveting tales, interactive play, props, and other techniques. Freeman writes in a fluent, conversational style, and the content is well organized, although the work would succeed better as a reference tool if its table of contents included the chapter subheadings. There are many books available on the art of storytelling. For example, many libraries already own the fourth edition of *Storytelling: Art and Technique,* by Ellin Greene and Janice M. Del Negro (see ARBA 2011, entry 597), which covers similar ground but overlaps less with *The Handbook for Storytellers* than one might expect. Both works belong in any public or school library with an active storytime program (ideally, one circulating copy and another for the librarians' bookshelf). Further, any academic institution that teaches storytelling to future librarians, K-12 teachers, or performers would do well to acquire this book and its companion volume.—**Susan E. Searing**

427.   Freeman, Judy, and Caroline Feller Bauer. **Handbook for Storytime Programs.** Chicago, American Library Association, 2015. 616p. index. $65.00pa.; $58.50pa. (ALA members). ISBN 13: 978-0-8389-1265-2.

The late Caroline Feller Bauer's *Handbook for Storytellers* (1977) and its revision, *New Handbook for Storytellers* (1993), influenced generations of youth services librarians, including Judy Freeman. Freeman (a former school librarian, teacher of storytelling, and herself the author of several books on storytelling and children's literature) collaborated with Bauer before her death to thoroughly update and expand the handbook, which they split into two distinct books. This volume focuses on library storytime programming for children and is divided into two parts. Part one, "Interactive Storytelling," covers the use of pictures and objects, puppetry, creative drama, music, magic, and so-called "fillers," such as fingerplays, tongue twisters, riddles, and rhymes. In addition to annotated lists of books and Websites for each technique, Freeman includes many ready-to-use examples and instructions. Part two is organized by audience level: preschool and primary school children (birth to age 7); and upper elementary and middle school children (ages 8 to 14). For the younger group, Freeman provides some 130 ideas for programs, alphabetically arranged by theme. The themes include familiar things in children's lives (e.g., bicycles, bullies, houses, pets, weather), holidays, real and fictional creatures, and concepts (e.g., honesty, resourcefulness, time). For each topic Freeman recommends several books to read aloud or retell, describes an appropriate activity, and includes a short poem. She also supplies lists of "the funniest picture books ever," Spanish-language stories, and professional books that contain additional storytime suggestions. For older children, Freeman reprints full stories of several types: stories about mysterious objects; narrative jokes; "think stories" that require the listeners to solve a puzzle; stories of the supernatural; funny stories; reinvented fairy tales; love stories; and tales about death. These are followed by briefer descriptions of 35 thematic programs, ranging from poetry slams, book clubs, and library scavenger hunts to hands-on programs about ice cream, mummies, and gardening. Each idea is accompanied by suggested activities and annotated book lists. Altogether, this volume recommends stories in approximately a thousand current books; it will save story-hunters enormous time and effort. Because the companion volume, published simultaneously with the title *The Handbook for Storytellers* (see ARBA 2016, entry 426), provides several hundred more sources for stories, along with tips for publicizing and conducting storytimes, the pair of volumes belong in both the circulating collection and the professional collection of nearly all public and school libraries. Freeman's fluent, conversational prose makes them enjoyable to read as well as to consult for practical storytime programming ideas.—**Susan E. Searing**

428.   MacMillan, Kathy, and Christine Kirker. **More Storytime Magic.** Chicago, American Library Association, 2016. 190p. illus. index. $52.00pa.; $46.80pa. (ALA members). ISBN 13: 978-0-8389-1368-0.

MacMillan and Kirker continue their successful formula for helping librarians and others who plan stories and activities for children aged two and up. Their previous works, also published by ALA Editions, include *Storytime Magic* (2008), *Kindergarten Magic* (2011), *Multicultural Storytime Magic* (2012), and *Baby Storytime Magic* (see ARBA 2014, entry 380). *More Storytime Magic* opens with a short chapter that lists practical tips for engaging young participants, aligning story programs with the Common Core educational standards for kindergarten (which are included in an appendix), and assuring that storytimes are accessible to children with special needs. The remaining 16 chapters focus on themes for programs: all about me; animals; around the world; at home; bugs and insects; concepts (e.g., colors, opposites); fairy tales and castles; family and friends; food;

holidays and celebrations; the natural world; people in my neighborhood; play; school and library; sing and dance; transportation. For every theme, the authors offer several songs and poems with accompanying movements, craft activities, and directions for flannel board stories and games, each keyed to one or more of the Common Core standards. Altogether there are 268 activities, ranging in complexity but all simple enough for a novice storyteller to undertake. Each chapter concludes with a brief unannotated list of recommended picture books related to the theme. The book includes hundreds of small black-and-white drawings that can be enlarged as patterns for flannel board stories and craft projects, but most readers will find it easier to download full-sized drawings from http://alaeditions.org/Webextras/. MacMillan and Kirker round out the volume with an appendix listing over 30 resource books for storytime planners (primarily collections of tales and activities) and an index of authors, titles, and subjects. Youth librarians are always looking for new ideas to enliven story hours for repeat attendees, so this book is a welcome addition for public and school library professional collections.—**Susan E. Searing**

429. **Storyteller's Sampler: Tales from Tellers around the World.** Margaret Read Macdonald, ed. Santa Barbara, Calif., Libraries Unlimited/ABC-CLIO, 2015. 185p. illus. index. $45.00pa. ISBN 13: 978-1-4408-3527-8; 978-1-4408-3528-5 (e-book).

Margaret Read MacDonald is a highly respected folklorist, storyteller, and author of more than 65 books. She has inspired many storytellers, especially children's librarians, to bring a global perspective to their craft. Since the 1990s, Libraries Unlimited has been in the forefront of publishing folktale collections in its World Folklore Series, which now numbers 40 volumes, each focused on a country or a culture. For this delightful sampler, MacDonald selected 54 tales from 30 of the series' volumes. The contents are presented alphabetically by country (e.g., Australia, Brazil, Russia), ethnic/cultural group (e.g., Hmong, Kurdish), or, in single instances, by a region (Siberia) and a continent (South America). Each chapter offers one or two stories, none longer than three pages. A typical story is accompanied by a citation to the original publication in the series, a brief list of similar stories, one or more suggestions for "playing with the story" using crafts or activities, and a short biography of the storyteller. The book's index allows for searching by topic or motif. Some of the stories echo tales that American children have heard before. For example, "Mother Frog and her Twelve Children," a Haitian story, shares plot elements and a moral with the story of the Little Red Hen, while the wood goblin in a Croatian story bears a strong resemblance to Rumplestiltskin. Most of these traditional tales, however, will be unfamiliar to American readers, and their charm lies in part in the glimpses they provide into other cultures. Libraries that possess all of the original volumes in the series will rightly view this new book as redundant, but it is worth acquiring as a one-stop source for beginning storytellers. It is highly recommended for public and school libraries without comprehensive storytelling collections and for academic libraries that support education and/or LIS curricula.—**Susan E. Searing**

Technical Services

430. Sandstrom, John, and Liz Miller. **Fundamentals of Technical Service.** Chicago, American Library Association, 2015. 213p. index. (ALA Fundamentals Series). $64.00pa.; $57.60pa. (ALA members). ISBN 13: 978-1-55570-966-2.

This new book in the ALA Fundamentals Series is a gem for anyone in need of an excellent briefing on Library Technical Services work. The basic functions of Technical Services are described clearly and understandably yet with enough detail to be useful. The book can be used as a textbook, for independent study, or as a reference tool.

Library Technical Services departments have seen many changes in recent years and like all areas of the library, they have been required to do more with less and do it faster. This book covers the changes, stressing the importance of communication and workflow at all levels. Each of the eight chapters is organized with: an introduction, "Before You Begin," "Specialized Terms," concise paragraphs for the body of the chapter, "Trends & Issues," "Final Thoughts," and a bibliography. Examples of helpful boxes include: "Care and Feeding of Vendors," "Approval Plans," and "Tips for Running an Efficient Meeting." Workflow charts and tables are found throughout. The book's appendix, glossary, and index are all exemplary.

This handy book on what goes on in Technical Services is written by experienced librarians who share their insights with helpful comments such as: "materials vendors can be your best friends, make sure you talk to your business office, licenses should be reviewed very carefully, and cataloging should always focus on the needs of the library users." Any library would benefit from this practical and well-written tool.—**Georgia Briscoe**

Publishing and Bookselling

Handbooks and Yearbooks

431.   Woll, Thomas. **Publishing for Profit: Successful Bottom-Line Management for Book Publishers.** 5th ed. Chicago, Chicago Review Press, 2014. 370p. index. $26.95pa. ISBN 13: 978-1-61374-973-9.

This fifth edition updates a book considered to be essential for those venturing into or already in the world of publishing. Since the first edition in 1998, the industry has undergone rapid change, most obviously the shift to digital; the entire publishing industry also faces new challenges, due largely to the availability of electronic information. While still concentrating on the business aspects of the industry, this title also includes updated publishing statistics and figures, a new profit and loss form that reflects the need to view print sales and e-book sales separately, a focus on metadata, and a discussion of digital formats. This handbook is directed at a practicing publishing firm, but can be utilized by anyone interested in the publishing industry.

Publishing for Profit is divided into three parts: "The World of Publishing," "Managerial Organization: Strategy and Techniques," and "Functional Organization: Strategy and Techniques," with chapters on such topics as cash flow, creating a board of directors, cash and accounts receivable, editorial acquisition, contracts, production schedules, sales, subsidiary rights, publishing software, and electronic publishing and marketing. Valuably, this title also has a number of lists and forms, including a publishing timeline, an organization chart, a production checklist, a basic marketing plan worksheet, and a book club pricing template.—**ARBA Staff Reviewer**

12 Military Studies

General Works

Atlases

432. Messenger, Charles. **The D-Day Atlas: Anatomy of the Normandy Campaign.** 2d ed. New York, Thames and Hudson, 2014. 176p. illus. maps. index. $24.95pa. ISBN 13: 978-0-500-29119-1.

The book is the second edition of the original published in 2004, and is now issued in paperback. The author, author of over 40 books on World War II, says in the preface that the volume is a straightforward account of what occurred rather than an in-depth study. But I would argue that it is the very best source that the interested lay person or a student could consult. The narrative is crisp and contains just the right amount of detail. However, the huge number of large color maps are what distinguish the volume. An abundance of photographs augment the narrative and maps. The volume is divided into five chapters—planning and preparation, fortress Europe, D-Day, the beachhead battles, and the post-invasion break out. The brief epilogue sums up the operation and its role in leading ultimately to V-E Day. Appendixes include code words connected with D-Day, diagrams of both the Allied High Command and the German High Command in June 1944, the divisions of all participants that fought in Normandy, a brief bibliography of some of the most useful studies of the event, and an index. At its very modest price for the high quality, glossy paperback, this is a book worthy of all libraries.—**Joe P. Dunn**

Biography

433. Tucker, Spencer C., ed. **500 Great Military Leaders.** Santa Barbara, Calif., ABC-CLIO, 2015. 2v. illus. index. $189.00/set. ISBN 13: 978-1-59884-757-4; 978-1-59884-758-1 (e-book).

"Selecting the 500 most important/noteworthy individuals in military history is no easy task," states Spencer Tucker in the preface, where Tucker admits that he wrote two-thirds of the entries himself, with the rest coming from other ABC-CLIO works that Tucker had edited. Tucker, a senior fellow at ABC-CLIO since 2003, certainly knows his subject. "Great" in the title is, however, misleading. There are entries for many leaders, such as

Alexander the Great, Julius Caesar, George Washington, Epaminondas, and Napoleon Bonaparte who, if not great, were very capable. Conversely other leaders, such as Adolf Hitler, George Armstrong Custer, Joseph Stalin, and Attila the Hun also have entries, being more infamous than great. Tucker not only includes prominent leaders such as Abraham Lincoln, Franklin Roosevelt, and Harry Truman, but also military reformers and administrators, military theorists, and logisticians and engineers. Women are represented with three entries: Boudicca, Joan of Arc, and Zenobia. There seems to be a good mix of ancient, medieval, and modern entries from around the world, but Tucker admits that the work is a bit skewed towards the twentieth century and America. Each entry has its own short bibliography; there is no general bibliography. For public, school, and undergraduate libraries.—**Michael W. Handis**

434.   Wagner, Frederic C., III. **Participants in the Battle of the Little Big Horn: A Biographical Dictionary of Sioux, Cheyenne and United States Military Personnel.** 2d ed. Jefferson, N.C., McFarland, 2015. 342p. index. $39.95pa. ISBN 13: 978-1-4766-6459-0; 978-0-4766-8439-6 (e-book).

The first edition of this book was published in 2011 (see ARBA 2012, entry 679). This second edition is divided into three main sections with nine appendixes, a bibliography, and an index. The first section lists soldiers of the Seventh Cavalry based on the 1876 regimental rosters. Each listing contains biographical details, including birth, death, and enlistment dates; physical appearance; and the individual's actions during the battle, including any major points of historical dispute. The following sections include similar information, with section two covering the Cavalry's civilians arranged by category (scouts, mule packers, etc.), and section three covering Native Americans opposing the Seventh. Although there are no footnotes the author often includes references to sources when discussing conflicting witness statements or facts that are in dispute.

The second edition extends the comprehensive listings of the first edition. A new appendix includes the names of some 5000 Native Americans who *could* have been in the encampment the Seventh Cavalry confronted on June 25. This is in addition to the approximately 1500 people *known* to have been at the battle who are listed, along with known biographical details, in section three. The new edition also includes additional birth dates and locations for soldiers born in Great Britain and continental Europe.

Other appendixes provide further detail relative to the battle: unit rosters, strength estimates for both sides, demographics, etc. This is a detailed and useful reference for those interested in researching particulars of the battle and those who took part in it.—**ARBA Staff Reviewer**

Dictionaries and Encyclopedias

435.   Tucker, Spencer C. **Wars That Changed History: 50 of the World's Greatest Conflicts.** Santa Barbara, Calif., ABC-CLIO, 2015. 609p. maps. index. $100.00. ISBN 13: 978-1-61069-785-9; 978-1-61069-786-6 (e-book).

As the author states in his preface "wars both fascinate and repel us." The esteemed encyclopedist Dr. Spencer Tucker gives his readers in *Wars that Changed History* everything a good encyclopedia should—the essential facts, clarity, and brevity. By using the selection criterion—that the included wars must have had "major impact on subsequent historical development, rather than being significant for costs, destruction, or new weapons" the reader is given a broad look at wars that traverse world geography from China to Mexico and time from 1479 B.C.E. to 2011.

For each war, Dr. Tucker goes over the causes, the course of the conflict, and the historical significance. A list of further reading accompanies each entry. Additionally, each war has a box with dates, locations, combatants, principal commanders, principal battles, and the outcome. Some even have maps.

The following are some of the many wars treated in this volume: The Peloponnesian Wars; The Punic Wars; The Qin Wars of Unification; Charlemagne's War; The Norman Conquest; The Thirty Years War; The War of Austrian Succession; The Napoleonic Wars; The Wars of Italian Unification; The American Civil War; The Russo-Japanese War; The Korean War; and the Iraq War.—**Scott R. DiMarco**

436.   **U.S. Conflicts in the 21st Century.** Spencer C. Tucker, ed. Santa Barbara, Calif., ABC-CLIO, 2016. 3v. illus. maps. index. $310.00/set. ISBN 13: 978-1-4408-3878-1; 978-1-4408-3879-8 (e-book).

Spencer C. Tucker, the master of military encyclopedias, offers another addition to his lengthy list of such volumes. Although it has a different name, in many ways this is an updated, leaner edition of Tucker's earlier five-volume *Encyclopedia of Middle Eastern Wars* (2010). Many of the entries are the same or updated from the previous publication. The difference is that the former encyclopedia was written while the wars were still in progress so the entries were interim reports. Also the earlier publication was more detailed with entries on all the countries and most of the military units involved. This latest encyclopedia has the advantage of addressing topics from the perspective of the supposed aftermath of the wars. Of course, none of the conflicts treated are really over in any substantive way.

No one does reference works better than ABC-Clio, and the military volumes employ a common model—lists of entries, documents, and maps; followed by preface, lengthy and valuable introduction essays, general maps, and the substantive essays themselves. As always, the entries are first-class. Appendixes include documents, chronology, glossary, bibliography, contributors, and an index.

These reference sources are excellent, expensive, and never-ending. Tucker's next volume, *The Roots and Consequences of 20th-Century Warfare: Conflicts That Shaped the Modern World,* which will overlap and duplicate some entries in the volumes discussed here, will be published later in 2016. Libraries have hard decisions concerning which of this array of encyclopedias to acquire.—**Joe P. Dunn**

Handbooks and Yearbooks

437.   Dixon, Jeffrey S., and Meredith Reid Sarkees. **A Guide to Intra-state Wars: An Examination of Civil, Regional, and Intercommunal Wars, 1816-2014.** Thousand Oaks, Calif., CQ Press / Sage, 2016. 801p. index. (Correlates of War Series). $175.00. ISBN 13: 978-0-8728-9775-5.

A Guide to Intra-State Wars: An Examination of Civil, Regional, and Intercommunal Wars, 1816-2014 is the latest volume in CQ Press' Correlates of War Series, which includes

Douglas Gibler's *International Military Alliances, 1648-2008* (see ARBA 2010, entry 629) and *Resort to War, 1816-2007* by Meredith Reid Sarkees and Frank Whelon Wayman (see ARBA 2011, entry 622). The authors of the respective volumes are all affiliated with the Correlates of War Project (COWP), which is dedicated to the study of warfare using quantitative data and scientific methodology.

The first two chapters introduce the reader to the methodology utilized in the work. The first, "The Correlates of War Project," details the nine different types of conflicts officially recognized by the COWP. The second chapter focuses specifically on the minutia of intra-state conflicts. Of particular importance are the distinctions that differentiate between civil, regional, and inter-communal wars. Also included is a breakdown and explanation of each component of an entry, which include: the assigned number of the conflict, the name(s) by which the war is known, participants, dates, battle-related deaths, initiator, outcome, war type, total system member military personnel, theater armed forces, antecedents, narrative, termination and outcome, coding decisions, and sources.

The heart of the work is found in the remaining six chapters, entitled "Intra-state Wars in North America," "Intra-state Wars in South America," "Intra-state Wars in Europe," "Intra-state Wars in the Middle East and North Africa," "Intra-state Wars in Asia and Oceania," and "Intra-state Wars in Sub-Saharan Africa." More than 400 conflicts are covered, beginning with the First Caucasus War of 1818 to 1822 to the ongoing Ukraine Separatists War that erupted in 2014. The work concludes with an appendix entitled "List of All Intra-state Wars in Chronological Order," an extensive bibliography, and an index. Since information about many of the conflicts included in this work is hard to locate, academic and large public libraries should definitely consider acquiring this work, especially if their constituencies include historians or political scientists.—**John R. Burch Jr.**

438.   Hughes-Wilson, John, and Nigel Steel. **The First World War in 100 Objects.** New York, Firefly Books, 2014. 448p. illus. maps. $39.95. ISBN 13: 978-1-77085-413-0.

Another entry in the "object analysis" genre of book launched by the 2011 Viking Press title, *A History of the World in 100 Objects,* by Neil MacGregor of the British Museum, Firefly's *The First World War in 100 Objects* stands out from similar titles with a compelling narrative organization and a strong selection of images. Suitable for high school, college undergraduates, and general readers, this collection consists of color images of 100 objects from the First World War accompanied by analysis of the specific object and the broader historical context associated with it. A photo of an aerial camera leads to a broader discussion about British intelligence during the war, for example. The connections drawn between the specific objects and bigger picture analysis of the war are fascinating, leading the reader to consider multiple aspects: social, political, economic, military, and more. A particular strength of the work is the chronological organization and narrative thread that runs through the entries. While some "objects" books tend toward thematic (or even more random) selections, this one's chronological structure tells the story of the war in a distinctive way. Most of the images are from the collections of the Imperial War Museums in the United Kingdom, and as a result, there is a definite U.K. emphasis here; more entries from France, Germany, and elsewhere would have provided a more diverse collection. The opening Contents pages list all of the objects with individual entry number, page number, and a phrase that indicates the broader theme that is connected to the object. Backmatter includes a collection of maps illustrating various phases and battles of the war, a list of further reading on the First World War, and an index.—**David Tipton**

439.   Ostrom, Thomas P., and John J. Galluzzo. **United States Coast Guard Leaders and Missions, 1790 to the Present.** Jefferson, N.C., McFarland, 2015. 211p. illus. index. $39.95pa. ISBN 13: 978-0-7864-9526-9; 978-1-4766-1805-0 (e-book).

The first chapters of *United States Coast Guard Leaders and Missions* discuss the United States Coast Guard (USGS) since the founding of the U.S. Revenue Marine (which later became the U.S. Revenue Cutter Service) in 1790; the history of the U.S. Lighthouse Service from 1789 until it was transferred to the jurisdiction of the USGS in 1939; and the U.S. Life-Saving Service from its founding in 1848 until it was integrated into the U.S. Revenue Cutter Service to form the USGS in 1915. During its lifetime, the USGS has passed from the jurisdiction of the Treasury Department to the Department of Transportation in 1967 to the Department of Homeland Security in 2003.

Over the long history of the USGS, leaders have been known as chiefs, captain-commandants, and commandants. The book highlights leaders and missions in chronological order starting with the Revenue Marine Chiefs (1843-1889). Along with biographies and evaluations of USGS leaders, the book considers the missions undertaken by the USGS during Prohibition, both world wars, the Vietnam War, the War on Terror, and more.

The book concludes with an appendix of leaders, notes, a bibliography, and an index. This title is not strictly a reference book, but with the aid of the index and the chronological organization, users can quickly find information on certain people, places, and events. Recommended for academic and public libraries.—**ARBA Staff Reviewer**

440.   **Pearl Harbor: The Essential Reference Guide.** Spencer C. Tucker, ed. Santa Barbara, Calif., ABC-CLIO, 2015. 274p. index. $89.00. ISBN 13: 978-1-4408-3718-0; 978-1-4408-3719-7 (e-book).

Seventy-four years after the Pearl Harbor attack, this catastrophic event remains a focal point in U.S. diplomatic, military, and political history which has received renewed attention in light of the December 2, 2015, Islamist terrorist attack in San Bernardino, California. This reference guide provides detailed coverage of the personalities, weapons, and events resulting in the Japanese attack on Pearl Harbor and its consequences.

This work describes the December 7, 1941, attack and it features an alphabetically arranged list of entries on this attack covering such topics as the *USS Arizona* navy battleship and memorial, Cordell Hull, Japanese Americans, Husband Edward Kimmel, Japanese and U.S. Pacific Theater naval strengths, the Pearl Harbor Survivors Association, radar, Rainbow Plans, the United States' Two-Ocean Navy Program, and Isoroku Yamamato. A second section includes the transcripts of oral history interviews with attack survivors such as *USS Maryland* seaman Edmund R. Chappell; Nurse Corps Lieutenant Ruth Erickson from the Pearl Harbor Naval Hospital; and Honolulu Fire Department firefighter Frederick Kealoha.

A third section includes primary source documents from participating governments such as the March 27, 1933, Japanese announcement of their withdrawal from the League of Nations; President Roosevelt's October 5, 1937, quarantine speech in Chicago; notes from a September 19, 1940, Imperial Conference in Japan seeking to work with Germany to achieve greater U.S. and British concessions to Japan in East Asia; a December 6, 1941, letter from Roosevelt to Emperor Hirohito; a memorandum from the Japanese government to the United States breaking off diplomatic relations on the same day; and Roosevelt's December 8, 1941, address to a joint congressional session asking for a declaration of war.

A final section discusses the enduring political controversy and historiographical debate over whether Roosevelt and the U.S. government were responsible for the Pearl Harbor attack, citing relevant historical literature on this topic. This section also addresses what might have happened if there had been a second Japanese strike on Hawaii and whether the Axis Powers contributed to their defeat by failing to coordinate their objectives and cooperate against the United States and its allies. It concludes with a chronology of events starting with the 1921-1922 Washington Naval Conference and ending with the December 23, 1941, capture of Wake Island by Japanese forces.

This is a valuable work which will benefit users in all libraries desirous of understanding the causes and consequences of Pearl Harbor. Many of the factors contributing to this tragedy remain present today in the military and intelligence preparation of multiple nations against current and emerging national and international security threats. Highly recommended!—**Bert Chapman**

441.   **Understanding U.S. Miltary Conflicts through Primary Sources.** Arnold, James R. and Roberta Wiener, eds. Santa Barbara, Calif., ABC-CLIO, 2015. 4v. index. $415.00/ set. ISBN 13: 978-1-61069-933-4; 978-1-61069-934-1 (e-book).

Editors Arnold and Wiener (noted authors of several history and journal editors) provide the reader with a unique and special tool—the ability to examine in a collected and organized manner the primary documents from United States military conflicts. While this may sound like no big deal, it is in fact, a time-saving resource. This four-volume set is extraordinary in not only its detail, but chronological organization. Starting with the American Revolution and ending with the War in Iraq, each major American conflict is represented and has a brief introductory essay; a timeline; individual primary source documents; and a bibliography.

A typical example is the sixth document of the American Revolution in volume two – "George Washington: Instructions to General Sullivan, May 31, 1779." Over two pages the reader is given the context of the document; the actual words of the document; and analysis to inform the reader of the consequences of this order.

This resource is well-researched, easy to use, and affordable. Highly recommended.— **Scott R. DiMarco**

442.   **Veterans History Project. http://www.loc.gov/vets/.** [Website] Free. Date reviewed: 2016.

This project was started in 2000 by the United States Congress in order to help future generations understand the realities of war. The project aims to collect, preserve, and make accessible the personal accounts of American war veterans who participated in major wars and conflicts. In addition to veterans, U.S. civilians who were actively involved in supporting war efforts may be found in the project database, including industry workers, USO workers, flight instructors, and medical volunteers.

An Experiencing War tab at the top of the page provides firsthand accounts of war in the form of audio, video, photos, and text. The Database tab allows users to search for veterans by name, service, rank, or ID number. In addition, users can limit the search by conflict or era, branch of service, gender, and type of material. A few veterans have published memoirs relating to their war experiences, and these can be found under the View Digitized Collection tab after a search is conducted. This is an excellent resource for upper-grade students studying wars and conflicts who are in need of primary sources.

The majority of the material on this Website is easy to read and informative. Students will benefit from reading memoirs and articles, and may even be able to locate friends and relatives previously in service. It is a recommended resource.—**ARBA Staff Reviewer**

Army

443.   Collins, Darrell L. **The Army of Northern Virginia: Organization, Strength, Casualties, 1861-1865.** Jefferson, N.C., McFarland, 2015. 388p. index. $49.95pa. ISBN 13: 978-0-7864-9997-7; 978-1-4766-2364-1 (e-book).

First under the command of General Pierre G.T. Beauregard and then General Joseph E. Johnston, the Army of the Potomac was tasked with the defense of Richmond, Virginia, which served as the capital of the Confederate States of America. On June 1, 1862, following the wounding of Johnston, General Robert E. Lee took command of the army, which he reorganized and formally named the Army of Northern Virginia. It became the most prominent of the Confederacy's armies through engagement in numerous battles, including Fredericksburg, Chancellorsville, Gettysburg, Petersburg, and Appomattox.

Darrell L. Collins, who has authored a number of books on the Civil War including *Major General Robert E. Rodes of the Army of Northern Virginia* (Savas Beatie, 2008) and *The Army of the Potomac: Order of Battle, 1861-1865, with Commanders, Strengths, Losses, and More* (McFarland, 2013), scoured the volumes of *The War of the Rebellion: A Compilation of the Official Records of the Union and Confederate Armies* (Government Printing Office, 1880-1901) to create this reference tool on the Army of Northern Virginia. It is divided into three sections: Organization Reports: With Army, Corps, Division, Brigade, Regiment, Battalion, and Battery Commander Timelines and Unit Organization Dates; Present for Duty Reports; and Casualty Reports. Also included are a Commander Index and Unit Index.

This work is designed for historians already familiar with the army. General users will face some challenges accessing the data due to the lack of a general index. This reference tool conveniently consolidates previously published information and is recommended for academic and public libraries supporting large Civil War collections. Genealogists will also find this a helpful resource.—**John R. Burch Jr.**

444.   Fish, Peter N. **Army Medical Officer's Guide.** Mechanicsburg, Pa., Stackpole Books, 2014. 150p. index. $16.95pa. ISBN 13: 978-0-8117-1184-5.

An Army Medical Officer generally approaches his or her time in the service differently than most commissioned officers, perhaps attending civilian medical schools, joining the military at an older age, or even bypassing basic training. This practical guide will help these officers (dental, veterinarian, psychiatric etc.) navigate the long-held customs, responsibilities, and regulations of contemporary Army life.

Three sections break down the information relating to the general, professional, and personal aspects of being an Army Medical Officer. Part one offers a short history of medical practice in the military, discussing such things as the heritage and mission of a medical professional in the military. The section defines an Army Medical Officer, details the organization of the corps and support branches, and describes contemporary military medical facilities and systems both domestic and overseas.

The second section covers professional development and new duty assignments and includes information on many topics, including ranks, evaluations, awards, training, and new unit integration. The last section helps readers navigate officer benefits like insurance, club membership, education scholarships, etc.

Within each section are many important details particular to the Army that will no doubt be helpful to any medical officer that might come to the service unconventionally, such as the nature of "dining in" or "dining out," the types of patients to expect, the components of a medical evacuation system, core organizations to join, like the Army Reserve Association, and much more.

Appendixes detail further information regarding pay, travel, and uniforms as well as a list of professional references and links to relevant media. There is also a helpful glossary for the plentiful acronyms and abbreviations employed by the military and an index.

This book serves as a worthy addendum to the more comprehensive *Army Officers Guide* by Col. Robert J. Dalessandro, USA (Ret.). It should also be noted that the book represents well-researched opinion gathered by the author from his own experience as well as from both active and retired medical officers; however, it is not officially sanctioned by the U.S. Army.—**Laura Herrell**

445.   Patterson, Benton Rain. **Lincoln's Political Generals: The Battlefield Performance of Seven Controversial Appointees.** Jefferson, N.C., McFarland, 2014. 234p. illus. index. $35.00pa. ISBN 13: 978-0-7864-7857-6; 978-1-4766-1681-0 (e-book).

What do Major General(s) John McClernand, Lew Wallace, John Fremont, Benjamin Butler, Nathaniel Banks, Stephen Hurlbut, and Franz Sigel all have in common? Besides serving the Union during the American Civil War, each was a political appointment by President Abraham Lincoln. Each was appointed, promoted, and kept in service due to political influence and not military skills. They were indeed controversial appointments, but were their positions, as stated by Union General-in-Chief Henry Halleck "It seems little better than murder, to give important commands to such men." Were they overreaching politicians and poor generals or just the scapegoats of professional officers and historians?

In the context of the tumultuous start of the American Civil War in 1861 and the sudden creation of a massive volunteer army from the very small pool of professional soldiers, it is little wonder that several were appointed as political plums to Lincoln supporters. Emeritus Professor Benton Rain Patterson (University of Florida) has written a piece to let the reader decide for themselves what the ramifications of these political generals are. The question of a great many readers of Civil War literature is often "how did he ever get to be a general?" This common question is explored in this work.

Each individual gets their own entry that includes: a brief biography, a bibliography, a version of the person's actions that are woven into the context of the war, pictures and sketches, and a brief bit about their lives after the war.

Overall, recommended.—**Scott R. DiMarco**

446.   Sweeting, C.G. **United States Army Aviators' Clothing, 1917-1945.** Jefferson, N.C., McFarland, 2015. 182p. illus. index. $55.00pa. ISBN 13: 978-0-7864-9396-8; 978-1-4766-1809-8 (e-book).

Authored by C.G. Sweeting, former Curator of Flight Material at the National Air and Space Museum, Smithsonian Institution, this monograph is a re-publication of *Combat Flying Clothing: Army Air Forces Clothing During World War II* (Smithsonian Institution,

1984). It is an exhaustive reference that not only includes information about flying suits, headgear, handgear, and footwear, but also about the research and testing that went into their construction. The text is supplemented by numerous black-and-white photographs and seven appendixes: "Program of the Personal Equipment Laboratory," *The Personal Equipment Officer* 2, no. 2 (c. 1946), p. 1; "Kit, Clothing and Equipment, Flyer," Technical Order no. 00-30-41, Headquarters, Army Air Forces, Washington, D.C., April 16, 1942; "Kit, Clothing and Equipment, Flyer," Technical Order no. 00-30-41, Headquarters, Army Air Forces, Washington, D.C., October 20, 1945; "Clothing–Refinishing Sheep Shearling Type Flying Clothing," Technical Order no. 13-1-10, Headquarters, Army Air Forces, Washington, D.C., October 16, 1943; "Preliminary Tests on Durability of Flying Clothing," Memorandum Report no. ENG-49-695-2S, Aero Medical Laboratory, Materiel Command, Wright Field, Ohio, April 22, 1944; Type Designation Sheets, Wright Field, Ohio, 1920s through World War II, and The Preservation of Vintage Flying Clothing and Accessories. The work concludes with a bibliography and index. This work is an essential purchase for libraries supporting research in aviation history or United States military history that do not already own the work in its prior incarnation.—**John R. Burch Jr.**

Navy

447.   Smith, Myron J., Jr. **Civil War Biographies from the Western Waters.** Jefferson, N.C., McFarland, 2015. 329p. illus. maps. index. $75.00pa. ISBN 13: 978-0-7864-6967-3; 978-1-4766-1698-8 (e-book).

Myron J. Smith, Jr., Director of the Library and Professor at Tusculum College, has authored a number of books on how the Civil War was fought on the waters of the Cumberland, Mississippi, Ohio, and Tennessee Rivers, including *The Fight for the Yazoo, August 1862-July 1864: Swamps, Forts and Fleets on Vicksburg's Northern Flank* (McFarland, 2012) and *Tinclads in the Civil War: Union Light-Draught Gunboat Operations on Western Waters, 1862-1865* (McFarland, 2010). His latest reference on that theater of conflict contains biographies of 956 individuals from both the Union and the Confederacy. The majority of the individuals profiled were military officers that held at least the rank of mate. The remaining entries focus on politicians, civilians that played a role in the war effort, Congressional Medal of Honor winners, or individuals who authored accounts of their experiences.

Most of the entries, which are alphabetically arranged, include the subject's date of birth and death, information about their lives before the outbreak of war, the name of the unit or boat on which they served, an account of their wartime experiences, and, if they survived, their postwar career. Some also include a portrait or photograph. The entries conclude with bibliographic information from sources such as *The War of the Rebellion: A Compilation of the Official Records of the Union and Confederate Armies* (Government Printing Office, 1880-1901) and *Official Records of the Union and Confederate Navies in the War of the Rebellion* (Government Printing Office, 1894-1922). The text is supplemented by three appendixes: "Individuals by Organization," "Campaigns, Battles, and Engagements," and "Ship Registers." The work concludes with a bibliography and index. This work fills an obvious gap in the historiography concerning the Civil War and should be acquired by libraries supporting research collections on United States history.—**John R. Burch Jr.**

448.   Williams, Greg H. **The Liberty Ships of World War II: A Record of the 2,710 Vessels and Their Builders and Namesakes, with a History of the *Jeremiah O'Brien*.** Jefferson, N.C., McFarland, 2014. 364p. illus. index. $75.00pa. ISBN 13: 978-0-7864-7945-0; 978-1-4766-1754-1 (e-book).

Liberty Ships—the unglamorous workhorses of World War II—are one of the war's most enduring symbols. Rallying to the cause of war, 18 American shipyards built 2,710 Liberty ships in four years, a truly amazing output within a short timeframe. This registry presents a listing of each Liberty cargo ship built and called to duty from United States shipyards.

The author presents a superb overview of the subject, which leaves no detail out. He begins with the brief history behind the American companies that came together to fulfill the first shipbuilding contracts from a desperate English delegation. In learning of the initial requirements to handle the orders, which included new company formations, land excavation, construction re-designs, training, financing, etc., readers can truly marvel over this immense undertaking.

The book then lists all Liberty ships, arranged by the shipyards where they originated. The listings may include information on the ship's namesake, the company that operated the ship, how the ship was used, the delivery date, the call sign, and more. Further information describes the steamship companies that operated the ships during wartime.

A highlight of this book is the full story of one Liberty ship in particular, the *Jeremiah O'Brien*. We read of the ship's namesake, a participant in what is regarded as the first naval battle of the American Revolution, as well as information about the ship's sponsor, crews, voyages, cargo, retirement, and restoration. The *Jeremiah O'Brien* is now one of only two Liberty ships remaining in the world.

Black-and-white photographs are sprinkled throughout the book, which concludes with an index. This book will serve as a reference for those interested in this remarkable piece of American history. Recommended for military and public libraries.—**Laura Herrell**

Weapons and Equipment

449.   Levy, Joel. **Fifty Weapons That Changed the Course of History.** New York, Firefly Books, 2014. 224p. illus. index. $29.95. ISBN 13: 978-1-77085-426-0.

Weaponry, like fashion, has always fascinated history lovers as an iconic time-stamp of an era. The longbow may mark medieval times the same way the atomic bomb may mark the nuclear age. This well-designed book takes a respectful and efficient look at 50 important weapons produced throughout history and shows how even a relatively basic piece of technology can play a role in the greater historical narrative.

From stone axes to robots, the book chronologically presents the weapons via a descriptive essay preceded by an introductory page. This page contains an illustration of the weapon juxtaposed with a number of visually engaging reference points, which may include a contextual quote, the year of the weapon's peak usage, type of weapon, name of weapon inventor, and type of impact the weapon had upon its time (from a choice of social, political, technical, and tactical).

Descriptive essays touch on a weapon's evolution, statistics, significant moment(s) in history, and more. It is interesting to see how even minor changes to a basic weapon design (e.g., the sword), can have a major impact. It is also interesting to note the inclusion of some unexpected weapon choices (e.g., the stirrup) among the 50 covered. Evocative photographs and illustrations accompany the essays. Some illustrations may highlight a weapon's design, exposing its technical make up and abilities.

While certainly not meant to be comprehensive, the book succeeds in educating readers on this very select slice of history through its knowledgeable but concise narrative and visually intriguing style. The book also includes ideas for further research and an index that facilitates quick searches.—**ARBA Staff Reviewer**

450.   Tucker, Spencer C. **Instruments of War: Weapons and Technologies that Have Changed History.** Santa Barbara, Calif., ABC-CLIO, 2015. 428p. illus. index. $89.00. ISBN 13: 978-1-4408-3654-1; 978-1-4408-3655-8 (e-book).

Military conflicts throughout history have seen combatant nations and groups produce, refine, and modify weapons to meet desired military objectives. This compendium by a prominent and prolific historian seeks to introduce readers to many historically significant weapons and technologies.

It begins with a listing of chronologically arranged entries and an alphabetical listing of profiled weapons. An introduction describes the historical evolution of weapons while also mentioning that this work contains descriptions of 270 weapons systems and technologies and 25 sidebars documenting how these weapons have been used in military tactics.

Weapons systems and technologies covered in this compendium include dagger (knife), shields, trireme, land mines and mining, steam warship, Dahlgren guns, poison gas, Molotov cocktail, radar, hydrogen bomb, Ohio-class U.S. Navy submarines, and unmanned aerial vehicles. Entries for each of these works are succinctly written and feature bibliographic citations. Sidebars are presented for topics as varied as Attempt to Assassinate Napoleon *I (1800), Torpedo Attack at Taranto (1940), First Successful Use of Poison Gas (1915), and the English ship Mary Rose* (1509-1545).

The work concludes with detailed bibliographic references.

This work serves as a very helpful introduction to undergraduates and public library users interested in introductory information on the origins of world weapons systems. It could be strengthened further with coverage of directed energy weapons, cyber warfare, suicide bombers, missile defense systems such as the U.S.' Patriot and Israel's Iron Dome, and emerging military uses of space besides satellites.—**Bert Chapman**

13 Political Science

General Works

Dictionaries and Encyclopedias

451. **Border Disputes: A Global Encyclopedia.** Emmanuel Brunet-Jailly, ed. Santa Barbara, Calif., ABC-CLIO, 2015. 2v. illus. maps. index. $294.00/set. ISBN 13: 978-1-61069-023-2; 978-1-61069-024-9 (e-book).

The entries seem to be well-researched, thorough, and concise, but the writing is awkward and the arrangement sometimes confusing, suggesting that more editing and proofreading was needed. The contents page is not very helpful, only repeating the same basic information about the arrangement and not including individual topics or page numbers. A list of entries presents the individual disputes that are discussed in each volume and another arranges them by areas (e.g., Central America, Europe), but each only gives the volume and not the page numbers where these discussions are located. The entries are arranged into three categories, which are each covered by a separate volume: territorial disputes (ca. 40 entries), positional disputes (ca. 30), and functional disputes (ca. 20). Volume one includes an overall discussion of border disputes and an explanation of the arrangement of the material presented here. Each entry includes a brief synopsis, an introduction, the disputed area's physical and topographical features and politics and culture, the current situation, a conclusion, and a bibliography. The text is enhanced with several black-and-white illustrations. Volume three offers excerpts from primary documents, directory of organizations, glossary, extensive bibliography, information on the editor and contributors, and an index. As the editor suggests, it is difficult to offer an all-encompassing discussion, since borders and the disputes that affect them are always changing. However, this selection will serve as a beginning place for further research.—**Martha Lawler**

452. **Encyclopedia of Modern Ethnic Conflicts.** 2d ed. Joseph R. Rudolph, Jr., ed. Santa Barbara, Calif., ABC-CLIO, 2015. 2v. index. $189.00/set. ISBN 13: 978-1-61069-552-7; 978-1-61069-553-4 (e-book).

The second edition of the *Encyclopedia of Modern Ethnic Conflicts* provides the college and university student with an up–to-date resource on late-twentieth- and early-twenty-first-century struggles between neighbors of differing identities. Indeed, 12 years have passed since the publication of the first edition and the revisions and additions to this new edition reflect how the world of ethnic conflict has changed over this period of time. The case studies for nations and regions that have changed borders and names have been updated, while other conflicts that have become more heated and global in scope have been added. For example, the Soviet Union is no longer a political entity in name, but its legacy can be read about in the case studies about Georgia and Armenia. Case studies added include conflicts pertaining to Guatemala, Kenya, and Christians in the Middle East to name a few. Generally the editor has attempted to include conflicts that have ongoing political importance in the twenty-first century. Given its ambitious scope—case studies cover conflicts in all continents with the exception of Australia—the encyclopedia cannot be comprehensive. Still, the articles reflect the variety of conflicts that derive from ethnonationalism and will provide the student with a solid understanding of the global ethnic conflicts that persist today.

The expanded room (from one to two volumes) allows for 44 case studies written by contributors of both genders from nine countries (Australia, Canada, England, Lebanon, Nigeria, Puerto Rico, Turkey, Wales, and the United States), all of whom are political scientists or have experience in military efforts and diplomacy in these areas. These case studies are alphabetically arranged, according to the country in which the given conflict takes place. For example, conflicts concerning Kurdish people are located in "Iraq: The Progress of the Kurdish movement in Iraq" and "The Middle East: The Kurds' Struggle for Kurdistan." The volumes no longer contain maps, but each one features the introduction, and there is an index at the end of the second.

Using the table of contents or index to locate a particular ethnic group as a topic for research, one first sees a timeline of events framing the conflict to be discussed in the case study. The case study then provides the following elements: a short introduction, which starts immediately after the timeline and does not have a heading; historical background; the conflict itself; the management of the conflict; and its significance. Most case studies also provide extensive end notes, suggested readings, and appendixes with primary source material. On the whole, this encyclopedia is recommended for colleges, universities, and other libraries supporting additional research of this kind.—**Amy Koehler**

453.   **Encyclopedia of Social Media and Politics.** Kerric Harvey, ed. Thousand Oaks, Calif., Sage, 2014. 3v. illus. index. $485.00/set. ISBN 13: 978-1-4522-4471-6.

This 1,500-page set explores the role, impact, and importance of social media in the realm of politics, both in the United States and the rest of the world. Entries such as Arab Spring, Middle East, China, and Latin America reflect the international scope of this work. Some of the entries will resonate more with younger readers of this work: Digg, Clicktivism, Vlogging, Ushahidi, etc. These articles, however, clearly present the importance of these "Web 2.0" sites and terms. Entries run from one to eight pages, with suggestions for further readings provided. Additional resources for users include a chronology, a glossary, a resource guide (bibliography) of books, journals, and Websites, a list of social media use by all 535 members of Congress, and an 80-page index.

Organized along the same clean lines as a number of other Sage encyclopedias published recently, the set (also available online) will be welcomed in public and academic libraries, as well as in many high school libraries, if they can afford it.—**Mark Schumacher**

Handbooks and Yearbooks

454.   **Global HIV/AIDS Politics, Policy, and Activism: Persistent Challenges and Emerging Issues.** Raymond A. Smith, ed. Santa Barbara, Calif., Praeger/ABC-CLIO, 2013. 3v. index. $194.00/set. ISBN 13: 978-0-313-39945-9; 978-0-313-39946-6 (e-book).

Emerging in the 1980's, AIDS and its parent virus HIV grabbed global headlines and sent fear through entire communities. Since then evolving awareness plus great strides in diagnoses and treatments have quieted the fear as well as the conversation and yet salient concerns remain. This comprehensive three-volume book contains contributions from an international network of thinkers working opposite the medical side of the HIV/AIDS conversation. Specifically, it presents 45 original essays covering the base politics, policies, and activism merging to drive the HIV/AIDS discussion forward.

Volume one–Politics and Government, discusses the politics of HIV prevention and treatment at international, national, and regional levels, and includes essays spotlighting several nations' successes (e.g., Brazil's "strategic internationalization") and failures (e.g., the infiltration of prejudice into crisis response), as well as the difficulties of creating national HIV prevention strategies.

Volume two–Policy and Policymaking, also addresses the range between international level and regional level policy debates, and includes topics concerning how policy shifts regarding Intellectual Property Rights can affect treatment costs and accessibility, how China tends to "exceptionalize" HIV/AIDS versus other communicable diseases in contrast to most other nations, and more.

Volume three–Activism and Community Mobilization, takes readers into the trenches of the HIV/AIDS discussion and includes pieces highlighting activism and its relationship to such issues as funding, education, and research. The volume notes the particular need for activists to pursue their agendas in countries such as Sudan where data is limited on program efficacy, and adapt to treatment program successes as part of a longer term public health movement, and much more.

The set shares solid biographical information about contributors, who range in expertise from university professor to advocate, and offers a truly eclectic mix of well-researched topics orbiting the HIV/AIDS sphere. Meticulously compiled, this set is an essential reference for anyone studying health epidemics, healthcare advocacy, policy-making, and more. Recommended for academic libraries.—**Laura Herrell**

455.   **InfoSci-Government Science and Technology. http://www.igi-global.com/e-resources/infosci-subject-databases/infosci-government/.** [Website] Hershey, Pa., Information Science Reference/IGI Global. Price negotiated by site. Date reviewed: 2016.

The *InfoSci-Government Science and Technology* database provides full-text access to over 100 e-books on government science and technology issues as they relate to and impact governmental issues around the world. This academic reference collection represents the scholarly research conducted on such topics as e-government, digital citizenship, law and policy, and social media uses and application—to name a few. Theoretical views (such as ethical considerations) as well as applied technical information (such as the engineering of structural control systems) are included.

The database provides three different research options including basic, advanced, and expert. The advanced search accommodates searches for full-text, keyword, title, author,

DOI, and publication date. The "expert" search option allows search terms to be excluded, included, and/or weighted. While this is interesting, it may not be heavily used, especially in a collection of this size.

Each full e-book has an annotated table of contents to facilitate ease of use and browsability. The collection has also been indexed and is searchable at the chapter level. Each book and chapter has a search box to help drill down to an even more granular level. Book chapters are provided in XML and PDF format for easy download. The database also provides the tools for citing the books and book chapters.

Lawmakers, policymakers, and anyone with technical service responsibilities at any level of government should know about this collection. Researchers in any of these fields as well as political and social scientists will find value in this collection. The titles are current, relevant, and timely. It is recommended as a source of authoritative and academic information the applications, implications, and impacts of technology and government.—**Kristin Kay Leeman**

456.   **The Politics Book: Big Ideas Simply Explained.** New York, DK Publishing, 2013. 352p. illus. index. $25.00; $9.99 (e-book). ISBN 13: 978-1-4654-0214-1; 978-1-4654-4107-2 (e-book).

"All men are created equal" wrote Thomas Jefferson in 1776. While sounding simple, these five words were both the culmination of a simmering resentment toward the British monarchy and a launching point towards proclaiming the universal rights of individuals. *The Politics Book: Big Ideas Simply Explained* is a wonderful collection of similarly challenging concepts that impacted contemporary and future societies around the world.

Seven sections, ranging from Ancient Political Thought to Postwar Politics highlight over one hundred "big ideas" and the thinkers behind them. Touching on philosophy ("What is a Woman?"), religion ("The objective of Islamic jihad is to eliminate the rule of an un-Islamic system"), militarism ("Political power grows out of the barrel of a gun"), and more, each idea receives a succinct yet robust explanation as well as historical background. The entries are conveyed chronologically, which helps readers trace idea development and influence. For example, the book clearly links the rise of communism to ideas germinating in 380 B.C.E. (Plato), sprouting throughout the nineteenth century (Hegel, Marx) and reaching full bloom in the twentieth (Lenin, Guevara, etc.). Shaded sidebars offer a timeline that puts each idea "In Context," reflecting its ideology, focus, and effects both before and after an idea's introduction to society. For example, in conveying Marsilius of Padua's medieval belief in secularism, we can refer to the crowning of Charlemagne as the Holy Roman Emperor five centuries prior as well as to Martin Luther's criticism of the Catholic Church 200 years after.

The design of the book is striking—large bold typeface demands that readers pay attention to each leading idea. Equally eye-catching graphics artistically render the essence of each concept, e.g., a silhouette of three climbers ascending a sharp black mountain peak via Friedrich Nietzsche's "will to power." The entries are cross-referenced and may include color illustrations, key works from notable thinkers, and clarifying diagrams of sometimes complex ideas.

The book includes a directory to provide additional information surrounding figures (George Washington, Adolf Hitler, etc.) who played a role in executing some of the "big ideas" but were not mentioned in their corresponding chapter. It also employs a generous glossary as well as section overviews, timelines, and an index. This dynamic book is a must read for any student of political science, history, philosophy and more. Highly recommended, especially given its price of $25.00 for a sturdy hardback title.—**Laura Herrell**

457. **Research Handbook on Climate Governance.** Karen Bäckstrand and Eva Lövbrand, eds. Northampton, Mass., Edward Elgar, 2016. 640p. index. $335.00. ISBN 13: 978-1-78347-059-4.

This timely and readable compendium of research on global efforts to combat climate change was proposed at Edward Elgar in 2013 and completed just a few months before the Paris climate summit in December 2015. Climate governance became a research topic only in the 1990s, and since that time has proliferated in response to increasing efforts to find a solution to humankind's effect on the changing climate. Editors Karin Bäckstrand (Professor of Environmental Social Science, Stockholm University) and Eva Lövbrand (Centre for Climate Change and Policy Research, Linköping University) have assembled 50 articles from 77 contributors, chiefly from Europe and the United States, representing a broad range of expertise and opinion. The seven parts of the book cover the theories, processes, and sites of climate governance, the relationship to climate governance of the state and of nonstate agents and institutions, the technologies and normative ideals of climate governance, and the future of climate governance. Among the many topics discussed are climate leadership in China, the United States, the European Union, and Brazil, the North-South divide on climate change governance, low-carbon economies, carbon accounting, environmental democracy, and reform options. Every chapter comes to one or more conclusions and is followed by notes and a bibliography. The book also has a list of figures and tables and a comprehensive index. This volume will serve as a valuable resource for students, policy-makers, and citizens concerned about the environment; recommended.—**ARBA Staff Reviewer**

458. Roth, Christopher F. **Let's Split: A Complete Guide to Separatist Movements and Aspirant Nations, from Abkhazia to Zanzibar.** Sacramento, Calif., Litwin Books, 2015. 626p. illus. maps. index. $75.00. ISBN 13: 978-1-936117-99-4.

Political change is ongoing throughout the world, constantly evolving over time and place. Groups want to remake countries, split into separate countries, areas want autonomy, states want borders changed, groups and individuals want sovereignty of local areas, or even social space on the Internet. All of these varying desires for a political rework of the current status are covered in this volume on separatist movements around the world. The author, who is a social-cultural and linguistic anthropologist, presents the material in a readable and enjoyable manner with a touch of humor thrown in for fun. Some users may question some of the implied humor depending on the user's place in the current political debate spectrum. This may say more to the user's apprehensions of objectivity than the author's political biases or neutrality in researching the volume.

Arranged by geographic region, starting in northern Europe and advancing eastward around the world, and subregion, if discussing a particular country or area, the work has a lengthy introduction to the region and country followed by the various political or organized groups desiring to split, the background and history to the movement, any territorial claims made in connection with the split, population affected by the split, images of flags associated with the group or movement, and prospects of current or future success. Maps for each section also help to explain the geopolitics discussed in the text. A selected bibliography grouped by region appears at the end. The work also has an extensive keyword index to round out the volume.

The volume will be useful in any academic, public, or high school library collection. Substantially bound, the work should withstand extended use by patrons. The information contained within will age faster than the binding itself. A planned update edition will be of importance to keep the information current with the fluid nature of political events around the globe.—**Gregory Curtis**

459. **World Political Yearbook, 2016.** Hackensack, N.J., Salem Press, 2016. 900p. maps. $125.00. ISBN 13: 978-1-61925-952-2.

This first edition of the *World Political Yearbook* from Salem Press publishes information on 233 national entities, grouped by regions: Africa; The Americas; Asia (including Russia, Australia and New Zealand); Europe; and the Middle East. The publisher's note informs us that the book "profiles every nation and self-governing territory around the world with material from the critically acclaimed *Nations of the World: A Political, Economic, and Business Handbook* by Grey House Publishing." The cover, introduction, and format are copyrighted by Grey House. Political, economic, and ethnographic data are given for each country, with the emphasis on the power structure, security issues, and, especially, the economy. Each entry has a country map and a highlighted box of "Key Indicators" such as population, GDP, unemployment, exports, imports, and trade balance. Each also has a box of "Key Facts" (official name, head of state, head of government, ruling party, area, population, capital, official language, currency, exchange rate, and more) and concludes with a political and economic risk assessment; for Muslim nations, there is also a highlighted box giving the percentage of Sunni and Shi'a Muslim inhabitants. There is little to no information on the cultural heritage of any nation, but a great deal on its security situation and economic viability. At over 1,000 pages, this compendium could be of value to a wide range of readers, from students to businessmen, journalists and policy-makers. Salem Press offers free access to its online database with every print purchase of this book.—**ARBA Staff Reviewer**

Ideologies

Dictionaries and Encyclopedias

460. Lamb, Peter. **Historical Dictionary of Socialism.** 3d ed. Lanham, Md., Rowman & Littlefield, 2016. 601p. (Historical Dictionaries of Religions, Philosophies, and Movements). $140.00; $139.99 (e-book). ISBN 13: 978-1-4422-5826-6; 978-1-4422-5827-3 (e-book).

This volume in the Historical Dictionaries of Religions, Philosophies, and Movements series provides foundational information on the particular topic of Socialism with the goal of acting as a catalyst for further, more in-depth research.

Over 500 compact entries document the various tenets, events, institutions, policies, people, and more associated with the Socialist movement. These entries are arranged alphabetically and are generously cross-referenced for ease of navigation. The paragraphs address big picture topics such as Marxism, Human Rights, or Religion, as well as precise, more obscure topics, such as Chartism, Bettino Craxi, or the Haymarket Affair. This third edition has been extensively updated with new entries, as well as expanded chronology, introduction, and bibliography sections. In particular, the extensive bibliography is highly organized, and the introduction section does well in defining Socialism as well as conveying its origins, development, and schisms that pushed it into the many-faceted force for social change it is regarded as today. The book also includes a helpful acronyms and abbreviations section, as well as a glossary.

While this resource offers limited context and detail within its entries, readers can absolutely benefit from the highly readable format and intelligent breakdown of its abundant material.—**Laura Herrell**

Handbooks and Yearbooks

461.   Zander, Patrick G. **The Rise of Fascism: History, Documents, and Key Questions.** Santa Barbara, Calif., ABC-CLIO, 2016. 219p. index. (Crossroads in World History series). $61.00. ISBN 13: 978-1-61069-799-6; 978-1-61069-800-9 (e-book).

This entry in ABC-CLIO's Crossroads in World History series, designed for high school students and undergraduates, provides a brief but thoughtful overview of the ideology of fascism, especially as it was practiced in Italy and Germany before and during World War II. Editor Patrick G. Zander, assistant professor of history at Georgia Gwinnett College, has set the discussion in the framework of European history from 1919 to the start of the Nuremberg Trials in November 1945. The 51 entries describe a limited number of key individuals, such as Benito Mussolini and Adolf Hitler; key events, such as the Abyssinian War, the Holocaust, and the Spanish Civil War; organizations, including the Blackshirts and the National Fascist Party; written works, such as Hitler's *Mein Kampf*; and significant places and concepts. Each entry is followed by a few suggestions for further reading. A selection of excerpts from primary sources gives the reader an up-close look at the factors that animated fascism. Among these sources are a 1925 speech by Mussolini and the testimony of a Nazi commandant at Auschwitz. A notable feature of the book is a set of three "key questions," each of which is answered by two scholars with differing viewpoints. Question two, for example, asks whether racism and anti-Semitism were an essential part of fascist ideology. The selected annotated bibliography contains online as well as print sources but is very limited in scope and content. The book has a timeline, beginning in 1871, and an index. Overall, it will give students a broader understanding of one of the twentieth century's most compelling and destructive political movements.—**Alice Chaffee**

Politics and Government

Canada

462.   **Governments Canada, 2016 Winter/Spring Edition.** Amenia, N.Y., Grey House Publishing, 2016. 1276p. illus. index. $424.00pa. ISBN 13: 978-1-61925-965-2; 978-1-61925-968-3 (e-book).

This large publication is the well-organized contact information source for all levels of government in Canada. The book is published twice a year in order to provide the most up-to-date information, particularly in reference to departmental restructuring in light of recent elections at all levels.

Opening pages provide excellent foundational material and include a description of government structure, charts reflecting government statistics, and highlights of significant changes at all levels—for example, the report of a record number of women and aboriginals elected to parliament in 2015. A quick reference guide alphabetically lists general areas of interest (adoption, agriculture, etc.) with the appropriate agencies and contact information noted beneath.

The bulk of the book is devoted to all government listings beginning with federal offices and working down through provincial/territorial listings (for all 10 provinces and three territories), and municipal listings. Each regional section includes a table of contents and is tabbed for ease of reference. Federal listings are organized by office, beginning with the office of the Governor General and Commander-in-Chief of Canada and including myriad other offices ranging from the Pest Management Regulatory Agency to the Canadian Human Rights Tribunal and much more. Information accompanying each listing may include a brief description of the body, acts administered, executive staff, and all contact information. Provincial/territorial listings are arranged alphabetically by province/territory, and municipal listings are arranged alphabetically within province/territory and are further classified by type of municipality. Following the municipal listings is a new section including key contact information for both foreign embassies and consulates in Canada and Canadian embassies and consulates abroad.

This resource concludes with two notable indexes: one listing acronyms commonly used throughout the book, and one listing more than 25,000 key contacts, organized alphabetically by last name, of organizations referenced in the book.

Recommended.—**ARBA Staff Reviewer**

Europe

463.   **Nations in Transit 2013: Democratization from Central Europe to Eurasia.** Sylvana Kolaczkowska-Habdank, ed. Lanham, Md., Rowman & Littlefield, 2014. 631p. $99.00; 99.99 (e-book). ISBN 13: 978-1-4422-3118-4; 978-1-4422-3119-1 (e-book).

This volume gathers reports for 29 Eastern European and Eurasian countries detailing the countries' democratic progress, or lack thereof. In compiling data for the reports, the volume looks at the issues and events occurring within these countries between January 1 and December 31 of 2012. It is the 17th collection of reports published by Freedom House.

The opening 50 pages of this book establish the methodology used in coming up with a country's final report. Each report addresses the following topics: National Democratic Governance, Electoral Process, Civil Society, Independent Media, Local Democratic Governance, Judicial Framework, and Independence and Corruption, and provides numerical ratings for each country to align with these topics. In determining a particular country's ratings, a series of questions is posed within the framework of each topic. For example, under the topic of National Democratic Governance, the report will answer questions such as "Is the legislature independent, effective, and accountable to the public?"

These opening pages additionally provide an overall assessment of the entire region (ranging from the Czech Republic in the west, Estonia to the north, Bulgaria to the south, and Russia to the east), which points out trends and other factors of note. A series of tables present each country's ratings history matched against the aforementioned topics.

Each report opens with a snapshot of a country's profile: the capital city, population, GNI/capita, and a table listing past ratings and scores. The reports themselves contain an executive summary for ease of reference and the main report which runs approximately 10 to 12 pages. Reports are followed by extensive notes.

While not intended to be regarded as absolute, the information in these reports would be highly valuable to researchers doing comparative analyses of countries or those seeking to make general, but well informed, assessments of these countries in terms of their path to democratization.—**ARBA Staff Reviewer**

United States

Atlases

464.   **Atlas of the 2012 Elections.** J. Clark Archer and others. Lanham, Md., Rowman & Littlefield, 2014. 306p. illus. maps. index. $75.00; $74.99 (e-book). ISBN 13: 978-1-4422-2583-1; 978-1-4422-2584-8 (e-book).

The 2012 elections in the United States saw the reelection of Barak Obama as president, but the elections also highlighted the partisan divides that still confront the country. This atlas provides in-depth analyses of not only the presidential election, but also selected state and local elections, several referenda, and specific issues that affected the results. In addition to covering the presidential election specifically, chapters are dedicated to the Republican primary elections, focusing on Iowa, Florida, and Ohio, and the Republican and Democratic campaigns which examined topics such as individual contributions to the candidates, campaign expenditures, campaign stops, and newspaper endorsements. Other chapters provide penetrating analyses of the outcomes of the presidential vote by state and county levels, by metropolitan area, by counties, and by selected suburbs. Regional analyses (Northeast, Appalachia, Southeast, Midwest, Great Plains, Mountain West, and Pacific Region) are included as are special reports on Hispanic and Asian American voting and the impact of religion on voting. The roles of health care and foreign policy on the outcome are also examined. Several state elections are covered including key senate elections in Virginia, Indiana, Wisconsin, North Dakota, and Montana, as well as the governor races in Massachusetts and Wisconsin. Votes on legalizing same-sex marriage in Maine, Minnesota, Maryland, and Washington, and the legalization of marijuana use in Colorado and Washington are discussed. Thus, this atlas provides a wealth of information on electoral politics during this important election cycle that will benefit students of political science, public administration, and public policy for years to come. The maps themselves provide excellent data in a clear and meaningful way and are the true heart of the book. By closely examining the maps, the bifurcation of the country can easily be seen, although the divide is not only Democrat/Republican, but also rural/metropolitan, liberal/conservative, Christian/non-Christian, white/nonwhite, and young/old. This atlas can be recommended for all academic libraries and for larger public libraries.—**Gregory A. Crawford**

Biography

465. **American Presidents.** 4th ed. Robert P. Watson, ed. Hackensack, N.J., Salem Press, 2015. 2v. illus. maps. index. $195.00/set. ISBN 13: 978-1-61925-940-9; 978-1-61925-941-6 (e-book).

A two-volume historical reference, *American Presidents* chronologically presents thorough biographies of all 43 U.S. presidents from George Washington to Barack Obama. This edition is the first to include the current president's biography, and has revised and updated entries for several recent presidents, the bibliography, and all appendixes. Many new photographs and illustrations enhance the publication and online access is newly available, as well.

Preceding the biographies are two excellent essays discussing the presidential office itself and touching on the general characteristics of its holders, as well as its origins, processes, duties, and evolution through modern times. Each biographical entry then offers rich information about the president's birth, education, political rise, election, time in office, postpresidency, and death. The particular administration's legacy is also assessed. Readers will find sufficient space given to a president's most remarkable moments, such as Lyndon B. Johnson's work with the Voting Rights Act of 1965, or Franklin Pierce's struggles with slavery and territorial expansion.

The book employs a number of tools which both organize and enhance the material. Shaded text boxes convey brief biographies of First Ladies and Vice Presidents, as well as important primary document excerpts such as Lincoln's Emancipation Proclamation. Each entry opens with listed administration information, such as years of term(s), birth and death dates and location, political party, and cabinet members. Essays conclude with updated, annotated bibliographies for further reference

The end of volume two offers a generous amount of supplementary information and include the U.S. Constitution and amendments, the Law of Presidential Succession, a timeline for each president, election returns, presidential libraries, a glossary, an index and much, much more.

This book works well as a companion to *American First Ladies,* third edition, published by Salem in 2015.—**ARBA Staff Reviewer**

Dictionaries and Encyclopedias

466. **American Governance.** Stephen L. Schechter, ed. New York, Macmillan Reference USA/Gale Group, 2016. 5v. illus. index. $700.00/set. ISBN 13: 978-0-02-866249-7; 978-0-02-866255-8 (e-book).

This encyclopedic treatment of government in the United States covers the historical development and evolving characteristics of American political life, key institutions, recurring and major issues, and the implications of governing structures for citizens and civil society. The interdisciplinary approach draws on political science, law, history, economics, sociology, and economics. Significant events, individuals, concepts, texts, and events illustrate aspects of four major themes: the intellectual foundations of the system; the constitutional and legal framework; government and public policy; and the expression of these designs through citizenship and participation in public life. Representative articles range from "Voting Behavior" and the history of "State Constitutions" to "Civil

Disobedience" and "Gender Discrimination," as well as important specifics such as *Roe v. Wade,* the Voting Rights Act and Magna Carta, plus concise biographies of selected presidents, jurists, and other leaders.

There are over 700 signed articles in alphabetical order, written by more than 400 contributors who are primarily American academics. The editor-in-chief is a widely published political scientist. The writing style is aimed at a college-level readership. Articles range in length from shorter definitions to longer essays on complex topics such as "Affirmative Action" or the stages of constitutional development. Historical coverage traces themes from classical Greece and medieval England to the present, with coverage as recent as the *Obergefell* v. *Hodges* court decision on gay marriage rights in June 2015. Most articles include citations for further reading, including scholarly books and articles published as recently as 2015. In print, this work consists of five volumes; it also is available in e-book format through the Gale Virtual Reference Library.

Ample additions support the text. An annotated Webliography identifies Websites for federal agencies, advocacy groups, think tanks, and collections of primary sources. Appendixes reprint the original Declaration of Independence, the Constitution, the Bill of Rights, and the later Amendments, as well as three issues of the *Federalist.* A case index covers court decisions and legal topics. A subject index deals with key politicians and statesmen, government entities and practices, ideology and concepts, legislation, advocacy groups, thinkers and writers, aspects of the Constitution, and topics in race, ethnicity, gender, and sexual orientation. Illustrations include maps, timelines, graphs, tables, and portraits based on engravings or photographs.

There are several comparable resources (sometimes with similar titles) that approach this general topic from different directions. *American Government* (see ARBA 2012, entry 724) is a database aimed at a high school audience, using primary and secondary sources to examine policies, leaders, and controversies. *Governing America: Major Decisions of Federal, State, and Local Governments from 1789 to the Present* (see ARBA 2012, entry 728) revolves around social, economic, and political policies and their impact. *Handbook to American Democracy* (see ARBA 2013, entry 631) consists of four volumes: an overview followed by separate volumes for each of the three branches of government, but these volumes are shorter than those of *American Governance.*—**Steven W. Sowards**

467. **American Political Culture: An Encyclopedia.** Michael Shally-Jensen, ed.; Mark J. Rozell and Ted G. Jelen, advisory eds. Santa Barbara, Calif., ABC-CLIO, 2015. 3v. illus. index. $310.00/set. ISBN 13: 978-1-61069-377-6; 978-1-61069-378-3 (e-book).

This three-volume encyclopedia from ABC-CLIO provides a unique and comprehensive description of political culture (or, more appropriately, cultures) within the United States throughout its most recent history. The nearly 200 entries range from broad issues such as war and politics to more contemporary topics such as an entry describing the rise of the Tea Party. The narrative of each entry follows the same general format: an introduction that defines the topic, a contemporary historical analysis that provides appropriate context, an extended explanation of why the topic is significant within the overall milieu of American politics, often accompanied by a breakdown of specific issues concerning the topics, and a conclusion that summarizes key points. Text boxes are used effectively to highlight a specific issue within an entry. Entries are written primarily by faculty and doctoral students from institutions in the United States representing a variety of social sciences disciplines beyond just political science. Entries average about 3,500 words and are arranged alphabetically throughout the encyclopedia. They include *see also* references to related terms and a bibliography of books, articles from scholarly and nonscholarly sources, and Websites that provide further readings about the topics. Most entries include nontextual elements such as photographs, charts, or illustrations. Front matter includes a list of all entries and an introduction to the encyclopedia. Back matter includes a complete bibliography, a list of contributors, and an index to be used for finding topics that are not main entries. Although there are entries on state and local politics and states' rights, the encyclopedia focuses on national, and, where appropriate, international political cultures. This is an impressive work and highly recommended for beginning researchers; it would be of value in any public, high school, or undergraduate library.—**Robert V. Labaree**

468.   **The Central Intelligence Agency: An Encyclopedia of Covert Ops, Intelligence Gathering, and Spies.** Goldman, Jan, ed. Santa Barbara, Calif., ABC-CLIO, 2015. 2v. illus. index. $189.00/set. ISBN 13: 978-1-61069-091-1; 978-1-61069-092-8 (e-book).

This two-volume encyclopedia from ABC-CLIO, edited by intelligence expert Jan Goldman of Georgetown University, aims to give students real information, in capsule form, about the workings of the Central Intelligence Agency (CIA) and to provide them with tools for further research. Volume one has 216 entries, arranged alphabetically from Afghanistan to Zenith Technical Enterprises and dealing with individuals, countries, operations, topics, and organizations with which the CIA was involved. There is good coverage of the CIA's role in the recent wars in Iraq and Afghanistan, of government directives on how the CIA should work, and of how the agency has used front organizations in its covert operations. This reviewer would have liked to see more entries on the CIA's role in Vietnam, and there is one notable omission from the Cold War era: Adolf Tolkachev, a senior Soviet engineer who gave the CIA a treasure trove of information. (Tolkachev's story is told in David E. Hoffman's book *The Billion-Dollar Spy* (Doubleday, 2015). Volume two contains 98 documents arranged chronologically, most of which were classified secret or above when issued and many of which are redacted in this publication, dating from the 1940's to 2014. Jan Goldman writes in his introduction that all these documents have now been declassified by the U.S. government and that readers can use them in their own research. The documents selected open a window into U.S. intelligence-gathering activities and their outcomes. One is the debriefing in 1962 of Francis Gary Powers, the U-2 pilot who was shot down and captured by the Soviets and later exchanged for a Russian spy. Another intriguing, if unsettling, document is titled "A Review of CIA Guatemala Assassination Proposals during 1952-54." Each document is preceded by an introduction that tries to put it in context. Another feature of this encyclopedia is the "Timeline of Central Intelligence Agency and Intelligence Activities, 1939-2015." Although it mainly emphasizes events since 2001, this section will give the careful reader a fairly coherent idea of how the agency has developed over time. The bibliography lists many excellent books and a number of Websites, but appears to include only one book published after 2012. Overall, the encyclopedia lives up to its promise—it does not purport to be a history of the CIA, but rather a usable introduction to the work and world of the spy agency and is recommended for school, academic, and general libraries.—**Alice Chaffee**

469.   Conley, Richard S. **Historical Dictionary of the U.S. Presidency.** Lanham, Md., Rowman & Littlefield, 2016. 503p. (Historical Dictionaries of U.S. Politics and Political

Eras). $130.00; $129.99. ISBN 13: 978-1-4422-5764-1; 978-1-4422-5765-8 (e-book).

This book, intended primarily for the general reader, provides an accessible and quite comprehensive outline of the presidencies of the 44 men who have held that office, from George Washington through Barack Obama. Author Richard S. Conley, associate professor of political science at the University of Florida, has written extensively on the presidency, including volumes on the Reagan-Bush, Clinton, and George W. Bush eras in the series of which this book is a part. Conley's introduction focuses on the evolution of executive power and its relationship to the other branches of government and the U.S. Constitution. The chronology which begins the book ranges from three lines for Zachary Taylor to nearly four pages for Franklin Roosevelt. The 200 plus entries in the dictionary section cover not only the presidents themselves but also their vice presidents, selected cabinet members, rivals, and other notable figures, as well as significant events. The bibliography has separate sections on each of the presidents and includes a list of presidential museum and library Websites. Perhaps the most notable feature of this volume is the series of 23 appendixes—over 120 pages—dealing with such matters as detailed election results, presidential approval data (beginning with President Truman), White House chiefs of staff, economic data, and much else. There is also a list of acronyms and abbreviations. The book contains essential information in a nutshell while also pointing the reader to more in-depth studies of the presidents and their times.—**ARBA Staff Reviewer**

470. **Contemporary Immigration in America: A State-by-State Encyclopedia.** Kathleen R. Arnold, ed. Santa Barbara, Calif., Greenwood Press/ABC-CLIO, 2015. 2v. index. $189.00/set. ISBN 13: 978-0-313-39917-6; 978-0-313-39918-3 (e-book).

This two-volume set is a creatively imagined resource that spans the breadth of history, politics, and culture in its study of immigration issues in the United States of America since 1945. In its unique focus on a state's particular experience with immigration (as opposed to conveying a national emphasis), the book aims to offer a thorough examination of its topic as well as open the door to further research.

As an encyclopedia, the volumes are structured to provide a state-by-state examination of the people, ideas, policies, and events that shape its own immigration story. From Alabama to Wyoming, each chapter presents a detailed chronology touching on historical events, a narrative historical overview, topical essays reflecting the state's current immigration situations, and notable figures/groups existing throughout the state's domain of immigration.

Delaware is a model example to share. This chapter begins with a timeline that notes the arrival of European explorers to the land of the Native American Nanticoke tribe and ends with the 2012 expiration-in-committee of Senate Bill 169 which would have allowed undocumented students to pay for higher education at the Delaware resident rate. The historical overview discusses the early conflicts between Scandinavian, Dutch, and English interests in the region, the importance of Irish immigration to economic growth, the state's current ethnic makeup, and more. Topical essays include pieces on how the economic growth spurred by transportation issues facilitated an immigration flux and how the 2003 Gay Rights Ordinance has also encouraged immigration. And the notable groups section points to La Esperanza, a faith-based community group providing several vital services to Latino/a immigrants.

Readers can focus on the individual states and their particular immigration story, or broaden the context by linking many of the contentious issues borne of immigration to what's in the news today, such as labor issues, education, LGBT politics, and detention. Volume one contains chapters from Alabama to Missouri, while volume two comprises Montana to Wyoming. Each chapter has its own bibliography, while the set includes a selected bibliography as well as black-and white-photos, tables, and an index. This timely and unique immigration-study resource will appeal to students, high school and above, and to anyone interested in the ways immigration has shaped and continues to shape each American state's destiny.—**Laura Herrell**

471.   **Encyclopedia of U.S. Intelligence.** Gregory Moore, ed. Boca Raton, Fla., CRC Press, 2014. 2v. illus. index. $675.75/set. ISBN 13: 978-1-4200-8957-8.

The Encyclopedia of U.S. Intelligence is an in-depth reference work offering an accessible overview of the history and workings of U.S. Intelligence. The encyclopedia is well-organized: the entries are arranged alphabetically by topic and by subtopic.

The encyclopedia covers a wide range of subjects going beyond terrorism and well-known federal government agencies to include criminal intelligence and analysis, legislation, historical events and figures, and education and training.

Each full-text entry includes an abstract to further assist readers in finding truly relevant information. Some abstracts are in-depth and detailed while others are concise, one-sentence descriptions. Author affiliations for each entry are also provided. This is especially useful as the book represents the combined contributions of both scholars and former intelligence professionals at many levels from both the public and private sector.

The online version is updated quarterly to keep up with this quickly changing discipline.

The Encyclopedia of U.S. Intelligence is useful in two specific ways. First, its table of contents provides an easy-to-grasp view of the history, breadth, geography, major events, and major players in U.S. Intelligence. Second, the entries themselves are authored by scholars and practitioners offering insightful analysis of topics often experienced first-hand. The blend of the scholarly, professional, public, and private sector viewpoints is interesting and offers serious students many avenues for further analysis.

This work is recommended for collections in academic, government, and law enforcement collections. It would also be a useful addition for large public libraries.—**Kristin Kay Leeman**

472.   **The 21st-Century Voter: Who Votes, How They Vote, and Why They Vote.** Guido H., III Stempel and Thomas K. Hargrove, eds. Santa Barbara, Calif., ABC-CLIO, 2015. 2v. illus. maps. index. $189.00/set. ISBN 13: 978-1-61069-227-4; 978-1-61069-228-1 (e-book).

The 21st-Century Voter: Who Votes, How They Vote, and Why They Vote introduces the mechanics of the modern American voting process. This two-volume book takes a broad look at the subjects concerning contemporary voting practices such as, but not limited to, campaign strategies, voting associations, and voter demographics. Authors Guido H. Stempel and Thomas K. Hargrove both have experience in research on voting, political campaigning, and governmental policies. The book's supplementary items include graphs, charts, further reading suggestions, a reference section, and an index..

Set up like a traditional encyclopedia, both volumes are arranged in a traditional A to Z format. Due to the length of the encyclopedia, the authors wisely divided the material into two volumes. Though the A to Z organization is quite logical, it may make readers less inclined to explore throughout the entire work. Moreover, users might have to do a little more legwork in order to find all the information on a given subject like voting habits. Different generations and their voting habits are covered in several in-depth analyses—baby boomers, the millennials, and generation X—but readers must go back and forth throughout the book to find all of the information. These concerns aside, the reader will become accustomed to the layout of the volumes, which in no significant way dilutes the value of the information.

This book is recommended for high school, academic, and public libraries.—**Sara Mofford**

473. Vile, John R. **Encyclopedia of Constitutional Amendments, Proposed Amendments, and Amending Issues, 1789–2015.** 4th ed. Santa Barbara, Calif., ABC-CLIO, 2015. 2v. index. $189.00/set. ISBN 13: 978-1-61069-931-0; 978-1-61069-932-7 (e-book).

In the foreword to this fourth edition of a book previously published in 1996, 2003, and 2010 (see ARBA 1997, entry 596; ARBA 2004, entry 535; and ARBA 2011, entry 436), Sanford Levinson of the University of Texas Law School identifies the book's sole editor, John R. Vile, as the recognized national expert on the amendments and proposed amendments to the U.S. Constitution. Levinson convincingly argues that Vile's work is "an essential book for scholars, but it is written in such an accessible style that anyone interested in the United States Constitution can profit from picking it up and reading entries basically at random." (p. xvii) Vile, professor of political science and dean of the University Honors College at Middle Tennessee State University, aims to provide an "indispensable tool for those who are interested in constitutional amendments, proposed amendments, and amending issues." (p. xix) The 2015 edition, now in two volumes, contains revised entries, new entries, and additional cross-references. It covers almost 12,000 proposed amendments together with major constitutional reforms introduced outside Congress, "influential individuals," "influential organizations," Supreme Court decisions, unresolved issues, and "miscellaneous" related topics such as the Articles of Confederation and Critical Elections.

Vile suggests that readers ranging from high school students to "advanced researchers in law, political science, and history" (p. xxiv) may explore entries ranging from George Washington to Phyllis Schlafly and Confederate Debt to Polygamy. Volume one features the A to Z list of entries from A to M and explains the features of this new edition. Volume two, entries N-Z, also offers four appendixes that include the Constitution and its amendments, the number of amendments by decade, and other key data, as well as an updated, wide-ranging bibliography of more than 40 pages, a list of cases, and a revised, comprehensive index. This authoritative set is essential for college, university, and law libraries. Its relatively low cost, impressive content, and clear writing style distinguish it from the other published studies of constitutional amendments carefully cited by Vile and also make it an important purchase for many high school and most public libraries.—**Julienne L. Wood**

474. **The War on Terror Encyclopedia: From the Rise of Al-Qaeda to 9/11 and Beyond.** Jan Goldman, ed. Santa Barbara, Calif., ABC-CLIO, 2014. 492p. index. $100.00. ISBN 13: 978-1-61069-510-7; 978-1-61069-511-4 (e-book).

The War on Terror Encyclopedia: From the Rise of Al-Qaeda to 9/11 and Beyond presents the history and course of modern terrorism from a U.S. perspective. The book's main concern is not terrorism in general; rather, it focuses on the people and policies involved on both sides of America's fight against different groups seeking to perpetrate violence and terror against the United States and its allies.

Its primary aim is to examine the U.S. war on terror from a policy perspective, rather than an academic perspective. Entries are drawn heavily from practitioners in the intelligence, defense, and security professions. The encyclopedia seeks to present a factual, neutral basis from which readers can formulate their own ideas and opinions.

The preface and introduction prepare the reader to understand an essential characteristic of the "war on terror"—namely that the enemy is not a nation-state (as in conventional warfare) and cannot be studied or understood in a conventional manner. As a result, the book is multidisciplinary: its entries touch upon policies, politics, doctrines, economics, sociology, warfare technologies, and individuals.

Entries are organized alphabetically and range from the Taliban to the Economic Impact of the September 11, 2001 Attacks and from the Bush Doctrine to Middle Eastern Television. There is a thorough index which also includes hyperlinked page numbers, making navigation to primary and related topics very easy. It would be ideal to have the *see also* options at the end of each entry similarly linked.

The entries are engagingly written and well presented. For example, entries on individuals (especially known terrorists) provide interesting biographical information, placing the individual in historical context, charting his activities, development, and connections in the terrorist world, as well as his current status today if he is still living. The author of each entry is included at the end of each entry along with *see also* entries and citations for suggested further reading.

Dr. Jan Goldman, editor, carries substantial credentials in this field. He has published several other well-received reference books about the CIA and the Intelligence Community The contributors are also listed with their respective affiliations.

This book is very strongly recommended for academic libraries and large public libraries. It should also find a place on the reading list for anyone in the defense, intelligence, and policy-making arenas (especially foreign and security policy). This is also a great read for anyone interested in a clearly presented, easy-to-digest history of recent events and topics that will continue to be very relevant for the foreseeable future. Anyone interested in strengthening their foundational knowledge in the study of terrorism will appreciate this book.—**Kristin Kay Leeman**

Directories

475.   **The Grey House Homeland Security Directory, 2015.** 11th ed. Amenia, N.Y., Grey House Publishing, 2015. 1141p. index. $195.00pa. ISBN 13: 978-1-61925-561-6.

With the growing interest in and concern with homeland security it is not unusual for patrons to go to their local public or college/university library to try to get contact information for federal and state employees working in this sector to express their concerns or to pursue research projects. However, finding this information can be a tricky feat since there are many federal and state agencies and subagencies that work in some way with issues related to homeland security and they may not be readily apparent to the librarian or the researcher. The 11th edition of *The Grey House Homeland Security Directory* helps fill this need in the reference collection for public and academic libraries. Information included in this comprehensive directory extends beyond governmental agencies and also includes entries for private sector companies which offer products and services related to homeland security issues and concerns, as well as a section for industry resources such as Websites, trade shows, publications, and other information resources.

This helpful directory is divided into five sections: Federal Agencies, State Agencies, Company Listings (provides information on companies that offer services and products to the consumer such as data security and emergency food and water rations), Industry Resources, and Indexes. In the first four sections, each of the 5,502 entries includes a brief description explaining how that entry relates to homeland security, contact information for the entry as a whole (department-level or company-level, for example), and the names and titles of important individuals (11,314 in total) and often their phone numbers and/or email addresses. A table of contents is useful for navigating this directory and section five is comprised of three indexes: entry name index, key personnel index, and products and services index to help the user find what they are looking for.

Length of entries and the level of information provided varies in section three: Company Listing. Shorter entries are often seen with smaller companies (less than 50 employees), but there are a few instances in which there is scant information provided on much larger companies. Despite the inconsistencies, this section is still very robust in the amount of information provided for the majority of companies profiled.

The most helpful section of this directory is section two: State Agencies. It can often be difficult to determine which state agencies play a role related to Homeland Security, and this directory clearly lists the applicable departments and includes a brief description in addition to contact information which is often buried on state Websites, if it is even listed at all.

Overall, the 11th edition of *The Grey House Homeland Security Directory* is very robust and a useful addition to public and academic libraries, especially those which are open to the public. It is a valuable reference tool, especially to libraries that have owned previous editions as contact information for many individuals has changed, more companies have been added to the Company Listing section, and Industry Resources have been updated and added.—**Julia Frankosky**

476.   **The New York State Directory, 2015/2016.** Amenia, N.Y., Grey House Publishing, 2015. 890p. maps. index. $155.00pa. ISBN 13: 978-1-61925-563-0.

The 2015/2016 edition of the *New York State Directory* is self-described as "a comprehensive guide to public officials and private sector organizations and individuals who influence public policy in the state of New York" With an easy-to-use arrangement, this directory is essential for anyone wishing to contact the decision-makers in the State of New York. The 45 chapters are divided into eight sections. Sections include the branches of New York government; public policy areas including the agencies and officials that formulate or implement public policy; government information from the federal level down to municipal; political parties, lobbyists, and Political Action Committees; a couple of chapters on business; news media; education from K-12 to higher education; and biographies of elected New York State officials on the federal and state level—including contact information. A great example of a typical entry is in section three, State & Local Government Public Information. In the chapter on Municipal Government users will find a listing for West Seneca, Town of, located in Erie County. On this page of the directory appears the names of key officials along with their email and telephone numbers.

Appendixes are also present that include color maps; three indexes; and a financial plan overview that has the cash disbursement by department projected to fiscal year 2019. This directory, by Grey House Publishing is a companion piece to *Profiles of New York State;* the two titles are available as a set.—**Scott R. DiMarco**

Handbooks and Yearbooks

477. **The American Presidency Project.** [Website] Free. Date reviewed: 2016.

The American Presidency Project is an online resource collecting the messages and papers of the presidents, public papers, and other presidential documents. The site is run by the University of California, Santa Barbara, and is a strong resource for documents related to the presidency.

The site allows quick access to materials such as data, documents, election information, and other forms of media. The wealth of the material is found in the documents section. Features include original texts of State of the Union Addresses, Inaugural Addresses, public speeches and appearances, and more. Documents are efficiently organized by topics, such as news conferences, proclamations, and a unique feature of a president's term in office, such as the Fireside Chats by Franklin D. Roosevelt.

The data section provides information on a president's popularity and approval ratings, although this section is limited to the more recent presidents. Election information includes voter preferences, how specific events or speeches affected voter support, and more. The database also lists which candidates were running in each election.

Finding the material beyond the top navigation is very intuitive and can allow a user to directly access the documents they are looking for, even specific press briefs or executive orders. The basic search function is small and hidden in the top left corner of the site, which could make it difficult for a user to find, if they do not have specific needs in mind. For further research, the project also includes links to presidential libraries and museums.—**ARBA Staff Reviewer**

478. **American President: A Reference Resource. http://millercenter.org/president.** [Website] Free. Date reviewed: 2016.

The *American President* Website is an information resource containing a wealth of material on each of the nation's 44 presidents. Maintained by the Miller Center of Public Affairs, a nonpartisan research affiliate of the University of Virginia that specializes in presidential scholarship and political history, the site is easy to navigate and attractively arranged. But it is the site's rich, deep, and authoritative content that gives it its distinctive value.

The *American President* home page features a standard search option, but many users will choose to explore the site's many treasures through its illustrated table of contents, which lists every president from Washington to Obama in chronological order. Each of these presidential links opens onto a home page for the president in question. On these home pages, users will find links to well-written and informative summaries of the president's personal background, his campaign and election experiences, his domestic and foreign triumphs and failures in the Oval Office, and his historical legacy.

In addition to these biographical essays, each presidential home page provides links to essays on key events of that president's administration, biographical profiles of the First Lady and key administration figures, transcripts of notable speeches and addresses, an image gallery, and Websites of historical sites and libraries devoted to the president in question. The site even includes video lectures from prominent historians on specific presidents of the nineteenth and early twentieth centuries.

The historical material available for every president is impressive, but students exploring the administrations of our more recent presidents will also have a terrific array of audiovisual materials at their disposal. These resources include Oval Office audio recordings from the Kennedy, Johnson, and Nixon administrations; audio recordings of important presidential speeches (beginning with Franklin D. Roosevelt); video recordings of important presidential speeches (beginning with John F. Kennedy); and an Oral Histories section where users can peruse the transcripts of interviews with leading officials and lawmakers from the Carter, Reagan, George H.W. Bush, Clinton, and George W. Bush administrations. The Oral History section for the Clinton presidency alone contains more than 60 interviews, including conversations with luminaries ranging from Secretary of State Madeleine Albright and Chief of Staff Leon Panetta to former Czech Republic president Vaclev Havel.

American President: A Reference Resource is a highly recommended site for high school, public, and academic libraries alike.—**ARBA Staff Reviewer**

479.   **America's National Park System: The Critical Documents.** Lary M. Dilsaver, ed. Lanham, Md., Rowman & Littlefield, 2016. 487p. index. $55.00pa.; $49.99 (e-book). ISBN 13: 978-0-8476-8440-3; 978-0-585-12121-5 (e-book)

This important collection of primary source documents highlights the founding, evolution, and challenges of one of the defining American institutions: The National Park Service. From the singular act of granting state stewardship to a granite cleft in California's Sierra Nevada, the National Park system has grown to confront millions of acres and hundreds of issues encompassing grazing rights, climate change, development, pollution, invasive species, recreational use, and much more. This book showcases 79 documents (some have been abridged) ranging from acts of Congress to fire management reports and advocacy letters which speak to the history of "America's best idea" and the diverse purposes it serves.

Nine chapters chronologically coalesce around the important documents of particular eras, allowing readers to connect the National Park situation to the national milieu. For example, "The New Deal Years 1933-1941" reflects issues of The Great Depression and racial desegregation via documents such as the Act for the Relief of Unemployment (CCC) and correspondence concerning equal, nondiscriminatory facilities in the national parks of the south. The author includes general context in each chapter preceding its particular documents.

This second edition has been updated with an additional chapter including documents produced from 1992 to present day, as well as supplementary material from the early years, such as the 1929 National Park Standards statement.

Some particular highlights include Frederick Law Olmsted's personal rendering of Yosemite in his quest for a philosophical approach to the management of the land ("At certain points the walls of rock are ploughed in polished horizontal furrows"), Bernard DeVoto's 1953 litany of maintenance issues which he believed should shut the parks down, and, of course, the many acts which elevated the land to icon status: the Preservation of

Historic Sites Act of 1935, the Wild and Scenic Rivers Act of 1968, the Native American Graves Protection and Repatriation Act of 1990, and many more.

Appendixes include summaries of lengthy documents and significant court rulings and opinions. An index rounds out the work.—**ARBA Staff Reviewer**

480.   **Congress.gov. https://www.congress.gov/.** [Website] Free. Date reviewed: 2016.

Congress.gov is a presentation of the Library of Congress and is the official Website for U.S. federal legislative information. Its dignified look and abundance of useful links fits perfectly with its mission.

Not only is *Congress.gov* a great place to see what's actually happening in the House and Senate on any given day, it's a very useful Website for students—or others—who are interested in learning more about important issues like how a bill becomes law. The Website includes some simple informational videos, a search engine that helps users find information among more than one million records, access to the entirety of the Congressional Record, and quick access to all bills being considered in the House and Senate. A glossary provides brief explanations of legislative terms used throughout the Website. A link to the crowd-sourced "top-10 most-viewed bills" provides an easy entrée into the complicated world of reading legislation.

A list of Congressional committees links to the committee proceedings, recent activity, and Websites of each committee. Information about each member of Congress (current and former) is easy to find along with important details like their contact information, remarks in the *Congressional Record,* and committee assignments. Content on the site is constantly being updated; for instance, a new video series called "Two-Minute Tips" teaches users how to get the most out of the Website. A link to Law Library of Congress resources on Supreme Court Nominations ties into current news. Users can even stream live floor proceedings when the House and Senate are in session.

Because people interested in the U.S. Congress might be recent immigrants or even users from other countries, a significant detriment is the paucity of Spanish-language (and other-language) resources.

Overall, *Congress.gov* is an easy-to-navigate site that does a great job of making Congressional legislation available and comprehensible to the average citizen. It's also an excellent starting place for links to other important Websites like all those connected with the Library of Congress, information about visiting the Capitol, and a gallery of study resources about significant primary source documents from American history.—**ARBA Staff Reviewer**

481.   **Council of State Governments. http://www.csg.org/.** [Website] Free. Date reviewed: 2016.

The Council of State Governments (CSG), founded in 1933, serves all three branches of state government in the formation of state public policy; the CSG also supports state government in fostering regional, national, and international opportunities. The CSG site hosts a wealth of freely accessible data. From the home page, users can click on myriad links: Economics & Finance, Education, Energy & Environment, Federal Affairs, Health, International, Interstate Compacts, Public Safety & Justice, Transportation, and Workforce Development. All these links lead to other information treasure troves. A click on Interstate Compacts, for example, takes users to a database that allows searches across

1,500 statutes—searches can be conducted through basic or advanced search functions or via an interactive map. Additional links on the home page take users to events, leadership development, the *Capitol Ideas Magazine,* and the venerable *Book of the States* (BOS), which since 1935 has provided pertinent data for all 56 territories, commonwealths, and states of the United States. The 2015 edition has 152 in-depth tables, charts, and figures along with 29 articles by policy experts and state leaders. Archived editions of the BOS are freely available and easy to download. Designed for policy-makers, this Website is equally valuable to students and researchers.—**ARBA Staff Reviewer**

482.   **Handbook of Social Choice and Voting.** Jac C. Heckelman and Nicholas R. Miller, eds. Northampton, Mass., Edward Elgar, 2016. 424p. index. $225.00. ISBN 13: 978-1-78347-072-3.

This offering from Edward Elgar examines the phenomenon of social choice as it pertains to voting behavior. Editors Jac C. Heckelman of Wake Forest University and Nicholas R. Miller at the University of Maryland Baltimore County have assembled 20 articles that look at the theory of social choice and its application to voting, with a heavy emphasis on theoretical models. The contributors are predominantly professors of political science at such institutions as the London School of Economics, the University of California, and the University of Chicago. The five parts of the book deal with perspectives on social choice, pairwise social choice, spatial models of social choice, social choice with multiple alternatives, and empirical social choice. Social choice, which derives ultimately from the field of rational choice and the subfield of public choice, focuses on collective decision-making. While the introduction acknowledges that many of the topics in this book are discussed in two earlier works, *The Elgar Companion to Public Choice* (2013) and the two-volume *Handbook of Social Choice and Welfare* (2002, 2011), it points out that most of the first book cited does not deal with voting behavior and the second work is designed for a specialist scholarly audience. The chapters in this book are followed by explanatory notes and references; a number of the chapters feature tables, graphs, and figures. The book contains a comprehensive index and also a glossary of technical terms relating to social choice theory and voting rules that will be of great help to readers with limited prior exposure in this field. *The Handbook of Social Choice and Voting* offers a helpful resource to students and researchers at a time when voting behavior is of enormous theoretical and practical interest, and should be considered by academic and general libraries.—**ARBA Staff Reviewer**

483.   Harris, Douglas B., and Lonce H. Bailey. **The Republican Party.** Santa Barbara, Calif., Greenwood Press/ABC-CLIO, 2014. 281p. illus. index. (Documents Decoded). $79.00. ISBN 13: 978-1-61069-645-6; 978-1-61069-646-3 (e-book).

Today's partisan political climate begs the scholar of American history to closely examine the nature of leading political parties. Specifically, how have the parties shaped American politics as we know them, and how have they evolved from their origins? This title in the Documents Decoded series traces the evolution of the Republican Party from its earliest association with the "order over anarchy" ideals of the Whigs, through the reform-minded ideas galvanized by Teddy Roosevelt and finally to its current characterization as a vehemently small government, socially conservative entity. The book's unique approach provides expert analysis of primary documents, facilitating an active relationship between readers and the material at hand.

Seven chapters delineate the major eras of Republican Party development, from "The Legacy of Abraham Lincoln" to "The Obama Years." The chapters organize a well-selected group of speeches, official party platforms, and other writings which encapsulate the ideas of key Republican leaders from Lincoln himself to Dwight Eisenhower, Ronald Reagan, Newt Gingrich, and many others. Here, for example, is an inaugural address from James A. Garfield calling for compromise between party ideologies, or President George W. Bush's media-driven 2003 "Mission Accomplished" speech. The chronology helps readers see the development of the Republican response to such issues as slavery, nationalism, communism, deficit spending, the military, and morality, while the historical contextualization enhances understanding. For example, the authors note that President Richard Nixon's hope of détente between the United States and the communist nations of China and The Soviet Union, as conveyed within his 1972 presidential nomination acceptance speech, would later be repudiated by President Reagan's policies.

The book concludes with a detailed timeline indicating events ranging from an 1854 meeting of Whig Party activists opposed to the expansion of slavery to the 2013 split between establishment and "Tea Party" Republicans, as well as sources for further reading and an index. Recommended for high school and academic libraries.—**Laura Herrell**

484.   LeMay, Michael C. **Illegal Immigration: A Reference Handbook.** 2d ed. Santa Barbara, Calif., ABC-CLIO, 2015. 382p. illus. index. (Contemporary World Issues). $60.00. ISBN 13: 978-1-4408-4012-8; 978-1-4408-4013-5 (e-book).

Author Michael LeMay, Ph.D., is a professor emeritus from California State University, San Bernardino, where he served as Director of the National Security Studies program as well as positions in the Department of Political Science and the College of Social and Behavioral Sciences. Le May has an extensive list of immigration writings, and also lectures on immigration history and policy.

Contemporary World Issues is a series well used as a starting point for studies on such contemporary issues as hate crimes, nuclear power, and immigration. This second edition of *Illegal Immigration: A Reference Handbook* explores the definition, history, and flow of unauthorized immigrants into the United States since 1970. This book, published in 2015, contains 400 pages starting with a concise table of contents. Like other books in this series, chapters are initiated with a black-and-white photograph. The glossary has a large list of terminology, which will be useful to those acquainting themselves with the immigration issue, and the index is comprehensive.

Chapters begin with an introduction, the topic text is followed by a conclusion or solution where warranted, and each chapter closes with references, both print and nonprint. The first chapter, "Background and History," describes how unauthorized immigration has come into being in the United States; the book comes full circle with the final chapter, "Chronology," providing an annotated timeline of important moments in immigration history. This book focuses on modern-day issues with immigration but historical information presents a contextual foundation.

Chapter three, "Perspectives," is a new addition to this second edition. Eight original essays give voice to all sides of the immigration issue. Groups who lobby for reform of polices or against those same policies are included here and will provide a strong springboard for discussion, debate, and further research. Chapter five, "Data and Documents," includes useful document resources for those looking for policy details and useable data. Tables like 5.4 "Unaccompanied Alien Children Encountered by Fiscal Year,

Country of Origin 2014" (p. 222) will give definition to report writing, though the Gallup polls offer less in the way of concrete data.

Focusing on trends and policies since 2000, *Illegal Immigration* will give researchers a place to discover the current problems and controversies of immigration, border security, and human rights issues. Readers will learn the issue is one of many layers and continues to plague politicians, policy makers, and policy implementers. Key issues will be found by readers and will spark research in a specific area; those looking for an overview with find this text will be a catalyst for narrowing the scope of study and resources to assist in the research. For more finite information on immigration, another series The International Library of Studies on Migration will give researchers a more detailed background on immigration and its global implications. This book is recommended for high school and college students, policy-makers, and those looking to better understand immigration issues in the United States.

Recommended.—**Janis Minshull**

485.   Rawal, Purva H. **The Affordable Care Act: Examining the Facts.** Santa Barbara, Calif., ABC-CLIO, 2016. 220p. index. (Contemporary Debates). $63.00. ISBN 13: 978-1-4408-3442-4; 978-1-4408-3443-1.

This book, from ABC-CLIO's new Contemporary Debates series intended for high-school and undergraduate students, examines the Affordable Care Act (ACA) from before its passage in 2010 to the present. Hailed by many as a signature achievement of the Barack Obama presidency, the act has been vilified by others, some of whom hope to overturn it if a Republican wins the White House in 2016. Each of the eight chapters features four to eight questions that are followed by answers, a detailed examination of the facts, and suggestions for further reading—these suggestions, often extensive, take the place of a formal bibliography. Author Purva H. Rawal, PhD, was working for a senator involved with the legislation when the ACA was passed and brings an intense commitment to getting accurate facts before the public. The questions cover the relationship of the ACA to the insurance industry, its effect on costs, the likelihood that it will improve the overall health of Americans, and much more. The answers are clearly stated and the facts cited show the complexity of the issues under discussion. The book has an index and a foreword by Dr. Len Nichols, director of the Center for Health Policy Research and Ethics at George Mason University. This book will help students and members of the public find both specific answers to questions about the ACA and food for thought about America's health care system.—**Alice Chaffee**

486.   Stanley, Harold W., and Richard G. Niemi. **Vital Statistics on American Politics 2015-2016.** Thousand Oaks, Calif., CQ Press / Sage, 2015. 448p. index. $135.00. ISBN 13: 978-1-4833-8031-5; 978-1-4833-8029-2 (e-book).

Vital Statistics on American Politics is a comprehensive compilation of statistics related to all areas of the federal government. The 2015-2016 edition is updated with the most current information available. As the title infers, this book covers statistics related to politics, such as voter turnout, election results, and campaign finance. However, it also goes beyond the obvious and provides information about the topics that surround and influence politicians in the areas of foreign, social, and economic policy.

More broadly, this book also provides statistics on how the American public gets its information and how we interact with American politics. Who reads newspapers? Who watches CNN or Fox News? How many people watch presidential debates? How has public opinion evolved on topics such as abortion, gay marriage, and gun control?

Students, researchers, historians, and everyday citizens will find useful information on the main subjects that surround politics and the entire political system.—**Lisa Schultz**

487.   **U*X*L Civics.** Rebecca Valentine, ed. Farmington Hills, Mich, Gale/Cengage Learning, 2015. 3v. illus. index. $272.00/set. ISBN 13: 978-1-5730-2962-9; 978-1-5730-2966-7 (e-book).

Like other UXL sets, these volumes feature excellent supporting documentation and ancillary materials. Each volume contains the complete table of contents and index for the set, as well as appendixes with the full text of founding American documents and student guides to civic engagement.

The American Government volume includes extensive historical detail pertaining to the development of democracy and republican forms of government, as well as discussion of political philosophy. Although information about how the branches of the U.S. government work overlaps with information in the second volume on rights and liberties, the second volume focuses specifically on American history. The final volume considers extensive contemporary international issues, such as the current crisis in the Ukraine and the goals of Boko Haram in Nigeria. Ample color photographs and visual aids complement the material and add to reader interest. These are suitable for both in-class use and inclusion in reference libraries.—**Delilah R. Caldwell**

488.   **Watchdogs and Whistleblowers: A Reference Guide to Consumer Activism.** Stephen Brobeck and Robert N. Mayer, eds. Santa Barbara, Calif., Greenwood Press/ABC-CLIO, 2015. 533p. index. $89.00. ISBN 13: 978-1-4408-2999-4; 978-1-4408-3000-6 (e-book).

As consumers have become increasingly proactive, there is a corresponding need for information that covers the most prominent U.S. consumer organizations and consumer action worldwide. Forty geographical regions in the world are featured here, including South America, the People's Republic of China, Central and Eastern Europe, Africa, and the Middle East. This one reference provides a wealth of information about how governments, commercial entities, and consumer organizations relate. As consumers increasingly seek to shape commerce, government regulations, and policies, the conflict between consumer and corporate values encourages whistleblowers and watchdogs to attempt to uncover and expose wrongdoing. Targets for change covered in this volume include health care, food safety, all-terrain vehicles, cosmetics, digital communications, and prescription drugs. As shown here, in many countries consumer activism is only beginning while in others it has a long and often distinguished history. The over 140 entries, from AARP to Barry Zigas, provide very useful background not easily found together elsewhere on consumer activists, organizations, and movements worldwide.

Recommended for public and academic libraries and for anyone interested in consumer activism.—**Diane J. Turner**

Public Policy and Administration

Handbooks and Yearbooks

489.   **Handbook of Critical Policy Studies.** Frank Fischer, Douglas Torgerson, Anna Durnova, and Michael Orsini, eds. Northampton, Mass., Edward Elgar, 2016. 544p. index. $240.00. ISBN 13: 978-1-78347-234-5.

Handbook of Critical Policy Studies introduces the basics of public policy while also injecting comprehensive commentary and research by some of the leading scholars in public policy. The book contains 24 essays contributed by 36 experts in their respective fields. These essays embody history, theoretical discussion, process, cultural significance, and trends. As clearly stated in the introduction the objective of this book is to "further advance the development of critical policy." With this objective the book opens the door to beginning students of public policies, but also provides experienced pupils with recent developments that broaden their knowledge of public policy. Divided into six parts the essays included cover Origins and Theoretical Development, Theoretical Perspectives, Discursive Politics, Policy Processes, The Politics of Policy Expertise, and Methodological Issues. With a large index and reputable secondary sources, the readers can further their research outside the book with the sources documented. There is no inclusion of any other type of supplementary materials (i.e. graphs, images, tables) other than the aforementioned index.

The book's focus on post World War II politics includes a strong concentration of Western public policy. Personal commentary and opinion about political science is limited in these essays. The essays are generally comprised of factual evidence discovered through reporting. Rather than focusing on examples of situations on public policies, the essays generally concentrate on notable figures, philosophy, and the theoretical process. In only one of the essays "Making Gender Visible: Exploring Feminist Perspective through the Case of Anti-Smoking Policy" by Stephanie Paterson and Francesca Scala does the concentration rely on an individual case study; the other essays mention specific cases briefly and do not expound on the connections between public policy and the real-life events. There is a large range of political science curriculum that can be taught from this book. There is also teachable content for those interested in subjects such as sociology, economics, research, environmental studies, international relations, and anthropology. While each of the essays has distinct writing styles provided by the diverse authors, the book is compiled in order that the reader can easily flow through the book without having to constantly adjust to the differences. This book is recommended to be used as a reference source for academic and high school libraries.

Highly recommended.—**Sara Mofford**

14 Psychology, Parapsychology, and Occultism

Psychology

Dictionaries and Encyclopedias

490. **Abuse: An Encyclopedia of Causes, Consequences, and Treatments.** Rosemarie Skaine, ed. Santa Barbara, Calif., Greenwood Press/ABC-CLIO, 2015. 330p. illus. index. $89.00. ISBN 13: 978-1-61069-514-5; 978-1-61069-515-2 (e-book).

This encyclopedia helps define abuse and takes a hard but composed look at the varying reasons behind it, effects stemming from it, and ways to prevent and treat it. Over 150 alphabetized entries, ranging in length from several paragraphs to several pages, provide the latest information concerning such topics as child abandonment, hate speech, animal abuse, and rape. Entries are well-detailed, and some, like rape, are further analyzed through more specific subentries (statutory rape, date rape, etc.) reflecting a nuanced approach to conveying the topic's broader meaning. The book does well to include some of the current implications of the Internet era, such as the devastating issues of cyberbullying and cyberstalking.

Importantly, the book gives significant weight to society's expanding awareness of the devastation caused by abuse, and includes entries on legislation and systems arising from particularly notorious examples, like the 1998 murder of Matthew Shepard and the creation of the Hate Crimes Prevention Act of 2009, or of the encouraging success of the AMBER alert system.

Abuse is certainly a difficult topic with which to engage. This encyclopedia, however, successfully offers a straightforward approach to educating readers on the many facets of this troubling issue and providing helpful keys to unlocking strategies and solutions with which to confront it. It includes *see also* references, suggestions for further reading, helpful Websites, contact information for associated organizations, and a concluding subject index.—**Laura Herrell**

491. **APA Dictionary of Psychology.** 2d ed. Gary R. VandenBos, ed. Washington, D.C., American Psychological Association, 2015. 1204p. $49.95. ISBN 13: 978-1-4338-1944-5.

Functionally, the new edition of the *APA Dictionary of Psychology* is very similar to its 2007 predecessor (see ARBA 2007, entry 649). The vast majority of the volume is dedicated to providing definitions of terms, arranged alphabetically. A brief "Guide to the Dictionary" provides basic information on how to use the source. Users familiar with other dictionaries will not need most of this content, but the section on "Hidden Entries" explains the protocol for locating related words–similar to cross-references–but these are terms in bold face in the text of the definitions and used in context. Entries also frequently include standard cross-references and brief etymological information as appropriate. A significant change is in the biographical information. In the 2007 edition, biographical entries were included in the text of the dictionary, with an index of biographical entries at the end of the volume. In the 2014 edition, these have been placed in a separate section at the end, but they have also been greatly shortened; the entry for Carl Rogers, for example, has gone from approximately 250 words to under 40. The preface notes, however, that this has enabled the editors to include far more biographies than in the previous edition. (p. vii) The remainder of the text has been updated to reflect current terminology and incorporate connections to the DSM-IV-TR and DSM-5. The volume concludes with lists of institutional entries, testing instrument entries, and techniques. Overall, this new edition is an excellent resource for students of all levels as well as practitioners. Recommended for high school, public, academic, and special libraries supporting researchers in mental health fields.—**Amanda Izenstark**

492.   de Young, Mary. **Encyclopedia of Asylum Therapeutics, 1750-1950s.** Jefferson, N.C., McFarland, 2015. 368p. illus. index. $55.00pa. ISBN 13: 978-0-7864-6897-3; 978-1-4766-1788-6 (e-book).

The mid-twentieth century ushered in a new place to go when confronted with issues of mental illness—the pharmacy. But the encapsulated therapies contemporary society takes for granted now are a far cry from the options patients had before then. *The Encyclopedia of Asylum Therapeutics* focuses on the sometimes surprising treatments conducted behind closed doors (and often behind locked gates) during the preceding two centuries, sweeping the cobwebs away from such therapies as Counterirritation or the Coercion Chair.

It was during the eighteenth century that asylums began to use therapies on their charges as opposed to merely confining them. This encyclopedia shares 35 entries covering major therapies with applicable subentries which aim to present an objective catalog. For example, the larger entry covering Hydrotherapy includes 29 subentries specifying particular types ranging from Cold Water Ingestion to Mustard Baths.

The author, a professor of sociology, has pored over numerous reports, studies, and fascinating personal accounts to provide detailed histories of this obscure topic and make for a truly interesting read. Such detail allows readers to glean much about the particular state of medical knowledge and societal attitudes taking hold during this historical time period. This well-referenced resource includes several striking black-and-white photographs and illustrations. There are references throughout the encyclopedia, which is rounded out by an index.—**Laura Herrell**

493.   **Encyclopedia of Social Deviance.** Craig Forsyth and Heith Copes, eds. Thousand Oaks, Calif., Sage, 2014. 2v. index. $250.00/set. ISBN 13: 978-1-4522-4033-6.

The 313 entries in this "broad and comprehensive" encyclopedia cover the theory, philosophy, and methodology of social deviance, as well as "substantive topics." The vast diversity of the subject is seen in the subjects covered: from "bead whores," "buckle bunnies" and "bug chasers" (sexual deviance) to civil disobedience, Black Panthers, atheism, and vegetarianism. At least 24 entries include "theory" in the title. Each article has a list of further readings, from both the journal and monographic literature. A 30-page index aids readers looking for specific terms.

This volume is clearly aimed at adults, mainly in the academic sphere; many of the articles are quite graphic, such as "Suspension" which discusses flesh hook suspension of individuals! Academic libraries, and some public libraries, would benefit from the information provided here.—**Mark Schumacher**

494. **Mental Health and Mental Disorders: An Encyclopedia of Conditions, Treatments, and Well-Being.** Sperry, Lee, ed. Santa Barbara, Calif., Greenwood Press/ ABC-CLIO, 2015. 3v. index. $310.00/set. ISBN 13: 978-1-4408-0382-6; 978-1-4408-0383-3 (e-book).

This three-volume encyclopedia provides a broad overview of various aspects of mental health relating to disorders, treatments, and well-being. The preface clearly states the work's intended purpose of providing a "wide-ranging reference source... written at a level accessible for upper high school and college students as well as for the layperson" (Preface, xxxvii) and offers a synopsis addressing the scope and features of the encyclopedia. This user-friendly resource contains 875 entries organized in the customary A-Z format and covering six main areas of emphasis: mental disorders and conditions, treatment, tests and assessment methods, common terms and concepts, influential individuals and organizations, and popular culture sources and events. Usability is enhanced by the definition of technical terms at the beginning of most entries and the inclusion of *see also* references and suggestions for further reading. Each volume contains a thematic guide to related topics, preface, and a cursory introduction to mental health. Volume three concludes with a glossary, biographical information about the contributors, and a comprehensive 47-page index. In addition, volume three includes a diverse list of relevant organizations and corresponding contact information as well as a bibliography of recommended resources for further exploration of mental-health-related topics.

The breadth of topics covered as well as the accessible writing and up-to-date, reliable resources are the encyclopedia's strongest features. Despite these strengths, the encyclopedia reveals drawbacks related to content. The connection between the pop culture entries and mental health is tenuous. Some entries briefly address the psychological influence of a particular pop culture phenomenon (see "Sixteen Candles") but many are merely plot summaries (see "South Park" and "The Sixth Sense"). In addition, contradictory information is found in the encyclopedia. The "Sex and Gender" entry states that "the terms 'sex' and 'gender' are often used interchangeably but are distinguishable" (p. 1015) while the "Transgender" entry notes that the term transgender "describes the self-identification of a person's sex (gender)" (p. 1149) thus implying that the terms are interchangeable. Although this encyclopedia offers limited usefulness for an academic audience (undergraduate students may find it a suitable starting point for research), it is an appropriate resource for high school students or the general reader. Although general in its depth of coverage, this set serves as an acceptable introduction to the vast topic of mental health.—**Lisa Morgan**

495. Neukrug, Edward S. **The SAGE Encyclopedia of Theory in Counseling and Psychotherapy.** Thousand Oaks, Calif., Sage, 2015. 2v. index. $375/set. ISBN 13: 978-1-4522-7412-6.

The SAGE Encyclopedia of Theory in Counseling and Psychotherapy is a comprehensive resource that provides readers with in-depth knowledge of contemporary counseling and theories in psychotherapy. A team of international researchers and practitioners combined their knowledge of modern theories and theorists to create the cultural and historical context students require to apply psychotherapy and counseling effectively. An informative and easy-to-read introduction distinguishes psychotherapy from counseling and expounds on the important role of theory in the field today. With over 1200 pages, this two-volume source may be overwhelming for those new to the study of psychology, but will undoubtedly prove useful for students in graduate or undergraduate psychology courses and counseling education programs.

The encyclopedia includes both bibliography and resource guides that provide additional resources such as books, journals, and organizations for students looking for more specialized information. Also included is a chronology to help readers place each theory in a historical context; this is extremely useful for beginning professionals and students in their first years of study to assist in setting the backdrop for the evolution of psychotherapy theories. Under the reader's guide are a detailed index and cross-reference pages that allow users to search for specific information within the text for both print and electronic formats. This title is highly recommended.—**ARBA Staff Reviewer**

496.   **Salem Health: Psychology & Behavioral Health.** 4th ed. Paul Moglia, ed. Hackensack, N.J., Salem Press, 2015. 5v. illus. index. $495.00/set; $495.00 (e-book single user). ISBN 13: 978-1-61925-543-2; 978-1-61925-544-9 (e-book).

Whether you are just starting out in psychology or doing some quick fact checking, a good subject encyclopedia can be a great tool. There are many choices out there, and the fourth edition of *Salem Health: Psychology & Behavioral Health* is among the best. The college student will find that this five-volume set provides context for the many diverse areas of psychology, while offering structure and needed grounding when crafting a paper or assignment for class. There are 650 articles, nearly 100 are new and on current topics such as DSM-V controversies, Hoarding, and Exercise addiction. Culturally diverse material is a welcome inclusion with 18 articles listed under the multicultural category index. Scope is wide ranging, covering most areas of psychology and including historical, biographical, clinical, cognitive, forensic, and behavioral topics, to name just a few. Articles are written clearly and structured in a way that will be helpful to students, providing the type of psychology, an abstract, and key concepts. A bibliography completes each article and cross-referencing to other articles within the set will help with navigation. There are a number of useful and substantial appendixes (glossary, directories) and among them the Mediagraphy is an interesting feature. In this section are annotations of feature films and other mass media describing their relevance to psychology. *Psychology & Behavioral Health* would be an excellent addition for academic and public libraries.— **Lorraine Evans**

Handbooks and Yearbooks

497.   Bannink, Fredrike. **101 Solution-Focused Questions Series Set.** New York, W. W. Norton, 2015. 3v. $39.95pa./set. ISBN 13: 978-0-393-71125-7.

This set of three multicolored books is an attractive addition to a budding therapist's literary collection. Each book provides 101 questions for clients suffering from anxiety, depression, or trauma in order to provide healing. Solutions-focused and cognitive behavior therapy are both evidence-based practices, and this title provides the kind of applicable information that may be appropriate for professionals who have more experience in research and academia and less in conducting therapy. While not an academic resource, this title will undoubtedly be helpful for some.

Each book is divided into the same 10 chapters. Diagrams and exercises are provided to aid clients in mentally reframing their situations. A references section lists all individuals and studies used, and a brief Websites page provides links for additional information. An index helps readers locate subjects. This is an excellent title for students in psychology or those new to the practice of therapy, though seasoned therapists will likely be familiar with a solutions-focused approach and may find it repetitive.—**ARBA Staff Reviewer**

498.   Cohen, Lisa J., comp. **The Handy Psychology Answer Book.** 2d ed. Canton, Mich., Visible Ink Press, 2016. 544p. illus. index. $21.95pa. ISBN 13: 978-1-57859-600-3; 978-1-57859-599-0 (e-book).

This second edition book is a useful contrast to much of the dull and dense material written in the field of psychology. A blend of academic research and interesting facts will keep readers hooked regardless of their background in the study. It is structured in a basic question-and-answer format and includes approximately 1,300 questions that are answered concisely in one or two paragraphs, allowing for the reader to choose whether to read it from cover to cover or to simply skim over the content they find most interesting. Students of psychology will find the content refreshing and straightforward to read, and the concepts are uncomplicated enough to be read by those entirely new to the field. Revised to the newest edition of the DSM-5 (Diagnostic and Statistical Manual of Mental Disorders), this title is guaranteed to be relevant.

The book is divided into 11 sections that cover various subjects from history to mental health to forensics. The table of contents also lists page numbers directly next to the chapters as well as the content covered in them in addition to a thorough index, making subject search easy. A helpful introduction covers basic information contained in the book and a further reading section will be useful for readers who want additional information on any given topic.—**ARBA Staff Reviewer**

499.   **Counseling   and   Therapy   Online: Current   Practices.   https://www. alexanderstreet.com/discipline/counseling-therapy.**   [Website]   Alexandria,   Va., Alexander Street Press. Price negotiated by site. Date reviewed: 2016.

Counseling and Therapy Online is an online multimedia collection of current resources designed to support the study and practice of counseling and therapy. The collection includes e-books, periodicals, real-life counseling session transcripts, and over 1500 hours of video (presentations, lectures, and instructional). Collection development and maintenance is guided by a scholarly editorial review board committed to delivering current information in all of these formats.

The main page offers a search box and promotes browsing by field-specific subject: Presenting Condition, Therapeutic Approach, Content Type, and Publisher. Selecting any one of these options then takes users to a screen with a wide array of options for narrowing the search such as therapist/psychologist, school of therapy, psychotherapy collection as well as standard criteria such as date, content type, and publisher. Users can also refine by format type (text, video).

The results list includes a thumbnail image (giving a nice visual aspect to navigation in general), a one-to-two sentence description, and links to save the result to a list, cite it, or share it via email or social media channels.

The really unique and useful feature of the collection is the recordings of actual client therapy sessions. These resources have application in both study and practice. These transcripts have loads of metadata for the researcher/student to mine such as age of therapist, therapeutic approach, specialized area of interest, counseling type, etc.

This thoughtful and powerful resource has obviously been built with both study and practice in mind. As a multimodal collection, it brings together a wealth of resources that address the real-life needs of practicing counselors and it appears to strive for currency with contemporary issues. It will be extremely valuable for students (both undergrad and graduate) and practitioners. It may also be a useful tool for large behavioral health centers as it provides not only case studies from real life counseling sessions, but it provides access to a lot of practical resources (tool boxes, handbooks, etc.)—**Kristin Kay Leeman**

500. Cozolino, Louis. **Why Therapy Works: Using Our Minds to Change Our Brains.** New York, W. W. Norton, 2016. 271p. index. (Norton Series on Interpersonal Neurobiology). $23.95. ISBN 13: 978-0-393-70905-6.

This book addresses the many ways therapy works for clients. From understanding brain programming and evolution to navigating the difficulties of anxiety and trauma, *Why Therapy Works* addresses a wide range of human behavior and phenomena from a psychological perspective. Students in the field will find this work helpful and illuminating, while those curious about the often mysterious mechanisms of therapy will find answers to their questions.

Chapters are divided into three parts addressing The Thinking Brain, The Social Brain, and Dissociation and Integration. Each chapter opens with a philosophical quote, encouraging readers to engage with the material in a more subjective and less theoretical manner. The book flows naturally and could easily be read in one sitting given its clean and accessible writing. Even newbies to the field will find the language easy to comprehend. For more difficult-to-understand concepts, readers can look to the textboxes entitled "Neuroscience Corner" throughout the pages to better grasp academic concepts, such as neuroplasticity or apoptosis. Though there is no glossary, an index will aid with keyword searching. This title will be most useful for students in the field of psychology and those looking to determine if therapy is right for them.—**ARBA Staff Reviewer**

501. France, Kenneth. **Crisis Intervention: A Handbook of Immediate Person-to-Person Help.** 6th ed. Springfield, Ill., Charles C. Thomas, 2014. 324p. index. $54.95pa.; $54.95 (e-book). ISBN 13: 978-0-398-08106-5; 978-0-398-08107-2 (e-book).

In the sixth edition of Kenneth France's *Crisis Intervention,* readers can expect to find effective solutions for crises ranging from suicide to confined disasters. In this updated edition, France draws on theories from renowned psychologists to explain common thought processes of individuals who create or contribute to crisis, and then provides proven methods based on academic research to inform interveners how they can best prevent a crisis from escalating as well as support victims who have already suffered from disastrous experiences. All examples are based on real-life scenarios. Chapters are followed by an extensive references section and both a name and subject index to assist in key word search. Also helpful are study questions at the end of each chapter that allow readers to apply the content to situations they may encounter in their own lives. There is no glossary, which would have been a useful tool for readers who are less familiar with psychology terminology and theories, but France does an adequate job of providing basic definitions of relevant vocabulary within the text.

This title is likely to be found in general circulation and would serve as an excellent resource for individual interveners such as caregivers, social workers, psychologists, and individuals employed in corrections.—**ARBA Staff Reviewer**

502.   Horovitz, Ellen G. **The Art Therapists' Primer: A Clinical Guide to Writing Assessments, Diagnosis, and Treatment.** 2d ed. Springfield, Ill., Charles C. Thomas, 2014. 380p. index. $74.95; $64.95 (e-book). ISBN 13: 978-0-398-08110-2; 978-0-398-08111-9 (e-book).

Dr. Ellen G. Horovitz's second edition of *The Art Therapist" Primer* is a helpful reference manual for those studying or already employed in the field of art therapy. The treatise is not only helpful for reference, but is also a clinical guide that provides a step-by-step methodology for therapists to use when conducting studies. As is referenced in the title of the book, readers will find helpful information related to writing assessments, diagnosis, and treatment. For those newer to the field, a helpful preface tells "how to use this book," and the straightforward table of contents is easy to navigate; it is divided into five sections that instruct on processing notes, implementing qualitative assessments, and the use of standardized instruments.

A DVD compatible with Windows and Mac OS is provided in the back of the book and includes the Appendix Forms (A-L), all images contained in the book by chapter, and three movies that instruct on how to conduct the CATA, ATDA, and BATA. Readers can find both a name and subject index for reference as well.

Because *The Art Therapists' Primer* is a collaborative effort that comprises the knowledge and insights of dozens of researchers, this manual will prove useful for art therapists at any stage of their careers. However, due to its specialized nature and advanced terminology, this would not be a helpful guide for those merely interested in art therapy with no plans for formal study or prior degrees in the field.—**ARBA Staff Reviewer**

503.   Korn, Leslie E. **Nutrition Essentials for Mental Health: A Complete Guide to the Food-Mood Connection.** New York, W. W. Norton, 2016. 464p. index. $42.50. ISBN 13: 978-0-393-70994-0.

Dr. Leslie Korn's comprehensive guide to food-mood connection is a much needed addition to the field of mental health. Few mental health professionals have training in nutrition, something that greatly affects behavior and emotions, and this guide will help them in a variety of ways. The title addresses why nutrition matters, nutritional culprits that wreak havoc on the body, assessment techniques for evaluating client nutritional needs, and more. Dr. Korn even discusses the effects of foods and nutrients on DSM-5 categories of illness, and addresses alternatives to medication through diet change.

The book is divided into nine highly detailed chapters. While there is some scientific language, all terminology is thoroughly explained and those already in the field will likely be familiar with most of it. Though the book is written by and for clinicians, clients and those interested in nutrition will also find this book accessible. Chapter three is particularly helpful for therapists, as it includes a clinician checklist, food journals, and sample dialogue with a client for those new to addressing nutrition in a clinical counseling session. This easy-to-read guide is an invaluable resource for mental health professionals and is highly recommended. The book includes appendixes, an index, and references for further reading.—**ARBA Staff Reviewer**

504.   Mondimore, Francis Mark, and Patrick Kelly. **Adolescent Depression: A Guide for Parents.** Baltimore, Md., Johns Hopkins University Press, 2015. 408p. illus. index. $21.95pa. ISBN 13: 978-1-4214-1790-5.

Adolescent Depression is a helpful title for parents or guardians who know or have a child suffering from depression early in life. In this book, psychiatrists Francis Mark Mondimore, MD, and Patrick Kelly, MD, explore the reasons for adolescent depression as well as effective treatments for it. Included are step-by-step instructions for getting care for adolescents with depression, finding best fit doctors for treatment, and aiding children in the recovering process. The authors also explore the differences and similarities between depression and personality disorders, as well as the interactions between depression and Asperger's syndrome, eating disorders, premenstrual disorders, ADHD, and disruptive mood regulation. The writing is clear and concise, and diagrams are incorporated sporadically throughout the book to support understanding of difficult concepts.

Resources in the back of the book will prove helpful for individuals looking for additional resources to assist in their research. A small subject index will prove useful for those who require information on specific disorders, medications, or behaviors. In addition, a few pages dedicated to suggested readings, Internet resources, and advocacy organizations will help parents and guardians decide on the next step in assisting their children. Because of its specialization, this book will provide significantly more applicable information than any general psychology text that covers a variety of mental health disorders.—**ARBA Staff Reviewer**

505.   **Oxford Clinical Psychology. http://www.oxfordclinicalpsych.com/.** [Website] New York, Oxford University Press. Price negotiated by site. Date reviewed: 2015.

This online database provides users access to more than 100 titles in Oxford University Press's global clinical psychology publishing program, which includes reference books, scholarly and research works, and therapist guides and workbooks from the Treatments That Work series. The database is designed for use by clinical psychologists in academic settings and in practice, for professors and instructors, and for students, interns, and trainees in clinical psychology. The regularly updated database will grow to include over 300 titles. The works are all written by accomplished, world-class authors and editors, giving users reassurance regarding the academic integrity of the information on the site.

In terms of navigation, the database is simple to use. Help tutorials and guidelines are provided, but most researchers will be able to skip these due to the intuitive design of the interface. From the main page, users can conduct a quick search from a simple search box, but searches can also be started by using one of three options. The first, Specialty, includes Geropsychology, Psychotherapy, School Psychology, and more. Disorders and Clinical Problems, the second option, allows users to choose from such topics as Anger Disorders, Hoarding Disorder, or Trauma. The third search option, Series, offers a choice of titles from Best Practices in Forensic Mental Health Assessments, Oxford Guides to Cognitive Behavioural Therapy, Programs That Work, Specialty Competencies in Professional Psychology, Treatments That Work, and Other. Searches can be narrowed further by using tools on the left-hand side of the page. For example, a quick search of hoarding will result in a list of 65 chapters and the three books in which they appear. From here, a click on the title of Gail Steketee and Randy O. Frost's book *Treatment for Hoarding Disorder:*

Therapist Guide (2 ed.) produces an index card with an abstract, keywords, bibliographic information, and two brief biographies of the authors. Below this is a list of chapters in the book and a column on the left-hand side of the page with further links and information. Alternatively these same three books on hoarding could be found using the Hoarding Disorder link under Disorders and Clinical Problems. An added bonus is the Oxford Index Underbar, which allows users to search across all Oxford University Press journals and scholarly works. A toolbar at the top of the screen enables users to print, email, save and cite results. MLA, APA, AMA, and Chicago citations are offered; citations can be exported in a Word document, EndNote, ProCite, ReferenceManager, RefWorks, BibTeX, and Zotero (BibTeX). The database also features the ability to enlarge and download images; forms and checklists in the Treatments That Work series can be downloaded, edited, and saved for use in classroom and clinical settings.

Oxford Clinical Psychology provides a place for students (upper-level undergraduate and above), professors and teachers, and practitioners to conduct a thorough secondary search of clinical psychology journals and books available from Oxford University Press. More than a research vehicle, however, the database provides users with a reliable place to access images, forms, checklists, and lecture materials. Highly recommended for medical and academic libraries.—**ARBA Staff Reviewer**

506.   Simpson, Chris. **Cutting and Self-Harm.** Santa Barbara, Calif., Greenwood Press/ABC-CLIO, 2015. 193p. index. (Health and Medical Issues Today). $39.00. ISBN 13: 978-1-61069-872-6; 978-1-61069-873-3 (e-book).

The Health & Medical Issues Today series is designed to be a concise, balanced, and informative source of the latest information regarding a number of the more sensitive issues in health care today. This volume in the series addresses cutting and self-harm, issues which have gathered significant interest over the last 30 years. It is important to note, as this book deals with serious medical issues, that its discussion of treatments, diagnoses, etc. is not meant to replace consultation with qualified medical professionals.

Three smartly arranged sections make the information easy to digest. The first section defines and analyzes the many aspects of cutting and other ways people choose to harm themselves. Five chapters manage the material here, with many brief, well-defined paragraphs within. Topics include the history and basic characteristics of self-harm, the many reasons (e.g., biological, environmental, etc.) for cutting or committing self-harm, how the acts relate to other conditions, such as eating disorders, how to respond to someone who self-injures, and how to treat and prevent the behaviors.

Section two deals with some of the debate which surrounds the acts of cutting and self-harm. Four chapters explore self-harm at school, the impact on relationships, the use of group counseling, and the use of medication. Particular topics describe the ethical and legal concerns which confront the school personnel who encounter a self-harm situation, how group therapy might be helpful or harmful, and how medication might affect brain chemistry.

The final section offers a number of resources including Websites, books, and research documents; relevant documents including an essay titled "Mythbuster: Sorting Fact from Fiction on Self-Harm"; a glossary; a timeline; a bibliography; and an index. The book also includes several tables and case examples throughout.—**Laura Herrell**

Parapsychology

Dictionaries and Encyclopedias

507.   **Ghosts, Spirits, and Psychics: The Paranormal from Alchemy to Zombies.** Matt Cardin, ed. Santa Barbara, Calif., ABC-CLIO, 2015. 409p. index. $89.00. ISBN 13: 978-1-61069-683-8; 978-1-61069-684-5 (e-book).

Though many consider stories of the occult, the paranormal, or their related aspects such as psychics and ghosts to be remnants of a bygone, more superstitious era, one will often find that such phenomenon have had an important contribution to various cultures and creative traditions. This work seeks to serve as an introduction to such topics and to broaden the reader's perspectives on how they have influenced different sections of society. This includes not only popular culture but also art, literature, religion, and even the beginnings of science.

Through a selection of 120 articles each written by experts in their respective fields, this title provides a comprehensive overview of paranormal topics including psychics, spiritualism, alien phenomenon, and magic as well as detailing important individuals and organizations that have contributed to the study of these fields. Entries are listed alphabetically and the book includes a detailed index for quick reference. Topics vary from individual phenomenon, individuals, or concepts to larger schools of thought or societies. Each entry also possesses references to other topics in the text and a brief bibliography for further reading. Other features contained in the book include a master timeline of important historical events, sidebars within entries for additional information, and a more general bibliography at the end of the text.

One does question the editor's choice as to how certain entries should be listed and thereby which information is deserving of an individual entry. Examples of this would be the lack of entries for such individuals as Aleister Crowley and Madame Helena Blavatsky. While there is information on these individuals contained in the entries for Occultism and Theosophy, respectively, it is curious that they were not given their own entries while other persons of interest did receive such attention. Despite this they are mentioned in the index which overall proves to be a more than adequate reference for the entire work. On the whole this work is good introductory reference for general readers, high school students, or entry-level college students.—**W. Cole Williamson**

15 Recreation and Sports

General Works

Dictionaries and Encyclopedias

508. Thompson, William N. **Gambling in America: An Encyclopedia of History, Issues, and Society.** 2d ed. Santa Barbara, Calif., ABC-CLIO, 2015. 505p. illus. index. $89.00. ISBN 13: 978-1-61069-979-2; 978-1-61069-980-8 (e-book).

Gambling in mainstream American life is a significant social and economic issue and *Gambling in America* is a concise encyclopedic look at what is a multimillion-dollar industry. This second edition (the first was published in 2001, see ARBA 2002, entry 824) presents 187 entries with nearly 100 covering nations, states, cities, and territories. Twenty-five feature individuals ranging from the well-known Howard Hughes to the lesser-known Moe Dalitz. Many entries are longer essays focusing on broader issues such as horse racing, sports betting, and lotteries. Entries are clearly written, avoid bias, and include reading references. There are generous illustrations, 10 tables, and an appendix with 13 major gambling legal cases. The comprehensive volume also includes a glossary, bibliography, and 20-page index—the last of which could be improved. Also of interest is a 17-page glossary of gambling events. Many individuals and events are embedded in larger entries such as the point shaving scandal at Boston College in college basketball and the many subsections in the entry on problem gambling. No one is more qualified than editor Thompson who has written widely on gambling in America for years. In all, this is a useful addition for reference collections on an often-overlooked social issue across the world.—**Boyd Childress**

509. Williams, Victoria. **Weird Sports and Wacky Games around the World.** Santa Barbara, Calif., Greenwood Press/ABC-CLIO, 2015. 369p. illus. index. $89.00. ISBN 13: 978-1-61069-639-5; 978-1-61069-640-1 (e-book).

While it is not likely that many of the somewhat stranger pastimes will take over the popularity of, say, World Cup Soccer, it is definite that readers will find *Weird Sports and Wacky Games around the World* highly informative and engaging. While primarily designed as a research tool, the book nonetheless encompasses a fun topic that even general readers will enjoy.

Over 100 alphabetized entries showcase obscure yet beloved sports and games from around the world. Each entry provides general rules, in addition to any relevant history, folklore, literature, politics, and more surrounding the topic. Individual entries range in length from just under two pages to several pages and are followed by *see also* references and suggestions for future reading. We learn of broader sports that have been adapted geographically, like Elephant Sports (that is polo, soccer, and racing with pachyderms), and we learn of a simple pub game called Shove Ha'Penny which, though a mere board game for two, has nonetheless managed to hold an annual world championship. Readers certainly take away elements of fun and entertainment. Who wouldn't want to try a rousing game of Sepak Takraw, a Southeast Asian game which adapts elements of volleyball, soccer, gymnastics, and martial arts? But readers are also able to see how play remains a vital part of the human experience well into adulthood and throughout all cultures.

The book begins with an alphabetical list of entries, a geographic guide to entry origins by region, and a thematic guide to entries. It also includes a few black-and-white photographs, a selected bibliography, and an index. This highly recommended title is a handy place for students of all ages to begin a research project; though organized as an encyclopedia the fascinating subject matter makes this a good candidate for a cover-to-cover read for both students and the general public.—**Laura Herrell**

Directories

510.   **The Sports Market Place Directory, 2015.** Amenia, N.Y., Grey House Publishing, 2015. 1800p. index. $265.00pa. ISBN 13: 978-1-61925-562-3.

Need names and organizations for the sports business, then look no further. This massive (and expensive) volume lists over 14,000 contacts covering 100 sports in over 2,000 pages. There are nine specific categories covering specific sports, college sports, media information, facilities, and trade shows—and others. There are indexes for main entries, executives, and a geographic index. Two specific examples help explain—the section on college sports has over 1,700 listings including conferences and schools in the NCAA and NAIA. Each entry includes key personnel with contact information, Websites, e-mail addresses, fax and phone numbers, and a brief summary of sports the institution sponsors. There are outdated entries due to changes in coaches and administrations but the contact information is invaluable. The other example is 300 pages of media information including newspapers, magazines, and the electronic media. A typical listing includes contacts, phone and fax numbers, e-mail and Website information, and a brief description of coverage. Once again some names are out of date due to personnel changes. But overall the information is as accurate as reasonably possible. Grey House has been publishing this sports market directory for over 30 years and the volume has been a must for collections serving a sports business audience. Much of the information is now accessible on the Internet but the location of so much sports business in one source makes this a useful reference volume.—**Boyd Childress**

Handbooks and Yearbooks

511.   Beckinsale, James. **The Triathalon Training Book.** New York, DK Publishing, 2016. 168p. illus. index. $19.95pa. ISBN 13: 978-1-4654-4417-2.

The interdisciplinary and intense nature of the triathlon can certainly make it seem daunting. After all, they don't call its ultimate event the Ironman for nothing. This book, however, does a great job of empowering readers to accept the challenge of a triathlon, whether it be the basic sprint or the mighty Ironman itself, by outlining clear training steps for each component of the race, then putting it all together for a solid race-day plan.

The book organizes the material by separating the components of the triathlon: swimming, cycling, and running, into sections or "labs." Chapters within address general topics such as anatomy, efficiency, or apparel and tie them to their specific event, so that readers learn how different muscle groups are used for different events, how different exercises will prepare those muscles, and so on. Other sections of the book mark steps in a complete plan to get readers through race day. Getting Started focuses on goals, nutrition, and more. Personalize Your Training helps readers create a training profile and then offers several distinct training programs. The Race focuses on final preparations, hydration tips, and tactics. A final section, Essential Maintenance, notes common complaints and injuries, with a glossary and index adding helpful reference.

Reflecting the publisher's signature style, the book contains a plethora of full-color photographs, tables, text boxes, Q & A, and more which enhance the material visually and make it memorable. In addition, the book makes for a dynamic read with its many tips, exercise demonstrations, training schedules, and more. Whether a seasoned athlete or a novice, it would be difficult not to be inspired by the information in and design of this book. Recommended.—**ARBA Staff Reviewer**

512.   Freedman, Lew. **The 100 Most Important Sporting Events in American History.** Santa Barbara, Calif., Greenwood Press/ABC-CLIO, 2016. 385p. illus. index. $89.00. ISBN 13: 978-1-4408-3574-2; 978-1-4408-3575-9 (e-book).

Lew Freedman has written dozens of books on sports history, including ones on baseball, football, basketball, auto racing, and dog sledding, so he is more than qualified to write on the variety of events selected here.

The 100 entries are not the necessarily the best or most significant games in history. In his selections, Freedman gave "more weight to sports developments that ultimately shaped individual habits or ways of thinking." (xvii) Many are not even specific events, but rather processes. For example, "Sports Come to Radio" is entry six and "Sports Come to Television" is entry seven. Other entries are devoted to individual athletes such as Jim Thorpe (entry 15), Joe Louis (entry four), or Jackie Robinson (entry one). The top-ranked contest is 1980's Miracle on Ice (entry two). Other high-ranking games include the 1958 NFL championship (entry 16), all-black Texas Western winning the NCAA basketball title (entry 20), and Don Larsen's perfect game in the World Series (entry 25).

By my rough count, 28 entries are just about sports, 21 deal with transcendental athletes, seven highlight innovators, five are concerned with tragedy, 13 involve culture, media, and politics, and 26 are focused on race, ethnicity, and gender. By sport, Freedman leans heavily to baseball. Twenty-eight entries are about that sport, with 19 on basketball, 14 on football, 10 on the Olympics, and the rest spread across many other sports.

Not surprisingly, the selections themselves are the controversial feature of the book. As noted above, there are twice as many entries on baseball as there are for football despite football being the nation's most popular and culturally omnipresent sport for approximately the last 50 years. In this dumbfounding light, the World Series is entry 12, but the Super Bowl is not listed at all! There is no more culturally ubiquitous event in American society, so its absence here is a gaping hole. This reviewer was surprised that several other essential topics are missing from this volume: steroids and performance-enhancing drugs; Arnold Palmer and his role both in the rise of golf and sports agents; the formation of the NCAA; Madden Football and gaming; Nike and its pervasive influence across sports; the modern political practice of pitting cities against one another to publicly finance new stadiums; the mergers of established and upstart leagues in football, basketball, and hockey in the 1960s and 1970s; plus several unmentioned giants such as Tom Brady, Joe Montana, Sugar Ray Robinson, and Sugar Ray Leonard.

Most entries run for three or four pages; each is thorough and lively and includes a bibliography and notes. Black-and-white photos illustrate several entries, and there is an index

Inspiring thought and discussion is a good thing. Freedman's book encourages reasoned disagreement and would be welcome in any sports collection.—**John Maxymuk**

513. **Sports-Reference.com. http://www.sports-reference.com/.** [Website] Free. Date reviewed: 2016.

Sports-Reference.com provides users with freely accessible, complete sports statistics. The site that began as *Baseball-Reference.com* has expanded to include football, basketball, hockey, and the Olympics. Users will find player indexes, team histories, draft information, and much more by clicking on the appropriate tab at the top of the page. Statistics extend back to different dates depending on the sport. In the case of baseball, data is available as far back as 1871. Navigation within a sport is simple and intuitive. For someone wishing to see the trade history between two baseball franchises, for example, it only takes a couple of clicks to land on a baseball team's encyclopedia.

While the advertisements on the free site are not intrusive, a modest $20/year fee will allow ad-free browsing of the entire Sports-Reference family of sites.—**ARBA Staff Reviewer**

Baseball

514. Cava, Pete. **Indiana-Born Major League Baseball Players: A Biographical Dictionary, 1871-2014.** Jefferson, N.C., McFarland, 2015. 247p. index. $39.95pa. ISBN 13: 978-0-7864-9901-4; 978-1-4766-2270-5 (e-book).

Indiana is a state famously known for basketball, but this book highlights the impact Hoosiers have had on major league baseball. It is a straight alphabetical listing of the 364 Indianans who have appeared in a major league baseball game since the start of the National Association in 1871 through 2014. Defunct leagues such as the Union Association, Players' League and Federal League are included, but the Negro Leagues are not, so Indiana-born Hall of Fame African American Oscar Charleston is not included, for example. There are 10 Hall of Fame players as well as 58 of the 174 inductees of the little-known Indiana Baseball Hall of Fame included here.

Each entry begins with basic biographical data, such as positions, teams, and years played, as well as summary major league statistics. This information is followed by a fairly detailed biography for each player.

The earliest entry I noticed was for Al Barker who was born in 1839 and played for Rockford of the National Association in 1871. Entries are filled with fascinating details:

Grover Lowdermilk was the single-season minor league strikeout king; Scott Sheldon was the first American-born player to play all nine positions in a game; Bert Shepard was the only man to play in the majors with an artificial leg. Even players who appeared in just one game in the big leagues, such as Jack Corriden, Dutch Fehring and Meow Gilmore, are given their full due here.

Cava's deep research has uncovered some telling nuggets and colorful quotes, For instance, Senators' manager Ossie Bluege summed up pitcher Red Cary in 1947 with: "He can't brush you back with his fastball, and his curve isn't the sharpest in the league, but he can thread the needle with that ball, and as soon as he learns a batter's blind spot, he's got him." Cary was back in the minors in 1948.

The book is extremely well-executed; its only flaw is that it occupies such a narrow niche of a market. There is a bibliography and an index, but no appendixes. An appendix listing the 58 members of the Indiana Baseball Hall of Fame indicated in the text would have been nice. It's also surprising that the author resisted the urge to name his own 25-man roster of the greatest of these Hoosier ballplayers. If anyone wants to read about the lives and careers of the Throwin' Kokomoan (Joe Thatcher), Hammond Hummer (Bob Anderson), Slinger from Servia (John Eubank), Terre Haute Terror (Art Nehf) or Hoosier Schoolmaster (Vic Aldridge), this is the place to do so.—**John Maxymuk**

515. Gorman, Robert M., and David Weeks. **Death at the Ballpark: More Than 2,000 Game-Related Fatalities of Players, Other Personnel and Spectators in Amateur and Professional Baseball, 1862-2014.** 2d ed. Jefferson, N.C., McFarland, 2015. 344p. illus. index. $39.95pa. ISBN 13: 978-0-7864-7932-0; 978-1-4766-2258-3 (e-book).

Today's baseball fans likely would be surprised to discover that in 1930 the *New York Times* declared baseball the "most dangerous recreation." (p.5) That this unusual book detailing some 2,000 baseball-related deaths is now published in a second edition is clear tribute to baseball fans' fascination with statistics of all varieties and to the determination and diligence of its authors who have pursued their unusual subject for almost 15 years. As Gorman and Weeks graciously note, two other researchers, Ed Morton and Chuck McGill, also mined old newspapers and related sources and contributed greatly to the compilation of more than 1,000 additional baseball death reports not printed in the first edition. Interestingly, the authors note that the office of the Commissioner of Baseball does not track fan injuries and they recommend several practical safety measures to protect fans of sandlot games, high school and college contests, semi-pro, minor league, and major league contests.

Here Gorman and Weeks repeat their goal as given in the preface to the first edition, to provide "a comprehensive study of game-related baseball fatalities among players, field personnel, and fans at all levels of play in the United States." Each death is placed in the context of contributing factors and subsequent changes in the game of baseball including "style of play, the development of protective equipment, crowd control, stadium structure, and so forth." (p. 2) The authors provide specific and detailed definitions of game-related deaths and include all fan deaths if the deaths occurred "on the grounds," defined as the stadium, field, or parking lot. Section one of the book contains nine chapters tallying specific forms of death ranging from beaning to weather and violence. Section two offers two chapters on the deaths of field personnel. Section three presents four chapters on the deaths of fans. Appendix A covers unconfirmed fatalities based on plausible but possibly unreliable newspaper accounts. Appendix B yields a chronology of all fatalities by decades, from the 1860s through September 2014. Detailed chapter notes cite sources used and the bibliography includes books, journal and magazine articles, newspapers by state and city, other documents, and online indexes and databases. The index permits readers to locate death reports by name of person, location, league, and team. Reproductions of black-and-white photographs and drawings enhance the text. This book belongs in large public library and college or university baseball collections but its distinctive subject matter will be of interest to a wide range of baseball fans as well as many baseball players of all ages and to researchers interested in the sociology of sports.—**Julienne L. Wood**

516.   Wirkmaa, Andres. **The Complete Baseball Scorekeeping Handbook.** Jefferson, N.C., McFarland, 2015. 256p. index. $35.00pa. ISBN 13: 978-0-7864-7994-8; 978-1-4766-1525-7 (e-book).

The Complete Baseball Scorekeeping Handbook is in some ways an updated version of the author's 2003 *Baseball Scorekeeping: A Practical Guide to the Rules.* It is, however, completely rewritten and presented in a new format; the new handbook also reflects Major League Baseball's rule changes. The author, a retired baseball coach and member of the Society for American Baseball Research, has worked as an official scorekeeper in the amateur baseball leagues and is a recognized baseball scorekeeping expert.

The book covers everything a baseball scorekeeper needs to know, from what appears on the card, to abbreviations used, to the official scorekeeping rules and their applications. All of this information is enhanced by black-and-white scorecard illustrations. The book concludes with a subject index. Recommended for public libraries.—**ARBA Staff Reviewer**

Boxing

517.   Fernandez, Robert F., Sr. **Boxing in New Jersey, 1900-1999.** Jefferson, N.C., McFarland, 2014. 194p. index. $29.95pa. ISBN 13: 978-0-7864-9476-7; 978-1-4766-1607-0 (e-book).

Jersey Joe Walcott. Smoking Joe Frazier. Rocky Graziano. If these names don't "ring a bell," then *Boxing in New Jersey 1900-1999* will provide an enjoyable and informative reminder of these boxing legends and more. The author calls upon his extensive background in the sport (he has been an amateur fighter, trainer and, memorabilia collector, among other things) to share highly engaging stories of the daring and dangerous men who earned their pay by "kayo."

The sport of boxing has developed along a winding path moving from ancient Mesopotamian origins through late-seventeenth-century British refinement and ultimately to what now is a glamorous multimillion-dollar industry. This book, centered on the gyms and boxing rings in the state of New Jersey, presents a unique perspective on what boxing meant to twentieth-century America. In chapters filled with the sweat of boxing gyms and the din of arenas, we are introduced to a colorful cast of characters. There are, of course, the famous names like Graziano, an "incorrigible punk" who used boxing to keep him on the right side of the law. But we also read of more obscure fighters like Chuck Wepner, who was known to bleed easily, or Charley Fusari, who looked like a Hollywood star and got into fighting shape by climbing stairs and carrying bottles in his day job as a milkman. In addition we meet the trainers, promoters, managers, and others who orbit the prizefighting world and were often as intriguing as their charges. In the background are various wars, the economic hardships of the Great Depression, the advent of television, and more.

Each chapter is filled with rich and abundant details, allowing readers the electric sensation of sitting ringside at each bout. We see the swollen eyes, the bloody noses, and the puffed faces. We hear the bells, the "boos," and the Bronx cheers. And we feel the elation and exhaustion accompanying each match. Writing in the gritty vernacular of one immersed in twentieth-century American boxing's hard-scrabble, adrenaline-fueled world ("they hotfooted around that ring with the Brown Bomber in hot pursuit"), the author demonstrates his abundant respect and passion for the sport and its "warriors" and "gladiators." Including 50 questions of boxing trivia, this book offers a hugely entertaining slice of American sporting lore that will engage boxing fans, history lovers, and others through and through.

Illustrations would have enhanced the lively text, but the reader is provided with an index that allows for a quick search of a book that could also be read cover to cover. Recommended for school and public libraries.—**Laura Herrell**

Chess

518. De Felice, Gino, comp. **Chess Competitions, 1971-2010.** Jefferson, N.C., McFarland, 2016. 368p. index. $49.95pa. ISBN 13: 978-1-4766-6207-7; 978-1-4766-2365-8 (e-book).

This book presents a dedicated, well-researched record of a variety of publications on chess competitions held globally between the years 1971 and 2010. An enormous undertaking, the book does not profess to be comprehensive. However, the author has amassed over 5,000 publications detailing nearly 4,000 chess competitions. These publications include books, bulletins, and competition programs.

With such material as this, organization is key. This book segments its information into five sections based on the type of chess competition described in the publication: Individual Tournaments, Individual Matches, Team Tournaments, Team Matches, and Correspondence Competitions. Competitions are numbered across all sections (e.g., the first competition in the second section will be numbered following the last competition in the first section). Publications are then numbered in accordance with their numbered competition. Competitions within each section are listed in alphabetical and chronological order. The listings are generously cross-referenced throughout all sections. Note that further organizational information is available in the book's introduction.

For the tournament sections, each entry lists the location of the tournament followed by the tournament date and name. Match sections first list the winner and loser followed by the year and location. Applicable publications are then listed, and may include publication name, issue number, author, place of publication, publisher, year, description, language, sources, and more.

Supplemental information will be extremely useful to finding and understanding entry particulars, and includes a list of abbreviations related to sources, a list of other abbreviations and symbols used, and an index of competitions arranged alphabetically by place.—**ARBA Staff Reviewer**

Cricket

519.   **Cricker: http://cricker.com/.** [Website] Free. Date reviewed: 2015.

Cricker is a recently updated informational Web page that provides information about cricket games. A useful News section at the top of the homepage provides the latest information about recent cricket matches around the world and reroutes users to ESPN to read in-depth articles about game highlights. The Scores page shows scores of games currently taking place, and users can click on the game they would like to view to be rerouted to ecb.co.uk. Here, they can see who won the toss, find out the names of the umpires and officials, obtain player information, and eventually learn the end score of the game.

Though the Website includes some distracting advertisements, it has a simple format and is straightforward to use.

Cricker's extensive glossary may be the best feature of the site, as it includes over a hundred cricket vocabulary words. The terms can be searched at the top of the page alphabetically, and any additional questions can be sent to *Cricker* representatives in the feedback section located on the About page.

Overall, *Cricker* is a great tool for avid cricket fans and those looking to improve their basic knowledge of cricket terminology, and perhaps follow their favorite teams. While the site is simple and free to use, it is easy for all age groups to navigate and is a recommended resource for those involved with cricket in any capacity.—**ARBA Staff Reviewer**

Hockey

520.   Fischler, Stan. **The Handy Hockey Answer Book.** Canton, Mich., Visible Ink Press, 2015. 369p. illus. index. $19.95pa. ISBN 13: 978-1-57859-513-6.

If readers ever doubted there was a lot to learn about the game of hockey, this volume in the Handy Answer series would certainly enlighten them.

Written with keen knowledge, genuine respect, and pure enthusiasm, *The Handy Hockey Answer Book* presents 14 chapters which begin with hockey's obscure origins (medieval ice golf, anyone?) then skate readers through the game's highlights and developments in each decade since the start of the twentieth century.

Like other works in this series, the story of hockey is presented in an engaging question-and-answer format. Chapters are arranged chronologically so readers can truly observe the sport's evolution. Questions run the gamut from "who is the highest scoring left-winger of all time" to "who was the shortest player to ever play in the NHL." Answers are thorough and very entertaining, and shed light on everything from common injuries, changes to the sport, coaches, dramatic victories, and stunning defeats. Even the casual fan will recognize the names of legends like Bobby Orr or Wayne Gretzky and teams like the L.A. Kings and Pittsburgh Penguins.

The book also includes black-and-white illustrations, a bibliography, two glossaries (one general and, interestingly, one devoted only to penalties), information on current NHL teams, the author's own list of the top 100 players, and an index.—**ARBA Staff Reviewer**

Outdoor Life

521.   Nyerges, Christopher. **How to Survive Anywhere.** 2d ed. Mechanicsburg, Pa., Stackpole Books, 2014. 296p. illus. index. $19.95pa. ISBN 13: 978-0-8117-1418-1.

One of the basic tents of modern survivalism holds that nature is everywhere. Another tenet posits that one should always be prepared for what nature throws at you. *How to Survive Anywhere* teaches basic survival skills for use in urban, suburban, and wilderness areas. Focusing on water, fire, food, shelter, clothing, and tools and weapons, the chapters offer easy to follow instructions and incorporate an abundant use of black-and-white photographs and illustrations (particularly helpful when demonstrating how to make something), comparison charts, and handy lists. Readers will also appreciate the delightful "in a nutshell" tips which offer quick summaries of each topic. The book also shares important material regarding navigation, hygiene, and first aid. A subject index also assists readers in finding information about particular topics.

The information is carefully considered against varying survival scenarios. For example, readers learn how to find and treat water sources in the wild, as well as how to store water in case municipal transports and sources are compromised. The second edition expands on chapter information and provides updates where necessary. An easy book to carry around, it is nonetheless filled with knowledge that anyone may find useful at any time, whether to enhance one's enjoyment of the great outdoors or to simply, as the Boy Scouts remind us, "be prepared."—**Laura Herrell**

Polo

522.   Laffaye, Horace A. **The Polo Encyclopedia. Second Edition.** Jefferson, N.C., McFarland, 2015. 411p. illus. $85.00pa. ISBN 13: 978-0-7864-9577-1; 978-1-4766-1956-9 (e-book).

This second edition of *The Polo Encyclopedia* updates the first edition in 2004 with the inclusion of approximately 8,000 more entries; previous entries were reviewed and corrected or deleted when necessary. The entries are cross-referenced and arranged alphabetically, providing a ready reference to more than 150 years of a game that is growing in popularity worldwide. The author, Horace A. Laffaye, has also written books on polo in Argentina, Britain, and the United States, as well as a book on how the sport has evolved. Users can find information on polo clubs worldwide, the rules of the game, individual riders, tournaments, technical polo terms, and more. The encyclopedia also has a generous sprinkling of black-and-white photographs, as well as several tables, like the one adjacent to the entry for the New Zealand Open that lists winners for the competition from 1977 to 2014. The cost of the book, $85.00 (paperback), and the breadth and quality of information makes this a good choice for libraries in need of information on this particular sport and for polo players and polo clubs everywhere.—**ARBA Staff Reviewer**

Soccer

523.   Dunmore, Tom. **Encyclopedia of the FIFA World Cup.** Lanham, Md., Rowman & Littlefield, 2015. 395p. index. $75.00; $74.99 (e-book). ISBN 13: 978-0-8108-8742-8; 978-0-8108-8743-5 (e-book).

Occurring every four years, the FIFA World Cup has come to be the world's largest staged sporting event, drawing soccer (or football) teams from over 200 eligible nations as well as hundreds of millions of television viewers. Producing many memorable moments from familiar players like Brazil's Pelé, England's Gary Lineker, or Germany's Thomas Müller, the competition continues to dazzle audiences and grow the sport. This encyclopedia is a necessary and thoroughly engaging companion to the sport that so many around the globe have come to adore.

Prefacing the alphabetical entries is an excellent and concise history of the tournament, beginning with the formation of the sport's governing body, FIFA (or the Fédération Internationale de Football Association), at the turn of the twentieth century. The preface touches on both moments of triumph, like the 1970 color television broadcast of Brazil's third tournament victory, and moments of controversy, such as the tournament's Eurocentric establishment or association with political propaganda. There is also a detailed tournament recap of each World Cup, including information such as host nation, number of matches, finalists, dates, and game highlights.

The entries themselves cover a wide range of players, countries, stadiums, coaches, awards, and other topics surrounding the tournament. Within the entries are fascinating facts and exciting moments from games worth reliving, such as American hero Landon Donovan's dramatic late goal against Algeria in the 2010 tournament, or French legend Zinedine Zidane's notorious red card received during the 2006 final. The book's encyclopedic format makes it easy for readers to track the ebbs and flows of a favorite player or home team. Including a number of appendixes to chart individual tournament award winners, the book offers entertaining, generous information about "the beautiful game" and its crowning tournament.—**Laura Herrell**

16 Sociology

General Works

Handbooks and Yearbooks

524. **The Sociology Book: Big Ideas Simply Explained.** New York, DK Publishing, 2015. 352p. illus. index. (Big Ideas Simply Explained). $25.00: $9.99 (e-book). ISBN 13: 978-1-4654-3650-4; 978-1-465445223 (e-book).

This survey starts with the founding fathers of sociology, like Auguste Comte, Karl Marx, and Emile Durkheim, and goes on to cover the broad spectrum of thought across the twentieth and into the twenty-first centuries. Essays encapsulate the key thoughts of a wide range of prominent sociologists with abundant graphics under the subject categories of Foundations of Sociology, Social Inequalities, Modern Living, Living in a Global World, Culture and Identity, Work and Consumerism, The Role of Institutions, and Families and Intimacies. Each section of essays starts with an introduction to set the context for the featured academicians. As a nice touch, each scholar's essay is cross-referenced to other relevant writers. A sociologist's work may be found in more than one category. For example, under the topic, Families and Intimacies, we learn about Michel Foucault's writings on how the advent of psychiatry melded with the longstanding Christian practice of confession to become a cultural obsession and means of therapy as seen in today's fixation on reality shows and social media. Foucault is then linked to Rousseau, Freud, and other thinkers. Foucault is also found in the category of Foundations of Sociology with his thoughts on power and in the category of The Role of Institutions with his comments on government. In addition to the featured sociologists, there is a directory with thumbnail sketches of additional scholars who have also contributed to the field. This episodic reference shows us an interesting cross-section of this field of study and helps us understand how our behavior is shaped and how changes come about in society.—**Adrienne Antink**

Family, Marriage, and Divorce

Handbooks and Yearbooks

525. Bakst, Dina, Phoebe Taubman, and Elizabeth Gedmark. **Babygate: How to Survive Pregnancy & Parenting in the Workplace.** New York, Feminist Press, 2014. 343p. $18.95pa. ISBN 13: 978-1-55861-861-9.

The practical issues of welcoming a baby are many: spit-up, sleepless nights, and mountains of diapers among them. But today's expectant mothers face other challenges stemming from the fact that many are employed, and the climate in which they work may not be supportive of them. *Babygate* addresses those issues which specifically arise at the intersection of work and family life and aims to educate women about their legal rights.

Four chapters work along the timeline of informing employers of the happy news, managing the job as you plan for parental leave, returning to work after the baby's birth, and dealing with subtle but no less damaging issues of workplace stigma and prejudice. The book helps readers walk through the labyrinth of legislation which may or may not be relevant, such as the Family and Medical Leave Act of 1993 (applicable only to companies employing over 50 people, for example), the Americans with Disabilities Act (ADA), and the Pregnancy Discrimination Act, among others. Chapters take care to share real-life scenarios as they discuss issues like interviewing for a job while pregnant, breastfeeding on the job, initiating a flexible work schedule, and much more. The authors make generous use of personal stories, Q & A's, shaded sidebars, checklists, and other tools to make this important information truly accessible and easy to remember.

The book also provides thorough notes and numerous resources to address specific concerns from filing a claim with the Department of Labor, finding the most family-friendly companies, and understanding child and dependent care tax credits. It concludes with a very helpful state-by-state guide detailing the applicable legal mandates and methods of recourse. The state-by-state guide employs illustrative symbols for easy reference.

This book works as a true ally in educating family-minded women about their legal rights in the workplace.—**ARBA Staff Reviewer**

526. Day, Lori, and Charlotte Kugler. **Her Next Chapter: How Mother-Daughter Book Clubs Can Help Girls Navigate Malicious Media, Risky Relationships, Girl Gossip, and So Much More.** Chicago, Chicago Review Press, 2014. 250p. index. $16.95pa. ISBN 13: 978-1-61374-856-5.

It is estimated that some five million adults participate in clubs wherein avid literature lovers gather to discuss a mutually agreed upon book they have all ostensibly read. Aside from improving one's literary comprehension, these groups offer added bonuses of good snacks and bonding. Enter the mother-daughter book group and the book *Her Next Chapter*, which highlights the many benefits of navigating this female and familial road via literature and other media.

Parenting coach and educational psychologist Lori Day, alongside her student-daughter Charlotte Kugler, have certainly exposed a delightful way to encourage mother-daughter quality time and a love of literature. But the key is what lies beyond the bonding—a fun, organic opportunity to address the big issues relevant to girls today, such as bullying, body image, premature sexualization, gender stereotyping, and more.

This book provides a host of diverse books, television shows, films, and other media that can serve as excellent launching points for solid discussion on these matters. Choices represent both sides of the coin: the authors may recommend watching the distressingly vapid *Toddlers and Tiaras* alongside reading the smart and serious *The Hunger Games* to address such issues as femininity and sexualization. In addition to the many recommendations, the authors include discussion questions, personal reflections, key takeaways, activities, and clear advice on how to go about setting up and maintaining a "book" club. Teachers, counselors, and others can also benefit from the book's motivating ideas. An index rounds out this recommended work.—**Laura Herrell**

527. **Domestic Violence Sourcebook.** 5th ed. Keith Jones, ed. Detroit, Omnigraphics, 2016. 620p. index. (Health Reference Series). $95.00. ISBN 13: 978-0-7808-1460-8; 978-0-7808-1459-2 (e-book).

This volume in the notable Health Reference Series is an invaluable reference regarding basic, comprehensible information about a wide range of issues connected to domestic violence. The book is designed to convey information to victims, their families, and others who have a personal interest in domestic abuse in a clear, straightforward manner. This fifth edition conveys the most up-to-date information on the many aspects of domestic abuse, including its definitions, risk factors, types, and much more.

The material is organized into six general parts which gather a profusion of specific topics: Facts about Domestic Violence; Stalking and Sexual Harassment; Intimate Partner Abuse; Abuse in Specific Populations; Preventing and Intervening in Domestic Violence; Emergency Management, Moving Out, and Moving On; and Additional Help and Information.

Each part is then broken down into manageable chapters housing well-defined topics. For example, part three—Abuse in Specific Populations—discusses child abuse, teen dating violence, digital dating abuse, elder abuse, workplace violence, and much more. Discussion of each topic is clear and concise, with a generous use of bullet points, Q & A's and short, well-demarcated paragraphs. Information conveyed for each topic is copious, but never overwhelming as this reference is targeted to the layperson.

Chapters in the last section include a glossary as well as hotlines, directories, and programs for easy access to proper assistance. An index rounds out the work.

This reference is not produced to replace professional counsel; however, it succeeds at providing intelligent, basic information about domestic abuse to consumers.

Recommended.—**ARBA Staff Reviewer**

528. **Handbook of Research on Work-Life Balance in Asia.** Luo Lu and Cary L. Cooper, eds. Northampton, Mass., Edward Elgar, 2015. 330p. index. $190.00. ISBN 13: 978-1-78347-508-7; 978-1-78347-509-4 (e-book).

This unique title provides a new perspective on work and life balance in Asia. It effectively makes use of theories and empirical research to explain why and how families choose to balance work and leisure, and how this affects their emotional, mental, and physical well-being. A previously underexplored topic, this title will help students navigate a rapidly changing culture that responds to global competition by increasing already long work hours in many Asian countries.

The book is divided into three parts. The first two provide Asian perspectives on negotiating work-life balance at individual and familial levels (part one) as well as the organizational and societal levels (part two). Part three addresses a cross-cultural perspective, which will be particularly helpful for students. Each chapter is authored by a different contributor, and includes a brief introduction outlining the research at the beginning as well as all references used at the end. The index is quite thorough. The accessible format makes it easy for students to locate the chapters most relevant to their studies, as reading cover to cover may prove challenging given the dense material. This book is recommended as an academic resource to upper-level scholars in Asian or cultural studies.—**ARBA Staff Reviewer**

Gay and Lesbian Studies

Handbooks and Yearbooks

529.   **Archives of Human Sexuality and Identity.** [Website] Farmington Hills, Mich., Gale/Cengage Learning. Price negotiated by site. Date reviewed: 2016.

The *Archives of Human Sexuality and Identity* is a digital archive collection of LGBTQ history and culture since 1940. The collection provides access to material from hundreds of institutions and organizations representing/participating in LGBTQ history. The collection contains gay and lesbian newspapers; meeting minutes, and administrative records from LGBTQ organizations worldwide; private correspondence; government reports and memoranda, and photographs. The collection is able to shed light on: the response to the HIV/AIDS crises, LGBTQ activism in several countries including the United States, Canada, and Britain; development of women's rights activism; and political and social organizations founded by LGBTQ individuals.

Materials from major collections and libraries around the world are included such as the Mattachine Society and Daughters of Bilitis (the earliest gay and lesbian groups in the United States). Also represented are the Gay, Lesbian, Bisexual, and Transgender Historical Society; Canadian Lesbian and Gay Archives; National Organization for Women; the Albany Trust; and the Gay Activists Alliance, among others.

Due to its scope, the collection is able to also provide access to documents by and about organizations that no longer exists such as the Q Spirit forum and the Southern California Council on Religion and the Homophile.

The collection can be searched by keyword or browsed by collection. The homepage provides a simple search box and a link for an advanced search that allows keywords to be combined and filtered by such things as content type, illustrated works, and source library.

The Term Frequency tool allows a user to enter a search term and see the frequency of its use in the collection over time plotted on a chart. Users can then click on a point in the graph to see documents. Further, there is a Term Cluster tool to allow users to interact visually with the search results and see which words and subjects are found most often in the text of the search results. It is a fun way to reveal unexpected connections, and it is a powerful way to dig into a primary document collection.

Searches can be saved and tagged. Saved and tagged search results can be saved or used by individuals or groups. The group function is a nice option to support collaborative work.

This is a very unique resource and represents a major and meaningful effort to support the study of LBGTQ issues. It is highly recommended for academic and large public libraries. It is carefully and thoughtfully constructed and enhanced with advanced search tools. It is invaluable to have all of these major sources of information in one place, and the addition of the powerful search features make it even more valuable.—**Kristin Kay Leeman**

530. **Proud Heritage: People, Issues, and Documents of the LGBT Experience.** Chuck Stewart, ed. Santa Barbara, Calif., ABC-CLIO, 2015. 3v. illus. index. $294.00/set. ISBN 13: 978-1-61069-398-1; 978-1-61069-399-8 (e-book).

This 2015 reference work, consisting of three volumes and over 1,300 pages, is at first glance a handsome addition to comprehensive LGBT reference collections. Yet it has a number of spelling errors and proofreading lapses, and is already out-of-date. The introduction to volume three, "State Laws and Issues Concerning LGBT Rights" states that "over 60%" of LGBT Americans "live in states where they can marry"—but same-sex marriage was legalized nationwide in June, 2015. Otherwise, volume three is a useful state-by-state roundup of statutes and laws, including those pertaining to custody, gender change on state IDs, schools, surrogacy, etc., and includes an overview of the history of LGBT issues in each state. Each chapter in volume three closes with legal citations and references to newspaper articles. Elaine Noble is correctly included as the first openly gay or lesbian individual elected to a state legislature (Massachusetts) yet she is not included in the index; her named is misspelled in a chronology of national and international events in volume one. Volume three also includes Recommended Resources, consisting of selective lists of books, organizational Websites, and publications.

Volumes one and two contain over 360 entries, each of which includes a bibliography. Volume one covers people, events, and issues, such as Larry Kramer, for whom a 2008 date of death is given; however, he is very much alive as of the writing of this review. Other entrants are Audre Lorde, Bayard Rustin, Adrienne Rich, Martina Navratilova, and "Chinese Early LGBTQ History in the United States." Poets Emily Dickinson and Amy Lowell do not have their own entries but are mentioned in an entry for Lillian Faderman. Two images of Gertrude Stein illustrate the entry for the "Alice B. Toklas Lesbian Gay Bisexual Transgender Democratic Club." One caption states that she was "one of the world's foremost novelists" but she does not have her own entry. There are a greater-than-expected number of entries about homophobic individuals (e.g. Pat Robertson, illustrated by three images, one of which consumes more than a half page) and movements (e.g. Exodus International). The documents in volume two, from the Old Testament (Sodom and Gomorrah) through 2014 (Arizona's attempt to allow discrimination based on religious freedom) draw from a wide variety of sources. These include an excerpted interview with Anita Bryant from a 1980 issue of *Ladies' Home Journal,* in which she "rethinks" her anti-gay stance; the text of Urvashi Vaid's speech given at the 1993 March on Washington; and "Transgender Rights and the ACLU," (2000) from an ACLU report.

This work, with its more-than-adequate number of black-and-white images, is clearly aimed at a high school and undergraduate audience. Due to its high cost and lack of comprehensiveness, libraries would do well to wait for a revised edition. Libraries that already own the *Encyclopedia of Lesbian, Gay, Bisexual, and Transgender History in*

America (2004), which *Library Journal* called "invaluable" (see ARBA 2005, entry 804) will definitely want to keep it.—**Martha E. Stone**

Men's Studies

Dictionaries and Encyclopedias

531.   **Cultural Encyclopedia of the Penis.** Michael Kimmel, Christine Milrod, and Amanda Kennedy, eds. Lanham, Md., Rowman & Littlefield, 2014. 251p. illus. $85.00; $84.99 (e-book). ISBN 13: 978-0-7591-2312-0; 978-0-7591-2314-4 (e-book).

Perhaps the most rudimentary image of the human body—the male body, to be specific—boils down to the penis. From prehistory to current times, its image has been painted on cave walls and bathroom stalls in an effort to convey a powerful message of invincibility, prowess, and success. This encyclopedia offers an excellent look at the many representations and associations of the penis, and hones in on its impact on our culture, our history, our health, and more.

With its wealth of scholarly contributors, the encyclopedia presents over 150 alphabetical entries covering a wide range of historical and current penis topics. There are the specific matters which may or may not ring a bell, such as Deep Throat, Viagra, or Lorena Bobbitt. Then there are the more general issues such as aging (social science perspective), fashion, transgender/transsexual, or Mythology and Old Norse religion. These diverse entries are thoughtfully constructed and cross-referenced. Readers can easily sort through the concise entries to construct a theme (e.g., the penis in art). Or readers can focus on the topic at hand—tattooing, perhaps. Each entry offers suggestions for further reading as well.

The large contingent of contributors, hailing from many areas of academia, lends the encyclopedia a broad perspective. The book's systematic yet scholarly approach to this fascinating and provocative subject will help engage casual readers and researchers alike.—**Laura Herrell**

Philanthropy

Alamancs

532.   Philanthropy Roundtable. **Almanac of American Philanthropy.** Washington, D.C., Philanthropy Roundtable, 2016. 1317p. illus. index. $25.00. ISBN 13: 978-0-9861474-5-6.

In the almanac, Karl Zinsmeister, series editor of the Wise Giver's Guides, of the Philanthropy Roundtable in Washington, D.C., and head of publication of that organization, provides an extensive, introductory analysis of the cultural importance of philanthropy to the success of the United States of America. The creative prose of this introduction belies the ostensibly parochial title, and provides a compelling platform for the almanac as a "living document,"—a description coined by Adam Meyerson, current President of The Philanthropy Roundtable.

This unique resource features 11 sections detailing information about American philanthropy from the years 1636 to 2015. The aforementioned introduction is followed by a section profiling great men and women of American philanthropy: prominent living donors and 56 donors who brought about change in the United States and the world through their private giving. The third chapter outlines major achievements in several areas including medicine, education, arts, religion, and public policy reform, just to name a few. The fourth section focuses on an annotated list of essential books and articles about philanthropy, followed by sections on an original 2015 national poll, statistics on United States generosity, details on who gives the most, and an explanation of tax protection. A comprehensive index begins on page 1195, and an informative, 22-page foldout features a timeline of American philanthropy (1636-2015).

Readers and researchers of all stripes would gain perspective about the vital role philanthropy plays in our day-to-day lives through the stories and facts presented in this reference work. It is highly recommended for corporate, foundation, public, community college, and academic libraries.—**Laura J. Bender**

Sex Studies

Handbooks and Yearbooks

533.   Helm, Katherine M. **Hooking Up: The Psychology of Sex and Dating.** Santa Barbara, Calif., Greenwood Press/ABC-CLIO, 2015. 239p. index. $38.00. ISBN 13: 978-1-61069-950-1; 978-1-61069-951-8 (e-book).

Hooking Up is the newest addition to The Psychology of Everyday Life series of books that discusses different aspects of everyday life in an accessible and approachable way. *Hooking Up* focuses on the psychology of sex and dating and is geared toward students of human sexuality.

Each book in this series is divided into the three parts. Part one discusses the topic in detail, using the who/what/when/where/why/how framework to organize the discussion. *Hooking Up* uses this section to discuss forms of sex, its importance, its effects, psychologists' theories about sex, sex throughout the life cycle, and sex around the world. Part two provides five real life scenarios and analyses of the different situations in order to provide some practical application of the information. Part three covers common controversies and debates (such as discussing sex with children, homosexuality, etc.), and includes two responses to each question. The book concludes with a directory of resources, a glossary, bibliography, and an index.

Hooking Up is a wonderfully approachable and informative text about the topic of human sexuality. Although the book is geared toward students of human sexuality, the content should prove helpful and instructional to anyone trying to learn more about the topic. The real stars of this book are parts two and three that address the real-life scenario and the common controversies, but unfortunately these sections are both relatively brief. That being said, *Hooking Up* would be a great addition to most collections.—**Tyler Manolovitz**

Social Work and Social Welfare

Dictionaries and Encyclopedias

534.   **Encyclopedia of Social Work. http://socialwork.oxfordre.com/.** [Website] New York, Oxford University Press. Price negotiated by site. Date reviewed: 2015.

The *Encyclopedia of Social Work* (ESW) is an online product that builds on the print version of the encyclopedia. Under the direction of Editor-in-Chief Cynthia Frankel, an editorial board vets each of the hundreds of articles.

The main page offers a search by such subfields as Criminal Justice, Gender and Sexuality, Mental Behavioral Health, Poverty, and Social Justice and Human Rights. A click on Gender and Sexuality, for instance, takes searchers to 37 articles, alphabetized by title. The search can be narrowed through the use of tools located on the left-hand side of the page. Articles are easily accessed with one click, which connects users to the full text, starting with a content box that contains the publication date, a list of subjects, and a Direct Object Identifier, followed by an abstract, keywords, and the text. On the left-hand side of the screen are an outline of the article, a list of related articles in the ESW (all linked), and Other Resources (New & Featured and Forthcoming articles). A list of references with links to online sources, suggestions for further reading, and the author biography appear at the end of the article. An added bonus is the Oxford Index Underbar, which links the ESW with all of Oxford University Press's related online content. For example, in the case of the article "Mental Health Courts," the Oxford Index Underbar produces links to "Mental Health Act," from the *Oxford Handbook of Mental Health Nursing* and the book *Parenting by Men Who Batter.*

For librarians, the ESW provides a trusted source of information; content is timely, regularly updated, and easy to find. This site is highly recommended to academic libraries.—**ARBA Staff Reviewer**

Substance Abuse

Handbooks and Yearbooks

535.   **Drug Information for Teens.** 4th ed. Keith Jones, ed. Detroit, Omnigraphics, 2016. 339p. index. (Teen Health Series). $69.00. ISBN 13: 978-0-7808-1358-8.

This book is designed to convey basic, up-to-date information about drug addiction, abuse, and treatment in regards to a variety of different substances. Its information is clear and highly organized in direct targeting of the teen market. This book appreciates the need to continue to educate teenagers about the risks of drug abuse on their mental and physical health even as drug use amongst them continues to decline.

The book is separated into eight major parts which are, in turn, filled with short topical chapters for ease of reference. Parts include: General Information about Addiction and Substance Abuse; Alcohol; Tobacco, Nicotine, and E-Cigarettes; Marijuana; Abuse of Legally Available Substances; Abuse of Illegal Substances; Other Drug-Related Health Concerns; and Treatment for Addiction. A ninth, concluding part lists National Organizations for Drug Information, Substance Abuse Hotlines and Helplines, and a State-by-State List of Alcohol and Drug Referral Phone Numbers.

The book employs a variety of tools for ease of comprehension, including black-and-white illustrations, charts, bullet points, shaded text boxes, and more. Material is straightforward and is primarily conveyed via an appealing question-and-answer format. For example, the chapter on alcohol asks a series of such questions as what is underage drinking, why is underage drinking dangerous, and what is binge drinking. Answers are concise and stick to the question at hand. A particularly insightful chapter connects substance abuse with auxiliary issues such as teen pregnancy, mental illness, infectious disease, violence, and suicide. In addition, the book makes every effort to provide up-to-date information; pointing to the latest substances like bath salts, using street names alongside chemical names, discussing the most current treatments like Adolescent Community Reinforcement Approach (A-CRA), etc.

The reference is not produced to replace professional medical counsel; however, it succeeds at providing intelligent, basic information about many facets of this problem to patients, families, caregivers, and others. Recommended.—**ARBA Staff Reviewer**

17 Statistics, Demography, and Urban Studies

Demography

Handbooks and Yearbooks

536.   **Handbook of Chinese Migration.** Robyn R. Iredale and Fei Guo, eds. Northampton, Mass., Edward Elgar, 2016. 330p. index. $190.00. ISBN 13: 978-1-78347-663-3; 978-1-78347-664-0 (e-book).

Handbook of Chinese Migration serves as a historical, political, economic, and sociological reference in regards to the continuing migration of the Chinese people. Providing a reference point that is up-to-date with twenty-first-century migration trends, this book covers the most recent developments and research concerning Chinese migration. The book discusses two kinds of migration—internal and international migration. The book is divided into the following two parts: one, trends in internal migration and, two, international migrants' identity and their relationship with the People's Republic of China. The contributors of this book offer a wide variety of commentary concerning geography, health, economics, anthropology, business, law, and sociology. The supplementary items in the book include an index, a list of commonly used abbreviations, graphs, images, and charts. After every essay the authors provide references that could lead the reader to further research resources.

Even though this book does provide research and commentary on international migration outside of China, the material primarily focuses on internal migration in China. The individual essays all provide a unique perspective on Chinese migration but are formatted to flow together nicely, so that the reader does not struggle with adjustments when reading. Many essays reference or address ideas that were mentioned in the previous essay. An example of this is an essay titled "Negative Native-Place Stereotypes and Discriminatory Wage Penalties in China's Migrant Laborers Markets" and the following essay which also deals with wage pensions titled "Determinants of Wage Arrears and Implications for the Socio-Economic Wellbeing of China's Migrant Workers: Evidence from Guangdong Province." The objective of this book is to provide timely information updates regarding the major trends that are affected by Chinese migration such as identity, well being, and their relationships. This book relies heavily on research in documenting these implications with most of the research cited being fresh and current with just a few citations dating back before 2010. The research is presented in such an appropriate and basic fashion that it would be a relevant to addition to any high school or academic library. An index rounds out the work.—**Sara Mofford**

Statistics

United States

537.   **America's Top-Rated Cities: A Statistical Handbook.** 22d ed. Amenia, N.Y., Grey House Publishing, 2015. 4v. maps. $295.00/set. ISBN 13: 978-1-61925-552-4; 978-1-61925-557-9 (e-book).

Now in its 22nd edition, this is a standard reference work in many libraries. With the addition of five cities (Palm Bay, FL; Roanoke, VA; Springfield, IL; Tyler, TX; and Winston-Salem, NC), the new edition covers 100 U.S. cities that have a population of at least 100,000. The entry for each city provides background information, rankings, and statistical tables. The background information summarizes the history of the area and touches upon the city's environment, politics, culture, and climate. For example, the entry on Boston includes its place in history, a survey of historic buildings, a listing of its major sports teams, and a discussion of the Boston Marathon. The rankings for each city are drawn from over 300 books, articles, and Internet sources that have been categorized into topics such as business/finance, dating/romance, education, environmental, health/fitness, and real estate. Specific rankings are as varied as most well-read, most wired, safest, most polite, most tax friendly, best for dogs, gayest, and most tattooed. The statistical tables are the heart of the entries and are divided into two broad categories: the business environment (such as city finances, demographics, economy, income, and employment) and the living environment (including cost of living, health, education, recreation, and climate). Each volume includes the same four appendixes: Comparative Statistics, Metropolitan Area Definitions, Government Type and County, Chambers of Commerce and Economic Development Organizations, and State Departments of Labor and Employment. The Comparative Statistics appendix includes 80 different charts which permit the user to compare the 100 cities on a wide variety of topics such as demographics, economy, income and poverty, employment and earnings, election results in the 2012 presidential election, housing, education, cost of living, health care, public safety, climate, and air quality. For most public libraries this set will be a well-used resource, especially for those examining business opportunities and for those who are considering relocating to other cities. For academic libraries, this set will be useful for many sociology and public policy courses.—**Gregory A. Crawford**

538.   **County and City Extra, 2014: Annual Metro, City, and County Data Book.** 22d ed. Deirdre A. Gaquin and Mary Meghan Ryan, eds. Lanham, Md., Bernan Press, 2014. 1404p. maps. (County and City Extra Series). $155.00; $154.99 (e-book). ISBN 13: 978-1-59888-719-8; 978-1-59888-720-4 (e-book).

County and City Extra 2014 is the fully updated, 22d annual edition of a guide to key demographic and economic data applied to various geographic subdivisions of the United States. Data has been grouped into five basic parts: States, States and Counties, Metropolitan Areas, Cities of 25,000 or more, and Congressional Districts of the 113th Congress.

Each part then presents copious data tables measuring information related to population, crime, income, housing, Social Security, agriculture, land area, employment, government finance, and much, much more. Each part opens with data "Highlights and Rankings" particular to that section, selecting points of comparison such as population, density, land area, and agricultural land value.

Preceding all the data tables is an overall introduction pointing to the newest sources of data—specifically the American Community Survey (replacing the census long form) and the 2010 census, as well as newly considered measurements such as "non-employer" (e.g., self-employed) businesses. The introduction also houses a subject summary, a colored map portfolio, and organizational information.

Appendixes provide excellent context for understanding the data in regards to Geographic Concepts and Codes, Metropolitan Statistical Areas (Divisions and Components), Core Based Statistical Areas (Divisions and Components), a Map of Congressional Districts and States, Cities by County and Source Notes, and Explanations.

This book is a greatly helpful resource for advanced students and professionals alike.—**Laura Herrell**

539.   **County and City Extra. Special Historical Edition, 1790-2010.** Deirdre A. Gaquin and Mary Meghan Ryan, eds. Lanham, Md., Bernan Press, 2015. 271p. $125.00. ISBN 13: 978-1-59888-804-1.

Using information from the U.S. Census, the Census Bureau's two-volume *Bicentennial Edition: Historical Statistics of the United States, Colonial Times to 1970,* and smaller bureau publications, this title supplies data from the earliest days of the republic into the early twenty-first century. Part A, United States, includes a short introduction, population statistics, life expectancy data, information on race, and more. It concludes with "Notes and Definitions," a section designed to help users understand and interpret the data, providing definitions for such things as housing unit, percent urban, and civilian labor force as well as explanations for how the measurement of urban areas or racial data have changed over time. States, part B, provides population data, percent change from previous censuses, percent Hispanic or Latino, personal income, farm income, etc., followed by "Notes and Definitions." Country population data is presented in part C, alphabetically by state and further by county. The "Notes and Definitions" after the data tables explain shifting boundaries, name changes, or other circumstances particular to each state. Part D, the final section, offers population data on the city level.

This handy reference compiles a wealth of data in one place; the graphs, tables, charts, and "Notes and Definitions" facilitate both use and comprehension.—**ARBA Staff Reviewer**

540.   **Patterns of Economic Change by State and Area: Income, Employment, & Gross Domestic Product.** 3d ed. Mary Meghan Ryan, ed. Lanham, Md., Bernan Press, 2015. 497p. $200.00pa.; $99.99 (e-book). ISBN 13: 978-1-59888-796-9; 978-1-59888-797-6 (e-book).

Patterns of Economic Change by State and Area, a special edition of *Business Statistics of the United States: Patterns of Economic Change,* is a complement to titles that include the *State and Metropolitan Area Data Book* and *County and City Extra. Patterns of Economic Change by State and Area* is arranged in three parts. Part A, Personal Income and Employment by Region, State and Metropolitan Area, includes annual data (some data going back to 1958) for farm and nonfarm earnings; payments to persons of dividends, interest, and rent; total personal income; population; per capita personal income and disposable income; and total number of jobs in state or area. Part A also includes a guide for researchers on "Notes and Definitions," as well income concepts. Tables are arranged by region (e.g., Far West, New England, Great Lakes); state, and metropolitan statistical areas (MSAs). Part B includes gross domestic product on a state-by-state basis. Part C includes the poverty rate by state (defined for a demographic group as the number of poor people in that group expressed as a percentage of the total number of people in the group). The appendix lists MSAs, metropolitan divisions, and components. Each MSA includes core-based statistical area number, state/county FIPS code, and a list of counties in the area. *Patterns of Economic Change by State and Area* fills a need for locating data on personal income, employment, and gross domestic product by region, state, and metropolitan statistical area. Recommended for larger public and academic libraries.— **Lucy Heckman**

541.   **State Profiles: The Population and Economy of Each U.S. State.** 6th ed. Shana Hertz Hattis, ed. Lanham, Md., Bernan Press, 2014. 554p. index. $165.00. ISBN 13: 978-1-59888-721-1; 978-1-59888-722-8 (e-book).

Finding statistics about states and the United States as a whole is not necessarily challenging for a librarian but it can be time-consuming and tedious to find answers to questions such as "which state uses the most energy?" Or, "how much money did the state of Arizona collect in taxes and what was the amount derived through property taxes?" At times it can also be tricky to remember which government agency would collect the information sought. The sixth edition of *State Profiles: The Population and Economy of Each U.S. State* does an excellent job of compiling basic economic and social statistics. From population counts through state government tax collection, this resource provides general statistics for each state and the District of Columbia in an easy to use volume.

Beginning with a textual summary about the United States, followed by statistical charts ranking each state based on a variety of topics (total population, median household income, and traffic fatalities, just to name a few examples), this volume is then organized alphabetically by state (including the District of Columbia). Each entry begins with a summary page, providing "Facts and Figures" such as location and size information; state motto, nickname, and song; date of statehood; and other basic facts. This page also includes a bulleted "At a Glance" section that highlights some key facts, such as rate of population growth, median household income, homeownership (actual bulleted points vary depending on the state), and the numerical ranking for the state for these factors. The rest of the entry consists of 16 tables, which are the same tables for every state and in the same order; a list of tables is provided following the contents page at the start of the book to enable users to easily see what information is provided for each state. In addition to tables, charts and graphs are provided for selected aspects.

A "Notes and Definitions" section at the end of the book provides information about each of the tables, such as the source of the data, definitions for the terminology used by the originating source, the source's methodology, and where to go for more information. One thing of note is the lack of citations for the statistics used for the United States Rankings in the first section of the volume. An index is included after the "Notes and Definitions" section, providing users with the specific page numbers for a particular state's statistical tables.

Statistical information was primarily collected from American FactFinder and other Census Bureau Websites. Additional sources include the Bureau of Labor Statistics (BLS),

Bureau of Economic Analysis (BEA), U.S. Department of Education, and Uniform Crime Reports from the Federal Bureau of Investigation (FBI). For this 2014 edition, data is predominantly from 2012, with some tables using 2010, 2011, and some 2013 information as well. While the most recent data at the time of publication was included, some tables also include older data (often 2000 and 2010) to show users change over time.

While all of the data used to create the statistical tables that make up this resource are freely available, knowing where to look and how to use the various government Websites can be laborious for users. Because of this, this volume is an excellent ready reference source for a library of any type and size and its ease of use allows it to be accessible to library patrons of all levels of research experience.—**Julia Frankosky**

542.　　**State Rankings 2015: A Statistical View of America.** Kathleen O'Leary and Scott Morgan, eds. Thousand Oaks, Calif., CQ Press / Sage, 2015. 603p. index. (State FactFinder Series). $100.00. ISBN 13: 978-1-4833-8504-4.

State Rankings 2015 "provides an easily accessible collection of data in a broad range of quality of life factors in the United States" and "compares data from the fifty states and the District of Columbia in 566 tables." Tables are arranged within the categories of: agriculture; crime and law enforcement; defense; economy; education; employment and labor; energy and environment; geography; government finances: federal; government finances: state and local; health; households and housing; population; social welfare; and transportation. Sources for data were selected by the editors from various government and private sector sources. Subjects are designated as positive or negative (e.g., high state crime rates negatively affect a state's comparison ranking). In addition to the tables listed within the subject categories, this reference source contains 2015 state rankings; the date each state was admitted to statehood; state fast facts (e.g. state flower, name of capital); a list of names, addresses, phone numbers, and URLs; and an index. Each table's years of coverage vary, dates range from 2010 to 2015 (for instance, estimated new cancer cases is for 2014 and enrollment in institutions of higher education is from 2012). Each table includes title, national rates or totals, and states listed in alphabetical order. Sources are designated for each of the tables. Researchers can locate diverse data by state, such as: Internal Revenue Service gross collections in 2013; unemployment rate in 2014; population per square mile in 2014; employees in leisure and hospitality in 2014; cattle on farms in 2015; and percent of population enrolled in Medicare in 2012. *State Rankings 2015* is a valuable reference source that provides a wealth of data for researchers and also is a starting point for locating further information—the list of sources is especially helpful. Recommended for larger public libraries and academic library collections.—**Lucy Heckman**

543.　　**Statistical Abstract of the United States 2015: The National Data Book.** Lanham, Md., Bernan Press, 2015. 1024p. maps. index. $179.00. ISBN 13: 978-1-59888-729-7.

Ignoring the protests of many librarians and citizens, the Census Bureau recently decided to discontinue publication of this reference tool, the standard source for accurate, comprehensive U.S. statistical information since 1878. Issued in August 2011, the 2012 *Statistical Abstract of the United States* was the last edition published by the U.S. Census Bureau. Beginning in 2012 ProQuest and Bernan Press assumed responsibility for publishing "the most used statistical reference tool in U.S. libraries" (p. v). This 2015 edition, issued in December 2014 with more than 1,000 pages in a large 8.5 x 11-inch format, presents statistics current as of early September 2014. It contains 45 new tables listed on page xi and a deleted tables list on pages xii-xiii as well as updated tables from the 2012 Census of Agriculture and the 2012 Economic Census. New or infrequent users will appreciate the "Guide to Tabular Presentation," pp. xiv-xv and the third appendix, "Limitations of the Data," pp. 947-948. Source notes below each table in this volume guide readers to other statistical publications as does the first appendix, "Guide to Sources of Statistics, State Statistical Abstracts, and Foreign Statistical Abstracts." The extensive index yields references to table numbers rather than page numbers.

While Bernan Press produces the print version of the book, ProQuest offers an online version of this title. Updated monthly, the online edition yields additional back year's data, spreadsheets corresponding to each table in the print edition, and the option to refine and manipulate data. It can be purchased alone or as a part of the publisher's ProQuest *Statistical Insight* package that includes "The Tables Collection," over one million tables published since 1999 on the basis of U.S. and foreign statistical sources and "over 100,000 statistical reports in PDF," to enable users to locate a specific table or number easily.

This essential print resource belongs at or near the reference center and/or government documents service desk of all public and academic libraries as well as in many high school libraries. Larger libraries with substantial government documents collections and a research-oriented constituency or libraries with more expansive collection development budgets may prefer the online *Statistical Insight* package.—**Julienne L. Wood**

Urban Studies

Handbooks and Yearbooks

544.   **The Comparative Guide to American Suburbs, 2015/2016.** 8th ed. Amenia, N.Y., Grey House Publishing, 2015. 2297p. maps. index. $210.00pa. ISBN 13: 978-1-61925-558-6.

Suburbs have grown to house more people and businesses than ever before. This comprehensive volume reports vital data covering over 3,000 suburban communities throughout the United States with populations of 10,000 or more and located within the 80 largest metro areas. It gathers most of its information from various versions of the U.S. Census Bureau's American Community Survey. This eighth edition has been updated with the data of 134 additional communities. Further, new topics are covered in their profiles: population growth, English-only speaking households, individuals with disabilities, veterans, and health insurance coverage.

There are three main sections of the volume: Metro Area Suburbs (which includes profiles and rankings), National Rankings, and Metro Area Rankings. Metro Area Suburbs alphabetically arranges all metro areas and includes state and suburb maps, a metro area profile, individual suburb profiles (also listed alphabetically), and data rankings by category. There are 71 categories ranked, which include poverty rate, ancestry, travel time to work, median home value, unemployment rate, educational attainment, city property taxes, and much more. The following National Rankings section compares data for all 3,000 plus communities, while Metro Area Rankings compares data for all 80 metro areas. National Rankings uses the 71 categories from the individual metro profiles. Metro Area Rankings use 51 categories, including religion, health insurance coverage, and air quality.

The volume also includes three helpful sections to help manage the material: a User Guide; a Metropolitan Area Index, which alphabetically lists all 80 metro areas with their states, counties, and suburbs; and, finally, a Suburb Index, which alphabetically lists all 3,022 suburbs analyzed.

This substantial volume is a definitive source for quality demographic and statistical insight into American suburban life.—**ARBA Staff Reviewer**

545.   **Handbook on Green Infrastructure.** Danielle Sinnett, Nick Smith, and Sarah Burgess, eds. Northampton, Mass., Edward Elgar, 2016. 496p. index. $290.00. ISBN 13: 978-1-78347-399-1.

This book focuses on the planning, design, and implementation of green infrastructure in urban environments. The three editors, all from the University of West England in the United Kingdom, have divided the handbook into five parts: the role of green infrastructure in the urban environment; strategic planning for green infrastructure; designing green infrastructure for all; implementation and management of green infrastructure; and looking forward. The 47 contributors come from both academia and the professional fields of urban planning, landscape architecture, water policy, land regeneration, and a host of other related specialties. Their experience covers not only the United Kingdom but also Western Europe, Australia, the United States, and South America. Each chapter is followed by a summary or conclusion and an extensive list of references and there is a single index at the end. Photographs, charts, graphs, and maps are used throughout the book. The emphasis is on the effect of green infrastructure—or the lack of it—on the lives of the people. Chapter topics include green infrastructure and health, the impact of green infrastructure on air quality and temperature, green infrastructure and biodiversity in the city, and ensuring green infrastructure for all. Photographs show examples of good and bad urban planning. Although the intended audience for this book is researchers, postgraduate students, and practitioners, the style is straightforward and accessible for undergraduates as well. Recommended for academic and public libraries.—**ARBA Staff Reviewer**

546.   **Immigration and America's Cities.** Joaquin Jay Gonzalez, III and Roger L. Kemp, eds. Jefferson, N.C., McFarland, 2016. 300p. index. $39.95pa. ISBN 13: 978-0-7864-9633-4; 978-1-4766-2379-5 (e-book).

This book from McFarland offers a wealth of information on how American cities are dealing with immigrants. It is designed to serve as a handbook for the development of good services at the country and municipal level. Editors Joaquin Jay Gonzalez, III, and Roger L. Kemp, both professors at Golden Gate University—Kemp also spent 25 years as a city manager—have pulled together contributions from 45 scholars, journalists, and public servants (including a police chief and several city administrators) that delve into major immigration issues and how they are being handled by local governments across the country. Chapters cover the growth of the immigrant population over the past decades and specific topics such as immigrants and the law, safe havens, language access, driver's licensing, employment, public safety, education, and voting. The 10 appendixes include a 2014 letter to Congress from the U.S. Conference of Mayors, a list of sanctuary cities, and a national immigration resource directory. There is an index and a description of the contributors. The book will be of interest to general readers and could provide a valuable resource for those seeking solutions to immigration issues.—**Alice Chaffee**

547.   **New York City Water and Transit Infrastructure in Photographs** http://digitalcollections.nypl.org/collections/metropolis-new-york-city-water-and-transit-infrastructure-in-photographs#/?tab=about. [Website] Free. Date reviewed: 2016.

This collection from the New York Public Library includes several archival collections of photographs in addition to supplemental published illustrated sources all relating to the transit and water infrastructure of New York City in the past 150 years.

The Web page is attractive and organized, and does offer a variety of reports and text documents related to the transit and water infrastructure. Students who are studying this specialized subject may find these items interesting, though many text documents are very dense and some are difficult to read due to the aging of the document. Each still image provides the user with the following information: type of resource, date issued, division, author, dates/origin, topics, notes, physical description, and citations (in MLA, APA, Chicago, and Wikipedia), as well as additional descriptive information. A timeline shows when the image was issued and digitized. Users can also download the images in a variety of sizes and resolutions. This highly specialized collection will be particularly useful for those interested in the history of New York City water and transit infrastructures.—**ARBA Staff Reviewer**

18 Women's Studies

Biography

548. **American First Ladies.** 3d ed. Robert P. Watson, ed. Hackensack, N.J., Salem Press, 2015. 459p. illus. index. $165.00. ISBN 13: 978-1-61925-942-3; 978-1-61925-943-0 (e-book).

A companion to *American Presidents,* fourth edition, published by Salem in 2015, this well-conceived volume provides concise biographies of the 47 First Ladies who have served the nation from Martha Washington to Michelle Obama. Black-and-white portraits or photographs enhance these biographical offerings. This third edition is the first to include an entry on Mrs. Obama, and has also updated and revised entries for several recent first ladies, as well as the bibliography and appendixes.

Each essay presents clearly formatted and engaging information regarding the First Ladies' "Early Life," "Marriage and Family," "Presidency and First Ladyship," and "Legacy." Shaded textboxes offer biographical summaries of the president, along with interesting anecdotes from the subject's time as First Lady. For example, we learn of Nellie Taft's unprecedented accompaniment of her husband between his inaugural ceremony and the executive mansion.

Special to this volume is a series of topical essays adding further depth to readers' understanding of the role of the First Lady. Subjects include "First Ladies and Social Causes," "Family Life in the White House," and more. The book also includes supplemental information for further reference, including chronological lists of First Ladies and Presidents; a selection of appropriate libraries, museums, historic sites and Websites; an annotated bibliography; and an index.—**ARBA Staff Reviewer**

Dictionaries and Encyclopedias

549. **Cultural Encyclopedia of the Breast.** Merril D. Smith, ed. Lanham, Md., Rowman & Littlefield, 2014. 288p. $85.00; $84.99 (e-book). ISBN 13: 978-0-7591-2331-1; 978-0-7591-2332-8 (e-book).

Whether we wish to acknowledge it or not, the breast appears everywhere. It is an image that conjures much from nourishment to sexuality and beyond. This encyclopedia is an engaging and informative way to realize the myriad impact that the breast has had. Beginning with a four-page chronology of selected breast events (such as Anne of Austria's 1665 breast cancer surgery), the book then presents nearly 150 alphabetized entries capturing the breast's significance in art, history, medicine, childcare, pop culture, and other arenas.

We read much, for example, of the brassiere and its ability to both adorn and support the breast. As entries are generously cross-referenced, readers can connect this particular topic to others such as corsets, Maidenform, sports bras, Wonderbra, Fredericks of Hollywood, and others. Serious subjects are treated respectfully: the topic of breast cancer is covered in a thoughtfully composed essay. And, of course, the lighthearted topics will certainly amuse as they evoke images of the Folies Bergère, topless protests, and Barbie Dolls.

The large contingent of contributors lends the encyclopedia a broad perspective; overall, the systematic yet scholarly approach to this subject will help the book to engage casual readers and researchers alike.—**Laura Herrell**

550.   Hendricks, Nancy. **America's First Ladies: A Historical Encyclopedia and Primary Document Collection of the Remarkable Women of the White House.** Santa Barbara, Calif., ABC-CLIO, 2015. illus. index. $100.00. ISBN 13: 978-1-61069-882-5; 978-1-61069-883-2 (e-book).

This reference describes the lives of our First Ladies, from Martha Washington to Michelle Obama. Reading this survey, we see how the position of First Lady, a role that is unofficial and still undefined by any governmental directive, has evolved to a unique platform to do good and to make a lasting mark on our society. Each chapter gives the traditional biographic information as to family life, education, etc., but what makes this collection so engaging are the stories that bring to life the amazing women who in their own ways contributed to their husbands' presidencies. For example, we all know Dolley Madison saved George Washington's portrait and important cabinet papers when the White House was attacked by the British during the War of 1812. But she also saved her favorite red velvet drapes which she later used to make the ball gown she wore often and proudly as a reminder of the United States's victory over Britain. Elizabeth Monroe, while her husband was ambassador to France, rescued General Lafayette's wife from prison thus saving her from execution during the French Revolution. Louisa Catherine Adams and her young son accompanied her husband, John Quincy Adams, to Moscow when he served as ambassador to Russia for six years. Hurriedly called to Paris to negotiate the Treaty of Ghent, Adams left Louisa to close their affairs at the embassy and to get herself and her son from Moscow to Paris during the last year of the Napoleonic wars. Traveling alone and often through battle lines, she had only her son's toy sword as a weapon. Harriet Lane, niece of James Buchanan, served as First Lady for her uncle. Harriet accompanied Buchanan when he served as ambassador to Great Britain and became a favorite of Queen Victoria. It was rumored at the time, that Queen Victoria's government refrained from officially recognizing the Confederacy because of the Queen's friendship with Harriet, an action that changed the course of the Civil War. Clearly America's First Ladies are not just pretty faces but women of substance to be respected.—**Adrienne Antink**

551.   Sheldon, Kathleen. **Historical Dictionary of Women in Sub-Saharan Africa.** 2d ed. Lanham, Md., Rowman & Littlefield, 2016. 489p. maps. (Historical Dictionaries of Women in the World). $135.00; $134.99 (e-book). ISBN 13: 978-1-4422-6292-; 978-1-4422-6293-5 (e-book).

In this second edition of the *Historical Dictionary of Women in Sub-Saharan Africa,* author Kathleen Sheldon updates the information in the first edition of her book, published in 2005. Dr. Sheldon is a research scholar at the University of California at Los Angeles and has written extensively on Africa. She is currently finishing a textbook on African women's history and serves on the editorial boards of *Oxford Bibliographies in African Studies* and the *Dictionary of African Biography*. Her introduction to this book discusses the major role that African women have traditionally played in African economic life and the ways they have exerted leadership. This edition of the historical dictionary has about 800 entries on individual women, women's organizations, historical events, and practices that have affected African women. While many entries deal with organizations or cultural practices, the majority of the entries give thumbnail biographies of outstanding African women. Among these are President Ellen Johnson Sirleaf of Liberia who won the Nobel Peace Prize in 2011, Kenyan actress Lupita Amondi Nyong'o, and Fatma Ahmed Ibrahim, the leading women's activist in South Sudan. Subject entries provide perspective on important features of African women's lives. For example, the entry on polygyny (many wives) shows both the negative and positive aspects of this deeply rooted practice. There are helpful entries on the effect of Shari'a law on women and on the practice of female genital cutting. Surprisingly, there is no entry on the Ebola epidemic of 2014-15, though Ebola is briefly covered under Health. The dictionary entries are preceded by a succinct chronology, beginning with the Queen of Sheba in the tenth century B.C.E. There is also a list of acronyms and abbreviations. The bibliography fills over 130 pages and will reward the scholar in search of original and thoughtful secondary sources dealing with women in Africa. This book is a valuable resource for persons with an interest in Africa and in women's issues.—**Alice Chaffee**

552.   **Women's Rights in the United States: A Comprehensive Encyclopedia of Issues, events, and People.** Wayne, Tiffany K. and Lois Banner, eds. Santa Barbara, Calif., ABC-CLIO, 2015. 4v. illus. index. $415.00/set. ISBN 13: 978-1-61069-214-4; 978-1-61069-215-1 (e-book).

This encyclopedia is unique in its breadth of coverage of women's issues, describing events, controversies, and people from 1776 to 2014. In 2016 it won important awards from *Choice* and RUSA as an outstanding reference source. The editors have doctorates in history and are well-published. Wayne is the editor or author of three earlier works in women's history and Banner is a university professor and author of several important academic texts. As a resource it is nearly flawless: so well-organized, comprehensive, and readable, one may be tempted to read its four volumes from cover to cover.

The set includes 650 signed entries by about 300 contributors, as well as 127 primary documents. The editors' broad understanding of history is demonstrated in the selection of topics and organization of volumes. The interrelationship between the women's movement and contemporaneous struggles are made clear, and are highlighted in the subtitles of volumes: one, *Moral Reform and the Woman Question (1776-1870)*; two, *Suffrage and a New Wave of Women's Activism (1870-1950)*; three, *Civil Rights and Modern Feminism (1950-1990)*, and four, *Third-Wave and Global Feminisms (1990-Present)*.

Each volume begins with a specific introduction, alphabetical list of entries, list of primary documents, and list of entries by topic, and ends with the primary documents in full text. Volume one also contains a preface to volumes one-four and a chronology of women's rights in America from 1776 to 2014. Volume four also contains a general bibliography, information about the editors and writers, and an index.

The entries focus on individuals and subjects related to women's rights and gender equality, including significant events, organizations, all types of media, legislation, and court cases. They have *see also* references to other entries and primary documents in all volumes. Most include well-selected references for further reading, including books, articles, Websites, and videos, and some have black-and-white illustrations. Examples of entries are Coverture, Harriet Tubman, Women and World War II, Lesbian Feminism, Women and the Civil Rights Movement, Hillary Clinton, and Same-Sex Marriage. Primary documents include "Aren't I a Woman?" by Sojourner Truth (1851); "If Men Were Seeking the Franchise," by Jane Addams (1913); *Toward a Female Liberation Movement,* by Beverly Jones and Judith Brown (1968); and *Sexual Violence in the World of Online Gaming* by Anita Sarkeesian (2012). The variety and breadth of the content cannot be overestimated. It is an outstanding choice for all types of libraries, and readers from high school to college graduates.—**Madeleine Nash**

Handbooks and Yearbooks

553.   **Canadian Women's History. http://eco.canadiana.ca/?usrlang=en.** [Website] Free. Date reviewed: 2016.

Canadiana is an independent, not-for-profit charity established in 1978. Its goal is to preserve and share hundreds of documents through a "virtual library that holds the most complete set of full-text historical content about Canada." Its *Canadian Women's History* collection includes memoirs, diaries, collected letters, drama, political pamphlets, and more, with topics ranging from poetry to fashion to medicine. Those looking for early writings of Canadian female authors can find a multitude of resources here published from the eighteenth century to the twentieth century. One such document is the captivity narrative (published in London in 1760) of Elizabeth Hanson, taken into Canada in 1725 from her home in New England. While the majority of the items are written in English, there are a fair number written in French, as one would expect.

The collection is easy to navigate, offering users a simple search bar that filters titles, creator names, subjects, and texts. Users can also select a date range to find works published within specified years. This is a highly recommended resource for scholars studying Canada and Canadian culture. It will also prove beneficial for educators instructing students on how to find and appropriately implement primary sources into their academic work.—**ARBA Staff Reviewer**

554.   Derks, Scott. **Working Americans 1810-2015. Volume VI: Women at Work.** 2d ed. Amenia, N.Y., Grey House Publishing, 2016. 600p. illus. index. (Working Americans). $150.00. ISBN 13: 978-1-68217-077-9; 978-1-68217-078-6 (e-book).

This is part of a multivolume series from Grey House Publishing purporting to examine the workplace history of Americans. This particular volume strives to examine American women at work covering domestic work at home as well as work in various professions outside the home.

The nineteenth-century section of this compilation is broken down by selected years covering a Western Kentucky estate matron in 1810; an 1827 Litchfield, Connecticut, school teacher; an 1881 Oswego, Wisconsin, educational reformer; and a Boston, Massachusetts, child prodigy composer. The twentieth- and twenty-first-century profiles are broken down into decadal sections such as a 1919 Harlem, New York, hair care business owner; a school librarian in Danville, Virginia, in 1933; a Nashville, Tennessee, psychologist and Head Start champion in 1965; an Atlanta, Georgia, hydrogen fuel cell visionary in 1994; and a San Diego, California, homeschooling mother in 2010.

Entries for these individual sections describe home and work life for these individuals, their interactions within their community, and a historical snapshot of key local, state, national, and international events in the year these women and their work was covered.

Entries are well-illustrated and aided by timelines, advertisements, selected prices for consumer goods, and biographical information on the individual profiles such as Sarah Walker, the owner of the hair care business in Harlem and Annie Rosewood, the homeschool mom in San Diego. A bibliography of secondary sources concludes the work.

This work will be most effective in public libraries in providing readers with an introductory overview of the environments in which women worked at various time periods in U.S. history. While entries mention various political and social issues women workers have dealt with, it provides no details on laws and litigation which have affected women's working status. It does not address topics such as governmental regulation, occupational safety, equal pay, sexual harassment, social media, and group identity politics which can still affect the working conditions of women. A work of this kind which seeks to examine working women that would be most useful for academic library users would cover these topics and include bibliographic references from governmental sources such as the Census Bureau, Department of Education, Department of Health and Human Services, Bureau of Labor Statistics, Occupational Safety and Health Administration, and congressional committee investigations.—**Bert Chapman**

555.   **Gifts of Speech: Women's Speeches from Around the World: http://www. giftsofspeech.org/.** [Website] Free: Date reviewed: 2016.

Gifts of Speech is a nonprofit project founded by Liz Kent León, Head of Digital Initiatives and Outreach at Sweet Briar College Library. This Website is dedicated to preserving and providing access to speeches given by influential and contemporary women across the world and is intended for secondary students and college undergraduates. Speeches are carefully researched in newspapers, magazines, Internet pages, reference works, news, documentaries, and educational media. All content on this Web page is used with permission. Most content has never been published in any paper-based format or speech index, and comes directly from the authors, though instructors should be aware that content is not vetted for accuracy and is not censored in any way, making some of the audio potentially inappropriate for younger users. Because online speeches can be difficult to find, this resource is excellent for students conducting research for projects and academia, especially debate.

Users can browse for content alphabetically by speaker name or by date under the browse tab; a How-to tab provides information on conducting searches on the site. The earliest speeches come from the 1848 Seneca Falls Convention and the most recent is from a 2009 by Huerta Muller, Nobel Prize winner in literature, entitled "Every Word Knows Something of a Vicious Circle." A Nobel Lectures page contains the Top 100 American Speeches of the 20th Century, as well a few dozen Nobel lectures by women laureates. A FAQ page should help to answer any questions. Overall, this is a very easy and helpful Website that is highly recommended.—**ARBA Staff Reviewer**

556. **Women in World History. http://chnm.gmu.edu/wwh/.** [Website] Free. Date reviewed: 2016.

Women in World History is a Website created by George Mason University's Center for History and New Media to aid high school and college teachers in developing course content in women's history and gender studies. Recognizing the challenges of finding and effectively using classroom resources on these topics, the site provides primary resources and curriculum material emphasizing global history and cross-cultural connections, thus helping teachers and students keep up to date on the latest research approaches.

The site's main components are easily accessed through the homepage. The "Primary Sources" section, which can be searched by region, time period, or topic, includes letters, newspaper articles, photographs, and more. Primary sources are available for various regions of the world and for ancient through modern time periods; however, the site could benefit from a larger collection (there are about 200). Two other sections, "Analyzing Evidence" and "Modules," provide guidance, suggestions, and examples for using primary sources in the classroom. The "Analyzing Evidence" section includes explanations of how historians use primary sources (such as census data, art, and oral histories) in their research, while "Modules" presents clear strategies for creating document-based lessons. A potential drawback of the "Modules" section is the limited number (14) of lesson plans provided; however, even teachers unable to use the specific plans provided can still use them as models for their own lessons. Another section, "Teaching Case Studies," is a collection of accounts in which educators describe their experiences using historical case studies in their courses. Finally, reviews of other Websites on women's history will be very helpful to teachers looking for assistance in assessing online resources and their usefulness in the classroom.

It is unclear how frequently the site is updated: the "About" page refers to the project's upcoming completion in 2006, and the most recent archived discussion in the teachers' forum is dated March 2006. Nevertheless, the site's content is of high quality and is recommended as a resource for teachers wishing to incorporate primary source studies into their women's history courses.—**ARBA Staff Reviewer**

557. **Women, War, and Violence: Topography, Resistance, and Hope.** Mariam M. Kurtz and Lester R. Kurtz, eds. Santa Barbara, Calif., Praeger/ABC-CLIO, 2015. 2v. index. (Praeger International Security). $184.00/set. ISBN 13: 978-1-4408-2880-5; 978-1-4408-2881-2 (e-book).

While we have learned a lot since gender studies was formalized as a discipline in the 1970s, there remains much to discover. This work takes a broader view of violence encompassing not only physical violence, but also psychological and emotional violence. The definition further extends to include structural and cultural violence (typically considered injustices). The introduction classifies violence as direct (perpetrated at the individual level), structural (perpetrated by the social system), cultural (perpetrated by the culture, and possibly endorsed by women themselves), and environmental (perpetrated towards the environment and adversely affecting women in particular). Gender is seen through the lens of a social construct (as in contemporary gender studies) rather than a biological construct. War is viewed more broadly as conflict, and is considered a manifestation of violence.

This two-volume work consists of 36 essays that explore the various facets of gender and violence. Most essays analyze sources of violence and possible solutions;

some provide an overview. Essays on sex trafficking, violence towards immigrants, and the need to support legislation with other reforms summarize current scholarship. Other essays on the tools women use to function in highly violent environments, spouses of PTSD veterans, models used to resist gendered violence, and sexual assault on women in the armed forces, provide fresh perspective to current scholarship. Violence against LGBT women is not covered. A single chapter on women protecting the ecosystem outlines how women are affected by adverse environmental changes. However the analysis does not address gendered roles in impacting the environment.

The essays provide a broad perspective on gender and violence–albeit with some gaps in coverage. It is an excellent collection summarizing the intersection between gender and violence. Recommended as a starting point for those addressing issues of gender and violence.—**Muhammed Hassanali**

Part III
HUMANITIES

19 Humanities in General

General Works

Bibliography

558.   Melton, J. Gordon and Alysa Hornick, comps. **The Vampire in Folklore, History, Literature, Film, and Television: A Comprehensive Bibliography.** Jefferson, N.C., McFarland, 2015. 380p. index. $45.00pa. ISBN 13: 978-0-7864-9936-6; 978-1-4766-2083-1 (e-book).

Prior to the age of zombies, vampires ruled the media landscape. A multitude of books and television series and movies, each featuring variations of the origins and abilities and vulnerabilities of those creatures of the night roamed the media landscape, hunted and feasted upon by fans whose hunger for vampire lore was never quenched. With the publication of *The Vampire in Folklore, History, Literature, Film and Television: A Comprehensive Bibliography,* even those who are merely peckish when it comes to vampire lore will appreciate the vampires' long reign and their supernatural ability to adapt their storyline to each new generation.

The bibliography, published in 2015 by McFarland and Company, Inc., was compiled by J. Gordon Melton and Alysa Hornick (with the assistance of six other bibliographers). The primary compiler, Melton, is a distinguished professor of American religious history at Baylor University in Waco, Texas, and wrote three previous books on the subject of vampires: *The Vampire Book: The Encyclopedia of the Undead* (originally published in 1994, revised in 1999 and 2010, reviewed by ARBA in 1995 and 2000 and 2011, see ARBA 2000, entry 1135 and ARBA 2011, entry 1037); Video Hound's *Vampires on Video,* 1997, (see ARBA 198, entry 1321); and *The Vampire Gallery: A Who's Who of the Undead,* 1998, (see ARBA 1999, entry 1214). The second compiler, Alysa Hornick, hosted *Whedonology: An Academic Whedon Studies Bibliography* online from 2005 to 2015 (as of June 2015, the Whedon Studies Association began hosting *Whedonology* on their official Website). The bibliography is divided into nine topic segments: Vampires and Vampirism: General Sources; Folklore and History; Literature; Vampires on Stage and Screen; Vampires on Television; Vampires in Music and Arts; The Metaphorical Vampire; The Contemporary Vampire Subculture; and Juvenilia. Each of the 6,018 citations listed are numbered for easier access when referring to the index. Taking the section Folklore and History as an example—that section is subdivided into the following sections: Folklore and Mythology; Historical Perspective; Vlad Tepes; Elizabeth Bathory; and Vampire Slayers. Melton precedes each of these subsections with an introduction that offers an analytical summary of the section's topic. For example, with the first section, Folklore and Mythology, Melton provides a thoughtful overview of the vampire's evolution—from female blood-sucking, pitiless creatures such as the lamia that roamed Ancient Greece to the present-day depiction of humanoid vampires, male and female, afflicted with conscience, remorseful beings for whom readers and viewers feel empathy. The citations, as noted, are numbered. However, they are listed alphabetically, by author, in each section. The citations provide the following information: author; article, book, or journal title; journal information; date; publisher; and Web location (if applicable). The majority of citations provide only that information...but there are annotated exceptions such as when Melton points out that the work cited is a dissertation or if the cited work won an award or if the cited work has historic or cultural significance.

Melton describes the citation format in his very thorough introduction. In that introduction, Melton explains that in an effort to prevent the bibliography from burgeoning out of control, sources such as newspaper articles and movie reviews were not included. On the other hand, Melton et al. strove to infuse this bibliography with scholarly sources about vampires. Finally, Melton not only guides the reader through the many origins and versions of vampires in his introduction, he also devotes an off-shoot of the introduction to a brief overview of vampire studies, tracing those studies' origins from the 1700s to the first "Slayage Conference on Buffy the Vampire Slayer" in 2004.

The bibliography offers a vampire timeline with special references to literature, stage drama, the cinema, and television, 1800-2013. Three appendixes are included: top grossing vampire movies; vampire series on television; and Buffy the Vampire Slayer Conferences (2002 - 2014). The book also includes a thorough index arranged alphabetically by subject with reference (citation) numbers instead of page numbers.

Would Giles include this in the Library...if Sunnydale had not been destroyed? Should you? Whether your library is located in academic setting or public setting...or over a hellmouth...this bibliography would make an excellent addition to a library's collection.—
Brian T. Gallagher

Dictionaries and Encyclopedias

559.   **Creative Glossary. http://www.creativeglossary.com/.** [Website] Free. Date reviewed: 2016.

Creative Glossary is a free-to-use site that is easy to navigate and relatively unobstructed by advertising. From the home page, users can select from the drop-down menus of several tabs: Art, Craft, Culinary/Gardening, Design, Fashion, Performance Art, Story Art, and Trade. If one prefers to search alphabetically, there is a clickable A-Z list that takes users to hundreds of terms.

There is a wide range of subcategories. Under Art, for example, the glossary is divided into 15 such narrower sections as Business Art, Calligraphy, Jewelry, Print Making, and Sculpture. Blown Glass, Carpets/Rugs, Leather, Measures, Mosaics, Paper, Quilting, and Textiles are listed under Craft. Culinary/Gardening reveals three subcategories: Cooking, Fermentation, and Gardening. Design is further subdivided into Architecture, Computer, Graphic Design, Interior Decorating, and Math. Fashion has one subcategory, while a click on Performance Art takes users to a glossary of terms for Dance. The drop-down menu for

Story Art takes the curious to glossaries for Animation, Anime/Manga, and Film. Trade, the last tab, reveals further links to Carpentry, Cosmetology, Furniture, and Welding.

The Story Art tab provides a good example of the site's functionality. If one is interested in Anime/Manga, a click on this link will reveal the 56 associated terms. If Cosplay, for instance, is selected, users will see that it is a general Anime/Manga term meaning costume play that is rooted in the custom of anime watchers putting on the costumes of anime characters. Cosplay can also be found using the alphabetical links on the home page.—**ARBA Staff Reviewer**

Handbooks and Yearbooks

560.   **Essential Library of Cultural History.** Minneapolis, Minn., ABDO Publishing, 2015. multivolume. illus. index. 23.95/vol.

This six-volume set features ample illustrations and insets with specific information about topics and individuals. Written by different authors, each book consists of eight to nine chapters with the first chapter serving as an introduction and the remaining chapters arranged chronologically. Although the titles are general, the focus is on western art forms and specifically on finding space to explain the development of each medium within the United States. The art volume includes discussions of John James Audubon and Thomas Cole as American examples within the chapter describing innovations by Caravaggio and Bernini.

The content embraces the causal interactions between culture and art, explaining that works by female artists were often attributed to men and that television coverage of the Civil Rights movement helped convince Americans to support political change. The up-to-date series includes very recent examples in order to analyze the contemporary relevance of each art form, noting the use of Netflix and including still images from *The Game of Thrones* in the volumes on film and television, and explaining the recent use of transgender models.

Because the books target an 8th-grade reading level, they contain sophisticated sentence structures and end notes. Each volume provides a timeline and brief glossary specific to its content. The set provides a remarkably lucid general introduction to each of the six areas, managing to hit the highlights in the long history of art, music, fashion, and dance, and providing careful detail in the examination of the history of film and television.—**Delilah R. Caldwell**

20 Communication and Mass Media

General Works

Directories

561. **Hudson's Washington News Media Contacts Directory.** 48th ed. Amenia, N.Y., Grey House Publishing, 2015. 262p. index. $289.00pa. ISBN 13: 978-1-61925-575-3.

It is the hub of our nation's government, and a significant source of the news affecting every American's life. In fact, Washington, D.C., maintains its long-held role as the home to the largest concentration of media in the world. This 48th edition of *Hudson's Washington Media Contacts Directory* is a highly valuable, one-stop resource for everyone from political consultants to public relations professionals and beyond who may be interested in and affected by the large and influential Washington, D.C., news network.

Over 3,000 news organizations (and their holdings) and over 4,000 major media contacts are distributed within seven general sections of the directory: News Services, Newspapers (DC Bureaus), Newspapers (DC Metro Area), Foreign News, Syndicates and Columnists, Radio and TV Stations, and Magazines and Periodicals. Within each section, listings are further subdivided as appropriate. For example, Magazines and Periodicals listings are subdivided by DC Bureau, Foreign, and DC Headquartered categories.

Listings may include such information as street address, fax, Website, social media accounts, and key contacts from publishers to staff writers and more. Large media companies will also list their holdings. For this edition, all listings have been updated with the most current contact information.

As found in prior editions, the directory includes a Geographic Index/Foreign Media which provides a home country and/or city guide to all D.C.-based foreign media. New to this edition are four other indexes: an Entry Name Index which alphabetically lists all main headings, a Personnel Index alphabetically (by last name) listing all key media contacts, a Magazine Subject Index which lists categories from Advertising to Urban Affairs, and an Assignment Locator Index which lists almost 100 topics with reference to specific correspondents.

The keen organization of the material, in addition to its comprehensive detail and unique focus, makes this book essential.—**ARBA Staff Reviewer**

Handbooks and Yearbooks

562. **BBC Video Collection. http://alexanderstreet.com/products/bbc-video-collection.** [Website] Alexandria, Va., Alexander Street Press. Price negotiated by site. Date reviewed: 2016.

The BBC is well known and respected for their informative, entertaining, and timely documentaries The Alexander Street *BBC Video Collection* provides access to 700 of the most popular BBC documentary films. The collection also includes a small selection of performances (e.g., opera, dance, theatre, etc.) and covers a wide range of subjects including history, science, technology, art, religion, and politics. Documentaries range from an in-depth analysis of Hitler's rise to power to the design of the Coca Cola bottle.

All of the videos are provided in full-length version, and each video is fully transcribed. The transcript is interactive and synced with the video time code allowing users to click on any word or phrase in the transcript and jump to the corresponding place in the video. The transcripts also enable full-text searching of the videos. Each video has a visual table of contents to help users easily navigate the videos by memorable scene. Users are allowed to add their own bookmarks to the videos, and they can cite and share the videos, save favorites to a playlist, and generate a permalink embed code—an option very useful for teaching. Users are also able to make and save their own video clips allowing many different and useful applications for both teachers and students such as building an engaging lesson, presentation or report.

The video collection can be by browsed by title, discipline, people, and series. It can also be searched by keyword. Searches can also be narrowed by persons and places discussed and by content type (i.e., documentary, interview, performance, instructional material, etc.).

As an engaging and entertaining medium, video is also gaining ground for instructional use. This collection is highly recommended for school and public libraries. Teachers and students alike will enjoy using it. The layers of tools provided for using this video collection take it to the next level. Academic libraries will also find this collection beneficial for undergraduates in history, political science, business, and a range of humanities.—**Kristin Kay Leeman**

563. **The Handbook of Lifespan Communication.** John Nussbaum, ed. New York, Peter Lang, 2014. 460p. index. (Lifespan Communication: Children, Families, and Aging. Volume 2). $55.95pa. ISBN 13: 978-1-4331-2265-1.

The Handbook of Lifespan Communication takes a unique and wise look at human communication. Specifically, this book tracks the changes and developments of one's communication abilities, approach, and needs within various life stages. It represents volume two of the Lifespan Communication: Children, Families and Aging series.

A variety of communications scholars have contributed essays which are organized into seven sections within the book. After the opening section, which discusses lifespan communication theories and the methodologies used in studying them, sections coalesce around particular eras of life: Early Childhood, Childhood, Adolescent, Emerging Adulthood, Middle Adulthood, and Older Adulthood.

Within each section, essays focus on age-relevant themes. In the Early Childhood section, Beth Bonniwell Haslett and Wendy Samter share "Parent-Infant Communication," and point out how these first significant interactions, from facial expressions to simple vocalizations, work to initiate the child's concept of self, acquisition of language, social aptitude, and more. Andrew C. High's timely essay "Friend Me, Poke Me, Then Comfort Me: An Explanation of Supportive Communication in Online Social Networking Sites" can be found in the Emerging Adulthood section, and discusses the many implications of "virtual" social support. And the essay "Health Care Interactions in Older Adulthood" by Carla Fisher and Mollie Rose Canzona details communication issues related to the emphasis on various health care concerns in the Older Adulthood stage of life. These are just some examples of the broad range of topics helping to illustrate the scope of *Lifespan Communication.*

Each essay concludes with a generous list of references. The book is thoroughly indexed and shares information about the contributors. This volume succeeds in showing how placing communication research into a context of lifespan development can be genuinely revelatory.—**ARBA Staff Reviewer**

564. **Media Violence and Children: A Complete Guide for Parents and Professionals.** 2d ed. Douglas A. Gentile, ed. Santa Barbara, Calif., Praeger/ABC-CLIO, 2014. 477p. index. $58.00. ISBN 13: 978-1-4408-3017-4; 978-1-4408-3018-1 (e-book).

In the 13 years since the publication of *Media Violence and Children,* edited by Douglass A. Gentile, not only has research in the field of violence and media evolved, but also our definition of media. Whereas the trends of the late 1990s and early 2000s focused on V Chips for censoring violence on television and presences of violence in video games, the dawn of social media and the new technology on which it became available has altered the focus of research. The interactive nature of the new media has created a host of new issues which made an update and reshaping of the original necessary.

Facebook, Instagram, smart phones, tablets, cyberbullying, and cyberstalking are all softwares, technologies, and issues that parents and researchers have faced in recent years. Gentile and his group of writers attempt to put these all new issues in perspective when understanding research in the field of media violence and children. In 15 essays the subject of media violence is explained both in historical terms ("Television Violence: Sixty Years of Research"), today's issues ("Cyberbullying"), and future approaches to the topic ("Media Violence and Public Policy").

Marketed as a complete guide for parents and professionals, this second edition would be an ideal companion to the first edition in academic and professional library collections. I am less convinced that parents would find this tool as useful. This is not a simple explanation of the issues involved with media violence and children—instead the essays are well researched and of a high academic standard.

I highly recommend purchasing for academic and professional collections.—**Rob Laurich**

Authorship

Style Manuals

565.   Mills, Elizabeth Shown. **Evidence Explained: Citing History Sources from Artifacts to Cyberspace.** 3d ed. Baltimore, Md., Genealogical Publishing, 2015. 892p. index. $59.95. ISBN 13: 978-0-8063-2017-5.

Evidence Explained: Citing History Sources from Artifacts to Cyberspace, now in its third edition, allows historians and other researchers to cite accurately almost every type of source, particularly those not covered in more traditional citation guides. The author encourages users of this hefty book to read the first two chapters, "Fundamentals of Evidence Analysis" and "Fundamentals of Citation" in their entirety and to reference individual types of works and citations as necessary. Each chapter begins with a list of "QuickCheck Models" followed by a list of "Guidelines & Examples" and source models. For instance, chapter 14 "Publications: Periodicals, Broadcasts & Web Miscellanea" delineates citation models for such sources as sound clips, podcasts, and blogs. Chapters are followed by a glossary, bibliography, index, and separate index for QuickCheck Models.

For libraries that already own a copy of the earlier editions (see ARBA 2007, entry 563 and ARBA 2009, entry 610), this may not be a necessary purchase. For other libraries, however, this source is an essential addition to the reference shelf, as it will quickly and easily allow users or librarians to find answers to tricky citation questions.—**ARBA Staff Reviewer**

566.   **MLA Handbook for Writers of Research Papers.** 8th ed. New York, Modern Language Association of America, 2016. 146p. index. $12.00pa. ISBN 13: 978-1-60329-262-7; 978-1-60329-265-8 (e-book).

This eighth edition of the Modern Language Association (MLA) handbook provides the updated guide to citing sources in scholarly writing. While seemingly simple in scope, the new edition offers valuable information that works well to adapt to the evolving landscape of research writing.

Since first experimented with in 1951, the MLA style sheet has undergone vast change. No longer does the manual need to remind writers to type their work; instead, the guide must deal with the proliferation of diverse sources and potentially complex rules. With mind to changes in literary studies, the needs of the modern student and certainly the advent of modern media, this eighth edition emphasizes a level of flexibility when creating the necessary source documentation.

The book is separated into two parts, dealing with Principles of MLA Style (covering such things as information gathering, organization, etc.) and Details of MLA Style (covering the nitty-gritty of quotations, numbering, abbreviations, punctuation, and much more). Information in this part is delivered in short, sectioned paragraphs with clear examples following. Aids such as highlighting, lists, cross-referencing, and a practice template help readers navigate the technical material.

The book is a must have for any student embarking on a path of academic writing and belongs in libraries of all sorts—public, middle and high school, academic, and personal.—**ARBA Staff Reviewer**

Journalism

Dictionaries and Encyclopedias

567.   Roth, Mitchel P. **The Encyclopedia of War Journalism, 1807-2015.** 3d ed. Amenia, N.Y., Grey House Publishing, 2015. 673p. index. $165.00. ISBN 13: 978-1-61925-745-0; 978-1-61925-746-7 (e-book).

The original edition entitled the *Historical Dictionary of War Journalism* (see ARBA 98, entry 881) contained more than 900 entries and this retitled third edition has more than 200 additional entries. The volume is divided into two sections: the first part contains alphabetical entries on many topics including correspondents, illustrators, photographers, periodicals, news organizations, among many other subjects. Each entry includes a reference source; the article length varies from one to several paragraphs and the quality of the content ranges from sparse to good. The second section contains 56 primary documents including article and book excerpts and also photographs. The 29 appendixes are useful and contain much hard-to-find information: lists of many war correspondents (no comprehensive list is possible) from the Mexican-American War through the wars in Afghanistan and Iraq, films that portray war correspondents, journalism award winners, lists of photographers and camera people, and names of correspondents killed in several wars. The timeline notes significant incidents but unfortunately, only includes the year but not the specific date of the event.

Although other journalism reference works discuss war journalism, this title solely devoted to the topic provides unique and readily-accessible information compiled from numerous sources.—**Donald Altschiller**

Handbooks and Yearbooks

568.   **Journalist's Resource. http://journalistsresource.org/.** [Website] Free. Date reviewed: 2016.

Journalist's Resource is a project of Carnegie-Knight Initiative of the Future of Journalism Education, and it is based at Harvard Kennedy School's Shorenstein Center. The team consists of Harvard faculty, staff members, researchers, and a developer, and is an open-access Website that curates scholarly studies and reports.

According to Tom Patterson, Acting Director at the Shorenstein Center, research and fact-based information are tools that today's journalists should use more frequently, and they form the basis for the articles on *Journalist's Resource*. This makes the site extremely beneficial for academics and educators who wish to avoid biased sources as well as anyone interested in or studying journalism. Though the information is often dense, this site will even be useful for younger students who need reputable sources for academic purposes. Many articles include bullet points that highlight important aspects of the piece, a feature that students can use to better understand the more advanced scholarly studies.—**ARBA Staff Reviewer**

Radio, Television, Audio, and Video

Dictionaries and Encyclopedias

569.   Street, Seán. **Historical Dictionary of British Radio.** 2d ed. Lanham, Md., Rowman & Littlefield, 2015. 391p. (Historical Dictionaries of Literature and the Arts). $115.00; $109.99 (e-book). ISBN 13: 978-1-4422-4922-6; 978-1-4422-4923-3 (e-book).

While the history of British radio for the most part is dominated by the British Broadcasting Corporation (BBC), this historical dictionary also covers the early advent of radio in the United Kingdom as well as contemporary independent stations, podcasts, and digital audio downloads. British broadcasting began in the spring of 1922 and will soon celebrate its centenary in 2022. The BBC was pioneering in a number of areas including women news readers in August of 1933 and foreign language broadcasting, starting initially with Arabic language broadcasts in January of 1938. The work begins with an excellent historical essay that covers the period from the late nineteenth century up until the present. The BBC has been both a major national presence and an international one. The book is arranged topically and covers such things as: radio personalities, programming, and electronic technical topics. Entries are confined to short paragraphs on the topic. There are no illustrations in the book. The first edition was published in 2006 (see ARBA 2007, entry 783) and this second edition will serve as a reference tool for the centenary. Also included are a list of acronyms and abbreviations, a chronology, and a classed bibliography containing materials up until 2013. The book will be essential for collections on the history of radio, British life and literature, and world history.—**Ralph Lee Scott**

Directories

570.   **Complete Television, Radio & Cable Industry Directory.** 3d ed. Amenia, N.Y., Grey House Publishing, 2015. 1601p. $350.00pa. ISBN 13: 978-1-61925-287-5.

This is the third edition of the *Complete Television, Radio & Cable Industry Directory* published by Grey House. For nearly 75 years, R. R. Bowker published previous editions of this reference work under the title *Broadcasting & Cable Yearbook.* This information-packed book begins with a chronology of electronic media, information about the FCC and its regulatory authority, a glossary of terms, and a list of abbreviations. Following are 10 sections: Broadcast Television—United States; Broadcast Television—Canada; Radio—United States; Radio—Canada; Cable—United States; Cable—Canada; Programming; Equipment Manufacturers & Production Services; Professional Services; Associations, Events, Education & Awards; and Government. The table of contents makes it easy to find information about such topics as the top 100 television shows of 2014 in the United States or special programming on radio stations in Canada. For libraries serving users in the broadcasting industry or for anyone working in these fields, this is a valuable assemblage of a massive amount of information. The purchase of the print edition provides buyers with a year's access to the online database at http://gold.greyhouse.com. Highly recommended.—**ARBA Staff Reviewer**

Handbooks and Yearbooks

571. **60 Minutes: 1997-2014.** [Website] Alexandria, Va., Alexander Street Press. Price negotiated by site. Date reviewed: 2016.

60 Minutes: 1997-2014 contains 482 hours of videos, comprising 3,415 reports and editorials shown on the CBS network since the late 1990s. The material is, because of the show's stature in American popular culture and politics at the time, historically important on its own terms. The main page offers the ability to search by keywords or to browse by titles, subjects, reporters, people, organizations, places, and events. The most active reporters are also listed on the main page, as is a subheading for the most popular subjects. Each subject includes the number of shows about that subject. The "Advanced Search" feature provides tools for more targeted searches. Because "Terrorism (150)" is far and away the most frequently referenced subject in this collection—a "9/11" search generates 179 items. Adding the term "Clarke," however, as in Richard Clarke, the terrorist expert in the White House at the time of the attacks, generates only four hits, including a two-part interview just before Clarke's congressional testimony on the attacks, a rebuttal by National Security Advisor Condoleeza Rice the following week, and another episode that referenced these interviews. For any scholar working on natural security and foreign diplomacy in the late twentieth and early twenty first centuries, these shows are crucial material.

The collection is structured in a way to make research and educational use easy. Each video page includes full documentation of the show's production and broadcast. The transcripts are also available and searchable, making it a snap to quote and cite interviews or editorials accurately. The transcript search feature also automatically forwards the video to that segment. This is quite useful for using this material in lectures as long as the teacher realizes that they will need to queue up the video beforehand, since loading is dependent on bandwidth. The videos are not downloadable; they are also at a lower resolution, and the width of the image was compressed on my tablet screen. This means that projection will result in a grainy and distorted image. Thus while the material in this video collection is interesting and occasionally historically important, and the collection is useful for research and some teaching formats, users must be aware that the image quality degrades rapidly the larger is it projected.—**Joseph E. Taylor III**

21 Decorative Arts

Collecting

572. **Benjamin K. Miller Collection of United States Stamps:** http://digitalcollections.nypl.org/collections/benjamin-k-miller-collection-of-united-states-stamps#/?tab=navigation. [Website] Free. Date reviewed: 2016.

This collection of stamps and other materials was donated to The New York Public Library in 1925 by Milwaukee attorney Benjamin K. Miller. These items are revered for being the first complete collection of U.S. stamps ever assembled and were displayed at the library for more than 50 years until a 1977 theft robbed the collection of 153 of its rarest stamps. They are now available for viewing on this Website, though students who are not specifically studying Benjamin K. Miller may not get much out of this Website academically. Each item data includes the Title, Collection, Library Locations, Genres, and Type of Resource.

Overall, this page would be most useful for historians and those specializing in stamp collections in the early 1900s, as well as for individual collectors.—**ARBA Staff Reviewer**

Crafts

573. Atkin, Jacqui. **Troubleshooting for Potters: All the Common Problems, Why They Happen, and How to Fix Them.** Hauppauge, N.Y., Barron's Educational Series, 2014. 144p. illus. index. $21.99pa. ISBN 13: 978-1-4380-0409-9.

This title provides users with guidance regarding problems associated with the creation of ceramics. The first chapter supplies 25 pages of diagnostic charts organized for quick reference that list common problems (clay that is too wet, shapes that warp, surface cracks, glaze that is too thick, blistering, uneven firing, etc) and solutions.

Clays; Forming and Bisqueware; Surface Decoration; and Firing are the subjects of the next four chapters; each is organized into two sections, best practices and fix it. So, for example, after learning about the nature of various clays in chapter two, readers can learn how to fix such difficulties as the tendency of standard porcelain to harden quickly or the formation of mold on stored paper clay. The same formula applies to chapter three, which outlines the best practices for forming and bisqueware but provides solutions to the common problems of collapsing shapes, cracking and splitting, and more. Chapter four treats the topic of surface decoration and what to do about blurred patterns, crazing, and holes in decals. The last chapter, "Firing," provides the pros and cons of different kiln types, ways to measure and control kiln temperature, and temperature tables.

Health and safety hints, a glossary, and an index follow the informative chapters. Recommended for public libraries and school libraries that support ceramics programs.—**ARBA Staff Reviewer**

Fashion and Costume

574.   Bent, James. **Asian Street Fashion.** New York, Thames and Hudson, 2014. 272p. illus. $24.95pa. ISBN 13: 978-0-500-54440-2.

Asian Street Fashion documents the quirky and elegant styles that decorate the streets of major cities such as Tokyo, Seoul, Hong Kong, and Singapore. With little text and nearly 300 photographs, this book will be a delight for those inclined to fashion or curious about new styles. Featuring loud patterns, chic black-and-white attire, edgy cuts, and everything in between, there is much to be celebrated within these pages. Apart from a few paragraphs that introduce each chapter, readers are left with only photos to experience the many approaches to fashion in Asian cities. A perfect gift or decoration for a coffee table, the book itself is even designed aesthetically, though some may find the vertical font difficult to read. It is a highly recommended photo book that readers will cherish.—**ARBA Staff Reviewer**

575.   **Clothing and Fashion: American Fashion from Head to Toe.** Mary D. Doering, Patricia Hunt-Hurst, Heather Vaughan Lee, and José Blanco F., eds. Santa Barbara, Calif., ABC-CLIO, 2016. 4v. illus. index. $415.00/set. ISBN 13: 978-1-61069-309-7; 978-1-61069-310-3 (e-book).

This comprehensive look at the way Americans have dressed covers over 400 years of history, from bodices, footwear, and hairstyles of the seventeenth century to the latest styles of the twenty-first. Each volume has a timeline and a historical overview of the period (1600-1785, 1785-1899, 1900-1945, and 1945-present) as well as chronological and alphabetical indexes. The social and cultural breadth of this work is reflected in articles such as "Jazz," "African-American Clothing, 1715-1785," "Man Ray," and "Native American Influence." Attention to detail is seen in the division of a single subject, such as "Jewelry," into chronological slices within a single volume, each entry written by different scholar.

Each entry includes a "Further Reading" list, which, for the earlier eras, refers the reader to other books of use on the topic, only rarely citing journal literature. The last volume's reading lists include magazines, newspapers, and Websites. Each volume also includes a 16-page section of excellent color plates illustrating clothes and fashion from the era, a glossary, and a comprehensive bibliography gathering together the works cited throughout the volume. Any library with patrons interested in these topics will find this set a valuable set to have.—**Mark Schumacher**

576.   **Dress & Fashion: Design & Manufacture. http://digitalcollections.nypl.org/ collections/dress-fashion-design-manufacture#/?tab=about.** [Website] Free. Date reviewed: 2016.

This collection from the New York Public Library contains contemporary and practical works relating to apparel manufacturing, industry, design, and aesthetics in the early 1900s. It is intended to provide users a window into the daily practices and resources of a manufacturing industry that is still thriving in New York City today. The collection will continue to expand in the next few years.

The Web page is attractive and organized, but does not offer much apart from clickable images. Each still image provides the user with the following information: type of resource, genre, date issued, division, publisher, engraver, cartographer, dates/origin, topics, notes, and citations (in MLA, APA, Chicago, and Wikipedia), as well as additional descriptive information. A timeline shows the approximate date the image was issued and digitized. Users can also download the images in a variety of sizes and resolutions. This collection is highly recommended those interested in the history of manufacturing and design but will likely serve a variety of users.—**ARBA Staff Reviewer**

577.   English, Bonnie. **A Cultural History of Fashion in the 20th and 21st Centuries.** 2d ed. New York, Bloomsbury Academic, 2013. 255p. illus. index. $29.95pa. ISBN 13: 978-0-85785-135-2.

Bonnie English argues that haute couture, from its recognition in the nineteenth century as a system of social and status markings to the late twentieth century, underwent a process of democratization that now leaves that term of limited utility. She creates an interesting and engaging history that connects many of the major socioeconomic and artistic trends to ultra-high-end clothing designers and the complex reciprocal relationships among designer, ready-to-wear, and what she terms street fashion. English, Associate Professor of Art History and Theory at the Queensland College of Art, is most effective describing how clothing designs reflect modernity as she seeks to break down the boundary between so-called fine art and the applied art of fashion, including a discussion of the many groundbreaking female artists who were also successful designers in the early twentieth century. She is somewhat less effective with the dawning of postmodernism, in part because that trend is much more difficult to define and perhaps too recent for perspective, but she closes with a strong summary of the trends that are emerging in the twenty-first century. Though the impact of globalization and the Internet may seem obvious, she links these factors to specific changes at specific fashion houses, which makes her analysis more persuasive. With its strong narrative thread, *A Cultural History of Fashion in the 20th and 21st Centuries* is most likely intended as a textbook but, with its comprehensive bibliography and index, it will also serve as a useful reference. Black-and-white figures and color plates help the reader to see fashion change over the years although an interested reader is likely to seek many more examples. If there is a third edition (a little more copyediting could remove a few annoying errors and repetitions), it will be interesting to see how present ideas of fashion change in the future.—**R. K. Dickson**

Interior Design

578.   **Empire and Regency: Decoration in the Age of Napoleon. http:// digitalcollections.nypl.org/collections/empire-and-regency-decoration-in-the-age-of-napoleon#/?tab=navigation.** [Website] Free. Date reviewed: 2016.

This collection from the New York Public Library contains books and plates from the Astor and Lenox Library Collections as well as from the private library of the architect Thomas Hastings. The vast majority of this collection consists of still images of Empire and Regency style furniture and décor dating back to the early 1800s. The images may appeal to those who are studying fashion and design in this time period, as well as history buffs curious about the origins of fashion. These pieces are particularly interesting given their ties to Napoleon I, whose ambitious art and design program lasted until the end of his reign in 1815 and was highly influential.

The easily navigable Website offers a series of clickable images that provide the user with the following information: type of resource, date issued, division, author, artist, topics, identifiers, and citations (in MLA, APA, Chicago, and Wikipedia), as well as additional descriptive information. A timeline shows when the creator of the image was born and died, when the image was issued, and when it was digitized. Users can also download the images in a variety of sizes and resolutions. This collection will be useful for those curious about Empire and Regency design, specifically in furniture and décor.—**ARBA Staff Reviewer**

579.   Jenkins, Alison. **300 Tips for Painting and Decorating: Tips, Techniques & Trade Secrets.** New York, Firefly Books, 2014. 176p. illus. index. $19.95pa. ISBN 13: 978-1-77085-452-9.

If you are looking for the impetus and inspiration to start that home improvement project you've been considering, look no further. *300 Tips for Painting and Decorating* is an easy-to-navigate source for many of your interior design and maintenance needs. The author has included 300 helpful tips aligning with particular home improvement tasks (e.g., sanding wooden floors) that are further organized into broader chapters.

The book gives plenty of space to the essential equipment, materials, planning, and preparation needed before beginning a project. It then delves into particular topics of décor and maintenance, from walls and floors to windows and doors, paying mind to practical concerns such as window security, as well as creative design approaches like marbleizing paint effects. The book also discusses overall maintenance issues pertaining to hardware, weather, and safety and points out when it may be worth it to hire a professional.

Within each chapter, readers will note the generous use of color photography and clear illustrations detailing toolbox must-haves, wall treatments, task demonstrations, and more. They will also find useful checklists, estimation and comparison charts, and "fix-it" and "try-it" panels revealing special tricks of the trade.

From the differences between grouts and sealants to painting dos and don'ts, *300 Tips* covers all the bases of a do-it-yourself approach to making a beautiful home. The book concludes with a glossary of useful terminology and an index. This would make a fine addition to the collection of a public library.—**Laura Herrell**

22 Fine Arts

General Works

Dictionaries and Encyclopedias

580. **The Bloomsbury Encyclopedia of Design.** Clive Edwards, ed. New York, Bloomsbury Academic, 2016. 3v. illus. index. $725.00/set. ISBN 13: 978-0-4725-2157-6.

This three-volume encyclopedia is a reference work for the general public, students, professionals, and scholars on the broad umbrella of design, which in a multidisciplinary world focuses on definitions, critiques, descriptions, and analyses of design culture, practices, and ideology for the last 150 years. There are over 1,800 entries written by 200 contributors and six editors, from simple definitions to short essays. Extensive cross-referencing is provided, along with a comprehensive index for each volume. Bibliographic references are included for each entry, as well as a bibliographic section for each volume. Black-and-white photos and pictures are included where appropriate. The introduction discusses some of the depth and breadth of the encyclopedia in terms of boundaries, history, people, concepts, ideologies, theories, practice, and geography. Overall, this work provides a basic knowledge on contemporary design worldwide, and would be an excellent addition to any reference collection.—**Bradford Lee Eden**

Architecture

581. **Archnet. http://archnet.org/.** [Website] Free. Date reviewed: 2016.

Archnet is the world's largest globally accessible online databank of Islamic architecture, art, and urbanism. Its mission is to provide access to visual and textual material that will help highlight the traditions and culture of Islam and assist students who lack resources for learning. It was developed in 2002 at the Massachusetts Institute of Technology (MIT) School of Architecture and Planning in partnership with the Aga Khan Trust for Culture.

This Website is highly aesthetic and organized and is free from advertisements. Interactive clickables allow users to explore timelines, a variety of archive collections, and a resources page that includes images, videos, drawings, publications, seminars, and academic articles. A course syllabi section allows users to access free material provided by faculty teachers about culture in the Muslim world. This is a perfect tool for students interested in Muslim studies who either do not have the resources to take formal upper-level courses, or those who want to try out the field without committing financially. The content of this site will best serve upper-level high school or college students as an academic resource, though the interactive pages will be fun for younger students to peruse as well.—**ARBA Staff Reviewer**

582. **Art and Architecture in Video. https://search.alexanderstreet.com/artv.** [Website] Alexandria, Va., Alexander Street Press. Price negotiated by site. Date reviewed: 2016.

An online media database, *Art and Architecture in Video* is a collection of 848 videos that provides information and opens doors to critical analysis of art forms. This assembly of videos contains over 500 hours from various visual media companies. Primarily the collection contains documentaries though there are also instructional videos, biographical videos, videos of interviews, and one book animation (*Hirsoshima no Pika* by Toshi Mauki).

The entire contents are easily accessible from a sidebar including: Browse, Subjects, and People. The advanced search box easily accesses your specific subject request and will include all videos that reference the selected subject matter. Having generated a subject list of videos, brief annotations help students determine which video is of interest. A simple click on the left photo brings you to the video. The Detail tab will provide more specifics on the video and this summary will give the strongest overview of the film. Where available, the Transcript tab shows the written text with narration highlighting. Options for e-mail, sharing, and saving are practical for collection of data for future review. The Cite link makes referencing the visual media easy as it includes necessary bibliographic data. Related Items links to other relevant videos.

Visual media can be a valuable tool for research, and in the area of art studies, visual media becomes a dynamic tool to understanding both theory and art forms. Art periods, styles, and critiques of work all contribute to art study via this video collection. Alexander Street Press has amassed a broad base of art, artists, architecture, and architects for an overview both historical and contemporary. The collection includes videos on well-known artists such as Auguste Renoir (*The Road to Impressionism: 19th Century France*) and less-well-known artists such as Man Ray.

Unfortunately, the quality of videos is not always consistent; *Louis Corinth-Self Portrait at his Easel 1914: Neve* has poor audio quality detracting from the video itself. Most videos are of a good quality and the information will be more useful to art students because of the visual aspect necessary for critical analysis of art.

Overall, *Art and Architecture in Video* is a collection of visual media that is a useful tool for undergraduate and graduate students researching a diverse array of art and architecture, historically or in the modern era. It will also be of use in multidisciplinary studies where researchers want to bring in an art/design/culture element.

Recommended.—**Janis Minshull**

583. **Carnegie Survey of Architecture of the South.** [Website] Free. Date reviewed: 2016.

The *Carnegie Survey of the Architecture of the South,* a Library of Congress collection, is a systematic record of American buildings and gardens photographed by

Frances Benjamin Johnston (1864-1952) primarily in the early 1930s. Users can browse more than 1,700 structures in this collection that focuses on rural and urban areas of Virginia, Maryland, North and South Carolina, Georgia, Alabama, Louisiana, Florida, Mississippi, and West Virginia. Johnston's photographs include grand mansions and public buildings as well as small houses and mills. Her initial work was funded privately; grants from the Carnegie Corporation funded the rest of the work based on the condition that the photographs be deposited in the Library of Congress. ARTstor digitized all the photographs in 2008.

This site contains a wealth of information about Johnston's history and photography methods, and the process of collecting and preserving her images. There are links to information about the background and scope of the collection, which includes listings of photographs by state. Users will also find a short bibliography and information about how the collection is organized. There are also links to related collections in the Library of Congress and other institutions. A subject index list will help users find specific information. The easy-to-use Website provides researchers in many disciplines with a trove of valuable information.—**ARBA Staff Reviewer**

584.   Panhorst, Michael W. **The Memorial Art and Architecture of Vicksburg National Military Park.** Kent, Ohio, Kent State University Press, 2015. 164p. illus. maps. index. $19.95pa. ISBN 13: 978-1-60635-219-9; 978-1-61277-866-2 (e-book).

Monuments to the Civil War abound in many areas of the country from small town centers to tucked away parks in large metropolitan areas. Perhaps one of the largest, collective groups of monuments is located at the Vicksburg National Military Park in Vicksburg, Mississippi. *Vicksburg National Military Park* is less about the battle in 1863 to control the vital location on the Mississippi River and more about the statuary and other monuments erected years after the battle to commemorate the military units and individuals that participated in the struggle. The work is not a catalog of the monuments and statues located within the park as much as a work on the techniques used by the sculptors and architects in creating the monuments. The work also discusses the planning, fundraising, and political negotiations which occurred prior to the actual construction of the art. Profusely illustrated with photographs, predominantly in color, along with maps, the book is meant to be read as background information prior to or in conjunction with a visit to the park. A chapter near the end of the work outlines driving routes that encompass most of the major memorials within the park boundaries. Brief biographical sketches of the known artists involved with the creation of the monuments appears as an appendix to the work.

Vicksburg National Military Park is a useful addition to collections supporting Civil War interests, art, and landscape architecture, as well as public projects. Written in a style that lends itself to extended reading by a wide range of individuals at all levels, placing the work in a circulating collection seems an appropriate approach to its location.—**Gregory Curtis**

585.   Radford, Anthony, Selen Morkoç, and Amit Srivastava. **The Elements of Modern Architecture: Understanding Contemporary Buildings.** New York, Thames and Hudson, 2014. 344p. illus. index. $50.00. ISBN 13: 978-0-500-34295-4.

Architects design buildings for the combination of order, space, form, and function, and interested readers can use this book to analyze how well they succeeded in particular instances. Fifty important buildings are covered here, from the Arab World Institute in Paris to the Menara UMNO in Penang, Malaysia. A wide variety of representative architecture is sampled here, with the earliest design being that of Frank Lloyd Wright's Guggenheim Museum in New York City (in this case, "contemporary" refers to the period after 1950). Some of these are quite striking, such as the Kunsthaus in Graz, Austria, while others are not quite so impressive on the outside. The exteriors might appear simple, but the interiors can be quite advanced. The photographs are all in black and white, so they are artistic statements in themselves as well as providing interesting views of the buildings.

The descriptions are brief, with most of the page space being taken up by over 2,500 illustrations. Floor plans, perspective views, landscape diagrams, and lots of drawings about the various structural details will prove attractive to architecture students. The book also discusses materials, lighting, and the various parts of each building, touching on the geographical context and public response (some of which had to be controversial). For each building there is also a map showing where on the globe and in a country the building is located.

At the end of the book is a bibliography divided up by building, with just a few important references for each structure. The endnote briefly discusses 15 common themes (e.g., ethics, identity, style, etc.) revealed by a study of these buildings. This reasonably priced book is suitable for the reference or circulating collections of public and academic libraries, as both experts and nonexperts can enjoy it. And it is attractive enough to sit on your coffee table as a conversation starter—**Daniel K. Blewett**

586.　Striner, Richard, and Melissa Blair. **Washington and Baltimore Art Deco: A Design History of Neighboring Cities.** Baltimore, Md., Johns Hopkins University Press, 2014. 243p. illus. index. $49.95. ISBN 13: 978-1-4214-1162-0.

When you think of Art Deco you automatically think of New York and Miami; however, Washington and Baltimore also have a history of hosting this amazing style. The authors, Striner and Blair explore the major remaining examples of Art Deco in Baltimore and Washington, while at the same time chronicling those which have been lost. This study is important because it explores the design history of two major east coast towns that are essentially interconnecting neighbors. One city had a major Federal New Deal construction spurt during the depression, while the other depended on commercial interests for their Art Deco treasures. In fact Baltimore's mayor resisted the New Deal and felt that it was a threat to real estate interests in the city. Private residences and apartment buildings in both cities were built in the Art Deco style and many remain in use today. The Federal Housing Administration attempted to provide homes for lower income citizens in both cities. The volume begins with two introductory essays: "The Spirit of Art Deco" (an overview of the movement) and "Washington and Baltimore in the Age of Art Deco." The rest of the book is devoted to chapters covering various Art Deco types in these two cities: Residential, Commercial, and Public/Institutional. The latter covers such impressive buildings as: the Enoch Pratt Free Library, the University of Maryland Hospital, Folger Shakespeare Library, Library of Congress Annex (John Adams Building), Bethesda Naval Medical Center, and Hoover Field (Reagan National Airport). The book ends with a "coda" pleading for preservation of existing buildings along with musing on building fate in various economic climates. Also included are a list of major architects, an essay on sources, footnotes, and an index. Overall the authors have taken a compelling topic and treated it in an outstanding manner. The volume is illustrated with matt finish photographs of a number of Art Deco examples in both cities. Most libraries will want to purchase this volume as it is a fascinating tale of two cities and how modern architecture shaped their future.—**Ralph Lee Scott**

Painting

587.   Bofkin, Lee. **Global Street Art: The Street Artists and Trends Taking Over the World.** New York, Firefly Books, 2014. 304p. illus. index. $29.95pa. ISBN 13: 978-1-77085-485-7.

Global Street Art is a gorgeous photo book documenting the subversive medium that has broken the boundaries of what global society considers to be true art. While it would be nearly impossible to showcase the expansive reach of this contemporary phenomenon, the author nonetheless has curated a brilliant and diverse collection of compelling examples from this vibrant scene.

Providing a brief perspective on the history and global evolution of street art, the book touches on the origins and meanings of graffiti, the selection of the appropriate "canvas," the pioneers of the movement, the constraints of the art form, and much more.

Mainly, however, the author lets the art tell its own story. Over 500 color photos from around the world offer an excellent representation of the various forms of street art today. The photos take readers from train yards to highway underpasses, from slums to sophisticated urban centers, and from London to Melbourne to Sao Paolo. We note recurring motifs from hip-hop culture and the animal world, and observe the skill with which artists integrate their work into public spaces. We also learn of unusual materials like yarn, metal, and stickers that have made their way into the street art landscape. An index of artists and their contact information adds further value for those wishing to pursue this subject more deeply.

From the gritty to the sublime, this book captures the essence of an art form that has altered the urban landscape and stoked the visual imagination of its population.—**Laura Herrell**

588.   Girst, Thomas. **The Duchamp Dictionary.** New York, Thames and Hudson, 2014. 224p. illus. $29.95. ISBN 13: 978-0-500-23917-9.

As the legend has it, Picasso was talking freely about his work to journalist Giovanni Papini in 1952. Never one to shy from tooting his own horn, Picasso said, "Today, as you know, I am famous, I am rich." Hardly news but he went to say he knew he was not one of the "[g]reat painters …like Giotto, Titian, Rembrandt, Goya." Rather he was, "[O]nly a public entertainer who has understood the times and has exploited as best he could the imbecility, the vanity and the greed of his contemporaries."

That's the legend because it appears he may well never have said such a thing. It is in dispute though one must say that he should have said it. The present volume makes it clear that for better or for worse, but mostly the latter, modern art has done more to push art to the background than anything any conservative government could have hoped to accomplish. This is not to say that modern art has no merit; it has some. But most of it has to be explained, and, like a joke that falls flat is no joke, art that requires explanation to be understood has failed in its most central mission. Alas, De gustibus non est and all that.

The Duchamp Dictionary makes a good case that Duchamp "challenged our understanding of art and thus forever changed the course of art history" as its introduction states, but it cannot get away from the fact that in making that challenge it may also have sowed the seeds of its own destruction. Girst is certainly well-suited for this task, himself a Duchamp scholar. From Duchamp's urinals, to his war with language, to his silly photographs with nude women, this well-wrought dictionary cannot get away from Duchamp's silliness and imbecility. The dictionary ranges far afield from art, of course, but also into philosophy, linguistics, and more. Its generous illustrations often give it a seventies collage feel, however.

The book does have its quirks. First, the introductory text is pink on beige paper. This is Duchamp-y, to be sure, but it's also damnably difficult to read. Further, the main body of the dictionary is in a lighter purple font which does make it easier to read, but parts of it are highlighted in a darker shade of pink, acting as colorful footnotes. Lastly, quixotry has its limits, as the illustration of Duchamp's most famous work, *Nude Descending a Staircase, No.2* is nothing at all like the real work (p.129). One can appreciate the irony, but only if one is already familiar with the actual work. Would we find it equally entertaining if we opened a dictionary in which the words were purposely ill-defined? How can we recommend it to the unwary?

While helpful in its intent to bring to a wider audience the unhinged nature of Duchamp's work and school of zany thought, these reservations must be noted as drawbacks.—**Mark Y. Herring**

589.   Kloosterboer, Lorena. **Painting in Acrylics: The Indispensible Guide.** New York, Firefly Books, 2014. 320p. illus. index. $35.00. ISBN 13: 978-1-77085-408-6.

Painting in Acrylics is a beautiful book filled with ideas and expertise related to the creation and exhibition (whether personal or professional) of acrylic paintings. The author uses her vast experience as an award-winning artist and exhibitor to teach all aspects of acrylic painting in a visually appealing, easy-to-navigate, and encouraging manner.

Organized into six chapters, the book opens with the basics. Readers explore the qualities of different types of acrylic paint, common materials, and equipment available for acrylic painting and main principles of color theory, mixing, and more. Ensuing chapters focus on a large variety of acrylic painting techniques (washes, spattering, or glazing to name but a few), and explore acrylics in relation to different painting categories, such as still lifes, landscapes, and more. A final chapter offers more inspiration related to how best to care for and market the final acrylic product, and touches on framing, handling criticism, copyright issues, and other important topics.

Within each chapter are helpful tools such as tables, charts, a section navigator, technique swatches, text boxes, and more which make the experience of reading this book appropriately visual and very easy to follow. Many of the techniques are explained via step-by-step instructions, both verbal and pictorial. In fact, a generous selection of striking color photographs really tells the story of acrylic painting, and demonstrates, in addition to technique, a range of vibrant color, subject matter, and finished works with an eye toward fine detail and inspiration. The book also includes a helpful glossary of art terms (as associated with acrylic painting) and an important Color Index (C.I.) Pigment Chart, detailing standardized pigment codes, names, color examples, and opacity.

From mixing your first acrylic colors to signing your finished work, this book will guide both beginning and experienced artists along a satisfying creative journey.—**Laura Herrell**

Photography

590. **Digital Photography Complete Course.** New York, DK Publishing, 2015. 360p. illus. index. $30.00. ISBN 13: 978-1-4654-3607-8.

This visual-centric book is designed to guide readers through a 20-week course on digital photography. The book uses a dynamic approach to convey its information, incorporating bright colors, assertive fonts, emphasized text, and, fittingly, an abundance of graphic images ranging from camera diagrams to stunning examples of photography.

Twenty chapters, or modules, are color coded for easy reference. Each presents a lesson overview, a visually engaging tutorial, and a module Q and A review to help readers mark progress. Modules cover such topics as getting the right exposure, using depth of field, how to compose, using natural light, black and white, and lenses. An introductory section explains the best way to use the book, a description of camera types, an explanation of how a camera works, and basic information on how to get started with a camera. A glossary and index complete the book.

The success of the book comes from the clear instruction juxtaposed with the wealth of visual aids; from varying samples of photography, to bulleted and boxed text, to technical diagrams and interactive "quizzes." Readers can easily find the appropriate information, work at their own speed, and track their progress. Even though the book is easy to use, its components are professional and appropriately technical. Whether the impetus is personal or professional, readers will find great value in the information and structure of this book.—**ARBA Staff Reviewer**

591. **Photographers' Identities Catalog. http://pic.nypl.org/.** [Website] Free. Date reviewed: 2016.

The *Photographers' Identities Catalog* (PIC) is an experimental interface from New York Public Library Labs. The catalog provides life dates; nationalities; dates and areas where the photographer, company, or studio was active; as well as links to museum and archival collections and further biographical information. The catalog currently (as of March 2016) contains information on 115,700 names related to the history of photography from 1687 to the present day.

The search feature allows the researcher to enter a name and/or to filter active dates or by such categories as nationality, country, format, process, or gender. A zoomable world map displays locations for birth, activity, business, and death for individuals, but moving from the map to finding the record associated with each dot on it is not easily accomplished, and the map was quite slow to load when zooming in on an area. That said, the catalog provides a starting point for a variety of research ranging from creating a list of female photographers who worked in a particular country or time period to dating a family photograph by finding when the photography studio was in business at the given address. This is a promising tool for photography researchers at various levels, though members of the public may be disappointed to find that it does not actually contain photographs but rather links to further information (including photographs) elsewhere online.—**ARBA Staff Reviewer**

23 Language and Linguistics

General Works

Handbooks and Yearbooks

592. **Collected Works of Braj B. Kachru.** Jonathan J. Webster, ed. New York, Bloomsbury Academic, 2015. 3v. $425.00/set; $424.99 (e-book). ISBN 13: 978-1-4725-3918-2; 978-1-4725-6767-3 (e-book).

Over centuries the English language has emerged as the central bridge between global cultures. Spoken today by over 750 million people, it is recognized as an "official language" in 57 sovereign states and 27 nonsovereign countries. English is a chief language of literature, government, commerce, and more. As a scholar of linguistics, Professor Braj B. Kachru has tracked the expansion and development of the English language throughout the world, pursuing a wide variety of perspectives and ideas along the way. The *Collected Works of Braj B. Kachru* comprises writings spanning roughly 30 years which cement the professor's reputation as a pioneer of the study of world Englishes.

Two volumes carry 20 essays arranged chronologically in an effort to best show the trajectory of Kachru's research on his subject. Throughout them, readers are exposed to signature concepts as well as in-depth analysis regarding such questions as to whether or not there should be an international standard for the language. A third volume focuses more specifically on his work regarding bilingual or multilingual societies.

Volume one highlights Kachru's earliest work in understanding the development of non-native varieties of the English language. Initial pieces isolate the hurdles of using English in a non-native context (such as native linguistic prejudices) and explore the interplay between non-native language usage and social engagement. Other essays examine attitudinal shifts toward the usage of non-native English, the realization of English language as power, and the use of literature in the language classroom.

Volume two focuses on Kachru's work during the last decade of the twentieth century. Here we learn how Kachru models the "diaspora" of English as concentric rings emanating from the inner circle of native speakers (e.g., England, the United States, etc.) through the outer circle of more recently institutionalized Englishes (India, Kenya, etc.) and finally through the expanding circle where English usage is ascending (Saudi Arabia, China, Israel, etc.) In "The Speaking Tree," Kachru cleverly invokes an ancient legend to dismiss a variety of myths surrounding the global spread of English, such as the Monoculture Myth whereby English is learned only as a gateway to adopting Judeo-Christian traditions.

Writings in this volume also touch on language teaching and the "culture wars" emanating from the global preeminence of English.

Volume three emphasizes broader work concerning bi/multiculturalism, which, Kachru observes, is the norm of the world. His essay "Linguisitc Schizophrenia and Language Census: A Note on the Indian Situation" uses Indian census data to determine the range of influence English and Hindi have in such a multilinguistic society. He also ruminates on the "creativity of multilinguals" via linguistic, literary and pedagogical analysis, discusses the subject of "code-mixing" and defines four different types of speech communities.

Connecting his research to bigger issues of communication, politics, teaching and more, Kachru's work is a touchstone for academics pursuing the study of linguistics. This collection does well to gather the writings of this distinguished and groundbreaking scholar. Each volume has a bibliography and an index to facilitate searching within the volumes and further study on the topic. This unique work is recommended for upper-level undergraduate and graduate students.—**Laura Herrell**

593.   **Students' Right to Their Own Language: A Critical Sourcebook.** Staci Perryman-Clark, David E. Kirkland, and Austin Jackson, eds. New York, St. Martin's Press, 2015. 506p. index. $44.65pa. ISBN 13: 978-1-4576-4129-9.

The Students' Right to Their Own Language (SRTOL) resolution at the 1974 Conference on College Composition and Communication marked the beginning of an intense discussion about how to teach writing to diverse students. The need for self-expression and creativity seemed to clash with the need to learn standard English in order to fit in and find work. This collection of papers documents the SRTOL movement and the issues that it raised. The editors present articles covering all sides of several topics related to the resolution. The book has six sections. They cover the foundations of SRTOL, the politics of language and memory, African American language, pluralism, SRTOL in the teaching of writing, and questions that remain. The papers are dense and jargon-filled, but they raise important, relevant questions about the teaching of language in a world that is dealing with educational disparity and diverse populations. Libraries supporting programs in education, ethnic studies, and linguistics will want to consider it.—**Barbara M. Bibel**

English-Language Dictionaries

General Usage

594.   **Fowler's Dictionary of Modern English Usage.** 4th ed. Jeremy Butterfield, ed. New York, Oxford University Press, 2015. 928p. $39.95. ISBN 13: 978-0-19-966135-0.

Once described as the "most famous book about English usage ever written," the lexicographer Henry Watson Fowler first compiled this venerable work in 1926. This fourth edition edited by the lexicographer and Oxford University Press author Jeremy Butterfield has added 250 new entries that have been coined or become more popular since the last edition (see ARBA 1997, entry 284; see ARBA 2010, entry 885). Among other discussions, these entries include how competing forms of a word can be used, e.g., "website" or "web site." The work relies heavily on the *Oxford English Corpus* which is based mainly on pages from the World Wide Web plus printed texts. It contains 2.5 billion words from twenty-first-century texts published since 2000. The introduction discusses the recurring debate among English usage scholars on prescriptive and descriptive language and this work skillfully navigates between those contentious linguistic poles. Unsurprisingly, this British work does not lack humor. An essential reference work which superbly complements the American usage manual *Garner's Modern American Usage: The Authority on Grammar, Usage, and Style* (see ARBA 2010, entry 843).—**Donald Altschiller**

Grammar

595.   Hult, Christine A. **The Handy English Grammar Answer Book.** Canton, Mich., Visible Ink Press, 2016. 419p. illus. index. $21.95pa. ISBN 13: 978-1-57859-520-4.

This clever volume offers an effective and engaging tool with which readers can explore the art of effective communication vis-à-vis the English language. It organizes its information into three major sections which migrate from a brief history of modern English, through a thorough examination of grammar basics, and ultimately into applying the best topic-targeted writing approach. Additionally, the author includes a generous appendix section with an excellent range of writing and common grammar examples. The book's readability is enhanced throughout by black-and-white illustrations, shaded text boxes, lists, intriguing anecdotes, and more.

Within each section are a number of chapters which hone in on more detailed matters such as sentence structure, punctuation, or business writing. If this seems a bit mundane at first glance, rest assured it is not! Each topic is presented as an answer to a question—a format both eye-catching and extremely readable. Further, the material is succinct and on point with topics moving smartly from one to another. One chapter deftly answers such questions as what is a noun, what is a pronoun, and what is a linking verb, as well as over 40 more queries relative to sentence structure alone.

Chapters also address matters of style like improving sentence variety and using action verbs. The author then puts all these pieces into place in the chapters regarding academic and business writing. Chapters discussing English as a second language and current electronic communication issues close out the book in advance of the appendix section and index.—**Laura Herrell**

Idioms, Colloquialisms, Special Usage

596.   **The Concise New Partridge Dictionary of Slang and Unconventional English.** 2d ed. Dalzell, Tom and Terry Victor, eds. New York, Routledge/Taylor & Francis Group, 2015. 864p. $88.95. ISBN 13: 978-0-415-52720-0; 978-1-315-75477-2 (e-book).

Every entry found in the new Partridge (an update of the 1984 edition) is included here, but without the original citations. The criteria for inclusion are words and expressions that lower the formality of language or express identity with a particular group and are used anywhere in the English speaking world after 1945. All senses of a word are combined in a single entry and some phrases that contain a similarity are combined under a shared concept (e.g., "roll the dice" and "roll on" are listed under "roll"). Entries are listed alphabetically and preceded with prefaces and an introductory essay, which describe the layout and intention of the entries and discuss the basic concept of unconventional English. Each entry is highlighted in bold print, as are any related terms. An indication of the part-of-speech (including if it is used as a nickname), brief definitions, an approximate date of first usage, a cultural or geographical place of origin, and any *see* references comprise the majority of each entry. The alphabetical listing is followed by a brief section of numeric slang. Many of the terms included are offensive, but offer a large cross-section of human expression. Not as thorough as previous editions, this version is a good source for quick reference or as a starting place for future research.—**Martha Lawler**

597.   Polashek, Timothy. **The Word Rhythm Dictionary: A Resource for Writers, Rappers, Poets, and Lyricists.** Lanham, Md., Rowman & Littlefield, 2014. 689p. index. $165.00; $164.99 (e-book). ISBN 13: 978-1-4422-3325-6; 978-1-4422-3326-3 (e-book).

"Embarrass" and "dilemma." "Napoleon" and "plutonium." "New York" and "outdoors." These are rhythm rhymes, or words and names with the same number of syllables and the same syllabic accents. The *Word Rhythm Dictionary,* a unique reference book by musician and music technologist Timothy Polashek, is designed for writers who want to add musicality to their prose, poetry, or lyrics.

Polashek delineates three methods for using this resource. The most obvious is to look up one's chosen word in the alphabetically arranged general index, which provides the page number(s) on which that word appears along with many others having the same rhythm. Alternatively, poets might turn to Appendix A, listing poetic feet such as iambs, dactyls, and anapests, to be directed to their rhythmic matches. In addition, lyricists might use Appendix B, listing music notations, to help them find terms that match musical rhythms. Words with more than one pronunciation, such as "progress," are followed by a plus sign.

The rhythm rhymes to which users are directed are organized first by number of syllables (from 1 to 14) and then by rhythm rhyme group number. For example, in the table of contents one can see that "7-Syllable Words" consists of 16 rhythm rhyme groups, each group being identified by syllabic emphasis, such as "u-S-u-P-u-S-u" for rhythm rhyme group 8 (u = unstressed, S = secondary stress, P = primary stress). Terms in each rhythm rhyme group are arranged by their sound—first by rhyming vowel, then by consonants— because, according to the author, "poets and lyricists often make use of similar sounding words, through the use of alliteration, assonance, and consonance."

Writers looking only for words that simply rhyme (black, back, stack, Jack) will also find them in this valuable resource—**Lori D. Kranz**

Thesauri

598.   **A Thesaurus of English Word Roots.** Danner, Horace Gerald. Lanham, Md., Rowman & Littlefield, 2014. 990p. index. $165.00; $164.99 (e-book). ISBN 13: 978-1-4422-3325-6; 978-1-4422-3326-3 (e-book).

More than 1,200 word roots across a range of disciplines are included in this large thesaurus. Here one can expand one's knowledge of English word meanings by learning their roots, or combining forms. The sheer volume of information provided here is unmatched by other word root thesauri, as most are limited to a single discipline or offer few examples of terms containing these roots.

By way of example, consider the word "liberate." In the thesaurus, one finds the element "liber," listing the original source as Latin, meaning free, and the Indo-European base as "leudh-," meaning to grow up or rise. In the second column are numerous examples of words with "liber" and their meanings, under categories such as Simple Root ("liberal," "liberty" and their synonyms), Prefixed Root ("illiberal"), Leading Root Compound ("liberticide"), and Prefixed Disguised Root ("deliver," "deliverance," "delivery"); plus discipline-related examples like Academic (liberal arts), Geographic ("Liberia"), Historical ("Liberty Bell"), and Place-Name ("Liberal, Kansas or Missouri"); foreign-language terms (French "liberté"); Notes ("The Anglo-Saxon base of 'friend' is also 'free'"); and Cross-References to elements with the same or a similar meaning ("eleuthero, fran, lys, solv"). Additional categories for word roots are Trailing Root Compound (such as "androgen" and "anthropogenesis" for the root "gen," meaning race, birth, or kind); Doublets, or two words with different meanings and spellings that originally were one word ("gentle:genteel"); and Cognates (such as "gasp" under word root "gap"). If a word is used in more than one discipline, it is categorized as interdisciplinary and is presented in all-capital letters along with its meaning(s). If a word does not belong to a listed group (e.g., "labile" under word root "lab"), it is so noted.

At the end of the volume is an English to Roots Index, which lists major meanings of word roots and guides the user to the word roots themselves. It would have been useful to include all single word roots in alphabetical order with a *see* reference, as some entries contain more than one root. For instance, the author of the foreword suggests looking up the word "lexicographical" in the index, but it is not listed there; and if one looks for "lex" in the main section of the thesaurus, it is grouped under "lect" and "leg." This is a small caveat for what is otherwise a comprehensive and fascinating reference work.—**Lori D. Kranz**

Non–English-Language Dictionaries

599.   Chafe, William. **A Grammar of the Seneca Language.** Oakland, Calif., University of California Press, 2015. 234p. (University of California Publications in Linguistics, Volume 149). $65.00pa. ISBN 13: 978-0-520-28641-2.

This volume is an advanced and detailed analysis of the language of the Seneca people of Western New York State, now spoken fluently by less than 150 individuals. Chafe is a scholar who has studied the language for 50 years, and has written frequently on the subject. The work is clearly organized, beginning with phonetics and phonology, followed by verb and noun morphology, syntax, and chapters on more focused topics such as kinship terms, clitics, questions, imperatives, and interjections. Four texts, recorded between 1956 and 1991, are also included, providing a bit of narrative setting for the language. A brief but useful bibliography is also included.

Designed for specialists in the Native American languages of the Iroquoian family, the volume will best serve academic libraries which support advanced linguistics programs or Native American studies.—**Mark Schumacher**

600.   Gimba, Alhaji Maina, and Russell G. Schuh. **Bole-English-Housa Dictionary and English-Bole Wordlist.** Oakland, Calif., University of California Press, 2015. 388p. maps. (University of California Publications in Linguistics, Volume 148). $65.00pa. ISBN 13: 978-0-520-28611-5.

Based on ongoing research dating back to the 1980's, this volume expands and revises earlier volumes from 2004 and 2009, by the same authors, dealing with the West Chadic language Bole, widely spoken in northeastern Nigeria. Introductory material discusses phonology, morphology, and syntax of the language, while the wordlist basically serves as an index to the dictionary. The latter provides numerous examples of usage, providing sentences in which the word is presented. A "verb form appendix" of 36 pages is also included.

Clearly a work designed for scholars in African languages and speakers of Bole, this work will be most appropriate for academic libraries supporting linguistic research in world languages at an advanced level.—**Mark Schumacher**

24 Literature

General Works

Bibliography

601. Errington, Philip W. **J.K. Rowling. A Bibliography 1997-2013.** New York, Bloomsbury Academic, 2015. 514p. illus. $128.00; $100.99 (e-book). ISBN 13: 978-1-8496-6974-0; 978-1-8496-6977-1 (e-book).

This exhaustive bibliography presents the works of J.K. Rowling in chronological order of title, providing complete descriptions of English-language editions published in the United Kingdom and the United States from 1997 to the end of 2013. The bibliography is separated into four sections, the first and largest of which is "Books and Pamphlets by J.K. Rowling." Here users will find transcriptions of title pages, collation and construction details, a measurement of page size, details of page contents, and notes on paper stock, running titles, illustrations, and more. Section B, "Books and Pamphlets with Contributions by J.K. Rowling" is comprised of the edition details of books and pamphlets published in the United Kingdom and the United States to which Rowling has contributed original material. This section is followed by original "Contributions to Newspapers and Periodicals" by Rowling, and the last section "Items Created Specifically for Sale at Auction" by Rowling. The title has a generous number of illustrations throughout, along with two eight-page, full-color plate sections.

This title will serve book dealers, collectors, auction houses, and anyone wishing to investigate the publishing history of the Harry Potter series and Rowling's other work. Highly recommended as the definitive source on the writings of J.K. Rowling.—**ARBA Staff Reviewer**

Dictionaries and Encyclopedias

602. **Cyclopedia of Literary Characters.** 4th ed. Magill, Frank N., ed. (original editions) Hackensack, N.J., Salem Press, 2014. 5v. $455.00/set. ISBN 13: 978-0-61925-497-8; 978-1-61925-498-5 (e-book).

The first edition of *Cyclopedia of Literary Characters* was published as two volumes in 1963, using material from *Masterplots;* it contained descriptions of 16,000 characters from 1,300 novels, plays, epics, and world literature. Subsequent editions of *Cyclopedia of Literary Characters* incorporated not only material from *Masterplots* but also from *Masterplots II* which covers twentieth-century North American and Latin American literature. The current edition of the cyclopedia covers 3,500 literary works and more than 29,000 characters in five volumes.

The arrangement of the entries makes information easy to find. Tables of contents appear in each volume, along with a list of contributors and a pronunciation guide. The articles appear alphabetically by title of work, and there are guide words at the top of each page. The titles of books appear in bold and are followed by author, date the work was first published, genre, locale, a classification of the plot (pastoral, psychological realism, historical, etc), and a time period. Character descriptions follow the ready-reference data— important characters receive more lines of text. The entries appear to average about a page in length. While the work could be used alone, it makes more sense to use it in conjunction with a resource like the Masterplots series, especially for those readers unfamiliar with the plot or main themes of the works in question.

Three indexes in volume five (which take up nearly 200 pages) round out the work and allow searches by work title, character, or author.—**ARBA Staff Reviewer**

Handbooks and Yearbooks

603.   Budick, Emily Miller. **The Subject of Holocaust Fiction.** Bloomington, Ind., Indiana University Press, 2015. 250p. index. $32.00pa. ISBN 13: 978-0-253-01630-0; 978-0-253-01632-4 (e-book).

The Holocaust is one of the most horrific events in modern history. Making sense of it is impossible. Fiction is one path to understanding it. The author, a professor at Hebrew University of Jerusalem, looks at the role of literature as a vehicle for understanding the Holocaust. She notes in her introduction that fiction provides a view of events through the eyes of the characters. This differs from a nonfiction historical account, but it is still an important vehicle for commemorating the events, mourning the victims, and considering the moral and ethical dilemmas presented. The book has three sections representing various aspects of Holocaust literature and approaches to writing about the events. She examines the work of many writers: Cynthia Ozick, Art Spiegelman, Aryeh Lev Stollman, Michael Chabon, and Aharon Appelfeld. She also looks at the work of non-Jewish authors such as William Styron and Bernhard Schlink. By examining the themes of mourning, memory, and love, and considering the relationship of the Holocaust to apartheid and animal slaughter, the author provides a framework for students of literature, history, religion, philosophy, and ethics. Academic libraries supporting programs in Jewish studies, Holocaust studies, and comparative literature will want to consider this volume.—**Barbara M. Bibel**

604.   **Critical Insights: Virginia Woolf & 20th Century Women Writers.** Kathryn Stelmach Artuso, ed. Hackensack, N.J., Salem Press, 2014. 324p. index. (Critical Insights). $95.00. ISBN 13: 978-1-61925-419-0; 978-1-61925-420-6 (e-book).

Through her modern novels and nonfiction, Virginia Woolf has had a great impact on women writers of the last century. In *Virginia Woolf & 20th Century Women Writers*, this influence is probed by scholars in essays about the work of more than a dozen women writers of fiction, autobiography, or poetry. The first third of the book, Critical Contexts, discusses Woolf's oeuvre against the backdrop of social, historical, and political events of her time, and her critical reception. Critical Insights then explores the works of later authors who, to paraphrase Woolf's feminist masterpiece, defied the patriarchy and made "a room of their own" in which to write about what mattered to them. These are authors who challenged war, colonialism, traditional gender roles, ethnic and racial stereotypes, not to mention literary conventions of narrative, style, theme, place, and temporality. The writing throughout is clear without lapsing deeply into theory or pedantry, though the occasional nonsensical phrase or sentence (presumably introduced by the publisher during scanning or the editorial process) interrupts the reading process.

Woolf's major works appear throughout the volume. For example, in "Narrative Forms and Feminist (Dis)Contents: An Intertextual Reading of the Prose of Toni Morrison and Virginia Woolf," Sandra Cox compares the careers of both authors, looking in particular at *Mercy* vs. *To the Lighthouse and Playing in the Dark* vs. *Three Guineas*. In "The Woolf Sting: Sylvia Plath Annotating Virginia Woolf," Amanda Golden discusses the poet's marginal notations in her personal copies of Woolf's books and mentions of Woolf's writings in her journals and class notebooks, all of which inform Plath's writing process. And in "Raced Bodies, Corporeal Texts: Narratives of Home and Self in Sandra Cisneros' *The House on Mango Street*," Shanna M. Salinas describes how both the author and the novel's protagonist find their identity in their home space.

The volume's back matter consists of a recommended reading list of twentieth-century women authors, a bibliography, brief descriptions of the contributors, and an index.—**Lori D. Kranz**

605. **Literary Criticism Online. http://www.literaryhistory.com/.** [Website] Free. Date reviewed: 2016.

As its name implies, *Literary Criticism Online* is an aggregator of links to Websites that offer a wide variety of both mainstream and academic literary criticism. As such, the site can be a handy resource for librarians, students, and teachers who need to find literary critiques quickly and easily. The main page features clickable headlines for 20th-Century Literary Criticism and 19th-Century Literary Criticism, which bring up alphabetical lists of author names. The left column of the main page begins with a topical commentary by the site's founder, Jan Pridmore (the February 1, 2016 entry is titled "The Anger Epidemic"), followed by a list of the most recent authors covered. Clicking on one of those authors— Wilkie Collins and Saul Bellow were at the top of the most recent edition—jumps to a full page divided into sections titled Introduction & Biography and Literary Criticism, pages whose content and format vary widely depending on the author. Some sections are focused on the author's titles (for Collins, for example, Literary Criticism *The Woman in White*), while other sections offer links to Websites and media. Links are displayed for sources as varied as *The New Yorker, The Guardian,* and academic journals. A major drawback, however, is that almost all the academic links merely connect to the JSTOR site, which requires registration and may be confusing to newer users. Otherwise, the site is easy to navigate. Pridmore launched the site in 1998, and has made little or no attempt to update its design to meet the standards of twenty-first-century Web design. In addition, the editorial inconsistency of the author pages themselves offers no illusions that the site is anything more than a simple aggregator. For example, the first subhead on the Wilkie Collins page reads Introduction & Biography, while the first subhead on the Saul Bellow page reads introduction and biography. The content of the author pages is very uneven, with some pages displaying long lists of links and some very short lists.—**ARBA Staff Reviewer**

606.   **Project Gutenberg: www.gutenberg.org/.** [Website] Free. Date reviewed: 2015.

Project Gutenberg is a volunteer effort to digitize cultural works and archive them on an accessible Website. It was founded in 1971 and is the oldest digital library today. The project contains over 50,000 full texts of public domain books that users can search and download easily. It is closely affiliated with an Internet-based proofreading community called Distributed Proofreaders comprised of volunteers committed to providing free literature to the public. Materials are added to the *Project Gutenberg* archive only if copyrights have expired or if it receives a copyright clearance, so as long as users download the literature within the United States, there is no danger of pirating information. Copyright laws outside the United States should be researched by users before downloading content.

The books on this Website are available in open formats that should be compatible with most computers. Users can download them in plain text as well as HTML, PDF, EPUB, MOBI, and Plucker. Though most titles are in English, users can use the search menu to locate books in German, French, Italian, and Portuguese, as well as a few other widely used languages. All the search tabs on the homepage are located either at the top or the left side, making navigation simple, though more links are included toward the bottom of the homepage for those who want additional information on digitized sheet music, free kindle books, offline catalogs, and much more. Search tabs allow for book searches by Popular, Latest, or Random, and a search bar in the top right corner makes it possible for users to search by title and/or author.

Project Gutenberg is a great resource for middle, high school, and college students who are studying the classics, such as Jane Austen's *Pride and Prejudice* or Dante's *Inferno.* Because this Website is easy to navigate, free to use, and provides access to some of the most popular literature read today, it is a highly recommended resource.—**ARBA Staff Reviewer**

Children's and Young Adult Literature

Bibliography

607.   **The Coretta Scott King Awards, 1970-2014: Fifth Edition.** 5th ed. Carole J. McCollough and Adelaide Poniatowski Phelps, eds. Chicago, American Library Association, 2015. 192p. illus. index. $50.00pa.; $45.00pa. (ALA members). ISBN 13: 978-0-8389-3610-8.

The Coretta Scott King book award was established in 1970 to honor and promote African American authors and illustrators of books for children. Under the auspices of the American Library Association, a committee of librarians annually selects two award-winning books, one for its literary merit and one for the excellence of its illustrations, and additionally designates Honor Books. The Coretta Scott King/John Steptoe New Talent Award is also given in most years. Since the first guide to the award books was published in 1994, updates have appeared every five years, making this volume the fifth edition. Compiled for the first time by McCollough and Phelps, coauthors of the recent *Coretta Scott King Award Books Discussion Guide: Pathways to Democracy,* it follows closely the format of earlier editions and features paragraph-long reviews of the winning books in reverse chronological order. Previous entries are reprinted without revision. The early entries are unsigned, but newer entries identify the experts on children's literature who contributed the reviews. Since 2000, the author award entries also include brief quotations from the works. Author awards and illustrator awards are covered in separate sections. Other components of the volume are: selected short biographies of award-winners; brief biographies of the reviewers; alphabetical lists of the authors and illustrators and their winning books; a subject index; a general index; and 14 colored plates. In a small change from the last edition, thumbnail photographs no longer appear in the biographical section, but many of the book entries are, for the first time, accompanied by black-and-white images of book covers. Whereas past editions included one or two short interviews with award winners, this edition's half-page interview with Gabrielle Douglas, an African American trailblazer in Olympic gymnastics, is superfluous. Any library owning the previous editions will want to purchase this update, which serves as an excellent selection tool for librarians, teachers, and parents desiring to share the best multicultural literature and art with young people.—**Susan E. Searing**

608.   Irwin, Marilyn, Annette Y. Goldsmith, and Rachel Applegate. **Autism in Young Adult Novels: An Annnotated Bibliography.** Lanham, Md., Rowman & Littlefield, 2015. 151p. index. $75.99; $74.99 (e-book). ISBN 13: 978-1-4422-5183-0; 978-1-4422-5184-7 (e-book).

This slim volume serves a vital need. As more diagnoses along the Autism Spectrum Disorder (ASD) are made, families, patients, and those in the medical community are looking for more ways to make sense of it. Literature is one of those ways. This book offers an academic analysis of the depiction of autism in young adult fiction with the goal of identifying accurate character portrayals and ultimately of finding the best fiction for use in autism education.

The first five chapters disseminate the authors' research about how the ASD is represented in young adult fiction. Using 100 young adult novels published between 1968 and 2013, the authors devised a series of questions regarding the characterization, schooling, and relationships of autistic figures (other parameters for the novel selection are explained in the book's introduction). For example, the authors asked which characters in the novels have ASD, if the autistic characters have friends, and with whom the autistic characters live. These short, academic chapters include a number of data tables to help visualize the analysis.

The second section of the book presents an annotated bibliography of the young adult fiction used in the authors' research. The listings are arranged alphabetically by author's last name, and include book title; publishing information; genre; plot synopsis and background; and a listing of criteria connected to the novel's handling of the autistic element/character: an Autism Content Scale, Autism Role in Story Scale, and a Literary Quality Scale. This is followed by a select bibliography of young adult novels where autism appears to be present but is never mentioned. As determined by the authors, the books are of very good or excellent literary quality. This bibliography is also alphabetical by author last name. Bibliographical information is followed by plot synopses.

Numerous appendixes classify the studied novels in a variety of ways: by the role of autism, by literary quality, by genre, by year of publication and by foreign press. The last appendix shares the coding sheets the authors used in their study. Recommended for school and public libraries, as well as personal libraries.—**ARBA Staff Reviewer**

609.   Phelps, Adelaide Poniatowski, and Carole J. McCollough. **Coretta Scott King Award Books Discussion Guide: Pathways to Democracy.** Chicago, American Library Association, 2014. 256p. index. $45.00pa.; $40.50pa. (ALA members). ISBN 13: 978-0-8389-3604-7.

Since 1970 the Coretta Scott King Book Awards have been given annually by the American Library Association to outstanding African American authors and illustrators of books for children and young adults that "demonstrate an appreciation of African American culture and universal human values" (ALA). Phelps and McCollough draw on their expertise as past members of the awards jury to map 244 award-winning books to the core values of American democracy: the common good, diversity, equality, justice, liberty, life, personal freedom, the pursuit of happiness, and the rule of law. (A quick Google search reveals that these values are often included in school curricula.) The authors expand on the discussion guides created over the years by the awards committees (recent guides are available at http://www.ala.org/emiert/coretta-scott-king-book-awards-educational-resources) and, by choosing the lens of democratic values to profile the titles, supplement other resources, such as lessons plans accessible at www.teachingbooks.net and publishers' Websites. Entries are arranged by grade in seven overlapping chapters (K-3, 2-4, 3-6, etc.); within each chapter, the books are alphabetized by title. The index provides additional access points by author, title, and core value. For each book, Phelps and McCollough provide basic bibliographic data and a black-and-white image of the cover; identify the core value that the book illuminates; summarize the work; and suggest several "discussion openers" to engage children. A brief section labeled "beyond the book" recommends learning activities and further avenues for student research. Finally, three to five additional books on similar topics are listed. With this focused guide in hand, K-12 teachers and school media specialists will have ample inspiration for incorporating the best youth literature about African Americans into civics education.—**Susan E. Searing**

Handbooks and Yearbooks

610.   Hammond, Heidi K. and Gail D. Nordstrom, eds. **Reading the Art in Caldecott Award Books: A Guide to the Illustrations.** Lanham, Md., Rowman & Littlefield, 2014. 280p. illus. index. $40.00pa.; $39.99pa. (e-book). ISBN 13: 978-1-4422-3923-4; 978-1-4422-3924-1 (e-book).

This guide is a useful tool for preparing to read and discuss Caldecott award-winning books with readers of all ages. Tips from ALSC's Caldecott Manual are included, giving readers a better understanding of how the Caldecott selection process works. Essays include a description of the artwork style and medium, analysis of the book's illustrations, thoughts for further consideration, an illustrator note, and a listing of sources consulted. Appendixes include; "Selected Sources about Picture Book Art," "Randolph Caldecott Medal: Terms, Definitions, and Criteria," "Bibliography of Caldecott Entries," and

"Caldecott Medal Winners 1938-2014." This is a must-have reference for librarians and children's literature enthusiasts. It is also a valuable resource for classroom teachers who wish to integrate award-winning books. The work also includes a glossary and an index.—**Amy Merrill**

Indexes

611.   **Children's Books in Print 2015.** 46th ed. Amenia, N.Y., Grey House Publishing, 2014. 2v. $605.00/set. ISBN 13: 978-1-61925-385-8.

This is the 46th edition of R.R. Bowker's *Children's Books in Print,* produced from the *Books in Print* database. This two-volume set begins with a usage guide, followed by publisher country codes, country sequence, language codes, and a list of abbreviations.

An alphabetical index of nearly 257,000 books published after 2003 from 16,583 U.S. publishers comprises the majority of volume one's 1,933 pages. Tens of thousands of these book listings have been added since the last edition. A shorter numeric title list completes the volume. In addition to standard publishing details, book entries include information about audience, grade level, and binding type. Publishers regularly review and correct (if necessary) book information, ensuring accuracy. Volume two contains author, illustrator, publisher, and wholesaler & distributor indexes. The author and illustrator indexes include references to the relevant pages numbers in volume one as well as *see* references. The publisher index indicates whether or not the publisher participates in the Cataloging in Publication Program of the Library of Congress and supplies ISBN prefixes, contact information, a Standard Address Number (SAN), and the names of distributors. Those publishers that also serve as distributors appear again in the wholesaler & distributor index where users can find ISBN prefixes, physical and Web addresses, SAN, and phone and fax information.

For those who want to search electronically, the entire *Books in Print* database is available online to customers. This venerable reference title is an important tool for librarians who work with children and young adults.—**ARBA Staff Reviewer**

612.   **Subject Guide to Children's Books in Print 2015.** 45th ed. Amenia, N.Y., Grey House Publishing, 2014. 2900p. $460.00. ISBN 13: 978-1-61925-388-9.

Used alongside the two-volume set *Children's Books in Print 2015* or as a stand-along reference, the *Subject Guide to Children's Books in Print 2015* serves as an essential reference for librarians serving youth populations. Parents and teachers looking for books will also appreciate a source that groups titles by topic.

The title begins with a usage guide, publisher country codes, country sequence, language codes, and a list of abbreviations before presenting listings (hundreds of thousands) grouped into 9,610 subject headings from nearly 16,600 publishers. Tens of thousands of these book listings are new since the last edition. The subject headings adhere for the main part to Library of Congress Subject Headings. This, plus the use of guide words and *see* references, facilitates searches for books on subjects from aardvarks to Zulus and every imaginable topic in between.

The book concludes with a publisher name index followed by a wholesaler & distributor name index, both of which provide such information as ISBN prefixes, physical and Web addresses, and phone and fax numbers.—**ARBA Staff Reviewer**

National Literature

American Literature

General Works

Bibliography

613.   Gunn, Drewey Wayne. **Gay American Novels, 1870-1970.** Jefferson, N.C., McFarland, 2016. 192p. index. $39.95pa. ISBN 13: 978-0-7864-9905-2; 978-1-4766-2522-5 (e-book).

This book offers a survey of over 250 novels, novellas, and other literary works which feature gay or bisexual men as prominent characters. Entries are organized chronologically, for the most part. However, if one author is responsible for more than one work of this nature, all works are examined under the same entry (organized by earliest work). In addition, two or more authors may share the same entry if their works are considered similar.

Entries convey author's name, title(s) of work, and publication date, then go on to deconstruct the plot with particular emphasis on the gay character(s) arc. Entries also examine the work's gay themes in context with the times in which it was published and/or in relation to the writer's particular experience. For example, the entry covering Dashiell Hammett's *The Maltese Falcon* exposes his editor's request to change the homosexual subtexts (Hammett did not). Each entry also includes brief biographical information and a bibliography.

Readers will be quite satisfied with the appearance of many well-regarded authors such as Hammett, Gore Vidal, Truman Capote, Carson McCullers, James Baldwin, and more alongside pulp writers and lesser-known literary figures. In addition, this guide points to a wide range of genres encompassing the gay character and themes, ranging from murder mysteries to historical romances to westerns and beyond.

The book's introduction does an excellent job of detailing the history and parameters of the literature. A postscript tracks the further evolution of this literature in the decade following this book's range of discussion. The book also includes a general bibliography and index.—**ARBA Staff Reviewer**

Dictionaries and Encyclopedias

614.   **Ethnic American Literature: An Encyclopedia for Students.** Emmanuel S. Nelson, ed. Santa Barbara, Calif., Greenwood Press/ABC-CLIO, 2015. 570p. illus. index. $100.00. ISBN 13: 978-1-61069-880-1; 978-1-61069-881-8 (e-book).

This diverse and important reference catalogs the major ethnic genres, figures, works, and themes emerging from the whole of the American literary tradition over the last two centuries.

Over 150 alphabetical entries by over 100 contributors are included and range from broader topics like Chinese American poetry to particular authors such as Sandra Cisneros, inspirations like the Civil Rights movement, works like *The Color Purple,* and themes like multiculturalism. While emphasizing four main ethnic groups (Native American, Asian American, African American, and Latino/a), the book pays clear attention to our America's rapidly changing demographics and allows a glimpse into newly emerging literary traditions such as Iranian American literature and its themes of exile, adjustment, and cultural pride.

The encyclopedia is directed at high school and community college students and teachers; its entries range in length from 750 words to 5,000 words and use clear language and an easy-to-follow A-Z arrangement. This is highly important when cataloguing topics as diverse as Hawaiian literature and jazz. Cross-referenced and with a plethora of ideas for further reading following each entry, this book is an excellent resource not only for students of American literature, but for lovers of history, writing, popular culture, and more. The title concludes with a selected bibliography, notes on contributors, and an index.—**Laura Herrell**

Handbooks and Yearbooks

615.   Connelly, Mark. **Saul Bellow: A Literary Companion.** Jefferson, N.C., McFarland, 2016. 222p. index. (Literary Companions). $39.95pa. ISBN 13: 978-0-7864-9926-7; 978-1-4766-2485-3 (e-book).

Author Saul Bellow, winner of both the Nobel Prize and Pulitzer Prize, is admired by many for his novels *The Adventures of Augie March, Herzog,* and *Humboldt's Gift,* as well as his many other writing pursuits. This book, one in McFarland's Literary Companions series, makes a fine, manageable source for gathering both facts and criticism about the author and his works.

An excellent chronology opens the book with a walk through Bellow's life and accomplishments, providing rich narrative detail rather than just names and dates. For example, we read how a young Bellow sought out the corpse of Leon Trotsky the day after he was assassinated in Mexico City. The main section of the companion then shares alphabetical entries covering the author's works, major characters, influences, and themes. Here readers will find diverse entries on Gunter Grass, the Holocaust, *Humboldt's Gift,* the anti-Semitic Marla Glyph character, his short story "Cousins," the city of Chicago, and much more. Following some entries are resources for further research.

The book also conveys a selection of insightful Saul Bellow quotes excerpted from various interviews conducted throughout his career. These excerpts are arranged by theme, and cover such topics as fame, religious faith, and, naturally, writing. An excellent addition to this book is an appendix offering 45 potential research questions that both students and teachers will find helpful. An extensive bibliography and index round out the book.—**ARBA Staff Reviewer**

616.   **Critical Insights: American Writers in Exile.** Birkenstein, Jeff and Robert C. Hauhart, eds. Hackensack, N.J., Salem Press, 2015. 300p. index. $95.00. ISBN 13: 978-1-61925-517-3; 978-1-61925-518-0 (e-book).

This volume in the Critical Insights series focuses on the intriguing idea of American writers in exile. Contributions examine, of course, the literal acts of writers removing themselves from their home country to gain different perspectives. But pieces also delve into motivating factors behind their exile, figurative ideas of exile, questions of national identity, and much more. Essays touch on an array of such writers as W.H. Auden, Ernest Hemingway, Paul Bowles, Jamaica Kincaid, and Hart Crane.

An opening essay by the editors helps define the many aspects of exile; it is an "act of exclusion and banishment," "a scattering or dispersion" and can be political or personal, for example. The four-essay Critical Contexts section then offers broad-based foundational essays touching on the general need for writers to distance themselves. Jeff Birkenstein's essay "Paris Between the Wars: Gertrude Stein, Ernest Hemingway, Hunger and Language" uses the example of two renowned writers situated in the right place (post-World War I Paris) to observe the beginnings of a new age while removed from their more conservative, American origins. Joseph J. Cheatle then discusses the exile of two African American writers, James Baldwin and Richard Wright, who physically removed themselves from America's racial tensions but never really left them behind.

Critical Readings then presents 11 diverse essays examining the unique manifestations of writers abroad. Charlotte Anne Fiehn writes about Henry James, whom readers may consider the prime example of the American expatriate. Her essay looks at his contrasting views of nineteenth-century Americans and Europeans, and establishes James' influence on future exiled writers. Ashley E. Reis, in her essay "Edward Abbey's Ecological Exile," discusses how the author's exile came in the form of his scathing antidevelopment views, which were completely at odds with postwar America.

The volume concludes with a listing of other works by these American writers in exile, and a bibliography, and an index.—**ARBA Staff Reviewer**

617.   **Critical Insights: Beloved.** Maureen N. Eke, ed. Hackensack, N.J., Salem Press, 2015. 260p. index. $95.00. ISBN 13: 978-1-61925-828-0; 978-1-61925-829-7 (e-book).

Published in 1987, Toni Morrison's Pulitzer Prize winning novel *Beloved* brought about a new and profound contemplation of slavery and its legacy. With its somewhat mythical style and intense narrative, the book inspires continuous critical debate. *Critical Insights: Beloved* gathers a good range of essays helping to advance the critical conversation into new areas, while at the same time providing significant context for the novel's success.

A Critical Contexts section presents four essays which provide excellent background for approaching the novel. Kristine Yohe, for example, revisits the true case of Margaret Garner, an escaped slave who allegedly murdered her own child rather than have her return to slavery (an incident said to inspire *Beloved*). Touria Khannous then surveys 30 years of *Beloved's* critical reception; pointing to many spokes—African American, feminist, modernist, etc., on the theoretical wheel.

Critical Readings then offers nine essays examining the book's themes and structure. In her piece "A Gathering of Trees: An Examination of Memory, Trauma and Embodiment in Toni Morrison's *Beloved*," Kokahvah Zauditu-Selassie writes of the healing influences of West African spirituality upon the book's afflicted characters. Lynne Simpson then points to the importance of regarding slavery as stories vsersus statistics in her essay "The Psychological Impact of Slavery and Separation in *Beloved.*" Two closing essays propose interesting ways in which to teach and disseminate the complex novel.

Concluding with a chronology of Toni Morrison's life, a listing of her works and a bibliography, *Critical Insights: Beloved* helps to confirm the novel's emotional appeal and universal importance.—**ARBA Staff Reviewer**

618.   **Critical Insights: Contemporary Immigrant Short Fiction.** Evans, Robert C., ed. Hackensack, N.J., Salem Press, 2015. 251p. index. $95.00. ISBN 13: 978-1-61925-832-7; 978-1-61925-833-4 (e-book).

Throughout American literature today, readers are hearing more diverse voices than ever before. This volume in the Critical Insights series devotes its pages to analysis of contemporary immigrant fiction, and showcases essays covering the works of such writers as Jhumpa Lahiri, Edwige Danticat, and Junot Diaz.

Emphasizing the short story form as key to the immigrant writer's literary aspirations, the volume's opening chapter "On Contemporary Immigrant Short Fiction" by Natalie Friedman provides an excellent foundation for understanding the origins and challenges of the genre.

The Critical Contexts section then presents historical contexts, critical surveys, and essays that emphasize the notion of the truly global nature of immigrant short fiction. In particular, Anupama Arora, in her essay "Forbidden Desires: Relationships in Chimamanda Ngozi Adichie and Jhumpa Lahiri's Short Fiction," compares the works of two successful immigrant short-fiction writers to show how they, of vastly different origins, can be concerned with similar issues (in this case, interracial relationships).The 10 essay Critical Readings section offers up insight naturally as diverse as this book's subject. Some highlights include King-Kok Cheung's "Somewhat Queer Triangles: Yiyun Li's 'The Princess of Nebraska' and *Gold Boy, Emerald Girl*," which exposes the added burdens placed on Chinese immigrant homosexuals so that their alienation is both sexual and ethnic, and Bridget Kevane's "Even the Dead Make Noises," which examines the need for the immigrant (in this case, the Puerto Rican of Spanish Harlem) to have his uniquely melded voice be heard.

The book also includes a chronological listing of recent contemporary immigrant short fiction as well as a bibliography and index.—**ARBA Staff Reviewer**

619.   **Critical Insights: David Foster Wallace.** Philip Coleman, ed. Hackensack, N.J., Salem Press, 2015. 322p. index. $95.00. ISBN 13: 978-1-61925-513-5; 978-1-61925-514-2 (e-book).

David Foster Wallace left behind a treasure trove of literature, both published and unpublished, upon his untimely death in 2008. A writer who employed unusual literary technique to explore themes of mindfulness, addiction, and more, he has always been a critical favorite due to his aesthetic choices and diverse subject matter. Prolific with short fiction and essays, he is perhaps best remembered as the author of the lengthy novel *Infinite Jest.* While that novel alone has inspired numerous critical observations, *Critical Insights: David Foster Wallace* divides its attentions among the broad scope of his work to promote an open, yet compact discussion.

The book begins with background on Wallace's life and career; painting a portrait of an intellectually and aesthetically restless creature whose talent in tennis, interest in philosophy, and trouble with women and addiction would all eventually make their way into his groundbreaking writing. We also learn of the cultural and critical landscape within which he wrote. Kiki Benzon's "David Foster Wallace and Millennial America," for example, aims to help readers place Wallace's work in relation to the historical, political, and social contexts from which it was born. This section also notes the influences of various literary progenitors upon Wallace's writing development.

Twelve essays then examine the breadth of his work and showcase a diverse array of critical analyses. Arranged more or less chronologically, pieces like Steve Gronert Ellerhof's "Proteus Bound: Pinning *Girl with Curious Hair* under Short Story Theory," examine the importance of a reader's acknowledgment of literary effort via Wallace's early short fiction, while Aine Mahon's "Difficulties of Reality in Cora Diamond and David Foster Wallace" points to the ultimate meeting of literature and moral philosophy as expressed throughout his writing.

Much, of course, is said of *Infinite Jest,* as it remains his definitive work. David Hering's essay "Form as Strategy in *Infinite Jest*" examines the novel's unique form in relation to its complex themes, while Alex Resar ponders the repeated re-imaginings held both within the novel and its analysis.

Including chronological and bibliographical resources, this book gathers a well-curated assortment of criticism that does well to capture the essence of a talented writer saturated in his own complex view of contemporary society. Recommended for academic libraries.—**Laura Herrell**

620. **Critical Insights: Harlem Renaissance.** Christopher Allen Varlack, ed. Hackensack, N.J., Salem Press, 2015. 335p. index. $95.00. ISBN 13: 978-1-61925-822-8; 978-1-61925-823-5 (e-book).

Thought to represent the most significant artistic period in African American history, the Harlem Renaissance gave voice to a unique culture. At the same time, the Harlem Renaissance challenged the assimilation (or the lack thereof) of this culture into greater society. This volume in the Critical Insights series serves this complex and long-studied artistic movement well by delving deeper into themes previously explored in the works of such icons as Zora Neale Hurston or Langston Hughes. The book also showcases more from lesser-known authors and critics to provide a truly fresh perspective.

The Critical Contexts section provides excellent foundational essays concerning a number of topics, including the multifaceted visions melding into the art of the Harlem Renaissance, the short-sighted "apathetic" criticism of the times, and, in Allyson Denise Marino's "Sugar Cane and Women's Identity in Selected Works of Zora Neale Hurston" the racial and economic oppression suffered by African American women during the 1920's.

Following this section are 14 essays making up the Critical Readings section. These essays are further subdivided into four sections covering the principal artistic and political sensibilities behind the Harlem Renaissance, racial passing, the rise of the new Negro woman in regards to both literary subject and author, and the more controversial or neglected works and/or approaches to them. Highlights of the Critical Readings section include Tiffany Austin's essay "'Blue Smoke' and 'Stale Fried Fish': A Decadent View of Richard Bruce Nugent," which re-examines the more obscure, and only openly gay Harlem Renaissance artist, and Seretha D. Williams' "'The Bitter River': Langston Hughes and the Violent South" which points out how Hughes' poetry transcends the period of the Harlem Renaissance to capture the ongoing subjugation of blacks.

An extensive chronology, complete list of Harlem Renaissance works, a bibliography, and an index round out this intelligently conceived, thought-provoking essay collection.—**ARBA Staff Reviewer**

621. **Critical Insights: LGBTQ Literature.** Robert C. Evans, ed. Hackensack, N.J., Salem Press, 2015. 347p. index. $95.00. ISBN 13: 978-1-61925-423-7; 978-1-61925-424-4 (e-book).

This volume in the Critical Insights series gathers a number of well-curated essays examining a genre of literature that has perhaps only been openly studied over the last half a century. With the crux of its focus on nineteenth- and twentieth-century American literature (although a few non-American works are considered), *Critical Insights: LGBTQ Literature* tracks the genre's challenges, dissemination, and evolution through this time.

The opening Critical Contexts section provides a necessary foundation for understanding the history of LGBTQ literature both from the perspective of its authors and critics. In two essays, Margaret Sönser Breen briefly catalogs the most well-known examples of LGBTQ work from the nineteenth century to the present, spotlighting such writers as Oscar Wilde, Frank O'Hara, and Patricia Highsmith. In doing so, she points out the ways these writers might have adapted to a potentially unwelcoming readership. For example, she notes that American author Ann Bannon managed to "affirm lesbian desire" in her pulp novels of the 1950's at a time when censorship defined lesbianism as "a deviant form of sexuality aligned with criminality and disease." Other essays in this section note helpful resources with which to pursue the thriving realm of LGBTQ scholarship, how "critical pluralism" may be an apt literary theory with which to approach LGBTQ literature, and how the marked sexual differences of two great writers, Gertrude Stein and Ernest Hemingway, affected their attitudes toward the devastating Great War.

Working chronologically from an analysis of James Fenimore Cooper's mid-nineteenth century work Jack Tier to more recent work by Sharon Dennis Wyeth, the essays in the Critical Readings section expose a number of compelling topics, including the use of cross-dressing, homo-erotic imagery, the advent of "openly" gay literature, the constraints of traditional gender roles, and more. For example, Lorna Raven Wheeler's essay entitled "The Fugitive Erotic in the Poetry of Mae V. Cowdery" adds another dimension to the study of the Harlem Renaissance via the cryptic but clearly sexual verse of this lesser-known poet.

The book finally presents a number of useful resources for further study of this burgeoning area of literature, including a listing of dramatic, fictional, and poetic works in the LGBTQ genre, a bibliography, and notes on contributors. As the world works towards better integration and understanding of its LGBTQ population, this book can be a discerning resource for further education at the public and academic level.—**Laura Herrell**

622. **Critical Insights: Little Women.** Gregory Eiselein and Anne K. Phillips, eds. Hackensack, N.J., Salem Press, 2014. 244p. index. $95.00. ISBN 13: 978-1-61925-427-5; 978-1-61925-428-2 (e-book).

In a canon dominated by bloody battlefield heroics and challenging political maneuvering, it is easy to forget that one of the foremost literary works of the U.S. Civil War period is a domestic drama. Louisa May Alcott's *Little Women* has stood the test of time as one of the most popular American novels. Encompassing issues of family, class, productivity, personal development and the transition from childhood into adulthood, the novel is a critic's delight. *Critical Insights: Little Women* collects a number of essays which work to uncover the roots and effects of the novel's great appeal.

The volume opens with a general assessment of the legacy of *Little Women*—a book that has never been out of print—in addition to a biographical essay on Louisa May Alcott. Gregory Eiselein and Anne K. Phillips note the importance of relating Alcott's particular upbringing (she was a neighbor if not an acolyte of Ralph Waldo Emerson and Henry David

Thoreau) as well as her keen ability to sense the tenor of her time to the establishment of *Little Women's* "unique place in literary and cultural history."

The following section then delves into the book's Cultural Contexts. Daniel Shealy deftly ties the contemporary national milieu, which included issues of immigration, women's rights, and more, to his extensive research on Alcott's family. And Beverly Lyon Clark, in her "Critical Reception of *Little Women,*" surveys opinion of the novel from first publication to the present.

The Critical Readings section of this book includes a good range of essays examining a variety of subjects. Two pieces examine the importance of written communication in the life of Victorian women and the conflicts between professional achievement and personal obligation. R. Eric Tippin explores the influence of organized religion within the novel in his piece titled "Up the Steep Hill by Trying." And three essays cover the novel's treatment of courtship and marriage, including Sarah Wadsworth's "Unsettling Engagements in *Moods*and *Little Women;* or, "Learning to Love Louisa May Alcott," which positions Alcott as progressive in response to nineteenth century romantic conventions and expectations.

Including a chronology of Alcott's life, a listing of her other works, and notes on this book's contributors, *Critical Insights: Little Women* provides thought-provoking analyses of one of the truly great works of American fiction. Recommended for upper-level high school students and undergraduate students.—**Laura Herrell**

623.   **Critical Insights: Louisa May Alcott.** Gregory Eiselein and Anne K. Phillops, eds. Hackensack, N.J., Salem Press, 2016. 260p. index. $95.00. ISBN 13: 978-1-61925-521-0; 978-1-61925-522-7 (e-book).

Beloved by millions for her novel *Little Women,* with its detailed examination of how the March family makes its way through the Civil War era, Louisa May Alcott is truly one of the keystone writers in American literature. Her views on domestic life and personal development, as well as her candid prose style, have provoked thought among casual readers and critics alike. In fact, readers may be familiar with another volume in the Critical Insights series which gathers criticism exclusively on *Little Women.*This book deals more intimately with the author and is able to shine a spotlight on her other, less-renowned works for a more complete portrait of her life and times.

The volume is separated into four sections: Career, Life and Influence, Critical Contexts, and Critical Readings and Resources. The first section shares two essays providing biographical context for Alcott's writing as they discuss her brief time as a Civil War nurse, her interest in Transcendentalism, and more. Critical Contexts then shares four essays providing a foundational understanding of the times in which Alcott wrote, including contemporary reaction to her work. John Matteson, who won a Pulitzer Prize for his biography of Alcott, contributes "When Rude Hands Shake the Hive: Louisa May Alcott and the Transformation of America," which posits the notion that Alcott's life moved parallel to America's coming of age.

Critical Readings carry the bulk of this volume, with 10 essays delving into an array of topics seeking to explore beneath Alcott's surface. Several essays place Alcott in juxtaposition to other examples of nineteenth-century literature. Christine Doyle, in her piece titled "American Girls and American Literature: Louisa May Alcott 'Talks Back' to Henry James," points out the similarities between Alcott and the younger James even as they promoted vastly different views of writing and womanhood. Other pieces highlight the progressive nature of Alcott's work. In "Polly, Pygmalion and the (Im)practicalities of an Independent Womanhood," Marilyn Bloss Koester introduces readers to the character of Polly Milton from Alcott's book *An Old-Fashioned Girl.* Polly has artistic friends and Koester establishes that Alcott foresees a future where women can explore artistic, alternative paths in accordance with their own ambition. Other Alcott works discussed include *Little Men, Eight Cousins,* and *Work.*

Each essay includes notes and a list of works cited. Critical Insights closes with a chronology of Alcott's life, a listing of all her works, notes on the book's contributors, and an index.—**ARBA Staff Reviewer**

624.   **Critical Insights: One Flew Over the Cuckoo's Nest.** Robert` C. Evans, ed. Hackensack, N.J., Salem Press, 2015. 293p. index. $95.00. ISBN 13: 978-1-61925-830-3; 978-1-61925-831-0 (e-book).

That one work could inspire such a variety of critical response attests to the provocative and compelling talent of its author. *One Flew Over the Cuckoo's Nest* came out at a time of rapid change, and represented the struggle of the individual against institutional authority. This volume in the Critical Insights series takes a close look at this particular work, focusing on its broader depictions of individualism and authoritarianism as well as some of the novel's lesser developed threads.

After a brief overview of the book and the life of its author, Ken Kesey, the Critical Contexts section offers four foundational essays which explore its historical background and critical reception in addition to noting the importance of a multiperspective critique and comparing the work with another iconic novel—*The Grapes of Wrath.*

The Critical Readings section exposes many themes within the novel, and presents 10 essays such as Ronald G. Billingsley's "American Minorities in One Flew Over the Cuckoo's Nest," which posits that the widespread use of minorities in the story relates to the author's view on the whole of humanity, and "One Flew Over the Cuckoo's Nest: A Survey of Commentary on the Film Adaption" which provides an important overview of the critical response to the 1975 film adaption, arguably the tool which cemented the book's stature.

Concluding with a chronology of Kesey's life, a listing of his works and adaptations of his works, a bibliography, and an index, *Critical Insights: One Flew Over the Cuckoo's Nest* succeeds in using this groundbreaking book as a magnifying glass on a truly significant time in America's past.—**ARBA Staff Reviewer**

625.   **Critical Insights: Robert A. Heinlein.** Rafeeq O. McGiveron, ed. Hackensack, N.J., Salem Press, 2015. 276p. $95.00. ISBN 13: 978-1-61925-826-6; 978-1-61925-827-3 (e-book).

This volume in the Critical Insights series devotes its pages to the author Robert A. Heinlein, creator of many essays, story collections, novels, and more, most notably in the genre of science fiction. In fact, Heinlein is considered to be one of the most influential authors in the contemporary version of the genre. Much of his work conveys themes of individual liberty, societal repression of nonconformist thought, the influence of organized religion on society, and more along similar lines.

Opening chapters introduce readers to Heinlein via a rather general discussion of his works and legacy, and a brief biography which takes him from his early-twentieth-century birth through the naval academy, three marriages, and ultimately to his prolific writing career. The Critical Contexts section then discusses a number of topics which help establish an understanding of Heinlein and his times, as well as the many different types of criticism he endured as an author.

The Critical Readings section is comprised of 10 essays which analyze the span of Heinlein's career starting with his shorter pieces published in pulp magazines and ending with his longer ruminating works. John J. Pierce writes a smart survey of Heinlein's "juveniles" in "Growing Up with Heinlein." Anna R. McHugh explores Heinlein's notion of extraterrestrial realities vis à vis a relatively new understanding of Einstein's theories in her piece "Compulsively Fruitful: Proliferation in the Short Fiction of Robert A. Heinlein, 1939-1952." Wolf Forest explores the ways philosophy, economics, and ethics are conveyed throughout 25 years of Heinlein's writing. And Ira Halpern looks at Heinlein's *Stranger in a Strange Land,* arguably his most famous work, as a disingenuously satirical, inadvertently (perhaps) utopian novel.

This volume concludes with a chronology of Heinlein's life, a listing of his many works, a bibliography, and an index.—**ARBA Staff Reviewer**

626.   **Critical Insights: Southwestern Literature.** William Brannon, ed. Hackensack, N.J., Salem Press, 2016. 239p. index. $95.00. ISBN 13: 978-1-61925-842-6; 978-1-61925-843-4 (e-book).

Literature of the Southwest has evolved along a unique path influenced by a stunning landscape and diverse peoples. This volume in the Critical Insights series gathers a good variety of essays which explore the many themes in and responses to Southwestern literature. The volume discusses works by such writers as Larry McMurtry, Willa Cather, Cormac McCarthy, and Sandra Cisneros.

Four essays in the Critical Contexts section provide foundational material to understanding the genre. The essays include a survey of major works and critical response, an introduction to the recurring elements and themes found throughout the literature, and more. Of particular note is the essay "Writing (and Righting) the Desert Southwest: Literary Legacies and the Restoration of Glen Canyon," by Laura Smith. This essay connects the literature to an ecological mandate by pointing out how the Glen Canyon Dam controversy inspired writers such as Edward Abbey and Ellen Meloy to the point where their literature impels the discussion.

The Critical Readings section houses 10 essays offering more pointed examinations of the genre. Essays may explore themes of culture clash or take on the view of a physical landscape that inspires both creativity and violence. For example, Maria O'Connell's "Of Judges and Fairybook Beasts: The Male Mentor and Violence in Cormac McCarthy's *Blood Meridian*" posits that the violence rendered within the story comes in response to the unrelenting need to exert control over the natural landscape. Three essays discuss Mexican American literature and spotlight writers María Ampara Ruiz de Burton and Ana Castillo as well as a variety of Mexican American memoirists. And two essays discuss how the environment influenced Willa Cather's visual sense. John Samson, for example, establishes how the simple elements of light, form, and color express this influence in his piece "Willa Cather and Southwestern Aesthetics." Each essay concludes with a list of cited works.

A Resources section of the volume contains a list of additional categorized examples of Southwestern literature, a bibliography, notes on contributors, and an index.

Recommended.—**ARBA Staff Reviewer**

627.   **Critical Insights: Tim O'Brien.** Robert C. Evans, ed. Hackensack, N.J., Salem Press, 2015. 313p. index. $95.00. ISBN 13: 978-1-61925-421-3; 978-1-61925-422-0 (e-book).

Critical Insights: Tim O'Brien presents a thorough analysis of the writer many consider to be the voice of the Vietnam generation. Author of many essays, articles, and works of fiction, he is perhaps recognized most as the author of *The Things They Carried,* a book notable for both its unique style and impactful content.

This volume first discusses Tim O'Brien via the approach to his work as a scholar, his early small Midwestern town upbringing, and his career-fueling war experience as well as other biographical information. Four essays in the Critical Contexts section then set the stage for further analysis, examining, for example, popular culture at the time in which O'Brien came of age, and in Stefania Ciocia's essay "Tim O'Brien, Ernest Hemingway and the Short Story Cycle Tradition," the particular use of the short story medium.

The Critical Readings section then hosts 10 diverse essays consisting of two general overviews of O'Brien's works, as well as essays focusing on particular pieces. In separate essays, Susan Farrell and Robert C. Evans take on *The Things They Carried,* discussing the book's handling of trauma and its critical reception, respectively. Meanwhile, Derek C. Maus discusses the unhinged attitudes of the 1960's in "Insanity and the Problem of Meaning in The Nuclear Age" while Owen Gilman, Jr., compares O'Brien's novel *Lake of the Woods* to Henry David Thoreau's Walden, examining the role of nature and use of narrative techniques.

A chronology of O'Brien's life and a listing of his many works, followed by a select annotated bibliography and an index, attest to the profound respect this writer commands in contemporary American literary scholarship.—**ARBA Staff Reviewer**

628.　De Roche, Linda. **The Jazz Age: A Historical Exploration of Literature.** Santa Barbara, Calif., Greenwood Press/ABC-CLIO, 2015. 237p. illus. index. (Historical Explorations of Literature). $61.00. ISBN 13: 978-1-61069-667-8; 978-1-61069-668-5 (e-book).

Linda De Roche's exploration of five 1920s novels—*Babbitt* by Sinclair Lewis, *The Great Gatsby* by F. Scott Fitzgerald, *Gentlemen Prefer Blondes* by Anita Loos, *The Sun Also Rises* by Ernest Hemingway, and *Passing* by Nella Larson—is an installment in a series aimed at students which views literature of important periods through a historical lens. Each work is summarized and accompanied by essays about its historical background, its author, its literary significance, and primary sources drawn mostly from contemporary periodicals which reflect the social and political themes relevant to each novel. The book also includes a high-level overview of the decade in question and a timeline of important events.

The selection of novels is a sound one. Hemingway and Fitzgerald are givens in any discussion of Jazz Age literature, but the others are just as essential to understanding this turbulent decade; even more so perhaps because they generally receive less exposure. The range of these works spans the entire decade and encompasses perspectives from different classes, races, genders, and geographic areas.

The historical themes highlighted and supported by primary resources are also apropos for an age when new music, new media, advancing technology, and the shadow of the Great War were overturning old mores: social unrest, race, gender, and class identity, capitalism, consumerism, and crime. The contextual background woven in tandem by the critical essays and historical documents permits a more nuanced appreciation of each individual work, as well as a broad grasp of this critical era in American history.

Other works in this series include *The Harlem Renaissance: A Historical Exploration of Literature* by Lynn Domina and *American Slavery: A Historical Exploration of Literature* by Robert Felgar.—**Autumn Faulkner**

629.   **Magill's Literary Annual 2015.** Emily Goodhue and Matthew Akre, eds. Hackensack, N.J., Salem Press, 2015. index. $195.00/set. ISBN 13: 978-1-61925-685-9; 978-1-61925-870-9 (e-book).

This annually produced reference selects and reviews the most compelling literature, both fiction and nonfiction, that has been published over the course of a particular year. Criteria for selection from the greater pool of published works include a book's general appeal, its reflection of publishing trends, and its ability to enhance a curriculum regarding authors explored in academia. Books selected run the gamut through biography, short story, debut works, young adult fiction, essays, and much more. Users of this reference (and of this specific edition) will recognize well-established authors such as David Mitchell or Joan Didion, and perhaps be introduced to up-and-coming writers like Kerry Howley.

Alphabetically arranged and produced as a two-volume reference, the reviews are standardized in that they, in an orderly fashion, provide a book's general information from the complete title down through the author's name, publisher, type of work, main characters, etc. The reviewers employ criticism from a variety of sources, referenced at the end of each review to present a balanced, well-researched essay.

The reviews make sure to note a book's intent and perspective, and further, whether an author has successfully met these particular literary goals. Reviews of fiction do well to generally examine plots and tone without revealing too much. Essays are mostly of equal, sufficient length and provide enough information for users to truly get a taste for the subject and quality of a book without overwhelming them with unnecessary opinion and detail.

In addition to the essays, the volumes contain supplementary information that will be of great interest to readers, including a brief author biography, an annotated list of titles, a category index whereby books are aligned by subject areas, a title index, and an author index. Volume one covers books titled A through K, while Volume two reviews titles L- Z. Magill's is a valuable, easy-to-use reference for any librarian, literature teacher, or avid reader among us.—**Laura Herrell**

British Literature

Individual Authors

William Shakespeare

630.   **Critical Survey of Shakespeare's Plays.** 2d ed. Joseph Rosenblum, ed. Hackensack, N.J., Salem Press, 2015. 363p. illus. index. $125.00. ISBN 13: 978-1-61925-864-8; 978-1-61925-865-5 (e-book).

Critical Survey of Shakespeare's Plays attempts to provide the essential information for basic Shakespeare research by providing a collection of essays about Shakespeare's life and works. Although not immediately apparent, this is a second edition having been updated after 17 years. As a result, the vast majority of the essays have been reprinted and reproduced from other publications. Interestingly, three of the four new essays are actually about Shakespeare's poetry and are located in a brief section near the end of the volume. In a text specifically dedicated to Shakespeare's plays, this poetry section seems a bit out of place.

Regardless, *Critical Survey of Shakespeare's Plays* does accomplish its goal and provides an excellent introduction into Shakespeare and his work. The text begins with a brief biography looking at Shakespeare the man, the dramatist, and the poet, while continuing to the main section discussing each of Shakespeare plays. Each essay provides a plot summary, a critical analysis, and a list for further reading. The reader will also find a brief history of Shakespeare studies, a guide to free online resources, United States Shakespeare festivals, bibliography, character index, quotation index, and subject index.

This volume does serve very well as a thorough introduction and students picking up this volume will have a great jumping off point in their research. However, the relative lack of new material about his plays (some of the essays date back to 1987) raises the question of whether this collection represents a significant step forward from the previous edition.—**Tyler Manolovitz**

631. **The Shakespeare Book: Big Ideas Simply Explained.** New York, DK Publishing, 2015. 352p. illus. index. $25.00; $9.99 (e-book). ISBN 13: 978-1-4654-2987-2; 978-1-4654-3902-4 (e-book).

This informative and interesting book offers detailed analyses of each of Shakespeare's plays as well as his narrative poems and sonnets, presenting them using the chronology laid out in the *Complete Oxford Shakespeare.* Each entry is several pages in length and has a list of principal characters, a timeline of the action by act and scene, a full plot synopsis, and information about the ongoing reputation and impact of the work.

The treatment of *Othello,* for example, introduces the characters of Othello, Iago, Desdemona, Cassio, Emilia, Roderigo, Brabanizo, Monano, Bianca, Lodovico, Graziano, and the clown. This is followed by a plot discussion that explicates the themes and contextualizes the story. A sidebar lists the pertinent themes (jealousy, loyalty, betrayal, love), the setting, sources of inspiration for Shakespeare, and notable dates associated with the play. Another sidebar looks at the black American actor, Ira Aldridge, who in 1825 became the first black person to play Othello on the London stage.

For students unfamiliar with Shakespeare's works, these scholarly, yet accessible entries are an ideal starting point. The color photographs, images, and layout of the book will also hold the reader's interest. Highly recommended for school and public libraries.—**ARBA Staff Reviewer**

632. **Shakespeare Online. http://www.shakespeare-online.com/.** [Website] Free. Date reviewed: 2016.

Shakespeare is central to the English literature curriculum at all levels, and this Website makes available a voluminous body of information related to his life and works.

The site includes the text of Shakespeare's plays along with explanatory notes, criticism, character analysis, and information about sources. The section for each play provides resources. Some of these are generic articles on how to read the plays, Shakespeare's reputation, and similar topics, while others are critical essays. For each scene of a play, study questions appear on the right and explanatory notes appear at the end of the scene. There are sections on the sonnets as well.

The site also includes reviews of a small number of books about Shakespeare and these reviews are generally a short paragraph without bibliographic information. There are also study guides for the major plays. Additional features include brief biographies of roughly 20 scholars active primarily during the late nineteenth and early twentieth centuries; excerpts from Shakespeare's sources; several timelines; information about Shakespeare's life; and an assortment of trivia questions.

Of special note is the attention the site gives to Shakespeare's language, with information about his words and imagery, a glossary, quotations in context, and a quotation of the day.

The Website would be most useful to students and general readers seeking an introduction to Shakespeare. Much of the material included was published in the early twentieth century or before then, including the texts of Shakespeare's works and the explanatory notes. While there is some critical material written expressly for the site, there do not seem to be excerpts from modern university press books and scholarly journal articles protected by copyright. The layout is attractive and engaging, but a serious drawback is that this free Website is littered with ads.—**ARBA Staff Reviewer**

633.   Vienne-Guerrin, Nathalie. **Shakespeare's Insults: A Pragmatic Dictionary.** New York, Bloomsbury Academic, 2016. 489p. index. (Arden Shakespeare Dictionaries). $172.00. ISBN 13: 978-0-8264-9833-5.

As one of the icons of English Literature, William Shakespeare has inspired innumerable forms of scholarship and classification. This volume, one in the Arden Dictionaries series, carefully catalogs one of the playwright's most effective devices—the insult. Throughout his works, Shakespeare has used this device to heighten the drama, expose one's character, and certainly to delight and excite the reader/theatergoer. This book examines Shakespeare's cutting words by exploring their origins, their usage, their impact on the particular play, and their influence on the wider culture.

Over 450 alphabetized entries detail words from "ab(h)ominable" to "zed." Entries include general definitions, specific Shakespearian references, and scholarly contexts, which is particularly helpful when considering such seemingly benign words as "acorn" or "maypole" as insults.

The dictionary also includes a bibliography, an index of Shakespeare's works with respect to insults, index of characters, a list of abbreviations, and a list of headwords for ease of reference. While it is certain that lines like "I cannot endure such a fustian rascal" (King Henry IV, Part I) make reading and performing Shakespeare quite delightful, this excellent resource provides the necessary context for their maximum effect.—**ARBA Staff Reviewer**

Chilean Literature

Handbooks and Yearbooks

634.   **Critical Insights: Roberto Bolaño.** Ignacio López-Calvo, ed. Hackensack, N.J., Salem Press, 2015. 267p. index. $95.00. ISBN 13: 978-1-61925-834-1; 978-1-61925-835-8 (e-book).

The late writer Roberto Bolaño, responsible for a number of poems, essays, and short stories as well as his prize-winning novel *The Savage Detectives,* was described by the *New York Times* as the "most significant Latin American literary voice of his generation." Exploring themes such as the artist's ability to comprehend the struggles of life, or the rampant violence particular to Latin America in the 1970's and 1980's, Bolaño passed away at the early age of fifty. This volume in the Critical Insights series gathers essays from a variety of Bolaño scholars which examine many aspects of his work, ranging from the relationship between his poetry and prose to a discussion of film adaptations of his works and more.

The book's opening chapters establish Bolaño's personal story: born in Chile to a lower-middle-class family, he grew up in a time of political upheaval and moved between his native country and Mexico where his affiliation with left-wing dissenters would ultimately influence his writing. His early works, mainly poems, were defined by the infrarealism movement, which he cofounded: marginal in the scheme of things and reactionary to the commercial and critical success of authors such as Octavio Paz, Isabel Allende, and others.

The book's Critical Contexts section then presents four essays delving more deeply into Bolaño's world. They describe the influence of Latin American history on his work, particularly the impact of the 1973 Chilean military coup, his reception from critics with mind to his early death, and publishing concerns, among other things.

The Critical Readings section is focused topically and examines thematic continuity within Bolaño's writings, the impact of U.S. literature on him, the presence of queer themes, the contrast between his *Una novelita lumpen* (2002) and its film adaptation *Il futuro* (2013), and more. For example, Rubén Medina's essay entitled "Bolaño and Infrarealism, or Ethics as Politics" discusses Bolaño's relationship to the literary movement and how it provides the foundation for comprehending his work.

A brief Resources section rounds out this book by providing a chronology of Bolaño's life, a listing of published works, a bibliography, and information on the contributors. This book goes far to elevate Bolaño's profile as one of Latin America's most compelling men of letters.—**Laura Herrell**

French Literature

Handbooks and Yearbooks

635.   **Critical Insights: Gustave Flaubert.** Tom Hubbard, ed. Hackensack, N.J., Salem Press, 2015. 300p. index. $95.00. ISBN 13: 978-1-61925-824-2; 978-1-61925-825-9 (e-book).

This volume in the Critical Insights series presents a wide array of discussion on the nineteenth-century novelist Gustave Flaubert. The book closely examines his work in addition to casting a wide eye over the literary concerns of his time. Opening essays by Tom Hubbard describe a man noted both for his painstaking attention to, and certain detachment from, precise storytelling. His signature novel *Madame Bovary* would come to signify a new approach to literature.

The Critical Contexts section of this volume provides four foundational essays which can help readers to understand the time in which Flaubert wrote, as well as acknowledge the criticisms he may have received. Priscilla Meyer does well in her essay "*Anna Karenina:* Tolstoy's Polemic with *Madame Bovary*" to contrast the two great works and highlight their artistic differences even as they share the plot vehicle of a scandalous adultery.

Critical Readings embarks on a more diverse set of objectives through 11 essays which cover everything from how Flaubert treats the concepts of time and memory to his influence on modernism and his artistic relationship to other writers. Mark Conroy's essay "Seduction by Story in Flaubert and Conrad," for example, considers Flaubert in contrast to Joseph Conrad relative to their unique ways of conveying their hero(ine)'s struggles. Apart from *Madame Bovary,* the essays in this section discuss Flaubert's *L'Education Sentimentale, Bouvard et Pécuchet, Salammbó* and more. Each essay comes with its own cited sources. In addition, the volume contains a chronology of Flaubert's life, a chronological listing of his published (some incomplete) works, a good bibliography, and an index.—**ARBA Staff Reviewer**

Italian Literature

Handbooks and Yearbooks

636.   **Dartmouth Dante Project https://dante.dartmouth.edu.** [Website] Free. Date reviewed: 2016.

An ongoing endeavor of inestimable scholarly value, the *Dartmouth Dante Project* is a searchable database containing the text of more than 70 commentaries on Dante's *Divine Comedy* along with Giorgio Petrocchi's modern edition of the 1321 text of the poem. The commentaries are in their original languages and range from Jacopo Alighieri's 1322 commentary on the *Inferno* to a 2003-2015 commentary by Nicola Fosca. The commentaries typically offer line-by-line explications of the poem, with some providing more sustained narrative interpretations. Many of the commentaries are difficult to obtain, and some are protected by copyright.

Through the database, a user can conduct Boolean searches for words appearing in the commentaries or poem. Searches can be limited to particular commentaries, canticas, cantos, and lines, and the database provides clear instructions for initiating and refining queries.

Despite its utility, the database does have its drawbacks. While particularly strong in representing the Renaissance commentary tradition, it lacks, for example, the commentaries of Hermann Gmelin (1954), André Pézard (1965), and Robert Durling and Ronald Maritnez (1996). Since the database is a versatile concordance, it indexes keywords rather than concepts. Thus a reader searching for what the Italian commentators said about Dante's giants would need to look up "giganti" (812 results) rather than "giants" (87 results). It would also be helpful if the database included all of Dante's canon rather than just the *Divine Comedy.* Nonetheless, the database fulfills its objective.

While an essential tool for scholars, the database is less useful to undergraduates, high school students, and general readers, since the text of the poem is in Italian and many of the commentaries are in Italian and Latin. Users might also be interested in the *Dartmouth*

Dante Lab http://dantelab.dartmouth.edu/, which builds on the *Dartmouth Dante Project* and allows users to compare commentaries; the *Princeton Dante Project* http://etcweb. princeton.edu/dante/index.html, which provides texts of Dante's works, critical material, and multimedia resources; and *The World of Dante* http://www.worldofdante.org/, a multimedia Website that includes texts, images, music, and teacher resources.—**ARBA Staff Reviewer**

Nonfiction

Handbooks and Yearbooks

637.   **Critical Insights: American Creative Nonfiction.** Jay Ellis, ed. Hackensack, N.J., Salem Press, 2015. 235p. index. $95.00. ISBN 13: 978-1-61925-417-6; 978-1-61925-418-3 (e-book).

This entry in the Critical Insights series provides an extensive overview of what editor Jay Ellis terms a "genre of genres" (p. vii)—American creative nonfiction. The volume opens with a detailed general summary of the book's contents followed by the editor's chapter outlining the history and challenges of studying a wide-ranging genre that encompasses several subgenres (memoir, captivity narratives, travel writing, nature writing, and illness narratives to name just a few). A Critical Contexts section presents four original essays reflecting on the background and critical reception of creative nonfiction as well as an in-depth consideration of Tim O'Brien's work in the genre. The Critical Readings section follows with 10 essays from scholars representing diverse educational interests. The essays build upon the material offered in the Critical Contexts section through their specific analyses of the creative nonfiction subgenres. Each essay in the volume concludes with endnotes and a works cited list. The volume concludes with a useful Resources section offering a general bibliography, a list of additional works of American creative nonfiction, entries on the professional credentials of the editor and contributors, and a subject index. The essays approach the genre from multiple critical perspectives (two notable examples include essays on African American autobiography as sociocultural criticism and the role of gender in nature writing) resulting in a well-rounded resource appropriate for an academic audience. Keeping in line with the aim of the Critical Insights series, this volume provides comprehensive, authoritative scholarship suitable for both students and teachers. This volume is recommended for academic collections and large public libraries.—**Lisa Morgan**

Poetry

Handbooks and Yearbooks

638.   **American Poets and Poetry: From the Colonial Era to the Present.** Jeffrey Gray, Mary McAleer Balkun, and James McCorkle, eds. Santa Barbara, Calif., Greenwood Press/ABC-CLIO, 2015. 2v. index. $189.00/set. ISBN 13: 978-1-61069-831-3; 978-1-61069-832-0 (e-book).

A modest two-volume set—though a single volume would not have been too thick—*American Poets and Poetry: From the Colonial Era to the Present* does just that, though it is by no means exhaustive. It provides a strong introduction or overview of key American poets and critical poetic concepts and movements—such as modernism and the Harlem Renaissance—in concise, critical entries. Biographical entries are anywhere from three to six pages in length and provide key biographical details relevant to the poet's life, development, and career; these entries also contain selected primary and secondary sources pertaining to the poet's work. Conceptual or movement-related entries contain critical events and figures and feature a listing for further reading. Some of these entries contain subheadings; many of these entries and some of the biographical entries would have benefitted from subheadings, given the density of the entries. The reader finds themselves facing walls of text when reading this title, unrelieved by graphics, illustrations, or photographs which would have contributed a great deal to an appreciation of both movements and individuals. In spite of this, the title is useful as an introductory critical title. It is highly recommended for secondary school libraries, public libraries, and undergraduate college/university libraries.—**Megan W. Lowe**

25 Music

General Works

Bibliographies

639. Gray, John. **Afro-Brazilian Music: A Bibliographic Guide.** Nyack, N.Y., African Diaspora Press, 2014. 585p. index. (Black Music Reference Series, Volume 5). $124.95. ISBN 13: 978-0-9844134-4-7.

This book is a comprehensive, multidisciplinary, and multilingual work for scholars, students, librarians, and writers on black music and musicians born outside of the African subcontinent. It focuses on four distinct but interconnected categories of black vernacular culture: secular and Afro-Catholic religious festivals, the music and dances associated with these festivals, folk and popular idioms associated with Brazilians of African descent, and liturgical musics performed in worship traditions. Coverage is from 1833 through 2012, with the bulk of the resources dating from the 1930s to the present. Information is presented in a modified MARC format familiar to those who use library catalogs, as much of the content has been scraped from OCLC/Worldcat along with a number of European and Brazilian libraries. The book is organized into seven sections: Cultural History and the Arts, Festivals and Carnival, General Works, Musical Instruments, Genre Studies, Regional Studies, and Biographical and Critical Studies. Sections five and six are rich in subsections such as Choro, Lundu, Reggae, and Zabumba, along with regional studies of Amapa, Goias, Pernambuco, and São Paulo, to name but a few. A number of indexes to help navigate the content are provided. A very useful and content-rich resource for this area of study.—**Bradford Lee Eden**

Dictionaries and Encyclopedias

640. Brown, Emily Freeman. **A Dictionary for the Modern Conductor.** Lanham, Md., Rowman & Littlefield, 2015. 421p. illus. (Dictionaries for the Modern Musician). $85.00; $84.99 (e-book). ISBN 13: 978-0-8108-8400-7; 978-0-8108-8401-4 (e-book).

Brown (director of orchestral activities and professor of conducting at Bowling Green State University) casts a very wide net, covering pretty much all aspects of music: orchestras, instruments, venues, festivals, and associations. Since most of these items can be found elsewhere in standard music sources (though perhaps not necessarily all under one cover), its true merit lies in the area most closely related to its purpose: conductors and conducting. A highlight is the keen insight into the legendary personalities of the world's most famous conductors, with which modern audiences may not be familiar. A sampling: Fritz Reiner "cultivated an intense stare bordering on the hypnotic"; Herbert van Karajan "sought total control over every element"; Leopold Stokowski "sought drama in performance whenever possible." Composers are included only if they were also conductors: Berlioz yes, Brahms no. In a field historically dominated by white males, Brown pays due homage to women (Marin Alsop, JoAnn Falletta), minorities (Henry Lewis, Isaiah Jackson) and both (Margaret Harris). On the conducting side, the dictionary provides illustrative notations of conducting technique, (e.g. the eleven dynamic signs) and multilingual entries in italics for French, German, Italian, and Spanish terms (though most without an English-language equivalent). For novice conductors, Brown includes Monteux's 5 "musts" and 12 "don'ts" for young conductors and Richard Strauss' 10 golden rules for a young conductor. All entries are listed in one straight alphabet with cross-references embedded within articles, even terms like conductor and orchestra. This extremely thorough and systematic system of cross-referencing often leads to overkill. For example, since the word "conductor" appears in every mention of the articles about conductors, when one turns to the definition for conductor, one finds simply "a person who conducts." A highly comprehensive thematic bibliography includes classics in the field as well as items published as recently as 2015. The dictionary concludes with several useful appendixes: six pieces that changed conducting, a two-page history of conducting, translations in French, German, Italian and Spanish of instruments and of pitch, interval and rhythmic terms, and a sample recitative from Così fan tutte. Although one would expect that the professional conductor would be familiar with this material, this volume would prove useful to the music school or conservatory student; the public library user or college student would certainly find the information informative, if not entertaining, but the title might dissuade said users despite its wealth of potentially useful general music information.—**Lawrence Olszewski**

Handbooks and Yearbooks

641. **Europeana Music. http://europeana.eu/portal/collections/music.** [Website] Free. Date reviewed: 2016.

Europeana is a wide-reaching digital library documenting books, paintings, films, objects, and audio recordings from museums, archives, and historical institutions across Europe. There are a variety of Europeana group projects: initiatives specializing in different disciplines. Europeana Sounds is behind the music collection housed on Europeana. From the site: "The Europeana Music Collections brings together a selection of the best music recordings, sheet music, and other music related collections from Europe's audio-visual archives, libraries, archives and museums. This month the spotlights have been carefully picked by the Danish Statsbiblioteket."

The site features an attractive, contemporary layout. The music collection also utilizes Soundcloud for curated listening lists as well as individual music pieces. The music collection boasts 184,698 images, 61,081 sound recordings, 19,995 texts, 11,318 videos, and five 3D objects. The site is arranged for both casual browsing and purposeful searching for professional, student, or recreational users.

The purpose of the collection is comprehensive historic documentation; therefore, it is most suited to vintage highlights rather than contemporary fads. For example, the above-mentioned Danish spotlight features sheet music from WWI, Irish Folk music, Jean Sibelius, Richard Strauss, Mongolian folk music recorded by a Danish explorer, and the early recordings of Robinson Crusoe. Also featured are exhibitions on musical instruments, and recording and playing machines.

Many of the sounds are downloadable, providing digitized primary sources directly to the user. Links to the institutional sources of the media are provided to explore more extensively if desired. This site is oriented toward researchers of primary documentation, so those seeking commentary, context, and explanation would need to refer to other resources.

The music collection on Europeana is a triumphant merger of contemporary technology with historic cultural preservation. Beautiful and informative, the site is rewarding and engaging for visitors. *Europeana Music* is a highly recommended immersive learning experience.—**ARBA Staff Reviewer**

642. Holoman, D. Kern. **Writing about Music: A Style Sheet.** Oakland, Calif., University of California Press, 2014. 126p. illus. $29.95pa. ISBN 13: 978-0-520-28153-0; 8-0-520-95881- (e-book).

Scope mirrors the previous editions (1988, 2008) that outlined issues facing writers about music: title strategies, materials in multiple languages, formats, and access methods, plus the recording of terminology and notation in writings. The author concisely lists principles that writers need in the digital age, and the prime sources of information to create their narratives and citations. The author hopes to simplify citations of Internet locators, provides examples of World Music, addresses page layout in the paperless world, and notes the multiple platforms available for publication and dissemination.

The pattern resembles the *Chicago Manual of Style* (Chicago: University of Chicago Press, 2010), cited as *CMS.* Holoman provides guidance in musical terminology, and methods of constructing a narrative essay.

He begins with "Music Terminology," where he defines titles of works, distinctive and generic, liturgical works, movement titles, numbering of works, diacritical marks, thematic catalogs, pitch names, chords, and rehearsal marks. He clarifies the use of apostrophes in the citation of names. The thematic catalogs indexed are the basic ones for freshmen, but this list scratches the surface. The "Narrative Text" chapter details the use of diacritics, punctuation, and other details critical to writing about music. "Citations and Credits" proves very useful for those citing digital materials and recordings. The author presents further advice on the displays of musical examples, tables, and the textual layout of concert programs.

Although there is no index, the author provides a detailed table of contents. *Writing About Music* is simpler for musicians to use than is the *Chicago Manual of Style,* and addresses their specific issues. This volume should be on music reference shelves, near the CMS and Kate Turabian's *A Manual for Writers of Research Papers, Theses, and Dissertations* (Chicago: University of Chicago Press, 2013).—**Ralph Hartsock**

643. Scott, Allen. **Sourcebook for Research in Music.** 3d ed. Bloomington, Ind., Indiana University Press, 2014. 497p. index. $35.00pa. ISBN 13: 978-0-253-01448-1.

Allen Scott takes a general approach similar to previous editions, to create an "introductory reference source...largely bibliographical, pertaining to research in the field of music." (p. xv) He concentrated on providing a selective representation rather than comprehensiveness. The editor expands and numerically systematizes many aspects of the previous editions' introduction, such as glossaries and classification systems. To the bibliographical terms in English, French, and German, Scott adds Italian terms. He then displays a summary of the Library of Congress classification for music and its literature. The Dewey classification guide for music is updated to show the 23d edition, followed by a guide to the 19th edition.

After this, the organization of the third edition departs from that used for the first and second. The editor created two large sections. Part one is literature about music, while part two cites specific sources to help users find the music itself.

The editor moves from general to specific in each chapter of part one: General Bibliographies, Dictionaries and Encyclopedias of Music, and Journals and Periodicals and Their Indexes. The meatiest portions in part one are the last two chapters. The fifth chapter covers musicology, ethnomusicology, music theory, education, music therapy, and music history. The next chapter presents sources relating to musical instruments, genres and forms, and repertory guides.

Part two begins with sources that describe early manuscripts, monuments, composers' complete works, and thematic catalogs. In this listing of monuments, the editor yields to George R. Hill's and Norris L. Stephens's mammoth volume, *Collected Editions, Historical Series & Sets & Monuments of Music: A Bibliography* (Berkeley, Calif: Fallen Leaf Press, 1997), for detailed descriptions. The second chapter of this part describes discographies.

Another departure from the second edition is the absence of miscellaneous sources, such as manuals of style, and general sources about the music industry. In this way, Scott focuses upon the sources for research in music, instead of processes. Those relevant to research are in the general bibliographies. The volume concludes with two indexes: one for persons, and the second for titles.

Those who desire fuller annotations of each title may still go to Vincent Duckles's and Ida Reed's *Music Reference and Research Materials,* 5th edition (Schirmer Books, 1997; see ARBA 98, entry 1189), up to that publication date. For major publications after 1997, Laurie Sampsel's *Music Research: A Handbook* (Oxford University Press, 2013) provides very useful annotations. Those who seek guidance in the processes of music research, citation of sources, and style manuals, should also consult Sampsel's volume and updated Website (http://global.oup.com/us/companion.websites/9780199797127/).

Scott did miss some significant titles about the blues: *Encyclopedia of the Blues,* by Gérard Herzhaft (Fayetteville: University of Arkansas Press, 1997; see ARBA 99, entry 1150); *The Big Book of Blues: A Biographical Encyclopedia,* by Robert Santelli (New York: Penguin Books, 2001; see ARBA 2002, entry 1167); and *Encyclopedia of the Blues,* edited by Edward Komara (New York: Routledge, 2006; see ARBA 2007, entry 1007). Readers will also find *100 Books Every Blues Fan Should Own,* by Edward Komara and Greg Johnson (Lanham, Maryland: Rowman & Littlefield, 2014; see ARBA 2015, entry 745) to be a useful source.

Nevertheless, Allen Scott has created a volume that is easy to use, which identifies titles important to the research of music. This is partially due to the numerical organization instituted by the compiler that resembles the organization of the *Chicago Manual of Style.* Libraries should keep a copy behind the desk for quick reference.—**Ralph Hartsock**

Instruments

Handbooks and Yearbooks

644.   Wilkinson, Philip. **The History of Music in Fifty Instruments.** New York, Firefly Books, 2014. 224p. illus. index. $29.95. ISBN 13: 978-1-77085-428-4.

This book is part of publisher Firefly's Fifty Things that Changed the World series that now includes volumes on machines, animals, plants, and foods. The author of this volume, Philip Wilkinson, is an English freelance writer of over 40 books with specialization in music, architecture, and history (e.g., *The British Monarchy for Dummies* from For Dummies Press in 2007). This volume traces the history of music-making through the production and evolution of 50 different musical instruments beginning in the 1300s with the creation of the lute and ending with the synthesizer in 1985, with stops along the way for 48 other creations. The length of the article depends on the importance of the instrument; for example, castanets (1845) and the harmonium (1842) get two pages each whereas the violin (1636), piano (1709), and baton (1812) have eight pages each. The text covers in lucid nontechnical prose such topics as the evolution and nature of the instrument, different types and their characteristics, the role and importance of the instrument in orchestral music, composers who wrote for this instrument, and famous art works in which the instrument is featured. Sidebars are used to give interesting tidbits of related material (e.g., the article on the English horn (1720) has a sidebar on how it got is name and the one on the violin features a list of great violin makers). Classical music is emphasized throughout although there are some references to jazz and folk music. The glory of this volume, however, is in its illustrations, mostly in color. They include diagrams of the instrument (often with labeled parts), other members of its family and their history, famous composers and instrumentalists associated with the instrument, and historical prints that feature the instrument. The book begins with an introduction that covers musical instruments and their families and ends with a bibliography for further reading, a list of important Websites, and a five-page index. This is an engaging, informative volume suitable for both reference and browsing.—**John T. Gillespie**

Musical Forms

Classical

645.   **Classical Scores Library Package.** http://alexanderstreet.com/products/classical-scores-library-package. [Website] Alexandria, Va., Alexander Street Press. Price negotiated by site. Date reviewed: 2016.

The Alexander Street *Classical Scores Library Package* provides access to approximately 51,000 in-copyright music scores for all major classical music genres from the "Middle Ages to the 21st century." All major composers (e.g., Bach, Mozart,

Beethoven, etc.) are included as well as lesser-known contemporary composers. The complete collection is divided into four volumes that can be purchased separately or as a package.

The collection includes full, study, voice, and piano scores. It has been thoroughly indexed allowing it to be searched by keyword and browsed by title, genre, instrument, people, publisher, time period, and composer.

A high-quality image copy of the music score is provided with a wealth of accompanying metadata (composer, date, language, publisher, etc.). The in-score navigation feature allows users to jump between movements. The viewing interface allows users to create custom playlists, annotate the music, and share the score and their notes. Recommendations for related works are included. All scores and movements can be easily cited using any one of the major citation styles (powered by EasyBib).

The collection will certainly "enhance the study of music history, performance, composition and theory for a variety of scholars"; thus, it is highly recommended. The ability to access such a large scope of music collected from a wide range of publishers is a major benefit to musicians and researchers. Any academic or public library committed to serving serious music scholars should have this resource. The collection has over 1.3 million printable pages and claims the shelf space needed to house such a collection is over 200 meters. This kind of space-saving is valuable in itself, but the added search tools, enhancements, and the ability to access the collection online makes this an indispensable, go-to tool.—**Kristin Kay Leeman**

646.   Murray, Lucy Miller. **Chamber Music: An Extensive Guide for Listeners.** Lanham, Md., Rowman & Littlefield, 2015. 427p. $85.00; $84.99 (e-book). ISBN 13: 978-1-4422-4342-2; 978-1-4422-4343-9 (e-book).

If music be the food of love, then chamber music is the food of angels who created that love. An excess of it would surely never whet any appetite for it for it is the breath of violets, the sweet odor of the beating, diaphanous wings. It is, in short, the language of God and hardly better understood than by Bach himself.

But it is, of course, more than Bach as these 600+ works attest. It is more far-reaching than Bach, too, since this collection covers the Classical through the Romantic and past the post-Modern. But that Bach is the only representative of chamber music in the Baroque period serves to validate the former assertions.

This current volume is a second edition of *Adams to Zemlinsky: A Friendly Guide* (Concert Artists Guild, 2006). This edition shakes off the alphabetic restrictions and focuses more on the wide expanse that is chamber music. The obvious in addition to Bach are here: Bartok, Beethoven, Brahms, Chopin, Debussy, and Mozart. But so are some that many general readers will never have heard of: Abramovic, Ades, Bridge, D'Rivera, Reger, and the modern composer Zorn. Each entry contains a survey of the composer's work, a note about the chosen piece (or pieces) of chamber music, and the author's personal assessment. Miller's personal viewpoints make the book since so much scholarly information is available online. Even she admits its quirkiness, as when she compares a moment in one of Beethoven's string quartets to a belly dance. But it is just this personalization that makes the book an interesting read and a must buy.

A detailed table of contents makes finding certain pieces simple and straight-forward. The book is laid out alphabetically, of course, for easy reference to the body of the chamber work by individual composers.—**Mark Y. Herring**

Folk Music

647.   Robb, John Donald. **Hispanic Folk Music of New Mexico and the Southwest: A Self-Portrait of a People.** Albuquerque, N.Mex., University of New Mexico Press, 2014. 891p. illus. index. $75.00. ISBN 13: 978-0-8263-4430-2; 978-0-8263-4432-8 (e-book).

The University of Oklahoma Press published the original version of this book in 1980. Now exclusively available from the University of New Mexico Press, this superior title is based on the author's recordings and transcriptions of New Mexican folk music, a labor of love 35 years in the making. A forward by Jack Loeffler and a prologue by Enrique Lamadrid contextualize both Robb and the enduring importance of *Hispanic Folk Music of New Mexico and the Southwest: A Self-Portrait of a People.*

The text is arranged in three parts: Secular Song Texts and Melodies; Religious Song Texts and Melodies; and Instrumental Melodies. Song texts appear in both Spanish and English and the book also includes music for the pieces. This is followed by five appendixes: Piano-Vocal Arrangements of Selected Songs; Song Literature of the Villages; Sampling of Despedidas; Songs with Chorus or Refrain; and Forum for Analysis of Folk Melodies. Definitions, a bibliography, a discography, an index of titles, an index of first lines, and a general index round out this work that also includes 31 black-and-white photographs. This priceless work is recommended to academic and public libraries.—**Melinda F. Matthews**

648.   Vigil, Cipriano Frederico. **New Mexican Folk Music/Cancionero del Folkor Nuevomexicano.** Albuquerque, N.Mex., University of New Mexico Press, 2014. 258p. illus. $45.00. ISBN 13: 978-0-8263-4937-8; 978-0-8263-4939-2 (e-book).

Cipriano Vigil, born in the northern New Mexican village of Chamisal in 1941, is regarded as one of the most important performers of traditional New Mexican folk music. Though not a traditional songbook, this wonderful title contextualizes and provides the bilingual texts of folk songs from northern New Mexico and southern Colorado. Vigil, who composes in traditional genres such as the romance, the décima, the cuándo, and the corrido, showcases and explicates the music from the perspective of an insider born and raised in this musical tradition. This book represents about one-quarter of Vigil's pieces and presents traditional material not seen before by scholars or students.

The book's preface is followed by 14 chapters and a conclusion. Although it does not provide an index, photographs and sketches enhance the text. A CD with 20 of Vigil's spectacular performances is also included. Vigil's use of side-by-side bilingual texts makes the work more accessible to readers of both English and Spanish. The superb masterwork is priceless for music, academic, and public libraries. Anyone researching New Mexican legendary melodies or Cipriano Vigil will be more than delighted with the brilliant superior resource.—**Melinda F. Matthews**

Orchestral

649.   Daniels, David. **Daniels' Orchestral Music.** 5th ed. Lanham, Md., Rowman & Littlefield, 2015. 885p. index. $85.00. ISBN 13: 978-1-4422-4537-2.

The fifth edition of this staple of music libraries has increased by one third in its number of pages, entries, and updates from the fourth edition, but its purpose and format remain basically unchanged. The work is an alphabetical listing by composer and work that includes information to help orchestras schedule rehearsals and plan concerts. To save space due to its complex and detailed nature, instrumentation is indicated by a series of codes; for those not familiar with them, an explanation in the preface explains their interpretation. For orchestra staff responsible for programming notes, the work provides skeletal composer biography, date of composition, and approximate duration. As a collection tool, publication information indicates the availability of scores for music libraries that want to expand their collections, especially of lesser-known composers and works.

Even without the requisite omission of operatic works, any such source must needs be selective; nevertheless, the inclusion of over 8000 works in the repertoire by composers worldwide is indeed impressive, incorporating all the symphonies of Haydn and Mozart and Bach's cantatas, to name just three complete series of works by prolific composers.

A gem of this work has always been the appendixes. Where else can one find programmable works that are under five minutes? One appendix will assist planners of tie-ins to local ethnic programming events, another to celebrate the significant anniversaries of composers through 2026, and yet another of works intended for young audiences.

This resource is also available by annual subscription through Orchestralmusic.com with monthly updates.

Besides the obvious target audience of music librarians, conductors, and orchestra programmers, it will also be useful for critics, concertgoers, and music collectors. However, this edition may be the last overseen by octogenarian Daniels, now retired from conducting and from the faculty at Oakland University.—**Lawrence Olszewski**

Popular Music

650.	**Bloomsbury Encyclopedia of Popular Music of the World, Volume X. Genres: Middle East and North Africa.** David Horn and John Shepherd, eds. New York, Bloomsbury Academic, 2015. 148p. illus. maps. index. (Encyclopedia of Popular Music of the World). $250.00. ISBN 13: 978-1-5013-1146-8; 978-1-5013-1148-2 (e-book).

Compilers noted a need for a comprehensive and reliable reference source on popular music. *The Bloomsbury Encyclopedia of Popular Music of the World* proposes to satisfy that need. Previously published are volumes on various topics (part one), geographical areas (part two), and the genres (part three). This volume belongs in the last named group.

The aim is to create a systematic resource in which related subjects are organized coherently, rather than being scattered alphabetically between volumes. Each volume has its own index, plus selected volumes contain combined indexes.

Part three, like part two, is organized geographically, as the regional basis proves most effective. Authors prefer to use the term genre rather than style, and define genres as "collective terms that are commonly used to refer to music with an identifiable function." Some citations in the discography are incomplete, intentionally. Editors chose to include partial information due to the importance of sound recordings in popular music. Four basic grayscale maps give referential geography for the volume.

For demographic groups, such as "Kurdish Folk in Turkey," contributors present social, political, and historical background, then musical qualities: melody, types of tunes, instruments played, and recent production of recordings. Various other "Underground

Music" movements are discussed, such as the Arabic, or Iranian. For genres, such as "Khaliji" or "Heavy Metal," the contributors define the term, pinpoint the geographical area in which it is prominent, note when the genre has been used, and identify principal performers of the genre. Bibliographies vary in size as do discographies.

This volume proves beneficial for those seeking interrelationships of political or cultural activities (such as folk dancing) with music.—**Ralph Hartsock**

651.   Moore, Mark A. **The Jan & Dean Record: A Chronology of Studio Sessions, Live Performances and Chart Positions.** Jefferson, N.C., McFarland, 2016. 454p. illus. index. $75.00pa. ISBN 13: 978-0-7864-9812-3; 978-1-4766-2290-3 (e-book).

This account of the musical careers of "Jan & Dean" (Jan Berry and Dean Torrence) provides a rich trove of information on the creation, work, and life of an important group in the 1960's Southern California music scene and beyond. Jan & Dean were responsible for such hits as "Surf City" and "The Little Old Lady from Pasadena" and they also recorded and produced the work of many other artists. The heart of the book is a detailed, almost day-by-day chronology, spanning some 350 pages, of their song writing, recording sessions, album releases, concerts, business ventures, and significant personal events—including the 1966 car crash that put a stop to Jan's career for many years. Author Mark A. Moore brings the story to life with reminiscences by family members, friends, and music business associates. His prologue takes the story of Jan & Dean up to 1958, when the chronology begins, and the epilogue describes their careers and lives after the accident. An introductory page explaining how to use the book will help those seeking specific information on recording sessions, performances, and on Jan & Dean's personal history. The book has a song index plus a general index, and there is a preface by Brian Wilson of the Beach Boys. Jan & Dean's story is illustrated by dozens of black-and-white photographs as well as reproductions of musical scores, receipts, contracts, and other miscellany. The book will interest many readers (including the generation that grew up listening to Jan & Dean) and those concerned with the history of popular music in America. Recommended.—**Alice Chaffee**

Rock

652.   **The 100 Greatest Bands of All Time: A Guide to the Legends Who Rocked the World.** David W. Moskowitz, ed. Santa Barbara, Calif., Greenwood Press/ABC-CLIO, 2015. 2v. illus. index. $189.00/set. ISBN 13: 978-1-4408-0339-0; 978-1-4408-0340-6 (e-book).

This biographical encyclopedia of 100 bands is edited by music historian David W. Moskowitz, with several additional contributors. The scope of the two volumes is primarily rock bands of the twentieth century in the English-speaking popular music industry. Solo performers are not included. Each entry includes the biography of the band's career, noting critical and commercial reactions, followed by a selected discography and additional sources. The biographical sections include the instrument specializations of the band's members and any lineup variations. The entries are arranged alphabetically by artist.

Moskowitz begins the encyclopedia with an introduction and 10 themed essays that aim to set the succeeding biographical entries in some context. The essays include themes such as women in rock, the Woodstock festival, the crossover of rap into the mainstream and the impact of MTV. These and other topics are posited as seminal events or trends that make the backdrop of Moskowitz's selections for the encyclopedia.

In the introduction, Moskowitz is frank about the subjectivity of a task like selecting the 100 greatest bands of all time. "Greatness," especially in the context of popular media, is surely a matter of taste with varying and occasionally arbitrary criteria. Moskowitz cites the book and film versions of *High Fidelity* as a touchstone for his approach, pointing to Nick Hornsby's characters' penchant for rock music list-making, in which they blend the personal and the (supposedly) universal to arrive at a top 5 or 10 songs or albums for a particular situation. Moskowitz also points to what he calls scientific factors like album sales and a band's overall impact, but even these variables can be difficult to weigh when assessing "greatness." Moskowitz is right to be up front about the inherent imprecision of deciding on the 100 greatest bands of all time, though doing so acknowledges the mixed value of a work in which the basis for inclusion or exclusion is not wholly defined.

As a biographical resource on rock bands, Moskowitz's efforts compete with many comparable or even superior reference sources, some of which are freely available online. Rovi Corporation's All Music Guide is one, and is even cited throughout the entries in these volumes. However, All Music Guide is a vastly more comprehensive resource; Moskowitz's work will be a more manageable entry point for identifying and contextualizing crucial bands. It seems most likely to serve this purpose in a high school or public library setting.—**Joshua Barton**

653.   Shumway, David R. **Rock Star: The Making of Musical Icons from Elvis to Springsteen.** Baltimore, Md., Johns Hopkins University Press, 2014. 244p. illus. index. $29.95. ISBN 13: 978-1-4214-1392-1; 978-1-4214-1393-8 (e-book).

Cultural theorist David Shumway leverages portions of biography of seven popular music acts from the twentieth century to support his argument for the Rock Star as a discrete cultural construct. Shumway posits the Rock Star as distinct from celebrities and the otherwise famous, the distinction being in Rock Stars' wielding of unique political and cultural significance, unwittingly or not. Shumway argues that the influence of the Rock Star is inaccessible to other varieties of celebrity and was unique to the conditions that manifested in the mid-1950s with the advent of rock-n-roll music, peaked in the 1960s, and has since declined.

Shumway's work consists of a preface, eight chapters, and a conclusion. The preface and chapter one set up Shumway's overarching argument, framing the succeeding chapters as case studies rather than biographies, though the case studies certainly draw on elements of biography. The case studies include Elvis Presley, James Brown, Bob Dylan, The Rolling Stones, The Grateful Dead, Joni Mitchell, and Bruce Springsteen. The conclusion closes out Shumway's argument. It should be understood that Shumway does not intend to create a reference work on the lives of these stars, but rather interpret portions of their work and legacies to serve his theory.

Each case study focuses on one or a few examples of the clout that these respective stars enjoyed, and/or the challenges that they posed to cultural norms. Challenges to gender norms are reviewed in several cases. Throughout, Shumway draws on lyrics, performances, and legends of the selected stars, adding further context with reference to music journalism, criticism, and a broad range of Shumway's fellow cultural theorists. These help characterize the serious treatment of rock music and stars that developed chiefly in the 1960s. However, Shumway seems to be disappointed in his observation of the decline of the Rock Star in contemporary times. He attributes this decline to audience fragmentation and argues that rock and pop stars now seem to be "mere" celebrities, with culture now lacking the conditions that allowed for the singular influence and power that Rock Stars wielded in earlier years.—**Joshua Barton**

26 Mythology, Folklore, and Popular Culture

Folklore

Dictionaries and Encyclopedias

654.   Redfern, Nick. **The Bigfoot Book: The Encyclopedia of Sasquatch, Yeti, and Cryptid Primates.** Canton, Mich., Visible Ink Press, 2016. 381p. illus. index. $19.95pa. ISBN 13: 978-1-57859-561-7.

In much of the world there exist folk tales and legends of large humanoid creatures resembling great apes. Whether it is the Kikomba of the Congo, the Yeti of Tibet, or the Sasquatch of North America these creatures possess many similarities with one another that have inspired explorers of various backgrounds to search for conclusive evidence of their existence. The purpose of this reference is to gather together in one accessible volume the various accounts and legends of these creatures along with the fictional tales that they've inspired in film and other media.

With a collection of over 230 articles the author details various world legends of Bigfoot both ancient, such as Alexander the Great and the great hairy wild men, and more modern accounts, including Alabama's Ape man. The text also talks about notable hoax stories as well as entries for various adaptations of these legends in film and literature ranging from horror to comedic tales. The entire collection is arranged alphabetically with each entry listed in the contents. Many entries possess references to additional topics within the text and the book itself possesses a comprehensive index as well as a list for further study on the topic.

While the index is quite extensive it would be primarily useful to individuals with a previous working knowledge of the materials within. Despite this the individual entries are understandably written and engaging and thus this would serve as an adequate introduction to the subject for general enthusiasts, high school students, or early college students.—**W. Cole Williamson**

Handbooks and Yearbooks

655.   **A Companion to Folklore.** Regina F. Bendix and Galit Hasan-Rokem, eds. Hoboken, N.J., Wiley-Blackwell, 2014. 660p. index. $54.95pa. ISBN 13: 878-1-118-86314-5.

A Companion to Folklore is a long-awaited, cohesive text on the study of folklore. With introductions to each chapter that bring together the topics of concepts and phenomena, location, reflection, and practice, this volume is an essential piece for folklore studies. Covering a wide scope and rich with information, editors Bendix and Hasan-Rokem have gathered thought-provoking and interdisciplinary scholars in a single volume. References and notes follow each chapter, allowing for an even deeper understanding of the discussion by the author and further research. Anyone interested in the current trends and outlook of folklore studies needs look no further, at the moment, than this volume. Covering information across time periods and continents, this truly is a multicultural and multidisciplinary approach to folklore studies.—**Michelle Martinez**

656.   Elswit, Sharon Barcan. **The Latin American Story Finder.** Jefferson, N.C., McFarland, 2015. 318p. index. $45.00pa. ISBN 13: 978-0-7864-7895-8; 978-1-4766-2229-3 (e-book).

This is the third book published by this author related to ethnic stories, the other two on East Asian and Jewish tales. This guide provides access to stories from 21 countries and over 75 indigenous tribes in Latin America after the arrival of Spanish and Portuguese colonials in the sixteenth century. These tales from native cultures such as the Maya and Quechua tribes were mixed with those of Sephardic Jews and Catholic missionaries, sprinkled with ancient Inca and Amazonian cultures along with Anansi stories from African slaves. The author divides this "soup" of stories into a number of categories, from journeys to other realms to supernatural seducers, from winning and losing with the gods to tricksters and fools, among many. The real power in this book are the indexes and appendixes, which include a glossary and listing of indigenous peoples by country with alternate names, along with a story title and subject index. An extensive bibliography makes this a unique resource on over 470 Latin American tales.—**Bradford Lee Eden**

657.   Sellen, Betty-Carol. **Self-Taught, Outsider, and Folk Art: A Guide to American Artists, Locations and Resources.** 3d ed. Jefferson, N.C., McFarland, 2016. 320p. index. $49.95pa. ISBN 13: 978-0-7864-7585-8; 978-1-4766-2304-7 (e-book).

Compared to the refined, formalized world of fine art, information on American Folk Art may be more difficult to accumulate due to its less-conventional nature. This book helps bring the more obscure world of self-taught, outsider, and folk art to the foreground of the discussion by offering a vital resource for those interested in viewing, buying, showcasing, or learning more about this special type of art. This third edition has been updated with the very latest contact information due to the many changes inherent in the folk art community: many resources have switched away from brick-and-mortar establishments to an online presence only or have adopted a greater social media presence, etc.

Chapters relay information on a variety of diverse venues, organizations, and other places where readers can find information, if not outright examples, of the art. Such venues include galleries, private dealers, fairs, auctions, museums, and libraries. Chapters also reference written information available on the art—such as books, exhibition catalogs, and magazines. Within each chapter, venues are listed alphabetically by state. Entries may include phone numbers, email address, street address, proprietor, venue profile, artists displayed, and more.

The largest chapter then presents an alphabetical catalog of select folk artists along with a brief biography which may include contact information. In examining these biographies it is interesting to note some personal details of the artist's life: Joseph Abrams, for example, started making newspaper hats when he was 80 years old, while Mercedes Jamison creates works which almost always include the image of a smiling sun.

Especially due to the fact that many folk artists are "outsiders" by definition and may be less prone to commercialize their work, this book is a valuable resource for anyone intrigued by their world. Recommended.—**ARBA Staff Reviewer**

Mythology

Handbooks and Yearbooks

658.   Aldhouse-Green, Miranda. **The Celtic Myths: A Guide to the Ancient Gods and Legends.** New York, Thames and Hudson, 2015. 207p. illus. index. $24.95. ISBN 13: 978-0-500-25209-3.

In recent history there has been a revival of interest in cultural traditions thought to originate with the Celtic peoples. Whether in the areas of music, the arts, or especially new age spiritual beliefs, many people are fascinated and drawn to this ancient culture both as a window into their own ancestry and as a rejection to many aspects of today's society. There is unfortunately a great disparity between what we sometimes ascribe to this civilization and what they actually thought and believed themselves. This is due in large part to a sizable dearth of information from their own point of view. Through painstaking archaeological and cultural research this guide seeks to piece together the actual legends and beliefs of this lost society.

In each chapter this book delves into various aspects of the Celtic traditions such as an examination of their surviving mythic tales, the cultural aspects of oral histories, legends of spirits, heroes, and enchanted lands, and finally how these tales evolved with the coming of Christianity. The chapters are divided in their focus with some homing in on individual locations such as Wales or Ireland, while others explore especially important practices in detail such as the celebration of significant events.

The arrangement of the text flows well and it includes an adequate if not exhaustive index. The real appeal in this work lies with its extensive use of beautiful photographs and highly informative charts strategically placed throughout the text. Special note may be given to a chart at the beginning that highlights pronunciation standards for proper names in the rest of the text that greatly aids the reader unfamiliar with linguistic intricacies. Overall this serves as an excellent guide to the richness of Celtic cultures for either the academic reader or general enthusiast.—**W. Cole Williamson**

Popular Culture

Dictionaries and Encyclopedias

659. **Holiday Symbols and Customs.** 5th ed. Detroit, Omnigraphics, 2015. 1437p. index. $133.00. ISBN 13: 978-0-7808-1364-9.

This large volume, a companion to *Holidays, Festivals, and Celebrations of the World Dictionary* (Omnigraphics, 2015) and an update to the fourth edition (see ARBA 2010, entry 1049), presents information about the activities and symbols of over 375 events of many sorts. Included, for example, are Christmas, the British Open (golf tournament), Tinkat (the Ethiopian celebration of Epiphany), Setsubun (a Japanese festival), and the Army-Navy Football Game. The symbols range from objects (crystals, masks, water lanterns, the moon) to activities within the celebration. Most entries include contact information and Websites, when available.

Besides the table of contents, other tools enhance access to the information herein: a list of entries by type of celebration, a list by symbols involved, listings of tourist information worldwide (including foreign chambers of commerce and consulates in the U.S.), and a 70-page general index. Libraries of all kinds would benefit from acquiring this volume, should budgets allow it.—**Mark Schumacher**

660. **Holidays, Festivals, and Celebrations of the World Dictionary.** 5th ed. Detroit, Omnigraphics, 2015. 1500p. $177.00. ISBN 13: 978-0-7808-1362-5.

This massive volume provides information on over 3,300 events of all kinds, from the World Santa Claus Conference (held annually in Denmark) and the Pitra Visarjana Amavasya ceremony in India, to the Fourth of July and Festivus (inspired by the "Seinfeld" show). Details of the history of the event and its various activities are included. Websites and addresses for additional information are also available in many cases.

Appendixes and indexes provide numerous ways to explore the volume—legal holidays by state and by country, an index by date throughout the year, and a subject index (arts, religious, sporting, etc.). There are also discussions of world religions and calendar systems, tourism resources, a 25-page bibliography, and a 120-page general index. This work is recommended to all libraries whose users are seeking resources on these celebrations, from school and public libraries to academic institutions.—**Mark Schumacher**

Handbooks and Yearbooks

661. **Comic Book DB.com. http://comicbookdb.com/.** [Website] Free. Date reviewed: 2016.

Comic Book DB is a fairly comprehensive database of comic book issues, creators, artists, publishers, and characters. The site is mostly useful for anyone researching a popular character or creator.

The database allows users to browse by various categories from an alphabetical list of characters, creators, publishers, and more. The amount of information available is heavily in favor of the major publishers (DC Comics, Marvel, Image Comics, etc.), creators, and characters. Character searches such as "Superman" or "Captain America" include exhaustive lists of titles and various appearances by the characters over time. Moreover, such well-known creators Stan Lee and Jack Kirby are accompanied by significant biographies. Each creator is also paired with a very detailed chronological list of credited works and awards, making it easy for a user to jump from that creator into his or her works and accolades. Pages on creators without the legacy of Lee and Kirby contain less biographical information, but most creators still come with a strong list of credited works and awards.

The site does contain issues that limit the ability to search. For example, a search of "Lee, Stan" will not actually lead to results including the creator because the site lists him as "Lee, Stan 'The Man' – 'Stanley Martin Lieber'." Also, it appears the Website allows users to update information, much like Wikipedia. Nevertheless, the ability to search creators, their credited works, and some biographical information makes the database is a good starting point for students looking to research comic books and their creators or characters.—**ARBA Staff Reviewer**

662.   **Earth Calendar. http://www.earthcalendar.net//index.php.** [Website] Free. Date reviewed: 2016.

This fun, simple site allows users to find holidays and celebrations around the world by date. Holidays are defined as any day that recognizes a cultural event. The site's copyright dates are listed as 1998-2008, but holidays and celebrations are searchable until 2020. *Earth Calendar* is freely accessible and nonprofit, but there is no advertising on the site.

Navigation is simple. From the home page, users can click a today tab that produces the day's holidays. Holidays and celebrations linked to March 11, 2016, for instance, include Commonwealth Day in Tuvalu and the celebration for the Restoration of Lithuania's Statehood. From March 11, users can navigate to previous and following days. Other search options include Holidays by Date, Holidays by Country, or Holidays by Religion. For the more creative, there is a link to lunar phases. A country search using Bermuda and 2016 revealed in addition to New Year's Day on January 1, that Bermudans will celebrate Peppercorn Day on April 23, Bermuda Day on May 24, Dame Lois Browne-Evans Day on November 11, Christmas Day on December 25, and Boxing Day on December 26. Each country also has a basic map powered by Graphic Maps that shows its place in the world and its geographic outline. Those wishing to search for holidays by religion can choose from Baha'i, Buddhism, Celticism, Christianity, Hinduism, Jainism, Judaism, Muslim/ Islamic, Paganism, Rastafarian, Shinto, Sikhism, Voudon, and Zoroastrian.—**ARBA Staff Reviewer**

663.   Nichols, Elizabeth Gackstetter, and Timothy R. Robbins. **Pop Culture in Latin America and the Caribbean.** Santa Barbara, Calif., Greenwood Press/ABC-CLIO, 2015. 402p. index. (Entertainment and Society around the World). $94.00. ISBN 13: 978-1-61069-753-8; 978-1-61069-754-5 (e-book).

Organized topically, this handbook is part of the ABC-CLIO "Entertainment and Society around the World" series, and covers music, literature, film, sports, television, fashion, and Internet and gaming culture in and Latin America and the Caribbean in the twentieth and twenty-first centuries.

Each chapter starts with an introductory essay that provides a broader historical and social context—a useful resource for beginning researchers—and a list of sources for further reading. The entries in each section highlight particular contemporary issues and people, with bibliographies citing reputable Websites as well as popular and trade publications. Many of the individuals and trends are easily recognizable, but the entries provide a greater context. For example, the entry for the Brazilian star Xuxa provides insight into her life prior to her rise to North American stardom, as well as what she has been producing in the years since her peak.

Its organization may be confusing to casual browsers, however. While the titles of the articles are clearly indicated at the tops of the pages, it would be useful to have chapter titles as well. The appendix includes a number of top 10 lists related to entertainment and culture, but they mostly focus on 2012-2014, which limits their usefulness for examining longer-term trends.

A more substantial bibliography at the end primarily refers to scholarly books that are excellent next steps for finding information. Written in a style accessible to high school and college-level researchers, this is a good introduction and suitable for most school, public, and academic libraries.—**Amanda Izenstark**

27 Performing Arts

General Works

Biography

664. Lentz III, Harris M. **Obituaries in the Performing Arts, 2014.** Jefferson, N.C., McFarland, 2015. 382p. illus. $49.95pa. ISBN 13: 978-0-7864-7666-4; 978-4-4766-1967-3 (e-book).

Collected from a variety of sources, *Obituaries in the Performing Arts, 2014* shares career highlights, biographical information, and death details of nearly 1200 global celebrities who passed away in 2014. While predominantly profiling novelists, playwrights, producers, actors, and the like, the book also pays respect to the more obscure celebrity, such as Jovian, the lemur known as Zoboomafoo on the PBS children's series of the same name, or Red Klotz, a coach of the Washington Generals, the basketball team known for inevitably losing to the Harlem Globetrotters. The book obviously includes celebrities of great fame and accomplishment, such as actor Robin Williams, but does well to include those lesser known as well, such as Paula Kent, marginally known for her acting but perhaps better known as the cofounder of Redken Laboratories, a beauty industry stalwart.

Though each entry is limited in scope to basic information, it is nonetheless interesting to consider each person's contribution to the performing arts: that familiar face from the cola commercial just may have extensive credits in theater and film. Each obituary is accompanied by one or more black-and-white photos. The entries are preceded by a reference bibliography, listing both print and online sources.—**Laura Herrell**

Dance

Dictionaries and Encyclopedias

665. Snodgrass, Mary Ellen. **The Encyclopedia of World Ballet.** Lanham, Md., Rowman & Littlefield, 2015. 424p. illus. index. $95.00; $94.99 (e-book). ISBN 13: 978-1-4422-4525-9; 978-1-4422-4526-6 (e-book).

In 377 pages, the world surrounding the global emergence and growth of ballet historically and thematically is described through dense, informative entries. Immensely useful in both organization and structure, entries include choreographers, companies, dancers, and key terminology, among other things. These entries display not only the rich internal history of the dance world and ballet specifically, but also the role and impact this world has had on the larger social structure. This is echoed in the colorful timeline—noting, for example, the 23 years of censorship of the Iranian National Ballet between 1979 and 2002. This volume is both an encyclopedic look at the elements that comprise ballet, as well as the unfolding of the larger philosophy of movement and dance. Because we are presented with this wider scope in a compact volume, the listing of entries (and rationale for their inclusion or exclusion) might not be intuitive to the nonexpert. A companion volume would have ensured a more comprehensive sweep. The index does indicate which terms are found within as complete entries, and this makes cross-referencing easier. Useful for students and practitioners of dance; anyone with a broad interest in the historiography of the humanities will find this necessary as well.—**Stephen J. Shaw**

Film, Television, and Video

Dictionaries and Encyclopedias

666. Hischak, Thomas S. **The Encyclopedia of Film Composers.** Lanham, Md., Rowman & Littlefield, 2015. 819p. illus. index. $95.00; $94.99 (e-book). ISBN 13: 978-1-4422-4549-5; 978-1-4422-4550-1 (e-book).

Paying homage to those often-forgotten composers whose music serves as the backdrop of film, this encyclopedia focuses on 252 composers who have contributed significantly to movie music. Some entries feature artists who composed songs, but this is predominantly a collection of composers of film scores. Major film composers are covered, but this work attempts to give attention to Hollywood and foreign film composers often left out of other treatments on the subject. Entries provide biographical information, descriptions of the composer's career and musical style, and a complete list of film score credits. Only films in which the individual is listed as the primary composer or one of two composers are listed. For the common reader, the encyclopedia provides a few surprises such as an entry on Charlie Chaplin, who scored some of his own films decades after their release. Familiar names in jazz appear as entries as well. Featured in this work is more than a century of composers who have provided original music for silent films to contemporary movies.—**Brian J. Sherman**

667. King, Lynnea Chapman. **The Coen Brothers Encyclopedia.** Lanham, Md., Rowman & Littlefield, 2014. 215p. illus. index. $80.00; $79.99 (e-book). ISBN 13: 978-0-8108-8576-9; 978-0-8108-8577-6 (e-book).

The phenomenal careers of brothers Joel and Ethan Coen as cowriters, directors, and producers of their own films began in 1984 with the crime story, *Blood Simple.* The author of this reference work, an English professor and film buff, concentrates on the brothers' collaborative work from this first feature through their 16th major work together, *Inside Llewyn Davis* of early 2014 (there is no mention of later work like script writing on Angelina Jolie's 2014 *Unbroken* or Steven Spielberg's 2015 *Bridge of Spies.* Each of these highlighted films is given a separate entry in the alphabetically arranged, double-columned reference work. The remaining 80-odd entries are about a page each in length and are almost all biographical in nature, focusing mainly on actors important in these films like Frances McDormand (Joel's wife and star of *Burn after Reading* and *Fargo*) and George Clooney (*Burn after Reading, Intolerable Cruelty,* and *O Brother Where Art Thou?* plus a few production personnel (designers, cinematographers). These entries concentrate on the subject's work with the Coens. The biographical entry for the brothers Coen (which includes a photograph) is nine pages in length and supplies extensive material on their professional and personal lives particularly outside of their collaborative film efforts. The heart of this work, however, is found in the entries for each of their films. Each of these is about five pages in length beginning with a box containing such basic data as production staff, cast members (actors and their roles), running time and release date, followed by a lengthy plot summary and character analysis. Material is then given on the genesis of each film, script writing details, casting considerations, production problems and solutions, critical reception, and a general evaluation. Each of these entries contains a black-and-white still from the film. In all of the book's entries, the author refers to a concluding section for each entry called "References." This section ends with an extensive *see also* list of related entries which helps supplement a concluding, bare bones name index. The appendixes also include a bibliography of 13 books suitable for further reading and a filmography of the Coen's movies in reverse chronological order. This is a highly readable, fascinating work that will be a suitable addition to both film and large library collections.—**John T. Gillespie**

668.   **The Routledge Encyclopedia of Films.** Sarah Barrow, Sabine Haenni, and John White, eds. New York, Routledge/Taylor & Francis Group, 2014. 665p. index. 205.00. ISBN 13: 978-0-415-68893-2; 978-7-315-77383-4 (e-book).

When applied to a book on a particular subject, the term "encyclopedia" usually means that it contains a comprehensive overview of that subject. This is not so with this volume although it deserves the attention of anyone interested in films because of its unique contents. The three editors with the help of almost 80 contributors (all film and media academics primarily in American and British institutions) have chosen almost 200 films that are considered among the most important, influential, trail-blazing, and also critically satisfying. Therefore, this is not the usual "best films" list (although some of the titles in this volume often appear on such lists). The films are arranged alphabetically by title and each entry is three double-columned pages in length. The coverage is truly international in scope—only about 50 (25% of the entries) are English-language films. These include such standards as *Citizen Kane* (1941), *On the Waterfront* (1954), and *Singin' in the Rain* (1952), as well as some questionable entries like those for *Mad Max* (1979) and *Moulin Rouge!* (2000). The remainder of the entries are for foreign-language films with particularly fine coverage for French, Italian, Spanish, and German films. Also included are films from such countries as Turkey, Senegal, and Burkina Faso. The most recent film included is *Milk of Sorrow* (2009) from Peru. Each entry is scholarly in tone and emphasizes material on why the film is important in cinematic history.

Entries begin with a listing of the cast and key production personnel and a brief plot synopsis. These are followed by an essay on the movie that includes a critical analysis of the film often with reference to particular scenes and performances and directorial techniques. Background material on social and political movements that affected the content of the film and its treatment are included. Sources of the script (novel, play, etc) and other influences on the film are covered as well as the material on the past (and future) of key personnel including the director and the stars. Each entry is signed and ends with a brief footnote-like section called "Notes." That is followed by a "Further Reading" bibliography that typically contains a list of four or five English-language sources. In addition to an excellent detailed index, the editors have provided lists of the films by both their English- and foreign-language titles and a chronology for films by their release dates (there are entries for 13 silent movies including *Birth of a Nation* (1915). This is a fascinating scholarly work that deserves a place in libraries needing quality material on movie history.—**John T. Gillespie**

669.   Umland, Samuel J. **The Tim Burton Encyclopedia.** Lanham, Md., Rowman & Littlefield, 2015. 283p. illus. index. $80.00; $79.99 (e-book). ISBN 13: 978-0-8108-9200-2; 978-0-8108-9201-9 (e-book).

After working for several years in Hollywood as a scenic designer and animator (chiefly with Disney), Tim Burton (b. 1958) directed his first full-length feature, *Pee-Wee's Great Adventure* in 1985. Since then he has directed and/or produced over two dozen ground breaking, blockbuster movies such as *Edward Scissorhands* (1990), *Batman* (1989) (plus two sequels), *Beetlejuice* (1988), and *Sweeney Todd* (2007). Most are fantasies that usually deal with the bizarre or macabre. In this volume, the author, an English professor, covers Burton's illustrious career in about 150 alphabetically arranged entries some of which have been written and signed by colleagues including the author's wife, Rebecca Umland. With the exception of the biographical entry for Burton, which is six double-columned pages in length, the longest articles are for each of his movies. These are three to four pages each. After a highlighted box containing cast and production names and running time, these entries contain a detailed plot summary, anecdotes on casting and production, critical assessments, and audience reactions. A few have additional entries on the original source material (e.g., Broadway's *Sweeney Todd*) or spinoffs like video games. The greatest number of the remaining articles are biographical in nature and average a page in length. They include important cast members like Johnny Depp and Michael Keaton as well as production personnel including composers, script writers, and designers. The coverage here is erratic (e.g., there are entries for writers Washington Irving and Roald Dahl but none for Stephen Sondheim or Hugh Wheeler, the originators of *Sweeney Todd.* All of the entries end with a section called "References" in which the books and articles used as sources for the entry are listed. Coverage ends in December of 2014 (there is mention of the breakup of Burton and long-time companion Helena Bonham-Carter in December of that year).The book lacks a filmography and cross-references but there are a few black-and-white photographs scattered throughout the text and a "Selected Bibliography" of about 40 books and articles for further reading. The book ends with a helpful 20-page name index. In spite of sloppy editing and inconsistent coverage, this is an interesting, valuable study of one of Hollywood's most innovative filmmakers.—**John T. Gillespie**

Filmography

670.   Blottner, Gene. **Columbia Noir: A Complete Filmography, 1940-1962.** Jefferson, N.C., McFarland, 2015. 283p. illus. index. $45.00pa. ISBN 13: 978-0-7864-7014-3; 978-

1-4766-1761-9 (e-book).

The author uses a broad definition of film noir, defining it as a dark, pessimistic mood rather than a genre. For that reason, many Westerns make the list in addition to some horror, science fiction, and even comedy films.

Author Gene Blottner has written four other books on Columbia or Universal studios. Going beyond the usual, though disputed, date of 1958's *Touch of Evil* as the end of the classic noir cycle, Blottner goes up to 1962, the year of *Cape Fear, The Manchurian Candidate,* and *Experiment in Terror* (only the last is from Columbia). Columbia Studios produced 169 films that the author calls noirs between 1940 and 1962. He has personally watched them all, so his commentary and synopsis is well informed.

Each entry includes release date, complete cast and credits, songs(!), production dates, running time (though running times may vary, the author used the time on the copy he watched), synopsis, commentary which includes information from the behind the scenes workings of Columbia, a few quotes from reviews, and a summation. In addition, many films include information on alternate titles, filming locations, and story source. Other notes include items such as "Color by Technicolor" or "Filmed in Cinemascope." Each film is given a page to a page and a half and there are black-and-white photographs about every two to four pages.

A preface and introduction explain the layout and context. Appendixes include a list of films alphabetically, a list of films chronologically, a bibliography, and a very complete index. While the cast and credit information can easily be found at Internet Movie Database (imdb.com), the story synopsis and commentary in *Columbia Noir* is much more thorough.—**Robert M. Lindsey**

671.   Sassen, Claudia. **Larry Semon: Daredevil Comedian of the Silent Screen: A Biography and Filmography.** Jefferson, N.C., McFarland, 2015. 252p. illus. index. $39.95pa. ISBN 13: 978-0-7864-9822-2; 978-1-4766-2027-5 (e-book).

In this publishing season there have been two important biographies of largely unsung giants of silent screen comedy. The first is Matthew Dessem's *The Gag Man: Clyde Bruckman and the Birth of Film Comedy* (Thomas Elrod, 2015) and the second is this volume on the life and work of Larry Semon (rhymes with lemon) who died at age 39 in 1928, immediately before the birth of talking pictures. This multitalented man (he was an accomplished magician and cartoonist as well as writer, director, producer, and actor in films) lived a roller-coaster, rags-to-riches (and back again) life where one year he was penniless and the next, he was signing a million-dollar contract with the Vitaphone company. In various capacities, he was significantly involved in over 200 movies, highlights being working with both Laurel and Hardy before they became a team and starring in the first film version of *The Wizard of Oz* (1925). The author, a cartoonist, linguist, college teacher, and Semon lover, devoted 20 years to the data collecting and writing of this biography which is admiring in tone but also candid and honest. It is filled with a wealth of personal anecdotes and fascinating behind-the-scenes details. Additionally, it contains a treasure trove of black-and-white illustrations—many are movie stills and lobby posters, while others are examples of Semon's artwork (several from the author's own collection).

The last 30 pages of this work will be of particular value for reference work. It is a chronologically arranged, very detailed filmography (compiled by two other Semon fans) of all the films in which he was involved in different capacities. Whenever possible, the data includes length, survival status, release date, copyright information, director, producer writer(s), distributors, actors with their cast names, a plot summary, and quotations from reviews. The book concludes with a chapter-by-chapter list of sources used listed in footnote fashion with good bibliographic information for each source. As well, there is an extensive seven-page bibliography that includes a separate list of newspapers and magazines. The book ends with a name index (to the biography section only) that indicates references to the illustrations by using bold type. This fascinating and enlightening work on this unsung genius of the silent era will be a fine addition to both reference and circulating collections.—**John T. Gillespie**

672.   Vogel, Michelle. **Marilyn Monroe: Her Films, Her Life.** Jefferson, N.C., McFarland, 2014. 209p. illus. index. $39.95pa. ISBN 13: 978-0-7864-7086-0.

While much has been written about the Hollywood icon who died of a drug overdose at the age of 36, this book sets itself apart by examining her filmography in close concert with her short and tumultuous life. Opening with an examination of the facts of her death, and emphasizing the mysterious circumstances surrounding it, the book establishes the context for analyzing her filmography: specifically, there was more to Marilyn than meets the eye.

The author then chronologically presents her filmography, from a brief appearance in 1947's *Dangerous Years,* to her award-winning performance in 1959's *Some Like It Hot,* and finally to the unfinished *Something's Got To Give.* The filmography includes such details as cast, crew, technical information, production details, promotion details, and a synopsis. As readers traverse the actress's filmography, they learn the concurrent story of her life and are thus able to create the connection between Monroe's personal issues and experiences and her portrayals onscreen.

Including a forward by award-winning talent George Chakiris, this book does well to present this catalog of 30 films and connect it to the strong image within filmgoers' minds about the Marilyn Monroe they thought they knew. A bibliography and an index round out this work.—**ARBA Staff Reviewer**

Handbooks and Yearbooks

673.   Berumen, Frank Javier Garcia. **Latino Image Makers in Hollywood: Performers, Filmmakers and Films Since the 1960s.** Jefferson, N.C., McFarland, 2014. 335p. illus. index. $55.00pa. ISBN 13: 978-0-7864-7432-5; 978-1-4766-1411-3 (e-book).

The stated purpose of *Latino Image Makers in Hollywood* "is to document the history of Latino film images and icons in the Hollywood film industry from the 1960s to the present." Berumen begins with a chapter on the origins of Latino stereotypes followed by decade-by-decade chapters on Latinos in films from the 1960s to the 2000s and a postscript "Beyond the 2000s: Looking Back and Looking Forward." In addition to Latino performers and filmmakers, the author studies non-Latino performers in Latino roles (e.g., Natalie Wood as Maria in *West Side Story*). The author has viewed most of the films mentioned in the book and consulted reviews of films, interviews with Latino performers and filmmakers, and works on film history, biographies, and newspapers and magazines. Discussed are early film performers such as Ramon Novarro, Gilbert Roland, Lupita Tovar, and Dolores del Rio. It should be noted that Beruman's earlier work, *Brown*

Celluloid: Latino/a Film Icons and Images in the Hollywood Film Industry (2003), documents the 1920s-1950s. Chapters profile and study key films and performers and analyze social and historical conditions of the times. For example, the 1960s focuses on major films such as *The Alamo, Che!, West Side Story,* and *The Wild Bunch* and profiles performers and filmmakers among which are Pedro Armendariz, Jr., Henry Darrow, Lalo Schifrin, and Raquel Welch. The following films are analyzed for subsequent decades: *State of Siege, La Bamba, Selena, Stand and Deliver, American Me, Frida,* and *Traffic.* Additionally, actors, actresses, and filmmakers profiled include Salma Hayek, Penelope Cruz, Javier Bardem, Carlos Avila, Jennifer Lopez, Benicio Del Toro, Antonio Banderas, Raul Julia, Jimmy Smits, Hector Elizondo, Luis Valdez, Mark Sanchez, Charlie Sheen, and Martin Sheen (Estevez). *Latino Image Makers in Hollywood* also contains copious illustrations, chapter notes, a bibliography, and an index. Highly recommended to public libraries and to college and university collections supporting programs in Latin American and Hispanic studies as well as motion picture history. It is recommended that libraries also purchase Brown's *Celluloid: Latino/a Film Icons and Images in the Hollywood Film Industry.*—**Lucy Heckman**

674.   Bliss, Michael. **Invasions USA: The Essential Science Fiction Films of the 1950s.** Lanham, Md., Rowman & Littlefield, 2014. 169p. index. $32.00pa.; $31.99 (e-book). ISBN 13: 978-1-4422-3651-6; 978-1-4422-3652-3 (e-book).

Post-World War II America was not what it seemed. While images of smiling, clean-cut families alongside their shiny cars and perfect houses prevail, was there perhaps something sinister lurking behind that white-picket fence? This book looks at a popular 1950's film genre—science fiction—and uses it to expose the very real insecurities and fears felt within American postwar society.

Examining 11 of the decade's most outlandish and outstanding science fiction films, the author positions Hollywood as providing the best articulation of America's underlying anxiety. Using such films as *The Day the Earth Stood Still, The Incredible Shrinking Man,* and *I Married A Monster from Outer Space,* the author exposes much fear in relation to conformity, militarism in the nuclear age, domesticity, totalitarianism, and more. For example, in his essay on *Invasion of the Body Snatchers,* Bliss rejects the notion that the film, depicting strange alien pods replicating human bodies, reflects the generally accepted anti-Communism message allotted to many artistic endeavors of the time, and suggests the story is truly indicative of man's fear of conformity to small town values and expectations—a genuine fear which has Miles, the protagonist, wind up stark raving mad at film's end. The author goes on to point out the many ways in which science fiction films of the 1950's promoted their ideas, from the use of emotionless aliens, to the protagonist's misogynistic view towards women, to the fact that the movies generally end bleakly.

Including a filmography listing such information as cast, crew, running time, release date and DVD information, the book also contains detailed notes, a bibliography, and an index.—**ARBA Staff Reviewer**

675.   Bradley, Edwin M. **Unsung Hollywood Musicals of the Golden Era: 50 Overlooked Films and Their Stars, 1929-1939.** Jefferson, N.C., McFarland, 2016. 225p. illus. index. $35.00pa. ISBN 13: 978-0-7864-9833-8; 978-1-4766-2400-6 (e-book).

The demand for easy entertainment was high in 1930's America, as the public craved distraction from the troubles of the Great Depression. Hollywood did its best to comply by producing many glitzy musical extravaganzas making stars of the likes of Bing Crosby, Ruby Keeler, and, of course, Fred Astaire and Ginger Rogers. While certain films and performers are indelibly etched in our movie-loving hearts, this book pays tribute to 50 of the lesser-known musical films from the era. In doing so, it unearths the stories of nearly forgotten directors, players, and productions which provides readers a more complete view of the musical genre.

Five chapters are arranged by themes, and explore musicals that survive from the earliest days of sound recording, showcase dubious talent, showcase rising talent, emerge from low-budget studios, and may generally be considered "oddities." We read, for example, of the comic duo of Myrt and Marge, whose eponymous musical film is now best remembered for the appearance of a comic trio: The Three Stooges. We also read of the adventurous *I Am Suzanne!* which involved dream sequences, marionettes, and many production mishaps afforded to its star, Lilian Harvey, who made a total of four Hollywood films before tearing up her studio contract.

The author writes with genuine knowledge of and admiration for the genre, as evidenced by the interesting behind-the-scenes production tales, honest criticism, and historical context. Each chapter shares filmographies which include release date, cast and crew, featured songs, a plot synopsis, and other miscellany. Fun black-and-white production stills are dotted throughout the book. It also includes notes, a bibliography, and a thorough index.—**ARBA Staff Reviewer**

676.   Coniam, Matthew. **The Annotated Marx Brothers: A Filmgoer's Guide to In-Jokes, Obscure References and Sly Details.** Jefferson, N.C., McFarland, 2015. 303p. illus. index. $39.95pa. ISBN 13: 978-0-7864-9705-8.

For lovers of Marx Brothers films, the author provides a guide to the in-jokes, obscure references, and sly details of 14 films starting with *The Cocoanuts* (1929) and moving chronologically through the following: *Animal Crackers* (1930), *Monkey Business* (1931), *Horse Feathers* (1932), *Duck Soup* (1933), *A Night at the Opera* (1935), *A Day at the Races* (1937), *Room Service* (1938), *At the Circus* (1939), *Go West* (1940), *The Big Store* (1941), *A Night in Casablanca* (1946), *Love Happy* (1949), and *The Incredible Jewel Robbery* (1959). To allow users to pinpoint the exact moment referred to in each film, the author uses time codes that appear in both NTSC and PAL format; the films used are the best official materials available in the United Kingdom. The book is illustrated throughout with black-and-white photographs and concludes with two appendixes, notes, a bibliography, and an index. This straightforward guide to references and humor in the Marx Brothers films will appeal in the main to aficionados but can be useful to a wider audience of those interested in or studying film, history, and popular culture.—**ARBA Staff Reviewer**

677.   Curti, Roberto. **Italian Gothic Horror Films, 1957-1969.** Jefferson, N.C., McFarland, 2015. 213p. illus. index. $39.95pa. ISBN 13: 978-0-7864-9437-8; 978-1-4766-1989-7 (e-book).

Focusing on the quirky niche genre of Italian gothic horror, this passionately researched filmography showcases an interesting collection of films released between the years 1957 and 1969. Characterized by musty, dark settings, lusty and vengeful characters, and atmospheric stories of evil, these films didn't have to work hard to gain a cult following.

Cataloging close to 40 films, the book provides thorough analysis of a film's inspiration, techniques, players, central themes, and critical reception. Some highlights include: the frequent appearance of Barbara Steele, an English actress who made her breakthrough in the 1960 film *Black Sunday* and went on to appear in six more prime examples of the genre; the recognition of recurring themes of vampirism, reincarnation, and marital infidelity; and the author's honest assessment of a film's capabilities ("the sets are slapdash, the lighting is passable at best, the dialogue abounds with absurdly inane lines…" he writes of 1965's *The Seventh Grave*).

Each entry lists cast and crew and provides a plot synopsis and notes. Black-and-white photos of production stills or marketing posters may also accompany the entries. A selected bibliography and an index conclude a book which every cinephile must read.—**ARBA Staff Reviewer**

678.   **Film Scripts Online Series. http://search.alexanderstreet.com/afso.** [Website] Alexandria, Va., Alexander Street Press. Price negotiated by site. Date reviewed: 2016.

Alexander Street Press' *American Film Scripts Online* is an online resource of English-language film scripts. These are shooting scripts, which contain not only dialog but camera and setting direction. The materials are drawn primarily from the American film industry, but they also feature scripts from several British studios. In all there are more than 1,100 screenplays that, while not exhaustive, do offer access to many important directors and writers from across the twentieth century. Because these are shooting scripts, they also provide a more comprehensive textual analysis of direction, although researchers will still want to hunt down the original notes and diary entries when available. The Website also makes available 37 monographs from the British Film Institute's Film Classics Series. Each is a book-length critique of a major film from the twentieth and early twenty-first centuries. Suggestive of the range of this material are such films as *Nosferatu, Citizen Kane, Cléo de 5 à 7,* and *Pan's Labyrinth.*

Research can be done several ways. The site offers featured collections such as scripts by Billy Wilder or from the famed Ealing Studios, a powerhouse of British cinema in the 1940s and 1950s. Users may also browse by broad categories such People, Genre, and Awards. The browse function is usually a coarse sieve, but in this collection the People category is subdivided into director, producer, writer, and performer. For example, "Huston, John" brings up 20 items: 12 as director, 1 as producer, 17 as screen writer, and none as performer; "Streisand, Barbra" reveals 1 item as a performer and 1 as a producer. This is pretty nifty. The Genre and Awards browse functions are coarser in this respect, although the latter is useful for exploring minor film festival awards. The advanced function allows for much more targeted searches. One caveat for libraries is that this is the third script offering by Alexander Street Press. The company has previously released two other volumes titled *Film Scripts Online:* volume one released more than 1,000 screenplays, and volume two provided an additional 500 screenplays. The present site seems to present a subset of the two previous collections along with some additional material.—**Joseph E. Taylor III**

679.   Garcia, Enrique. **Cuban Cinema after the Cold War: A Critical Analysis of Selected Films.** Jefferson, N.C., McFarland, 2015. 222p. $40.00pa. ISBN 13: 978-0-7864-9910-6; 978-1-4766-2060-2 (e-book).

With the late-twentieth-century demise of the Soviet Union came a re-imagining of the arts throughout its satellite nations. Cuba was no exception. With its vibrant island culture left to simmer behind more pressing economic and ideological tribulations, Cuba and its filmmakers nonetheless began to set aside their revolutionary scripts and explore new ways of telling visual stories. This book employs a diverse range of post-Cold War Cuban films and analyzes their ability to make a distinctly Cuban artistic statement in the world of global cinema.

The book initially provides the necessary background for understanding the trajectory of Cuban cinema. Tracing its roots to the heavy influence of Hollywood musicals, Mexican melodrama, and a "folklorist vision" of Cuba, we then note the revolution of 1959 and its establishment of the Cuban Film Institute, or the ICAIC, with the intent of promoting the island's new ideology and in direct opposition to the prevailing sense of international exploitation.

The crux of the book then focuses on films made when the collapse of the Soviet Union diminished its influence upon the Latin American nation. Garcia provides in-depth discussion of hard-to-find films such as *Alice in Wondertown* (1991), *Strawberry and Chocolate* (1993), *Paradise under the Stars* (1999), *Juan of the Dead* (2011), and more. In his analysis, he raises issues regarding the breakdown of the restrictive socialist narrative, the redefinition of what it means to be Cuban, the changing view of race via Cuban musicals (many of which were internationally coproduced), and the further emergence of genre films that employ satire, horror, and more to distance themselves from authoritarian ideas. A highlight of Garcia's work is the chapter titled "Ideology, Realism and Fantasy in Juan Padrón's Animated Franchises *Elpidio Valdés* and *Vampires in Havana* Before and After the Special Period" which connects and contrasts the art and narrative behind Cuban animation with such icons as Walt Disney.

Although the work is not illustrated, it concludes with chapter notes, a bibliography, a filmography, and an index and would be a useful source for libraries that support film studies or related programs.—**Laura Herrell**

680.   Linder, Shirley Ayn. **Doc Holliday in Film and Literature.** Jefferson, N.C., McFarland, 2014. 200p. illus. index. $40.00pa. ISBN 13: 978-0-7864-7335-9; 978-1-4766-0330-8 (e-book).

One of the more enigmatic figures of the old west, Doc Holliday has been immortalized many times over in books and film. This book seeks to corral many of the Doc's depictions and works to separate the man from the many myths that have sprung from both Hollywood and the world of fiction.

The opening chapter attempts to establish the truth of Holliday's life: a young tubercular from Civil War-ravaged Georgia, Holliday nonetheless goes on to graduate from the Pennsylvania College of Dental Surgery before pursuing a life of gambling, drinking, and gunslinging out west. Subsequent chapters then chronologically deconstruct the legend surrounding his appearance in Tombstone, Arizona, as disseminated through the contemporary media, and then later through books, film, and television. Some of the books and movies discussed include the 1927 book by Walter Noble Burns titled *Tombstone: An Iliad of the Southwest* (the first to mention Holliday in print aside from salacious newspaper accounts); the 1939 film *Frontier Marshall,* where the Doc figure hails from Illinois, is a doctor rather than a dentist, and has an initial fondness for milk; and the 1993 film *Tombstone,* which the author cites as offering "the most authentic cinematic Doc Holliday characterization ever." Many, many other films, television shows, magazine articles, etc. are discussed.

The book includes extensive notes, a filmography including films made for the cinema and for television, an excellent bibliography, photographs, and an index. Recommended.—**ARBA Staff Reviewer**

681.   McKenna, Michael. **The ABC Movie of the Week: Big Movies for the Small Screen.** Lanham, Md., Scarecrow, 2013. 365p. index. $88.00; $87.99 (e-book). ISBN 13: 978-0-8108-9156-2; 978-0-8108-9157-9 (e-book).

The popularity of television movies soared during the late 1960s to the mid-1970s. The American Broadcasting Company (ABC) capitalized on the trend by airing a Movie of the Week. At the time, devoting 90 minutes during prime time was considered a risky move. With the network in third place, it was struggling to catch up to the two leading networks of CBS and NBC. The Movie of the Week was so successful for the ABC network that they were able to program an additional night for a movie of the week. Many of these movies are remembered by viewers today including, *That Certain Summer, Don't Be Afraid of the Dark,* and *The Over The Hill Gang.*

In the book, the author devotes each chapter to every season that the Movie of the Week was broadcast. Movies that were successful and not so successful and what led to their success are discussed. The book also talks about key executives involved in getting the project off the ground like future Paramount Pictures chief Barry Diller. A very important and particularly useful feature of the book is the alphabetical filmography of all 240 movies including credit information and a plot summary. Promotional advertisements from several movies are included in the book. Another interesting facet to this book is the list of pilots, some that evolved into popular shows, and some that did not come to fruition. These included the very popular *The Six Million Dollar Man, Starsky and Hutch,* and *Kung Fu.*

This would be an appropriate title to add to large public and academic library collections. Readers will enjoy this interesting and easy read.—**Holly Skir**

682.   Meuel, David. **The Noir Western: Darkness on the Range, 1943-1962.** Jefferson, N.C., McFarland, 2015. 216p. illus. index. $40.00pa. ISBN 13: 978-0-7864-9452-1; 978-1-4766-1974-3 (e-book).

In *The Noir Western: Darkness on the Range, 1943-1962,* David Meuel examines 21 western films that incorporate such noir influences as flawed heroes and dark and fatalistic themes. Meuel organizes individual chapters around directors, some of them more well-known than others, starting with William Wellman, followed by Raoul Walsh, André de Toth, Robert Wise, Sam Fuller, Henry King, Anthony Mann, Allan Dwan, Delmer Daves, Budd Boetticher, and John Ford. The 21 movies analyzed are: *The Ox-Bow Incident, Yellow Sky, Track of the Cat, Pursued, Colorado Territory, Ramrod, Day of the Outlaw, Blood on the Moon, I Shot Jesse James, Forty Guns, The Gunfighter, The Bravados, Devil's Doorway, The Naked Spur, Man of the West, Silver Lode, 3:10 to Yuma, The Hanging Tree, The Tall T, Ride Lonesome,* and *The Man Who Shot Liberty Valence.* A generous number of black-and-white photographs enhance the text.

The book concludes with a list of 50 "noir-ish" westerns worth seeing, chapter notes, a bibliography, and an index. This title would more likely be found in the circulating collection, but also has value as a reference work. Recommended for general readers and for students, high school and above.—**ARBA Staff Reviewer**

683.   **The Movie Book: Big Ideas Simply Explained.** New York, DK Publishing, 2016. 352p. illus. index. (Big Ideas Simply Explained). $25.00. ISBN 13: 978-1-4654-3799-0.

Part of DK's "Big Ideas Simply Explained" series, *The Movie Book* provides a nice overview of "the movies that best capture cinema," as it's put in the introduction. The book discusses 100 films, organized chronologically in six sections: Visionaries (1902-1931), A Golden Age in Black and White (1931-1949), Fear and Wonder (1950-1959), Rebel Rebel (1960-1974), Angels and Monsters (1975-1991), Small World (1992-Present). Each section includes a brief timeline and introduction. Each film entry begins with an "In Context" fact box with credits, noting related movies that preceded and followed the film, then discusses such topics as the inspiration for and origins of the film, production, and the wider impact of the film. Each film is also accompanied by a brief "What else to watch" list, and many have sidebars with director or actor profiles. Throughout the book are numerous photos (in color and black and white) and movie posters; infographics and quotes are also distributed evenly. *The Movie Book* includes a nice selection of widely recognized classics (*Casablanca,* 1942) along with some less obvious choices (*To Be or Not to Be,* 1942) that will benefit those without extensive knowledge of film history. As with any volume that seeks to single out key films in the history of cinema, film buffs might disagree with some of the choices (and omissions), but they may enjoy comparing their "essentials" to the authors'. Recommended for high school and public libraries.—**ARBA Staff Reviewer**

684.   Parish, James Robert. **Pirates and Seafaring Swashbucklers on the Hollywood Screen: Plots, Critiques, Casts and Credits for 137 Theatrical and Made-for-Television Releases.** Reprint ed. Jefferson, N.C., McFarland, 2013. 228p. index. $25.00pa. ISBN 13: 978-0-7864-7742-5.

McFarland has a tradition of publishing specialized reference tools such as this one. Eighteen years after the hardcopy version was published, McFarland has issued a reprint in paperback format. The time period covered is 1914 to 1992, so unfortunately it does not include *The Pirates of the Caribbean* series and the renewed popular interest in pirates generated since the 2003 release of that Disney movie series colossus. For each entry the author provides a synopsis of the film's plot, along with an evaluation of the quality of the movie. The various details about the making of the movie add a little something extra to description. Since the price is right, and the book is of a comfortable size, this item is suitable for all circulating and reference collections of those public and academic libraries that do not have the hardcopy edition. One just wishes that it had been updated and expanded.—**Daniel K. Blewett**

685.   Roots, James. **The 100 Greatest Silent Film Comedians.** Lanham, Md., Rowman & Littlefield, 2014. 432p. illus. index. $95.00; $94.99 (e-book). ISBN 13: 978-1-61069-832-0; 978-1-4422-3650-9 (e-book).

Ranking of the arts is always fraught with landmines. Here, author James Roots, a deaf man and disabilities advocate, takes on the challenge of ranking silent movie comedians in a bold manner.

Each entry includes the name of the comedian or comedy team, birth and death dates, a good sized black-and-white picture, and a rating which includes subscores for Funny, Creativity, Teamwork, Timelessness, Appeal, and Intangibles added up to a total score of 100 possible points. Charlie Chaplin and Buster Keaton tie at 99 points for first place.

Cliff Bowes is at number 100 with 21 points. Then each article has a partial list of films for that act, an opinionated essay ranging from a couple of paragraphs to a several pages, and finally a list of films available on DVD at the time of printing. Many of these films are shorts and are included in compilation DVDs rather than as individual titles.

There is an appendix of also-rans, an annotated bibliography for both general books on the topic and for individual comedians, and an index. Websites are not included as they tend to change. An appendix of the available DVDs in one place and possibly ranked would have been nice and perhaps helpful in purchasing decisions.

Roots' deep knowledge of, and appreciation of, these films allows him to address many controversial topics and counter several generally received opinions about these artists, their contributions, and behind-the-scenes controversies. He is well read in the field and is not afraid of taking on well-known critics and their opinions and uses an entertaining writing style to make his points.

With the strongly subjective essays, this might be a better choice for a general circulating collection than reference. Recommended for all libraries with film studies collections or interest in the history of film.—**Robert M. Lindsey**

686.   Terrace, Vincent. **Internet Comedy Television Series, 1997-2015.** Jefferson, N.C., McFarland, 2016. 380p. illus. index. $45.00pa. ISBN 13: 978-0-7864-9760-7; 978-1-4766-2393-1 (e-book).

This anthology addresses one of the more quirky examples of global media culture: the Internet comedy television series. Made with little cash, sometimes questionable production values, and likely no star power, some of these series have nonetheless become cult favorites or have even made the leap to network or cable television (e.g., *Drunk History* or *Annoying Orange*). One of a series on Internet television, this book catalogs over 1,000 comedy series for those looking for the latest in entertainment options or perhaps studying the medium in general.

Numbered and alphabetical entries provide the Website in which the series appears, production date, a brief plot synopsis, cast and crew, general critique, and episode list. Some entries come with black-and-white photos.

Perusing the entries, readers can discern the wide variety of Internet comedy offerings, from tales of inanimate objects come to life to talk show hosts from outer space and everything in between, although some of the more popular series themes include the comparatively mundane superheroes, careers, and love.

The book includes an index relating to entry number. Recommended.—**ARBA Staff Reviewer**

687.   Terrace, Vincent. **Internet Lesbian and Gay Television Series, 1996-2014.** Jefferson, N.C., McFarland, 2015. 226p. illus. index. $45.00pa. ISBN 13: 978-0-7864-9805-5; 978-1-4766-2126-5 (e-book).

The current work is the third in an ongoing series that "examines television programs produced exclusively for the Internet," in the words of prolific author Terrace, although "television programs" on the Internet seems incongruous. Regardless, this volume alphabetically arranges 335 LGBT-themed series from 1996 to 2014, with each half-page entry containing a brief but detailed storyline, episode descriptions, cast and credits, years of production, and commentary. Terrace also notes the series genre–reality, comedy, drama, etc.–but a breakdown at the conclusion of the book would have been helpful for anyone seeking just one genre. Most of the series are or were created in the United States, but Terrace also includes some he could identify in other languages. Although the author also strives to provide as much locating information as possible, the reader is sometimes simply left with "Youtube.com" as the URL, which doesn't help in pinpointing the series in that massive video collection. Considering also the "here today, gone tomorrow" nature of the Internet, readers should not be surprised that they cannot retrieve some of the series. However, despite those issues, the current book does a great service for anyone researching not only LBGT and/or popular culture history but also those interested in tracing the development of the phenomenon of Web-based series. Considering the work's narrow scope, however, it is recommended primarily for comprehensive popular culture and LBGT collections.—**Anthony J. Adam**

Theater

Dictionaries and Encyclopedias

688.　Fisher, James. **Historical Dictionary of American Theater: Beginnings.** Lanham, Md., Rowman & Littlefield, 2015. 525p. (Historical Dictionaries of Literature and the Arts). $135.00; $129.99 (e-book). ISBN 13: 978-0-8108-7832-7; 978-0-8108-7833-4 (e-book).

Historical Dictionary of American Theater: Beginnings is the first in a series of historical dictionaries of the theater in America. The series has been divided into three periods: Beginnings, defined as the first known historical mention of the performance of a play in 1538 to 1880, Modernism (1880-1930), and Contemporary (1930-present). *Beginnings* is the last published but the first chronologically and is a highly unique resource, which provides the basic historical context for early American theater and references many known but lost works. This volume is structured in four sections: a concisely written chronology (xv-xliv), an introduction (pp. 1-20), dictionary entries listed alphabetically (pp. 21-485), and an extensive bibliography (pp. 487-523). The chronology provides a timeline of important developments in theater and helps the reader trace influences and effects. The introduction surveys this period in sections with the following headings: Beginnings to the American Revolution, Revolutionary Theater, The Drama of a New Nation, Finding a Voice, The Nation Divided, Broadway, and The Theater as a Profession. The introduction establishes for the reader how the progress of theater in America either halted or slowed during the Revolutionary and Civil Wars, providing examples of issues surrounding these conflicts being reflected through artistic expression. The researcher will also find a succinct explanation for how Broadway became the center of theater in the United States after the conclusion of the Civil War. The dictionary entries cover a range of topics, from individual practitioners and plays to major events and dramatic genres and issues. Entries are thoroughly cross-referenced, often to entries in one or both of the other volumes of the dictionary. The bibliography itself is an excellent resource as it has been carefully provided with its own introduction and table of contents. Researchers are provided with lists of bibliographies and general reference works, as well as historical and critical studies about a range of topics such as melodrama, minstrels, and Native

Americans. This is followed by lists of biographies and memoirs of theater artists, plays and anthologies of plays, and theater practice, management, technology, and terminology. As most entries are cross-referenced with entries in the other two volumes, researchers will get the best use if they are additionally available. This historical dictionary would be an excellent resource for an academic collection supporting research in either American history or theater studies.—**Todd Simpson**

689.   Leiter, Samuel L. **Historical Dictionary of Japanese Traditional Theatre.** 2d ed. Lanham, Md., Rowman & Littlefield, 2014. 766p. illus. (Historical Dictionaries of Literature and the Arts). $165.00; $164.99 (e-book). ISBN 13: 978-1-4422-3910-4; 978-1-4422-3911-1 (e-book).

The Historical Dictionary of Traditional Japanese Theatre is a densely rich resource with an acute focus on the four classical genres of no, kyogen, bunraku, and kabuki. The chronology of this new updated edition covers events, people, and plays central to these traditions from 1301 to 2013, spanning ancient origins to modern relevance, such as the effect of the 2011 earthquake and tsunami. The introduction is particularly helpful with its four concise histories of each genre.

The alphabetically arranged dictionary entries, ranging from a sentence to a couple of pages, often contain a considerable amount of cross-references. There are *see* references for other entries on the same topic, and *see also* references for related terms. Terms that appear in boldface type have entries of their own. There are English-language entries for topics such as "Literary Sources" and subjects like "Puppeteers," and there are photographs and illustrations throughout. Entries on plays often include histories as well as plot summaries. Appendix A is a list of play titles and their translations; plays with full entries are marked with an asterisk. Appendix B is a simplified table of Japanese historical periods. The appendixes are followed by a 22-page glossary of terms and an extensive bibliography that begins with its own table of contents and introduction.

The subject is hard to penetrate and all the more intimidating for a novice to the Japanese language; however, Mr. Leiter does an admirable job of carefully demystifying the evolution of terms and word origins. He has a deft sense for charting the ebb and flow of fashions over time and updated this edition so that it includes modern innovations such as the introduction of female performers and the melding of genres. This dictionary is appropriate for both undergraduate and graduate researchers and would be a solid addition to any reference collection that covers the humanities in general and theatre specifically.—**Todd Simpson**

Handbooks and Yearbooks

690.   **Brazilian Theater, 1970-2010: Essays on History, Politics and Artistic Experimentation.** Eva Paulino Bueno and Robson Correa de Camargo, eds. Jefferson, N.C., McFarland, 2015. 265p. index. $55.00pa. ISBN 13: 978-0-7864-9703-4; 978-1-4766-2024-4 (e-book).

Brazil is a country well known for its vibrant and passionate cultural personality. This certainly extends to the world of Brazilian theater. And yet there was a time when the country's theatrical voice teetered on the edge of silence. This book takes a look at 40 years of Brazilian theater and follows its path through the dark years of political oppression to its ultimate arrival at a place of ample creativity and new meaning.

The introduction provides a good overview of the longer history of Brazilian theater and begins with the story of an early playwright executed in Portugal for questioning religious authority. Mapping the country's theater identity from that point to modern times shows a trajectory fraught with economic struggle, political pressure, and other obstacles.

Two sections then house 13 scholarly essays which refer to such obstacles, as well as the resultant art. The first section, "Establish Historical Markers" shares seven essays which focus on historical issues, such as the conflict between larger established theaters which operated with a more commercial mindset and the smaller theater groups which emphasized the art. Tin Urbinatti's essay "Factory Workers on Stage: The Creation of Grupo de Teatro Forja in São Paulo's Industrial Region" discusses the challenges and successes of Grupo Forja, a theater group comprised of steel mill workers whose creativity helped raised awareness of labor issues.

Section two, "Practices and Experiments," contains essays which focus on the results of hard-won artistic freedom. Eduardo Jose Reinato writes about Grupo Máskara and their distinctly Brazilian reinterpretation of Samuel Beckett in his essay "Beckett with Curupira Feet: Group Máskara, Readings and Receptions to Beckett in the Interior of Brazil." Other topics explored in this section include the curious emphasis on accents, the dramatic impact of the "incomplete" character, and much more.

Each essay provides notes and a list of cited works. The book also includes a section about the contributors and an index.—**ARBA Staff Reviewer**

691.   Frome, Shelly. **Playwriting: A Complete Guide to Creating Theater.** Jefferson, N.C., McFarland, 2014. 179p. index. $25.00pa. ISBN 13: 978-0-7864-7747-0.

This is a word-for-word reprint of the well-received title originally published in 1990 by McFarland. Such important present-day writers as Tony Kushner, Craig Lucas, and Beth Henley, therefore, are not mentioned in the text. This is, however, only a minor limitation to an otherwise quality work. The author, a former actor and academic, has also written widely with works that include several mysteries and a companion work. *The Art and Craft of Screenwriting Fundamentals.* (McFarland, 2009). The purpose of the playwriting volume is to supply the reader with an understanding of the steps in the writing and development of a dramatic play (e.g., specific theatrical genres like musicals or solo performances are not included) from sources of inspiration like a poignant memory or a story of a social injustice, to the eventual marketing and possible rewrites of the finished product. The chapters in between outline in step-by-step logical sequence the creation of a play and cover such topics as the importance and use of setting, the creation of both central and secondary characters, plot development, scene construction, dialogue writing, types of evaluation, and the importance of possible rewrites. Throughout the text, there are numerous examples from important plays including Shakespeare's *Hamlet,* Ibsen's *A Doll's House,* and Chekhov's *The Sea Gull,* but most are from mid-to-late twentieth-century American playwrights like O'Neill, Williams, and Arthur Miller. The author's comments and writing style range from the practical to the pretentious, but mostly the former. Particularly valuable are the quotes from interviews that the author has had with many theatrical people including an agent, a director, and several such playwrights as Alfred Uhry (*Driving Miss Daisy* and A.R. Gurney (*The Dining Room*). There are four appendixes: Professional Playscript Format, A Selected Bibliography, A Directory of

Market Information, Agents and Support, and notes on sources. These are followed by a brief index. There are many useful guides to playwriting in print, including even a *Playwriting for Dummies* (2011). This reprint deserves to be included with the best of these guides.—**John T. Gillespie**

692.　Lachman, Marvin. **The Villainous Stage: Crime Plays on Broadway and in the West End.** Jefferson, N.C., McFarland, 2014. 254p. index. $45.00pa. ISBN 13: 978-0-7864-9534-4; 978-1-4766-1875-3 (e-book).

Unlike Amnon Kabatchnik's chronological approach in his Blood on the Stage series (2008-2014), Lachman treats the generally neglected history of crime plays thematically. Considering both popular and obscure works, Lachman looks at such topics as historical mysteries, series detectives, crooks, psychological mysteries, courtroom dramas, whodunits, romantic triangles, spies, criminal justice, race, ethnicity, religion, spoofs, musicals, and adaptations of fiction. Chapters are also devoted to plays featuring Sherlock Holmes and plays by and adapted from Agatha Christie. A typical examination of a play is the 2005 stage version of *The 39 Steps,* drawn from both John Buchan's 1913 spy novel and the 1935 Alfred Hitchcock film. Lachman briefly discusses the play's plot, origins, casting, staging, title changes, and number of performances. Lachman also frequently provides critical commentary, as when he explains why *Murderer,* Anthony Shaffer's flop following the huge success of his *Sleuth,* failed. Despite the book's subtitle, Lachman looks at several plays never performed on Broadway or in the West End. Although his comments about each play are brief, Lachman demonstrates that the crime play has had a more extensive history than might have been expected. There are notes for Lachman's sources, a short bibliography, and a name-and-title index.—**Michael Adams**

693.　Leland, John, and Alan Baragona. **Shakespeare's Prop Room: An Inventory.** Jefferson, N.C., McFarland, 2016. 217p. illus. index. $35.00pa. ISBN 13: 978-1-4766-6336-4; 978-1-4766-2343-6 (e-book).

To those not familiar with the theater, a prop is a small object such as a weapon or a book used by an actor or used as part of a scene. In Shakespeare's plays, props play a significant role in advancing the plot, the action, and actual stage direction. *Shakespeare's Prop Room: An Inventory* is a very informative book that discusses the significance of props used in Shakespeare's plays, dialogue related to the props, and description of what it might have been like to see these plays at theaters in England. The book opens with a foreword by Ralph Alan Cohen, cofounder and director of mission at the American Shakespeare Center. Included in the book are some very high-quality illustrations; chief among them is one of Shakespeare's busts located in Stratford-upon-Avon. In addition to the importance of props, the authors also discuss some of the costumes worn by the characters and the reasoning behind why they were dressed in such a way. The book is broken up into 13 chapters and each chapter has a theme based on a line of dialogue. For example, chapter six "Come on, then, let's to bed" discusses the plays that Shakespeare wrote that include bedroom scenes. The book includes notes, a bibliography, and an index. The index is especially helpful for finding a specific prop related to a scene. Based on the content, this book would be an appropriate title for most academic libraries as well as some special libraries. Shakespearean scholars and actors will find it most useful in learning more about Shakespeare.—**Holly Skir**

694.   **Musicals: The Definitive Illustrated Story.** New York, DK Publishing, 2015. 360p. illus. index. $40.00. ISBN 13: 978-1-4654-3886-7.

"Definitive" is arguably the wrong term to describe this glossy coffee-table volume on the Anglo-American musical (with occasional forays into Continental European works). Spanning the past one hundred or so years of stage and film musical history, *Musicals* seems more of a book in search of an audience. The editors indeed cover a lot of ground, offering a chronological but generally shallow history of the genre with a focus on roughly 100 (according to the book jacket) "of the most successful and pivotal musicals of all time." That being said, one would think Sondheim's *Company,* one of the seminal musicals of the century, would take pride of place. But no, the editors give more space to *Legally Blonde* and *Shrek the Musical,* neither of which have moved the genre forward an inch (except at the box office). With the U.K. emphasis throughout, one would also expect to see more about West End musicals, although Lloyd Webber and Elton John both are featured prominently. Twenty musicals receive special treatment through "Storylines" which pinpoint where in the plot different songs appear, although what real purpose these "Storylines" serve overall is questionable. Most disturbing, or at least annoying, is the reliance throughout on images from execrable film versions of musicals, ranging from *Kismet, Hello, Dolly!,* and *Mame* to *Nine* and *A Little Night Music*—any novice to the genre who viewed these films might be turned off from musicals forever! Couldn't the editors find better production stills from the stage shows? Additionally, although the editors highlight a number of composers, the information provided in the texts is much less than comprehensive. In sum, *Musicals* is glossy and pretty, but far from "definitive." Recommended for general readers.—**Anthony J. Adam**

695.   **Theatre in Video.** http://www.alexanderstreet.com/products/theatre-video-series. [Website] Alexandria, Va., Alexander Street Press. Price negotiated by site. Date reviewed: 2016.

Theatre in Video is a collection of hundreds of hours of theater performances and documentaries of the world's most famous and important plays. Full-length performances of plays from Sophocles to Shakespeare and contemporary writers like Troy Mink and Jeff Nevers are included. The collection represents not only theater, but it is also a unique record of twentieth-century theater performance in the form of live broadcasts, classic works, experimental performances, and cinematic productions. Recently added volume two of the collection includes an additional 400 hours of video expanding the collection's focus to include more contemporary and international works and performances.

The video collection also includes interviews with actors and directors, and behind-the-scenes looks at dozens of performances. The documentaries bring another dimension to the study of theater telling the story behind the stage. There are also videos focusing on nearly every aspect of bringing a play to the stage from auditioning to costume and lighting design.

The collection provides both simple and advanced text searching as well as many ways to browse the collection by title, people, production company, discipline, publisher, genre, and content type. All of these categories can be combined to refine and create a very specific search.

Each video is fully transcribed, and the transcript is synced with the video time code. This allows users to click on any word or phrase in the transcript and jump to the corresponding place in the video. Each video has a visual table of contents to help users easily navigate the videos by memorable scene. Users are allowed to add their own bookmarks to the videos, and they can cite and share the videos, save favorites to a playlist, and generate a permalink embed code—an option very useful for teaching. Users are also able to make and save their own video clips allowing many different and useful applications for both teachers and students such as building an engaging lesson, presentation, or report.

The scope, depth, and usefulness of the collection is very impressive. This is a highly recommended resource for theatre and performing art programs. Students at any level will find their study and enjoyment of theatre much increased by using this collection.—**Kristin Kay Leeman**

28 Philosophy and Religion

Philosophy

Dictionaries and Encyclopedias

696.   Ariew, Roger and others. **Historical Dictionary of Descartes and Cartesian Philosophy.** 2d ed. Lanham, Md., Rowman & Littlefield, 2015. 388p. illus. (Historical Dictionaries of Religions, Philosophies, and Movements Series). $115.00; $109.99 (e-book). ISBN 13: 978-1-4422-4768-0; 978-1-4422-4769-7 (e-book).

Descartes is known as "the father of modern philosophy" and is a central figure in the study of rationalist philosophy in the pantheon including Spinoza, Leibnitz, and Kant. His philosophical and metaphysical works are part of the focus of philosophy study today overshadowing his many other considerable influences and accomplishments in mathematics, physics, and science (known then as "natural philosophy"). These were the major sources of his influence in European intellectual and religious circles of the seventeenth century.

The second edition of the *Historical Dictionary of Descartes and Cartesian Philosophy* builds upon the first (see ARBA 2005, entry 1228) by adding new material and expanding the first edition from 302 pages to 388 pages, covering over 300 entries. New material is primarily historic, detailing biographical and intellectual information about those historical persons who corresponded with Descartes on subjects of scientific or philosophical interest, including friends, supportive Cartesians, religious personages, or critics of Cartesianism. The expanding influence of Descartes and the Cartesianist movement is given a context in the historical milieu of church, science, intellectual debate, and conflict that opens philosophy and science to the modern era. New entries, for example, such as Anti-Cartesianism, Authority, Cartesianism, Catholicism, and Union of Mind and Body, have been added.

Enhancements include: an expanded chronology of events relevant to Descartes's life and the Cartesian movement; an introduction with subheadings and additional material on Descartes's place in modern philosophy; expanded biographical entries; footnotes at the end of each alphabetical section; bolded topics that point to separate entries; *see* and *see also* cross-references. The bibliography has been expanded from 40 to 49 pages. Subsections in the Bibliography with expanded entries are: Texts of Descartes, Texts and Editions, and Works on Descartes, and a new entry: Other Internet Resources.

These improvements to the second edition significantly enhance this valuable resource for the historical study of this essential modern philosopher.—**William Shakalis**

697.   Pasanek, Brad. **Metaphors of Mind: An Eighteenth-Century Dictionary.** Baltimore, Md., Johns Hopkins University Press, 2015. 372p. maps. index. $49.95. ISBN 13: 978-1-4214-1688-5; 978-1-4214-1689-2 (e-book).

Ever since the groundbreaking work of Auerbach's *Mimesis,* literary theorists have tried to improve upon that hallowed ground. Auerbach took two basic texts, Homer's *Odysseys* and the Bible's *Genesis,* to look at two ways in which authors view the reality of the world and how they go about that imitation. The book carried the day for a very long while, and still influences those who take the time to read it.

Pasanek has been involved in a similar but slightly different approach: how Enlightenment writers use various figures of speech to characterize the mind as it perceives reality, that part of philosophy that deals with both ontology and epistemology. Pasanek has one advantage over Auerbach by virtue of living in the twenty-first century: he has applied the vast ability of technology to distill the works in question to their discrete parts. Thus, from the gigantic database of the *Mind Is a Metaphor* (http://metaphorized. net) comes this volume on metaphorics.

Pasanek with his digital archive is able to bring to each chapter more than a smattering of quotations. He provides context and character of the works allowing readers insight not only on Enlightenment thinkers but also on today's digital natives. The book challenges assumptions about what Enlightenment thinkers meant by certain metaphors, as well as raises questions—if not hackles—about digital readers and their soi-distant "shallow" and/ or "surface" reading.

It takes some getting used to Pasanek's style: "This valedictory critical exercise further demonstrates how distant reading supports close interpretation by indicating the range of metaphors by which figure and ground may be defined." Or, "Because this dictionary arrays four-square superimpositions of mind and matter, metaphor and meaning, eighteenth-century thought and its social context, each becomes an excuse to say something about the other." While many of us will luxuriate in the style and panache, other readers may find it hard slogging. The conclusion is, however, worth the preamble.

The book has 11 chapters of metaphors broken down in broad terms such as animals, coinage, empire, fetters, metal, mirrors, room, writing, and so on. Within each chapter are various metaphors used by writers. For example, under animals we find man or beast, duck or rabbit, birds and flights of fancy, and so on. The conclusion, "The Mind Is a Metaphor" sums up Pasanek's findings and is worth the price of the book. While the book is not meant to be read as a monograph but as a dictionary, many well-versed readers will be tempted to do so anyway, so rich and lush are both language and litany.—**Mark Y. Herring**

Handbooks and Yearbooks

698.   Burns, William E. **The Enlightenment: History, Documents, and Key Questions.** Santa Barbara, Calif., ABC-CLIO, 2016. 197p. index. (Crossroads in World History). $63.00. ISBN 13: 978-1-61069-845-0; 978-1-61069-846-7 (e-book).

Spanning the bulk of the eighteenth century, the Enlightenment was a time when reason and science began to assert a strong influence upon the status quo in particular with regards to Western religion and government. It followed a long period of absolutism in those regards and paved the way for the tumult of revolutions to come. This insightful book concisely and creatively assembles the most essential ideas, people, and events behind the Enlightenment era and produces a go-to reference ideal for students.

Breaking the information down into easily digestible sections, the book begins with a brief historical overview. It then segues into an A-Z encyclopedia section filled with both general ("Economics") and specific ("Voltaire") entries, a selection of primary source document excerpts such as from the 1776 American Declaration of Independence, and a section posing three "Key Questions" accompanied by "pro/con" responses which serve to encourage readers' own critical thinking.

Supplementary information includes both an alphabetical and topical list of entries, a timeline of major events running from the 1662 founding of London's Royal Society up through the 1798 passing of the decidedly unenlightened Alien and Sedition Acts in the United States, and a well-organized bibliography.—**Laura Herrell**

699.   **Electronic Enlightenment. http://www.e-enlightenment.com/.** [Website] New York, Oxford University Press. Price negotiated by site. Date reviewed: 2015.

Electronic Enlightenment (EE), a project of the Bodleian Libraries, University of Oxford, contains nearly 68,000 letters and documents in 11 languages from over 8,300 correspondents representing 52 nationalities across Europe, Asia, and the Americas. The project succeeds admirably in its aim to create a dynamic online network of Enlightenment correspondents and correspondence and is a boon to researchers.

Users can easily find letters with a simple word search or by utilizing a variety of fields (language, writer, recipient, location, etc.). A separate browse option allows users to search letters by decade or correspondents by surname, occupation, or nationality. Searchers can also access letters by locations or edition. "Locations" currently links over 32,000 letters to the corresponding source location. Letters themselves are titled and include a set of linked tabs underneath the letter heading—document (the default tab), enclosures, related, versions, and parent—that are enabled when applicable. On the left-hand side of every document page is a series of metadata that include editorial information, biographical information about the writer and recipient, and, when available, letter dates, location where the letter was written, location where the letter was sent, and information about the envelope. There is also information on instances (manuscript, digital, print) and annotations (authorial notes, textual notes, editorial notes, language notes, and remarks) of which there are over 300,000 in EE. A citation for the letters is available in the most common humanities styles—Chicago, MHRA, and MLA. Moreover, EE now participates in CrossRef so there is a Digital Object Identifier for all the EE letters, documents, and people.

The EE Coffee-House and EE Print-House add further value to this online resource. In the Coffee-House, users can find the EE classroom, which contains lesson plans and talking points; the EE Map Room, with such resources as EE's own atlas; and the Reading Room, with complimentary links to encyclopedias, dictionaries, biographies, and journals. In the Coffee-House, users can also find information about projects, such as EE's collaboration with leading graduate translation programs in North America and Europe. The Print-House has links to significant anniversaries, miscellany, the Fact-Sheet, and the Letterbook, which, among other things, will serve as a place for scholars to present their research findings in an informal setting.

Librarians receive free MARC21 records, quarterly updates, usage statistics, and technical support. Subscription and purchase prices depend on the size and type of institution. Personal and free trial subscriptions are also available. This online product offers upper-level undergraduates, graduate students, and scholars access to an unparalleled wealth of information. Highly recommended for academic libraries, large public libraries, and to individuals doing intensive research in the period.—**ARBA Staff Reviewer**

700. **The Routledge Companion to Phenomenology.** Sebastian Luft and Soren Overgaard, eds. New York, Routledge/Taylor & Francis Group, 2014. 716p. index. (Routledge Philosophy Companions). $68.95pa. ISBN 13: 978-0-415-85841-0; 978-0-203-81693-6 (e-book).

As one of the core ideas in modern philosophy, phenomenology and its discourse demands to be encapsulated for the contemporary student. *The Routledge Companion to Phenomenology* brings together over 50 chapters from leading contributors around the globe that expound upon this dynamic topic.

At its root, phenomenology addresses the role perception plays in comprehending and participating in the world around us. This sturdy companion highlights the many facets of phenomenology and examines such ideas as the self, the body, intentionality, subjectivity, being, and methods. Contributions are sorted into five sections that outline the most prominent thinkers in the movement, (Husserl, Derrida, and Merleau-Ponty, among others), focus on the most vital areas of discussion within the phenomenological movement, illustrate the ways in which phenomenology has worked within the greater philosophical realm, highlight areas where phenomenology intersects with other disciplines, and observe its study through a historical lens. In part three, for example, James Dodd writes how phenomenology can be the bridge to understanding the roots of political exchange, while in part four, Helen A. Fielding explains the mutual reliance phenomenology shares with feminism.

This generously referenced book emphasizes the importance of phenomenology to contemporary thought when applied over a vast array of ideas, from art and literary appreciation to logic and morals. It is simply a must-have for any student of contemporary philosophy.—**Laura Herrell**

Religion

General Works

Dictionaries and Encyclopedias

701. **Miracles: An Encyclopedia of People, Places, and Supernatural Events from Antiquity to the Present.** Patrick J. Hayes, ed. Santa Barbara, Calif., ABC-CLIO, 2016. 478p. index. $89.00. ISBN 13: 978-1-61069-598-5; 978-1-61069-599-2 (e-book).

Depending upon an individual user's personal beliefs, a book focusing on the existence of miracles should or should not be included in their library's collection.

However, when a reader approaches any book, that reader runs the risk—or, encounters the opportunity—of reshaping his or her beliefs, expanding his or her world view. One can surmise that this was the intent of the 82 authors (including the editor) who contributed to *Miracles: An Encyclopedia of People, Places, and Supernatural Events from Antiquity to the Present.* Their entries traverse historical eras and geographic regions, gathering and presenting information on such topics as the role of dirt in miracles, hagiography, the representation of miracles in movies, and people such as Baruch Spinoza. Published in 2016 by ABC-CLIO and under the editorial stewardship of Patrick Hayes, archivist for the Redemptorists (founded in Italy in 1732) of the Baltimore Province, based in Philadelphia, Pennsylvania, this encyclopedia, based upon a cursory search in WorldCat, appears to be the first encyclopedia to focus specifically upon miracles and, more important, examine them philosophically, historically, and culturally. Hayes edits and contributes to the online publication *Redemptorist North American Historical Bulletin.* He wrote *A Catholic Brain Trust: The Catholic Commission in Intellectual and Cultural Affairs, 1945 - 1965,* published in 2011 by University of Notre Dame Press. Most recently, Hayes coedited *Realist's Church: Essays in Honor of Joseph Komonchak* which was published by Orbis Books in 2015. With this book, the passion Hayes and his authors feel for this topic is clearly evident in the scope of the research, the adherence to details. Each entry in this encyclopedia provides the reader with sources for further reading and Hayes ends this single-volume encyclopedia with an extensive bibliography. Hayes also offers the reader a timeline and a detailed introduction about miracles. Along with an alphabetical listing of the entries, Hayes provides a guide to related topics such as [miracles] by era, [miracles] by geographic location, and, [miracles] by religious community. However, despite all these attributes, a glaring flaw does exist in this book: subjective tone. For example, under "Caribbean, Miracles in the," page 67, the following is written concerning Haiti: "Within that time the epidemic subsided and Perpetuel Secours [sic] secured a place in the popular Catholic imagination both as a powerful healer and positive proof that a Catholic icon trumped any voodoo cult." Further, under "England, Miracles in," page 118, last paragraph, first sentence, the author, writing about the Reformation, describes the treatment of those who chose to remain true to their religious convictions as "reprehensible." Yet, on page 107, under "Dominicans and Miracles," the same author writes, "Dominic's abilities to convert the inhabitants of southern France were aided considerably by the Albigensian Crusade, which forcibly and horrifically turned the people away from their heretical views, some of which included the denial of the Holy Trinity and the promotion of vice. Saint Dominic had the ability to ferret out and control the demonic tendencies of anything or anyone he encountered." Based on this reviewer's reading, the tone of these entries, and others, come across as evangelical and culturally biased. Do the aforementioned attributes outweigh these flaws? Should this book be added to your collection? As stated earlier, every reader runs a risk—or, encounters the opportunity—of reshaping his or her beliefs, expanding his or her world view when they pull a book from the shelf—whether that book is deemed flawed or perfect. As some people place faith in miracles, librarians must place faith in their readers' ability to question what they read and their desire to seek answers to those questions by pursuing further reading.—**Brian T. Gallagher**

702.   **Religion and American Cultures: Tradition, Diversity, and Popular Expression.** 2d ed. Gary Laderman and Luis Leon, eds. Santa Barbara, Calif., ABC-CLIO, 2015. 4v. illus. index. $399.00/set. ISBN 13: 978-1-61069-109-; 978-1-61069-110-9 (e-book).

This title was first published in 2003 (see ARBA 2004, entry 1187). In its second edition, this four-volume set casts a wide net in attempting to understand the "religious terrain" of American culture. Knowing a comprehensive survey would be a challenging task, the editors instead provide a selected scan of the conjoining concepts, covering the broad landscape as it currently exists (volume one), and then selecting specific touch points in volume two to drill down and explore (Autopsies, End Times, and Shopping Malls, etc.). These first two volumes have similar topics to the first edition (updated by the original authors), and the final volume is comprised of "primary documents" (broad definitionally—lyrics from a Klezmatics song are found), incorporating some new selections. The new third volume, however, provides a more thoughtful counterpoint to the second. Here we find longer, reflective historical essays on topical concerns, instead of shorter sociological snapshots. These serve to cogently frame the previous two volumes. The overall content is not intended to be exhaustive (the Episcopal Church is mentioned as an aside, and in the context of a specific American offshoot from the branch), but the points of view are challenging and vital, speaking to the present dynamic dialogue unfolding on our soil.—**Stephen J. Shaw**

703.   **Religion in Southeast Asia: An Encyclopedia of Faiths and Cultures.** Jesudas M. Athyal, ed. Santa Barbara, Calif., ABC-CLIO, 2015. 396p. illus. index. $89.00. ISBN 13: 978-1-61069-249-6; 978-1-61069-250-2 (e-book).

From less than 1% of the total U.S. population in 1965, Asian Americans increased to 5.8% (or 18.2 million) in 2011, according to the U.S. Census. Buddhists and Hindus together account for about the same share of the U.S. public as do Jews (roughly 2%). Buddhism alone is growing among Americans born in the United States. The number of adherents rose by 170% between 1990 and 2000, according to the American Religious Identity Survey. These statistics help to explain why ABC-CLIO has come out with *Religion in Southeast Asia: An Encyclopedia of Faiths and Cultures.*

This is admittedly an ambitious undertaking for only one volume. Like many "encyclopedias" that are really handbooks on enormous topics, *Religion in Southeast Asia* is a quirky assortment of entries (125) arranged alphabetically, signed by one of over 40 contributors, and concluded with several bibliographical references to further reading.

In the preface, the editor, Jesudas M. Athyal, notes that *Religion in Southeast Asia* is aimed at high school students in the United States. But the unique collection of topics (Christian Conference of Asia, Localization of Hinduism in Indonesia, Reynaldo C. Ileto) and the advanced reading level in selected entries: "Southeast Asia has ... competing religious belief-systems and syncretism...," makes this volume more appropriate for college students. And the large number of contributors (most with doctorates) yields a range of writing styles and reading levels. A careful reading of the Introduction also shows that the themes of the work go beyond the average high school student's comprehension.

The topic selection appears to be somewhat arbitrary. Students interested in feminism, for example, will have to be satisfied with "Feminism and Islamic Traditions." The entry on "Humanism" includes the subtopics of "Humanism and Contextualization" and "Capacity to Address Humanist Concerns." Although the editor claims that the volume "provides a comprehensive introduction to the complex world of the faiths and practices of the Southeast Asians," this is hardly possible in only 362 pages.

Given the increased population of Asian Americans and the popularity of Asian religions in the United States, students of world religions will be pleased to have a handbook exclusively on this topic. But most high school librarians will want to examine the handbook more closely before adding it to their collection for the reasons mentioned above.—**John P. Stierman**

Handbooks and Yearbooks

704.   **Migration and Religion.** James A. Beckford, ed. Northampton, Mass., Edward Elgar, 2016. 2v. (International Library of Studies on Migration). $790.00/set. ISBN 13: 978-1-78347-257-4.

Publication #18 of the series The International Library of Studies on Migration, this two-volume set is a collection of global articles and studies identifying relationships between migration and religion. The volumes are divided into 14 sections with each part representing one migration topic. The organization of these scholarly articles shows some overlap as to where articles could be, but, overall, the organization is succinct.

Each study starts with an abstract where appropriate and contains tables, charts, and figures in support of the research. Interestingly, all articles are reprinted in their original format, so font size varies throughout. The level of study and documentation varies from article to article. Bibliographic references conclude each segment. Articles provide well-documented and footnoted research.

Currently and historically, migrations coincide with religious beliefs and persecution. Examining migration with a religious focus, articles discuss class, society, and culture at different points in time, in different global locations, and in different theological frameworks, factoring in the variables of ethnicity, gender inequality, age, generation, and socioeconomic status. Juxtaposition of articles such as "Beyond Migration: Islam as a Transnational Public Space" with "Migration as Preservation and Loss: The Paradox of Transnational Living for Low German Mennonite Women" provides a paradigm of the long-reaching expanse of studies included in these volumes.

Volumes one and two explore religion as a catalyst for migration and, additionally, examine the redistribution of world religions globally. This shifting of religions has major implications for cultures and creates a global effect for all peoples. Some of the research here delves into those implications; some is more implicit.

This assemblage of research studies is most suitable for advanced degree students. These volumes are best for students, professors, and researchers involved with history, religion, world issues, or social sciences and would work well for interdisciplinary studies. For academic libraries in need of more depth in their migration or religion reference offerings, or for those interested in garnering this complete series, this collection of papers is a valuable resource. Recommended.—**Janis Minshull**

705.   **Religion: Sources, Perspectives, and Methodologies.** Jeffrey J. Kripal, ed. New York, Macmillan Reference USA/Gale Group, 2016. 418p. illus. index. (Macmillan Interdisciplinary Handbooks). $179.00. ISBN 13: 978-0-02-866287-9; 978-0-02-866288-6 (e-book).

This primer is the first in a 10-volume series entitled The Macmillan Interdisciplinary Handbooks on Religion, with the other nine forthcoming. As Kripal (Rice University) points out, the series is an ambitious attempt to offer an interdisciplinary narrative spun around a variety of perspectives to the study of religions, ranging from sociology, psychology, philosophy, ethics, history, literary and cultural studies, and anthropology. In fact, Kripal avoids a clear definition of the final product, which is part reference guide, part original research, part textbook. He characterizes it as a "multidimensional object," a "story" of multiple ideas and perspectives. It is up to the reader, he argues, to draw conclusions or choose the direction to move through in this labyrinthine construction. Granted the "openness" of the methodological démarche and the exegetic involvement of the reader, it is this openness that actually constitutes the main weakness of the book. The chapters do not read in the same fashion, some being expository, scholarly, and neutral, in the fashion of encyclopedia entries, while others venture onto new, creative territory that often crosses into personal and even questionable interpretation. The book's more traditional chapters, dealing with the sociological, historical, comparative, or philological study of religions offer a valuable, although unimpressive overview of the existing scholarship and methods. The more original chapters, however, use postmodern concepts and ideas uncritically and without the necessary interpretative context, offering little scholarly insight to a readership of beginners.—**Rares G. Piloiu**

706.   **The Routledge Handbook of Research Methods in the Study of Religion.** Michael Stausberg and Steven Engler, eds. New York, Routledge/Taylor & Francis Group, 2014. 546p. index. $59.95pa. ISBN 13: 978-0-415-71844-8.

Since the literature on religion is so vast, it is difficult to fathom that there had been no comprehensive handbook to research methods for the study of religion in English until the publication of this title in hardback in 2011. Now, this handbook is available in paperback at a price that is accessible to most students. The goal of the work is to increase the importance of theoretical models as applied to the study of religion. As the editors say, "In the light of theories, methods construct, collect and/or generate the data for scholarly work" (p. 4). Thus, the contributors strive to provide information that has both practical and critical value to students, especially graduate students, and researchers. The first section provides general information related to methodology such as, epistemology, research design, and research ethics. The second section is the heart of the work and provides 22 chapters that detail specific research methods from content analysis and hermeneutics to semiotics and surveys. The final section includes five chapters that discuss materials such as auditory materials and visual culture. Although the structure of the chapters varies, of necessity, by the topics covered, each chapter provides a brief summary, helpful comments, references, and key concepts. Thus, although the work stands as a whole, each chapter can be used independently for background on specific methods. The index provides good access to the contents of the book. For academic and seminary libraries, this is a must purchase that will receive much use. Finally, there is an excellent sourcebook on methods for undertaking research in religion!—**Gregory A. Crawford**

707.   **Spirit Possession around the World: Possession, Communion, and Demon Expulsion across Cultures.** Joseph P. Laycock, ed. Santa Barbara, Calif., ABC-CLIO, 2015. 414p. illus. index. $89.00. ISBN 13: 978-1-61069-589-3; 978-1-61069-590-9 (e-book).

In 2014, the Catholic Church increased the number of priests trained in the rite of exorcism due to a spike in public demand. As Joseph Laycock points out in his introduction, spirit possession is not an antiquated human response to the forces of nature; rather it is a diagnostic model for filtering culture. In this introductory primer, Laycock has brought together leading scholars to provide an overview of spirit possession across geographical, religious, and historical boundaries. More importantly, *Spirit Possession around the World* intentionally underscores spirit possession in the twenty-first century to demonstrate its melding and adaptation into today's pervasive digital culture. Coupled with a chronology, a detailed and thorough introduction contextualizes spirit possession with a larger narrative of historical and cultural relevance. Entries are arranged alphabetically and span across countries, religious traditions, historical events, court cases, and persons of interest. Though varying in length and scope, each entry averages one to three pages and includes a small bibliography for further reading. Moreover, to facilitate searching, related entries are cross-referenced and indexed. Though representations of spirit possession in popular culture are mentioned in entries on television, film, and music, this facet of the subject is woven into larger entries where possible. Of particular interest are the original translations of several primary religious texts included throughout. In addition to the smaller bibliographies included with each entry is a larger bibliography of works, delineated by religious and cultural tradition. Overall, this is a well-researched and expertly edited addition to the interdisciplinary subject of spirit possession. Coupled with Matt Cardin's *Ghosts, Spirits, and Psychics: The Paranormal from Alchemy to Zombies,* this is both a timely and necessary addition to any library's reference collection.—**Josh Eugene Finnell**

Bible Studies

Handbooks and Yearbooks

708.   **The Book of Revelation and Its Interpreters: Short Studies and an Annotated Bibliography.** Ian Boxall and Richard Tresley, eds. Lanham, Md., Rowman & Littlefield, 2016. 282p. index. $80.00; $79.99 (e-book). ISBN 13: 978-0-8108-6153-4; 978-1-4422-5513-5 (e-book).

The New Testament Book of Revelation, often known as Revelation or The Apocalypse of John, combines apocalyptic (heavenly secrets) and prophetic (divine orations) genres which play a central role in Christian eschatology (theology of last events). Exegetically, the book is associated with various Roman and Jewish events of the apostolic period (first century). Passages relate to Roman imperial maltreatment of Jesus-believers. They also point to Christ-laden redemptive history whose visionary appeal draws heavily from Jewish sources (Isaiah 6, Ezekiel, Daniel, 1 and 2 Enoch), parallels elements in contemporary apocalypses Baruch and Ezra, and references Second Temple Judaism (Jerusalem with and without Temple, priesthood, twelve tribes of Israel, dietary laws, holy-war ideology, and so forth). Over time, a plethora of views (pretext, context, history, futurist, symbolic, idealist) has emanated in Church history and interpretation related to the meaningfulness of this focused on the Second Coming of Jesus Christ. However, this volume is primarily concerned with pre-1700 data. The very detailed annotated bibliography covering commentaries on Revelation until 1700, including most of the early illuminated Apocalypses, by Richard Tresley (147 pages) set the perimeter. Short chapters on the figure of John of Patmos (Ian Boxall), reception history (Christopher Rowland), visualizations of Revelations (Natasha O'Hear), and Church Fathers Tyconius on Rev 4-5 (Sean Michael Ryan) and Chromatius of Aquileia on John 21:22 and Rev 10:11

complement this valuable reference work.—**Zev Garber**

709.   Fishbane, Michael. **The JPS Bible Commentary: Song of Songs.** Lincoln, Nebr., University of Nebraska Press, 2015. 400p. $55.00. ISBN 13: 978-0-8276-0741-5.

This volume begins with an introduction that describes the literary genre of Song of Songs as well as the four types of meaning utilized in the commentary. After an interlinear Hebrew-English text of the book follows commentary verse by verse, each with explanation of the text according to the four types of meaning: Peshat or the plain sense of the text, Derash or midrashic exegesis, Remez or thematic content, and Sod or the mystical aspect. The volume concludes with a review of historical interpretation of the Song of Songs and a bibliography of sources consulted.—**Arthur Quinn**

710.   Sokolow, Moshe. **Tanakh: An Owner's Manual: Authorship, Canonization, Masoretic Text, Exegisis, Modern Scholarship, and Pedagogy.** Brooklyn, N.Y., KTAV Publishing House, 2015. 219p. index. $23.00. ISBN 13: 978-965-524-176-1.

As described in the subtitle, there are six sections that constitute this book beginning with authorship, or the identity of the writers and editors of Tanakh according to Jewish tradition. Canonization, or recognition of the books of Tanakh as inspired, is acknowledged as a process that lasted several centuries, reaching its culmination at the end of the Second Temple Period. The Masoretic or traditional text was compiled in medieval times to preserve the known pronunciation of the Hebrew text, adding spaces between words, and dividing the text into verses and chapters. Exegesis in modern times was influenced by medieval techniques including comparative study of Semitic languages, Ancient Near Eastern texts, and early translations. Modern scholarship in the Jewish tradition views the documentary hypothesis with skepticism although acknowledges Ancient Near Eastern influence on biblical literature. Finally, pedagogy of Tanakh ought to include an understanding of Hebrew as well as interpreting Scripture through the eyes of the original writers. While relatively brief considering the broad topic being examined, this book is a well-organized introduction to biblical scholarship in the Jewish tradition and is recommended for any collection that includes biblical studies.—**Arthur Quinn**

Buddhism

Handbooks and Yearbooks

711.   **Digital Library of Northern Thai Manuscripts. http://lannamanuscripts.net/en.** [Website] Free. Date reviewed: 2016.

Presents more than 4,200 manuscripts from four collections. The Preservation of Northern Thai Manuscripts Project contains digitized microfilms with a focus on indigenous and secular traditions, including what are possibly the oldest Pali manuscripts in Southeast Asia. The Digital Library of Northern Thai Manuscripts features color images of manuscripts identified but not filmed during the aforementioned project and includes texts from eight temples. The Dokumentarische Erfassung literarischer Materialien in den Nordprovinzen Thailands (DELMN) collection contains digitized microfilm that was part of the first comprehensive survey of Lan Na manuscripts in the eight northernmost provinces of Thailand. The Harald Hundius Handwritten Collection contains color images of temple manuscripts copied by temple scribes during the DELMN project in the 1970s. Among the highlights, the digital library includes the entire library collection at Wat Sung Men, which became a center of Pali and Buddhist studies in the early nineteenth century. The digital library can be searched by simplified title, category, language, script, material, author, date, location, and other criteria. The manuscripts are primarily bilingual (Pali and Northern Thai) and written in Tham or Dhamma script, but additional vernacular languages and scripts are also represented. This collection will primarily be of interest to scholars studying the religious and secular literature of Northern Thailand from the fifteenth to the twentieth centuries.—**ARBA Staff Reviewer**

Christianity

Dictionaries and Encyclopedias

712.   **The Concise Encyclopedia of Orthodox Christianity.** John Anthony McGuckin, ed. Hoboken, N.J., Wiley-Blackwell, 2014. 568p. $49.95pa. ISBN 13: 978-1-118-75933-2.

Here at last is an encyclopedia about Orthodoxy, written by scholars with expertise in both the academy and the contemporary Church! The one-volume *Concise Encyclopedia of Orthodox Christianity* does exactly what the title suggests: it provides succinct articles that cover a range of topics and are written in a way that is both readable and authoritative and scholarly. The list of contributors reveals a global network of scholars who write and teach about Orthodoxy every day. High school and college students as well as lay parishioners can easily pick up the text, navigate to an article and get immersed in its facts, and then continue their study by following the short References and Suggested Readings Bibliographies. Before doing so, however, it is worth the time to read through the artfully crafted Preface. This tells the intellectual history and impact of Orthodoxy with a passion directed not to cultivate sympathy, though it may, but an eagerness to appreciate its traditionalism and its relevance in the World today.

At the same time, readers will gain the most from the book if they come to it with a general understanding of the Orthodox tradition. There is no introduction to acquaint the novice with key terms or to justify why certain persons, places, and ideas are chosen while others are omitted by the editors. One misses an entry or cross-references for Orthodoxy itself, but does find distinct entries for Coptic Orthodoxy, Africa, Orthodoxy in, and the councils, all of which assume prior knowledge that the student may not hold. A simple introduction could, for example, instruct or perhaps remind the student of the Great Schism and then perhaps lead them by way of a historical timeline to the current complexities of Global Orthodoxy.

Still, the encyclopedia fills an important gap in the reference literature of the Orthodox Church. The features of the work enhance the content with beautiful illustrations, maps, a useful index, and list of entries. Finally, articles cross-reference and also provide short bibliographies for further reading.—**Amy Koehler**

713.   **Encyclopedia of Ancient Christianity.** Angelo Di Berardino, Thomas C. Oden, Joel C. Elowsky, and James Hoover, eds. Downers Grove, Ill., InterVarsity Press, 2014. 3v. $360.00/set. ISBN 13: 978-0-8308-2943-9.

The *Dizionario patristico e di antichità cristiane* (DPAC) was published in 1983-1988 by Casa Editrice Marietti. In 1992, James Clarke & Co. in Great Britain and Oxford University Press in the United States published an English translation as the *Encyclopedia of the Early Church (EEC)*. A second edition in Italian, the *Nuovo dizionario patristico e di antichità cristiane* (NDPAC), was published in 2006-2010. The EEC served as the standard source in English until the publication of the *Encyclopedia of Ancient Christianity* (EAC), an English translation of the NDPAC.

The EAC contains 3,200 articles by 266 contributors from 26 countries, an expansion of 35 percent from the original DPAC. The EAC offers a wide range of articles from the archaeological, philosophical, historical, geographical, and theological arenas; uses more work from art historians, linguistic experts, epigraphers, and papyrologists; provides better representation of Eastern European and Syriac traditions; and includes new entries from Arabic, Coptic, Armenian, and Gothic experts.

The work is grouped into three volumes, each of which contains notes on how to use the encyclopedia, a contributor list, a key to biblical and bibliographical abbreviations, and a complete list of articles. Coverage extends from the first century through the eighth century. Entries vary in length from a short paragraph to multiple pages. Contributors' names appear at the end of the entries, along with valuable bibliographical information. Cross-references, indicated by asterisks, enhance navigation throughout the three volumes. In the entry for Acesius, for example, an asterisk appears before Novatianist, Constantinople, Nicaea, Catholics, apostasy, and Constantine. While the editors did not choose to cross-reference the terms that one would expect in an encyclopedia of early Christianity, the complete list of articles included in each volume can assist searchers. People or places with the same name are distinguished. For example, the encyclopedia includes a Palladius of Helenopolis, Palladius of Ireland, Palladius of Saintes, Palladius of Suedin, and Palladius of Ratiaria. Guide words at the top of each page also facilitate navigation throughout this large work.

This encyclopedia is an unparalleled collection for anyone working in this period and is highly recommended for academic and larger public libraries.—**ARBA Staff Reviewer**

714.   **Jesus in History, Legend, Scripture, and Tradition: A World Encyclopedia.** Leslie Houlden, general editor, and Antone Minard, ed. Santa Barbara, Calif., ABC-CLIO, 2015. 2v. illus. index. $189.00/set. ISBN 13: 978-0-61069-803-0; 978-1-61069-804-7 (e-book).

It is not necessarily easy to disentangle the historical figure of Jesus from the larger narrative of Christianity. However, in 2003, Leslie Houlden successfully navigated these waters producing a multidisciplinary encyclopedia that did just that. Here, in this updated version of the two-volume encyclopedia, Houlden and Minard both expand and revise the scholarship contained in the first volume to reflect an even broader approach to the influence of Jesus on history, thought, and culture. The juxtaposition of the current introductory essay with the 2003 introduction, also included in this updated edition, reflects the editors' shift in scope. Entries are arranged alphabetically but are also grouped into a topical list of entries to enable quick references to specific historical periods and countries. Though varying in length, each entry is substantial and includes a bibliography of further reading.

Moreover, to facilitate searching, each entry is cross-referenced. Though by no means exhaustive, entries range from the very general (art) to narrower points of interest (feminist theology). A glossary, cross-referenced to relevant entries, and an extensive index of terms are particularly useful for quick reference. Of particular interest is the inclusion of several primary documents, such as the Epistle of Ignatius of Antioch to the Smyrnaeans. These documents augment several entries within the encyclopedia as well as represent recent discoveries in the scholarship on Jesus. Overall, Houlden and Minard, though admittedly selective in their scholarship choices, should be commended for their efforts to create a concise, yet comprehensive, encyclopedia on such an expansive and controversial topic. Unlike Delbert Burkett's *Blackwell Companion to Jesus,* which often exposes the philosophical and religious bias of the contributors, this encyclopedia manages to weave a multiplicity of perspectives and sources into an excellent primer on one of the world's most intriguing historical figures.—**Josh Eugene Finnell**

Islam

Dictionaries and Encyclopedias

715.   **Encyclopedia of Islam and the Muslim World.** 2d ed. Richard Martin, ed. New York, Macmillan Reference USA/Gale Group, 2016. 2v. illus. maps. index. $489.00/set. ISBN 13: 978-0-0286-6272-5.

This encyclopedia of over 540 articles, prepared by over 350 scholars from around the world, explores the religious, social, political, and cultural realms of Islam over the last 14 centuries. There appears to be considerable "evolution" from the 2004 edition. For example, the articles "American Culture and Islam," "Americas, Islam in the," and numerous biographies are no longer present, while many new entries, such as "Australia and New Zealand," "Byzantines," "Damascus," "ISIS," and "Intifada" now appear. Broad articles exploring art, architecture, and literature exist alongside specialized topics of the Islamic faith and Muslim history.

Numerous maps and color photos enhance the work considerably, as do the bibliographies at the end of each article. Students and scholars of the Muslim world will find much useful information here. Academic and public libraries will benefit from having this set, as could high school libraries. Librarians might consider retaining the 2004 volumes as well.—**Mark Schumacher**

716.   Glassé, Cyril. **New Encyclopedia of Islam, Fourth Edition.** Lanham, Md., Rowman & Littlefield, 2013. 736p. maps. $105.00. ISBN 13: 978-1-4422-2348-6.

The third edition of *The New Encyclopedia of Islam* was published in 2008 (see ARBA 2009, entry 1117). The fourth edition has more entries and expanded (although not necessarily updated) existing entries from the previous edition. Entries pertaining to Islamic intellectual traditions and diverse Muslim communities still lack depth and can be misleading. While the entries are more heavily cross-referenced, the absence of an index is a serious impediment to using this reference. Treatment of the subject matter is too basic for most undergraduate work. The chronology is updated to December 2012.—**Muhammed Hassanali**

Handbooks and Yearbooks

717. **Oxford Islamic Studies Online.** http://www.oxfordislamicstudies.com/.
[Website] Price negotiated by site. Date reviewed: 2015

Oxford Islamic Studies Online (OISO), is under the direction of Editor-in-Chief John
L. Esposito, Georgetown University, assisted by Deputy Editor, Natana J. DeLong-Bas,
Boston College, senior editors, senior consultants, an editorial advisory board, and a
library advisory board. Updated three to four times a year, OISO provides thousands of
A-Z reference entries, approximately a thousand biographies, chapters from scholarly and
introductory texts, Qur'anic materials, primary sources, images and maps, and timelines
that can serve students, governments, community groups, librarians, scholars, and anyone
interested in Islam.

OISO content is discoverable in many ways. Users can conduct a quick search from
the home page or utilize the five main headings also available on the main page—Advanced
Search, Browse, Qur'anic Studies, Timelines, and Learning Resources. Advanced Search
allows users to seek information by a Main Search, Biography Search, Image & Map
Search, Primary Source Search, Bibliography Search, Qur'an Search, and Concordance
Search. Under the Browse button, researchers can search content across the whole site or
by subject entry, biographies, chapter works, primary sources, or images & maps. Three
works are searchable under the Qur'anic Studies button: two Oxford classics, M.A.S.
Abdel Haleem's *The Qur'an* and A.J. Arberry's *The Koran Interpreted,* and Hanna Kassis'
Concordance of the Qur'an. Two timelines can be accessed via the eponymous button, one
a timeline of world events and one a timeline of events in Islam. Both timelines are linked
with related content throughout the OISO site. The Learning Resources button connects
users to a wealth of information via the following sublinks: Thematic Guides, Teaching
Islam, Internet Resources, Geography of the Islamic World, What Everyone Needs to
Know about Islam, Glossary, Lesson Plans, Interviews, the Arab Sprint, Reference Works,
and Further Reading. Once an entry is accessed, users can highlight and search within
OISO for related terms. While reading an entry on Mu'ammar al-Qaddafi, for instance,
you can highlight Qur'an, click "Look it Up" on the toolbar above the entry, and be taken
to a new list of 41 entries on the Qur'an.

OISO core content comes from *The Oxford Handbook of Islam and Politics, The
Grove Encyclopedia of Islamic Art and Architecture, The Oxford Encyclopedia of the
Islamic World, The Islamic World Past and Present, The Oxford Dictionary of Islam, The
Oxford History of Islam, What Everyone Needs to Know about Islam, Teaching Islam,
Makers of Contemporary Islam,* and the three Qur'anic texts mentioned above. Documents
are drawn from the following Oxford collections: *Islam in Transition, Modern Islam,* and
Liberal Islam. Primary sources have been carefully selected and all are contextualized by
introductory editorial comments. *The Oxford Encyclopedia of the Modern Islamic World*
is included in full on the site and archived articles can be excluded or included during
the search process. Results are easily printed or emailed. Citations in Chicago and MLA
are provided, and citations can be exported to EndNote, ProCite, ReferenceManager, or
RefWorks.

OISO is available via annual subscriptions to institutions and individuals; individuals
can also subscribe monthly. Librarians also have free access to downloadable MARC
records. Given the importance of the subject matter, the features and functionality of the
site, and the breadth and depth of the source material, OISO is highly recommended to

large public libraries and academic libraries.—**ARBA Staff Reviewer**

Indexes

718.   **Index Islamicus Online. http://bibliographies.brillonline.com/browse/index-islamicus.** [Website] Boston, Brill Academic, 2015. Price negotiated by site. Date reviewed: 2015.

Edited by Heather Bleaney, Pablo García Suárez, and Susan Sinclair at the editorial offices in the Library, School of Oriental and African Studies, University of London, and the Insituto de Lenguas y Culturas del Mediterráneo y Oriente Próximo in Madrid, the *Index Islamicus Online,* consisting of more than 475,000 records drawn from over 3,000 journals along with conference proceedings, monographs, and book reviews, continues to be the leading international classified bibliography of publications written in European languages on the Muslim world and Islam. Coverage areas include but are not limited to history, religion, law, literature, politics, economics, and archaeology. The classification scheme uses broad subject area headings such as education, Israel, and philosophy as well as subcategories. There are also indexes of names and subjects, searches on the article and author level, and article- and chapter-level indexing for journals and books. Users can also take advantage of personal tools for saving, alerting, sharing, and exporting. The *Index Islamicus Online* is updated quarterly. Libraries can choose to subscribe or to purchase the index outright. On the Brill site, potential purchasers can view a list of consulted periodicals as well as options for purchasing access for a day, a week, or a month. Proquest and Ebsco also host the *Index Islamicus Online;* purchasers can request trial subscription access through either of these providers.—**ARBA Staff Reviewer**

Judaism

Handbooks and Yearbooks

719.   **The Commentators' Bible: Deuteronomy. The Rubin JPS Miqra'ot Gedolot.** Michael Carasik, ed., translator, annotator Lincoln, Nebr., University of Nebraska Press, 2015. 296p. $75.00. ISBN 13: 978-0-8276-0939-6.

Contemporizing the input of Rashi, Ibn Ezra, Nachmanides, Rashbam, and other medieval Bible commentators (e.g., Kimhi, Sforno Hizkuni, and, especially, Abarbanel) and source texts on Deuteronomy for readers of little or no Hebrew background is no easy task. Inspired by the format of the 500-year-old Miqra'ot Gedolot (Classic "Rabbinic Bible"), the page layout contains several verses in Hebrew from the book of Deuteronomy, surrounded by both the 1917 and the 1985 JPS translations and by new contemporary English translations of the major commentators. Emendations, editing, and insightful notes help navigate the reading and understanding of text, context, and intertext of the cited rabbinic commentators. The book also includes introductory material, a glossary of terms, a list of names used in the text, notes on source texts, essays on special topics, and resources for further study. Particularly helpful are the editor's suggestions on how to read the commentators, notations to distinguish the biblical text within the rabbinic commentary, and the editor's comments interspersed therein. Due to this mix, the separation of the editor's voice from the biblical and medieval voices is of high importance. An expected guide to transliterating Hebrew (academic or popular) is wanting. In sum, an excellent guide to medieval Torah study and commentary.—**Zev Garber**

720.   Eisenberg, Ronald L. **Essential Figures in Jewish Scholarship.** Northvale, N.J., Jason Aronson, 2014. 379p. $65.00; $64.99 (e-book). ISBN 13: 978-0-7657-0993-6; 978-0-7657-0995-0 (e-book).

The Jews are known as the People of the Book for a reason. They have a tradition of studying and commenting upon religious texts. The result is many volumes of commentary interpreting the Torah, the Talmud, and other important works of scholarship. Ronald L. Eisenberg, a physician who also holds a doctorate in Jewish studies, offers a useful source with information about approximately 400 great Jewish scholars who lived and worked from around 600 C.E. to the present.

After a brief introduction that summarizes the relevant history, the book is divided into five sections covering major historical periods. Within each section, there are alphabetical entries with brief biographies of scholars from each era. The entries range in length from one paragraph to three pages and provide information about their lives and major works. The chapters cover the Geonic period (589-1038), the rishonim ("first ones," late tenth century to late fifteenth century), the acharonim ("last ones," 1492 through the sixteenth century), the modern period (eighteenth century to the present), and Hasidism (a separate section covering the sages of this mystical movement). Since many of these early scholars were known by acronyms based on their Hebrew names, there is a list of them, divided by historical period, at the beginning of the book. A series of appendixes offers a complete list of the scholars by period, a list of major works, a glossary, and a list of important sources. Among the scholars covered are Saadia Gaon, Moses Maimonides (Rambam), Samuel ben Israel (Rashi), Isaac Luria (Ari), the Vilna Gaon, the Baal Shem Tov, and Nachman of Bratislav.

This is a useful resource for synagogue, day school, and public libraries in need of introductory material on classic Jewish scholarship.—**Barbara M. Bibel**

721.   Fraenkel, Avinoam. **Nefesh HaTzimtzum, Volume 1: Rabbi Chaim Volozhin's Nefesh HaChaim with Translation and Commentary.** Jerusalem, Urim Publications/ Independent Publishers Group, 2015. 811p. $31.00. ISBN 13: 978-965-524-165-5.

Nefesh HaTzimtzum (two volumes) provides a general yet comprehensive gateway to the teachings and world view of Rabbi Chaim Volozhin ("Volozhiner"), a leading disciple of Rabbi Elijah b. Solomon Zalman, the Gaon of Vilna, as presented in his magnum opus, *Nefesh HaChaim* (Vilna and Grodno, 5584 [1824]), arranged and published posthumously by his son and successor, Rabbi Yitzchak. The title's double entendre ("soul of Chaim" and "soul of life") speaks to the ideology of these volumes: fear of God brings life and intense love of Torah purports its sacred destiny at the highest attainable spiritual level. Following an introduction by Rabbi Yitzchak, the volume is parsed into Four Gateways, containing multiple chapters and additional notes by Rabbi Chaim: (1) God, Soul, and Man created in the image of God can change/repair the world; (2) Prayer, turning upward and inward to the Source of Life; (3) Presence (*Makom*/Place) of God in, from, about Creation; *yetser ha-tov* and *yester ha-ra'* (good and bad inclinations) in Man; doing Torah *lishmah* (for its own sake) diminishes evil inclination; (4) Torah study, the ultimate refinement of self-purpose and identity. Avinoam Fraenkel's research, translation, and commentary are essential components to making this classic of *Mitnaged* (non-Hasidic) Ashkenazi Orthodoxy accessible to the English reading audience.—**Zev Garber**

722.   Fraenkel, Avinoam. **Nefesh HaTzimtzum, Volume 2: Understanding Nefesh HaChaim through the Key Concept of Tzimtzum.** Jerusalem, Urim Publications/ Independent Publishers Group, 2015. 757p. index. $31.00. ISBN 13: 978-965-524-177-8.

The Four Gateways of *Nefesh HaChaim* are introduced and discussed in *Nefesh HaTzimzum,* volume one. They speak respectfully of the power of human actions, speech/ prayer, and thought in transforming self and world with metaphysical repercussions. *Nefesh HaTzimtzum,* volume two, is exclusively focused on sections of Gateway Three which discusses God's Being (essence, existence, metaphysics) as developed in the Kabbalistic doctrine of *Tzimtzum,* that is, the contractions of the Infinite Being to create, penetrate, and sustain a finite universe. Doctrinal issues embrace experiential and transcendental response. Rationally, can an absolute Infinite Being be contracted to Finite Being; if God's presence is everywhere in creation then in what way is creation an independent entity and Man's function therein; if God as God does not contract does this embrace associated attributes, such as God's Will and Glory, and so on. Of particular significance, Fraenkel's attempt by introduction, insightful notes, use of additional writings of Rabbi Chaim and others to adjudicate differences between *Mitnagdim* and *Hasidim* on the language, ideology, and salvific role of *Tzimtzum* as mediator between holy and profane. Nonetheless, the Yeshiva *Weltanschauung* (Gateway Four) is extant. Rabbi Chaim's understanding of *Torah Lishma* is less communion (*devekut*) and intention (*kavvanah*) with Heaven than performance of *mitzvah lishma* done in the context of Torah and *halakhah.* Historical overview, proper Hebrew-English layout, and intensive index are helpful.—**Zev Garber**

723.   **The Jewish Year Book 2015: 5775-5776.** Elkan D. Levy and Derek Taylor, eds. Portland, Oreg., Vallentine Mitchell, 2015. 496p. index. $69.95. ISBN 13: 978-0-85303-978-5.

This venerable reference source for British Jewry begins with a preface that evaluates Jewish life and culture in the previous year called "2014: A Lose-Lose Situation." This is followed by seven essays: "Jews in Unexpected Places," "Women in Jewish Law," "UK/Israel Trade," "25 Years of Jewish Care," "The First World War Centenary," "The Jewish Film Festival," and "The Belfast Jewish Community." The majority of the book contains a wide range of information on Anglo-Jewish institutions and organizations, international and British; Jewish communities around the world, arranged alphabetically by country; historical information on British Jewry; a Who's Who; an abridged Jewish/ British calendar for 2015; an index; and much more. Recommended for public libraries, as well as academic and institutional libraries.—**ARBA Staff Reviewer**

724.   Langer, Ruth. **Jewish Liturgy: A Guide to Research.** Lanham, Md., Rowman & Littlefield, 2015. 264p. index. (Illuminations: A Rowman & Littlefield Series of Guides to Research in Religion). $85.00; $84.99 (e-book). ISBN 13: 978-0-8108-8616-2; 978-0-8108-8617-9 (e-book).

Jewish liturgy has a deep, rich tradition. Although rooted in ancient biblical texts, it has undergone change throughout history. Ruth Langer has compiled an annotated bibliography of English-language sources on the origins and history of this liturgy. She is a professor of Jewish studies and associate director of the Center for Christian-Jewish Learning at Boston College. The book is intended as a guide for Christian seminary students interested in the origins of their liturgy, but it is a useful resource for anyone wishing to learn more about the topic.

The 14 chapters cover a wide range of topics: rabbinic literature, the structure of the prayer book, historical and chronological overviews of liturgy, the synagogue as an institution, women in the synagogue, medieval and modern liturgy, and more. The differences in Orthodox, Conservative, and Reform rites, weekday, Sabbath, and High Holiday prayers, and prayers for life-cycle events are covered as well. The entries are brief with a bibliographic citation and one or two sentences about the content. A glossary, a section listing resources cited multiple times, and a detailed index make it easy for users to find materials. Information about liturgical poetry, music, mysticism, and comparisons with early Christian liturgy make this a very useful resource. Academic libraries supporting programs in religious studies, Jewish studies, and seminary programs will want to add this to their collections.—**Barbara M. Bibel**

Shamanism

Dictionaries and Encyclopedias

725.   Harvey, Graham, and Robert J. Wallis. **Historical Dictionary of Shamanism.** 2d ed. Lanham, Md., Rowman & Littlefield, 2016. 366p. (Historical Dictionaries of Religions, Philosophies, and Movements). $100.00; $99.99 (e-book). ISBN 13: 978-1-4422-5797-9; 978-1-4422-5798-6 (e-book).

In 2016, Itzhak Beery will be the featured shaman in a new television show entitled, *Soul Search.* This newest representation of shamanism, coupled with characters in World of Warcraft and numerous Twitter accounts, in the popular culture canon further underscores the cultural impact of the shamanism in the twenty-first century. As Graham Harvey and Robert J. Wallis point out in the introduction, the appropriation of shamanism by western culture is both a challenge and an opportunity to demonstrate the diversity of shamans around the world. In this second edition of the dictionary, Harvey and Wallis continue to challenge a western-centric approach to both a global and localized historical movement. Unlike most dictionaries in the series, the chronology is not a Eurocentric, linear conception of time; rather, it is an overview of events and dates that help underscore the longevity of shamanism throughout history. Entries are arranged alphabetically and span countries, cultures, and individuals. Most entries are fairly concise. However, to facilitate searching, related entries are cross-referenced in bold—eliminating the need for an index. The brevity of each entry allows for a breadth of coverage, spanning continents, cultures, and history. Perhaps most impressive about this updated edition is the extensive bibliography, spanning nearly 100 pages in length, delineated by regions and themes. Intentionally, the one term lacking an entry in this dictionary is emblazoned across the front cover: shamanism. Always contextualized within a specific, culture, locale, and historical period, shamanism continues to be an evolving practice, identity, and experience that defies simple characterization. What Harvey and Wallis have accomplished in this updated edition is to show how that identity continues to transform and elude a reductionist characterization.—**Josh Eugene Finnell**

Part IV

SCIENCE AND TECHNOLOGY

29 Science and Technology in General

Dictionaries and Encyclopedias

726. **U*X*L Doomed: The Science behind Disasters.** K. Lee Lerner and Brenda Wilmoth Lerner, eds. Farmington Hills, Mich., Gale/Cengage Learning, 2015. 3v. illus. maps. index. $272.00/set. ISBN 13: 978-1-4103-1774-2; 978-1-4103-1778-0 (e-book).

The three volumes in this excellent set cover 100 natural and man-made disasters occurring since 1900, beginning with a hurricane in Galveston and ending with faulty ignitions in General Motors vehicles. Each volume includes a complete chronology, glossary, table of contents, thematic table of contents, and detailed index. Alphabetically arranged entries within the volumes sometimes require consultation of the table of contents, chronology, or index to ascertain the title being used for a specific event. For example, the Challenger disaster is found under "Space Shuttle Challenger Explosion."

Some entries include primary source documents such as excerpts from government reports. Individual primary source documents are listed in the index, so readers can go directly to entries featuring such documentation if that is of especial interest. Most entries include both photographs and insets with information about related events or extended discussions of concepts causally involved in the disaster, such as building resonance.—**Delilah R. Caldwell**

727. **U*X*L Encyclopedia of Science.** 3d ed. Amy Hackney Blackwell, ed. Farmington Hills, Mich., U*X*L/Gale, 2015. 10v. illus. $780.00/set. ISBN 13: 978-1-4144-3075-1; 978-1-4144-3086-7 (e-book).

In a world overflowing with information, finding good, concise research sources in clear language can be a difficult task. This is especially true with science. U*X*L has produced an encyclopedia set that helps the battle. In the Reader's Guide portion of the *U*X*L Encyclopedia of Science, Third Edition,* the editors perfectly state the objective of the work as "an alphabetically organized 10-volume set that opens up the entire world of science in clear nontechnical language" (ix). The set easily accomplishes this goal. Certainly no work is all inclusive, but the encyclopedias cover topics relevant to today from "physical, life and earth sciences, as well as health and medicine, mathematics, engineering, technology, and the environment" (ix). Each volume starts with an "Entries by Scientific Field" section with pertinent subtopics listed along with volume and page number. An example of a main entry is "Artificial Intelligence" with subheadings "Artificial Intelligence," "Automation," and "Robotics." This part of the set alone is useful for providing key words in subject areas a person might not know much about. The volume listings follow. Each volume contains the same "Where to Learn More" section at the end listing scientific books, periodicals, and Websites for further study. Volume 10 contains a cumulative general index for quick reference. Throughout each volume, entries are supplemented with colorful photographs, drawings, Words to Know sidebars, and cross-references. As a side note, the color choice for sidebars and headings is visually pleasing and makes navigation easier. The *U*X*L Encyclopedia of Science, Third Edition,* a good addition to any public or school library, would be useful for anybody just wanting general information and/or a place to start their research.—**Sue Ellen Knowlton**

Handbooks and Yearbooks

728.   Barel, André O., Marc Paye, and Howard I. Maibach. **Handbook of Cosmetic Science and Technology.** Boca Raton, Fla., CRC Press, 2014. 725p. illus. index. $199.95; $139.97 (e-book). ISBN 13: 978-1-84214-564-7; 978-1-84214-565-4 (e-book).

The first and second editions of this handbook provided a useful formulation guide and a source of ideas for the development of modern cosmetics; the third edition switched its focus to the mode of action and the science behind cosmetic products, ingredients, and methodology. This fourth edition expands on the third and also provides up-to-date information on the regulatory context. As the introduction points out, cosmetic science involves chemistry, physics, biology, bioengineering, dermatology, microbiology, statistics, and other fields. While other texts in the Cosmetic Sciences and Technology series cover these topics in depth, this title strives to provide cosmetic manufacturers with a better scientific- and evidence-based assessment of the safety and efficacy of their products based on sound science and not on unreliable information.

The breadth of this handbook and its ease of use facilitate achievement of this goal, while the table of contents and index make it easy to find information. The book is organized into 64 chapters of varying length arranged into nine sections covering different skin types and their specificities, skin hydration, skin barriers and skin pH, skin aging and skin care products, skin perception, skin tolerance, skin color and appearance, the application of cosmetics to specific parts of the body, and ethics and regulation. The chapters cover a fascinating array of topics, including ethnic differences in skin properties, tests for sensitive skin, human skin buffering capacity, skin aging, UV filters, skin whitening agents, baby care products, cosmetics for the elderly, oral cosmetics, and trends in regulation in the European Union and the United States. The contributors (all listed in the front matter) are area experts. Each chapter ends with references.

While this is an obvious contender for the libraries of cosmetic companies, the information makes it a recommended title for academic libraries and larger public libraries.—**ARBA Staff Reviewer**

729.   **Handbook of Toxicology.** 3d ed. Michael J. Derelanko and Carol S. Auletta, eds. Boca Raton, Fla., CRC Press, 2014. 1022p. illus. index. $169.95; $118.97 (e-book). ISBN 13: 978-1-4398-9013-4; 978-1-4398-9014-1 (e-book).

Approximately 20 years after the publication of the first edition comes this third edition of the *Handbook of Toxicology.* Despite the wealth of information available on the Internet, the editors determined that the handbook still provides users with a quick source of reliable data without the hassle of weeding through numerous Websites.

The editors reviewed all the chapters in the second edition, a process that resulted in several updates and changes. The chapters on histopathology, clinical pathology, and renal toxicology were reprinted in their entirety while most other chapters received minor to major changes. The immunotoxicology, endocrine toxicology, and reproductive and developmental toxicology chapters were completely rewritten. The data on inhalation toxicology, neurotoxicology, and regulatory toxicology formerly presented as several chapters was updated and consolidated into single chapters for each specialty. There are new chapters on chemical and pharmaceutical toxicology, juvenile toxicology, and safety pharmacology. A further enhancement is the addition of a separate glossary with toxicological terms presented alphabetically and by toxicology subspecialty.

To facilitate use, chapters begin with a list of all major topics covered; headings appear at the top of each page. The detailed table of contents also allows searchers to locate topics quickly and can be used as a supplement to the index. There are 23 chapters covering such subjects as laboratory animal management, dermal toxicology, ocular toxicology, neurotoxicology, renal toxicology, endocrine toxicology, carcinogenesis, chemical toxicology, and regulatory toxicology. Following these are appendixes A-I, followed by a subject glossary, an alphabetical glossary, and an index.

Recommended for practicing toxicologists and academic libraries.—**ARBA Staff Reviewer**

730. **Science In Context. http://solutions.cengage.com/InContext/Science/.** [Website] Farmington Hills, Mich, Gale/Cengage Learning. Price negotiated by site. Date reviewed: 2016.

Science In Context is an online database that integrates science reference content with news, videos, academic journals, and more. The goal of the tool is to illustrate the connection between real-world life and science issues thus making science more appealing to students. This aim is illustrated by the layout of the homepage which is dominated by rotating images linking to recent and/or newsworthy scientific events.

The scope of the collection encompasses all the branches of science: natural, formal, social, and applied. A sampling of topics includes black holes, 3D printing, gene expression, cognitive behavioral therapy, etc. Information about these topics is collected from the spectrum of source types ranging from general reference to academic journals. Videos, images, audio files (e.g., NPR clips), magazine and news articles, and Websites are also included. All of these sources are presented together, curated on one page for a holistic view of the topic in question. This approach creates an information "command center" experience that is quite compelling.

The database can be searched by keyword or browsed by topic. There are so many topics to browse that a helpful filter for category (e.g., Chemistry, Health and Medicine, New and Updated, etc.) is also included. An advanced keyword search option allows users to combine keywords with article and/or publication title and limit their search to full-text or peer-reviewed journals, specify a desired document type (e.g., map, cover story, pamphlet, or video among many options), or content type (book, journal, experiments, Websites, etc.). Teachers will especially appreciate the ability to search by content level (beginner to advanced) and Lexile level. Educators will also appreciate the curriculum standards provided in the site. Curriculum standards for not only the United States (both national and state) are provided, but the standards for other English-speaking countries like Canada, Australia, New Zealand, Ireland, and the countries of Great Britain are included as well.

The database integrates with Google apps including Google Drive and Google Classroom making it easy for both students and teachers to save documents to their own Google drive. The ability to save research to a central location is a very useful feature. Any highlights and notes made in the database can be retained when the document is saved to Google Drive. Teachers have the added ability to save a document to their Google Classroom as an announcement or an assignment.

This is a fantastic resource, and it is highly recommended for school and public libraries. It brings a fresh and engaging perspective to the study of science by powerfully illustrating its place at the heart of our day-to-day lives and by demonstrating this through engaging multimedia resources. Students and teachers alike will find this a "go-to" resource for anything science-related. By including the typical database tools (save and share search results, citation tools, etc.) this becomes a tool everyone will want to use. Rather than going to many different places to find this information, it is all now available in one powerful, user-friendly dashboard.—**Kristin Kay Leeman**

731.   **TryNano. http://trynano.org/.** [Website] Free. Date reviewed: 2016.

TryNano is a freely accessible, easy-to-navigate site sponsored by IEEE (the Institute of Electrical and Electronics Engineers), IBM, TryScience, and the New York Hall of Science. The information is aimed at students, parents, teachers, and guidance counselors.

From the top of the page, users can select from five main links. The first, Nanomaterials, provides a general explanation of the field and further links to specific nanomaterial types, including carbon nanotubes, graphene, inorganic nanowires, dendrimers, nanoparticles, and quantum dots; all of the explanations have helpful color illustrations. Applications, the second link, discusses ways that nanotechnology is already being used in information and communications, in materials and manufacturing, in the biomedical field, in transportation, in consumer goods, and in energy and engineering. Again, color illustrations enhance the material. The following link takes users to 36 interviews with nano experts from a variety of backgrounds. For those wanting more information on companies, universities, and government organizations, there are links to: Drexel University; IBM; Industrial Technology Research Institute (Taiwain), Johns Hopkins Institute of NanoBio Technology; Keithley Instruments, Inc.; Korea Institute of Science and Technology; Lockheed Martin; Nanofilm; Nano-Tex, Inc.; National Institute of Advanced Industrial Science and Technology (Japan), National Nanotechnology Center (NANOTEC) (Thailand); the National Nanotechnology Initiative; the Network for Computational Nanotechnology; POSTECH (Korea); Rice University; and Zyvex Instruments. The resources tab links to an image gallery, a glossary, nano games, worldwide universities with nano programs or coursework, nano standards and guidelines, and nanotechnology-related links. To top it off, teachers can find six lesson plans under the resources tab for students ages 8 to 18. Although not listed on the top of the page, there is a "what's new" tab on the left-hand side of the home page that reveals an impressive collection on newsworthy events in the nano world from 2009 to the present. The latest news feature from March 17, 2016, reports the findings of Washington University nano researchers on a nanoparticle that may help impact tumor growth.

Altogether http://TryNano.org/ is a multifaceted and very useful site.—**ARBA Staff Reviewer**

30 Agricultural Sciences

Food Sciences and Technology

Atlases

732.   Braatz, Dieter, Ulrich Sautter, and Ingo Swoboda. Kevin D. Goldberg. **Wine Atlas of Germany.** Oakland, Calif., University of California Press, 2014. 280p. illus. maps. index. $60.00. ISBN 13: 978-0-520-26067-2.

This book is simply the next best thing to exploring the wine regions of Germany in person. Full of viticulture history, geology, and frank opinion, readers will learn much about climate, soils, grape varieties, and the history of winemaking throughout Germany's 13 official wine regions. Shaded text boxes house the most pertinent information: wine classifications (from the common Deutscher Wein to the peculiarly created Eiswein), grape varieties (like the famous Riesling or the comparatively obscure Tauberschwarz), and of course the most important information of all, the "Best Vineyards" within each winemaking region.

Maps, of course, take center stage in this book, and are used liberally to clarify wine regions and the vineyards within. Any traveler, armchair or otherwise, would appreciate that vineyards are color-coded to represent quality and villages are labeled in bold if they happen to be next door to a vineyard. Color photographs beautifully spotlight sloping golden hills carpeted with grapevines at harvest, angular green waves of vines approaching charming villages, and bracing close-ups of earth and grape. The book concludes with a vineyard index, a village index, and a list of major producers, which enhances the book's reference value. Appeasing both the wine lover and the viticulture student, the *Wine Atlas of Germany* would beautify any coffee table while serving as an outstanding reference on the subject of German wines.—**Laura Herrell**

733.   Hoffman, James. **The World Atlas of Coffee: From Beans to Brewing—Coffees Explored, Explained and Enjoyed.** New York, Firefly Books, 2014. 256p. illus. maps. index. $35.00. ISBN 13: 978-1-77085-470-3.

Broken into three parts, *The World Atlas of Coffee* introduces the curious to worldwide varieties, production methods, and growing regions. The book focuses on specialty coffees rather than commodity coffee.

In part one, Introduction to Coffee, the author introduces readers to Arabica and robusta, types of coffee trees, various harvesting methods, the manner in which coffee is graded, shipped, and traded, and more. From Bean to Cup, part two, details the harvesting processes, professional tasting, tasting at home, purchasing and storing, grinding, and brewing. Part three, Coffee Origins, takes readers on a worldwide tour of coffee-producing countries. African countries covered include Burundi, Ethiopia, Kenya, Malawi, Rwanda, Tanzania, and Zambia. Asian countries include India, Indonesia, Papua New Guinea, Vietnam, and Yemen. Bolivia, Brazil, Colombia, Costa Rica, Cuba, the Dominican Republic, Ecuador, El Salvador, Guatemala, Hawaii, Honduras, Jamaica, Mexico, Nicaragua, Panama, Peru, and Venezuela represent the Americas. Each country gets its own brief introduction that provides details about such things as the history of coffee cultivation and a taste profile. Readers will also find out about growing regions as well as population and production statistics.

The book is packed with color maps and beautiful color illustration, which makes this a visually appealing read. The book concludes with a glossary and an index but does not have a bibliography, sources notes, or suggestions for further reading. Recommended for public libraries.—**ARBA Staff Reviewer**

Dictionaries and Encyclopedias

734.   **Archaeology of Food: An Encyclopedia.** Karen Bescherer Metheny and Mary C. Beaudry, eds. Lanham, Md., Rowman & Littlefield, 2015. 2v. illus. maps. index. $195.00/ set; $104.99 (e-book). ISBN 13: 978-0-7591-2364-9; 978-0-7591-2366-3 (e-book).

This two-volume set provides 284 articles on a wide range of information on topics "including eras, places, cultural groups, specific foodstuffs, landmark sites, analytical techniques, methodology, pioneers in the field, innovations, theories, issues, controversies, and more." (p. xxvii) Scholars from around the world explore the history of food over the last 40,000 years. Whether discussing sweet potatoes or rye, explaining the significance of a Mesolithic site in England, or describing the value of scanning electron microscopy, the entries provide a rich introduction to the archaeological history of food.

While some of the entries are somewhat technical, many are accessible to all readers. For students and faculty, or anyone interested in the history of our food, these volumes will provide useful, and often fascinating, information. One nice feature: the contents and index are included in both volumes.—**Mark Schumacher**

735.   Buckingham, John, and V. Ranjit N. Munasinghe. **Dictionary of Flavonoids with CD-ROM.** Boca Raton, Fla., CRC Press, 2015. 1199p. index. $759.00; $531.30 (e-book). ISBN 13: 978-1-4665-5434-4; 978-1-4822-8250-4 (e-book).

Over 20,000 different flavonoids have been characterized. Flavonoids are known as the basis of plant colors but more recently colorless flavonoids have been linked to important plant functions. Organized alphabetically, this dictionary of flavonoids is a major, up-to-date summary of all known flavonoids and their literature. It is intended to complement major flavonoid literature, which is listed in the introduction. The dictionary is searchable by name, substructure, and physical and other properties. Entries are also searchable by type of compound codes; type of organism codes enable searches across plant families. The CD-ROM, which comes with the purchase of the book, provides even more powerful search functions. Extensive bibliographies accompany the individual entries.

The book concludes with a name index and a type of compound index. The introduction discusses the classification of flavonoids, nomenclature, how the entries are structured, the type of compound classification schemes, flavonoid types, and strategies for using the dictionary on CD-ROM. The dictionary is part of CRC Press's Chemical Database; a large component of the database is the *Dictionary of Natural Products* (DNP). The database is updated regularly and re-released biannually on DVD and online. A team of specialists produced this dictionary by reviewing, updating, or expanding relevant entries from the DNP database. The dictionary will be updated but will also fall under the umbrella of DNP updates.

This specialized dictionary is highly recommended for academic libraries.—**ARBA Staff Reviewer**

736. Cumo, Christopher. **Foods That Changed History: How Foods Shaped Civilization from the Ancient World to the Present.** Santa Barbara, Calif., ABC-CLIO, 2015. 451p. illus. index. $100.00. ISBN 13: 978-1-4408-3536-0; 978-1-4408-3537-7 (e-book).

This 7-by-10-inch, 451-page, hardbound book starts with an alphabetical list of 90 food entries, followed by lists of the same food items categorized according to their topics, a preface, and an extensive introduction. Next is a timeline that indicates when these food items became part of the diet. I have been in the food industry for over 60 years and was shocked as to how long these items had been utilized; the main portion of the book next goes through an alphabetical discussion of the individual foods. Most of these entries are several pages in length (in most books, these entries would be equivalent to chapters), often with highlighted areas that indicate notable facts. Often figures of the item and subchapters of the various factors that have influenced their usage are emphasized. This is followed by further reading recommendations. After the individual food items have been discussed, the book provides a lengthy bibliography and an extensive index. The binding is average and the font size is a little small but acceptable for short reading assignments. I would strongly recommend this book for most general libraries and particularly for individuals who are interested in history and/or foods.—**Herbert W. Ockerman**

737. Mariani, John F. **The Encyclopedia of American Food and Drink.** 5th ed. New York, Bloomsbury USA, 2013. index. $35.00; $24.99 (e-book). ISBN 13: 978-1-6204-0160-6; 978-1-6204-0161-3 (e-book).

This is the fifth edition of Mariani's *Encyclopedia of American Food and Drink,* a book that illuminates the origins, variety, creativity, and originality of food and drink in the United States. This review is based on the electronic version of the book, made available in 2014. The book's thoroughly informative introduction provides readers with a lively narrative of American food history that extends back to the colonial period and emphasizes how American fare, like food everywhere, has been shaped by a mix of cultural influences. Following the introduction, a guide discusses the goal the encyclopedia, which aims to demonstrate the array of American food and drink, how Americans speak about food and drink, how it is consumed, and how Americans have created a unique food and drink culture.

The main entries are arranged alphabetically and can contain other terms, types of food, or regional variations, so it is important to use the index. Words in boldface type within an entry have their own main entry. The list of food and drink is interesting, fun, and extensive. There are such foods as apple pie, baked Alaska, halibut, oysters Rockefeller, eggs Benedict, bonefish, the peanut, and Twinkies. Drinks include the fuzzy navel, the Alabama slammer, milk, sauvignon blanc, and pinot noir. There are also conceptual entries for topics like African American food, New American cuisine, tailgate party, and TV dinner. An added bonus is the new-to-this edition biography section with brief summaries of Julia Child, Charles Krug, James Beard, Clarence Birdseye, Martha Stewart, and many others.

In addition to the index, the book is rounded out by a bibliographic guide to what the author considers the most important and best resources—a great place for further research.—**ARBA Staff Reviewer**

738.   **The SAGE Encyclopedia of Food Issues.** Albala, Ken, ed. Thousand Oaks, Calif., Sage, 2015. 3v. index. $395.00/set; $316.00 (e-book). ISBN 13: 978-1-4522-4301-6; 978-1-5063-1730-4 (e-book).

This 8.5-by-11-inch, three-volume encyclopedia has 1506 pages. It contains 11,784 entries on food related history and facts, all under the editorship of Ken Albala, professor of history at the University of the Pacific and Director of the Food Studies MA in San Francisco. All of the more than 300 contributors are in positions of authority in the food area. The book's contents include an alphabetical list of entries, a reader's guide, information on the editor and contributors, an introduction, and an index. Most of the entries range from three-quarters of a page to more than a page in length. The encyclopedia treats the subject of food broadly across the social sciences. Users will find material on the environment, health, government, retail and shopping, hunger, and so much more. The entries themselves are interesting and informative and have cross-references and suggestions for further reading. The binding and paper are of average quality, and the font is small but adequate for short-term reading. I would recommend this book for all libraries and for anyone with a food interest.—**Herbert W. Ockerman**

Handbooks and Yearbooks

739.   Barnes-Svarney, Patricia, and Thomas E. Svarney. **The Handy Nutrition Answer Book.** Canton, Mich., Visible Ink Press, 2015. 374p. illus. index. $21.95pa. ISBN 13: 978-1-57859-484-9; 978-1-57859-553-2 (e-book).

This fact-filled and exhaustive work on nutrition contains the following chapters: "The Basics of Nutrition: Micronutrients," "The Basics of Nutrition: Macronutrients and Non-nutrients," "Food Chemistry and Nutrition," "Nutrition in Eating and Drinking Choices," "Food Preservation and Nutrition," "Nutrition and Allergies, Illnesses, and Diseases," "Nutrition Throughout the Centuries," "Modern Nutrition," "Controversies with Food, Beverages, and Nutrition," "Nutrition Throughout Life," and "Nutrition and You." Approximately 152 black-and-white pictures marvelously intrigue the reader. About 53 charts enhance the superb discussion. The text is a book a reader does not want to put down. The index is precise. Appendix one, "Food Safety Websites," discloses 12 Websites like FoodSafety.gov. Excellently, appendix two, "Nutrition Websites," shares 11 Websites such as Nutrition.gov. Outstandingly, appendix three, "Comparing Diets," exposes the advantages and disadvantages of diets presented in three sections. The further reading section points out 30 other fabulous texts on nutrition. The invaluable glossary defines 120 informative terms. Vital for academic, public, and school libraries, as well as people researching nutrition.—**Melinda F. Matthews**

740. **Biopesticides Handbook.** Leo M. L. Nollet and Hamir Singh Rathore, eds. Boca Raton, Fla., CRC Press, 2015. 308p. illus. index. $135.96; $111.97 (e-book). ISBN 13: 978-1-4665-9652-8; 978-1-4665-9653-5 (e-book).

This handbook, international in scope, distills an amazing array of information about biopesticides into one very accessible resource, starting with an introduction that lays out the case for the use of biopesticides to promote crop vitality.

The book is arranged into five sections: Biopesticides: Types, Metabolism, and Modes of Action; Biopesticide Residues; Biopesticides, Regulatory Schemes; Biochemical Biopesticides; and, Plant Extracts, Wastes and Fungi as Pesticides. Readers can peruse the book cover to cover or quickly focus on a particular topic, like the history of biopesticides, biopesticide regulations, the impact of biopesticides on bodies of water, the drawbacks to using petroleum products as biopesticides, and a wide range of other issues.

All of the chapters are authored by field experts. Figures and illustrations enhance the text, and an index facilitates searches within the volume. This essential resource is a necessary addition to academic libraries and will find wide use by students and researchers in a number of fields.—**ARBA Staff Reviewer**

741. **Food in Time and Place: The American Historical Association Companion to Food History.** Paul Freedman, Joyce E. Chaplin, and Ken Albala, eds. Oakland, Calif., University of California Press, 2014. 395p. index. $49.95. ISBN 13: 978-0-520-28358-9; 978-0-520-95934-7 (e-book).

Interest in food and cooking is increasing rapidly. Cooking shows on television, magazines, and cookbooks covering a wide range of cuisines are everywhere. It is not surprising that food history is a growing academic discipline. The role of food in culture is important, so this interdisciplinary field calls on scholars from diverse areas. This volume edited by three academics includes essays by scholars, food writers, cookbook authors, and curators. The essays demonstrate different approaches to food history. Regional histories examine the food of a geographic area. There are chapters on premodern Europe, China, India, the Middle East, Africa, and America as well as a paper about migration and transnational cuisines. The section about cuisine is broader, covering topics such as restaurants, cookbooks as resources for social history, and the invention of modern cuisine by the French. The final part, Problems, looks at food and popular culture, postmodern food developments, and the search for artisanal and local foods rather than bland, mass-marketed brands. All of the papers have bibliographies for those seeking further information. This diverse collection will intrigue scholars working in the fields of history, anthropology, and culinary arts.—**Barbara M. Bibel**

742. **Food Studies Online. http://alexanderstreet.com/products/food-studies-online.** [Website] Alexandria, Va., Alexander Street Press. Price negotiated by site. Date reviewed: 2016.

Food Studies Online advertises itself as a one-stop provider of a wide variety of food-related resources for researchers and activists. The collection is comprised of an assortment of proprietary and public materials. Users will gain access to several bodies of privately controlled materials through the Alexander Street Ephemera Collection, Prendismo Small Farm Interview Collection (28 hours, some interviews with industry figures), and an array of documentary films that seem to have little thematic continuity. The remainder of the collection is fleshed out with materials available elsewhere, including the Discovery Menu Collection (23,000 items drawn from the New York and Los Angeles Public Libraries) and food- and agriculture-related photographs drawn from the National Archives and Records Administration's collections. These are primarily English-language materials and they are overwhelmingly focused on the United States since 1900.

Research in these materials can be done several ways. The site offers featured collections and a set of broad themes such as Titles, Subjects, Publishers, and Archival Collection. All seem to channel users toward proprietary materials. The videos contain transcripts that can be searched by keywords, and viewers can fast forward to the relevant text. This is very useful function, but the keyword searches also revealed a major weakness in the collection, which its provincialism. When I typed in the terms "organic" and "California," for example, I expected more than the 29 hits that the search generated (a similar search on Google Scholar generated 2.6 million hits). Close examination of the *Food Studies Online* material showed that most materials actually focused on the food industry in upstate New York. The advanced search function allows for more targeted searching capabilities, but the result, when I used the same terms, was zero entries. The phrase "French cuisine" generated 11 hits. This is not to say that the materials in this collection are without merit, but there is a regional bias towards the Northeastern United States and the contents are, even on those terms, more limited than items freely available elsewhere, including the New York Public Library, Los Angeles Public Library, and the American Memory site at the Library of Congress.—**Joseph E. Taylor III**

743.   **Handbook of Plant Nutrition.** 2d ed. Barker, Allen V. and David J. Pilbeam, eds. Boca Raton, Fla., CRC Press, 2015. 773p. illus. index. $149.95; $104.97 (e-book). ISBN 13: 978-1-4398-8197-2; 978-1-4398-8198-9 (e-book).

Advances in many aspects of plant nutrition necessitated the publication of the second edition of this title first published by CRC Press in 2007. There is some repetition with the first edition, but this is minimized by several things. First, most of the chapters are written by different experts. Second, the content reflects current interests within plant nutrition; most chapters contain less on the discovery of essentiality or beneficial action, and there are fewer tables on elemental composition of different plants and different plant parts. Third, there is more known now about the importance of lanthanides in plant nutrition, so this topic gets its own chapter.

The handbook is organized into five sections: an introductory first section is followed by the second section, "Essential Elements: Macronutrients," with chapters on nitrogen, phosphorus, potassium, calcium, magnesium, and sulfur. Section three, "Essential Elements: Micronutrients," has chapters on boron, chlorine, copper, iron, manganese, molybdenum, nickel, and zinc. Chapters on aluminum, cobalt, lanthanides, selenium, silicon, sodium, and vanadium comprise the fourth section, "Beneficial Elements." A final section contains the conclusion, which is followed by an index and an insert of figures and color photographs of plants suffering from nutrition deficiencies.

This guide to plant nutrition is geared to an academic audience and is highly recommended to college and university libraries, even to those that already own a copy of the first edition.—**ARBA Staff Reviewer**

744.   McLean, Alice L. **Asian American Food Culture.** Santa Barbara, Calif., Greenwood Press/ABC-CLIO, 2015. 211p. illus. index. (Food Cultures in America). $49.95. ISBN 13: 978-0-313-34144-1; 978-1-56720-690-6 (e-book).

This selection in the Food Cultures in America series focuses on how major Asian culinary traditions have permeated American commercial and home kitchens. Specifically emphasizing Chinese, Japanese, Korean, Filipino, and Vietnamese cuisine, the book's opening historical overview examines how each ethnicity came to America and how they adapted their culinary tastes and skills to a new land. We learn of the small successes and numerous hurdles faced by the immigrants in their desire to maintain and share their food traditions. For example, we read how the US Department of Agriculture once classified water spinach, a Southeast Asian dietary staple, as a "noxious weed," prompting a ban (since rescinded) on its cultivation and hurting the livelihoods of Asian American farmers, wholesalers, and more. The overview does an excellent job of relaying the impacts of such things as war, politics, disease, and famine on the development of Asian American food culture.

Other chapters detail the main ingredients in the selected cuisines, from the common grain of rice to unusual flavorings like galangal root. They discuss particular cooking philosophies and techniques, such as pickling and fermenting, as well as special equipment like the wok. The chapters then survey typical home meals, i.e., what is served, how it is served, etc., as well as restaurant and special occasion meals. The book also touches on the Asian perspective concerning the relation between food, medicine, and health.

As if this were not satisfying enough, the author generously includes a varied sampling of recipes, a glossary of each ethnicity's food terms, an excellent resource guide, bibliography, index, and a lengthy chronology covering everything from the Spanish occupation of the Philippine Islands to the opening of the first P.F. Chang's Bistro. In taking readers on a journey from the simplicity of a single bowl of rice to the cultural crossroads of a salmon sushi burrito, this book will have your mouth watering with knowledge of a rich and delicious Asian American food culture.—**Laura Herrell**

745.   Newton, David E. **GMO Food: A Reference Handbook.** Santa Barbara, Calif., ABC-CLIO, 2014. 336p. index. (Contemporary World Issues). $58.00. ISBN 13: 978-1-61069-685-2; 978-1-61069-686-9 (e-book).

The multidimensional debate surrounding genetically modified organism crops (GMOs), is addressed in this volume of the Contemporary World Issues series.

Beginning with a comprehensive history of genetic science and its agricultural implications, the book then provides a balanced look at the issues surrounding genetically modified foods, such as how public opinion differs from Europe to America, how GMOs can benefit or harm human health, or whether or not to label GMO foods.

In addition, writers from fields as diverse as biology, pharmacology, law, and farming weigh in with strong research and varied personal opinions on multiple aspects of the subject. For example, organic farmer Tony Owen's essay defines the GMO debate as political rather than scientific. The book also profiles a number of leading figures and organizations on both sides of the debate, such as biologist and Genentech founder Herbert W. Boyer, environmental watchdog group Food and Water Watch, and the often newsworthy Monsanto. With ample access to data and documents such as court cases and government protocols, in addition to an annotated bibliography, helpful glossary, and a detailed timeline, this book is a go-to resource on the globally vital subject of GMOs.—
Laura Herrell

746.   Pessarakli, Mohammad. **Handbook of Plant and Crop Physiology.** Boca Raton, Fla., CRC Press, 2014. 1031p. illus. index. $209.95; $146.97 (e-book). ISBN 13: 978-1-4665-5328-6; 978-1-4665-5329-3 (e-book).

New data in the field of plant and crop physiology necessitated this third edition of the handbook in which approximately 90 percent of the material is entirely new— the remaining 10 percent is updated and modified. Edited by Mohammad Pessarakli, a professor in the School of Plant Sciences, College of Agriculture and Life Sciences at the University of Arizona, Tucson, the handbook contains contributions from 105 specialists, scientists, and researchers from 17 countries. The result is a title designed to serve as a resource for university courses and for research.

The handbook itself is over 1,000 pages in length, but information is quickly accessible via the subject index or the table of contents. The book is broken into nine parts: Physiology of Plant/Crop Growth and Development Stages; Cellular and Molecular Aspects of Plant/Crop Physiology; Plant/Crop Physiology and Physiological Aspects of Plant/Crop Production Processes; Physiological Responses of Plants/Crops under Stressful (Salt, Drought, Heat, Nutrient Deficiency, and Other Environmental Stresses) Conditions; Physiological Responses of Plants/Crops to Heavy Metal Concentration and Agrichemicals; Physiology of Plant/Crop Genetics and Development, Bioinformatics and Using Computer Modeling in Plant Physiology; Plants/Crops Growth Responses to Environmental Factors and Climatic Changes; and Future Promises: Plants and Crops Adaptation and Biotechnological Aspects of Plants/Crops Improvement. Chapters in these sections cover a plethora of topics: seed dormancy, the growth orientation of underground shoots, the role of nitric oxide in plant development, physiology of crop productivity in cold climates, drought physiology of forage crops, arsenic toxicity and tolerance mechanisms in crop plants, carbon dioxide, climate change, crops in the twenty-first century, and the use of sewage in agriculture and related activities.

This important title is recommended for academic libraries, even those that own a previous edition of the handbook.—**ARBA Staff Reviewer**

747.   **Routledge International Handbook of Food Studies.** Ken Albala, ed. New York, Routledge/Taylor & Francis Group, 2014. 408p. index. (Routledge International Handbooks). $65.95pa. ISBN 13: 978-1-138-01949-2; 978-1-203-81922-7 (e-book).

Interest in food and nutrition is growing rapidly. Cookbooks, diet books, and popular books on nutrition are best sellers. Academic studies in these areas are also very popular. Students and scholars are examining food in different cultures, eating habits, food history, as well as nutrition, health, and public health. Food studies, an interdisciplinary program, is emerging as an academic field. This new title in Routledge's International Handbooks series provides an introduction to food studies for students and professionals interested in pursuing careers in this area.

The editor, a professor of history at the University of the Pacific, has collected articles from more than 30 scholars working in various areas related to food. They are from all over the world. Chapters covering the social sciences, the humanities, interdisciplinary food studies, and special topics in food studies demonstrate the broad range of topics in this field: anthropology of food, food and communication, journalism, food and literature, food and American studies, food museums, culinary arts and food service management, food justice, and food and the senses. Each article contains a brief history of food research in the discipline, information about research methodologies, ideologies, and theories, resources for research, and a bibliography. Students will also find information about archives, grants, and fellowships. This is a very useful resource for academic libraries supporting any food-related programs.—**Barbara M. Bibel**

748.   Sarkar, Prabir K., and M.J. Robert Nout. **Handbook of Indigenous Foods Involving Alkaline Fermentation.** Boca Raton, Fla., CRC Press, 2014. 629p. illus. index. $179.95; $125.97 (e-book). ISBN 13: 978-1-4665-6529-6; 978-1-4665-6530-2 (e-book).

Indigenous alkaline-fermented foods (AFFs) are widely (and almost exclusively) consumed in Africa and Asia. This self-described "reference-cum-textbook" is the first work devoted solely to AFFs. It records AFFs, documents the preparation processes, and discusses AFF properties, culinary use, nutritional quality, and benefits. Though some AFFs are produced on an industrial scale or for export, the majority are still produced on a small scale or at home.

The introduction provides a history of fermentation, its role as a preservation agent, and its other advantages, focusing specifically on AFFs. This is followed by nine chapters: "Diversity of Plant-Based Food Products Involving Alkaline Fermentation," "Diversity of Animal-Based Food Products Involving Alkaline Fermentation," "Microorganisms Predominating in Alkaline-Fermented Foods," "Quality Aspects of Alkaline-Fermented Foods," "Safety Aspects of Alkaline-Fermented Foods," "Challenges Associated with Technological Aspects for Modernization of Alkaline-Fermented Foods," "Value-Added Products from Alkaline-Fermented Foods or from Microorganisms Predominating Therein," "Future of Alkaline-Fermented Foods for Traditional Markets," and "Outlook," followed by an index. Each chapter concludes with a list of references.

The book is directed at an academic and professional audience—graduate students, researchers in food science and technology, and those working in nutrition, dietetics, food microbiology, and related disciplines. Highly recommended for academic libraries.—**ARBA Staff Reviewer**

749.   Thurston, Robert W., Jonathan Morris, and Shawn Steiman. **Coffee: A Comprehensive Guide to the Bean, the Beverage, and the Industry.** Lanham, Md., Rowman & Littlefield, 2013. 416p. illus. index. $61.00. $59.99 (e-book). ISBN 13: 978-1-4422-1440-8; 978-1-4422-1440-8 (e-book).

This could have been a glitzy (appropriately enough) coffee table book on the subject of coffee, but instead the editors have produced a comprehensive, scholarly (but not stuffy) volume on the subject that covers exhaustively all aspects of the product from its cultivation and marketing to its various manifestations and its world-wide consumption (there is even a concluding chapter, "How to Make a Great Cup of Coffee"). The book consists of 63 individually signed chapters of about five to eight pages each in length that are grouped into five different parts. The first and largest part (with 18 chapters) is called "The Coffee Business" and deals with general contemporary conditions, like the nature of the coffee plant, cultivation concerns, pickers, processing problems, and specialty coffees. The second part contains articles specifically on the contemporary coffee trade followed by profiles of seven major coffee-producing countries, including India, Vietnam, and Brazil, that stress the importance of coffee in each economy. This section ends with similar material on nine such countries as Russia, the United States, and France that are important consumers of coffee. Part three deals with a history of coffee and its effects on social life (e.g., the importance of coffee houses in English history). Part four contains nine chapters on the varieties and qualities of coffee and health concerns related to coffee. The last part contains five chapters on the future of coffee that covers topics like genetically modified coffees. The three editors also wrote many of the chapters (e.g., the editor-in-chief, Robert Thurston, wrote over a dozen). Their credentials and those of the other contributors are given in a separate appendix. Most are academics or people related directly to the coffee trade. Throughout each article important terms are given in bold type. Each of these terms is defined in a special glossary that is followed by a seven-page index. Although there is no general bibliography, each chapter concludes with a notes section that contains material on sources used. Scattered about the text are a few black-and-white photographs. This is an attractive, important, and fascinating sourcebook on one of the world's favorite beverages.—**John T. Gillespie**

Horticulture

Handbooks and Yearbooks

750. **The Gardener's Year.** New York, DK Publishing, 2015. 320p. illus. index. $24.95pa.. ISBN 13: 978-1-4654-2457-0.

Lifelike DK photography and organization make this a worthy investment in horticultural reference. The drawings, instructions, and models explain seed and stock selection, planting, and harvesting of a broad range of flowers and edibles, including dwarf fruit trees. By arranging data and colorful landscapes by season, the work promotes variety, as with trees and shrubs that produce appealing, textured stems for winter viewing. Identification of flora by both common and botanical names increases likelihood of purchasing the same varieties shown in photos. The six-page index lists primary and secondary topics, as with bedding plants for summer and dwarf rootstock. A practical coffee table book for gifts to hobby gardeners and new homeowners and a reasonably priced resource for public, high school, and community college libraries. Highly recommended—**Mary Ellen Snodgrass**

31 Biological Sciences

Biology

Dictionaries and Encyclopedias

751.   **The SAGE Encyclopedia of Stem Cell Research.** 2d ed. Eric E. Bouhassira, ed. Thousand Oaks, Calif., Sage, 2015. 3v. index. $475.00/set. ISBN 13: 978-1-4833-4768-4; 978-1-4833-4766-0 (e-book).

The SAGE Encyclopedia of Stem Cell Research (2d ed) is a three-volume reference source containing over 250 articles covering various topics related to stem cell science research as well as religious, ethical, legal, social, and political perspectives. The target audience for this source would include upper-level secondary students and undergraduate students seeking basic stem cell biology information, as well as information on clinical trial updates, legislative information, and information on the ethics of stem cell research.

Each volume contains a comprehensive alphabetical list of all articles. Volume one also contains a reader's guide (broad topics and their specific entry names), an introduction from the editor, a list of contributors, and a short chronology of key events. Articles continue in volumes two and three; volume three concludes with a resource guide, appendixes of key U.S. Presidential Executive Orders on stem cell research (2007 and 2009), a U.S. Senate Hearing report (2010), and a complete topic index to all volumes. There is a brief glossary.

Main entry narratives average two to four pages in length; some entries are divided into subcategory topics. Broad categories for articles include topics related to adult and nonadult stem cells, animal models, cancer stem cells, clinical trials in the United States and worldwide, industry and educational research institutions, methods to study stem sells, key organizations and people, stem cell applications, and stem cell legislation or information related to country or U.S. state. The tone and reading level for articles is academic, and not intended to be comprehensive. (The editor states in the Introduction that a fully comprehensive view of the subject was not possible). Articles conclude with *see also* cross-references to other articles and a further readings bibliography. Selective entries have medical images, charts, tables, or illustrations.

A minor criticism would be a lack of a comprehensive index at the end of volumes one and two for ease of use. *The SAGE Encyclopedia of Stem Cell Research* (2d ed) offers a basic introduction and overview to key topics related to stem cell science and research. Most appropriate for high school libraries and college libraries that have a need for academic material on the topics presented.—**Caroline L. Gilson**

Anatomy

Handbooks and Yearbooks

752.   Barnes-Svarney, Patricia, and Thomas E. Svarney. **The Handy Anatomy Answer Book.** 2d ed. Canton, Mich., Visible Ink Press, 2016. 370p. illus. index. $21.95pa. ISBN 13: 978-1-57859-542-6.

This volume in the Handy Answer series offers a close, system-by-system look at human anatomy. While focusing on descriptions and primary functions of each component of our body's system, the book shares other material readers may find helpful regarding the history, statistics, diseases, and more about human anatomy, physiology, and pathology. This second edition has been updated to reflect the most current science related to human anatomy.

Tabbed for easy reference, each chapter focuses on a particular body system, such as the skeletal system, with additional chapters discussing the history of anatomy, human growth and development, and helping human anatomy. A unique question-and-answer format makes the material extremely navigable and easy to comprehend. Questions are sensibly connected, for example, "what are the functions of platelets," "where are platelets produced," and "what happens if blood does not clot." The book houses over 1,200 of these questions and their concise, but scholarly answers.

The generous use of color illustrations, shaded text boxes, tables, and charts make the abundant material truly engaging. Supplementary material includes a list of books and Websites for further study, a glossary, and an index. The book is perfect for younger students in particular.—**ARBA Staff Reviewer**

753.   **Student's Anatomy of Stretching Manual.** Hauppauge, N.Y., Barron's Educational Series, 2014. 192p. illus. index. $24.99pa. ISBN 13: 978-1-4380-0391-7.

The Student's Anatomy of Stretching Manual is a comprehensive guide focused on helping readers understand the mechanics and benefits of proper stretching. It accomplishes this via a well-organized collection of important stretching techniques highlighted by vivid, full-page anatomical illustrations sure to capture the reader's eye.

The manual is organized into four main sections. The Anatomy Overview depicts body regions and the systems (muscular, skeletal, nervous, and circulatory) and movements most directly relevant to stretching. The Principles of Stretching section provides a clear definition of stretching as well as key information, including stretching safety, types of stretching, parts of the body affected by stretching, and how stretching benefits people with different needs.

The Basic Stretches section includes fifty stretches affecting eight regions of the body, such as the shoulder, back, leg, and foot, etc. Succinct text descriptions explain how to properly perform each stretch, point out variations, and target the specific muscles. But what stands out are the excellent anatomical illustrations clearly marked to guide readers to the involved muscles. These pages also include text boxes highlighting stretching safety considerations.

The book concludes with a Coloring Workbook and glossary that students can use to further their understanding of and familiarity with the muscular, skeletal, and nervous systems. Athletes, young and old, and anyone studying sports medicine, human anatomy, physical therapy, and more will refer to this outstanding manual again and again.—**Laura Herrell**

754. Wilsdon, Christina, Patricia Daniels, and Jen Agresta. Illustrated by Cynthia Turner. **Ultimate Bodypedia: An Amazing Inside-Out Tour of the Human Body.** Washington, .C., National Geographic Society, 2014. 272p. illus. index. $24.99. ISBN 13: 978-1-4263-1722-4.

Whether interested in human anatomy or, perhaps, "grossed out" by it, who hasn't wanted to take an inside-out tour of the human body? National Geographic Kids *Ultimate Bodypedia* offers lots of irresistible and fun facts about how a body functions. Full-color photography and state-of-the-art graphics dominate the pages and entice readers to truly examine the body and all of its systems from the external to the cellular.

The authors have crafted a convivial yet clear examination of body parts and systems, including organs, nerves, and more. We learn, for example, of all the pieces within our respiratory system working as we breathe in and out, a seemingly simple action which requires a trachea, bronchioles, alveolar sacs, capillaries, and other things. The authors also make sure to provide a broader perspective by adding historical facts. Readers will enjoy learning, for example, how the ancient Greeks and Romans assumed one's personality depended on the balance of their bodily fluids; someone quick to anger was most likely overflowing with bile! The book is also adept at conveying how the body systems function in the real world, e.g., the impact of exercise on muscle fibers, the achievement of organ transplants, etc.

In addition to truly amazing illustrations and photographs, which showcase our insides from the tiny DNA molecule to our complex brain, colorful text boxes and bold fonts highlight a dynamic design that appeals to readers young and old. The book also provides a glossary and a directory including multimedia resources for learning more about the fascinating world of the human body. An index rounds out the text.—**Laura Herrell**

Botany

Handbooks and Yearbooks

755. Beidleman, Linda H., and Eugene N. Kozloff. **Plants of the San Francisco Bay Region: Mendocino to Monterey.** 3d ed. Oakland, Calif., University of California Press, 2014. 455p. illus. index. $39.95pa. ISBN 13: 978-0-520-27859-2.

Home to over 2,000 species of trees, shrubs, flowers and other plant life, California's San Francisco Bay Area is a verdant and diverse botanical region. This book is a newly updated visual guide to the abundant plant life residing within the valleys, coastlines, marshes, woodlands, and hills of this region. The book covers the nine counties that ring the San Francisco Bay, from Monterey in the south to Mendocino in the north.

An introductory section establishes how best to use this guide, and includes information on geographic ranges, common versus scientific names, plant measurement, how to read keys, and more. Supplemental information provides tips on how to grow native plants as well as the current state of conservation efforts.

Preceding the guide is a lovely color-plate section which helps to expose a plant's physical details such as color, texture, flower, seeds, and/or foliage. The descriptive guide itself arranges plants into three major groups: nonflowering plant species and families, flowering plant families, and flowering plant species. Further differentiations are provided as needed. Descriptions will generally include excellent line drawings as well.

This third edition has added 21 new plant families and 155 new species to its catalog and has updated over 300 scientific names where necessary. While the photographs make this guide user-friendly, its scientific categorizations make this quite valuable to professionals and students alike.—**ARBA Staff Reviewer**

756.   Helyer, Neil, Nigel . Cattlin, and Kevin C. Brown. **Biological Control in Plant Protection: A Colour Handbook.** Boca Raton, Fla., CRC Press, 2014. 276p. illus. index. $124.95; $87.47 (e-book). ISBN 13: 978-1-84076-117-7; 978-1-84076-601-1 (e-book).

This second edition is a completely revised version of the 2003 publication and includes a number of new color photographs, additional pest and beneficial organisms, a new section on the practical aspects and application of biological control, and a final chapter that puts biological control in perspective. The original objective of the first edition remains the same in the second: to create a handbook with profiles and color photographs of as many biological control organisms as possible.

Six chapters comprise the book. The first, "The Practice and Application of Biological Control," discusses parasites and parasitoids, predators, pathogens, strategies for biological control, Integrated Crop/Pest Management (ICM/IPM), practical aspects of biological control, and pest monitoring. "Biological Control in Various Crop Systems," follows and covers arable new crops, fruit, and protected crops. "Biology of Some Common Target Pests," chapter three, disseminates information about slugs and snails, spider mites, woodlice, millipedes, leafhoppers, whitefly, aphids, caterpillars, and beetles, among others. The longest section of the book is chapter four "Arthropod biological control agents." Species characteristics, life cycle, crop/pest association, and influence of growing practices are given for several varieties of spiders, insects, beetles, wasps, and more. For instance, readers learn that the wolf spider is identified by the position of the eyes and by color and amount of hair. Wolf spiders are active in the day and night, and a female wolf spider may reproduce three times a season (early summer onward). These hunting spiders feed on a variety of small insects or mites on the ground and do not normally climb plants. Wolf spiders are more commonly found in humid areas among crops that offer shelter. In chapter five, readers learn about beneficial pathogens like bacteria and fungi. The final chapter, "Biological Control in Perspective," covers such topics as the control of foreign plants and foreign pests, the regulation of biological control, and the future of biological control. A glossary, references, further reading section, list of useful Websites, and an index round out the work.

This handbook is recommended to public and academic libraries but would also be of interest to individuals interested in biological controls for gardens large and small.—**ARBA Staff Reviewer**

757.   Littlefield, Larry J., and Pearl M. Burns. **Wildflowers of the Northern and Central Mountains of New Mexico: Sangre de Cristo, Jemez, Sandia, and Manzano.** Albuquerque, N.Mex., University of New Mexico Press, 2015. 389p. illus. maps. index. $29.95pa. ISBN 13: 978-0-8263-5547-8; 978-0-8263-5548-5 (e-book).

Intended as a guide for anyone interested in the more common flora of the northern and central mountains of New Mexico, *Wildflowers of the Northern and Central Mountains of New Mexico* is the result of a collaborative effort by two well-respected experts. Pearl Burns teaches wildflower identification courses and leads hikes for various groups, including the United States Forest Service. Larry Littlefield is professor emeritus of plant pathology and volunteers at the Sandia Mountain Natural History Center.

The introduction contains basic information on using the book and descriptions of the topography of the Sangre de Cristo, Jemez, Sandia, Manzano, San Pedro, Ortiz, and Manzanita Mountains. This is followed by entries on 350 wildflowers and flowering shrubs, arranged by color. Each entry includes several color photographs featuring the entire plant and close-ups of its flowers; family common name; scientific name; physical description; flowering period (selected); and habitat. The text ranges from approximately 150 to 180 words each. The work concludes with text and illustrated glossaries, references, and indexes of common names and scientific names.

Hikers, amateur botanists, or anyone interested in identifying wildflowers in their native habitats in the northern and central mountains of New Mexico will find this book useful—especially since there are not many books of its kind. Libraries in New Mexico and Colorado should purchase.—**January Adams**

Zoology

General Works

Handbooks and Yearbooks

758.   **Animal Ethics. http://animalethics.org.uk/.** [Website] Free. Date reviewed: 2015.
The *Animal Ethics* Website offers users basic information on animal rights issues. The Website provides access to a free online book that outlines the author's animal rights ideology and provides statistics in the form of illustrations to teach users about the extent of animal abuse that occurs worldwide.

The book is titled *How to do Animal Rights* and is separated by chapter on the home page. As the user scrolls down, he can access additional chapters and print illustrations that provide facts and information predominantly relating to factory farming. The author of this book is a self-proclaimed animal rights activist and has degrees in biology and psychology, as well as a doctorate in animal behavioral psychology. The writing is often pathetical, but informative as it includes a variety of statistics and facts.

The homepage is not complicated to navigate and there are many additional resource sites included on the left side of the page. There is no glossary to reference, but the author provides definitions within the online book for words that students may not immediately recognize.

Though this material may be useful for students and activists hoping to understand how to become an advocate for animal rights, it is not ideal for students who are not already interested in the subject matter. Overall, it is an adequate and well-priced resource.—**ARBA Staff Reviewer**

759.   Baker, Lawrence W. **Animal Rights and Animal Welfare: A Documentary and Reference Guide.** Santa Barbara, Calif., Greenwood Press/ABC-CLIO, 2015. 351p. illus. index. (Documentary and Reference Guides). $100.00. ISBN 13: 978-1-61069-942-6; 978-1-61069-943-3 (e-book).

Are animals creatures with feelings and souls or simple beasts "destitute of reason?" How do the answers to questions like those bear on animal welfare—specifically the human care of animals participating in research, exhibition, etc., and animal rights, or the idea that all animals should have the same rights as humans? This collection of 51 varied primary source documents relates to all sides of the animal rights and animal welfare debates. Intended as a solid launching point for further study, the book does well in its clear and chronological exploration of a number of topics ranging from the superiority of the vegetarian diet to the infliction of pain upon animals used in scientific research.

The documents include book excerpts, acts of government, proclamations, news articles, court testimony, and much more. The selections can be riveting, such as the testimony of Lisa Lange, a vice president for the animal rights organization PETA, as she confronts a fast-food restaurant chain's accusation of illegal harassment, or the excerpt from Upton Sinclair's *The Jungle.* Each carefully sourced piece is accompanied by background and analysis, as well as ideas for further reading. With contributions from philosophical giants like Aristotle and Tolstoy, to recent U.S. presidents and leaders in the literary, political, or scientific worlds that orbit animal concerns, this book offers intelligent and eye-opening perspectives.—**Laura Herrell**

760.   **Endangered Animals of the World.** Chicago, World Book, 2015. 8v. illus. maps. index. $209.00/set. ISBN 13: 978-0-7166-5620-3.

Seven volumes in this set are dedicated to examinations of samples of 20-30 species from geographic areas (Africa, Asia, Australia and Pacific Islands, Europe, North America, South America, and the oceans) while an eighth book focuses on an examination of both categories of extinct animals (carnivorous and herbivorous dinosaurs) and individual species such as the dodo and the passenger pigeon. Each volume begins with an introductory essay either explaining why animals go extinct or why wildlife in the region is threatened. The area-specific volumes include legends explaining the symbols used to mark the primary causes of endangerment such as hunting, pollution, and global warming. Maps depict the natural range for each threatened species, and a diverse range of illustrations accompany each entry. In many cases, photographs are used, but drawings, reproductions of prints, and photographs of museum exhibits also appear. Glossaries specific to the text of each individual volume do not include pronunciation guides.

Although the writing throughout the set consistently offers clarity and parenthetical comments to explain complex ideas to younger readers, the volumes offer an opportunity to work on more advanced research skills. Each of the seven area-specific volumes features an explanation of the different organizations which assess the threat-level to the species in that work, noting that different criteria are often used, resulting in disagreement about the status of any given species. Since the titles use the word "endangered" and the introductory essays call the species "threatened," readers need to be able to distinguish between the use of broad terms and more technical scientific appellations. The selection of species can seem arbitrary, ranging from little-known invertebrates like the Giant weta to well-known endangered species such as gorillas and blue whales.

Advanced elementary school readers and all middle school readers could benefit from the material in the works, which include lists of books, Websites, and organizations with additional information on the topics in each volume.—**Delilah R. Caldwell**

Birds

Handbooks and Yearbooks

761. Baldassarre, Guy A. **Ducks, Geese, and Swans of North America.** Rev. ed ed. Baltimore, Md., Johns Hopkins University Press, 2014. 2v. illus. maps. index. $69.95/set; $69.95 (e-book). ISBN 13: 978-1-4214-0751-7; 978-1-4214-0808-8 (e-book).

The 2014 edition of *Ducks, Geese and Swans of North America* is the latest update of perhaps the most well-known and respected text on North American waterfowl. This series was first published in 1942 and has been updated several times since. This two-volume set covers all native species of waterfowl that breed in North America, as well the introduced Mute Swan. Volume one covers swans, geese, and dabbling ducks while volume two covers diving ducks and sea ducks.

Each chapter in the book covers one species and includes information on virtually every aspect of the species. The information is divided among 11 topics: Identification; Distribution; Migration Behavior; Habitat; Population Status; Breeding Biology; Rearing of Young; Recruitment and Survival; Food Habits and Feeding Ecology; Molts and Plumages; and Conservation and Management. The standardized format makes it very easy for the reader to find specific information. Each chapter has several color drawings and photographs plus maps of each species' breeding and wintering ranges. All of the information presented in the volumes is meticulously documented and referenced. Literature cited is included on a CD-ROM accompanying the books, apparently to reduce the size of the books, as the citations run to an impressive 104 additional pages of text!

The Ducks, Geese and Swans of North America series has long been one of the "gold standard" references to these species and this latest edition continues that tradition. It has been carefully updated with the latest information from the most recent studies and surveys up to about 2010. While waterfowl are generally well-studied and much information about them is fairly well-known, there is still a great deal of new information in this edition. I found it particularly interesting to read about the latest population trends among species, as waterfowl are carefully managed to try to protect their numbers.

The extensive information on a relatively limited topic may make this book more suitable for a college library or a scientific library with a similar focus. Certainly no library at a college with a wildlife management program or biology program should be without it. However, it would be an excellent addition to any library or the bookshelf of any individual interested in North American waterfowl.—**David Hawksworth**

762.　Day, Leslie. Illustrated by Trudy Smoke. Photographs by Beth Bergman. Foreword by Don Riepe. **Field Guide to the Neighborhood Birds of New York City.** Baltimore, Md., Johns Hopkins University Press, 2015. 378p. illus. index. $24.95pa. ISBN 13: 978-1-4214-1618-2; 978-1-4214-1619-9 (e-book).

This guide focuses on the 90 bird species commonly seen in New York City. This diversity of species illuminates the importance an urban area can have to bird conservation. Besides supporting a large human population, many readers may be surprised at the critical habitat for birds provided by New York City with its many large parks and its position along the Atlantic Flyway, a major migration route. Following some basics of bird anatomy and terminology, the majority of the guide is made up of species accounts arranged taxonomically. Each account lists where and when to find particular birds, origins of the name, description, size, nests and eggs, behavior, voice, and ecological role. Multiple high-quality photographs accompany each account and illustrate appearance as well as behaviors. The last part of the guide lists birding hot spots to visit, bird organizations, and resources.

Some unusual facts are interspersed in the species accounts, which adds interest. For example, the yellow-rumped warbler account notes this warbler's ability to digest the wax in bayberries, which allows them to stay the winter. There are no summary pages with multiple birds for a quick comparison among similar species that most bird guides employ. Readers need to be somewhat familiar with bird species or flip through pages to identify an observed species. The omission of a map emphasizes the guide's focus on city residents rather than visitors. Overall, this guide is not just a source of information, but fosters an appreciation for the wildlife that surrounds us every day.—**Karen Bagne**

763.　Eastman, John. **Birds Nearby: Getting to Know 45 Common Species of Eastern North America.** Mechanicsburg, Pa., Stackpole Books, 2015. 188p. illus. index. $24.95pa. ISBN 13: 978-0-8117-1484-6.

This highly enjoyable, regional guide elevates the stories of the ordinary, easily sighted birds residing in eastern North America through the use of gorgeous color photography and interesting facts. The author conveys his great appreciation for the natural world in compiling this guide, which showcases 45 common species of birds ranging from the ubiquitous American Crow to the ever noble Great Horned Owl. Simply organized as a bird-by-bird catalog, the author nonetheless provides ample information noting specific behavior, name origins, diet, breeding range, migratory habits, vocal characterizations, and much more. From details such as the favorite nesting sites of the American Goldfinch (dogwoods, shrub willows, and hawthorn thickets, if you please), we glean the author's tremendous respect for his subjects. Readers may also delight in the occasional obscure tidbit of birding lore, including, for example, how the writer Henry David Thoreau took joy in the "delicious sound" of crows in winter, or how a cofounder of American ornithology, the Scotsman Alexander Wilson, was inspired to compile descriptions of new world bird species immediately upon shooting a red-headed woodpecker the day he arrived in America.

Stunning and intimate photographs capture birds in their element, whether perching or taking to the air. This simple, yet lovely book can be enjoyed by avid birders or the casual nature lover alike.—**Laura Herrell**

764.　Elphick, Jonathan. **The World of Birds.** New York, Firefly Books, 2014. 608p. illus. maps. index. $75.00. ISBN 13: 978-1-77085-304-1.

The World of Birds is a very informative introductory book on all aspects of birds and bird biology. Approximately the first half of the book is divided up into chapters covering various topics on birds such as anatomy, flight, breeding, migration, and bird habitats. One particularly eye-opening and rather startling chapter is entitled "Birds and Humans" and reveals many of the reasons why many bird species are declining due to the actions of people. On a more hopeful note, it also covers some of the ways people are trying to help save birds. All of these sections are richly illustrated with many fine color photographs and clear, easy-to-understand, drawings.

The second half of the book contains brief descriptions of all of the world's bird families. For each family, there is an information box with general information on the characteristics of the birds in that family such as number of species, size, range, nest type, number of eggs, preferred habitat and, typically, a listing of the species in the family that are threatened or endangered. The text for each family provides additional information for each of the families and highlights many of the more well-known or unusual species in each family. Obviously there are far too many bird species to go into great detail, but it does a very good job of describing what makes each bird family and its members unique. It details many unusual facts and characteristics about the various species. Every page of the bird family description section has one or more superb color photographs of species in that family.

The book also includes an index, a glossary, and an appendix describing The International Union for Conservation of Nature's criteria for rating the vulnerability of Threatened and Endangered Species. In addition, a list of suggested readings provides further information on each of the book's subjects and a list of organizations to contact for additional information on birds and bird conservation.

The book had only a few slight drawbacks. Some of the taxonomy is not up-to-date, but, of course, it's almost impossible for any book to be completely accurate with new research constantly revising the taxonomy of birds. The author is English, so the English bird names and English spelling of words may be unfamiliar to North American readers (although, in all cases, the scientific names of birds are also included).

However, these minor flaws don't begin to diminish the overall excellent quality of the book. I found it to be full of good information for people interested in learning about birds as well as many interesting facts about unusual species. The excellent photographs will be intriguing for any reader and expect it will make them more interested to learn more about the birds depicted. believe it would make an excellent addition to any general library and be an excellent resource to help people learn about birds and their many fascinating habits.—**David Hawksworth**

765.   Garrigues, Richard. **Photo Guide to Birds of Costa Rica.** Ithaca, N.Y., Cornell University Press, 2015. 256p. illus. maps. index. $24.95pa. ISBN 13: 978-1-5017-0025-5.

Casual travelers and bird-watchers will delight in this handy *Photo Guide to Birds of Costa Rica.* The book is designed as a small, portable guide that is easier to carry than larger, more verbose field guides. It is a companion guide to the more extensive *The Birds of Costa Rica,* but differs in its photographic focus and emphasis on the birds a traveler is most likely to see, or the rarer species one desires to see in the beautiful country of Costa Rica.

Opening pages do an excellent job of explaining the structure and information within the book. Readers will find birds demarcated by their family description. The species accounts then include the following: species name, measurements, field marks, habitat and behavior, voice, and status and distribution. In addition, each bird comes with a thumbnail map of Costa Rica which is color-coded in regard to a species' range.

The most wonderful feature of this book, of course, is the high-quality color photography. Some species may be accompanied by more than one photo if there are significant physical differences between male/female or adult/juvenile birds. The photographs do well to highlight the field marks of each species and are truly a pleasure to look at for experienced and novice bird watchers alike. It is also important to note that the order in which the birds are presented may slightly differ from the order in *The Birds of Costa Rica* due to design issues.

Additional material includes a two-page map of Costa Rica, an illustrated guide to a bird's anatomical features, a glossary, and a species index. In spite of the book's seemingly narrow focus, a variety of readers would find it interesting: travelers, photography buffs, and, of course, bird lovers.—**ARBA Staff Reviewer**

766.   Leseberg, Nick, and Iain Campbell. **Birds and Animals of Australia's Top End.** Princeton, N.J., Princeton University Press, 2015. 272p. illus. maps. index. $27.95pa. ISBN 13: 978-0-691-16146-4.

Birds and Animals of Australia's Top End is part of the WILDGuides Wildlife Explorer Series. The Top End refers the northern region of Australia's Northern Territory near Darwin. The region is ecologically diverse and a popular destination for tourists. Following general maps of the area, the guide provides a brief summary of regional geography, geology, and weather. The guide is well suited for travelers and provides practical tips on how to find and watch wildlife, including nocturnal species, as well as a short synopsis of the area's popular national parks and reserves. Descriptions of wildlife come next making up the bulk of the guide. Animal groups are first covered broadly with a brief description followed by the individual species accounts representative of some of the most observable and interesting species. Although the focus is on birds, from shorebirds to nightjars to parrots, the guide also covers mammals, reptiles, and amphibians. Headers at the top of each page make it easy to flip to the correct section. Additionally helpful is the use of a full and a short index. Each species account includes high quality photographs, identification tips, brief life history, and a section on where to find them. Rather than a comprehensive guide to animals, the authors have created a practical and easy to use wildlife guide to enhance any trip to the region. The concise text, beautiful photography, appealing layout, and a focus on conspicuous species successfully merge the best features of a travel guide and a picture book for browsing at your leisure.—**Karen Bagne**

767.   Stallcup, Rich, and Jules Evens. **Field Guide to Birds of the Northern California Coast.** Oakland, Calif., University of California Press, 2014. 294p. illus. maps. index. $24.95pa. ISBN 13: 978-0-520-27617-8; 978-0-520-95838-8 (e-books).

In this important selection from the California Natural History Guides we have a handy, user-friendly reference for both amateur and expert birdwatchers. Focusing on Northern California's coastal counties the book conveys the necessary ecological detail behind the lands and waters frequented by many diverse avian species. The book initially explores the hows and whys of bird watching, particular climates and habitats of the Northern California coastal birding range, and general information regarding birding ethics, seasons, and migration. The introduction also considers the complex and highly mutable factors behind bird taxonomy, or their systematic sorting based on physical characteristics, habitat, etc.

All of this background provides an essential structure for the subsequent family and species accounts of nearly 250 birds both common and obscure. Accounts may detail physical attributes, nesting habits, mating behavior, and other information particular to the species. For example, we read of the "Western" Snowy Plover, a small federally threatened shorebird with unusual mating habits, or the curiously named Rhinoceros Auklet, a seabird very difficult to sight from land.

The guide culminates in an outstanding reference section, which includes maps and information on the region's best birding sights and nature centers, easy to read occurrence charts, a glossary, and beautiful color photographs of many of the aforementioned birds. Produced with real knowledge, care and affection, this guide serves as a wonderful companion for both the casual nature lover and the serious bird watcher. Its small size makes it easy to carry along on birding excursions. Recommended for private collections as well as public and school libraries.—**Laura Herrell**

768.   West, George C. **North American Hummingbirds: An Identification Guide.** Albuquerque, N.Mex., University of New Mexico Press, 2015. 233p. illus. index. $24.95pa. ISBN 13: 978-0-8263-3767-2; 978-0-8263-4561-5 (e-book).

North American Hummingbirds is an attractive book with copious photographs and illustrations of the creatures that often appear to the uninitiated as tiny, colorful blurs. George C. West is professor emeritus of zoophysiology at the University of Alaska, Fairbanks, the author of numerous scientific papers, and the coauthor of various other books. His expertise on the physiology and ecology of birds shines through in this pocket guide.

The introduction contains basic information on identifying hummingbirds of North America using size; shape and proportions; gorget color and shape; body color; wing feather patterns; behavior; and voice. A helpful discussion of scientific names and species codes is also included. This is followed by four sections titled "large hummingbirds," "medium sized hummingbirds," "small hummingbirds," and "accidentals" (the eight species of hummingbirds rarely seen in North America). Each of these sections is divided by entries on specific birds. The information includes the common name; Latin name and its meaning; basic identification; descriptions of adults and juveniles; voice; similar species; distribution and migration; courtship and nesting; and nutrition and molt. Each entry is supplemented with eight colored illustrations and over ten photographs. The abundance of drawings and close-up photographs from different angles makes the work very user friendly. The text ranges from approximately 600 to 1,000 words each.

The book concludes with Measurements and Weights of Adult Hummingbirds, Diagrams and Glossary of Hummingbird Characteristics and Terms, References, and an index.

The work more than fulfills its intended purpose of helping birders and banders identify, age, and sex the 17 species of hummingbirds found in North America. Anyone interested in identifying hummingbirds will find this lovely book indispensable. As this book is probably most useful outside library walls, libraries may also wish to obtain a circulating copy.—**January Adams**

Mammals

Handbooks and Yearbooks

769.   Feldhamer, George A. and others. **Mammalogy: Adaptation, Diversity, Ecology.** 4th ed. Baltimore, Md., Johns Hopkins University Press, 2015. 749p. illus. index. $110.00; $110.00 (e-book). ISBN 13: 978-1-4214-1588-8; 978-1-4214-1589-5 (e-book).

The fourth edition of *Mammalogy: Adaptation, Diversity, and Ecology* is a thorough introduction to the animals in the large and diverse Class Mammalia. Written by five leading mammalogists, along with contributions from numerous experts in the field, this text offers in-depth information on a very broad and rapidly changing field. Chapters are divided into five main parts: history of the field and current research, biological functions and physical structures, adaptations and diversity, behavior and ecology, and special topics including diseases, domestication, and conservation. New to the fourth edition are taxonomic revisions, newly discovered species, updated photos and figures, and citations to recent literature. The chapters on behavior and ecology especially have been updated to reflect recent advances in the field. This book offers a very comprehensive introduction to the study of mammals and should be required reading for students interested in the field.

This text is nicely laid out and while figures are somewhat lacking in color they are concise and nicely illustrate the topic at hand. A summary is provided at the end of each chapter, along with a short list of suggested readings and discussion questions. A much longer and detailed reference list is included at the end of the book. Although written as a textbook for a mammalogy course each chapter stands on its own and can be read independent of the others without a loss in understanding on the part of the reader. Written for an upper-level undergraduate or graduate audience, this book is best suited for the academic library.—**Andrea C Kepsel**

Marine Animals

Handbooks and Yearbooks

770.   Santhanam, Ramasamy. **Nutritional Marine Life.** Boca Raton, Fla., CRC Press, 2014. 290p. illus. index. $119.95; $83.97 (e-book). ISBN 13: 978-1-4822-6205-6; 978-1-4822-6206-3 (e-book).

Nutritional Marine Life fills a gap in the literature due to its focus on the nutritional qualities of edible marine life. Aimed at undergraduates and graduates in fisheries science, marine biology, aquatic science, and marine biotechnology, the book also serves doctors and dieticians and anyone involved in seeking ways to provide people in developing and underdeveloped countries with highly nutritious, accessible food.

An introduction is followed by chapters on phytoplankton, seaweeds and marsh plants, jellyfish, crustaceans, mollusks, echinoderms (starfish, sea urchins, sea cucumbers), prochordates (sea squirts), fish, turtles, and mammals. For each animal or plant, the book includes a color photograph, phylum, class, order, family, common name, area of distribution, habitat, description, and nutritional facts. So, in chapter seven, for instance, readers can easily locate the sea urchin, Tripneustes gratilla, which lives on the sea bottom in the Indo-Pacific, Hawaii, and the Red Sea; from Mozambique to the Red Sea; and off the west end of Australia. Its nutritional properties include protein and several amino acids and dipeptides.

The book concludes with references and an index. This high-quality reference source deserves a spot in every academic library, particularly those institutions supporting marine biology or fisheries programs.—**ARBA Staff Reviewer**

Reptiles and Amphibians

Handbooks and Yearbooks

771.   **Amphibians and Reptiles of the US-Mexico Border States.** Julio A. Lemos-Espínal, ed. College Station, Tex., Texas A&M University Press, 2015. 1056p. illus. maps. index. (W.L. Moody Jr. Natural History Series). $90.00. ISBN 13: 978-1-62349-306-6; 978-1-62349-313-4 (e-book).

In the first bilingual text on the herpetofauna of the 10 states bordering the U.S.-Mexico region, Julio A. Lemos-Espenal describes more than 600 species of frogs, toads, salamanders, sea turtles, alligators, lizards, and snakes. The 10 states making up this region include four in the United States—California, Arizona, New Mexico, and Texas—and six in Mexico—Baja California, Sonora, Chihuahua, Coahuila, Nuevo Leon, and Tamaulipas. Each chapter is dedicated to a specific state, with the first two providing an introduction to the book and justification for the nomenclature used, particularly when there have been disagreements in the literature about species names. The chapters begin with an introduction to the states that includes an overall description of species richness and broad geographical characteristics that influence species distribution. Next is a section covering previous herpetological studies, including an overview of major survey expeditions undertaken, the people and organizations responsible for the establishment of key herpetological collections, and significant publications. Finally, the bulk of each chapter is made up of the physiographic characteristics of the state and how this has influenced the distribution of the herpetofauna. This section provides an overview of the biotic communities, geography, hydrology, climate, and geological history that has shaped the present-day environment for amphibians and reptiles. Also, discussion includes the number of amphibian and reptile species present in each of the ecozones of the state, including those that are endemic and those that reside on both sides of the border. Six hundred colored plates of individual species are provided at the dividing point between the English and Spanish versions of the book. An appendix provides a checklist of all the species discussed in the book, followed by a 57-page list of references, organized by state, and approximately a 100-page index. Unlike other guides to reptiles and amphibians, this book does not provide biological or ecological information on individual species, but rather emphasizes how herpetofauna distribution is shaped by environment influences. Although written by a faculty member at the University of Mexico, the text is accessible to the common reader, and recommended for libraries in border states.—**Kevin McDonough**

772.   **The Leatherback Turtle: Biology and Conservation.** James R. Spotila and Santidrián Pilar Tomillo, eds. Baltimore, Md., Johns Hopkins University Press, 2015. 219p. illus. maps. index. $45.00. ISBN 13: 978-1-4214-7108-0; 978-1-4214-1709-7 (e-book).

This book comes at a crucial time, as this ancient and extraordinary animal—the largest reptile in the world, faces great challenges to its survival. The book expertly gathers contributions from an array of scientific disciplines (marine biology, environmental science, zoology, etc.) which provide readers with a multipronged understanding of the Leatherback and the issues it is facing. Writings thoroughly explore the animal's evolutionary biology, physiology, reproductive biology, geographical range, diving and nesting behavior and much more.

Experts offer exhaustive detail in terms of background, analysis, and conclusions regarding a particular topic with the goal of establishing the most comprehensive tool for understanding and protecting these unique creatures. For example, part two, Life History and Reproduction, relays extensive work on the turtle's reproductive biology and behavior. It examines such topics as male and female systems and cycles, nesting patterns, and egg and hatchling development. With the overarching threats of human encroachment on the turtle's nesting beaches and commercial fishing, each section further incorporates existing analysis of other potential threats to the Leatherbacks, such as climate variability, overfishing, egg pronged harvesting, beach erosion, etc. In laying out these threats, the writers then work to create a conservation strategy with which to restore the turtles back to a significant population.

Detailed graphs and tables pinpoint meticulously gathered data. Color photographs highlight the magnificence of these sea creatures in regards to their size, their behavior, and their habitats. Despite the dire issues facing the Leatherback, the book shows tremendous respect for its subject and a genuine, educated commitment to save the remarkable Leatherback.—**Laura Herrell**

773.   Moore, Robin. **In Search of Lost Frogs: The Quest to Find the World's Rarest Amphibians.** New York, Firefly Books, 2014. 255p. illus. index. $35.00. ISBN 13: 978-1-77085-464-2.

This book creatively mixes the rigors of science with the excitement and mystery of an epic quest as it chronicles a series of international expeditions in search of lost frogs. The author, director of the Amphibian Program at Conservation International, has written an intelligent and very personal tome brimming with genuine wonder and admiration for the elusive creatures.

A key component of the book is the generous use of beautiful color photographs. Documenting various aspects of the many varieties of amphibian, as well as the surprisingly diverse landscapes the author traversed in his quests, the photos are a truly stunning gift to readers.

Three sections organize the material with the first—Unravelling a Mystery—providing foundational information about frogs, the author's developing interest in them, and the alarming disappearance of some of the more unusual specimens. The second and largest part—The Search—documents the origins and actions of the massive task of dispatching over 100 researchers on a quest to find these "missing" animals. Chapters here discuss organizational issues, share diary-like entries, and detail the successes and setbacks of the difficult challenge. Part three—A Journey's End—discusses some of the immediate and long-term concerns for the existence of the amphibians, but ends with a message of hope in the creatures' resilience. The book also lists the expeditions covered, organized by country, and has an index. Recommended.—**ARBA Staff Reviewer**

32 Engineering

General Works

Handbooks and Yearbooks

774. **Careers in Science & Engineering.** Michael Shally-Jensen, ed. Hackensack, N.J., Salem Press, 2015. 379p. illus. index. $95.00. ISBN 13: 978-1-61925-860-0.

This book provides a compact resource for examining the wide variety of careers in science and engineering. Readers will learn general information about this booming sector, as well as more targeted information regarding particular jobs.

Alphabetically arranged chapters guide readers through 25 different jobs, ranging from aerospace engineer to zoologist. Within each chapter, readers will find ample and varied information detailing specific work duties, the expected work environment, occupation specialties (e.g., an agricultural engineer may specialize in research, equipment or tech), educational requirements, earnings and advancement potential, and much more. The use of bullet points, shaded sidebars, tables, and an index make the material easy to navigate. Some special features include projected employment trends, "fun facts," a typical day in the life on the job, interviews with professionals, a "snapshot" of the job, and a listing of applicable organizations readers can consult for more information. The book also includes a list of selected schools which offer highly regarded programs in the particular field. An appendix explains the "Holland Code," which provides a useful tool to help potential job seekers match their personalities with career possibilities.

Compiled in a positive, straightforward manner, this book will appeal to those pursuing a science- or engineering-based university program, embarking on their first job search, or considering a shift into this dynamic job sector.—**ARBA Staff Reviewer**

775. **Engineer Girl. http://www.engineergirl.org/.** [Website] Free. Date reviewed: 2015

This freely accessible Website is made available through sponsorship and is a service of the National Academy of Engineering (NAE). The site grew out of the NAE Committee on Diversity of the Engineering Workforce and is overseen by the EngineerGirl Steering Committee.

The information on the site is easily navigated and organized under three main links. The first, Engineers, connects users to interviews with women engineers; information on a typical day of a woman engineer; short, alphabetically organized biographies; biographies of historical women engineers; and a place to ask an engineer a question. The second link, What They Do, takes users to fun facts; lets them "try on a career" by clicking on several categories like civil engineer or environmental engineer; and has Cool Links to other information. How To Get There, the third link, instructs users in how to apply for internships; hosts an essay contest; provides information about clubs and programs; offers links to quizzes and polls; and provides scholarship information. The site also includes further resources for teachers, parents, and students.—**ARBA Staff Reviewer**

776. **TryEngineering. http://tryengineering.org/.** [Website] Free. Date reviewed: 2016.

TryEngineering has something to offer parents, teachers, career counselors, and students K-12 and beyond. IBM, Career Cornerstone Center, the Institute of Electrical and Electronics Engineers (IEEE), and Teachers Try Science sponsor the site which is free to use and free of advertising.

From the main page, users can choose from four main search options: Become an Engineer, Find a University, Lesson Plans, and Play Games. For students getting ready to pick a school, the Find a University section links to over 3,500 universities in 75 countries; simple or advanced searches are available. The Lesson Plans link offers 126 PDF files of curriculum for students ages 4 to 18. The plans can be narrowed by topic and student age. A sample search of robotics lesson plans for students age 16 to 18 produced three plans as of the date of this review. The link for Games takes users to approximately 30 engineering games like Park World (build a thrill ride) and Build a Lifeboat. The information in the Become an Engineer section is the most extensive. Once the link is accessed, users can choose from different majors via a drop-down menu—options include chemical, civil, computer, electrical, mechanical, and more. Selecting mechanical engineering, for example, will take users to a page that has a description of mechanical engineering, career guidance suggestions, and information about the course of study for mechanical engineers. There are also links to camps, internships, scholarships, competitions, and projects related to mechanical engineering. Further links to profiles of practitioners and students of mechanical engineering add value because users can get first-hand insight into a career. A great resource for those interested in a STEM career.—**ARBA Staff Reviewer**

Biomedical Engineering

Handbooks and Yearbooks

777. **The Biomedical Engineering Handbook.** 4th ed. Joseph D. Bronzino and Donald R. Peterson, eds. Boca Raton, Fla., CRC Press, 2014. 4v. illus. index. $339.96/set. ISBN 13: 978-1-4398-2533-4.

This massive compendium of biomedical engineering information is the latest edition of Bronzino's handbook (previous editions in 1995, 1999, and 2006). It now consists of four hefty stand-alone volumes: *Biomedical Engineering Fundamentals, Medical Devices and Human Engineering, Biomedical Signals, Imaging, and Informatics,* and *Molecular, Cellular, and Tissue Engineering,* running in total to almost 5500 pages and hundreds of thoroughly researched entries, each including necessary formulae, charts, illustrations, and substantial bibliographies. Each volume contains a CD with selected illustrations in PDF format. The entries are almost completely rewritten from earlier editions, with significant additions of new material, including a section on ethics in the final volume. Each volume contains a preface, list of contributors (mostly from significant universities in the United States, but with some international contributors), and a volume-specific index. The breadth and depth of the material is exhaustive, and, given the intertwined nature of the material covered, a set-wide index would be a welcome addition. While this resource should be useful to anyone interested in biomedical engineering or the many related fields, it has become so immense over 20 years of development that it practically demands to be reworked as an online resource rather than continuing in an increasingly unwieldy print format. Recommended for libraries with a biomedical program, especially given its competitive price.—**Peter Larsen**

Environmental Engineering

Handbooks and Yearbooks

778.   Spellman, Frank R. **Handbook of Environmental Engineering.** Boca Raton, Fla., CRC Press, 2015. 726p. index. (Applied Ecology and Environmental Engineering). $186.98; $153.97 (e-book). ISBN 13: 978-1-4987-0861-6; 978-1-4987-0862-3 (e-book).

Scientific and technical handbooks are useful references readers can use to locate overviews of specific topics, reference materials, and data. *The Handbook of Environmental Engineering* (HEE) by Frank R. Spellman is an essential reference handbook on environmental engineering; engineering students and professionals in environmental engineering will find this book useful for their work. The book is published by CRC Press, a well-known publisher of scientific handbooks and references.

The HEE has 11 chapters and could be (but isn't) divided into two parts. Chapters one through six introduce and review the basics of environmental engineering (definition of pollution and its tie to technological advancement, causes of pollution, and more) and the fundamental engineering and quantitative skills (advanced algebra, statistics, model development, and the use of models, unit conversions, etc.) required. Chapters 7 through 11 provide a thorough, but not exhaustive, discussion of air, water, and soil pollution, the problem contaminants, and remediation techniques. Major environmental laws (e.g., Clean Water Act and Amendments, Clean Air Act, NEPA) and regulations are discussed when appropriate. Water pollution receives the most in-depth coverage of any topic, with over 200 pages devoted to surface waters, groundwater, and wastewater contaminants and treatment technologies. The chapter on industrial hygiene provides an informative discussion of the environmental problems in the work place, (airborne chemical and particulate contaminants, radiation, noise, and more) as well information on relevant government agencies and their requirements, workplace monitoring, and more.

Spellman, a retired professor of environmental engineering and author of over 100 books, has successfully written a handbook that is both accessible to environmental engineering students and informative for professionals and researchers in the field. Scientific and technical handbooks frequently tend to be dry reading. Spellman's conversational tone makes this a very readable text, especially for less-experienced readers in environmental engineering. Both the conversational tone of the book and the examples and anecdotes help to draw readers into a topic and to illustrate the author's points.

HEE provides readers with excellent access to content through its very detailed table of contents and index. The major sections of each chapter are listed in the table of contents, while the index provides a very detailed subject list of the content. In the index, contaminants are listed by name and include acronyms when applicable.

The book is illustrated with black-and-white line drawings and flow charts, and also includes data and unit reference tables and some graphs. One of the most eye-catching illustrations is a 3D rendering of an environment illustrating the origin and fate of a class of contaminants in that environment (p. 317). The book also includes a glossary of environmental engineering terms in an appendix. In addition, many of the chapters contain topical terminology lists that provide the definitions of more specialized terms. Both of these are especially valuable for students because, as Spellman points out, it is "… necessary to learn the core vocabulary…" (p.4).

In lieu of a bibliography at the end of the book, the author has included a list of "References and Recommended Reading" at the end of each chapter. It is very helpful for the references to be done this way since the citations are associated with the specific topic to which they apply. If the citations were collected into one long list at the end, readers would have a hard time finding pertinent items. The references used include documents from relevant government agencies, articles from research journals, books, and newspapers, and more.

The HEE is a welcome addition to the reference literature in this field. It is very timely, providing detailed information on both emerging (e.g., pharmaceuticals in drinking water) and established environmental topics. This book is recommended for academic and special libraries serving students, professionals, and researchers working in environmental engineering.—**Theresa Calcagno**

33 Health Sciences

General Works

Dictionaries and Encyclopedias

779. **Adolescent Health & Wellness.** Paul Moglia, ed. Hackensack, N.J., Salem Press, 2015. 3v. index. $395.00/set. ISBN 13: 978-1-61925-545-6.

This three-volume encyclopedia covers a wide range of topics that relate to or may be of interest to adolescents and teens. Articles comprise topic areas such as biology and psychological or social issues. Job hunting, substance abuse, and the environment are examples of the diverse range of subjects that the reader will find. Each volume is divided into broad categories such as "Diversity" and "School and Jobs: Skills for Success." This formatting is easy to navigate and there is a useful subject index. Most articles are two to three pages, with a few longer entries that top out at six pages.

There are a few concerns, however, that need to be considered when examining this as a potential resource. The range of topics included in the three volumes is very broad. The downside of this is that there is a clear feeling of scope creep. One could argue that all topics relate to the interest of adolescents. But there are many sources for immediate and current information about composting, hydraulic fracking, and rice. Keeping the focus more narrowly defined would have made this a more useful and accessible source. Most of the articles are clearly appropriate and useful for the adolescent information consumer, but too many articles contain a rehash of information readily available on the open Web. A tighter grip on content would be an important improvement for future editions. There are at least four separate articles related to alcohol: teens and alcohol abuse, binge drinking, alcohol and its effects, and alcohol poisoning. These titles certainly suggest duplicative content.

Also, the target audience or possibly the purpose of the encyclopedia seems to be somewhat confused. Some of the articles read like advice columns. These articles clearly target the teens themselves. Other articles seem to be written for the student looking to write a short paper for a class assignment. These are more traditional in voice and presentation of facts. The information is presented clearly, but many articles do not have a lot of depth. This further limits the potential audience. More careful editing is needed throughout. There are numerous errors in wording and typeset.

Despite these issues, this set may be of use to libraries in the K-12 system or public libraries. It does have a wide range of topics and the writing should be within reach of middle-school-aged students. Older teens may find articles to be a useful entry point for further research.—**Lorraine Evans**

Directories

780. **American Hospital Directory. https://www.ahd.com/.** [Website] Louisville, Ky., American Hospital Directory, Inc., 2016. Price negotiated by site. Date reviewed: 2016.

This subscription-based Website, created and maintained by the privately owned company, American Hospital Directory Inc., provides users with data on more than 6,000 national hospitals. Information is discoverable by using a quick search screen or a criteria-based search. There is also a link for state and national hospital statistics, so a user can find the number of hospitals, number of staffed beds, total discharges, patient days, and gross patient revenue for each state. A click on the name of the state provides specific information about the hospitals within that state. While some basic information is freely available, a subscription is necessary to access the full site. For example, the free profile for Santa Barbara Cottage Hospital provides such things as the address, patient satisfaction rating, total patient revenue, clinical services offered, and inpatient and outpatient utilization statistics. More detailed information about salaries or bed size, for example, require a subscription. Data is drawn from a variety of sources, like Medicare cost data and private hospital reports. Included in the hospital profiles are data on accreditation, services provided, and more. An updates tab and sources tab provide copious details about both. For subscribers the site offers a variety of data services as well as advanced search tools, list creation, and detailed online reporting. Subscribers can also choose from a variety of apps, like a clinical cost analyzer and a market analysis app.—**ARBA Staff Reviewer**

781. **The Complete Directory for Pediatric Disorders, 2015-16.** 8th ed. Amenia, N.Y., Grey House Publishing, 2015. 1108p. index. $165.00pa. ISBN 13: 978-1-61925-551-7.

This award-winning reference is a smartly organized source for medical descriptions, resources, and support services covering 213 pediatric disorders. This eighth edition has been generously updated with the most current information, including contact data listing address, phone, fax, Website, email, and key executives. All listed disorders are clearly explained and report the most current diagnoses and treatments. Also included in the eighth edition is the new entry on Violence in Children and Teenagers, incidences of which have doubled over the past 30 years.

The bulk of this book's information falls into four sections. Section one alphabetically lists over 200 major disorders ranging from Achondroplasia to Wilson Disease. Entries begin with a detailed but comprehensible description of the disorder, including primary symptoms, potential cause, body system affected, and treatment. Entries then list a number of disorder-specific resources, such as federal and state agencies, support groups, associations, Websites, camps, and many others.

Section two includes over 1,000 entries regarding general resources such as government agencies, support groups, newsletters, and youth organizations. These listings may not be limited to a specific disorder, and some but not all entries may be familiar from the first section.

Essays in the third section detail components and functions of 14 body systems, such as the digestive system, or medical categories. This information offers a quick reference in regards to fully understanding a disorder's impact on a particular body system.

Section four provides three indexes for information accessibility: an entry Index, a geographic Index listing entries by state, and an alphabetical disorder and related term index.

Supplementary material rounds out this generous resource, and includes a glossary of medical terms and acronyms, a list of guidelines to follow when pursuing additional information, a list of disorders by biological system, and a timely essay on bullying and its impact on health. An index completes the work.—**ARBA Staff Reviewer**

782. **The Complete Directory for People with Chronic Illness, 2015/2016.** 12th ed. Amenia, N.Y., Grey House Publishing, 2015. 909p. index. $165.00. ISBN 13: 978-1-61925-548-7.

This book represents the 12th edition of the directory presenting a comprehensive look at 90 chronic illnesses, briefly describing the afflictions and offering many resources for support and education. This edition has been updated with a new entry on Post-Traumatic Stress Disorder.

Introductory pages convey helpful material for ease of reference and to promote greater understanding of the nature of chronic illness. These pages include a chart which matches the illness to the affected body system; a listing of body systems with applicable disorders categorized beneath them; an essay titled "Accepting and Coping with a Chronic Illness"; and a gentle but informative guide to moving on from a diagnosis, including questions to ask a doctor, how to seek out information and more.

The entries themselves run alphabetically, covering conditions such as Arthritis, Celiac Disease, Fibromyalgia Syndrome, Obesity, and Thyroid Disease. Some entries reflect general categories such as Mental Illness, Allergies, Growth Disorders, etc. Condition descriptions within each entry are very brief but offer a solid medical explanation of the affliction, its symptoms, and treatment. Following the description is a well-organized listing of national and state resources, support groups, hotlines, research centers, literature (including children's literature if applicable), and media such as audio, video, or Websites. State agencies and associations are listed alphabetically by state. Resource listings will generally include the name of the association, address, phone number, e-mail address, executive representatives, and a general mission statement. Note that each listing, including the condition description, is numbered continuously throughout the directory (for a total of over 10,000 listings). The numbering is of great assistance in organizing a directory of this size.

Closing sections include a listing of general resources (e.g., The American Academy of Pediatrics, The National Rehabilitation Information Center, etc.), a listing of wish foundations, and a listing of resources covering death and bereavement. Two indexes close out the book: an entry name index and a geographic index.

This well-organized and complete resource provides access to immediate information useful to patients, families, caregivers, and more.

Recommended.—**ARBA Staff Reviewer**

783. **HMO/PPO Directory, 2016.** Amenia, N.Y., Grey House Publishing, 2015. 700p. index. $325.00pa. ISBN 13: 978-1-61925-754-2.

This softcover text is comprehensive, well-written, and timely. The publisher and editors have created a detailed and informative resource on the topics of Health Maintenance Organizations (HMO) and Preferred Provider Organizations (PPO). This text spans more than 500 pages.

The cover is professionally designed. It includes color graphics and images that are health care related. The text on the cover and the spine is easy to read; similarly, the text is laid out in a logical format that makes it easy to find information.

The text begins with an introduction and user guide. This provides the user with an overview of the guide including a description of how the HMO/PPO guide is formatted. Key features of the Affordable Care Act (By Years) is presented next. This includes topics such as new consumer protections, improving quality and lowering costs, and increasing access to affordable care. An overview of health insurance coverage in the United States (2014) is provided followed by state statistics and rankings. Throughout this text, tables are effectively used to summarize information. For example, the state statistics and rankings section includes an overview of public and private insurance coverage by state and age brackets, as well as managed care organizations by state, organization, and plan type.

HMO and PPO profiles by state are presented over the next 400 pages. Each state's HMO/PPO section begins with a single page that includes a table summarizing insurance coverage status and coverage by age. Next, detailed content is presented for the respective state with the HMO/PPO companies listed alphabetically. The myriad information includes insurer name, address, Website, subsidiary, year founded, ownership, health plan and services defined, coverage, payment plans offered, geographic areas served, report card publication status, key personnel, and specialty managed care partners.

The appendixes are presented next. Here users will find a glossary of terms and references to industry Websites. Additionally, a plan index directs readers to sources for dental, HMO, Medicare, multiple, PPO, and vision plans. This is followed by a list of providers and the organizations for which they work. Several indexes are included: membership enrollment, primary care physician, and referral/specialty physician. These sections include the organization's name, the number of members, and a useful reference to the organization's location in the text. Black-and-white tables and charts are present throughout this text.

This text will appeal to a wide variety of individuals who are interested in or involved with any aspect of HMO/PPOs. Similar to other health care texts, readers should consider this text as one of many resources that may be consulted. This text will likely complement professional libraries, with an emphasis on organizations that are involved in the delivery of health care including access to care, the delivery of care, and health care payment and reimbursement.—**Paul M. Murphy III**

784. **Medical and Health Information Directory: A Guide to Organizations, Agencies, Institutions, Programs, Publications, Services, and Other Resources.** 29th ed. Farmington Hills, Mich, Gale/Cengage Learning, 2014. 4v. $340.00/set. ISBN 13: 978-1-56995-948-0.

The 29th edition of the *Medical and Health Information Directory* (MHID) presents an updated directory of selected health and medical organizations. Information on each of the organizations listed includes basic directory information. Some entries include descriptive information about the organization. The entire work is comprised of one volume divided into four separate parts with a total of 19 chapters. Volume one, part one contains the descriptive listings for national and international organizations. Part two covers state and regional organizations listed alphabetically first by 45 selected topics, such as autism, and then alphabetically by state. Entries in this section only provide directory information. Also included in volume one, part two is a list of funding agencies that include both directory and descriptive information, and a section covering consultants and consulting agencies listed alphabetically by state with some entries providing both directory and descriptive information and some only providing directory information. Volume one, part three covers a number of agencies or organizations by type, such as quality improvement or managed health care. Each type of agency comprises a separate chapter. Some of the entries in part three include both directory and descriptive entries while others provide just directory information. For example, Chapter 16, "University-Related & Other Nonprofit Research Centers," includes both directory and descriptive information while Chapter 15, "State Government Agencies," only provides directory information. Part four contains three more chapters with directory information including a list of medical and allied health schools by subject area, i.e., nursing, and a list of hospitals. Part four also contains the alphabetical name and keyword index. Consistent with part three, some of the entries in part four include description and directory information while others only provide directory information. For example, Chapter 17, "Federal Government Research Agencies, Facilities & Programs," contains both, while Chapter 18, "Medical & Allied Health Schools," only provides directory information. Chapter 19, "Hospitals," providing a selected list of hospitals by state and city, supplies only directory information and appears incomplete.

There is a wealth of information in the MHID but much of this information can be located in other resources. For example the American Hospital Association has an online and searchable directory of hospitals in the United States. A subject directory would be a welcome addition over the keyword index, which, upon closer inspection, is not inclusive of all the entries. For example, in part one there is an entry for the Academy of Eating Disorders, but checking the keyword index to see a list of other organizations related to eating disorders shows only two, neither of which is the Academy of Eating Disorders. The MHID also appears to lack comprehensiveness. For example, a Web search on "eating disorders and .org" retrieves the National Association of Eating Disorders, which does not appear to be included in this directory.

The directory is intended for both the practitioner and the public but the arrangement of information appears overly complex. The table of contents and user guide, which appear at the beginning of each part, is necessary to navigate the content. The variation in providing directory and descriptive information for organizations is puzzling. There is no explanation for why some entries include descriptive information and others do not. The lack of comprehensiveness to this resource makes using it questionable. For example, in the listing of hospitals some of the states omit entries for larger cities but includes smaller cities. Closer inspection of this anomaly suggests that some listings of hospitals may have been truncated as the listing of hospitals in Indiana stops after Muncie. This resource is now online which will likely be the preferred method of access for most.—**Susan E. Thomas**

Handbooks and Yearbooks

785.   Callahan, Alice Green. **The Science of Mom: A Research-Based Guide to Your Baby's First Year.** Baltimore, Md., Johns Hopkins University Press, 2015. 304p. illus. index. $19.95pa. ISBN 13: 978-1-4214-1732-5; 978-1-4214-1733-2 (e-book).

Representing a genre known for hosting fervent debate, *The Science of Mom* stands out from the crowd. Key to the book's success is its approach. Writing in a learned, but gentle voice, the author provides a measured scientific foundation behind the basics of caring for a newborn throughout his or her first year. Keeping its focus squarely on the most essential information, as opposed to attempting to address too many topics, the book is an easy to read, certifiable resource.

Chapters mainly explore issues surrounding newborn medical procedures, the umbilical cord, feeding, sleeping and the current hot button topic of vaccinations. The chapter on vaccines, in particular, emphasizes the science behind how they work, any risk potential, and how they are monitored for safety. While the author includes anecdotal information in her writing, she reminds readers to differentiate between stories and facts, and causation and correlation. Charts, text boxes, appendixes, and an index enhance the value of this concise, knowledgeable source.—**Laura Herrell**

786.   **Centers for Disease Control and Prevention. http://www.cdc.gov/.** [Website] Free. Date reviewed: 2016.

The official Website of the Centers for Disease Control and Prevention (CDC), a government agency under the Department of Health and Human Services, is a comprehensive educational resource for a wide range of health topics.

The Website is organized by topics that fall under a series of broad categories, including "Diseases & Conditions," "Healthy Living," "Traveler's Health," and "Emergency Preparedness." Each topic leads to its own separate page that offers in-depth information. The main page for diabetes (under "Diseases & Conditions"), for example, provides articles that give a general overview of the condition as well as treatment strategies; studies published by the CDC; data and statistics; and multimedia resources. For teachers, each page offers fact sheets, pamphlets, diagrams, and educational videos that can be useful tools in the classroom.

The CDC's site also serves as a hub for health-related news, such as recent scientific findings and public announcements. For instance, the front page lists recent infectious outbreaks that are being investigated by the agency.

Although the subjects of health, disease, and nutrition can be complex, the site's material is generally accessible to a broad audience. Articles are written in such a way that scientific or medical terms are clearly explained. It should be noted, however, that some publications or studies that are hosted on the site are specifically targeted to scholars or health professionals.

Because the CDC offers such a wide breadth of information, navigating the Website and its many subsections may at first seem overwhelming. Fortunately, the Website offers various ways to search through its content. All topics are additionally organized in an alphabetical index that can be accessed on the front page, and there is also a search bar for users who want to look up a specific subject.

Overall, the official Website for the CDC is highly recommended for high school or college students, teachers, or individuals looking for reliable and up-to-date information on health and wellness.—**ARBA Staff Reviewer**

787.   Fischer, Karen. **28 Days to Younger Skin: The Diet Program for Beautiful Skin Including More Than 50 Recipes.** Toronto, Robert Rose, 2014. 253p. index. 24.95pa. ISBN 13: 978-0-7788-0480-2.

With the knowledge that it takes 28 days for new skin cells to emerge to the surface of one's skin, this book offers an inspired and informative way to ensure that those skin cells do their job of creating a healthier, better you. With a background in nutrition and health science, the author has devised a 28-day program that works to incorporate nutrition into one's standard skincare routine. Beginning with essential knowledge relating to skincare including physiological basics, aging factors, the effects of "good" foods and "bad foods" upon the skin, and much more, the book then lays out a 14-day meal plan (designed to be repeated for a total of 28 days) that helps improve the look of one's skin.

Key to this plan is the understanding of how certain elements in foods affect one's skin. The book provides ample information about AGE's, or Advanced Glycation End products, and how it is important to reduce their influence on skin by choosing the right foods and cooking methods. Readers also learn about which foods are alkalizing and which are acidizing, and how to get their balance right.

Filled with FAQ's, lists, charts, and questionnaires, readers will find the book interactive and the program highly accessible. An added bonus is the range of easy-to-prepare, delicious recipes, such as a quinoa and pomegranate salad or spiced sweet potato soup. The book ends with references and an index and would be a welcome resource for anyone looking to naturally enhance their beauty and health routine. Highly recommended for the collections of public libraries.—**Laura Herrell**

788.   **HealthCare.gov. https://www.healthcare.gov/.** [Website] Free. Date reviewed: 2016.

The health insurance exchange Website is a necessary page for those living in the 36 U.S. states that opted not to create their own exchange. While this is not an optimal source to gather academic information, it is helpful for those seeking to obtain health insurance and find answers for frequently asked questions relating to individual and family plans.

The exchange provides the most information on issues that users tend to face when applying for coverage, such as uploading documents, applying for Medicaid, open enrollment, and exemption qualification. Students may benefit from perusing the site to gain insight about the health care process and how complicated it can be. This site will not, however, be useful for students looking for educational information apart from a thorough glossary under the "Still Have Questions?" tab.

Consequently, this Website is recommended for those seeking to obtain health coverage for themselves and their families, but is not recommended as an academic resource for students, scholars, and researchers.—**ARBA Staff Reviewer**

789.   **InfoSci-Medical, Healthcare, and Life Science and Technology. http://www.igi-global.com/e-resources/infosci-subject-databases/infosci-medical/.** [Website] Hershey, Pa., Information Science Reference/IGI Global. Price negotiated by site. Date reviewed: 2016.

IGI's *InfoSci-Medical, Healthcare, and Life Science and Technology* collection provides full-text access to nearly 200 e-books of scholarly study and reference materials on a wide range of topics related to technology and the study, practice, and delivery of medicine. Titles in the collection address subjects ranging from the development of e-health services and telemedicine to tools for image analysis and mining technologies for improving health outcomes. Not all titles are exclusively focused on technology; some books are the result of research on new/shifting models of delivering care and tackling health-related issues.

The database provides a basic, advanced, and "expert" search option. The advanced search option allows users to combine keywords with author, title, and publication date parameters. The expert search option allows for search terms to be included, excluded, and weighted which allows users to rank the term within the search results. The expert search option also provides an "inflectional" search feature that includes a dictionary and thesaurus to provide all forms and tenses of the search term. This is a really interesting feature, and the especially direct or simply curious will enjoy it. Search results found using any of the three options can be refined by content type, copyright year, subject, or subject topics. The books are indexed and searchable at the chapter level further facilitating ease-of-access to the collection.

Each book has an annotated table of contents for easy access and browsability. A search box to search within the text is also provided for each book. Book chapters are provided in HTML and PDF formats for easy download. The database also provides tools for citing the books and book chapters.

This resource is highly recommended for health care practitioners, administrators, policy-makers, and students. This is an important collection for anyone with interest in the impact/potential impact of technology on the health care field. The electronic resource is especially recommended, as new titles are made available more quickly than the print copy.—**Kristin Kay Leeman**

790.   Kelly, Evelyn B. **The 101 Most Unusual Diseases and Disorders.** Santa Barbara, Calif., Greenwood Press/ABC-CLIO, 2015. 287p. index. $89.00. ISBN 13: 978-1-61069-675-3; 978-1-61069-676-0 (e-book).

As its title suggests, this book catalogs medical disorders and diseases that fall within the spectrum of rare, unexplained, and outright strange. Blending solid medical expertise with straightforward descriptions in simply structured entries, the book tackles conditions such as Bigorexia, Trench Foot, Stockholm Syndrome, Ichthyosis, and more.

The book is partitioned into five sections which categorize the conditions as follows: Unusual Genetic Disorders, Unusual Mental Health Disorders, Unusual Environmental Diseases and Disorders, Unusual Infectious Diseases and Unusual Diseases, and Disorders with Other or Unexplained Origins. Each section opens with a helpful introduction providing general information about the specific group of conditions to follow. Each entry then provides anecdotal context, definitions, signs and symptoms, diagnosis, treatment, and resources for further information.

Some of the entries are particularly timely, spotlighting diseases like Ebola or conditions like Tech Neck Syndrome. Some are, of course, outright bizarre like the elusive Morgellons, a condition with specific characteristics of an itchy burning sensation with threadlike fibers appearing on the skin, which the medical profession does not believe exists. All entries are fascinating to read, and may be enhanced with patient testimonials, prevention tips, case stories, and other supplemental information.

The book includes a list of numerous resources for further study and an index.—**Laura Herrell**

791.   **KidsHealth. http://kidshealth.org/.** [Website] Free. Date reviewed: 2016.

KidsHealth is a group of Websites that provide accessible and easy-to-understand health resources for children, teenagers, parents, and teachers. The site is managed by the Nemours Center for Children's Health Media, a branch of the nonprofit health organization The Nemours Foundation. All material featured on *KidsHealth* is reviewed by a board of medical professionals.

The front page of *KidsHealth* serves as a portal to four different Websites that each cater to a specific demographic (parents, kids, teens, or educators). With the exception of the site for educators, the *KidsHealth* Websites are structured similarly; the main page of each site features a sidebar that lists broad health topics, such as "Diseases and Conditions" or "Staying Safe." Clicking on one of these topics will lead to a new page in which articles, videos, and other educational resources are listed under further subcategories.

The Website for educators is distinct from the other sites in that it offers teacher guides, posters, worksheets, and quizzes that can be used in the classroom instead of educational articles. Teaching materials are organized by grade level (preschool to high school) and topic ("Human Body," Health Problems," and "Personal Health.").

Generally, all the *KidsHealth* Websites are designed to be approachable and are easy to navigate. Each site also features a search bar in which users can look up resources for specific topics.

For the Websites aimed at kids, teens, and parents, covered health topics are specified to its targeted demographic. For example, the site for parents offers articles on pregnancy and care for newborns, while the site for teens includes articles on such school issues as bullying or study habits. The articles are easy to understand, and technical or medical terms are clearly defined. Furthermore, the kids' Website includes an alphabetical dictionary of medical terms that can be accessed on the sidebar. Each site also features a special Q&A section for commonly asked health questions as well as a library of recipes catered to those with specific nutritional needs.

Overall, *KidsHealth* is an excellent and comprehensive online resource for parents and young students. In addition, *KidsHealth* can be a useful tool for health teachers.—**ARBA Staff Reviewer**

792. Niel-Asher, Simeon. **The Concise Book of Trigger Points: A Professional and Self-Help Manual.** 3d ed. Berkeley, Calif., North Atlantic Books, 2014. 235p. illus. index. $29.95pa. ISBN 13: 978-1-58394-849-1; 978-1-58394-850-7 (e-book).

This third edition of the *Concise Book of Trigger Points* has been updated with the latest research, evidence, and techniques that can help readers isolate and treat their chronic pain.

Specifically, trigger points refer to the spot deep within muscle bands from which a general pain may radiate. They may appear due to a wide variety of reasons, such as repetitive activity, poor posture, whiplash, etc., and can be best characterized as tight lumps, cords, or nodules. This book provides readers with ample information about such things as muscle systems, trigger point diagnoses, and pain maps with the goal of self-healing, education, and care. It is important to note, however, that the techniques and diagnoses in this book should not be used in exclusion of other professional medical advice.

Opening chapters lay the foundation of trigger point physiology and general treatment procedures. Chapters seven through twelve then pinpoint clearly delineated muscle groups with anatomical descriptions, referred pain patterns, and more.

Within each chapter, readers will find illustrations, practitioner and self-help techniques, and frequently asked questions to help guide them through the information. Combined with a visual attention to detail, the wealth of material in this book provides a perfect reference for the experienced practitioner as well as the untried but eager to learn layperson.—**Laura Herrell**

793.   Pez, Catherine. **The 5-Minute Facial Workout: 30 Exercises for a Naturally Beautiful Face.** Toronto, Robert Rose, 2013. 192p. illus. index. $19.95pa. ISBN 13: 978-0-7788-0471-0.

The face is certainly an individual's primary source of expression and interaction, and yet how often has one thought to exercise it? This book aims to enlighten readers about the benefits of a facial "work out" by gathering exercises designed to improve the fitness of over 50 muscles of the face. These "facial gymnastics," as the author refers to them, offer a natural and economical way to combat the effects of aging, injury, and other damaging elements.

The author employs detailed anatomical illustrations to help teach readers about the principle muscles of the face. She further explains essential information regarding skin structure, cell renewal, topical skin treatments, and more. What follows from here are clear instructions accompanied by full-page, color photographs demonstrating proper technique, recommended repetitions, and effects of 30 unique facial exercises. The exercises work to pinpoint particular areas of the face, such as the cheeks, the upper eyelids, the jowls, etc., and can be performed individually or together as part of a whole face program. An additional section conveys the benefits and methods of facial massage. An index makes it easy to locate particular topics like frown lines and exercises for a sagging neck.

Recommended for personal and public libraries.—**Laura Herrell**

794.   Prinster, Tari. **Yoga for Cancer: A Guide to Managing Side Effects, Boosting Immunity, and Improving Recovery for Cancer Survivors.** Rochester, Vt., Healing Arts Press, 2014. 308p. illus. index. $15.96pa. ISBN 13: 978-1-62055-272-8.

Statistics show that survivors of traumatic disease have an increased chance of a better recovery if they have solid support in place. *Yoga for Cancer* is definitely a book cancer survivors will need in their network of support. The author presents 53 traditional yoga poses with easy to follow instructions which she seamlessly connects to particular issues of cancer recovery. She does this by conveying modifications to the poses based on the practitioner's ability and by explaining the targeted benefits of each pose, which may range from simply increasing flexibility to detoxification after chemotherapy.

Preceding the poses are chapters sharing the author's personal story of dealing with cancer and turning to yoga. She discusses the science which connects yoga practice to physical and psychological recovery and provides a strong foundation for those wishing to establish a safe home yoga practice.

Written with a gentle and knowledgeable voice, *Yoga for Cancer* empowers survivors to take a strong role in their health and recovery. The book also includes a bibliography and index in addition to a number of resources for survivors, teachers, and caretakers.—**Laura Herrell**

795.   Rao, Vani, and Sandeep Vaishnavi. **The Traumatized Brain: A Family Guide to Understanding Mood, Memory, and Behavior after Brain Injury.** Baltimore, Md., Johns Hopkins University Press, 2015. 224p. index. $18.95pa. ISBN 13: 978-1-4214-1795-0; 978-1-4214-1796-7 (e-book).

Caregivers, family, and patients living with traumatic brain injury will find this book highly informative and welcoming. Authors Vani Rao and Sandeep Vaishnavi write with a sense of warmth and care that is certain to help those who want to learn more about a timely subject. In this fairly concise book the reader will understand how a complex set of symptoms may be manifested after injury. Recognition of these systems is a vital step to management and recovery. The clarity in which the complex subject of neuroscience is presented is impressive. The book is comprised of five sections—the brain and types of injury, and the emotional, behavioral, cognitive, and physical problems that may arise from brain injury. Sections contain a short, case-study-type narrative and discussion of symptoms and treatment. It is interesting and educational throughout. There is a glossary, index, and a listing of resources. It is very accessible for a wide range of readers and an excellent resource.—**Lorraine Evans**

796.   Richardson, Daniel, Fraser Smith, and Susan Hannah. **The pH Balance Health & Diet Guide for GERD, IBS, & IBD: Practical Solutions, Diet Management, Plus 175 Recipes.** Toronto, Robert Rose, 2014. 288p. index. $24.95pa. ISBN 13: 978-0-7788-0492-5.

For those looking to treat poor digestive health or maintain a balanced pH, *The pH Balance Health & Diet Guide for GERD, IBS & IBD* is an outstanding resource. The book is separated into five parts that cover: pH Basics, GI Basics and Therapies, The pH Diet Program, Meal Plans for the pH Balance Diet Program, and Recipes for the pH Balance and Diet Program. The latter section comprises over half the book and includes health tips on every page. In the first four sections, interesting graphics provide helpful breaks in material that may otherwise seem dense, and charts with frequently used terms will prove useful for readers who are new to the subject matter.

For those looking for more information on pH balance after reading this title, the Resources page offers many Websites to scour for specific material. In addition, the References and Background Reading section is lengthy and offers books, journal articles, and Web articles for reference. While the chapters are structured intuitively, with the first two chapters providing answers to frequently asked questions and the last three devoted to learning about and incorporating a healthy and pH balanced diet, the Index is an excellent tool that will allow readers to search for any key words in the text as well as for specific ingredients in the Recipes section.

Readers who suffer from any of the described conditions in this book, or know someone who does, will find this resource helpful, easy to read, and informative. This title will be found in general circulation in Food and Health.—**ARBA Staff Reviewer**

797.   Smith, Fraser, and Ellie Aghdassi. **Keep Your Brain Young: A Health & Diet Program for Your Brain, Including 150 Recipes.** Toronto, Robert Rose, 2014. 384p. index. $24.95pa. ISBN 13: 978-0-7788-0472-7.

Dr. Fraser Smith and Dr. Ellie Aghdassi's *Keep Your Brain Young* is an excellent informational health guide that will prove useful for an increasing population of seniors. This holistic approach to mental wellness is outlined in five parts: Understanding Brain Diseases, Smart Nutrients, Standard Care for Dementia, The 12-Step Healthy Brain Diet Program, and Menus and Recipes for a Healthy Brain. The extensive menu plan includes many recipes that can be altered to fit vegetarian, vegan, and gluten-free diets.

Keep Your Brain Young gives simple explanations about disorders and nutrition but also provides information on managing and preventing certain disorders, making it a useful tool for those seeking knowledge, prevention advice, or both. The table of contents includes key information covered in each chapter and therefore readers can access desired content quickly. Two pages of academic references may serve useful for readers who are intrigued by the book's content and want further information on a specific subject. An index also makes key word search simple, and even includes foods for those hoping to find recipes containing certain ingredients. Since half the book is dedicated to recipes, this is a useful feature.

Readers should look to parts one and two for information, and to parts three and four for tips and advice. *Keep Your Brain Young* is most likely to be found in general circulation, but its chapters on brain diseases and standard care make it a useful resource for users looking to find basic information on a variety of aging-related issues.—**ARBA Staff Reviewer**

798.   Sothern, Melinda S. **Safe and Effective Exercise for Overweight Youth.** Boca Raton, Fla., CRC Press, 2014. 374p. illus. index. $99.95; $69.97 (e-book). ISBN 13: 978-1-4398-7288-8; 978-1-4398-7289-5 (e-book).

Overweight and obese children and adolescents are part of a growing epidemic. There are numerous obstacles to kids getting appropriate and necessary levels of physical exercise despite evidence about the multiple benefits. Based on vast amounts of scientific research and the author's 24 years of clinical experience, this reference resource addresses this escalating problem and dispenses valuable guidance to health care providers, educators, public health personnel, and fitness professionals who work with youth populations. This guide is intended to complement the *Handbook of Pediatric Obesity: Clinical Management*(2006), coauthored by Sothern.

Chapters one through five review the scientific literature that supports tailored exercise for overweight and obese youth, providing illustrations, exercise instruction, and sample lesson plans. Chapters six through nine include such essential items as a 40-week exercise curriculum and discuss such fundamental matters as the importance of medical monitoring and self-monitoring, clinical and field protocols, realistic expectations for youth struggling with weight issues, and current recommendations for physical activity and fitness. Chapter 10 provides a summary of current studies, aiming to support future research.

Data is well-documented and topics are easily found within the text due to the book's organization and index. In addition to exercise curriculums, the title offers talking points, charts, tables, leveled activities, sample classes, and sidebars with key points and case studies. There are also handouts and forms, which are printable at http://publichealth. lsuhsc.edu. This portal additionally supplies users with further resources, including videos. As the incidence of obese and overweight youth increases, busy professional will need to consult a reliable reference. Thus, this book is highly recommended for academic and medical libraries.—**ARBA Staff Reviewer**

799.   **Worldmark Global Health and Medicine Issues.** Brenda Wilmoth Lerner and K. Lee Lerner, eds. Farmington Hills, Mich., Gale/Cengage Learning, 2016. 2v. illus. maps. index. $310.00/set. ISBN 13: 978-1-4103-1752-0; 978-14103-1755-1 (e-book).

Worldmark Global Health and Medicine Issues is a two-volume reference source which offers 90 topical entries broadly addressing medical and public health issues within a global health context. Narrative entries address not only public health information but also the connections between health and social, economic, political, and ethical impacts. The target audience for this source would include high school and undergraduate students seeking an introduction to global health topics.

Entries are four to six pages in length and are arranged alphabetically. Each entry has six parts: Introduction, Historical Background, Impacts and Issues, Future Implications, a bibliography, and a sidebar which discusses a related topic such as a key organization or historical event. Some entries also contain an excerpt from a relevant historical text or contemporary article illustrating the entry topic. *See also* references to other entries are also given. Most entries have charts and graphs and/or color photos. Primary source material is also highlighted at the end of selected entries.

Also included are a glossary of terms and a chronology of events (at the beginning of both volumes), a list of selected organizations and advocacy groups, and a general resources bibliography of books, articles, and Websites (at the end of the second volume). The set concludes with a general index, referring readers to main entries or entries with primary source material.

Worldmark Global Health and Medicine Issues offers an introductory academic overview to global health and medical issues that broadly incorporates social, economic, political, and ethical issues as well. Most appropriate for school and academic libraries that field global health questions or teach global health courses.—**Caroline L. Gilson**

Medicine

General Works

Dictionaries and Encyclopedias

800.   **The Gale Encyclopedia of Medicine.** 5th ed. Jacqueline L. Longe, ed. Farmington Hills, Mich., Gale/Cengage Learning, 2015. 9v. illus. $1,200.00/set. ISBN 13: 978-1-4103-1730-8; 978-1-4103-1739-1 (e-book).

The Gale Encyclopedia of Medicine, Fifth Edition is a nine-volume reference source with over 2,000 full-length articles covering common medical disorders, conditions, and diseases and tests, treatments, and drugs. The target audience for this source would include users seeking general health and treatment information. It is intended to be comprehensive, not definitive and to be a supplementary source to a consultation with a physician or health care provider.

Each volume begins with a comprehensive table of contents and an alphabetical list of all entries (which this reviewer very much appreciates for ease of use). Volumes one through eight contain main entry content. The ninth volume contains a brief chronology of major medical advances, events, and discoveries, a list of organizations listed in the Resources section of the main entries, a glossary, and a complete topic index to all volumes.

Main entries are arranged alphabetically and have been written by medical experts. Entries fall into one of three broad categories: Diseases & Conditions; Tests, Treatments, Therapies and Other Procedures; and Drugs, Herbs and Supplements. Entry lengths vary from 500 to 4,000 words. Some entries have accompanying color images, including photos, charts, tables, or illustrations. Within each entry, information is broken down into subcategories such as Definition, Precautions, Causes, and Symptoms, Treatment, Prognosis, and Prevention. Bolded terms within entries indicate they have their own main entry listing. Specific key vocabulary terms are defined within individual entries. Brief bibliographies and cross-references to related topics follow most entries. All entries are signed. Content is introductory and easy to read and offers a good overview to the topics addressed. In addition, the fifth edition offers articles covering alternative therapies and features specific Alternatives sections for diseases and conditions that may be helped by complementary therapies.

The Gale Encyclopedia of Medicine, Fifth Edition offers general medical information on diseases, disorders, and treatments in an accessible writing style that is not too technical for average readers. As with other medical reference sources, it should not be a substitute for professional medical care. Appropriate for school and public libraries.—**Caroline L. Gilson**

801.   **The Gale Encyclopedia of Senior Health: A Guide for Seniors and Their Caregivers.** 2d ed. Farmington Hills, Mich., Gale/Cengage Learning, 2015. 5v. illus. index. $859.00/set. ISBN 13: 978-1-57302-746-5; 978-1-57302-752-6 (e-book).

The second edition of this four-color, five-volume set continues to be a highly readable, jargon-free, and beautifully illustrated reference on all aspects of senior health. Aimed at 9th grade to college senior readers, according to the publisher, these and other qualities make it a desirable addition to high school, college, and public libraries, as well as special libraries for seniors and health professionals. However, its high cost and continuing use of previously published material from other Gale encyclopedias also indicate it is probably not an essential purchase, at least not in its print edition and/or for holders of the first edition (see ARBA 2010, entry 1272).

Entries follow the format of other Gale health and medical encyclopedias. The scope of topics is wide and holistic, including diseases and conditions (about 50 percent of content); tests and procedures; drugs, herbs and vitamins; nutrition, exercise and diet; recovery and rehabilitation; professions; devices and tools, and other aging issues.

With 664 alphabetical entries, 73 are new and 229 updated. They are written and signed by medical writers and health care professionals. The publisher calls updates "classic entries," and notes they have updated bibliographies and statistics "so that every entry has at least some added value over the last edition." Many entries also duplicate or are very similar to entries in the Gale encyclopedias of medicine (see ARBA 2000, entry 1413; ARBA 2003, entry 1437; ARBA 2007, entry 1249; ARBA 2012, entry 1263) and nursing and allied health (see ARBA 2002, entry 1506; ARBA 2007, entry 1278, ARBA 2014, entry 1229). Positively, however, entries include *see also* references, and many have lists of resources (books, articles, Websites, and organizations) and/or boxes with key terms and questions to ask your doctor or pharmacist.

Additionally, there are 105 new color images and 179 new or updated tables, charts, and graphs. There is also a foreword and a list of entries grouped by 50 themes, ranging from addiction to women's health. These, as well as features from the first edition (introduction, alphabetical list of entries, and list of contributors) are included in each volume. The fifth volume also contains a list of organizations, a glossary of key terms, and an index. In summary, this is an attractive, comprehensive and easy to use reference that is highly desirable but a bit of a luxury.—**Madeleine Nash**

802.   **The Pregnancy Encyclopedia.** Chandrima Biswas and Paula Amato, eds. New York, DK Publishing, 2016. 351p. illus. index. $40.00. ISBN 13: 978-1-4654-4378-6.

This comprehensive encyclopedia is a welcome addition to the childbirth education canon. Uniquely conceived, its copious information is well-organized into 10 chapters which follow the major stages of pregnancy, delivery, and the postpartum period as well as the fundamental issues that accompany them. The distinct approach of addressing over 300 topics via question-and-answer segments is immensely readable and lends a personal appeal. Some examples from the Planning Your Care chapter include "What is a doula and how can they help with my labor and birth?," "Will I still need a doctor if I have a doula?," and "Can I have my older children present at my home birth?" Answers are concise but well-informed. Other topics range from breastfeeding concerns to pain relief to special needs and more.

To convey information, the book employs a dynamic visual style that includes many color photographs and illustrations, a variety of eye-catching typefaces, textboxes, scientific renderings, and charts. A notable highlight is the 14-page pregnancy timeline leading readers visually and textually from the moment of conception through to 40 weeks gestation. Thoughtfully crafted by leading experts in the field, this excellent reference also includes a glossary, an up-to-date listing of many useful resources, and an index.—**ARBA Staff Reviewer**

Handbooks and Yearbooks

803.　**Gastrointestinal Diseases and Disorders Sourcebook.** 3d ed. Keith Jones, ed. Detroit, Omnigraphics, 2016. 731p. index. (Health Reference Series). $95.00. ISBN 13: 978-0-7808-1457-8; 978-0-7808-1458-5 (e-book).

A volume of the notable Health Reference Series published by Omnigraphics, this book is an invaluable reference regarding basic, comprehensible information about a wide spectrum of disorders affecting the gastrointestinal system. The reference is designed to assist nonmedical professionals, patients, caregivers, and others who are not schooled in these issues but may take a genuine, personal interest in the information. Eight sections organize a profusion of topics, beginning with an overview of the digestive system (how it works, common symptoms, etc.) and then moving into diagnostic procedures, upper tract disorders, lower tract disorders, liver and pancreas disorders, cancers, and food intolerances and infections. A closing section offers a lengthy glossary of specialized terms and a useful directory of organizations working in the realm of gastrointestinal health.

Within each section are detailed chapters addressing all known gastrointestinal disorders and subdisorders. The book gives plenty of emphasis to many common disorders, such as Peptic Ulcers, Appendicitis, Colon Cancer, Gallstones, and Cirrhosis of the Liver. It additionally addresses congenital and pediatric conditions, such as Hirschsprung disease or Omphalocele. Discussion of each disorder is clear and concise. Paragraphs are mainly set up in a question-and-answer format (e.g., "What is indigestion?," "How is indigestion diagnosed?," etc.), and with the addition of diagrams, bullet points, and other visual aids, readers will find the format extremely navigable. Information conveyed for each disorder is copious, but never overwhelming as this reference is clearly targeted to the layperson. Beyond defining the disorder, chapter information may include causes, risk factors, forms of the disorder, prevention, associated conditions, diagnoses, treatment, dietary recommendations, and more.

This third edition conveys the most up-to-date information in regards to treatment, diagnosis, disorder classifications etc., relative to the rapid advancements in medical research happening as we write this.

This reference is not produced to replace professional medical counsel; however, it succeeds at providing intelligent, basic information about gastrointestinal disorders to patients, families, caregivers and, others.—**ARBA Staff Reviewer**

804.   Post, Linda Farber, and Jeffrey Blustein. **Handbook for Health Care Ethics Committees.** 2d ed. Baltimore, Md., Johns Hopkins University Press, 2015. 413p. index. $49.95pa. ISBN 13: 978-1-4214-1657-1.

Aimed at individuals who may not have had a formal background in the field–including community representatives who are included in some institutions' ethics committees–this work's first edition came out eight years ago with the goal of assisting ethics committee members in their roles in education, consultation, and policy development. This edition, written by Linda Farber Post (bioethics, Hackensack University Medical Center; associate professor, Rutgers New Jersey Medical School and St. Georges University School of Medicine) and Jeffrey Blustein (bioethics, philosophy, City College of New York), contains updates, new chapters (on reproduction, disability, and the elderly) and specific information for those serving on ethics committees outside the traditional acute care hospital or medical center settings. The bulk of the book is a 12-chapter curriculum to introduce the fundamentals of bioethics. Other sections include information about ethics consultation, education, organization codes of ethics, key legal cases, sample ethics policies and procedures, and the transcript of a sample ethics committee meeting. There is also useful nuts-and-bolts information such as how to prepare for an Ethics Grand Rounds (including the suggestion of "reviewing a list of relevant articles suggested by a medical library lit search") Though many chapter references are current, and are mainly from medical and scientific literature and associated Websites, some are in need of an overhaul. For example, in the chapter "Special Decision-Making Concerns of Minors," the 1991 edition of Furrow et al.'s *Health Law: Cases, Materials and Problems* is cited. However, the seventh edition of that book was published in 2013. In the "Privacy" section of the chapter "Key Legal Cases," mention is made of an "eventual repeal" of the Defense of Marriage Act (DOMA); it was repealed June 26, 2013.

The Handbook is also available as an e-book. This book is suitable for any medical, hospital, academic, or large public library. Its relatively modest price, straightforward writing, and generous use of case studies make it a book that any nonspecialist with interest in the field would find compelling.—**Martha E. Stone**

805.   Prendergrast, Stephanie A., and Elizabeth H. Rummer. **Pelvic Pain Explained: What Everyone Needs to Know.** Lanham, Md., Rowman & Littlefield, 2016. 213p. index. $35.00; $34.99 (e-book). ISBN 13: 978-1-4422-4831-1; 978-1-4422-4832-8 (e-book).

Pelvic pain can be indicative of many things, and tends to be associated with difficult diagnoses and treatments. This book helps lead both patients and practitioners through the intricate realm of pelvic pain by offering straightforward solutions. The book is structured into three general sections which cover the definitions of pelvic pain, how to treat pelvic pain, and how to maintain pelvic health. These sections are further broken down into concise and effective chapters with paragraphs that make generous use of subheadings for ease of reference.

The material is presented logically and clearly. For example, the material in Pelvic Pain: A Road Map moves from defining the pelvic floor through common pain symptoms, difficulties of diagnoses, contributing factors, and so on. A judicious use of charts, bulleted lists, black-and-white illustrations, tables, personal stories and more will be very helpful to readers. Readers may find some information surprising; for example, that treatment may be best handled via an interdisciplinary approach, that men are also susceptible to pelvic pain, and that there is significant support out there for this particular condition, from the Happy Pelvis online support community to, well, this first-rate book.

Appendixes convey a very good list of pelvic pain resources, including books, products, blogs, and more, as well as a basic evaluation interview which is a good starting point on the path to recovery from this condition. Detailed notes, a bibliography, and an index follow.—**ARBA Staff Reviewer**

Alternative Medicine

Dictionaries and Encyclopedias

806.   **The Gale Encyclopedia of Alternative Medicine.** 4th ed. Laurie Fundukian, ed. Farmington Hills, Mich., Gale/Cengage Learning, 2014. 4v. illus. index. $714.00/set. ISBN 13: 978-1-57302-730-4.

The use of alternative medical therapies is increasing as people seek more holistic care. Many insurance providers now cover chiropractic and acupuncture. The fourth edition of *The Gale Encyclopedia of Alternative Medicine* reflects this with an article about the Patient Protection and Affordable Care Act (Obamacare) and how it will impact alternative care practitioners. This edition of the encyclopedia contains 800 signed, alphabetical entries. Fifty are new. All have resource lists and definitions of key terms in colored text boxes.

The entries cover therapies (acupuncture, chiropractic), herbs/remedies (milk thistle, vitamins), and diseases/conditions (breast cancer, osteoarthritis). Articles about therapies include their history, description, benefits, precautions, and side effects. Those about herbs and remedies include their general use, types of preparation, side effects, and interactions. Entries for diseases and conditions contain a definition, description, causes and symptoms, diagnosis and treatment, allopathic treatment, expected results, and prevention. The contributors provide evidence-based information about the effectiveness of the therapies. A list of organizations and a glossary help readers find further information.

The Gale Encyclopedia of Alternative Medicine is an excellent resource for health information collections in public and consumer health libraries.—**Barbara M. Bibel**

807.   Group, David W. **Encyclopedia of Mind Enhancing Foods, Drugs and Nutritional Substances.** 2d ed. Jefferson, N.C., McFarland, 2015. 400p. index. 75.00pa. ISBN 13: 978-0-7864-4142-6; 978-1-4766-1915-6 (e-book).

This, the second edition of the encyclopedia (see ARBA 2002, entry 1486), has been significantly expanded and revised to include more entries as well as the most up to date research. For example, the inclusion of "Energy Drinks" lists the most currently popular brands (5-Hour Energy, Monster Energy, etc.) and notes any controversies surrounding them. Fourteen categories, beginning with the most basic and least engineered foods, herbs and spices, culminate with the more obscure but newly researched entheogens and nootropics. These categories provide a framework for the more than 1,000 entries that range in length from one paragraph to several pages. Each entry is then described in applicable terms, including common names, food sources, effects, dosages, precautions and more. For example, the entry of Ylang Ylang under the main category of Essential Oils contains its Latin name, describes its effects of slowing the heart rate and relieving stress and depression, points to synergistic oils, and discusses any precautions to use. Each section is prefaced with an overview that summarizes the latest research on any health benefits or concerns particular to that category as well as any notable debates. A bibliography and an index round out the work.

While not meant to be comprehensive or a tool for self-diagnosis (you'll find little in the way of history, noncognitive benefits, or issues, etc.), the encyclopedia nonetheless provides ample information regarding a nascent subject and acts as an excellent resource for further research.—**Laura Herrell**

Handbooks and Yearbooks

808.   **Complementary and Alternative Medicine Sourcebook.** 5th ed. Keith Jones, ed. Detroit, Omnigraphics, 2015. 623p. index. (Health Reference Series). $95.00. ISBN 13: 978-0-7808-1378-6; 978-0-7808-1404-2 (e-book).

The numbers of people turning to nontraditional forms of health care is rapidly growing, whether due to such things as spiraling medical costs, drug scandals, or bureaucratic snags. A volume of the notable Health Reference Series published by Omnigraphics, this book is an invaluable reference offering basic, comprehensible information about a wide spectrum of topics related to complementary and alternative medical treatments. The reference is designed to assist nonmedical professionals, patients, caregivers, and others who are not schooled in these issues but may take a genuine, personal interest in alternative therapies whether for general well-being or targeted health concerns.

Six sections organize the essential topics, beginning with a generous overview of Complementary Alternative Medicine, or CAM. The overview defines CAM, highlights frequently asked questions, discusses CAM relative to children and adults, addresses CAM in relation to current insurance policy, and more. Following sections address current CAM systems (acupuncture, naturopathy, and others), current CAM therapies (vegetarianism, meditation, massage, etc.), dietary supplements (herbs, vitamins, minerals, etc.), and targeted afflictions (cancer, asthma, mental health disorders, etc.). A closing section provides a glossary of specialized terms and offers a useful directory of organizations that provide information and assistance regarding CAM.

As previously suggested, each section is further divided into detailed chapters addressing the particulars of its topic. Section two, for example, discusses acupuncture at length; defining it, applying it to various medical issues, and more. The vegetarianism chapter in section three discusses types, how to derive nutrients from a vegetarian diet, and more. All this information is presented clearly and concisely. Paragraphs make prolific use of headings, and with the addition of diagrams, Q & A's, shaded text boxes and bullet points, readers will find the format extremely navigable. Information is copious, but never overwhelming as this reference is clearly targeted to the layperson. What is notable about this volume is the care with which it reminds readers of the science, benefits, and risks of CAM, a relatively new and rapidly advancing realm of treatments.

This fifth edition conveys the most up-to-date information in regards to complementary and alternative medicine relative to the rapid advancements in research. The reference is not produced to replace professional medical counsel; however, it succeeds at providing intelligent, basic information about many facets of CAM to patients, families, caregivers, and others.—**Laura Herrell**

Specific Diseases and Conditions

Arthritis

809. **Arthritis Sourcebook.** 4th ed. Amy L. Sutton, ed. Detroit, Omnigraphics, 2015. 704p. index. (Health Reference Series). $95.00. ISBN 13: 978-0-7808-1350-2; 978-0-7808-1401-1 (e-book).

A volume of the notable Health Reference Series published by Omnigraphics, this book is an invaluable reference regarding basic, comprehensible information about a wide spectrum of topics related to arthritis. The reference is designed to assist nonmedical professionals, patients, caregivers, and others who are not schooled in these issues but may take a genuine, personal interest in the issues of the all-too-common condition.

Six sections organize the essential topics, beginning with an overview of the joint disorder which points to statistics, risk factors, and affected joints. Following sections address types of arthritis and related rheumatic diseases, medical treatments, self-management strategies, and affiliated issues. A closing section provides a glossary of specialized terms and offers a useful directory of organizations working to assist those who suffer from this disease and their families.

Each section is further divided into detailed chapters addressing the particulars of its topic. Section two, for example, breaks down the great varieties of arthritis and related conditions, such as Rheumatoid Arthritis, Tendonitis, Bursitis, Carpal Tunnel Syndrome, Fibromyalgia, Lupus, and much more. Section three discusses drug therapies, joint surgeries, nonsurgical management, and more, while section four discusses diet, herbal supplements, and other complementary approaches. All this information is presented clearly and concisely. Paragraphs are mainly set up in a question-and-answer format (e.g., "Who provides care for people with Osteoarthritis?," etc.), and with the addition of diagrams, shaded text boxes, and bullet points, readers will find the format extremely navigable. Information is copious, but never overwhelming as this reference is clearly targeted to the layperson. Beyond basic topic information, chapters may include early signs, causes, risk factors, different forms of the disorder, prevention, associated conditions, diagnoses, treatment, latest research, and more. This particular volume is notable for its generous attention to arthritis treatment and pain management strategies.

This fourth edition conveys the most up-to-date information in regards to arthritis treatment, diagnosis, etc., relative to the rapid advancements in medical research. The reference is not produced to replace professional medical counsel; however, it succeeds at providing intelligent, basic information about many facets of this painful and all-too-common joint affliction to patients, families, caregivers, and others.—**Laura Herrell**

Autism

810.   Shane, Howard C. and others. **Enhancing Communication for Individuals with Autism: A Guide to the Visual Immersion System.** Baltimore, Md., Paul H. Brookes Publishing Co., 2015. 326p. illus. index. $49.95pa. ISBN 13: 978-1-59857-221-6.

Two main deficit areas that make up the diagnostic criteria of autism spectrum disorders (ASD) according to the *Diagnostic and Statistical Manual of Mental Disorders* (DSM-5) (American Psychiatric Association, 2013) are social communication and social interaction across contexts; and the other area is restricted, repetitive patterns of behaviors, interests, or activities. Because all individuals diagnosed with autism have deficits in social communication, it is imperative that effective techniques to increase communication skills are designed. The Visual Immersion System (VIM) as described by Shane and colleagues provides an approach to communication intervention that is visually based, thus supporting the acquisition of communication skills through associations made with visual images. Though there are other methods to teach language skills to individuals with autism spectrum disorders, the VIM "focuses on the visual modality to deliver communication intervention" (Shane, et al, 3). Use of visual graphics may be pivotal for individuals with moderate to severe ASD to acquire and adapt to spoken language.

From beginning to end this book provides clear, sequential information about how to assess language across domains in order to identify current skills and deficits and then to be able to utilize effective intervention based on research and clinical experience of the authors. Major objectives are effectively met through the detailed description of the Visual Immersion System, and each chapter defines one of the seven communicative functions, provides information regarding the means of environmental control and a rationale for that function, along with detailed information on how to teach that skill in a variety of settings. Targeted questions to elicit responses and communicative replacements used to express language of control using VIMs are provided, and the final chapter on Social Pragmatics provides culminating support for each of the communication function chapters.

This book provides comprehensive assessment and organized treatment information for experienced professionals to teach language to individuals with ASD. Some knowledge of the terminology and techniques described would be important in order to be effective with VIMs. It would be helpful to include the materials that can be downloaded after purchasing this book. It is a bit frustrating to want to use information in this book, but not be able to get started without the files in the downloadable materials. Overall, this book provides excellent information and guidance to assist professionals who want to find a more effective method of teaching language to individuals with ASD.—**Donna J Kearns**

811.   Smith, R. Garth, Susan Hannah, and Elke Sengmueller. **ASD: The Complete Autism Spectrum Disorder Health & Diet Guide: Includes 175 Gluten-Free and Casein-Free Recipes.** New York, Firefly Books, 2014. 408p. index. $24.95pa. ISBN 13: 978-0-7788-0473-4.

ASD: The Complete Austism Spectrum Disorder Health & Diet Guide is a comprehensive resource book that is sure to be valued among parents, caregivers, and health professionals alike. This title is an educational tool that will help readers better understand what autism is, how it is caused, and most importantly, ways that ASD symptoms can be mitigated through health and diet. Approximately half the book is comprised of recipes free of gluten or casein, naturally occurring proteins that are suspected to increase negative effects of ASD. In addition to providing practical knowledge and research about autism, the book also addresses common health concerns such as weight gain or nutrition deficiency in children with autism. The recipes included will not only appeal to picky eaters, but provide adequate nutrition and meet caloric needs. A helpful index allows for key word search of both academic terms as well as ingredients within the recipes. A comprehensive References and Background Reading section includes books, journal articles, and Web articles for additional information.

This health guide, written by a Developmental Pediatrician, a Health Author, and a Clinical Dietician, is a wonderful reference source that will greatly benefit individuals who know or have children with ASD. It will likely be found in general circulation in Food and Health.—**ARBA Staff Reviewer**

Brain disorders

812. **Brain Disorders Sourcebook.** 4th ed. Keith Jones, ed. Detroit, Omnigraphics, 2015. 688p. index. (Health Reference Series). $95.00. ISBN 13: 978-0-7808-1352-6; 978-0-7808-1397-7 (e-book).

A volume of the notable Health Reference Series published by Omnigraphics, this book is an invaluable reference regarding basic, comprehensible information about a wide spectrum of disorders affecting the brain. The reference is designed to assist nonmedical professionals, patients, caregivers, and others who are not schooled in these issues but may take a genuine, personal interest in the matters.

Nine sections organize a profusion of topics, beginning with an overview of the brain (mainly its development and the effects of toxins upon it) and then moving into degenerative disorders, infections, trauma, congenital disorders, tumors, seizures, and other brain disorders. A closing section organizes updated research on brain disorders, provides a glossary of specialized terms, and offers a useful directory of organizations working in the realm of brain disorders.

Within each section are detailed chapters addressing every known brain disorder and subdisorder. The book gives plenty of emphasis to many common disorders, such as Parkinson's Disease, Alzheimer's Disease, Meningitis, Concussion, Stroke, Tumors, Epilepsy, Headache, and much more. It additionally addresses many of the more obscure disorders known to the medical community, such as Batten Disease, Iniencephaly, or Friedreich's Ataxia. Discussion of each disorder is clear and concise. Paragraphs are mainly set up in a question-and-answer format (e.g., "What is Cerebral Palsy?," "What Causes Cerebral Palsy?," etc.), and with the addition of diagrams and bullet points, readers will find the format extremely navigable. Information conveyed for each disorder is copious, but never overwhelming as this reference is clearly targeted to the layperson. Beyond defining the disorder, chapter information may include early signs, causes, risk factors, different forms of the disorder, prevention, associated conditions, diagnoses, treatment, and latest research.

This fourth edition conveys the most up-to-date information in regards to treatment, diagnosis, disorder classifications, etc., relative to the rapid advancements in medical research.

This reference is not produced to replace professional medical counsel; however, it succeeds at providing intelligent, basic information about brain disorders to patients, families, caregivers, and others.—**Laura Herrell**

813. **The Brain, the Nervous System, and Their Diseases.** Jennifer L. Hellier, ed. Santa Barbara, Calif., Greenwood Press/ABC-CLIO, 2015. 3v. index. $294.00/set. ISBN 13: 978-1-61069-337-0; 978-1-61069-338-7 (e-book).

Neuroscience is a broad topic that includes research on how the brain and the nervous system work. *The Brain, the Nervous System, and their Diseases* includes a broad variety of topics, diseases, and issues within the complex field of neuroscience. This is a three-volume set, compiled by 73 authoritative experts including neuroscientists, family physicians, psychologists, and public health professionals who all work in this innovative and complex field. The books are easy to use as they are organized in the A-Z format. Entries range from popular issues such as Concussion and Alcoholism to more scientific topics such as Blood-Brain Barrier or Prions. The articles are written in a style that makes them useful to people working in the sciences, students working on research at colleges and universities, and the public. Each volume includes the alphabetical list of entries and the guide to related topics. Each entry includes *see also* references and includes citations for further reading on the topic. The third volume has a section at the end titled Experiments and Activities. This unique section includes hands-on activities and other experiments that could be completed in a classroom or school laboratory setting. Each experiment references the encyclopedia entry that is associated with the experiment. The experiments also include citations for further reading. Learning outcomes would augment the interactive educational component of this encyclopedia set. *The Brain, the Nervous System, and their Diseases* would enrich a university collection for undergraduates and graduates in the sciences, as well as the science collection in a public library.—**Amy B. Parsons**

814. Petraglia, Anthony L., Julian E. Bailes, and Arthur L. Day. **Handbook of Neurological Sports Medicine.** Champaign, Ill., Human Kinetics, 2015. 401p. illus. index. $92.00; $49.00 (e-book). ISBN 13: 978-1-4504-4181-0; 978-1-4504-9697-1 (e-book).

Current medical research along with evidence-based practice has made significant advances in how trainers and medical staff treat sports-related injuries. This handbook focuses on the spectrum of neurological injuries in sports. Chapter one describes neurological injuries that are possible in 39 different sporting activities. American football, wrestling, and boxing are obvious violent sports that are discussed. Also included are less violent sports such as bowling, ballet, archery, cheerleading, and many more. There is a detailed discussion of the legal ramifications of closed head injuries and concussions in chapter two, including detailed cases of interest. Part two of the book consists of sports-related head injuries including pathophysiology descriptions, detailed medical definitions, frameworks, evaluations, symptom checklists, and syndromes. Part two also includes a chapter on natural neuroprotective remedies for concussions. The third part of the book focuses on the spine and peripheral nervous system. An important element in the field of sports medicine is "return to play" assessments. These are described and discussed in part three. Lastly, part four includes other sports-related neurological issues with a lengthy chapter on headaches and heat illnesses. All chapters have bibliographical references. Appendixes include sport concussion assessment tools for both adults and children, as well as the American Spinal Injury Association (ASIA) Standard classification of Spinal Cord injury. The *Handbook of Neurological Sports Medicine* would be a rich addition to any academic library collection that supports a health and sports sciences program, undergraduate or graduate level.—**Amy B. Parsons**

Cancer

815.   Adler, Elizabeth M. **Living with Lymphoma: A Patient's Guide.** 2d ed. Baltimore, Md., Johns Hopkins University Press, 2016. 480p. illus. index. $26.95pa. ISBN 13: 978-1-4214-1810-0; 978-1-4214-1811-7 (e-book).

This book provides a focused, intelligent breakdown of the multifaceted disease of lymphoma. Author Elizabeth Adler offers a unique voice in addressing this topic as she melds a scientific researcher's meticulous eye to her own personal experience with the disease.

The structure of the book is key for readers as the material is approached from a very science-based point-of-view, even as the tone is patient-friendly. The book organizes the material into three parts: Living with Lymphoma, Treating Lymphoma, and Understanding Lymphoma. Within each part, chapters partition all the current information into more digestible pieces. Treating Lymphoma, for example, presents chapters on Chemotherapy, Radiation and Surgery, Monoclonal Antibodies, and Other Magic Bullet Therapies, Stem Cell Transplants, Unconventional Therapies, and Survivorship. A chapter may then break down therapy, procedures, side effects, and more.

The material in this second edition has been updated with 10 years of new research applicable to all parts of the book. While some material has been added, e.g., new or improved therapies (such as the use of medical marijuana), some has been removed. In a good sign, more emphasis in this edition has been placed on surviving lymphoma.

The author is generous in sharing her personal experience with lymphoma, which balances the medical language and enhances the reading experience throughout. The book includes helpful supplementary material such as illustrations, tables, suggestions for further reading, a lengthy glossary, and an index.—**ARBA Staff Reviewer**

816.   **The Gale Encyclopedia of Cancer: A Guide to Cancer and Its Treatments.** 4th ed. Kristin Fust, ed. Farmington Hills, Mich., Gale/Cengage Learning, 2015. 3v. illus. index. $526.00/set. ISBN 13: 978-1-4103-1740-7; 978-1-4103-1744-5 (e-book).

This hardcover encyclopedia set is comprehensive and well written. The editor, Advisory Board, and contributing authors have created a useful and informative clinical resource. This set of three encyclopedias spans more than 2000 pages.

The cover of each text is professionally designed. The layout is consistent among the three texts. The cover includes color graphics and images that are medical or scientific in nature. The text on the cover and spine of the book is easy to read.

This encyclopedia set consists of three volumes. Volume one includes "A-E," volume two includes "F-O," and volume three includes "P-Z." Each text begins with identical content. This includes listing the Advisory Board, Contents, Please Read-Important Information section, Foreword, Introduction, Alphabetical List of Entries, Contributors, and Illustrations of Body Systems.

The Please Read-Important Information section informs the reader that this encyclopedia set is intended to be one resource of many that may be used when researching or learning more about cancer. Similar to other medical conditions, it is often recommended that more than one resource be consulted or researched.

The content of each text is detailed and comprehensive. Volume one includes topics "Abarelix" through "Extragonadal germ cell tumors"; volume two includes "Familial cancer syndromes" through "Ovarian epithelial cancer"; volume three includes "Paget disease of the breast" through "Zolpidem".

The flow of the text is presented in a consistent manner throughout each text. For example, medical procedure information includes: Definition, Purpose, Description, Demographics, Preparation, Aftercare, Risks, Results, Morbidity and Mortality Rates, Alternatives, and Health Care Team Roles. Medical conditions include: Definition, Description, Demographics, Causes and Symptoms, Diagnosis, Treatment team, Clinical Staging, Treatment, Prognosis, Coping with Cancer Treatment, Clinical Trials, Prevention, Special concerns. Medication information includes: Definition, Purpose, Description, Recommended Dosage, Precautions, Side Effects, and Interactions. Following each topic resources are listed including Websites, references to specific books and periodicals, and related organizations. This format is very useful.

Text boxes, which are easy to read, are presented throughout the books. Examples include "Key Terms" and "Questions To Ask Your Doctor." Numerous colored illustrations and pictures are included throughout each of the texts.

The end of volume three includes detailed lists of organizations including "Organizations: National Cancer Institute–Designated Comprehensive Cancer Center" and "Organizations: Support Groups, Government Agencies, and Research Groups." Volume three also includes a detailed glossary and index.

This encyclopedia set is well written and detailed. It will likely appeal to a wide variety of individuals who are interested the topic of cancer. This text touches on numerous aspects of cancer, including assessments, treatment, and associated medical conditions. This encyclopedia set will likely complement personal or professional libraries, including those in academic and health care settings.—**Paul M. Murphy III**

817.   **A Guide to Survivorship for Women Who Have Ovarian Cancer.** 2d ed. Robert E. Bristow, Terri L. Cornelison, and F. J. Montz, eds. Baltimore, Md., Johns Hopkins University Press, 2015. 320p. index. $19.95pa. ISBN 13: 978-4-4214-1754-7.

Few new editions are more deserving of the expression "Expanded, Revised, and Enlarged" than *A Guide to Survivorship for Women Who Have Ovarian Cancer.* First published in 2011 (though in the planning stages for many years prior), this second edition has twice the number of pages, 14 tables (none of which appeared in the original edition), and almost double the number of chapters. Editors Robert E. Bristow (University of California), Terri L. Cornelison and F. J. Montz (both Johns Hopkins) are joined by contributing physicians and nurses, the majority of whom are from Johns Hopkins, and who take a conservative approach to treatment; for example, in the chapter titled "Surgery for Ovarian Cancer" they warn of the consequences of minimally invasive approaches such as laparoscopy for the purposes of surgical staging. Ovarian cancer stages I through IV-B are described in an accompanying table. The 17 chapters include essential concepts, treatment options, recovery (both physical and emotional), surveillance, social needs, genetic testing (including current information about protection against genetic discrimination), recurrence, and decision-making around end-of-life care. It should be noted that contributors are realistic about remission, recurrence, and death rates. The book incorporates brief "Personal Perspectives" into most chapters. The authors of these essays are not identified beyond their names. An Internet search revealed that the Ovarian Cancer National Alliance worked with editor Bristow to "include a series of patient perspectives on topics such as chemotherapy, side effects and survivorship" as per http://www.

ovariancancerannualreport.org/, accessed 1/27/16.

Some of the references from major medical journals seem older than necessary; a few are very current. The list of Web-based resources has been brought up-to-date from the earlier edition but surprisingly does not include two Johns Hopkins sites: http://ovariancancer.jhmi.edu/ (from Johns Hopkins Pathology) and http://ovariancancercenter.org (from the Johns Hopkins Ovarian Cancer Center for Excellence.)

It is clearly written, and will be a valuable tool for health care providers, patients, and anyone with an interest in the topic; it is suitable for all libraries and highly recommended for consumer health collections. This title is also available as an e-book.—**Martha E. Stone**

818.　Silver, Julie K. **Before and After Cancer Treatment.** Baltimore, Md., Johns Hopkins University Press, 2015. 296p. index. $18.95pa. ISBN 13: 978-1-4214-1794-3; 978-1-4214-1777-6 (e-book).

With gentle, positive, and well-informed advice, this book guides readers through the many aspects of the cancer healing process. The author, a cancer survivor, professor, and medical doctor specializing in rehabilitation, lends targeted expertise to a number of topics relative to this difficult but ultimately restorative process.

The book excels in pointing out particular struggles such as fatigue, depression, and pain in addition to providing a variety of studied approaches to mitigating them. Early chapters focus on understanding the overall concept of what it means to heal, and thus provide good background information regarding specific treatments, adopting the proper mindset, setting goals, and more. The author establishes, for example, the importance of setting goals by pointing out a three-step plan for doing so (make short term and long term goals, keep them realistic, and write them down).

Further chapters then provide the action plans with which to engage on the road to recovery. Such topics as conventional healing therapies, Eastern and other alternative medical systems, exercise, diet, medications, family support, and spirituality are covered. For example, the "Nourish Your Body" chapter discusses the healing benefits of a good diet as well as the red flags of substances survivors may innately turn toward, like alcohol, fats, or nicotine.

Chapters are not too long and information within them is well demarcated by subheadings for optimal comprehension. They each contain a list of references. Charts, tables, bullet points, and more supplement the material, as does an appendix listing many sources of information and help. An index also makes it easy to find particular topics. The key to the book's success, however, is the mixture of compassionate wisdom and intelligent advice derived from the author's unique perspective.—**ARBA Staff Reviewer**

Hepatitis

819.　Thuluvath, Paul J. Hepatitis C: **A Complete Guide for Patients and Families.** Baltimore, Md., Johns Hopkins University Press, 2015. 288p. index. $19.95pa. ISBN 13: 978-1-4214-1757-8; 978-1-4214-1758-5 (e-book).

This straightforward, smartly presented book provides a wealth of information about Hepatitis C, a viral disease now affecting over three million people in the United States alone. Balancing the need for sound medical explanation with compassionate advice, the book expertly walks readers through symptoms, treatments, related diseases, causes, and more. It is important to note that the information in the book should be considered a supplement to a patient's ongoing dialogue with medical personnel, and not a replacement.

The material is organized into three sections. Understanding Hepatitis C, Liver Disease, and Liver Cancer uses 12 concise chapters to discuss different manifestations of Hepatitis C (e.g., chronic, acute, in children, etc.) and the related conditions of liver disease and liver cancer. The chapters also help to explain the different varieties of the Hepatitis virus (A-E). Part two—Hepatitis C Management and Liver Transplantation—presents six chapters which help readers navigate treatment options including the use of interferons, other antiviral drugs, and combination therapies. Two chapters in this section also discuss liver transplants and the potential for Hepatitis C recurrence post-transplant. A brief third section discusses the relatively new considerations of alternative medicine in the treatment of this disease, such as herbs and acupuncture.

Tables, diagrams, bulleted summaries, and more are extremely helpful in comprehending the material and particularly useful with the complex information on drug therapies and side effects explained in part two. The book contains a list of patient resources, including national organizations related to education, clinical trials, transplants, etc., and an index. Recommended.—**ARBA Staff Reviewer**

Lyme Disease

820.   Barbour, Alan G. **Lyme Disease: Why It's Spreading, How it Makes You Sick, and What to Do about It.** Baltimore, Md., Johns Hopkins University Press, 2015. 315p. maps. index. $22.95pa. ISBN 13: 978-1-4214-1721-9; 978-1-4214-1722-6 (e-book).

Lyme Disease: Why It's Spreading, How it Makes You Sick, and What to Do About It provides evidence-based information on the history, diagnosis, treatment, preventive measures, and natural course of Lyme disease. It is an update to the 1996 work (also written by Barbour) titled *Lyme Disease: The Cause, the Cure, the Controversy.* In the 2015 text Preface, Barbour addresses the question why a new edition of the book now? "There are new diagnostic tests, greater appreciation of the long-term consequences of the infection and better understanding of what could be effective measures to control Lyme disease." Also, there are other infections that are transmitted by the same ticks that carry Lyme disease, and these other diseases are worthy of discussion and attention.

The revised text includes 13 chapters on Lyme disease in its early stage and in its later stage, the biology of the microbe, information on diagnosis, test result interpretation, treatment strategies, and disease prevention. The author draws heavily from updated research studies and established case studies. Understanding the ecology and transmission of Lyme disease were two chapters of interest, as well as medical treatment and discussion of protection and prevention. Chapters are written in a narrative style with boldface-labeled topic divisions. There are two pages of color photographs of Lyme disease rashes and the disease-carrying tick. There are also maps showing the progression of Lyme disease in the United States and also reports of ticks in U.S. state parks. The text ends with a list of Websites for further information and a glossary of selected terms. There are extensive footnotes and an index.

The strength of this source is the detail of sources cited and the current research and information given about Lyme disease; like other medical texts, it is not meant to be a substitute for professional medical care. Most appropriate for public libraries and academic libraries that field medical and disease-related questions.—**Caroline L. Gilson**

821.   Buhner, Stephen Harrod. **Natural Treatments for Lyme Coinfections: Anaplasma, Babesia, and Ehrlichia.** Rochester, Vt., Healing Arts Press, 2015. 440p. index. $19.95pa. ISBN 13: 978-1-62055-258-2.

Lyme disease is the most common tick-borne disease in the northern hemisphere, estimated to affect over a quarter million people a year in the United States. As common as it is, people may not know that many cases of Lyme disease are misdiagnosed due to the presence of other, more obscure tick-borne infections. This book delves into three of these coinfections with the ultimate intent of enlightening both clinicians and patients about their manifestations and the variety of natural treatments used to combat them.

The prolific author has a keen ability to take complex material and make it accessible to his readers, whom he refers to as "members of the Lyme community." He opens the book with an overview of the latest research on the nascent organisms which can develop into coinfections. He then divides the next chapters into general information on the specific organism (e.g., how Babesia infects a human, how a Babesia infection is diagnosed, etc.), more technical information on the organism (e.g., how Babesia works with active compounds in tick saliva, etc.), and finally information related to the natural healing of the coinfections. The book also includes a chapter about advanced infections, including sepsis and septic shock, as well as a detailed chapter—*The Materia Medica*—describing the many foundational and supportive herbs recommended for use against Lyme coinfections (with particularly detailed elucidation on Danshen, or Salvia miltiorrhiza). This chapter includes information on herb preparation, dosage, side effects, and more.

The book also provides resources for obtaining herbs (if you're not following the author's recommendation to grow them yourself), contact information for several practitioners, a glossary of the book's acronyms, an extensive bibliographical information, and an index. Since Lyme disease is often a chronic condition, this book will be of value to patients as well as to those in the medical/natural medicine profession.—**Laura Herrell**

Obesity

822.   **Handbook of Obesity.** George A. Bray and Claude Bouchard, eds. Boca Raton, Fla., CRC Press, 2014. 2v. illus. index. $279.76 (book and e-book). ISBN 13: 978-1-4822-1067-5; 978-1-4822-5786-1 (e-book).

The third edition of the *Handbook of Obesity,* volume one, and the fourth edition of *Handbook of Obesity,* volume two, are available either as a set or individually in both print and e-book formats.

The third edition of volume one contains 60 chapters, up from the 43 chapters in the second edition published in 2004. Scientific discoveries necessitated the publication of this new volume, which is organized into five parts: History, Definitions, and Prevalence (7 chapters); Biological Determinants of Obesity (20 chapters); Behavioral Determinants of Obesity (9 chapters); Environmental, Social, and Cultural Determinants of Obesity (8 chapters); and Consequences of Obesity (16 chapters).

Volume two of the *Handbook of Obesity* is in its fourth edition and focuses on diagnosis, evaluation, prevention, and treatment. Like the first volume, this one reflects the massive changes in the field, noting major developments since the third edition that include two American clinical trials which demonstrated the limit of long-term behavioral treatment for obesity and the important potential health benefits that flow from these efforts; the removal of one of two medications from the market and the approval of two new agents by the U.S. Federal Drug Administration; and the analysis of health benefits of weight loss as observed in patients treated surgically for obesity. This volume also contains five sections: Prevention of Obesity (5 chapters); Evaluation of the Overweight or Obese Patient (5 chapters); Medical Treatment of Obesity and Weight Management Issues in the Treatment of Obesity: Behavior, Diet, Exercise, and Medications (18 chapters); Surgery (6 chapters); and Epilogue, comprised of two chapters, one on the economic assessment and cost-effectiveness of obesity treatments and the other on international views of obesity and government responses to its prevalence.

Both these well-documented and well-researched volumes reflect the most current trends in obesity studies internationally. The organization of the volumes and the indexes only enhance the usefulness of this handbook. These volumes, separately or as a set, are highly recommended for academic and medical libraries, even for those that already own a copy of earlier editions (see ARBA 2004, entry 1447).—**ARBA Staff Reviewer**

823.   **School Nutrition and Activity: Impacts on Well-Being.** Hassan, Areej, ed. Boca Raton, Fla., CRC Press, 2015. 454p. illus. index. $139.95; $97.97 (e-book). ISBN 13: 978-1-7718-8107-4; 978-1-4987-2173-8 (e-book).

School Nutrition and Activity is designed to address the growing epidemic of overweight and obese youth. Following an introduction that discusses the role of school intervention in treatment and prevention are chapters that provide schools with a strong, science-backed basis for policies and practices that support healthy eating and regular physical activity. The volume targets the issue of overweight and obese children and adolescents on three levels by addressing the effects of unhealthy eating and lack of exercise, relaying successful small-and large-scale, school-based interventions, and synthesizing current literature along with a translation into specific guidelines and recommendations.

Each chapter begins with a citation because chapters were previously published in various places and in various formats. Chapters use tables and figures to support the text, and each chapter concludes with references. An index rounds out the work.

This volume is not a ready reference but under the editorship of Hassan, an instructor in pediatrics at Harvard Medical School and an attending physician at Boston Children's Hospital, it arranges in one place a vast amount of literature on an increasingly important topic. Directed at a professional audience, this book is recommended for academic libraries and medical libraries.—**ARBA Staff Reviewer**

824.   Stern, Judith S., and Alexandria Kazaks. **Obesity: A Reference Handbook.** 2d ed. Santa Barbara, Calif., ABC-CLIO, 2015. 362p. index. (Contemporary World Issues). $60.00. ISBN 13: 978-1-4408-3804-0; 978-1-4408-3805-7 (e-book).

The Contemporary World Issues series is known for its ability to provide a well-rounded approach to a variety of timely and important topics. This volume in the series focuses on the worldwide concern of obesity.

Seven chapters organize the material into sensible categories. "Background and History," chapter one, discusses a variety of reasons for, and shifting attitudes about, obesity. It highlights scientific, social, and economic issues relative to obesity. Such topics as the formulas for assessing healthy body weight, discrimination, and a growing health care expenditure are examined.

"Problems, Controversies and Solutions," chapter two, pinpoints areas of debate within the topic. Paragraphs take a neutral approach to considering whether obesity is a disease and/or an epidemic and also reflect on the efficacy of certain treatments, such as diets, medication, programs, and more. The section also looks at the health care industry's approach to obesity, discussing such issues related to the Affordable Care Act as labeling mandates.

The following chapter, "Perspectives" then offers a series of essays reflecting the individual views of a number of scholars and medical personnel covering their own connections to the issue via research or personal experience. Rajiv Narayan, for example, writes how his 100-pound weight loss inspired his entry into the field. "Profiles," chapter four, spotlights the leading figures and organizations within the field, e.g., Dr. Elizabeth Applegate, Jenny Craig, Weight-Control Information Network, and others.

The "Data and Documents" chapter has myriad tables, charts, and diagrams outlining much of the latest research on the topic. It also shares excerpts from federal guidelines, legislation, and reports such as 2011's Strategic Plan for NIH (National Institute of Health) Obesity Research. "Resources for Further Research," chapter six, has references to relevant databases and Websites, reports, books, magazine and journal articles, and more. The last chapter is a chronology, which is followed by a glossary, index, and information about the authors.

Recommended.—**Laura Herrell**

Pharmacy and Pharmaceutical Sciences

Dictionaries and Encyclopedias

825.   **The Gale Encyclopedia of Prescription Drugs: A Comprehensive Guide to the Most Common Medications.** Kristin Fust, ed. Farmington Hills, Mich., Gale/Cengage Learning, 2015. 2v. illus. index. $499.00/set. ISBN 13: 978-1-57302-742-7; 978-1-57302-745-8 (e-book).

Since there is so much information about medications available on the Internet for both consumers and health professionals, why bother with a print publication? The flip answer is because some consumers (dare I say older) still want it. This drug guide for the consumer is an excellent choice for public libraries to purchase.

The book includes entries on the top 300 drugs written by pharmacists, physicians, nurses, researchers, and other health care personnel. All articles are signed and give the author's credentials. The language is simple but does not talk down to the reader in the way consumer drug information books often do. Key terms such as bradycardia or triglycerides are defined clearly and the writers have accomplished their goal of providing an understandable yet comprehensive drug guide.

Unfortunately most users will skip the foreword, which provides a clear but concise explanation of the drug discovery process, clarifies the difference between adverse and side effects, and explains brand and generic drug equivalency. Drugs are listed alphabetically by generic name with an index of brand and alternative names. Entries include each drug's description, definition, and purpose including off label uses, dosage, precautions, side effects, and interactions. There are also a few sentences on the origins of the drug which provide a brief history in case anyone wants to know how long a product has been around.

After each entry there is a list of resources that includes articles, Websites, and books. The books and articles are geared for the professional but the Websites give consumers excellent sources of further information.

Four appendixes include a list of recommended questions for the pharmacist, the Institute of Safe Medicine Practices list of commonly confused drug names, a list of health organizations, and a glossary. This encyclopedia is a credible, easy to read place for the public to find basic drug information.—**Natalie Kupferberg**

Handbooks and Yearbooks

826.   Nicholson, Timothy RJ, and Donald RJ Singer. **Pocket Prescriber 2015.** Boca Raton, Fla., CRC Press, 2015. 308p. illus. index. $23.00; $16.79 (e-book). ISBN 13: 978-1-4987-4784-4; 978-1-4987-4786-8 (e-book).

This handy little guide offers a quick and important reference tool for novices in the medical profession, including those starting out as doctors, nurses, pharmacists, etc. Listing roughly 500 of the most commonly prescribed drugs, the small guide literally fits into a pocket, providing vital information at the user's fingertips.

Main drug entries are alphabetized for ease of reference, and include key abbreviated codes regarding use, drug classification, contraindications, side effects, dosage, and much more. As the information is highly specialized, the book opens with a vital section on how to use the book that includes definitions of the aforementioned codes, symbols, dosage information, administration routes, and a comprehensive list of abbreviations.

In addition to the entries, the book includes broader information relative to drug selection (e.g., in reference to a particular infection), complicated prescriptions (e.g., insulin), medical emergencies (e.g., overdoses), and more.

The added bonus of a fold-out cover, which maps algorithms for the European Resuscitation Council for cardiac arrest, stroke, etc., makes this book rather indispensable for those relatively new to the world of medicine and health care.—**Laura Herrell**

34   Technology

General Works

Handbooks and Yearbooks

827.   Balaban, Naomi, and James Bobick. **The Handy Technology Answer Book.** Canton, Mich., Visible Ink Press, 2016. 431p. illus. index. $21.95pa. ISBN 13: 978-1-57859-563-1; 978-1-57859-595-2 (e-book).

This timely volume in the Handy Answer series offers an exploration of how different types of technology have affected and continue to affect so many aspects of the world in which we live. From the obvious example of computers to the things we take for granted like clocks and cars, the book does well to trace the many diverse ways technology impacts the ways people live today.

Thirteen sections address everything from the origins of technology through a wide variety of specific innovations, and ultimately to an assessment of technology's greater influence on a number of diverse fields.

Each section is further broken into chapters discussing narrower topics. What truly sets this publication apart is the unique question and answer format, which enables readers to quickly find their particular topic of interest, connect these topics to broader ideas, and pique their curiosity for more. In rapid succession, for example, we learn the answers to questions about which elements are metals and the importance of aluminum, along with much more relative to mining, minerals, and manufacturing. The book amasses nearly 1,200 of these incisive questions, covering such topics as computers, time, and energy.

Closing chapters highlight the impacts of technology on the environment, genetics, and medicine. The book, perfect for younger students, in particular, closes out with an index and many ideas for further reading on the fascinating subject of technology.—**Laura Herrell**

Computers

Handbooks and Yearbooks

828.   **Code Academy. http://www.codeacademy.com.** [Website] Free. Date reviewed: 2015.

Code Academy is a free, interactive educational tool that allows users to practice coding. The company strives to create a beneficial online learning experience and operates under the knowledge that classroom learning has changed drastically over time and therefore teaching methods must shift accordingly. *Code Academy* offers a unique "net native education" and mimics the experiences of social media rather than a classroom in order to effectively teach students how to code.

The Website is minimalist and easy to navigate, providing links to coding tutorials at the bottom of the homepage. Here, users can choose to create their own interactive Websites based off the format of AirBnB. *Code Academy* offers tutorials on Javascript, AngularJS, HTML, CSS, and much more. Instead of lengthy text explanations, the tutorials begin with activities and are completely interactive from the start, guaranteeing that students will not fall asleep on the keyboard.

In addition to online instruction, users can read success stories from people around the world who have benefited from the site and have learned to code without prior knowledge of the subject material. Videos provide answers to frequently asked questions, such as "How can coding help you?"

This Website is a perfect tool for students who are easily distracted and would like minimal instruction before diving in to the coding process. Teachers will find this great educational tool to be helpful in the classroom as well. *Code Academy* is a highly recommended resource.—**ARBA Staff Reviewer**

829.   **Code.org. http://code.org/.** [Website] Free. Date reviewed: 2015.

The makers behind *Code.org* believe that every student worldwide should be offered the opportunity to learn how to code. *Code.org* is a phenomenal nonprofit organization that seeks to provide computer science resources to women and students of color, both underrepresented groups in the computer science field. The Website offers an introduction to computer science through the Hour of Code, a free hour-long, self-guided introduction to subject basics that takes place during the second week of December.

Those interested in the Hour of Code can sign up on the Website and even organize an event at school to encourage more students to participate.

Code.org is partnered with Outlier Research & Evaluation at the University of Chicago. Together they work to find more effective ways to reach students and spark curiosity in technology as well as provide them with opportunities to explore their interests. The organization is funded through *Indiegogo.com* and raised over $5 million to reach 100 million students worldwide in 2014, making their campaign the most successful in *Indiegogo* history.

Both students and teachers can create accounts to access coding videos and tutorials appropriate for all ages, and users can even practice coding with *Frozen* characters Anna and Elsa. Other tutorials teach users to make apps or games, create Websites, and even provide access to university-level coding courses. Teachers can set up a free classroom coding course through available for their K-8 classes.

The courses are available in over 30 languages and are used in over 180 countries. *Code.org* is a top-notch resource for teachers and students alike.—**ARBA Staff Reviewer**

830.　**InfoSci-Computer Science and Information Technology. http://www.igi-global. com/e-resources/infosci-subject-databases/infosci-computer-science/.** [Website] Hershey, Pa., Information Science Reference/IGI Global. Price negotiated by site. Date reviewed: 2016.

The InfoSci series is a comprehensive collection of academic databases incorporating the sciences and technology. A user profile will make it possible to access all tools for research. A user guide and help tab will provide instruction on using the databases and detail search options and features of the electronic resources. Found in a handy sidebar, search functions are: Basic, Advanced, Expert, and Classic. The larger sidebar provides options for further navigation forward or to return to a previous segment. Citing, favorites, and saved search tabs are essential for the researcher. Additionally, InfoSci offers this research feature—citings are found in MLA, ALA, and Chicago style.

The database *InfoSci-Computer Science and Information Technology* is a considerable collection of reference books available as e-books or hardcopy text. The format options are either HTML or PDF. Information is easily accessed by the series tools mentioned above, and further filtering may be necessary as there are 458 books in this grouping. Information on Web design, environmental impacts, big data, robotics, high performance and smart computing, artificial intelligence, and applications and systems are some of the areas covered in this database.

The 10-volume set of the *Encyclopedia of Informational Science and Technology* (3d edition) provides a full range of concepts, issues, methods, technologies, and trends and may be a good place for researchers to begin to define their focus of study. Other encyclopedia options are available. Some resources are practical like *Design Solutions for Improving Website Quality and Effectiveness.* Published in 2016, this covers analytics, metrics, usage, and security aspects of Web environments which may be useful for those involved in improving Web designs. There are several texts that describe expectations for trends in computer science and technology; *Emerging Innovations in Agile Software Development* provides research-based solutions for contemporary software development.

As with any technology-related data, the shelf life can be short. The four entries from 2000 will most likely be useful from a historical background only. Occasionally, older text is off-putting because of the age of it; *Information Technology Evaluation Methods and Management* (2001), Chapter 9 states "as information and communication technologies have rapidly developed in the 1990s, enormous changes have taken place everywhere," and unless looking for background on information technology, this will not be current enough for timely research or practical application.

InfoSci-Computer Science and Information Technology is strong in the range of technology subject areas and the tools will expedite the process of sifting through the content easily. Most book resources are current, offering information entrenched in practical and trending ideas on computer science and information technology. This database will be useful for high-level academic research, engineers, and others working in the IT industry. This database is relevant for any academic reference collection.

Recommended.—**Janis Minshull**

35 Physical Sciences and Mathematics

Physical Sciences

Chemistry

831. **Chemistry Guide.** http://www.chemistryguide.org/. [Website] Free. Date reviewed: 2016.

This is a free-to-use aggregator of chemistry-related Websites. It is authored by Andry Frolov, who holds a Ph.D. in chemistry and has years of experience in organic synthetic chemistry. It is supported by the Moscow-based Exclusive Chemistry Ltd. and by Aurora Fine Chemicals, LLC. Its basic structure makes it easy to navigate.

A navigation bar includes tabs for Home, Top 10 Sites, Newly Added, Links to Us, About Us, Contact Us, and Privacy Policy. The heart of the data is found under the Home tab, which provides links to Websites grouped into 23 such subcategories as Analytical Chemistry, Chemical Dictionaries, General Chemistry, Green Chemistry, Organic Chemistry, Periodic Table of the Elements, and Polymer Chemistry. The Top 10 Sites link includes several related to chemistry jobs as well as an interactive periodic table, a site on analytical chemistry basics, and more. The newly added sites include three purporting to assist students in the writing of research papers, along with many others including a chemistry blog and an amino acids guide.—**ARBA Staff Reviewer**

832. **Dynamic Periodic Table.** http://www.ptable.com/. [Website] Free. Date reviewed: 2016.

Dynamic Periodic Table, created by Michael Dayah, is an interactive, user-friendly Website that provides reliable source data curated from primary sources on the elements. The home page opens to a periodic table which, when mousing over the elements, highlights whether the element is a nonmetal, metal, metalloid, noble gas, transition metal, etc. Tabs at the top of the home page take the user to a demo that walks one through the many options available and how to make the most of the site. There are also "properties," "orbitals," "isotopes," and "compounds" tabs and, as is the case with the homepage periodic table, mousing over the element brings up more information about that element. This Website is an excellent source of information on the elements and will be of great use to teachers, students, and librarians.

Earth and Planetary Sciences

Astronomy and Space Sciences

833.   **Encyclopedia of the Solar System.** 3d ed. Tilman Spohn, Doris Breuer, and Torrence V. Johnson, eds. San Diego, Calif., Elsevier Science, 2014. 1336p. illus. $180.00. ISBN 13: 978-0-12-415845-0.

Edited by Tilman Spohn, director of the Institute of Planetary Research of the German Aerospace Center in Berlin and professor of planetology; Doris Breuer, head of the Department of Planetary Physics at the Institute of Planetary Research of the German Aerospace Center in Berlin and an associate professor; and Torrence V. Johnson, a specialist on icy satellites and a senior research scientist at Jet Propulsion Laboratory, the third edition of the *Encyclopedia of the Solar System,* contains 57 chapters by more than 75 eminent authors.

The book's 57 chapters are organized into nine sections: The Solar System; Fundamental Planetary Processes and Properties; The Sun; Earthlike Planets; Earth and Moon as Planets; Asteroids, Dust, and Comets; Giant Planets and Their Satellites; Beyond the Planets; and Exploring the Solar System. For the most part, the authors from the second edition updated their own work. Moreover there are important additions in this third edition. In light of the increased importance of geophysical tools for the exploration of planets and the increase in the theoretical knowledge of the inner workings of planets, there is a chapter on geophysical exploration tools in general and on exploration of the Moon and potential landing sites on Mars. There is also a new chapter on rotation of the planets and using its observation to constrain models of the interior of terrestrial planets. Chapters on the interiors of Mars and the Moon have been added along with theoretical chapters pertaining to the inner workings of terrestrial planets—the generation of their magnetic fields and the relation between the thermal evolution, convection in the interior, and their tectonics. There is also a new chapter on high resolution and stereoimaging tools of planetary exploration. Added to the suite of chapters on space exploration is a new chapter describing strategies that nations have jointly developed in the International Space Exploration Initiative.

There is also a glossary with *see* references and an extensive appendix, comprised of four tables: Selected Astronomical Constraints; Physical and Orbital Properties of the Sun, Planets, and Dwarf Planets; Physical and Orbital Properties of the Satellites of Planets and Dwarf Planets; and Solar System Exploration Missions. The latter table has data on missions to the sun, Mercury, Venus, the Moon, Marsh asteroids, Jupiter, Saturn, Uranus, Neptune, dwarf planets, comets, and the Kuiper Belt.

Tables, figures, and illustrations help readers understand the amazing amount of material in this highly recommended book.—**ARBA Staff Reviewer**

834.   **Exploring Space: http://www.pbs.org/exploringspace/mars/index.html.** [Website] Free. Date reviewed: 2015.

PBS's *Exploring Space: The Quest for Life* is a national public television show that explores space, recent discoveries, and the quest for life outside planet earth. To introduce this content to those who haven't seen the show, the Exploring Space Website is an exceptional tool that allows users to access information by reading articles, taking quizzes, and playing with games and interactive simulations.

This Website is best for students who may be studying space in the classroom and require additional sources or are looking to learn and play simultaneously. The sidebar on the homepage includes links for users to follow meteorites and stay updated on recent Mars discoveries. For those interested in alien life, the Designs of Alien Life page is a fun read for all ages.

An Essays page provides articles written by NASA scientists and researchers on the forefront of new discoveries in space. These short essays and opinions have the potential to be excellent nonfiction reading for student projects or papers.

Students can also simulate their own journeys to Mars. First, they create a schedule of events, then track their health based on the decisions they make in space while travelling thousands of miles per day. This creative simulation allows students to practice time management and understand the importance of balancing work with relaxation to stay in tip-top shape physically and mentally. It also highlights the challenges astronauts face in balancing their physiological and psychological needs in space. Additional activities include matching games and quizzes about Europa and Mars, complete with spectacular visuals.

The Web page has an attractive layout and is sure to hold the attention of younger readers as they play with the interactive tools and learn more about planets, moons, comets, and stars. A brief trailer of the PBS show on The Program page may even peak student interest and entice them to watch the show for even more information about the fascinating workings of space.—**ARBA Staff Reviewer**

835.   Scagell, Robin. **Urban Astronomy: Stargazing from Towns & Suburbs.** New York, Firefly Books, 2014. 208p. illus. index. $19.95pa. ISBN 13: 978-1-77085-325-6.

Light saturation, air pollution, and other obstacles interfere with those urban residents who want to study the planets and stars. This small but smart book presents a number of ways around such obstacles so that city-dwellers, too, can enjoy the wonders of the night sky.

The book lays out a multipronged attack on poor visibility, with eight efficient chapters focused on "knowing your enemy" (weather and surface light) and "choosing targets, weapons and ammunition." Specifically these latter chapters address what urban astronomers should be looking for in the night sky, what tools they should be using to look at the sky, and how they should adapt these tools to enhance their visibility. While some information can be quite technical, the author makes excellent use of beautiful color photographs and helpful illustrations throughout.

Other chapters explain further alternatives for urban astronomers, such as Internet astronomy, indoor astronomy, mobile astronomy, and more. Charts pinpointing the best deep-sky objects such as double stars, nebulae, and supernovas close out this effective guide.—**Laura Herrell**

Climatology and Meteorology

836. **U*X*L Encyclopedia of Weather and Natural Disasters.** 2d ed. Amy Hackney Blackwell, ed. Farmington Hills, Mich., U*X*L/Gale, 2016. 5v. illus. maps. index. $436.00/set. ISBN 13: 978-1-4103-3290-5.

Outstanding ancillary materials complement the smart choices of entries in these five volumes to produce a first-rate encyclopedia set covering meteorology and the effects of weather on living systems. Although the emphasis on human death tolls and the destruction of cities by historic events such as volcanic eruptions, floods, and storms is evident from the title, the set includes an overview of such issues as mass extinctions in planetary history and the impact of tectonic movements and climate change on biological systems more generally. Topics range over both basic terms such as drought and cloud to less-known terms such as foehn and mesoscale convective complex.

Each volume includes a complete table of contents, list of entries according to scientific field, glossary, index, and practical guides to activities and further research. Individual entries contain microglossaries, and most include visual aids such as photographs and full-color diagrams of various cycles.—**Delilah R. Caldwell**

Geology

837. Hinga, Bethany D. Rinard. **Ring of Fire: An Encyclopedia of the Pacific Rim's Earthquakes, Tsunamis, and Volcanoes.** Santa Barbara, Calif., ABC-CLIO, 2015. 402p. illus. maps. index. $89.00. ISBN 13: 978-1-61069-296-0; 978-1-61069-297-7 (e-book).

Framed within the context of plate tectonic activity in and around the Pacific Ocean, author Hinga provides encyclopedia entries describing the region's major volcanic eruptions, earthquakes, and tsunamis along with information about affected nations and influential geoscientists. Descriptions of related geologic terms are provided as well. To orient readers, two lists of entries are provided including an alphabetical listing and a listing by name of the related geologic event or natural disaster. Oddly, the listings do not include page numbers which would direct readers to the corresponding entries in the text. Following the listings are a brief preface, an informative introduction about the Pacific Rim's geographic and geologic settings, and a handy timeline of significant geologic events or natural disasters dating back to 1815. Each article entry is very well written using easy-to-understand language and some include black-and-white photographs. Regrettably, maps, which could help readers understand the location of a geologic event or disaster in relation to the Pacific Rim, were not included with the entries. All entries are cross-referenced to other relevant entries and are accompanied with a short list of suggested further reading. Finally, an extensive bibliography is located after the entries along with a comprehensive index. Overall, the value of the encyclopedia is in its treatment of the Pacific Rim's major geologic events or natural disasters, using nontechnical language, all within the context of plate tectonic theory.—**Jennifer Brooks Huffman**

General Works

Dictionaries and Encyclopedias

838. Calaprice, Alice, Daniel Kennefick, and Robert Schulmann. **An Einstein Encyclopedia.** Princeton, N.J., Princeton University Press, 2015. 347p. illus. index. $39.95. ISBN 13: 978-0-691-14174-9.

Few scholarly reference works focused on the very famous can described as "delicious" reads, but that is the case here. Beautifully written and illustrated, this compact but rich single volume beautifully celebrates the 100th anniversary of Albert Einstein's general theory of relativity (and by chance is all the more timely, considering recent confirmation of Einstein's gravitational waves theory). Here one can explore his rich biography, and what influenced his life-long intellectual and personal interests. The authors chose wisely to avoid a rigid, alphabetic encyclopedia format. Instead, they address Einstein's life in three very accessible sections: the intimately personal and biographical; key scientific works and collaborations; and, last, the progression of his philosophical/political leanings and affiliations. So in addition to focusing on Einstein's work as a scientist, a different, intriguing portrait of the man is also revealed—painted in personal photos, snippets of poetry and letters, stories of his love of sailing, his family life, friendships, romantic interests, and so forth. These insights into Einstein's world view, via historical ephemera and anecdotes, bring the man to life. He is revealed as a whole human being, versus the quirky, enigmatic science genius of public perception. Among supplementary features are a chronology of Einstein's significant life events, and a deeply detailed index that follows three appendixes. The last of these offers a chronological, selective, annotated bibliography for those who wish to dig deeper into key lectures and seminal publications—since the goal this work was not to provide comprehensive coverage of Einstein's research in physics (impossible), here the authors have supplied additional resources for the scholarly reader to pursue. In summary, the authors have contributed to the literature a reverent, meaty, intriguing, and scholarly encyclopedia that is accessible to most readers. It truly honors the life and work of the world's most-renowned scientist. A much earlier reference book on Albert Einstein—*An Einstein Dictionary* (see ARBA 1997, entry 1409)— pales in comparison to this new title.

Highly recommended.—**Judith Matthews**

Handbooks and Yearbooks

839. **Skeptical Science. http://www.skepticalscience.com/.** [Website] Free. Date reviewed: 2016.

Skeptical Science is a combination blog-Website with the self-described mission of "get[ting] skeptical about global warming skepticism." It was created and continues to be maintained by John Cook, a Climate Communication Fellow for the Global Change Institute at the University of Queensland in Australia. Entirely funded by private donations, *Skeptical Science* asserts that it seeks to entirely remove political considerations and viewpoints from the issue of climate change and focus only on our evolving scientific understanding of the issue. The site has been endorsed by many influential researchers and journalists studying the issue of global warming, and in 2011 it received the Australian Museum's Eureka Prize in the category of Advancement of Climate Change Knowledge.

The most prominent element of *Skeptical Science's* home page is its blog, in which Cook and a team of contributors comment on news and developments in the global warming field. But the top of the home page also provides gateway tabs to a wide range of information on climate change, from updates on the latest scientific research related to global warming to refutations of various arguments and talking points that have been offered up by skeptics and denialists over the years. The heart of the Website's offerings, though, is "Arguments," which pairs more than 175 "climate myths" with summaries of "what the science says." These "what the science says" analyses, which distill the findings of studies published in peer-reviewed scientific literature, are offered in different versions tailored to basic, intermediate, and (sometimes) advanced reader levels.

Another tab on the home page, identified as "Resources," provides access to a broad array of additional information on climate science, including graphs and charts, a search engine to find the latest climate-related articles and papers published around the world, a glossary of terms, and a handbook authored by Cook called *The Scientific Guide to Global Warming Skepticism* (available in 19 languages).

Other Websites are more elegantly designed than *Skeptical Science.* Nonetheless, it contains a wealth of information on the true state of climate change research, and is thus a recommended resource for high school, public, and academic libraries.—**ARBA Staff Reviewer**

Physics

Handbooks and Yearbooks

840.   Haché, Alain. **Slap Shot Science: A Curious Fan's Guide to Hockey.** Baltimore, Md., Johns Hopkins University Press, 2015. 192p. $28.95. ISBN 13: 978-1-4214-1792-9; 978-1-4214-1793-6 (e-book).

In *Slap Shot Science: A Curious Fan's Guide to Hockey,* Alain Haché discusses the science and technology involved in the sport of hockey. This work follows up on his 2002 publication, *The Physics of Hockey* (Johns Hopkins University Press), but excludes the complicated mathematics, making the content more accessible to a general reader. *Slap Shot Science* addresses many of the questions the author received interacting with the hockey community after publication of his first book, and new developments in equipment, rules, and training. It is a small book (176 pages with index) and is not meant to be encyclopedic, but rather tries to provide different perspectives on the science of hockey. The book begins by covering the key components of hockey: the rink, skates, sticks, and basic techniques. Chapter one discusses the science of ice, followed by techniques for making and maintaining ice conditions. Chapter two examines skates and skating, including blade shape and sharpening techniques, and the mechanics of skating. Shooting is covered in chapter three, from techniques to the aerodynamics and spin effects on puck trajectory. The next four chapters look at players and performance hockey, including hockey injuries, goaltending, and the fastest skaters or players with the hardest shots. The final chapter delves into statistics—team production, individual production, effects of skill versus chance and more—to distinguish between meaningful numbers and random occurrences. Three appendixes are provided to convert metric to standard units, list the symbols and acronyms used throughout the book, and present a formula for calculating a team's chances of winning. Although this book is based on science, the text is very accessible and engaging for any hockey fan. Recommended for all public libraries.—**Kevin McDonough**

Mathematics

Handbooks and Yearbooks

841.   **The Best Writing on Mathematics 2015.** Mircea Pitici, ed. Princeton, N.J., Princeton University Press, 2016. 392p. illus. $24.95pa. ISBN 13: 978-0-69116-965-1.

This absorbing book is the sixth volume in a series of anthologies of mathematical essays for nonmathematicians. There are essays on particular problems, recreational mathematics, philosophy of mathematics, statistics and probability, math education, and applied mathematics. The introduction includes an overview of 2014 nonspecialist mathematical books, supplemented by a Website. The book concludes with a bibliography of 2014 articles not included in this book. The essays are accessible without advanced math education although real concentration is often required.

An attractive purchase for any public or academic library.—**Frederic F. Burchsted**

842.   **The Princeton Companion to Applied Mathematics.** Nicholas J. Higham, ed. Mark R. Dennis, Paul Glendinning, Paul A. Martin, Fadil Santosa, and Jared Tanner, associate eds. Princeton, N.J., Princeton University Press, 2015. 1032p. illus. index. $99.50. ISBN 13: 978-0-691-15039-0.

This very useful book supplements *The Princeton Companion to Mathematics* (2008) which covers pure mathematics. Applied mathematics includes the use of mathematical methods in a wide variety of areas, including physics, biology, medicine, finance, social science, computer science, and other fields. The book's over 180 articles are arranged in eight sections on concepts, major equations and laws, areas of applied mathematics, specific example problems, etc.

Applied mathematics is composed of numerous specialist topics, and it is impossible for one person to have thorough knowledge of, or keep up to date with, all of them. This book is designed to allow applied mathematicians to acquaint themselves with areas outside their specialties. It will also serve as an introduction to interested lay people or to scientists in other fields. Substantial mathematical education is required for full understanding of the articles, but most of the articles have sufficient verbal explanation to allow the nonmathematical to garner the basic ideas.

Essential for college/university libraries and a useful addition to large public libraries.—**Frederic F. Burchsted**

36 Resource Sciences

Energy

Dictionaries and Encyclopedias

843. **Encyclopedia of Energy Engineering. Second Edition.** Sohail Anwar, ed. Boca Raton, Fla., CRC Press, 2015. 4v. illus. index. $1,320.00/set. ISBN 13: 978-1-4665-0673-2.

The *Encyclopedia of Energy Engineering and Technology,* second edition, is an informative reference work that will appeal to energy researchers, engineers, policy-makers, and graduate and undergraduate students interested in the field. The encyclopedia can assist students working on an energy research paper or project, provide active researchers with a quick review of a specific topic, process, or technology, and provide policy-makers with an overview of the economic implications of various energy solutions.

This compendium of information on energy resources explores all aspects of energy engineering and technology from the theoretical to current applications and possible solutions to issues. Contributors to this edition represent many regions of the world and are active in academia, business, industry, and environmental groups. This second edition of the encyclopedia (four volumes) is 40 percent larger than first edition (three volumes, 2007) resulting from the expansion of several sections and the addition of new articles. Mirroring energy research interests in recent years, the section on Renewable Energy has the largest number of new articles and is three times larger than its first edition counterpart. Other sections with significant increases in content are: Energy, Energy Sources and Energy Use, and Principles of Energy Analysis and Systems/Economic Analysis of Energy Systems.

The encyclopedia is arranged alphabetically by article title, and each volume features both alphabetical and topical tables of contents covering all four volumes. The topical table of contents is very helpful as a discovery tool as it brings together related articles from all volumes, allowing the reader to explore the subject in depth. Each volume also contains a detailed index for the entire encyclopedia. Most articles are five to seven pages long, but article length varies. Of the articles reviewed, the shortest was just over four pages, while the longest was 27 pages. The encyclopedia is illustrated and articles include black-and-white photographs, diagrams, and graphics. Some articles also provide nomenclature charts containing explanations of units and abbreviations or acronyms used by the authors.

The energy topics covered in the encyclopedia range from well-established energy technologies and sources (e.g., coal-to-liquid conversion) to developing technologies (large-scale solar and wind projects) to theoretical energy solutions (e.g., ocean thermal energy conversion). In addition, there are articles that discuss renewable energy education as well as the management, accounting, and auditing practices for the efficient use of energy in buildings and industrial plants. The topic coverage may not always be comprehensive, however. In the discussion of hydroelectricity, only small-scale (low head) and pumped storage options are included and large-scale hydropower dams are ignored. While large dams such as Hoover Dam have fallen out of favor for many reasons, they still exist and coverage of their operations and efficiencies would be of interest to readers.

All the encyclopedia articles reviewed are objective and provide a good balance between the technical and nontechnical information. Most are well written and edited, with very few grammatical or other errors noted. Generally, the content covered will be understood easily by experts, and will be accessible to novices who will be able to develop a high-level understanding of a topic. Although many of the technology and process discussions are easily understood (e.g., Water and Wastewater Treatment), nonexperts may need to reread some passages to completely understand the more complicated technologies and models discussed (e.g., Bio-mass Based Hydrogen Production). The structure of individual articles is essentially the same throughout the encyclopedia: abstract, introduction, overview and/ or detailed discussion of the topic, conclusions, and references, helping readers to know what to expect as they move from article to article. The history and development of a topic through time are usually discussed, providing context for the reader. The references can be helpful to readers providing them with additional sources on the topic. Not all articles were updated in this edition, however, so some of the Website references in these articles may no longer be valid.

Several drawbacks to this edition are the lack of color illustrations and a table of the nomenclature and units. While the quality of most photographs and illustrations is quite good, there are some that would be much easier to read and understand if they were in color. In "Alternative Energy Technologies: Price Effects," there are several graphics that clearly were in color in the original form. In this article, however, the contrasting colors are now just shades of grey making interpretation more difficult. Color graphics would make this a more expensive print resource but perhaps it can be added to future online versions.

The lack of an overall nomenclature and units table for the encyclopedia was a disappointment. While experts may recognize all the acronyms and know what a "quad" is, some users will not, and including this type of table makes this resource much more accessible. It was a feature of the first edition and it would certainly be helpful to include it in future editions.

The *Encyclopedia of Energy Engineering and Technology* is recommended for research libraries in academic, industry, business, and government whose users are working on or are interested in research in energy sources as well as their efficient use and management.—**Theresa Calcagno**

844.   **Oil: A Cultural and Geographic Encyclopedia of Black Gold.** Xiaobing Li and Michael Molina, eds. Santa Barbara, Calif., ABC-CLIO, 2014. 2v. illus. maps. index. $189.00/set. ISBN 13: 978-1-61069-271-7; 978-1-61069-272-4 (e-book).

Despite all the talk of alternative and renewable energy resources, oil remains the most widely used energy source throughout the world. Globally, it is established as a four trillion dollar per year industry, while the United States alone consumes more oil than any other country. *Oil: A Cultural and Geographic Encyclopedia of Black Gold* provides a wealth of context for truly understanding the importance of this viscous and vital substance.

Two volumes organized alphabetically by topic and country offer over two hundred entries, most several pages in length, written by experts from many fields and countries and detailing major concepts, terms, historical events, organizations, and individuals related to oil and its production, economy, and use. In volume one, we learn how oil affects and is affected by broad-scale politics, business, technology, and social behavior through entries ranging from the particular mechanics of a drillship to the devastating effects of disasters like the 2006 Guimaras oil spill and further to the wider subjects of globalization and energy consumption.

Volume two provides a catalog of all the countries who are the major oil producers, exporters/importers, and consumers in addition to conveying historical, economic, and political points relevant to each nation. We trace, for example, the late nineteenth century discovery of oil in Egypt through the establishment of various international partnerships at the country's production heyday through the oil embargo of the 1970s and finally to the current shift to natural gas exploration as a result of declining oil production, all set against the backdrop of war and political instability.

Each entry concludes with *see also* and source references. A list of contributors and an index complete the two volumes.—**Laura Herrell**

Handbooks and Yearbooks

845. **Energy Choices: How to Power the Future.** Robin Morris Collin and Robert William Collin, eds. Santa Barbara, Calif., Praeger/ABC-CLIO, 2014. 2v. $110.00/set. ISBN 13: 978-0-313-39719-6; 978-0-313-39720-2.

The study of energy is one of the fastest growing areas of research throughout the globe. The world we have built up to this point depends greatly on newer and stronger sources of energy. This two-volume book explores past and future energy choices with the goal of facilitating broader economic and business understanding of the challenges of matching energy sources to contemporary and future market demand. Numerous contributors from a variety of backgrounds contribute thought-provoking essays raising issues of population, sustainability, national security, the role of government, and more, all of which impact both the global research and consumption of energy.

Volume one explores the business of conventional sources of energy; namely, petroleum, natural gas, coal, and nuclear power. Conventional sources—mainly oil— remain the most widely used energy source throughout the world. While their use is widespread, they are undergoing interesting market challenges and transitions. For example, although nuclear power is so firmly established in global markets (and thus considered a conventional energy source), new technologies may mitigate its waste issues to the point where it becomes fully sustainable. The volume also includes a thorough discussion of all conventional energy sources, such as coal mining (featuring its methods and impacts on the environment and health) and the role of government regarding fossil fuel sources.

Volume two provides similar analyses of the latest renewable energy sources, including solar energy, ocean energy, wind energy, and other new and exciting processes like "cold" fusion. "The Business Case for Wind Energy," for example, is an excellent chapter explaining methodology, distribution, policy etc. of this new technology. Other ideas in this volume again circulate around the role of government, research, funding, and environmental challenges.

Each chapter concludes with lists of further readings and online resources. The book contains two appendixes: an appendix of acronyms and specialized terms and one that reproduces President Dwight D. Eisenhower's "Atoms for Peace" address to the UN General Assembly. An index rounds out the work. This set is recommended for general readers as well as students, high school and above.—**Laura Herrell**

846.   Newton, David E. **Wind Energy: A Reference Handbook.** Santa Barbara, Calif., ABC-CLIO, 2015. 348p. index. (Contemporary World Issues). $58.00. ISBN 13: 978-1-61069-689-0; 978-1-61069-690-6 (e-book).

The Contemporary World Issues series is known for its ability to provide a well-rounded approach to a variety of timely and important topics. This volume in the series focuses on wind energy, an exciting realm in the world of energy research.

Seven chapters organize the material into sensible categories. "Background and History" takes a concise look at the history of wind power and the development of technologies used to harness it. It also discusses the fluctuating interest levels of government research on the technology and highlights global developments. The next chapter, "Problems, Controversies, and Solutions," pinpoints areas of debate within the topic. Areas covered include costs, government policies, wind farm issues, public attitudes, and more. "Perspectives" then offers a series of essays reflecting the topical interest of a number of scholars and experts in the field of wind energy. Pieces discuss the varied (and rather fascinating) opposition to wind farms in Australia, the importance of properly siting a wind farm, and more. In the fourth chapter, "Profiles," readers will find information on leading figures and organizations within the field, such as inventor Anton Flettner, General Electric, and Women of Wind Energy. "Data and Documents," chapter five, provides myriad tables, charts, and diagrams outlining much of the latest research on the topic. It also shares excerpts from U.S. policy, guidelines regarding turbine design, site development, litigation, and more. This is followed by a chapter on resources for further research and a final chapter, "Chronology," which starts with a ca. 5000 B.C.E.-2013 timeline. A glossary, an index, and author information round out the book.—**Laura Herrell**

Environmental Science

Dictionaries and Encyclopedias

847.   Collin, Robert William. **Trash Talk: An Encyclopedia of Garbage and Recycling around the World.** Santa Barbara, Calif., ABC-CLIO, 2015. 484. illus. index. $100.00. ISBN 13: 978-1-61069-508-4; 978-1-61069-509-1 (e-book).

Based on his introduction, author Robert Collin intended this encyclopedia to serve as a review of waste management and recycling practices in countries from around the world. Written at a basic level, it serves as an entry-level resource for global information in these topical areas. Organizationally, the book contains a preface, a well-written introduction, eight "thematic essays," and articles on waste management processes for 173 countries. Articles include a brief narrative with supporting statistics; their lengths vary, but typically range from one to three pages. Each article sets the stage for a reader by very briefly describing each nation's population characteristics and geography followed by information on current waste management practices, emission sources and levels, and major waste issues. Each article also identifies suggested further readings. Black-and-white photographs accompany a few of the articles, as do some sidebar stories; but there is a noticeable lack of supporting tables, charts, or graphs. Finally, a basic glossary identifying key terms is provided, as is a bibliography and an index.

Overall, this encyclopedia should provide readers with a very basic understanding of waste management and recycling practices worldwide.—**Jennifer Brooks Huffman**

848.   **Encyclopedia of Natural Resources.** Yeqiao Wang, ed. Boca Raton, Fla., CRC Press, 2014. 2v. illus. maps. index. $1,560.00/set. ISBN 13: 978-1-4398-5258-3.

The earth's natural resources are crucial for maintaining life and the study of these topics reaches beyond a single discipline and requires input from across the scholarly spectrum. The two-volume *Encyclopedia of Natural Resources* provides the necessarily broad coverage of topics related to natural resources. The volumes are divided by subject, with volume one dedicated to topics related to land while volume two focuses on water and air. These volumes are well organized and feature both standard and topical tables of contents for efficient article locating. As stated in the preface, this reference work aims to deliver authoritative information across the multidisciplinary set of topics related to natural resources including science, technology, and societal impact. To that end, this encyclopedia is successful, offering informative articles on topics ranging from biodiversity and ecosystems, management and sustainability, hydrology, meteorology, and climate change written by subject experts in each field. Noticeably absent, however, is any discussion of energy. Considering the environmental and societal implications associated with coal and oil extraction or wind and solar energy, excluding the energy sector is a significant omission for a resource aiming for coverage in natural resources. Although expressly written to appeal to general readers, academics, and professionals alike, the writing in some articles is more appropriate for a scholarly audience and this encyclopedia is therefore recommended for academic and research libraries.—**Eric Tans**

849.   **Environmental and Natural Resources Economics: An Encyclopedia.** Timothy C. Haab and John C. Whitehead, eds. Santa Barbara, Calif., Greenwood Press/ABC-CLIO, 2014. 372p. index. $89.00. ISBN 13: 978-1-4408-0119-8; 978-1-4408-0120-4 (e-book).

As the climate change conversation becomes more "heated" and the idea of sustainability pops up everywhere from building design to farming, it is safe to say that environmental challenges are at the core of the future economy. Such challenges are causing economists to think outside the box. This unique encyclopedia offers over 130 entries devoted to providing a structural understanding of the interrelationship between our environment and our economy. These entries highlight the people, places, concepts, events, and more surrounding economic issues as they pertain to environmental concerns and vice versa. Many experts in a number of related fields have contributed concise yet informative entries which stem from basic tenets of environmental and natural resource economics, including market failure, economic policy, and applied welfare economics. Fortunately these well-written entries in a quickly expanding field are accessible to specialists and nonspecialists alike. Recommended for school, public, and academic libraries.—**Laura Herrell**

850.   **U*X*L Sustainable Living.** Everett, Jason M., ed. Farmington Hills, Mich., U*X*L/Gale, 2016. 3v. illus. index. $272.00/set. ISBN 13: 978-1-4103-1783-4.

Although the title might imply a merely practical guide, this sophisticated encyclopedia also tackles concepts like the carbon cycle and intergenerational responsibility and concrete events such as the passage of the US Farm Bill and the UN Conference on Environment and Development. Each volume includes excellent ancillary materials such as a list of entries according to which component(s) of sustainability the topic represents (environmental, economic, or social), chronology of events, general glossary, list of relevant organizations, and thorough index. Individual entries include their own miniature glossaries and list resources, both Websites and books, for further study.

The encyclopedia does contain useful resources for readers interested in practical applications. Many sidebars provide information that can be used to research options. For example, the entry on Nongovernmental Organizations includes information about *The Charity Navigator* Website. Current events, such as the Fukushima disaster, are also covered in sidebars and referenced in the index.—**Delilah R. Caldwell**

Handbooks and Yearbooks

851.   **Ecological Forest Management Handbook.** Guy R. Larocque, ed. Boca Raton, Fla., CRC Press, 2015. 604p. illus. maps. index. (Applied Ecology and Environmental Management). $169.96; $139.97 (e-book). ISBN 13: 978-1-4822-4785-5; 978-1-4822-4786-2 (e-book).

From the potential benefits of mangrove forests and the threat root rot poses to the coveted clutch tree, this collection ties together rich and tantalizing lines of research. So wide is the expert reach of the multiple authors that the pluses and minuses of palm oil plantations, some of the philosophical debate over European beech forests (as in strive for diversity or not), and even John Haldane's canary are here. The product-yielding and cultural dimensions of forests both receive solid treatment. The complexity of managing forests benefits from models that provide guidance about how to manage; and authors from different geographical regions summarize the many existing models while fully describing some. The "wake effect" is a valuable concept that suggests when forests are managed well for wood production, other gains accrue, such as protection of watersheds and wildlife. Each entry is supported by a robust list of references and there is an index. Because many authors are not writing in their native language, there are errors, such as leave for leaf and boarders for borders, and some verbosity and repetition. Quibbles aside, the most serious omission in the volume is a direct focus on the role of the human population, which has more than quadrupled since 1900. In fact, the world's population is not "an ecological indicator of stress on the world's forests" (page 365). The world's population actually puts direct pressure on forests. On the whole, coverage and content are good. The volume merits a place in a research library.—**Diane M. Calabrese**

852.   **Ecopsychology: Advances from the Intersection of Psychology and Environmental Protection.** Darlyne G. Nemeth, set editor, Robert B. Hamilton, and Judy Kuriansky, volume eds. Santa Barbara, Calif., Praeger/ABC-CLIO, 2015. 2v. index. (Practical and Applied Psychology). $131.00/set. ISBN 13: 978-1-4408-3172-0; 978-1-4408-3173-7 (e-book).

Ecopsychology is an innovative field of study that combines the science of ecology and psychology. Ecopsychology incorporates two significant concepts: ecodynamics, which considers how humans affect the environment, and ecokinetics, which investigates environmental influences on humans. The field of psychology provides support and assists in shaping our destiny and protecting the planet's ecology system. Implementing positive environmental policies promotes awareness and appropriate proactive action. This two-volume anthology explores the survival of the planet and our species. It seeks to achieve holistic planning goals and supports the viewpoint that the planet's future resides in humanity's resilience and its desire to safeguard the planet. Providing valuable information on how we should preserve the earth for future generations and improve our legacy for all living things, the pages encourage the requirement for national and international leaders to develop definitive action plans that halt distressing earth's environmental balance and harming its inhabitants. Editors and contributors meet the standards for academic excellence. Moreover, the editors provide a useful framework to identify and address environmental issues.

The first volume, *Ecopsychology: Science and Theory,* emphasizes empirical science and theory, addressing myriad issues, including why many individuals do not understand environmental issues; the principles of the earth's formation, evolution, and basic survival needs; complications associated with population growth and limited resources; and the impact of social and political changes. Volume two addresses successful interventions and related policies. The contributors offer admirable perspectives on developing conservation strategies and new perspectives. The role of psychology lies in communication and promoting desirable behaviors. Discouraging undesirable behaviors is the essence of the climate-change mitigation, adaptation, and sustainability. Psychologists must participate with scientists and other professionals to achieve environmental protection. This professional cooperation offers educational and environmental opportunities. Psychology can make significant contributions in identifying myths. Its influence lies in reconciling human differences and managing the future. Some psychologists may serve as robust leaders for promoting an environmental message banner.

Effective direction for the future requires dynamic leadership. A few gifted leaders may have charismatic and altruistic qualities that help gather supporters. The core of the environmental mission includes holistic planning. The plan incorporates an analysis of present conditions and an examination of unintended consequences. The management of environmental change targets specific goals and objectives. One particular difficulty is building the human incentive to take planned actions. The authors hypothesize that the failure to act now creates a domino effect that may result in the total destruction of our species. The research content is enlightening concerning our role and interactions within the ecosystem.

Ecopsychology warrants praise for readability, organization, and relevant information. It presents thoughtful passages and documented research. The two-volume set represents essential reading for public libraries. High school, community college, and university library colleagues are duty-bound to consider adopting this futuristic message. In addition, the adoption of this two-volume set of books will benefit a related special topics course on the university level. This contribution would serve as an excellent textbook for joint psychology and science seminars.—**Thomas E. Baker**

853.   **The Environmental Resource Handbook, 2015-2016.** 8th ed. Amenia, N.Y., Grey House Publishing, 2015. 1000p. maps. index. $155.00pa. ISBN 13: 978-1-61925-560-9.

Largely a compilation that derives heavily (and verbatim) from information provided by such open sources as the U.S. Environmental Protection Agency and the Centers for Disease Control and Prevention, this volume also includes some original research by the editors. For example, there is a section on the recycling practices (voluntary or not, curbside or not, etc.) of 100 major U.S. cities. Fingertip access to a glossary of environmental terms and to acronyms and abbreviations will be useful in some work settings. So, too, will the index to all entries in the volume by name (group, association), the index to entries by state (and Canada), and the subject index. Financial resources, consultants, and green products catalogs are among the subheads for the section on resources. The resources include a wide range of entities ranging from the Chlorine Institute to Numi Organic Tea; the nugget description attached to each entry varies from none to a robust sentence or two. Statistics from agriculture, children's health and environment, air quality, energy, and more are presented via maps, graphs, and tabulations derived almost wholly (and without modification) from open sources of information at federal agencies. An online database, which is sold separately, allows searches of compiled information by keyword as well as ability to save and organize search results. Those immersed in environmental work of any kind will find the activity of reading entries on resources a way to both identify new links with kindred groups and to assess work that needs to be done.—**Diane M. Calabrese**

854.   **Environmental   Studies   in   Video.   http://alexanderstreet.com/products/ environmental-studies-video.** [Website] Alexandria, Va., Alexander Street Press. Price negotiated by site. Date reviewed: 2016.

Environmental Studies in Video is an Alexander Street Press product offering online access to what should eventually be about 500 hours of environmental-themed videos. The films currently available vary in scholarly orientation. A random sample of films ranged from quite nuanced explorations of current environmental issues to simple advocacy pieces. All the films seem to be English-language with a strong focus on North America and the United Kingdom, but there is indeed global coverage in the collection as a whole. Similarly, the disciplinary thrust is primarily toward the social sciences, law, and planning. The platform advertises 330 films related to the environmental science, but a sampling of these materials suggests that many dwell only lightly on actual science. Database searches revealed many films on climate change, pollution, energy, food, and sustainability, but much of this material tends to inform viewers about the problems rather than the praxis of researching and managing pollution, energy, etc. There were few hits for terms such as "evolution" and "carbon cycle," and, surprisingly, none for any variant of the term "locavore." Thus there is a hit-and-miss feel to the materials, which are also overwhelmingly focused on recent events. Historical approaches to environmental issues are few and far between.

Overall, the collection seems most appropriate for teaching undergraduate courses in environmental studies, especially those that will stress social science approaches. The database is searchable by keyword or advanced search platforms, but it can also be browsed by topic and location. Each film provides a transcript that is searchable, making these resources a particular boon to students wanting to track down specific information, quotes, or themes. As products to watch, however, the online films are grainy and not conducive to projection by digital projectors, and sometimes the films do not run smoothly on a desktop computer. Thus this product is likely to find its strongest appeal with small colleges lacking extensive video libraries, and with institutions conducting lots of online courses. Conversely, *Environmental Studies in Video* offers little for scholarly researchers. The transcript search function is handy for tracking down text, but the films are few in number, recent in production, thematically scattered, and qualitatively uneven. There is almost no primary source material, so the collection will not be a very compelling acquisition for a research library.—**Joseph E. Taylor III**

855. **Handbook of Research Methods and Applications in Environmental Studies.** Ruth, Matthias, ed. Northampton, Mass., Edward Elgar, 2015. 534p. index. (Handbook of Research Methods and Applications). $290.00. ISBN 13: 978-1-78347-463-9.

Human life and well-being depend on the use of natural resources, while the utilization of those resources often results in environmental degradation. Environmental studies, as a discipline, exists as an examination of human interactions with the natural world and the tension between necessary use and damaging exploitation. Divided between sections on the social context and scientific modeling, the *Handbook of Research Methods and Applications in Environmental Studies* illustrates this tension while making clear that the very nature of environmental studies is interdisciplinary and multimodal. Each chapter introduces a research method concept or practice and then describes the practical application in the form of case studies. With an emphasis on mixed methods research, part one's social context section includes chapters on conducting cross-cultural research, constructing structured mental models, and fuzzy cognitive mapping, among other methods. The chapters in part two describe models for calculating, understanding, and predicting energy and water use, life cycle assessments, ecosystem dynamics, valuing ecosystem services, and gaming. Written for scholars and practitioners of environmental science research, this handbook succeeds in compiling not only the theoretical concepts behind interdisciplinary research methods in environmental studies, but also examples of practical applications of those same methods.

Recommended for research libraries.—**Eric Tans**

856. **Handbook of Sustainable Apparel Production.** Muthu, Subramanian Senthilkannan, ed. Boca Raton, Fla., CRC Press, 2015. 556p. illus. index. $144.46; $118.97 (e-book). ISBN 13: 978-1-4822-9937-3; 978-1-4822-9939-7 (e-book).

The *Handbook of Sustainable Apparel Production* covers in 23 chapters the environmental impacts of apparel production at all stages in the supply chain and offers ways to make the industry more sustainable. Each chapter is written by area experts who use well-documented research, tables, graphs, scientific studies, and illustrations to convey essential information.

The first section, Sustainable Textile Raw Materials and Manufacturing Processes for Apparel Manufacture, addresses in six chapters such things as sustainable flame-retardant finishing of textiles and sustainable UV-resistant protective clothing. In the four chapters of section two, Environmental and Social Assessment of Apparel Manufacturing, readers learn about the carbon footprint of textile and clothing products, the social impacts of the clothing and fashion industry, and more. Three chapters comprise section three and cover the importance of consumer behavior in the sustainability of the clothing field, consumer behavior in the fashion field, and textile sustainability. Assessment of Sustainable Apparel Production, the fourth section, contains six chapters that examine topics including the industrial processes used in the textile industry and pollution output, the environmental aspects of natural dye processing, and apparel supply chains and the role of developing nations in apparel manufacturing. The final section, Sustainability and Fashion, explicates myriad topics like creating new business models for sustainable fashion, product service systems, and how to transform the fashion industry into one that is more sustainable.

This subject is fascinating enough to compel a cover-to-cover read but the table of contents and index allow users to quickly hone in on a particular topic. This handbook is highly recommended for academic libraries, the libraries of fashion schools, and business libraries.—**ARBA Staff Reviewer**

857.   **InfoSci-Environmental Science and Technology. http://www.igi-global.com/e-resources/infosci-subject-databases/infosci-environmental-science/.** [Website] Hershey, Pa., Information Science Reference/IGI Global. Price negotiated by site. Date reviewed: 2016.

The InfoSci series provides information for research studies relating to science and technology. Students attending schools that own these databases will want to create a profile to access full use of the tools. A user guide and help tab will provide instruction on using the databases and detail search options and features of the electronic resources. Search functionality options are: Basic, Advanced, Expert, and Classic. Classic search also offers a more traditional search using keywords and subjects. All of these are located on a high-left sidebar for ease of access. The main sidebar provides options for forward or backward navigation. Citing, favorites, and saved search tabs are essential for the researcher. InfoSci offers these features with scholarly options; citings are found in MLA, ALA, and Chicago style and choices include HTML or PDF for full-text format.

InfoSci-Environmental Science and Technology has 71 reference books. Each page can be sorted via titles or copyright dates. Date ranges of 2001 (1) through 2016 (14) will provide historical and contemporary studies on environmental science and technology. Subtopics are many and examples may include: climate change, energy harvesting, meat consumption, sustainability, and water pollution. E-book resources vary in geographical impact from the finite (*Impact of Climate Change on Food Security in Small Island Developing States*) to those with a broader scope (*Marine Technology and Sustainable Development: Green Innovations*). Most books contain introductions, acknowledgements, references, author and contributor information, and indexes. Because this database is a collection of independent resource texts, there is not uniformity in access. Case in point, *Impact of Meat Consumption on Heath and Environmental* appears to have no index.

Chapters are easily accessed by clicking on the chapter heading. As an environmental title is accessed, a search bar will allow further filtering for specifics within the clear listing of chapters. Because of the complexity of some studies, the search bar will be extremely useful for further filtering. Chapters are well documented, and tables, charts, and other data structures are followed immediately by sourcing. Information may be saved by chapter or the entire book.

InfoSci-Environmental Science and Technology provides detailed research for college students, researchers, engineers, scholars, government officials, and other practitioners seeking to understand and make a difference in the care and treatment of the environment.

Recommended.—**Janis Minshull**

858.   Newton, David E. **Fracking: A Reference Handbook.** 2d ed. Santa Barbara, Calif., ABC-CLIO, 2015. 362p. illus. index. (Contemporary World Issues). $58.00. ISBN 13: 978-1-61069-691-3; 978-1-61069-692-0 (e-book).

The Contemporary World Issues series features works on such topics as genetic engineering, GMO foods, and biodiversity. Author David E. Newton has written several of the titles in this series. In *Fracking: A Reference Handbook,* he investigates this newer process for attaining oil and gas for energy use.

Newton has a master's degree in education from the University of Michigan and an education doctorate in science education from Harvard University. As a professor, he taught sciences and mathematics. He has also authored more than 400 textbooks, encyclopedias, resource books, research manuals, laboratory manuals, trade books, and other educational materials.

Chapters begin with a black-and white-photograph. The text includes tables and lists where appropriate; tables such as Table 1.4 Petroleum Consumption (p. 36) provide clear data for researchers. Each chapter closes with a conclusion where warranted and a detailed list of print and nonprint resources that correlate to the preceding topic. A table of contents and index make it easy for users to navigate to a precise place in the book.

Starting with an overview of the subject of fracking, the text then moves into the first chapters which give background on the history and development of the gas and oil industries. Industry terminology is included in chapter one, yet would be more useful as an appendix to be easily referred to throughout the reading. By the second chapter, "Problems, Controversies and Solutions," the stage is set for the controversy that fracking has brought to the United States and other countries who use this process.

In the second half of the book, the reference aspect of this book expands with extensive resources for further research. There are biographical sketches and industry profiles, facts and data or documents, and authoritative essays which are all referenced. Charts and tables add to the informative text; specifics such as gas wells in the Marcellus Play in Pennsylvania establish facts with specific site data. Various drilling sites are included as part of this text. The plethora of hydraulic fracking and directional drilling concerns are presented, legislative remedies discussed, and the weight of independent energy sourcing versus deleterious effects on plants and animals represented.

Fracking is a complicated issue; *Fracking: A Reference Handbook* gathers a multitude of resources for further study whether on the social, political, environmental, economic, or health angle of this practice of expelling oil and gas from the ground. This is definitely a starting point for academic fracking research for high school and college students, scholars, and general readers such as legislators and activists who are seeking a collection of resources for further study. Recommended.—**Janis Minshull**

859.   Stanwix, William, and Alex Sparrow. **The Hempcrete Book: Designing and Building with Hemp-Lime.** Cambridge, England, Green Books, 2014. 368p. illus. index. $49.95pa. ISBN 13: 978-0-8578-4120-9.

This book provides detailed information about the use of hempcrete in building. Hempcrete, comprised of the chopped stalks of the industrial hemp plant mixed with a lime-based binder, is a green building product developed in France in the 1980s and used in residential and commercial buildings in Europe and increasingly in Canada, Australia, and South Africa. Hempcrete has many advantages—it is breathable, sustainable, fireproof, and capable of regulating humidity. The book's examples focus on the United Kingdom where the authors operate Hemp-LimeConstruct.

This thorough how-to covers all aspects of building with hempcrete in three parts: Principles of Building with Hempcrete, Hempcrete Construction, and Designing a Hempcrete Building. In these sections, users will find information on such things as tools and equipment, building a hempcrete wall, mixing hempcrete, and design fundamentals. Color photographs and figures clarify instructions and concepts.

The book ends with notes, a glossary, a list of resources on where to find further information about hempcrete, a bibliography, and an index. This book will serve contractors, architects, or anyone interested in green building and alternative materials and building techniques.—**ARBA Staff Reviewer**

860.   **Wildlife Habitat Conservation. Concepts, Challenges, and Solutions.** Michael L. Morrison and Heather A. Matthewson, eds. Baltimore, Md., Johns Hopkins University Press, 2015. 185p. index. $75.00; $75.00 (e-book). ISBN 13; 978-1-4214-1610-6; 978-1-4214-1611-3 (e-book).

Amidst the burgeoning population of the twenty-first century lies a greater awareness of environmental issues. From grammar school through university graduation core ideas like sustainability, ecosystems, and habitat are introduced, discussed, debated, and defined. This collection of academic essays focuses on the specific idea of habitat and provides a scientific assessment of its tenets, boundaries, and challenges in order to more effectively ensure its healthier existence.

While not meant to be comprehensive, the contributions provide rigorous analyses of broader questions concerning wildlife habitat. Organized into three sections, the essays lay a foundation for reconceptualizing the idea of habitats, addressing threats to habitats and furthering habitat research and conservation.

Part one redirects the idea of habitat using new knowledge related to demographics, behavioral processes, and more, and points to the need for resource managers to adapt to a habitat's more complex concepts. Part two highlights a number of challenges facing habitat management beyond the well-documented loss of vegetation issues, such as the intrusion of non-native sounds, lights, plants, and animals. Part three discusses solutions and offers ways to prepare for future issues. It suggests a more dynamic role for wildlife managers, i.e., having them move from simple caretaking to proactive planning, managing, and restoring of wildlife habitats.

The "Literature Cited" sections at the end of each chapter further enhance the usefulness of this well-organized collection designed for both university students and professionals in land management.—**Laura Herrell**

861.   Worldwatch Institute. **State of the World 2014: Governing for Sustainability.** Washington, D.C., Island Press, 2014. 294p. illus. index. $23.00pa; $22.99 (e-book). ISBN 13: 978-1-61091-541-0; 978-1-61091-542-7 (e-book).

The Worldwatch Institute, an organization long dedicated to transitioning the world into an era of sustainability, has produced this book with the aim of addressing ways in which global governments and their citizens can work better to incorporate and promote sustainability. Highlighting the uphill battle faced when pursuing government action, this thought-provoking report gathers numerous writings from political, economic, and academic leaders in sustainability thinking.

Following introductory essays examining the key difficulties in fostering productive change in environmental legislation (e.g., complex global bureaucracies, climate change denial) the report then explores both political and economic paths leading toward the common goal of governance in mind of sustainability. The Political Governance section presents chapters on such topics as the need to promote an ecological literacy among whole communities in the hopes of creating sound public policy, while the Economic Governance section includes chapters defining the global financial system as a public service rather than as an industry, inviting labor unions into a partnership with environmental advocacy, and championing businesses which incorporate environmental and community "well-being" into their bottom line.

Richly infused with tables, black-and-white photographs, and insightful text boxes, this book does well to clarify and advance this all-important discussion on our globe's current and future environmental challenges and the need for governments to step up their response to them.—**Laura Herrell**

37 Transportation

General Works

Handbooks and Yearbooks

862. **The Business of Transportation.** Darren Prokop, ed. Santa Barbara, Calif., Praeger/ABC-CLIO, 2014. 2v. maps. index. $110.00/set. ISBN 13: 978-0-313-39735-6; 978-0-313-39736-3 (e-book).

The business of moving goods is complex and competitive. This two-volume set offers a nuts-and-bolts examination of our most common transportation systems in regards to business, productivity, and trade. With an overall eye to giving readers a grounded understanding of the interrelation of all modes and markets and applications, these volumes provide clear and factual contributions from a number of experts in various related fields.

Volume one (Modes and Markets) introduces the five modes of transportation: motor carriers, rail, airline, ocean shipping, and pipelines. Chapters provide a general overview of each mode's infrastructure, technologies, and markets allowing readers to note key similarities and differences. The volume also discusses transportation intermediaries and introduces the concept of "intermodalism" whereby we see more cooperation between certain transportation modes in order to reduce costs and improve service.

Volume two (Applications) brings more of a magnifying glass to the systems which make the transportation business hum. It takes a closer look at airports, roadways, and other hubs, and raises issues along the line of privatization, public-private partnerships, and complete public control. The volume also addresses international issues, technology, legal issues, politics, security, and environmental concerns.

Concisely written, with the helpful additions of a glossary, charts, graphs, and an index, these volumes provide a solid base for understanding the latest ideas in transportation management and are recommended for academic libraries.—**Laura Herrell**

863. **Handbook on Transport and Development.** Robin Hickman, Moshe Givoni, David Bonilla, and David Banister, eds. Northampton, Mass., Edward Elgar, 2015. 698p. index. $335.00. ISBN 13: 978-0-85793-725-4; 978-0-85793-726-1 (e-book).

This work contains 45 chapters, each devoted to analyzing current and emerging thinking among an international group of scholars about the relationships between transportation planning and development. Part one of the book is a brief introduction that reviews the topic of urban planning and travel and outlines the contents of the book. The remaining chapters are organized into four themes. Part two consists of chapters that focus on the built environment and movement of people, including the social, economic, spatial, cultural, demographic, and other variables that influence travel. For example, Xinyu (Jason) Cao uses a case study of Northern California to investigate attitude-related "self-selection" and travel behavior. Part three includes 16 chapters that examine the spatial dimensions of investments in transportation. Essays include analysis of freight distribution as an economic driver, high-speed trains as contributors to inter- and intraregional inequalities, and the impact of cargo and passenger air transport on global commerce. Many of the chapters in this section include important historical analysis that grounds their assumptions about the linkages among economies and the spatial distribution of modes of transportation. The 14 chapters in part four explore broader themes of analysis from a multidisciplinary social and cultural perspective, focusing on nonphysical dimensions of mobility and the influence of technology on travel. The book concludes with a summary chapter that reviews important advances in understanding transport and development and suggests new avenues of research. Chapters include notes, references, and a variety of nontextual elements. Considered collectively, this handbook provides a thorough, multidisciplinary examination of transport and development and is highly recommended for advanced students, scholars, and practitioner researchers who seek to understand these issues.—**Robert V. Labaree**

864.   **Urban Transportation Innovations Worldwide.** Roger L. Kemp and Carl J. Stephani, eds. Jefferson, N.C., McFarland, 2015. 252p. index. $39.95pa. ISBN 13: 978-0-7864-7075-4; 978-1-4766-1827-2 (e-book).

Urban transportation planning has never been more exciting, and more important. As populations have swelled, planners are both embracing ideas from the past in developing more pedestrian and bicycle-friendly avenues and considering the future with advanced technologies, renewable resources, and alternative fuels and designs. This book presents an array of best practices from communities outside the United States which highlight the ability to meld the simplicity of the past with the promise of the future and ultimately devise the best transportation solutions for their citizens.

The book divides its information into three sections which focus on the general topic of urban transportation planning, specific case studies of successful planning from cities around the world, and the great potential of urban transportation planning as it faces a rapidly evolving future.

Chapters in International Transportation Planning point to many of the issues driving urban transportation planning today, e.g., restoring natural environments, reducing dependence on fossil fuels, reducing traffic congestion, and more. The second and largest section—The Best Practices—shares over 35 case studies from diverse global communities which creatively address many of the issues raised in the first section. For example, readers learn how Copenhagen, Denmark, employed a 10-step program to make its city center safer, cleaner, more pedestrian-friendly, and more aesthetically pleasing. Readers also learn how Nagano, Japan, applies the Intelligent Transportation Systems (ITS) technology to traffic management and trip planning. Many more examples, from the promotion of nonmotorized transportation in Bogota, Colombia, and Monrovia, Liberia, to the redesign of public spaces in London, England, are showcased.

The Future speaks more generally to the need to meet tomorrow's demands. Topics discussed include improving current transportation services, adapting roadways to new uses, finding funding, and understanding and implementing "New Urbanism."

Appendixes offer a good variety of supplemental information, including a periodicals bibliography, glossary, list of acronyms and abbreviations, and several resource directories.—**ARBA Staff Reviewer**

Author/Title Index

Reference is to entry number.

Subject Index

Reference is to entry number.